Ryan Stephens
Ron Plew
Arie D. Jones

D1366157

Sams **Teach Yourself**

SQL

in **One Hour** a Day

SAMS | 800 East 96th Street, Indianapolis, Indiana 46240

Sams Teach Yourself SQL in One Hour a Day

Copyright © 2009 by Pearson Education Inc.

ISBN-13: 978-0-672-33025-4
ISBN-10: 0-672-33025-3

Library of Congress Cataloging-in-Publication Data:

Stephens, Ryan K.
  Sams teach yourself SQL in one hour a day / Ryan Stephens, Ron Plew, Arie D. Jones. — 1st ed.
      p. cm.
  Previously published under title: Sams teach yourself SQL in 24 hours.
  Includes indexes.
  ISBN 978-0-672-33025-4 (pbk.)
  1. SQL (Computer program language) I. Plew, Ronald R. II. Jones, Arie. III. Stephens, Ryan K. Sams teach yourself SQL in 24 hours. IV. Title.
  QA76.73.S67P554 2009
  005.13'3—dc22
                          2009014482

Printed in the United States of America
First Printing: June 2009

Trademarks

Warning and Disclaimer

Bulk Sales

Sams Publishing offers excellent discounts on this book when ordered in quantity for bulk purchases or special sales. For more information, please contact

U.S. Corporate and Government Sales
1-800-382-3419
corpsales@pearsontechgroup.com

For sales outside of the U.S., please contact

International Sales
international@pearson.com

Editor-in-Chief
Mark Taub

Acquisitions Editor
Trina MacDonald

Development Editor
Songlin Qiu

Managing Editor
Kristy Hart

Senior Project Editor
Matthew Purcell

Copy Editor
Seth Kerney

Indexer
Lisa Stumpf

Proofreader
Language Logistics, LLC

Technical Editor
Clayton Rardin
Steven Romero

Publishing Coordinator
Cindy Teeters

Book Designer
Gary Adair

Compositor
Nonie Ratcliff

Contents at a Glance

NOTE

Register this book at www.samspublishing.com/register for convenient access to updates, errata, and downloads for the book, including Appendixes E and F in PDF format, as well as source code and files from the book's examples.

Table of Contents

PART II: Database Design

LESSON 8: Database Normalization   **229**

PART VIII: Appendices

Online Appendixes

NOTE

Register this book at www.samspublishing.com/register for convenient access to updates, errata, and downloads for the book, including Appendixes E and F in PDF format, as well as source code and files from the book's examples.

About the Author

For more than 10 years, the authors have studied, applied, and documented the SQL standard and its application to the critical database systems in this book. **Ryan Stephens** and **Ron Plew** are entrepreneurs, speakers, and co-founders of Perpetual Technologies, Inc. (PTI), a fast-growing IT management and consulting firm. PTI specializes in database technologies, primarily Oracle and SQL servers running on all UNIX, Linux, and Microsoft platforms. Starting out as data analysts and database administrators, Ryan and Ron now lead a team of impressive technical subject matter experts who manage databases for clients worldwide. They authored and taught database courses for Indiana University-Purdue University in Indianapolis for five years and have authored more than a dozen books on Oracle, SQL, database design, and the high availability of critical systems.

Arie D. Jones is the Principal Microsoft Consultant for PTI in Indianapolis, Indiana. Arie leads PTI's team of experts in the planning, design, development, deployment, and management of database environments and applications to achieve the best combination of tools and services for each client. He is a regular speaker at technical events and has authored several books and articles pertaining to database-related topics. His most recent book is *SQL Functions Programmer's Reference* from Wrox Publishing.

Dedication

This book is dedicated to my parents, Thomas and Karlyn Stephens, who always taught me that I can achieve anything if determined. This book is also dedicated to my brilliant son, Daniel, and to my beautiful daughters, Autumn and Alivia; don't ever settle for anything less than your dreams.

—Ryan

This book is dedicated to my family: my wife, Linda; my mother, Betty; my children, Leslie, Nancy, Angela, and Wendy; my grandchildren, Andy, Ryan, Holly, Morgan, Schyler, Heather, Gavin, Regan, Caleigh, and Cameron; and my sons-in-law, Jason and Dallas. Thanks for being patient with me during this busy time. Love all of you.

—Poppy

I would like to dedicate this book to my wife, Jackie, for being understanding and supportive during the long hours that it took to complete this book.

—Arie

Acknowledgments

Thanks to all the people in our lives who have been patient during all editions of this book—mostly to our wives, Tina and Linda. Thanks to Arie Jones for stepping up to the plate and helping so much with this edition. Thanks also to the editorial staff at Sams for all of their hard work to make this edition better than the last. It has been a pleasure to work with each of you.

We Want to Hear from You!

As the reader of this book, *you* are our most important critic and commentator. We value your opinion and want to know what we're doing right, what we could do better, what areas you'd like to see us publish in, and any other words of wisdom you're willing to pass our way.

You can email or write me directly to let me know what you did or didn't like about this book—as well as what we can do to make our books stronger.

Please note that I cannot help you with technical problems related to the topic of this book, and that due to the high volume of mail I receive, I might not be able to reply to every message.

When you write, please be sure to include this book's title and author as well as your name and phone or email address. I will carefully review your comments and share them with the author and editors who worked on the book.

E-mail: feedback@samspublishing.com

Mail: Mark Taub
            Editor-in-Chief
            Sams Publishing
            800 East 96th Street
            Indianapolis, IN 46240 USA

Reader Services

Visit our website and register this book at informit.com/register for convenient access to any updates, downloads, or errata that might be available for this book.

Introduction

Over the past decade the landscape of information technology has drastically shifted to a data-centric world. More than ever companies are looking for ways in which they can leverage their own data networks to make intelligent business decisions. This includes the ability to gather, store, and report effectively over possibly large sets of data in multiple formats. So the role of database administrators and developers have become strategically important in the proper implementation and care of these systems.

The cornerstone to any database project is the language that will be used in order to interact with the system. Fortunately, a consortium of entities has enacted a standard query language for database environments known as the ANSI SQL standard. This provides a commonality between all database querying languages by following this known standard and allows developers to learn the standard and then work on any given number of database systems with minor adjustments.

This book takes a focused approach on getting the reader the basics of the SQL language in order to allow them to have a solid foundation for future learning. Often in today's business environment, there is very little time to learn new things as our day-to-day functions consume large amounts of our time. By focusing on smaller lesson plans and logically segmenting the sections in a stepping stone fashion, the book allows readers to learn the SQL language at their own pace and within their own schedules.

Who Should Read This Book?

This book is for people who want to learn the fundamentals of Structured Query Language (SQL) quickly. Through the use of countless examples, this book depicts all the major components of SQL, as well as options that are available with various database implementations. You should be able to apply what you learn here to relational databases in a traditional business setting.

How Is This Book Organized?

This book is divided into seven parts, which logically break down the structure of ANSI SQL into easily learnable sections:

- Part I, comprised of the first seven lessons, discusses the basic concepts behind SQL and mainly focuses on the SQL query.

- Part II includes topics on the art of database design, such as creating databases and database objects properly, which is often the foundation of RDBMS application development.

- Part III focuses on data manipulation and using SQL to perform UPDATEs, INSERTs, and DELETEs of data within your database. These will be the staple commands that you will use on a day-to-day basis.

- Part IV is dedicated to database administration, which covers such topics as security, management, and performance, enabling you to maintain the integrity and performance of your database instance.

- Part V focuses on more advanced SQL objects such as triggers and stored procedures. Using these objects will allow you to perform more sophisticated data manipulation techniques that would otherwise be difficult in standard SQL syntax.

- Part VI covers more advanced SQL programming. Advanced SQL programming will allow you to perform more advanced queries and manipulation of the data within your database.

- Part VII presents you with SQL in various database implementations. SQL extensions such as PL/SQL allow you to take advantage of unique attributes within a particular database environment, such as Oracle.

- This book also contains four appendices, which provide you with not only the answers to the exercises in each lesson but also the code examples to create and populate the tables used in the book. Two additional appendices are located at http://www.informit.com/store/products.aspx?isbn=0672330253 under the extras tab.

After studying this book, you should have an excellent understanding of SQL and should know how to apply SQL in the real world.

> **NOTE**
>
> If you are familiar with the basics and history of SQL, we suggest you skim the first lesson and begin in earnest with Lesson 2 "Introducing the Query."

The syntax of SQL is explained and then brought to life in examples using MySQL, which is the closest implementation of the ANSI SQL standard syntax, as well as Oracle Express edition, which demonstrates some of the extensions to ANSI SQL.

Conventions Used in This Book

This book uses the following typeface conventions:

- Menu names are separated from menu options by a comma. For example, File, Open means select the Open option from the File menu.

- New terms appear in italic.

- In some listings, we've included both the input and output (**Input/Output** ▼). For these, all code that you type in (input) appears in **boldface monospace**. Output appears in standard monospace. The Combination icon indicates that both input and output appear in the code.

- The **Input** ▼ and **Output** ▼ icons also identify the nature of the code.

- Many code-related terms within the text also appear in monospace.

- Placeholders in code appear in *italic monospace*.

- When a line of code is too long to fit on one line of this book, it is broken at a convenient place and continued to the next line. A code continuation character (➥) precedes the continuation of a line of code. (You should type a line of code that has this character as one long line without breaking it.)

- Paragraphs that begin with the **Analysis** ▼ icon explain the preceding code example.

- The **Syntax** ▼ icon identifies syntax statements.

- Special design features enhance the text material:

NOTE	Notes explain interesting or important points that can help you understand SQL concepts and techniques.

TIP	Tips are little pieces of information that will help you in real-world situations. Tips often offer shortcuts to make a task easier or faster.

CAUTION	Cautions provide information about detrimental performance issues or dangerous errors. Pay careful attention to Cautions.

Using MySQL for Hands-on Exercises

We have chosen to use MySQL for hands-on exercises in this edition. In previous editions, we left it up to the reader to obtain access to any SQL implementation. We decided that it would be better to provide the reader with an open-source SQL database that allowed all readers to start on the same level with the same software. We chose MySQL because it is the most popular open-source database available today, and it is easy to download and use.

Unfortunately, MySQL does have its limitations. There are several features of standard SQL that are not supported by MySQL. We have attempted to distinguish between the exercises that support MySQL and those that do not. Those exercises that do not will mainly focus on using Oracle Enterprise edition, instead. The beauty of SQL is that it is a standard language, although each implementation does have its differences. After using MySQL to understand the basic fundamentals of SQL, you should be able to easily apply the concepts you have learned to any SQL implementation.

About the Book's Source Code

In the appendices, you will find the source code for creating all of the objects used throughout the book. This includes all of the tables and data that is used. Additionally, the source code will be available for download from the publisher's website. This will allow you to simply cut and paste entries into your interface instead of spending the majority of your time typing and enable you to focus more clearly on the material.

LESSON 1
Getting Started with SQL

Welcome to your first lesson in teaching yourself SQL. This lesson will start your learning with a brief history of SQL and databases and will provide you with a foundation that will help you through the rest of the book. More specifically, you will learn the following:

- The history of SQL and databases.

- Dr. Codd's 12 rules for a relational database model.

- How to design a database structure.

- Popular SQL implementations.

- Why open database connectivity (ODBC) is important.

A Brief History of SQL

The history of SQL began in an IBM laboratory in San Jose, California, where SQL was developed in the late 1970s. The acronym *SQL* stands for *Structured Query Language*, and the language itself is often referred to as "sequel." It was originally developed for IBM's DB2 product (a relational database management system, or RDBMS, that can still be bought today for various platforms and environments). In fact, SQL makes an RDBMS possible. SQL is a nonprocedural language, in contrast to the procedural or third-generation languages (3GLs) such as COBOL and C, that had been created up to that time.

NOTE

Nonprocedural means *what* rather than *how*. For example, SQL describes what data to act upon rather than how to act upon the data.

The characteristic that differentiates a DBMS from an RDBMS is that an RDBMS uses a set-oriented database language. For most RDBMSs, this set-oriented database language is SQL. *Set-oriented* refers to the way that SQL processes data—in *sets* or *groups*.

Two standards organizations—the American National Standards Organization (ANSI) and the International Standards Organization (ISO)—currently promote SQL standards to industry. The ANSI SQL standard is the standard for the SQL used throughout this book. Although these standard-making bodies prepare standards for database system designers to follow, all database products differ from the ANSI standard to some degree. In truth, although the ANSI standard has grown quite large, the amount that needs to be implemented by a particular RDBMS to be considered compliant is quite small. Most systems provide some proprietary extensions to SQL that extend the language into a true procedural language.

Various RDBMSs are discussed throughout this book, and the various flavors of the SQL language for specific implementations are reviewed in more detail in Part 7, "SQL in Various Database Implementations."

A Brief History of Databases

A little background on the evolution of databases and database theory will help you understand the workings of SQL. Database systems store data in every conceivable business environment. From large tracking databases such as airline reservation systems to a child's baseball card collection, database systems store and distribute the data that you depend on. Just a couple of decades ago, large database systems could be run only on large mainframe computers. These machines were traditionally expensive to design, purchase, and maintain. However, today's generation of powerful, inexpensive workstation computers enables programmers to design software that maintains and distributes data quickly and inexpensively.

The most popular data storage model is the relational database, which grew from the seminal paper "A Relational Model of Data for Large Shared Data Banks" by Dr. E.F. Codd, written in 1970. SQL evolved to service the concepts of the relational database model. Dr. Codd defined 13 rules, oddly enough referred to as Codd's 12 rules, for the relational model:

0. A relational DBMS must be able to manage databases entirely through its relational capabilities.
1. Information—All information in a relational database (including table and column names) is represented explicitly as a value in tabular format.
2. Guaranteed access—Every value in a relational database is guaranteed to be acces-

sible by using a combination of the table name, primary key value, and column name.

3. Systematic null value support—The DBMS provides systematic support for the treatment of *null values* (unknown or inapplicable data), which are distinct from default values, and independent of any domain.

4. Active, online relational catalog—The description of the database and its contents is represented at the logical level in tabular format and can therefore be queried using the database language.

5. Comprehensive data sublanguage—At least one supported language must have a well-defined syntax and be comprehensive. It must support data definition, manipulation, integrity rules, authorization, and transactions.

6. View updating—All views that are theoretically updatable can be updated through the system.

7. Set-level insertion, update, and deletion—The DBMS supports not only set-level retrievals but also set-level inserts, updates, and deletes.

8. Physical data independence—Application programs and ad hoc programs are logically unaffected when physical access methods or storage structures are altered.

9. Logical data independence—Application programs and ad hoc programs are logically unaffected, to the extent possible, when changes are made to the table structures.

10. Integrity independence—The database language must be capable of defining integrity rules. These rules must be stored in the online catalog, and they cannot be bypassed.

11. Distribution independence—Application programs and ad hoc requests are logically unaffected when data is first distributed or when it is redistributed.

12. Nonsubversion—It must not be possible to bypass the integrity rules defined through the database language by using lower-level languages.

Most databases have had a "parent/child" relationship; that is, a parent node would contain file pointers to its children (see Figure 1.1).

This method has several advantages and many disadvantages. In its favor is the fact that the physical structure of data on a disk becomes unimportant. The programmer simply stores pointers to the next location, so data can be accessed in this manner. Also, data can be added and deleted easily. However, different groups of information cannot be easily joined to form new information. The format of the data on the disk cannot be arbitrarily changed after the database is created. Doing so would require the creation of a new database structure.

FIGURE 1.1
Codd's relational
database manage-
ment system.

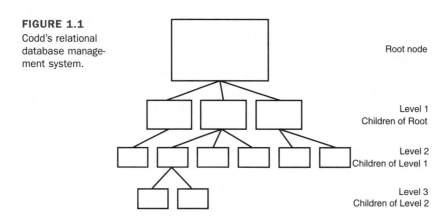

Root node

Level 1
Children of Root

Level 2
Children of Level 1

Level 3
Children of Level 2

Codd's idea for an RDBMS uses the mathematical concepts of relational algebra to break data into sets and related common subsets.

Because information can naturally be grouped into distinct sets, Dr. Codd organized his database system around this concept. Under the relational model, data is separated into sets that resemble a table structure. This table structure consists of individual data elements called *columns*, or *fields*. A single set of a group of fields is known as a *record*, or *row*. For instance, to create a relational database consisting of employee data, you might start with a table called EMPLOYEE that contains the following pieces of information: EMP_ID, LNAME, FNAME, and DOB. These four pieces of data make up the fields in the EMPLOYEE table, shown in Table 1.1.

Table 1.1   The EMPLOYEE Table

EMP_ID	LNAME	FNAME	DOB
1	HIGGINS	JOHN	25-JUL-75
2	SMITH	MICHAEL	16-MAR-80
3	BULLSWORTH	JENNIFER	27-MAY-67
4	SANDERS	CHRISTINA	01-MAR-69
5	WILLIAMS	MAC	14-FEB-85
6	STACKHOUSE	GERALD	17-JUN-71
7	MILLER	REGINALD	22-OCT-52
8	DORKSMART	BARTHALOMEW	25-DEC-68

The eight rows are the records in the EMPLOYEE table. To retrieve a specific record from this table—for example, Mac Williams—a user would instruct the database management system to retrieve the records in which the LNAME field was equal to Williams. If the DBMS had been instructed to retrieve all the fields in the record, the employee's EMP_ID, LNAME, FNAME, and DOB would be returned to the user. SQL is the language that tells the database to retrieve this data. A sample SQL statement that makes this query is

```
SELECT *
FROM EMPLOYEE;
```

Remember that the exact syntax is not important at this point. We cover this topic in much greater detail beginning in the next lesson.

Because the various data items can be grouped according to obvious relationships (such as the relationship of Employee LNAME to Employee DOB), the relational database model gives the database designer a great deal of flexibility to describe the relationships between the data elements. Through the mathematical concepts of JOIN and UNION, relational databases can quickly retrieve pieces of data from different sets (tables) and return them to the user or program as one "joined" collection of data (see Figure 1.2). The join feature enables the designer to store sets of information in separate tables to reduce repetition.

Figure 1.3 shows a union. The union would return only data common to both sources.

FIGURE 1.2
The join feature.

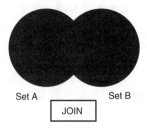

FIGURE 1.3
The union feature.

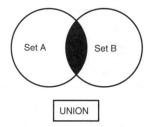

Here's a simple example that shows how data can be logically divided between two tables. Table 1.2 is called DEPENDENTS and contains five columns: EMP_ID, LNAME, FNAME, SEX, and RELATIONSHIP.

Table 1.2   The DEPENDENTS Table

EMP_ID	LNAME	FNAME	SEX	RELATIONSHIP
1	HIGGINS	MARY	F	WIFE
1	HIGGINS	TODD	M	SON
1	HIGGINS	CELIA	F	DAUGHTER
2	SMITH	TERRI	F	WIFE
2	SMITH	BILL	M	SON
3	BULLSWORTH	MIKE	M	HUSBAND
3	BULLSWORTH	BILL	M	SON
3	BULLSWORTH	CINDY	F	DAUGHTER
3	BULLSWORTH	BOB	M	SON
3	BULLSWORTH	JULIE	F	DAUGHTER
4	SANDERS	SANDOR	M	HUSBAND
7	MILLER	CHRISTY	F	WIFE
8	DORKSMART	ELIZABETH	F	WIFE

It would be improper to duplicate the employee's EMP_ID, LNAME, FNAME, and DOB fields for each record. Over time, unnecessary duplication of data would waste a great deal of hard disk space and increase access time for the RDBMS. However, if EMP_ID and data pertaining to family members were stored in a separate table named DEPENDENTS, the user could join the DEPENDENTS and EMPLOYEE tables on the EMP_ID field. Instructing the RDBMS to retrieve all fields from the DEPENDENTS and EMPLOYEE tables in which the EMP_ID field equals 3 would return the data in Table 1.3.

Table 1.3   Return Values from Retrieval in Which EMP_ID Equals 3

LNAME	FNAME	FNAME	RELATIONSHIP
BULLSWORTH	JENNIFER	MIKE	HUSBAND
BULLSWORTH	JENNIFER	BILL	SON
BULLSWORTH	JENNIFER	CINDY	DAUGHTER
BULLSWORTH	JENNIFER	BOB	SON
BULLSWORTH	JENNIFER	JULIE	DAUGHTER

More detailed examples of joins begin in Lesson 5, "Joining Tables."

Today's Database Landscape

Computing technology has made a permanent change in the ways businesses work around the world. Information that was at one time stored in warehouses full of filing cabinets can now be accessed instantaneously at the click of a mouse button. Orders placed by customers in foreign countries can now be instantly processed on the floor of a manufacturing facility.

Although 20 years ago much of this information had been transported onto corporate mainframe databases, offices still operated in a batch-processing environment. If a query needed to be performed, someone notified the management information systems (MIS) department, and then the requested data was delivered as soon as possible (although often not soon enough).

In addition to the development of the relational database model, two technologies led to the rapid growth of what are now called *client/server database systems*. The first important technology was the personal computer. Inexpensive, easy-to-use applications such as Lotus 1-2-3 and WordPerfect enabled employees (and home computer users) to create documents and manage data quickly and accurately. Users became accustomed to continually upgrading their systems because the rate of change was so rapid, even as the price of the more advanced systems continued to fall.

The second important technology was the *local area network (LAN)* and its integration into offices around the world. Although users were accustomed to terminal connections to a corporate mainframe, now word processing files could be stored locally within an office and accessed from any computer attached to the network. After the Apple Macintosh introduced a friendly graphical user interface (GUI), computers were not only inexpensive and powerful but also easy to use. In addition, they could be accessed from remote sites, and large amounts of data could be offloaded to departmental data servers.

During this time of rapid change and advancement, a new type of system appeared. Called *client/server development* because processing is split between client computers and a database server, this new breed of application was a radical change from mainframe-based application programming. Among the many advantages of this type of architecture are the following:

- Reduced maintenance costs
- Reduced network load (processing occurs on database server or client computer)
- Multiple operating systems that can interoperate as long as they share a common network protocol
- Improved data integrity owing to centralized data location

In *Implementing Client/Server Computing,* Bernard H. Boar defines client/server computing as follows:

> Client/server computing is a processing model in which a single application is partitioned between multiple processors (front-end and back-end) and the processors cooperate (transparent to the end user) to complete the processing as a single unified task. A client/server bond product ties the processors together to provide a single system image (illusion). Shareable resources are positioned as requester clients that access authorized services. The architecture is endlessly recursive; in turn, servers can become clients and request services of other servers on the network, and so on and so on.

This type of application development requires an entirely new set of programming skills. User interface programming is now written for graphical user interfaces, whether it be MS Windows, IBM OS/2, Apple Macintosh, or the UNIX X Window system. Using SQL and a network connection, the application can interface to a database residing on a remote server. The increased power of personal computer hardware enables critical database information to be stored on a relatively inexpensive standalone server. In addition, this server can be replaced with little or no change to the client applications.

A Cross-Product Language

You can apply the basic concepts introduced in this book in many environments. For example, Microsoft Access running on a single-user Windows application or SQL Server running with 100 user connections. One of SQL's greatest benefits is that it is truly a cross-platform language and a cross-product language. Because it is also what programmers refer to as a high-level or fourth-generation language (4GL), a large amount of work can be done in fewer lines of code.

Early Implementations

Oracle Corporation released the first commercial RDBMS that used SQL. Although the original versions were developed for VAX/VMS systems, Oracle was one of the first vendors to release a DOS version of its RDBMS. (Oracle is now available on more than 70 platforms.) In the mid-1980s, Sybase released its RDBMS, SQL Server. With client libraries for database access, support for stored procedures, and interoperability with various networks, SQL Server became a successful product, particularly in client/server environments.

One of the strongest points for both of these powerful database systems is their scalability across platforms. C language code (combined with SQL) written for Oracle on a PC is virtually identical to its counterpart written for an Oracle database running on a VAX system.

1

SQL and Client/Server Application Development

The common thread that runs throughout client/server application development is the use of SQL and relational databases. Also, using this database technology in a single-user business application positions the application for future growth.

An Overview of SQL

SQL is the de facto standard language used to manipulate and retrieve data from these relational databases. Through SQL, a programmer or database administrator can do the following:

- Modify a database's structure
- Change system security settings
- Add user permissions to databases or tables
- Query a database for information
- Update the contents of a database

NOTE

> The term *SQL* can be confusing. The *S*, for *Structured*, and the *L*, for *Language*, are straightforward enough, but the *Q* is a little misleading. *Q*, of course, stands for *Query*, which—if taken literally—would restrict you to asking the database questions. But SQL does much more than ask questions. With SQL you can also create tables, add data, delete data, splice data together, trigger actions based on changes to the database, and store your queries within your program or database.
>
> Unfortunately, there is no good substitute for *Query*. Obviously, Structured Add Modify Delete Join Store Trigger and Query Language (SAMDJSTQL) is a bit cumbersome. In the interest of harmony, we will stay with SQL. However, you now know that its function is bigger than its name.

The most commonly used statement in SQL is the SELECT statement (see Lesson 2, "Introducing the Query"), which retrieves data from the database and returns the data to the user. The EMPLOYEE table illustrates a typical example of a SELECT statement situation. In addition to the SELECT statement, SQL provides statements for creating new databases, tables, fields, and indexes as well as statements for inserting and deleting records. ANSI SQL also recommends a core group of data manipulation functions. As you will find out, many database systems also have tools for ensuring data integrity and enforcing security (see Lesson 14, "Controlling Transactions") that enable programmers to stop the execution of a group of commands if a certain condition occurs.

Popular SQL Implementations

This section introduces some of the more popular implementations of SQL. Implementations differ, each having its own strengths and weaknesses. Whereas some implementations of SQL have been developed for PC use and easy user interactivity, others have been developed to accommodate very large databases (VLDB). This section introduces selected key features of some implementations.

> **NOTE**
>
> In addition to serving as a SQL reference, this book also contains many practical software development examples. SQL is useful only when it solves your real-world problems, which occur inside your code.

MySQL

Examples of MySQL are used in this book to demonstrate command-line SQL syntax. MySQL (available at http://www.mysql.com/) downloads and installs with relative ease and is gaining popularity as a DBMS. Detailed steps for getting and installing MySQL are included as an appendix to this book. Refer to Appendix D, "Using MySQL for Exercises," for information about obtaining and installing MySQL on your computer.

Oracle

We use Oracle, which represents the larger corporate database world, to demonstrate command-line SQL and database management techniques. (These techniques are important because the days of the standalone machine are drawing to an end, as are the days when knowing one database or one operating system was enough.) In *command-line SQL* simple, standalone SQL statements are entered into Oracle's SQL*Plus tool. This tool then returns data to the screen for the user to see, or it performs the appropriate action on the database.

Most of the examples are directed toward the beginning programmer or first-time user of SQL. We begin with the simplest of SQL statements and advance to the topics of transaction management and stored procedure programming. The Oracle RDBMS comes with graphical tools for database, user, and object administration, as well as the SQL*Loader utility, which is used to import and export data to and from Oracle.

We chose the Oracle RDBMS for several reasons:

- It includes nearly all the tools needed to demonstrate the topics discussed in this book.

- It is available on virtually every platform in use today and is one of the most popular RDBMS products worldwide.

- A 30-day trial copy can be downloaded from Oracle Corporation's World Wide Web server (http://www.oracle.com).

1

Figure 1.4 shows SQL*Plus from this suite of tools.

FIGURE 1.4
Oracle's SQL*Plus.

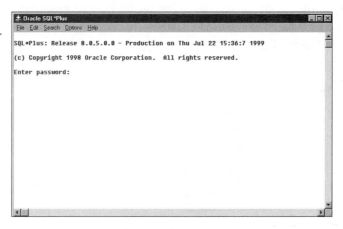

```
Oracle SQL*Plus                                                  _ □ X
File  Edit  Search  Options  Help

SQL*Plus: Release 8.0.5.0.0 - Production on Thu Jul 22 15:36:7 1999

(c) Copyright 1998 Oracle Corporation.  All rights reserved.

Enter password:
```

TIP

Keep in mind that nearly all the SQL code given in this book is portable to other database management systems. In cases where syntax differs greatly among different vendors' products, examples are given to illustrate these differences.

Microsoft SQL Server and Sybase

Sybase produced the original SQL Server implementation, which was originally designed for the OS/2 operating system. Later it entered into a code-development agreement with Microsoft, which ported the OS/2 application to its Windows platform. In 1993, the two companies decided to part ways. Now Sybase has renamed its product Sybase Adaptive Server Enterprise, and Microsoft has released a 2008 version of the SQL Server system.

IBM DB2

IBM originally developed SQL in the late 1970s for its DB2 platform. As the world's leading hardware vendor, IBM has also transformed its DB2 platform into what is known as the Universal Database line.

Open Database Connectivity

Open Database Connectivity (ODBC) is a functional library designed to provide a common Application Programming Interface (API) to underlying database systems. It communicates with the database through a library driver, just as Windows communicates with a printer via a printer driver. Depending on the database being used, a networking driver might be required to connect to a remote database. The architecture of ODBC is illustrated in Figure 1.5.

FIGURE 1.5
ODBC structure.

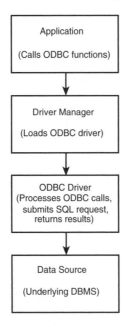

Application
(Calls ODBC functions)

Driver Manager
(Loads ODBC driver)

ODBC Driver
(Processes ODBC calls, submits SQL request, returns results)

Data Source
(Underlying DBMS)

The unique feature of ODBC (as compared to the Oracle or Sybase libraries) is that none of its functions is database-vendor specific. For instance, you can use the same code to perform queries against a Microsoft Access table or against an Informix database with little or no modification. Once again, it should be noted that most vendors add some proprietary extensions to the SQL standard, such as Microsoft's and Sybase's Transact-SQL and Oracle's PL/SQL.

You should always consult the documentation before beginning to work with a new data source. ODBC has developed into a standard adopted into many products, including Visual Basic, Visual C++, FoxPro, Borland Delphi, and PowerBuilder. As always, application developers need to weigh the benefit of using the emerging ODBC standard, which enables you to design code without regard for a specific database, versus the speed gained by using a database-specific function library. In other words, using ODBC will be more portable but slower than using the Oracle or Sybase libraries.

Embedding SQL in Application Programming

SQL was originally made an ANSI standard in 1986. The ANSI 1989 standard (often called SQL-89) defines three types of interfacing to SQL within an application program:

- Module Language—Uses procedures within programs. These procedures can be called by the application program and can return values to the program via parameter passing.
- Embedded SQL—Uses SQL statements embedded with actual program code. This method often requires the use of a precompiler to process the SQL statements. The standard defines statements for Pascal, FORTRAN, COBOL, and PL/1.
- Direct Invocation—Left up to the implementer.

Before the concept of dynamic SQL evolved, embedded SQL was the most popular way to use SQL within a programming environment. Embedded SQL, which is still used, uses *static* SQL—meaning that the SQL statement is compiled into the application and cannot be changed at runtime.

The principle is much the same as a compiler versus an interpreter. The performance for this type of SQL is good; however, it is not flexible—and cannot always meet the needs of today's changing business environments. Dynamic SQL is discussed shortly.

The ANSI 1992 standard (SQL-92) extended the language and became an international standard. It defines three levels of SQL compliance: entry, intermediate, and full. The new features that SQL-92 introduced include the following:

- Connections to databases
- Scrollable cursors
- Dynamic SQL
- Outer joins

The largest ANSI standard revision (SQL3) has five interrelated documents. Other documents may be added in the near future. The five parts are as follows:

- Part 1—SQL/Framework specifies the general requirements for conformity and defines the fundamental concepts of SQL.
- Part 2—SQL/Foundation defines the syntax and operations of SQL.
- Part 3—SQL/Call-Level Interface defines the interface for application programming to SQL.
- Part 4—SQL/Persistent Stored Modules defines the control structures that then define SQL routines. Part 4 also defines the modules that contain SQL routines.
- Part 5—SQL/Host Language Bindings defines how to embed SQL statements in application programs that are written in a standard programming language.

The SQL standard has two levels of minimal conference that a DBMS may claim: Core SQL Support and Enhanced SQL Support.

This book covers not only all these extensions but also some proprietary extensions used by RDBMS vendors. Dynamic SQL allows you to prepare the SQL statement at runtime. Although the performance for this type of SQL is not as good as that of embedded SQL, it provides the application developer (and user) with a great degree of flexibility. A call-level interface, such as ODBC or Sybase's DB-Library, is an example of dynamic SQL.

Call-level interfaces should not be a new concept to application programmers. When using ODBC, for instance, you simply fill a variable with your SQL statement and call the function to send the SQL statement to the database. Errors or results can be returned to the program through the use of other function calls designed for those purposes. Results are returned through a process known as the *binding* of variables.

Summary

This lesson covers some of the history and structure behind SQL. Because SQL and relational databases are so closely linked, this lesson also covers (albeit briefly) the history and function of relational databases. As you learned, databases are used by most organizations in one form or another to manage important corporate data. Without databases, organizations would be forced to continue storing all data in hard-copy format. Without a standard database language such as SQL, users would lack the robust and easy-to-use interface that allows communication with the database environment. Also, remember Dr. Codd's rules of the relational database model as they are the basis for all relational database management systems (RDBMSs). Lesson 2 is devoted to the most important component of SQL: the query.

Q&A

Q Why should I be concerned about SQL?

A Until recently, if you weren't working on a large database system, you probably
had only a passing knowledge of SQL. With the advent of client/server development tools (such as Visual Basic, Visual C++, ODBC, Borland's Delphi, and
Sybase's PowerBuilder) and the movement of several large databases (Oracle and
Sybase) to the PC platform, most business applications being developed today
require a working knowledge of SQL.

**Q Why do I need to know anything about relational database theory to
use SQL?**

A SQL was developed to service relational databases. Without a minimal understanding of relational database theory, you will not be able to use SQL effectively,
except in the most trivial cases.

**Q All the new GUI tools enable me to click a button to write SQL. Why should I
spend time learning to write SQL manually?**

A GUI tools have their place, and manually writing SQL has its place. Manually-
written SQL is generally more efficient than GUI-written SQL. Also, a GUI SQL
statement is not as easy to read as a manually-written SQL statement, and more
complex queries might be more cumbersome using a GUI tool than by writing the
query manually. Finally, knowing what is going on behind the scenes when you use
GUI tools will help you get the most out of them.

**Q So, if SQL is standardized, should I be able to program with SQL on any
database?**

A No, you will be able to program with SQL only on RDBMS databases that support
SQL, such as Microsoft Access, Oracle, Microsoft SQL Server, Sybase, and
Informix. Although each vendor's implementation will differ slightly from the oth-
ers, you should be able to use SQL with very few adjustments.

Workshop

The Workshop provides quiz questions to help solidify your understanding of the material covered, as well as exercises to provide you with experience in using what you have
learned. Try to answer the quiz and exercise questions before checking the answers in
Appendix A, "Answers."

Quiz

1. What makes SQL a nonprocedural language?
2. How can you tell whether a database is truly relational?
3. What can you do with SQL?
4. Name the model that separates data into distinct, unique sets.

Exercise

Refer to Appendix D. Download and install MySQL on your computer to prepare for hands-on exercises in the following lessons. We will be using MySQL for as many exercises as possible in this book because MySQL is mostly ANSI-compliant, free, and easy to download and use. Some MySQL exercises might utilize syntax that is slightly different than the Oracle examples we used. We will do our best to point out any differences or noncompliance with the ANSI standard that exist in MySQL.

LESSON 2
Introducing the Query

Welcome to Lesson 2! By the end of this lesson, you will be able to do the following:

- Understand what a query is and how it is used.

- Understand the syntax and use of SELECT and FROM.

- Select and list all rows and columns from a table.

- Select and list specific columns from a table.

- Select and list columns from different tables.

Exploring SQL's Background

To fully use the power of a relational database as described briefly in Lesson 1, "Getting Started with SQL," you need to communicate with it. The ultimate communication would be to turn to your computer and say, in a clear, distinct voice, "Show me all the left-handed, brown-eyed bean counters who have worked for this company for at least 10 years." A few of you might already be doing so (talking to your computer, not listing bean counters). Everyone else needs a more conventional way of retrieving information from the database. You can make this vital link through SQL's middle name, "Query."

As mentioned on Lesson 1, the name *Query* is really a misnomer in this context. A SQL query is not necessarily a question to the database. It can be a command to do one of the following:

- Build or delete a table

- Insert, modify, or delete rows or fields

- Search several tables for specific information and return the results in a specific order

- Modify security information

A query can also be a simple question to the database. To use this powerful tool, you need to learn how to write a SQL query.

Learning Basic Query Syntax

As you will find, the SQL syntax is quite flexible, although there are rules to follow as in any programming language. A simple query illustrates the basic syntax of a SQL SELECT statement. Pay close attention to the case, spacing, and logical separation of the components of each query by SQL keywords.

Syntax ▼

```
SELECT NAME, STARTTERM, ENDTERM
FROM PRESIDENTS
WHERE NAME = 'LINCOLN';
```

Analysis ▼

In this example, everything is capitalized, but it doesn't have to be. The preceding query would work just as well if it were written as follows:

Syntax ▼

```
select name, startterm, endterm
from presidents
where name = 'LINCOLN';
```

Analysis ▼

Notice that LINCOLN appears in capital letters in both examples. Although actual SQL statements are not case sensitive, references to data in a database are. For instance, many companies store their data in uppercase. In the preceding example, assume that the column name stores its contents in uppercase. Therefore, a query searching for "Lincoln" in the name column would not find any data to return. Check your implementation and/or company policies for any case requirements.

NOTE   Commands in SQL are not case sensitive.

Take another look at the sample query. Is there something magical in the spacing? Again, the answer is no. The following code would work as well:

Syntax ▼

```
select name, startterm, endterm from presidents where name = 'LINCOLN';
```

However, some regard for spacing and capitalization makes your statements much easier to read. It also makes your statements much easier to maintain when they become part of your project.

Another important feature of the sample query is the semicolon at the end of the expression. This punctuation mark tells the command-line SQL program that your query is complete.

2

If the magic isn't in the capitalization or the format, then just which elements are important? The answer is *keywords,* or the words in SQL that are reserved as a part of syntax. (Depending on the SQL statement, a keyword can be either a mandatory element of the statement or optional.) The keywords in the current example are

- SELECT
- FROM
- WHERE

Check the table of contents to see some of the SQL keywords you will learn and in which lessons. In this lesson, you learn about the SELECT and FROM keywords.

The Building Blocks of Data Retrieval: SELECT **and** FROM

As your experience with SQL grows, you will notice that you are typing the words SELECT and FROM more than any other words in the SQL vocabulary. They aren't as glamorous as CREATE or as ruthless as DROP, but they are indispensable to any conversation you hope to have with the computer concerning data retrieval.

This discussion starts with SELECT because most of your statements will start with SELECT:

Syntax ▼

```
SELECT   <COLUMNS NAMES>
```

NOTE

> Throughout this text there are examples of code and the results of that code. Examples that begin with
>
> ```
> sql>
> ```
>
> were created using Oracle. Examples that begin with
>
> ```
> mysql>
> ```
>
> were created using MySQL. These are known as PROMPTs. Examples of code that have no prompt are illustrations of syntax.

The basic SELECT statement couldn't be simpler. However, SELECT does not work alone. If you type just SELECT into your system, you might get the following response:

Input/Output ▼

```
SQL> SELECT;

SELECT
     *
ERROR at line 1:
ORA-00936: missing expression
```

If you were working in a MySQL database, the error might look something like this:

Input/Output ▼

```
mysql> select;
ERROR 1064: You have an error in your SQL syntax near '' at line 1
```

Analysis ▼

The asterisk under the offending line indicates where Oracle thinks the offense occurred. The error message tells you that something is missing. That something is the FROM clause:

Syntax ▼

```
FROM <TABLE>
```

Together, the statements SELECT and FROM begin to form a valid SQL statement. To clarify, the statement is the highest level of SQL syntax. A valid SQL statement is formed at the base level by SQL keywords that form clauses. So, in the following example

Syntax ▼

```
SELECT NAME FROM PRESIDENTS;
```

We would have the following logical breakdown:

Syntax ▼

```
Statement: SELECT NAME FROM PRESIDENTS;
Clause: SELECT NAME (SELECT clause)
            FROM PRESIDENTS (FROM clause)
Keywords: SELECT
                FROM
```

Now that you understand the basic syntax of a simple SQL statement, we will begin to put this knowledge into action.

Applying Query Concepts

Before going any further, look at the sample database that is the basis for the following examples. You can find a database table diagram, as well as the code examples for creating the tables, in Appendix B, "Code Examples to Create Tables." This database illustrates the basic functions of SELECT and FROM. In the real world, you would use the techniques described on Lesson 11, "Manipulating Data," to build this database, but for the purpose of describing how to use SELECT and FROM, assume it already exists. This example uses the CHECKS table to retrieve information about checks that an individual has written.

The CHECKS table in Oracle:

Output ▼

```
CHECK# PAYEE                  AMOUNT REMARKS
------ ----------------       ------- ------------------
     1 Ma Bell                   150 Have sons next time
     2 Reading R.R.           245.34 Train to Chicago
     3 Ma Bell                200.32 Cellular Phone
     4 Local Utilities            98 Gas
     5 Joes Stale $ Dent         150 Groceries
     6 Cash                       25 Wild Night Out
     7 Joans Gas                25.1 Gas
```

The CHECKS table in MySQL:

Output ▼

```
+--------+------------------+---------+---------------------+
| check  | payee            | amount  | remarks             |
+--------+------------------+---------+---------------------+
|      1 | Ma Bell          | 150.00  | Have sons next time |
|      2 | Reading R.R.     | 245.34  | Train to Chicago    |
|      3 | Ma Bell          | 200.32  | Celluar Phone       |
|      4 | Local Utilities  |  98.00  | Gas                 |
|      5 | Joes Stale $ Dent| 150.00  | Groceries           |
|      7 | Joans Gas        |  25.10  | Gas                 |
|      6 | Cash             |  25.00  | Wild Night Out      |
+--------+------------------+---------+---------------------+
```

NOTE	There are some obvious differences in the output between the two implementations. MySQL presents the output in a sort of framework, whereas Oracle presents the output in a more simple manner.

Writing Your First Query

The following SQL statement will select all columns from the CHECKS table. The asterisk (*) means "all."

Input ▼

```
SQL> select * from checks;
mysql> select * from checks;
```

It is important to understand that a SELECT is almost always accompanied by a FROM. As we progress through the lessons, you will begin to see patterns emerging that will allow you to more easily write your own queries in the future using the proper syntax.

The output from this SQL statement is the following, shown first in Oracle and then in MySQL:

Output ▼

```
CHECK# PAYEE                 AMOUNT REMARKS
------ ----------------      ------- -------------------
     1 Ma Bell                  150 Have sons next time
     2 Reading R.R.          245.34 Train to Chicago
     3 Ma Bell               200.32 Cellular Phone
     4 Local Utilities           98 Gas
```

```
     5 Joes Stale $ Dent          150 Groceries
     6 Cash                        25 Wild Night Out
     7 Joans Gas                 25.1 Gas

7 rows selected.

mysql> select * from checks;
+-------+------------------+--------+--------------------+
¦ check ¦ payee            ¦ amount ¦ remarks            ¦
+-------+------------------+--------+--------------------+
¦     1 ¦ Ma Bell          ¦ 150.00 ¦ Have sons next time¦
¦     2 ¦ Reading R.R.     ¦ 245.34 ¦ Train to Chicago   ¦
¦     3 ¦ Ma Bell          ¦ 200.32 ¦ Celluar Phone      ¦
¦     4 ¦ Local Utilities  ¦  98.00 ¦ Gas                ¦
¦     5 ¦ Joes Stale $ Dent¦ 150.00 ¦ Groceries          ¦
¦     7 ¦ Joans Gas        ¦  25.10 ¦ Gas                ¦
¦     6 ¦ Cash             ¦  25.00 ¦ Wild Night Out     ¦
+-------+------------------+--------+--------------------+
7 rows in set (0.20 sec)
```

2

Analysis ▼

The output looks just like the code in both examples. Notice that in the first example, columns 1 and 3 in the output statement are right-justified and that columns 2 and 4 are left-justified. This format follows the alignment convention in which numeric data types are right-justified and character data types are left-justified. In the MySQL example, column 1 is right-justified, but column 3 is centered even though they are of the same data type. Data types are discussed in Lesson 9, "Creating and Maintaining Tables." Be mindful to look at the documentation of the database platform you are using to ensure that you understand what other conventions they follow that might differ from what is shown in this book.

The asterisk (*) in SELECT * tells the database to return all the columns associated with the given table described in the FROM clause. The database determines the order in which to return the columns. This is an important thing to remember. The database is the ultimate determiner of what order the rows are returned to the user unless explicitly "told" how to return them. You cannot assume that the data will be returned to you in any order. For example, if you enter a set of employees into an Employee table of the database in the order of their birthdays and then turn around and write a SELECT * against that same table, there is a chance that the data will be returned to you in a different order. Later you will learn how to use the ORDER BY clause to force the returned dataset into a properly ordered sequence.

Terminating a SQL Statement

In some implementations of SQL, the semicolon at the end of the statement tells the interpreter that you are finished writing the query. For example, Oracle's SQL*Plus won't execute the query until it finds a semicolon (or a slash). MySQL will only execute the command if the interpreter finds the semicolon (;). On the other hand, some implementations of SQL do not use the semicolon as a terminator. For example, Microsoft SQL Server will execute the statement whether a semicolon terminator exists or not. So, the following set of queries would execute just the same in SQL Server:

Input ▼

```
> select * from checks;
> select * from checks
```

Selecting Individual Columns

Suppose you do not want to see every column in the database. You used SELECT * to find out what information was available, and now you want to concentrate on the check number and the amount. You type

Input ▼

```
SQL> SELECT CHECK#, amount from checks;
```

which returns

Output ▼

CHECK#	AMOUNT
1	150
2	245.34
3	200.32
4	98
5	150
6	25
7	25.1

7 rows selected.

Now you have the columns you want to see. Notice the use of uppercase and lowercase in the query. It did not affect the result.

What if you needed to order the columns differently from what is shown here?

Changing the Order of the Columns

Some of the preceding examples of a SQL statement used the * to select all columns from a table, the order of their appearance, from left to right in the output being determined by the database. To specify the order of the columns, you could type something like the following:

Input ▼

```
SQL> SELECT payee, remarks, amount, check# FROM checks;
mysql> select payee, `check`, remarks, amount from checks;
```

Analysis ▼

Notice that each column name is listed in the SELECT clause. The order in which the columns are listed is the order in which they will appear in the output. Notice the commas that separate the column names as well as the space between the final column name and the subsequent clause (in this case, FROM). The output would look like this:

Oracle:

Output ▼

```
PAYEE                REMARKS                 AMOUNT   CHECK#
---------------      --------------------    ------   ------
Ma Bell              Have sons next time        150        1
Reading R.R.         Train to Chicago        245.34        2
Ma Bell              Cellular Phone          200.32        3
Local Utilities      Gas                         98        4
Joes Stale $ Dent    Groceries                  150        5
Cash                 Wild Night Out              25        6
Joans Gas            Gas                       25.1        7

7 rows selected.
```

MySQL:

Output ▼

```
+-------------------+-------+--------------------+---------+
| payee             | check | remarks            | amount  |
+-------------------+-------+--------------------+---------+
| Ma Bell           |     1 | Have sons next time | 150.00 |
| Reading R.R.      |     2 | Train to Chicago    | 245.34 |
| Ma Bell           |     3 | Celluar Phone       | 200.32 |
| Local Utilities   |     4 | Gas                 |  98.00 |
| Joes Stale $ Dent |     5 | Groceries           | 150.00 |
| Joans Gas         |     7 | Gas                 |  25.10 |
| Cash              |     6 | Wild Night Out      |  25.00 |
```

2

Another way to write the same statement follows:

Oracle:

Input ▼

```
SELECT payee, remarks, amount, check#
FROM checks;
```

MySQL:

Input ▼

```
mysql> select payee, amount, remarks, `check`
    -> from checks;
```

Analysis ▼

Notice that the FROM clause has been carried over to the second line. This convention is a matter of personal taste when writing SQL code, but works to make your code much more readable. The output would look like this:

Oracle:

Output ▼

```
PAYEE               REMARKS               AMOUNT   CHECK#
----------------    ------------------    ------   ------
Ma Bell             Have sons next time     150       1
Reading R.R.        Train to Chicago     245.34       2
Ma Bell             Cellular Phone       200.32       3
Local Utilities     Gas                      98       4
Joes Stale $ Dent   Groceries               150       5
Cash                Wild Night Out           25       6
Joans Gas           Gas                    25.1       7

7 rows selected.
```

MySQL

Output ▼

```
+------------------+--------+--------------------+-------+
| payee            | amount | remarks            | check |
+------------------+--------+--------------------+-------+
| Ma Bell          | 150.00 | Have sons next time |   1  |
| Reading R.R.     | 245.34 | Train to Chicago    |   2  |
```

```
¦ Ma Bell             ¦ 200.32 ¦ Celluar Phone        ¦   3 ¦
¦ Local Utilities     ¦  98.00 ¦ Gas                  ¦   4 ¦
¦ Joes Stale $ Dent   ¦ 150.00 ¦ Groceries            ¦   5 ¦
¦ Joans Gas           ¦  25.10 ¦ Gas                  ¦   7 ¦
¦ Cash                ¦  25.00 ¦ Wild Night Out       ¦   6 ¦
+-------------------+--------+--------------------+------+
```

Analysis ▼

The output is identical because only the *format* of the statement changed. Now that you have established control over the order of the columns, you will be able to specify which columns you want to see.

Selecting Different Tables

Suppose you had a table called DEPOSITS with this structure:

Output ▼

```
DEPOSIT# WHOPAID                 AMOUNT REMARKS
-------- -----------             ------ -----------------
       1 Rich Uncle                 200 Take off Xmas list
       2 Employer                  1000 15 June Payday
       3 Credit Union               500 Loan
```

You would simply change the FROM clause to the desired table and type the following statement:

Input ▼

```
SQL> select * FROM deposits
```

The result is

```
DEPOSIT# WHOPAID                 AMOUNT REMARKS
-------- -----------             ------ -----------------
       1 Rich Uncle                 200 Take off Xmas list
       2 Employer                  1000 15 June Payday
       3 Credit Union               500 Loan
```

333 rows selected.

With a single change, you have a new data source.

Selecting Distinct Values

If you look at the original table, CHECKS, you see that some of the data repeats itself. For example, if you looked at the AMOUNT column using

Input ▼

```
SQL> select amount from checks;
```

you would see

Output ▼

```
    AMOUNT
---------
       150
    245.34
    200.32
        98
       150
        25
      25.1

7 rows selected.
```

Analysis ▼

Notice that the amount 150 is repeated. What if you wanted to see how many different amounts were in this column? Try this:

Input ▼

```
SQL> select DISTINCT amount from checks;
```

The result would be

Output ▼

```
    AMOUNT
---------
        25
      25.1
        98
       150
    200.32
    245.34

6 rows selected.
```

Analysis ▼

Notice that only six rows are selected. Because you specified DISTINCT, only one instance of the duplicated data is shown, which means that one fewer row is returned. Now what happens if you want to add an additional column to the result set?

Input ▼

```
SQL> select DISTINCT ,payee, amount from checks;
```

The result would be

2

Output ▼

```
PAYEE                 AMOUNT
------------          ---------
Ma Bell                   150
Reading R.R.           245.34
Ma Bell                200.32
Local Utilities            98
Joes Stale $ Dent         150
Cash                       25
Joans Gas                25.1

7 rows selected.
```

Analysis ▼

In this example, the DISTINCT keyword returned the distinct set of combinations of the columns—an important note to remember as we begin to write more complex statements.

The ALL keyword is implied in the basic SELECT statement. You almost never see ALL because SELECT <Column> FROM <Table> and SELECT ALL   <Column> FROM <Table> have the same result.

Try this example—for the first (and only!) time in your SQL career:

Input/Output ▼

```
SQL> SELECT ALL AMOUNT
  2>  FROM CHECKS;
    AMOUNT
---------
       150
    245.34
    200.32
        98
       150
```

```
     25
     25.1
```

```
7 rows selected.
```

It is the same as a SELECT AMOUNT. Who needs the extra keystrokes?

Summary

The keywords SELECT and FROM enable the query to retrieve data. You can make a broad statement and include all columns with a SELECT * statement, or you can rearrange or retrieve specific columns. The keyword DISTINCT limits the output so that you do not see duplicate values in either a column or set of columns. Lastly, the ALL keyword implies that you would want to see all results and is the default convention. In the next lesson, you learn how to make your queries even more selective.

Q&A

Q Where did this data come from and how do I connect to it?

A The data was created using the methods described on Lesson 11. The database connection depends on how you are using SQL. The method shown is the traditional command-line method used on commercial-quality databases. These databases have traditionally been the domain of the mainframe or the workstation, but recently they have migrated to the PC.

Q Okay, but if I don't use one of these databases, how will I use SQL?

A You can also use SQL from within a programming language. Embedded SQL is normally a language extension, most commonly seen in COBOL, where SQL is written inside of and compiled with the program. Microsoft has created an entire Application Programming Interface (API) that enables programmers to use SQL from inside Visual Basic, C, or C++. Libraries available from SQL Server and Oracle also enable you to put SQL in your programs. Borland has encapsulated SQL into database objects in Delphi. The concepts in this book apply to all these languages and more.

Workshop

The Workshop provides quiz questions to help solidify your understanding of the material covered, as well as exercises to provide you with experience in using what you have learned. Try to answer the quiz and exercise questions before checking the answers in Appendix A, "Answers."

Appendix B contains the CREATE TABLE statements that are needed for you to proceed. Appendix C, "Code Examples to Populate Tables," contains the INSERT statements that put data into your tables. Although we have yet to discuss the principles surrounding these statements, it is a good idea gain exposure to them as we progress. So, with that in mind, if you are using a MySQL database, type the following:

```
mysql> show databases;
+----------+
¦ Database ¦
+----------+
¦ PAYMENTS ¦
¦ matt     ¦
¦ mysql    ¦
¦ test     ¦
+----------+
4 rows in set (0.00 sec)
```

The databases mysql and test are standard with MySQL. We have created the databases matt and PAYMENTS as well. If you have not yet created your own database in MySQL, you can do so now. The name of the database can be your first name, your cat's first name—anything you like for right now. The next statement creates a database called BOB.

```
mysql> create database BOB;
```

Here is the result of the CREATE DATABASE statement:

```
Query OK, 1 row affected (0.00 sec)
```

To verify what you have just done, reissue the SHOW DATABASES command.

```
mysql> show databases;
+----------+
¦ Database ¦
+----------+
¦ BOB      ¦
¦ PAYMENTS ¦
¦ matt     ¦
¦ mysql    ¦
¦ test     ¦
+----------+
5 rows in set (0.00 sec)
```

To work within a database, you must tell MySQL that you want to use the specified database.

```
mysql> use BOB
Database changed
```

To see the tables in the database, type

```
mysql> show tables;
Empty set (0.00 sec)
```

We have no tables, so we cannot continue without creating them. The tables will do us little good, however, if there is no data in the table, so we will also have to put data in the table.

If you have access to an electronic version of the CREATE TABLE and INSERT statements, such as from the publisher's website, you can copy and paste them to your MySQL prompt. Otherwise, here is the syntax for the CREATE TABLE CHECKS statement:

```
mysql> create table checks
    ->(`check`         numeric(6)      not null,
    ->payee            varchar(20)     not null,
    ->amount           decimal(6,2)    not null,
    ->remarks          varchar(20)     not null);
```

The result you should receive in MySQL is

```
Query OK, 0 rows affected (0.05 sec)
```

Here are the INSERT statements:

```
insert into checks values
('1', 'MA BELL', '150', 'HAVE SONS NEXT TIME');
insert into checks values
('2', 'READING R.R.', '245.34', 'TRAIN TO CHICAGO');
insert into checks values
('3', 'MA BELL', '200.32', 'CELLULAR PHONE');
insert into checks values
('4', 'LOCAL UTILITIES', '98', 'GAS');
insert into checks values
('5', 'JOES STALE $ DENT', '150', 'GROCERIES');
insert into checks values
('6', 'CASH', '25', 'WILD NIGHT OUT');
insert into checks values
('7', 'JOANS GAS', '25.1', 'GAS');
```

Congratulations! You should now have successfully created and populated your first database.

Quiz

1. Do the following statements return the same output?

```
SELECT * FROM CHECKS;
select * from checks;
```

2. None of the following queries work. Why not?

   a.
   ```
   Select *
   ```

   b.
   ```
   Select * from checks
   ```

   c.
   ```
   Select amount name payee FROM checks;
   ```

3. Which of the following SQL statements will work?

   a.
   ```
   select *
   from checks;
   ```

   b.
   ```
   select * from checks;
   ```

   c.
   ```
   select * from checks
   ```

4. Write a SQL statement to return only the check number and amount from the CHECKS table.

5. Write a SQL statement to return only the DISTINCT payee names from the CHECKS table.

6. Write a SQL statement in the MySQL database to return the DISTINCT set of payee names and amounts from the CHECKS table. Does the order of the columns matter?

7. Is the ordering of either the column names from left to right or the ordering of the data guaranteed by using the following statement?

```
select * from checks;
```

2

Exercises

1. Using the CHECKS table from earlier in this lesson, write a query to return just the check numbers and the remarks.

2. Rewrite the query from exercise 1 so that the remarks will appear as the first column in your query results.

3. Using the CHECKS table, write a query to return all the DISTINCT remarks.

4. Write a query that presents only the CHECK and AMOUNT columns from the CHECKS table.

5. In MySQL, show all databases.

6. In MySQL, use another database.

7. In MySQL, show all tables in the current database.

8. In MySQL, go back to or use your original database (the one that has the CHECKS table in it).

LESSON 3
Expressions, Conditions, and Operators

In Lesson 2, "Introducing the Query," you used SELECT and FROM to manipulate data in interesting (and useful) ways. In this lesson, you learn more about SELECT and FROM. You will expand the basic query with some new terms, a new clause, and a group of handy items called *operators*. By the end of this lesson, you will

- Know what an expression is and how to use it.

- Know what a condition is and how to use it.

- Be familiar with the basic uses of the WHERE clause.

- Be able to use arithmetic, comparison, character, logical, and set operators.

- Have a working knowledge of some miscellaneous operators.

NOTE	We used Oracle and MySQL to generate this lesson's examples. Other implementations of SQL might differ slightly in the way in which commands are entered or output is displayed, but the results are basically the same for all implementations that conform to the ANSI standard.

NOTE	This lesson is one of the longest in the book and also one of the most important as it lays the foundation for most of the other lessons. In this lesson we provide many examples for you to absorb. Do not try to remember every specific example but rather learn the concepts behind them. The lessons to follow will give you plenty of practice in implementing what you will learn.

Working with Query Expressions

The definition of an expression is simple: An *expression* returns a value. Expression types are very broad, covering different data types such as String, Numeric, and Boolean. In fact, pretty much anything following a clause (SELECT or FROM, for example) is an expression. In the following example, AMOUNT is an expression that returns the value contained in the AMOUNT column:

Syntax ▼

```
SELECT AMOUNT FROM CHECKS;
```

Of course, the following is also considered a numerical expression. Remember that the key to an expression is that it returns a value.

Syntax ▼

```
SELECT AMOUNT*10 FROM CHECKS;
```

In the following statement, NAME, ADDRESS, PHONE, and ADDRESSBOOK are expressions:

Syntax ▼

```
SELECT NAME, ADDRESS, PHONE
FROM ADDRESSBOOK;
```

Now, examine the following WHERE clause:

Syntax ▼

```
WHERE NAME = 'BROWN'
```

It contains a condition, NAME = 'BROWN', which is an example of a Boolean expression. NAME = 'BROWN' will be either TRUE or FALSE, depending on the condition =.

Placing Conditions on Queries

If you ever want to find a particular item or group of items in your database, you need one or more conditions. Conditions are contained in the WHERE clause. In the preceding example, the condition is

Syntax ▼

```
NAME = 'BROWN'
```

To find everyone in your organization who worked more than 100 hours last month, your condition would be

Syntax ▼

```
NUMBEROFHOURS > 100
```

Conditions enable you to make selective queries. In their most common form, conditions comprise a variable, a constant, and a comparison operator. In the first example, the variable is NAME, the constant is 'BROWN', and the comparison operator is =. In the second example, the variable is NUMBEROFHOURS, the constant is 100, and the comparison operator is >. You need to know about two more elements before you can write conditional queries: the WHERE clause and operators.

The syntax of the WHERE clause is

Syntax ▼

3

```
WHERE <SEARCH CONDITION>
```

SELECT, FROM, and WHERE are the three most frequently used clauses in SQL. WHERE simply causes your queries to be more selective. Without the WHERE clause, the most useful thing you could do with a query is display all records in the selected table(s)—for example,

Input ▼

```
SQL> SELECT * FROM BIKES;
```

lists all rows of data in the table BIKES.

Output ▼

NAME	FRAMESIZE	COMPOSITION	MILESRIDDEN	TYPE
TREK 2300	22.5	CARBON FIBER	3500	RACING
BURLEY	22	STEEL	2000	TANDEM
GIANT	19	STEEL	1500	COMMUTER
FUJI	20	STEEL	500	TOURING
SPECIALIZED	16	STEEL	100	MOUNTAIN
CANNONDALE	22.5	ALUMINUM	3000	RACING

6 rows selected.

If you wanted a particular bike, you could type

Input ▼

```
SQL> SELECT *
  2 FROM BIKES
  3 WHERE NAME = 'BURLEY';
```

which would yield only one record:

Output ▼

NAME	FRAMESIZE	COMPOSITION	MILESRIDDEN	TYPE
BURLEY	22	STEEL	2000	TANDEM

1 rows selected.

These simple examples show how you can place a condition on the data that you want to retrieve.

Learning How to Use Operators

Operators are the elements you use inside an expression to articulate how you want specified conditions to retrieve data. Operators fall into six groups: arithmetic, comparison, character, logical, set, and miscellaneous. SQL utilizes three types of operators: arithmetic, comparison, and logical.

Arithmetic Operators

The arithmetic operators are plus (+), minus (-), divide (/), multiply (*), and modulo (%). The first four are self-explanatory. Modulo returns the integer remainder of a division. Here are two examples:

```
5 % 2 = 1
6 % 2 = 0
```

The modulo operator does not work with data types that have decimals, such as Real or Number.

If you place several of these arithmetic operators in an expression without any parentheses, the operators are resolved in this order: multiplication, division, modulo, addition, and subtraction. For example, the expression

```
2*6+9/3
```

equals

```
12 + 3 = 15
```

However, the expression

```
2 * (6 + 9) / 3
```

equals

```
2 * 15 / 3 = 10
```

Watch where you put those parentheses! Sometimes the expression does exactly what you tell it to do, rather than what you want it to do. The same holds true for SQL.

The following sections examine the arithmetic operators in some detail and give you a chance to write some queries.

3

Plus (+)

You can use the plus sign in several ways. Type the following statement to display the PRICE table:

Input/Output ▼

```
SQL> SELECT * FROM PRICE;
ITEM            WHOLESALE
--------------- ---------
TOMATOES              .34
POTATOES              .51
BANANAS               .67
TURNIPS               .45
CHEESE                .89
APPLES                .23
6 rows selected.
```

Now type

Input ▼

```
SQL> SELECT ITEM, WHOLESALE, WHOLESALE + 0.15
  2 FROM PRICE;
```

Here the + adds 15 cents to each price to produce the following:

Output ▼

```
ITEM            WHOLESALE WHOLESALE+0.15
--------------- --------- ---------------
TOMATOES             .34             .49
POTATOES            .51             .66
BANANAS             .67             .82
TURNIPS             .45             .60
CHEESE              .89            1.04
APPLES              .23             .38
6 rows selected.
```

Analysis ▼

What is this last column with the unattractive column heading WHOLESALE+0.15? It's not in the original table. SQL allows you to create a virtual or derived column by combining or modifying existing columns.

Retype the original entry:

Input ▼

```
SQL> SELECT * FROM PRICE;
```

The following table results:

Output ▼

```
ITEM            WHOLESALE
--------------- ---------
TOMATOES             .34
POTATOES            .51
BANANAS             .67
TURNIPS             .45
CHEESE              .89
APPLES              .23
6 rows selected.
```

Analysis ▼

The output confirms that the original data has not been changed and that the column heading WHOLESALE+0.15 is not a permanent part of it. In fact, the column heading is so unattractive that you should do something about it.

Type the following:

Input ▼

```
SQL> SELECT ITEM, WHOLESALE, (WHOLESALE + 0.15) RETAIL
  2 FROM PRICE;
```

Here's the result:

Output ▼

```
ITEM            WHOLESALE    RETAIL
--------------- ---------    ------
TOMATOES             .34       .49
POTATOES             .51       .66
BANANAS              .67       .82
TURNIPS              .45       .60
CHEESE               .89      1.04
APPLES               .23       .38
6 rows selected.
```

Analysis ▼

This is wonderful! Not only can you create new output columns, but you can also rename them on the fly. You can rename any of the columns using the syntax <column_name> <alias>. (Note the space between the column_name and alias.)

For example, the query

Input ▼

```
SQL> SELECT ITEM PRODUCE, WHOLESALE, WHOLESALE + 0.25 RETAIL
  2 FROM PRICE;
```

renames the columns as follows:

Output ▼

```
PRODUCE         WHOLESALE    RETAIL
--------------- ---------    -------
TOMATOES             .34       .59
POTATOES             .51       .76
BANANAS              .67       .92
TURNIPS              .45       .70
CHEESE               .89      1.14
APPLES               .23       .48
6 rows in set (0.00 sec)
```

NOTE

Some implementations of SQL use the syntax <column name = alias>. The preceding example would be written as follows:

```
SQL> SELECT ITEM = PRODUCE,
  2 WHOLESALE,
  3 WHOLESALE + 0.25 = RETAIL,
  4 FROM PRICE;
```

Alternatively, the SQL standard allows you to use the AS keyword, which is implemented in many database systems and looks like the following:

```
SQL> SELECT ITEM AS PRODUCE,
  2 WHOLESALE,
   3 WHOLESALE + 0.25 = RETAIL,
   4 FROM PRICE;
```

Check your implementation for the exact syntax.

NOTE

MySQL allows you to present your column alias in mixed case.

You might be wondering what use aliasing is if you are not using command-line SQL. Fair enough. Have you ever wondered how report builders work? Some day, when you are asked to write a report generator, you'll remember this and not spend weeks reinventing what Dr. Codd and IBM have wrought.

In some implementations of SQL, the plus sign does double duty as a character operator. You'll see that side of the plus sign a little later in this lesson.

Minus (-)

Minus also has two uses. First, it can change the sign of a number. You can use the table HILOW to demonstrate this function.

Input/Output ▼

```
SQL> SELECT * FROM HILOW;
STATE          LOWS     HIGHS
-----          ----     -----
CA             -50       120
FL              20       110
LA              15        99
ND             -70       101
NE             -60       100
```

For example, here's a way to manipulate the data:

Input/Output ▼

```
SQL> SELECT STATE, - LOWS, - HIGHS
  2 FROM HILOW;
STATE          LOWS     HIGHS
-----          ----     -----
CA               50      -120
FL              -20      -110
LA              -15       -99
ND               70      -101
NE               60      -100
```

NOTE	Notice that the minus sign was reversed on the temperatures.

3

The second (and obvious) use of the minus sign is to subtract one column from another—for example,

Input/Output ▼

```
SQL> SELECT STATE,
  2  LOWS,
  3  HIGHS,
  4  (-HIGHS - LOWS) DIFFERENCE
  5  FROM HILOW;


STATE          LOWS    HIGHS   DIFFERENCE
-----          ----    -----   ----------
CA              -50      120          170
FL               20      110           90
LA               15       99           84
ND              -70      101          171
NE              -60      100          160
```

If you accidentally use the minus sign on a character field, you get something like this:

Input/Output ▼

```
SQL> SELECT -STATE FROM HILOW;

ERROR:
ORA-01722: invalid number
no rows selected
```

The exact error message varies with implementation. Here is an example using MySQL:

Input/Output ▼

```
mysql> select -state
    -> from hilow;
+--------+
| -state |
+--------+
|      0 |
|      0 |
|      0 |
|      0 |
+--------+
4 rows in set (0.00 sec)
```

MySQL evaluated the SELECT statement, but as you can see, the results are rather meaningless.

Divide (/)

The division operator has only the one obvious meaning. Using the table PRICE, type the following:

Input/Output ▼

```
SQL> SELECT * FROM PRICE;
ITEM            WHOLESALE
--------        ---------
TOMATOES              .34
POTATOES             .51
BANANAS              .67
TURNIPS              .45
CHEESE               .89
APPLES               .23
6 rows selected.

mysql> select * from price;
+----------+-----------+
| item     | wholesale |
+----------+-----------+
| TOMATOES |      0.34 |
| POTATOES |      0.51 |
| BANANAS  |      0.67 |
| TURNIPS  |      0.45 |
| CHEESE   |      0.89 |
| APPLES   |      0.23 |
+----------+-----------+

6 rows in set (0.26 sec)
```

You can show the effects of a two-for-one sale by typing the next statement:

Input/Output ▼

```
SQL> SELECT ITEM, WHOLESALE, (WHOLESALE/2) SALEPRICE
  2  FROM PRICE;
ITEM            WHOLESALE SALEPRICE
--------------- --------- ---------
TOMATOES              .34       .17
POTATOES              .51      .255
BANANAS               .67      .335
TURNIPS               .45      .225
CHEESE                .89      .445
APPLES                .23      .115
6 rows selected.
```

The same example in MySQL would be:

Input/Output ▼

```
mysql> select ITEM, WHOLESALE, (WHOLESALE/2) Saleprice
    -> from price;
+----------+-----------+-----------+
| ITEM     | WHOLESALE | Saleprice |
+----------+-----------+-----------+
| TOMATOES |      0.34 |    0.1700 |
| POTATOES |      0.51 |    0.2550 |
| BANANAS  |      0.67 |    0.3350 |
| TURNIPS  |      0.45 |    0.2250 |
| CHEESE   |      0.89 |    0.4450 |
| APPLES   |      0.23 |    0.1150 |
+----------+-----------+-----------+
6 rows in set (0.26 sec)
```

The use of division in the preceding SELECT statement is straightforward (except that coming up with half pennies can be tough).

Multiply (*)

The multiplication operator is also straightforward. Again, using the PRICE table, type the following:

Input/Output ▼

```
SQL> SELECT * FROM PRICE;
ITEM            WHOLESALE
--------------- ---------
TOMATOES              .34
POTATOES              .51
```

3

```
BANANAS              .67
TURNIPS              .45
CHEESE               .89
APPLES               .23
6 rows selected.
```

The output from this query reflects an across-the-board 10% discount. The actual data in the table has not changed.

Input/Output ▼

```
SQL> SQL> SELECT ITEM, WHOLESALE, WHOLESALE * 0.9 NEWPRICE
   2 FROM PRICE;

ITEM              WHOLESALE  NEWPRICE
---------------   ---------  --------
TOMATOES               .34      .306
POTATOES               .51      .459
BANANAS                .67      .603
TURNIPS                .45      .405
CHEESE                 .89      .801
APPLES                 .23      .207
6 rows selected.
```

The same example in MySQL would be:

Input/Output ▼

```
mysql> select Item,
    -> Wholesale, Wholesale * 0.9 "New Price"
    -> from price;
+-----------+-----------+-----------+
¦ Item      ¦ Wholesale ¦ New Price ¦
+-----------+-----------+-----------+
¦ TOMATOES  ¦      0.34 ¦      0.31 ¦
¦ POTATOES  ¦      0.51 ¦      0.46 ¦
¦ BANANAS   ¦      0.67 ¦      0.60 ¦
¦ TURNIPS   ¦      0.45 ¦      0.41 ¦
¦ CHEESE    ¦      0.89 ¦      0.80 ¦
¦ APPLES    ¦      0.23 ¦      0.21 ¦
+-----------+-----------+-----------+
6 rows in set (0.00 sec)
```

NOTE   One last thing about aliases: You can give your column a two-word heading by using quotes to surround your aliases. Sometimes this will be single quotes and sometimes it will be double quotes. Please check your specific implementation's documentation to see what it allows.

These operators enable you to perform powerful calculations in a SELECT statement.

Modulo (%)

The modulo operator returns the integer remainder of the division operation. Using the table REMAINS, type the following:

Input/Output ▼

```
SQL> SELECT * FROM REMAINS;
NUMERATOR   DENOMINATOR
---------   -----------
       10             5
        8             3
       23             9
       40            17
     1024            16
       85            34
6 rows selected.
```

The same example in MySQL would be:

Input/Output ▼

```
mysql> select * from remains;
+-----------+-------------+
| numerator | denominator |
+-----------+-------------+
|        10 |           5 |
|         8 |           3 |
|        23 |           9 |
|        40 |          17 |
|      1024 |          16 |
|        85 |          34 |
+-----------+-------------+
6 rows in set (0.43 sec)
```

You can also create a new output column, REMAINDER, to hold the values of NUMERATOR % DENOMINATOR:

Input/Output ▼

```
SQL> SELECT NUMERATOR,
  2 DENOMINATOR,
  3 NUMERATOR%DENOMINATOR REMAINDER
  4 FROM REMAINS;

NUMERATOR DENOMINATOR REMAINDER
```

3

```
        10            5            0
         8            3            2
        23            9            5
        40           17            6
      1024           16            0
        85           34           17
6 rows selected.
```

The same example in MySQL would be:

Input/Output ▼

```
mysql> select numerator, denominator, numerator%denominator remainder
    -> from remains;
+-----------+-------------+------------------------+
| numerator | denominator | remainder              |
+-----------+-------------+------------------------+
|        10 |           5 |                      0 |
|         8 |           3 |                      2 |
|        23 |           9 |                      5 |
|        40 |          17 |                      6 |
|      1024 |          16 |                      0 |
|        85 |          34 |                     17 |
+-----------+-------------+------------------------+
6 rows in set (0.01 sec)
```

Analysis ▼

Some implementations of SQL implement modulo as a function called MOD (see Lesson 7, "Molding Data with Built-in Functions"). The following statement produces results that are identical to the results in the preceding statement:

Input/Output ▼

```
SQL> SELECT NUMERATOR,
   2 DENOMINATOR,
   3 MOD(NUMERATOR,DENOMINATOR) REMAINDER
   4 FROM REMAINS;

NUMERATOR DENOMINATOR REMAINDER
--------- ----------- ---------
        10            5            0
         8            3            2
        23            9            5
        40           17            6
      1024           16            0
        85           34           17
6 rows selected.
```

The same example in MySQL would be:

Input/Output ▼

```
mysql> select numerator, denominator,
    -> mod(numerator,denominator) remainder
    -> from remains;
+-------------+--------------+-----------------------------+
| numerator   | denominator  | remainder                   |
+-------------+--------------+-----------------------------+
|          10 |            5 |                           0 |
|           8 |            3 |                           2 |
|          23 |            9 |                           5 |
|          40 |           17 |                           6 |
|        1024 |           16 |                           0 |
|          85 |           34 |                          17 |
+-------------+--------------+-----------------------------+
6 rows in set (0.00 sec)
```

Precedence

Precedence is the order in which an implementation will evaluate different operators in the same expression. This section examines the use of precedence in a SELECT statement. Using the table PRECEDENCE, type the following:

Input/Output ▼

```
SQL> SELECT * FROM PRECEDENCE;
        N1         N2         N3         N4
   -------    -------    -------    -------
         1          2          3          4
        13         24         35         46
         9          3         23          5
        63          2         45          3
         7          2          1          4
5 rows selected.

mysql> select * from precedence;
+----+----+----+----+
| n1 | n2 | n3 | n4 |
+----+----+----+----+
|  1 |  2 |  3 |  4 |
| 13 | 24 | 35 | 46 |
|  9 |  3 | 23 |  5 |
| 63 |  2 | 45 |  3 |
|  7 |  2 |  1 |  4 |
+----+----+----+----+
5 rows in set (0.00 sec)
```

3

Use the following code segment to test precedence:

Input/Output ▼

```
SQL> SELECT
  2 N1+N2*N3/N4,
  3 (N1+N2)*N3/N4,
  4 N1+(N2*N3)/N4
  5 FROM PRECEDENCE;
N1+N2*N3/N4 (N1+N2)*N3/N4 N1+(N2*N3)/N4
----------- ------------- -------------
        2.5          2.25           2.5
    31.26087     28.152174      31.26087
        22.8          55.2          22.8
          93           975            93
         7.5          2.25           7.5

5 rows selected.
mysql> select n1+n2*n3/n4,
    -> (n1+n2)*n3/n4,
    -> n1+(n2*n3)/n4
    -> from precedence;
+-------------+-------------+-------------+
| n1+n2*n3/n4 |(n1+n2)*n3/n4| n1+(n2*n3)/n4 |
+-------------+-------------+-------------+
|       2.50  |          9  |        2.50  |
|      31.26  |       1295  |       31.26  |
|      22.80  |        276  |       22.80  |
|      93.00  |       2925  |       93.00  |
|       7.50  |          9  |        7.50  |
+-------------+-------------+-------------+
5 rows in set (0.00 sec)
```

Notice that the first and last columns are identical. If you added a fourth column
`N1+N2*(N3/N4)`, its values would also be identical to those of the current first and last
columns. The rules for precedence follow the usual algebraic set in that values are normally executed in the following order moving left to right.

1. Parentheses
2. Multiplication/division
3. Addition/subtraction

Analysis ▼

Quite simply, values inside parentheses are computed first, then multiplication or
division operations are performed, and lastly addition and subtraction operations are

performed. These rules are important to remember as you start to write more complicated calculations to analyze data.

Comparison Operators

True to their name, comparison operators compare expressions and return one of three values: TRUE, FALSE, or UNKNOWN. Wait a minute! Unknown? TRUE and FALSE are self-explanatory, but what is UNKNOWN?

To understand how you could get an UNKNOWN, you need to know a little about the concept of NULL. In database terms, NULL is the absence of data in a field. It does not mean that a column has a zero or a blank in it. A zero or a blank is a value. NULL means nothing is in that field.

If you make a comparison such as Field = 9 and the only acceptable value for Field is NULL, the comparison will come back UNKNOWN. Because UNKNOWN is an uncomfortable condition, most flavors of SQL change UNKNOWN to FALSE and provide a special operator, IS NULL, to test for a NULL condition.

Here's an example of NULL: Suppose an entry in the PRICE table does not contain a value for WHOLESALE. The results of a query might look like this:

Input/Output ▼

```
SQL> SELECT * FROM PRICE;

ITEM            WHOLESALE
---------       ---------
TOMATOES            .34
POTATOES            .51
BANANAS             .67
TURNIPS             .45
CHEESE              .89
APPLES              .23
ORANGES

7 rows selected.
```

Analysis ▼

Notice that no value appears in the WHOLESALE field position for ORANGES. The value of the field WHOLESALE for ORANGES is NULL. The NULL is noticeable in this case because it is in a numeric column. However, if the NULL appeared in the ITEM column, it would be impossible to tell the difference between NULL and a blank.

Try to find the NULL:

Input/Output ▼

```
SQL> SELECT *
  2 FROM PRICE
  3 WHERE WHOLESALE IS NULL;
ITEM             WHOLESALE
--------         ---------
ORANGES

1 rows selected.
```

As you can see by the output, ORANGES is the only item whose value for WHOLESALE is NULL, or does not contain a value. What if you use the equal sign (=) instead?

Input/Output ▼

```
SQL>SELECT *
  2 FROM PRICE
  3 WHERE WHOLESALE = NULL;

no rows selected
```

Analysis ▼

You wouldn't find anything because the comparison WHOLESALE = NULL returned a FALSE—the result was unknown. It would be more appropriate to use an IS NULL instead of =, changing the WHERE statement to WHERE WHOLESALE IS NULL. In this case, you would get all the rows where a NULL existed.

This example also illustrates both the use of the most common comparison operator (=) and the playground of all comparison operators, the WHERE clause. You already know about the WHERE clause, so here's a brief look at the equal sign.

Equal Sign (=)

Earlier today you saw how some implementations of SQL use the equal sign in the SELECT clause to assign an alias. In the WHERE clause, the equal sign is the most commonly used comparison operator. Used alone, the equal sign is a very convenient way of selecting one value out of many. Try this:

Input/Output ▼

```
SQL> SELECT * FROM FRIENDS;
LASTNAME         FIRSTNAME        AREACODE PHONE    ST ZIP
--------         ---------        -------- -------- --------
BUNDY            AL                    100 555-1111 IL 22333
```

```
MEZA            AL                      200 555-2222 UK
MERRICK         BUD                     300 555-6666 CO 80212
MAST            JD                      381 555-6767 LA 23456
BULHER          FERRIS                  345 555-3223 IL 23332
5 rows selected.
```

Let's find JD's row. (On a short list this task appears trivial, but you might have more friends than we do—or you might have a list with thousands of records.)

Input/Output ▼

```
SQL> SELECT *
  2 FROM FRIENDS
  3 WHERE FIRSTNAME = 'JD';

LASTNAME        FIRSTNAME       AREACODE     PHONE        ST      ZIP
--------        ---------       --------     --------     ----    ----
MAST            JD                   381     555-6767     LA      23456
1 rows selected.
mysql> select * from friends
    -> where firstname = 'JD';
+----------+-----------+----------+----------+----+-------+
¦ lastname ¦ firstname ¦ areacode ¦ phone    ¦ st ¦ zip   ¦
+----------+-----------+----------+----------+----+-------+
¦ MAST     ¦ JD        ¦      381 ¦ 555-6767 ¦ LA ¦ 23456 ¦
+----------+-----------+----------+----------+----+-------+
1 row in set (0.37 sec)
```

We got the result that we expected. Try this:

Input/Output ▼

```
SQL> SELECT *
  2 FROM FRIENDS
  3 WHERE FIRSTNAME = 'AL';
LASTNAME        FIRSTNAME       AREACODE PHONE     ST ZIP
--------        ---------       -------- --------  -- -----
BUNDY           AL                   100 555-1111  IL 22333
MEZA            AL                   200 555-2222  UK
2 rows selected.
```

NOTE

Here you see that = can pull in multiple records. Notice that ZIP is blank on the second record. ZIP is a character field (you learn how to create and populate tables in Lesson 9, "Creating and Maintaining Tables"), and in this particular record, the NULL demonstrates that a NULL in a character field is impossible to differentiate from a blank field.

3

Here's another very important lesson concerning case sensitivity:

Input/Output ▼

```
SQL>  SELECT FIRSTNAME FROM FRIENDS
   2 WHERE FIRSTNAME = 'BUD';

FIRSTNAME
---------------
BUD
1 row selected.
mysql> select firstname from friends where firstname = 'BUD';
+-----------+
¦ firstname ¦
+-----------+
¦ BUD       ¦
+-----------+
1 row in set (0.00 sec)
```

Now try this:

Input/Output ▼

```
SQL> select FIRSTNAME from friends
   2 where firstname = 'Bud';

no rows selected.
mysql> select firstname
    -> from friends
    -> where firstname = 'bud';
+-----------+
¦ firstname ¦
+-----------+
¦ BUD       ¦
+-----------+
1 row in set (0.01 sec)
```

Analysis ▼

Even though SQL syntax is not case sensitive, data within it is, at least in some implementations. As you can see in the preceding examples, data stored in an Oracle database (SQL*Plus) is case sensitive, whereas the MySQL example demonstrates the opposite.

Most companies prefer to store data in uppercase to provide data consistency. I recommend that you always store data either in all uppercase or in all lowercase, regardless of what type of database you are working in. Mixing case might create difficulties when you try to retrieve accurate data through comparisons in the WHERE clause.

Greater Than (>) and Greater Than or Equal To (>=)

The greater than operator (>) works like this:

Input/Output ▼

```
SQL> SELECT *
  2 FROM FRIENDS
  3 WHERE AREACODE > 300;
LASTNAME        FIRSTNAME      AREACODE PHONE    ST ZIP
--------        ---------      -------- -------- -- ------
MAST            JD                  381 555-6767 LA 23456
BULHER          FERRIS              345 555-3223 IL 23332
```

```
2 rows selected.
```

This example found all the area codes greater than (but not including) 300. To include 300, type this:

Input/Output ▼

```
SQL> SELECT *
  2 FROM FRIENDS
  3 WHERE AREACODE >= 300;
LASTNAME        FIRSTNAME      AREACODE PHONE    ST ZIP
--------        ---------      -------- -------- -- -----
MERRICK         BUD                 300 555-6666 CO 80212
MAST            JD                  381 555-6767 LA 23456
BULHER          FERRIS              345 555-3223 IL 23332
3 rows selected.
```

```
mysql> select * from friends
    -> where areacode >= 300;
+----------+-----------+----------+----------+----+-------+
| lastname | firstname | areacode | phone    | st | zip   |
+----------+-----------+----------+----------+----+-------+
| MERRICK  | BUD       |      300 | 555-6666 | CO | 80212 |
| MAST     | JD        |      381 | 555-6767 | LA | 23456 |
| BULHER   | FERRIS    |      345 | 555-3223 | IL | 23332 |
+----------+-----------+----------+----------+----+-------+
3 rows in set (0.34 sec)
```

With this change you get area codes starting at 300 and going up. You could achieve the same results with the statement AREACODE > 299.

NOTE	Notice that no quotes surround 300 in either of the two prior SQL statements. Number-defined fields do not require quotes.

Less Than (<) and Less Than or Equal To (<=)

As you might expect, these comparison operators work the same way as > and >= work, only in reverse:

Input/Output ▼

```
SQL> SELECT *
  2 FROM FRIENDS
  3 WHERE ST < 'LA';
LASTNAME          FIRSTNAME          AREACODE PHONE     ST ZIP
.........         .........          ........ ........  .. .....
BUNDY             AL                      100 555-1111 IL 22333
MERRICK           BUD                     300 555-6666 CO 80212
BULHER            FERRIS                  345 555-3223 IL 23332
3 rows selected.

mysql> select * from friends where st < 'LA';
+----------+-----------+----------+----------+----+-------+
| lastname | firstname | areacode | phone    | st | zip   |
+----------+-----------+----------+----------+----+-------+
| BUNDY    | AL        |      100 | 555-1111 | IL | 22333 |
| MERRICK  | BUD       |      300 | 555-6666 | CO | 80212 |
| BULHER   | FERRIS    |      345 | 555-3223 | IL | 23332 |
+----------+-----------+----------+----------+----+-------+
3 rows in set (0.00 sec)
```

> **NOTE**　In an Oracle database, if the column has only two characters, the column name is shortened to two characters in the returned rows. If the column name had been COWS, it would come out CO. The widths of AREACODE and PHONE are wider than their column names, so they are not truncated.

Analysis ▼

Wait a minute. Did you just use < on a character field? Of course you did. You can use any of these operators on any data type. The result varies by data type. For example, use lowercase in the following state search:

Input/Output ▼

```
SQL> SELECT *
  2 FROM FRIENDS
  3 WHERE STATE < 'la';
LASTNAME          FIRSTNAME          AREACODE PHONE     ST ZIP
.........         .........          ........ ........  .. .....
BUNDY             AL                      100 555-1111 IL 22333
MEZA              AL                      200 555-2222 UK
```

```
MERRICK          BUD                      300 555-6666 CO 80212
MAST             JD                       381 555-6767 LA 23456
BULHER           FERRIS                   345 555-3223 IL 23332
5 rows selected.

mysql> select * from friends where st < 'la';
+----------+-----------+-----------+-----------+----+-------+
| lastname | firstname | areacode  | phone     | st | zip   |
+----------+-----------+-----------+-----------+----+-------+
| BUNDY    | AL        |       100 | 555-1111  | IL | 22333 |
| MERRICK  | BUD       |       300 | 555-6666  | CO | 80212 |
| BULHER   | FERRIS    |       345 | 555-3223  | IL | 23332 |
+----------+-----------+-----------+-----------+----+-------+
3 rows in set (0.00 sec)
```

Uppercase is usually sorted before lowercase; therefore, the uppercase codes returned are less than la. Again, to be safe, check your implementation.

3

TIP   To be sure of how these operators will behave, check your language tables. Most PC implementations use the ASCII tables.

To include the state of Louisiana in the original search, type

Input/Output ▼

```
SQL> SELECT *
  2 FROM FRIENDS
  3 WHERE STATE <= 'LA';
LASTNAME         FIRSTNAME       AREACODE PHONE    ST ZIP
--------         ---------       -------- -------- -- -----
BUNDY            AL                   100 555-1111 IL 22333
MERRICK          BUD                  300 555-6666 CO 80212
MAST             JD                   381 555-6767 LA 23456
BULHER           FERRIS               345 555-3223 IL 23332
4 rows selected.

mysql> select * from friends where st <= 'LA';
+----------+-----------+-----------+-----------+----+-------+
| lastname | firstname | areacode  | phone     | st | zip   |
+----------+-----------+-----------+-----------+----+-------+
| BUNDY    | AL        |       100 | 555-1111  | IL | 22333 |
| MERRICK  | BUD       |       300 | 555-6666  | CO | 80212 |
| MAST     | JD        |       381 | 555-6767  | LA | 23456 |
| BULHER   | FERRIS    |       345 | 555-3223  | IL | 23332 |
+----------+-----------+-----------+-----------+----+-------+
4 rows in set (0.00 sec)
```

Inequalities (< > or !=)

When you need to find everything except for certain data, use the inequality symbol, which can be either < > or !=, depending on your SQL implementation. For example, to find everyone who is not AL, type this:

Input/Output ▼

```
SQL> SELECT *
  2 FROM FRIENDS
  3 WHERE FIRSTNAME <> 'AL';
LASTNAME        FIRSTNAME        AREACODE PHONE     ST ZIP
--------        ---------        -------- --------  -- -----
MERRICK         BUD                  300 555-6666 CO 80212
MAST            JD                   381 555-6767 LA 23456
BULHER          FERRIS               345 555-3223 IL 23332
3 rows selected.

mysql> select * from friends where firstname <> 'AL';
+----------+-----------+----------+----------+----+-------+
| lastname | firstname | areacode | phone    | st | zip   |
+----------+-----------+----------+----------+----+-------+
| MERRICK  | BUD       |      300 | 555-6666 | CO | 80212 |
| MAST     | JD        |      381 | 555-6767 | LA | 23456 |
| BULHER   | FERRIS    |      345 | 555-3223 | IL | 23332 |
+----------+-----------+----------+----------+----+-------+
4 rows in set (0.00 sec)
```

To find everyone not living in California, type this:

Input/Output ▼

```
SQL> SELECT *
  2 FROM FRIENDS
  3 WHERE STATE != 'CA';
LASTNAME        FIRSTNAME        AREACODE PHONE     ST ZIP
--------        ---------        -------- --------  -- -----
BUNDY           AL                   100 555-1111 IL 22333
MEZA            AL                   200 555-2222 UK
MERRICK         BUD                  300 555-6666 CO 80212
MAST            JD                   381 555-6767 LA 23456
BULHER          FERRIS               345 555-3223 IL 23332
5 rows selected.

mysql> select * from friends where st != 'CA';
+----------+-----------+----------+----------+----+-------+
| lastname | firstname | areacode | phone    | st | zip   |
+----------+-----------+----------+----------+----+-------+
| BUNDY    | AL        |      100 | 555-1111 | IL | 22333 |
| MEZA     | AL        |      200 | 555-2222 | UK|        |
```

```
¦ MERRICK  ¦ BUD       ¦        300 ¦ 555-6666 ¦ CO ¦ 80212 ¦
¦ MAST     ¦ JD        ¦        381 ¦ 555-6767 ¦ LA ¦ 23456 ¦
¦ BULHER   ¦ FERRIS    ¦        345 ¦ 555-3223 ¦ IL ¦ 23332 ¦
+----------+-----------+----------+----------+----+-------+
5 rows in set (0.00 sec)
```

> **NOTE**   Notice that both symbols, <> and !=, can express "not equal" in the two implementations we have shown you.

Character Operators

You can use character operators to manipulate the way character strings are represented, both in the output of data and in the process of placing conditions on data to be retrieved. This section describes two character operators: the LIKE operator and the ¦¦ operator, the latter of which conveys the concept of character concatenation.

LIKE

What if you wanted to select parts of a database that fit a pattern but weren't quite exact matches? You could use the equal sign and run through all the possible cases, but that process would be boring and time-consuming. Instead, you can use LIKE. Consider the following:

Input/Output ▼

```
SQL> SELECT * FROM PARTS;
NAME            LOCATION        PARTNUMBER
-----------     -----------     ----------
APPENDIX        MID-STOMACH              1
ADAMS APPLE     THROAT                   2
HEART           CHEST                    3
SPINE           BACK                     4
ANVIL           EAR                      5
KIDNEY          MID-BACK                 6
6 rows selected.
```

How can you find all the parts located in the back? A quick visual inspection of this simple table shows that it has two parts, but unfortunately the locations have slightly different names. Try this:

Input/Output ▼

```
SQL> SELECT *
  2 FROM PARTS
  3 WHERE LOCATION LIKE '%BACK%';
```

```
NAME            LOCATION        PARTNUMBER
-------         ---------       ----------
SPINE           BACK                     4
KIDNEY          MID-BACK                 6
2 rows selected.
```

Analysis ▼

You can see the use of the percent sign (%) in the statement after LIKE. When used inside a LIKE expression, % is a wildcard. What you asked for was any occurrence of BACK in the column location. If you queried

Input ▼

```
SQL> SELECT *
  2 FROM PARTS
  3 WHERE LOCATION LIKE 'BACK%';
```

you would get any occurrence that started with BACK:

Input/Output ▼

```
NAME            LOCATION        PARTNUMBER
-----           ---------       ----------
SPINE           BACK                     4

1 rows selected.
mysql> select * from parts where location like 'BACK%';
+-------+----------+------------+
¦ name  ¦ location ¦ partnumber ¦
+-------+----------+------------+
¦ SPINE ¦ BACK     ¦          4 ¦
+-------+----------+------------+
1 row in set (0.00 sec)
```

If you queried

Input ▼

```
SQL> SELECT *
  2 FROM PARTS
  3 WHERE NAME LIKE 'A%';
```

you would get any name that starts with A:

Output ▼

```
NAME           LOCATION      PARTNUMBER
-----------    -----------   ----------
APPENDIX       MID-STOMACH            1
ADAMS APPLE    THROAT                 2
ANVIL          EAR                    5
3 rows selected.
```

Is LIKE case sensitive in *both* Oracle and MySQL? Try the next query to find out.

Input/Output ▼

```
SQL> SELECT *
  2 FROM PARTS
  3 WHERE NAME LIKE 'a%';

no rows selected

mysql> select * from parts where name like 'a%';
+-------------+-------------+-------------+
¦ name        ¦ location    ¦ partnumber  ¦
+-------------+-------------+-------------+
¦ APPENDIX    ¦ MID-STOMACH ¦           1 ¦
¦ ADAMS APPLE ¦ THROAT      ¦           2 ¦
¦ ANVIL       ¦ EAR         ¦           5 ¦
+-------------+-------------+-------------+
3 rows in set (0.00 sec)
```

The answer is yes in Oracle and no in MySQL. References to data are dependent upon the implementation you are working with.

What if you want to find data that matches all but one character in a certain pattern? In this case you could use a different type of wildcard: the underscore.

Underscore (_)

The underscore is the single-character wildcard. Using a modified version of the table FRIENDS, type this:

Input/Output ▼

```
SQL> SELECT * FROM FRIENDS;
LASTNAME       FIRSTNAME        AREACODE PHONE     ST ZIP
--------       ---------        -------- --------  -- -----
BUNDY          AL                    100 555-1111  IL 22333
MEZA           AL                    200 555-2222  UK
MERRICK        BUD                   300 555-6666  CO 80212
MAST           JD                    381 555-6767  LA 23456
```

```
BULHER          FERRIS                  345 555-3223 IL 23332
PERKINS         ALTON                   911 555-3116 CA 95633
BOSS            SIR                     204 555-2345 CT 95633
7 rows selected.
```

To find all the records where ST starts with C, type the following:

Input/Output ▼

```
SQL> SELECT *
  2 FROM FRIENDS
  3 WHERE ST LIKE 'C_';
LASTNAME        FIRSTNAME               AREACODE PHONE    ST ZIP
--------        ---------               -------- -------- -- -----
MERRICK         BUD                          300 555-6666 CO 80212
PERKINS         ALTON                        911 555-3116 CA 95633
BOSS            SIR                          204 555-2345 CT 95633
3 rows selected.

mysql> select * from friends where st like 'C_';
+----------+----------+----------+----------+----+-------+
¦ lastname ¦ firstname ¦ areacode ¦ phone    ¦ st ¦ zip   ¦
+----------+----------+----------+----------+----+-------+
¦ MERRICK  ¦ BUD      ¦      300 ¦ 555-6666 ¦ CO ¦ 80212 ¦
¦ PERKINS  ¦ ALTON    ¦      911 ¦ 555-3116 ¦ CA ¦ 95633 ¦
¦ BOSS     ¦ SIR      ¦      204 ¦ 555-2345 ¦ CT ¦ 95633 ¦
+----------+----------+----------+----------+----+-------+
3 row in set (0.00 sec)
```

You can use several underscores in a statement:

Input/Output ▼

```
SQL> SELECT *
  2 FROM FRIENDS
  3 WHERE PHONE LIKE'555-6_6_';
LASTNAME        FIRSTNAME               AREACODE PHONE    ST ZIP
--------        ---------               -------- -------- -- -----
MERRICK         BUD                          300 555-6666 CO 80212
MAST            JD                           381 555-6767 LA 23456
2 rows selected.
```

The previous statement could also be written as follows:

Input/Output ▼

```
SQL> SELECT *
  2 FROM FRIENDS
  3 WHERE PHONE LIKE '555-6%';
```

```
LASTNAME        FIRSTNAME         AREACODE PHONE    ST ZIP
--------        ---------         -------- -------- -- -----
MERRICK         BUD                    300 555-6666 CO 80212
MAST            JD                     381 555-6767 LA 23456
2 rows selected.
```

Notice that the results are identical. These two wildcards can be combined. The next example finds all records with L as the second character:

Input/Output ▼

```
SQL> SELECT *
  2 FROM FRIENDS
  3 WHERE FIRSTNAME LIKE '_L%';
LASTNAME        FIRSTNAME         AREACODE PHONE    ST ZIP
--------        ---------         -------- -------- -- -----
BUNDY           AL                     100 555-1111 IL 22333
MEZA            AL                     200 555-2222 UK
PERKINS         ALTON                  911 555-3116 CA 95633
3 rows selected.
```

3

Concatenation (||)

The || (double pipe) symbol concatenates two strings. Try this:

Input/Output ▼

```
SQL> SELECT FIRSTNAME || LASTNAME ENTIRENAME
  2 FROM FRIENDS;
ENTIRENAME
--------------------
AL          BUNDY
AL          MEZA
BUD         MERRICK
JD          MAST
FERRIS      BULHER
ALTON       PERKINS
SIR         BOSS
7 rows selected.
```

Analysis ▼

Notice that || is used instead of +. If you use + to try to concatenate the strings, the SQL interpreter used for this example (Oracle) returns the following error:

Input/Output ▼

```
SQL> SELECT FIRSTNAME + LASTNAME ENTIRENAME
  2  FROM FRIENDS;

ERROR:
ORA-01722: invalid number
```

It is looking for two numbers to add and throws the error invalid number when it doesn't find any.

> **NOTE**
>
> Some implementations of SQL, such as Microsoft SQL Server, use the plus sign to concatenate strings. Check your implementation.

> **NOTE**
>
> MySQL can be set up to allow the || for concatenation; however, this is not the default when MySQL is installed. concat() is the default. Any number of variables may be passed to the function concat(), and it is quite easy to use. Should you desire to change the parameters in MySQL to allow the use of the || for concatenation, first please research the subject in the documentation provided with MySQL.

Input/Output ▼

```
mysql> select concat(firstname," ",lastname)Entirename from friends;
+---------------+
| Entirename    |
+---------------+
| AL BUNDY      |
| BUD MERRICK   |
| JD MAST       |
| FERRIS BULHER |
| AL MEZA       |
| ALTON PERKINS |
| SIR BOSS      |
+---------------+
7 rows in set (0.00 sec)
```

Here's a more practical example using concatenation:

Input/Output ▼

```
SQL> SELECT LASTNAME || ',' || FIRSTNAME NAME
  2  FROM FRIENDS;

NAME
----------------------------------------------
BUNDY     , AL
MEZA      , AL
MERRICK   , BUD
MAST      , JD
BULHER    , FERRIS
PERKINS   , ALTON
BOSS      , SIR
7 rows selected.

mysql> select concat(lastname,",","," " ",firstname)Name from friends;
+----------------+
| Name           |
+----------------+
| BUNDY, AL      |
| MEZA, AL       |
| MERRICK, BUD   |
| MAST, JD       |
| BULHER, FERRIS |
| PERKINS, ALTON |
| BOSS, SIR      |

+----------------+
7 rows in set (0.00 sec)
```

The Oracle statement inserted a comma between the last name and the first name. This was done because Oracle (and other implementations) accounts for the entire length that a column may be when it concatenates to the other string. This creates a natural spacing between the values of the columns/strings. The MySQL statement inserted a comma and a space between the two columns. MySQL automatically runs the values of the columns/strings into one; thus, any "natural" spacing between the values is lost.

NOTE	More on this space issue: Notice the extra spaces between the first name and the last name in the Oracle examples. These spaces are actually part of the data. With certain data types, spaces are right-padded to values less than the total length allocated for a field. See your implementation. Data types will be discussed in Lesson 9. Additionally, if you try to concatenate a NULL value to a string, the result will be a NULL value for the entire expression. In these instances, you would possibly want to use a built-in function to remove the NULL values. This will be discussed in Lesson 7.

3

So far you have performed the comparisons one at a time. This method is fine for some problems, but what if you need to find all the people at work with last names starting with P who have less than three days of vacation time? Logical operators can help in this case.

Logical Operators

Logical operators separate two or more conditions in the WHERE clause of a SQL statement.

Vacation time is always a hot topic around the workplace. Say you designed a table called VACATION for the accounting department:

Input/Output ▼

```
SQL> SELECT * FROM VACATION;

LASTNAME         EMPLOYEENUM    YEARS LEAVETAKEN
---------------  -----------    ----- ----------
ABLE                     101        2          4
BAKER                    104        5         23
BLEDSOE                  107        8         45
BOLIVAR                  233        4         80
BOLD                     210       15        100
COSTALES                 211       10         78
6 rows selected.
```

Suppose your company gives each employee 12 days of leave each year. Using what you have learned and a logical operator, find all the employees whose name starts with B and who have more than 50 days of leave coming.

Input/Output ▼

```
SQL> SELECT LASTNAME,
  2  YEARS * 12 - LEAVETAKEN REMAINING
  3  FROM VACATION
  4  WHERE LASTNAME LIKE 'B%'
  5  AND
  6  YEARS * 12 - LEAVETAKEN > 50;
LASTNAME        REMAINING
--------        ---------
BLEDSOE                51
BOLD                   80
2 rows selected.


mysql> select lastname,
```

```
        -> years*12 - leavetaken remaining
        -> from vacation
        -> where lastname like 'B%'
        -> and years*12 - leavetaken > 50;
+----------+-----------+
| lastname | remaining |
+----------+-----------+
| BLEDSOE  |        51 |
| BOLD     |        80 |
+----------+-----------+
2 rows in set (0.00 sec)
```

Analysis ▼

This query is the most complicated you have done to date. The SELECT clause (lines 1 and 2) uses arithmetic operators to determine how many days of leave each employee has remaining. The normal precedence computes YEARS * 12 - LEAVETAKEN. (A clearer approach would be to write (YEARS * 12) - LEAVETAKEN.)

LIKE is used in line 4 with the wildcard % to find all the B names. Line 5 uses the > to find all occurrences greater than 50.

The new element is on line 5. You used the logical operator AND to ensure that you found records that met the criteria in lines 4 *and* 5.

AND

AND requires that both expressions on either side be true to return TRUE. If either expression is false, AND returns FALSE. For example, to find out which employees have been with the company for 5 or fewer years and have taken more than 20 days leave, try this:

Input/Output ▼

```
SQL> SELECT LASTNAME
   2 FROM VACATION
   3 WHERE YEARS <= 5
   4 AND
   5 LEAVETAKEN > 20 ;
LASTNAME
--------
BAKER
BOLIVAR
2 rows selected.

mysql> select lastname from vacation
    -> where years <= 5
    -> and leavetaken > 20;
```

3

```
+----------+
¦ lastname ¦
+----------+
¦ BAKER    ¦
¦ BOLIVAR  ¦
+----------+
2 rows in set (0.00 sec)
```

If you want to know which employees have been with the company for 5 years or more and have taken less than 50 percent of their leave, you could write:

Input/Output ▼

```
SQL> SELECT LASTNAME WORKAHOLICS
   2 FROM VACATION
   3 WHERE YEARS >= 5
   4 AND
   5 ((YEARS *12)-LEAVETAKEN)/(YEARS * 12) < 0.50;
WORKAHOLICS
-----------
BOLD
COSTALES

2 rows selected.


mysql> select lastname Workaholics
   -> from vacation
   -> where years >= 5
   -> and ((years * 12) - leavetaken) / (years * 12) < 0.50;
+-------------+
¦ Workaholics ¦
+-------------+
¦ BOLD        ¦
¦ COSTALES    ¦
+-------------+
2 rows in set (0.00 sec)
```

Check these people for burnout. Also check out how we used the AND to combine these two conditions.

OR

You can also use OR to sum up a series of conditions. If any of the comparisons are true, OR returns TRUE. To illustrate the difference, run the last query with OR instead of with AND:

Input/Output ▼

```
SQL> SELECT LASTNAME WORKAHOLICS
  2 FROM VACATION
  3 WHERE YEARS >= 5
  4 OR
  5 ((YEARS *12)-LEAVETAKEN)/(YEARS * 12) < 0.50;


WORKAHOLICS
-----------
BAKER
BLEDSOE
BOLD
COSTALES


4 rows selected.
```

```
mysql> select lastname
    -> from vacation
    -> where years >= 5
    -> OR ((years*12)-leavetaken)/(years*12) < 0.50;
+----------+
| lastname |
+----------+
| BAKER    |
| BLEDSOE  |
| BOLD     |
| COSTALES |
+----------+
4 rows in set (0.00 sec)
```

The original names are still in the list, but you have three new entries (who would probably resent being called workaholics). These three new names made the list because they
satisfied one of the conditions. OR requires only that one of the conditions be true for data
to be returned.

NOT

NOT means just that. If the condition it applies to evaluates to TRUE, NOT makes it FALSE.
If the condition after the NOT is FALSE, it becomes TRUE. For example, the following
SELECT returns the only two names not beginning with B in the table:

Input/Output ▼

```
SQL> SELECT *
  2 FROM VACATION
  3 WHERE LASTNAME NOT LIKE 'B%';
```

```
LASTNAME        EMPLOYEENUM     YEARS LEAVETAKEN
--------        -----------     ----- ----------
ABLE                    101         2          4
COSTALES                211        10         78
2 rows selected.
```

```
mysql> select * from vacation
    -> where lastname not like 'B%';
+----------+-------------+-------+------------+
| lastname | employeenum | years | leavetaken |
+----------+-------------+-------+------------+
| ABLE     |         101 |     2 |          4 |
| COSTALES |         211 |    10 |         78 |
+----------+-------------+-------+------------+
2 rows in set (0.00 sec)
```

NOT can also be used with the operator IS when applied to NULL. Recall the PRICE table where we put a NULL value in the WHOLESALE column opposite the item ORANGES.

Input/Output ▼

```
SQL> SELECT * FROM PRICE;

ITEM            WHOLESALE
--------------- ---------
TOMATOES             .34
POTATOES             .51
BANANAS              .67
TURNIPS              .45
CHEESE               .89
APPLES               .23
ORANGES
7 rows selected.
```

To find the non-NULL items, type this:

Input/Output ▼

```
SQL> SELECT *
  2 FROM PRICE
  3 WHERE WHOLESALE IS NOT NULL;
ITEM            WHOLESALE
--------------- ---------
TOMATOES             .34
POTATOES             .51
BANANAS              .67
TURNIPS              .45
```

```
CHEESE              .89
APPLES              .23
6 rows selected.
```

Set Operators

In Lesson 1, "Getting Started with SQL," you learned that SQL is based on the theory of sets. The following sections examine set operators. *Set operators* are used to combine different sets of data returned by different queries into one query, and ultimately, one data set. There are various set operators available in SQL that allow you to combine different data sets to meet your data processing needs.

UNION **and** UNION ALL

UNION returns the results of two queries minus the duplicate rows. The following two tables represent the rosters of teams:

Input/Output ▼

```
SQL> SELECT * FROM FOOTBALL;

NAME
----------------
ABLE
BRAVO
CHARLIE
DECON
EXITOR
FUBAR
GOOBER
7 rows selected.
SQL> SELECT * FROM SOFTBALL;

NAME
----------------
ABLE
BAKER
CHARLIE
DEAN
EXITOR
FALCONER
GOOBER
7 rows selected.
```

How many different people play on one team or another?

3

Input/Output ▼

```
SQL> SELECT NAME FROM SOFTBALL
  2 UNION
  3 SELECT NAME FROM FOOTBALL;
NAME
---------------
ABLE
BAKER
BRAVO
CHARLIE
DEAN
DECON
EXITOR
FALCONER
FUBAR
GOOBER
10 rows selected.
```

UNION returns 10 distinct names from the two lists. How many names are on both lists (including duplicates)?

Input/Output ▼

```
SQL> SELECT NAME FROM SOFTBALL
  2 UNION ALL
  3 SELECT NAME FROM FOOTBALL;
NAME
---------------
ABLE
BAKER
CHARLIE
DEAN
EXITOR
FALCONER
GOOBER
ABLE
BRAVO
CHARLIE
DECON
EXITOR
FUBAR
GOOBER
14 rows selected.
```

Analysis ▼

The combined list—courtesy of the UNION ALL statement—has 14 names. UNION ALL works just like UNION except that it does not eliminate duplicates. You need to remember that the UNION and UNION ALL statements will only work if all SELECT statements have the same columns. Otherwise, an error message will be returned. Now show me a list of players who are on both teams. You can't do that with UNION—you need to learn INTER- SECT.

INTERSECT

INTERSECT returns only the rows found by both queries. The next SELECT statement shows the list of players who play on both teams:

Input/Output ▼

```
SQL> SELECT * FROM FOOTBALL
  2 INTERSECT
  3 SELECT * FROM SOFTBALL;
NAME
----------------
ABLE
CHARLIE
EXITOR
GOOBER

4 rows selected.
```

In this example, INTERSECT finds the short list of players who are on both teams by com- bining the results of the two SELECT statements. INTERSECT has the same limitations as the UNION and UNION ALL statement, in as much as the SELECT statements that it is bind- ing must contain the same columns.

MINUS (Difference)

MINUS returns the rows from the first query that were not present in the second. For example:

Input/Output ▼

```
SQL> SELECT * FROM FOOTBALL
  2 MINUS
  3 SELECT * FROM SOFTBALL;
NAME
----------------
BRAVO
DECON
FUBAR

3 rows selected.
```

The preceding query shows the three football players who are not on the softball team. If you reverse the order, you get the three softball players who aren't on the football team:

Input/Output ▼

```
SQL> SELECT * FROM SOFTBALL
  2 MINUS
  3 SELECT * FROM FOOTBALL;
NAME
-------------------
BAKER
DEAN
FALCONER

3 rows selected.
```

Miscellaneous Operators: IN and BETWEEN

The two operators IN and BETWEEN provide a shorthand for functions you already know how to do. If you wanted to find friends in Colorado, California, and Louisiana, you could type the following:

Input/Output ▼

```
SQL> SELECT *
  2 FROM FRIENDS
  3 WHERE ST= 'CA'
  4 OR
  5 ST ='CO'
  6 OR
  7 ST = 'LA';
```

LASTNAME	FIRSTNAME	AREACODE	PHONE	ST	ZIP
MERRICK	BUD	300	555-6666	CO	80212
MAST	JD	381	555-6767	LA	23456
PERKINS	ALTON	911	555-3116	CA	95633

```
3 rows selected.
```

Or you could type this:

Input/Output ▼

```
SQL> SELECT *
  2 FROM FRIENDS
  3 WHERE ST IN('CA','CO','LA');
```

```
LASTNAME        FIRSTNAME       AREACODE PHONE    ST ZIP
--------        ---------       -------- -------- -- -----
MERRICK         BUD                  300 555-6666 CO 80212
MAST            JD                   381 555-6767 LA 23456
PERKINS         ALTON                911 555-3116 CA 95633
3 rows selected.


mysql> select * from friends
    -> where st in ('CA','CO','LA');
+----------+-----------+----------+----------+----+-------+
| lastname | firstname | areacode | phone    | st | zip   |
+----------+-----------+----------+----------+----+-------+
| MERRICK  | BUD       |      300 | 555-6666 | CO | 80212 |
| MAST     | JD        |      381 | 555-6767 | LA | 23456 |
| PERKINS  | ALTON     |      911 | 555-3116 | CA | 95633 |
+----------+-----------+----------+----------+----+-------+
2 rows in set (0.20 sec)
```

The second example is shorter and more readable than the first. You never know when you might have to go back and work on something you wrote months ago. IN also works with numbers. Consider the following, where the column AREACODE is a number:

Input/Output ▼

```
SQL> SELECT *
  2 FROM FRIENDS
  3 WHERE AREACODE IN(100,381,204);
LASTNAME        FIRSTNAME       AREACODE PHONE    ST ZIP
--------        ---------       -------- -------- -- -----
BUNDY           AL                   100 555-1111 IL 22333
MAST            JD                   381 555-6767 LA 23456
BOSS            SIR                  204 555-2345 CT 95633
3 rows selected.
```

If you needed a range of data from the PRICE table, you could write the following:

Input/Output ▼

```
SQL>  SELECT *
  2   FROM PRICE
  3   WHERE WHOLESALE > 0.25
  4   AND
  5   WHOLESALE < 0.75;

ITEM            WHOLESALE
--------        ---------
TOMATOES             .34
```

```
POTATOES              .51
BANANAS               .67
TURNIPS               .45
4 rows selected.
```

Or using BETWEEN, you would write this:

Input/Output ▼

```
SQL> SELECT *
  2 FROM PRICE
  3 WHERE WHOLESALE BETWEEN 0.25 AND 0.75;
ITEM            WHOLESALE
--------        ---------
TOMATOES            .34
POTATOES            .51
BANANAS             .67
TURNIPS             .45
4 rows selected.
```

```
mysql> select * from price
    -> where wholesale between .25 and .75;
+----------+-----------+
| item     | wholesale |
+----------+-----------+
| TOMATOES |      0.34 |
| POTATOES |      0.51 |
| BANANAS  |      0.67 |
| TURNIPS  |      0.45 |
+----------+-----------+
4 rows in set (0.08 sec)
```

Again, the second example is a cleaner, more readable solution than the first.

NOTE	If a WHOLESALE value of 0.25 existed in the PRICE table, that record would have been retrieved also. Parameters used with BETWEEN are inclusive.

Summary

At the beginning of this lesson, you knew how to use the basic SELECT and FROM clauses. Now you know how to use a host of operators that enable you to fine-tune your requests to the database. You learned how to use arithmetic, comparison, character, logical, and set operators. This powerful set of tools provides the cornerstone of your SQL knowledge. In Lesson 4, you learn to increase the data-mining power of the SQL query by integrating other clauses such as the WHERE clause into your queries to perform operations involving grouping and ordering.

Q&A

Q How does all this information apply to me if I am not using SQL from the command line as depicted in the examples?

A Whether you use SQL in COBOL as Embedded SQL or in Microsoft's Open Database Connectivity (ODBC), you use the same basic constructions. You will use what you learned in these first lessons repeatedly as you work with SQL.

Q Why are you constantly telling me to check my implementation? I thought there was a standard!

A There is an ANSI standard (the most recent version was released in late 2008); however, most vendors modify it somewhat to suit their databases. The basics are similar if not identical, and each instance has extensions that other vendors copy and improve. We have chosen to use ANSI as a starting point and to point out the differences as we go along.

Workshop

The Workshop provides quiz questions to help solidify your understanding of the material covered, as well as exercises to provide you with experience in using what you have learned. Try to answer the quiz and exercise questions before checking the answers in Appendix A, "Answers."

Here are the CREATE TABLE statements and INSERT statements for the FRIENDS and PRICE tables. Type the following code into MySQL if you have not already done so.

```
create table friends
(lastname      varchar(15)     not null,
 firstname     varchar(15)     not null,
 areacode      numeric(3)      null,
 phone         varchar(9)      null,
 st            char(2)         not null,
 zip           varchar(5)      not null);

insert into friends values
('BUNDY', 'AL', '100', '555-1111', 'IL', '22333');

insert into friends values
('MEZA', 'AL', '200', '555-2222', 'UK', NULL);
```

```
insert into friends values
('MERRICK', 'BUD', '300', '555-6666', 'CO', '80212');

insert into friends values
('MAST', 'JD', '381', '555-6767', 'LA', '23456');

insert into friends values
('BULHER', 'FERRIS', '345', '555-3223', 'IL', '23332');

insert into friends values
('PERKINS', 'ALTON', '911', '555-3116', 'CA', '95633');

insert into friends values
('BOSS', 'SIR', '204', '555-2345', 'CT', '95633');

create table price
(item          varchar(15)    not null,
 wholesale     decimal(4,2)   not null);

insert into price values
('TOMATOES', '.34');

insert into price values
('POTATOES', '.51');

insert into price values
('BANANAS', '.67');

insert into price values
('TURNIPS', '.45');

insert into price values
('CHEESE', '.89');

insert into price values
('APPLES', '.23');
```

Quiz

Use the FRIENDS table to answer the following questions.

LASTNAME	FIRSTNAME	AREACODE	PHONE	ST	ZIP
BUNDY	AL	100	555-1111	IL	22333
MEZA	AL	200	555-2222	UK	
MERRICK	BUD	300	555-6666	CO	80212
MAST	JD	381	555-6767	LA	23456
BULHER	FERRIS	345	555-3223	IL	23332
PERKINS	ALTON	911	555-3116	CA	95633
BOSS	SIR	204	555-2345	CT	95633

1. Write a query that returns everyone in the database whose last name begins with M.

2. Write a query that returns everyone who lives in Illinois with a first name of AL.

3. Given two tables (PART1 and PART2) containing columns named PARTNO, how would you find out which part numbers are in both tables? Write the query.

4. What shorthand could you use instead of WHERE a >= 10 AND a <=30?

5. What will this query return?

```
SELECT FIRSTNAME
FROM FRIENDS
WHERE FIRSTNAME = 'AL'
  AND LASTNAME = 'BULHER';
```

6. What is the main difference in the result set when using UNION versus UNION ALL?

7. What is the primary difference between using INTERSECT and MINUS?

3

Exercises

1. Using the FRIENDS table, write a query that returns the following:

```
NAME            ST
-----           -------
AL              FROM IL
```

2. Using the FRIENDS table, write a query that returns the following:

```
NAME                 PHONE
---------------      -----------
MERRICK, BUD         300-555-6666
MAST, JD             381-555-6767
BULHER, FERRIS       345-555-3223
```

3. Select all columns from the PRICE table where the column WHOLESALE is greater than .50.

4. What results do you get from the following query?

```
mysql> select *
   -> from price
   -> where item like '%ATO%';
```

5. Does MySQL support set operators such as UNION, UNION ALL, INTERSECT, and MINUS?

6. What is wrong with the following query?

```
SELECT FIRSTNAME,LASTNAME FROM FRIENDS_1
UNION
SELECT FIRSTNAME  FROM FRIENDS_2;
```

LESSON 4
Clauses in SQL Queries

This lesson's topic is clauses. Clauses are the piece of the SQL statement that grant you fine grained control over your result set. By the end of this lesson, you will understand and be able to use the following clauses:

- WHERE

- ORDER BY

- GROUP BY

- HAVING

To get a feel for where these functions fit in, examine the general syntax of a SELECT statement:

Syntax ▼

```
SELECT [DISTINCT | ALL] { *
                | { [schema.]{table | view | snapshot}.*
                | expr }  [ [AS] c_alias ]
              [, { [schema.]{table | view | snapshot}.*
                | expr } [ [AS] c_alias ]  ] ... }
FROM [schema.]{table | view | snapshot}[@dblink] [t_alias]
[, [schema.]{table | view | snapshot}[@dblink] [t_alias] ] ...
    [WHERE condition ]
    [GROUP BY expr [, expr] ... [HAVING condition] ]
    [{UNION | UNION ALL | INTERSECT | MINUS} SELECT command ]
    [ORDER BY {expr|position} [ASC | DESC]
         [, {expr|position} [ASC | DESC]] ...]
```

The MySQL equivalent is

Syntax ▼

```
SELECT [STRAIGHT_JOIN] [SQL_SMALL_RESULT] [SQL_BIG_RESULT] [SQL_BUFFER_RESULT]
      [HIGH_PRIORITY]
      [DISTINCT | DISTINCTROW | ALL]
   select_expression,...
   [INTO {OUTFILE | DUMPFILE} 'file_name' export_options]
   [FROM table_references
      [WHERE where_definition]
      [GROUP BY {unsigned_integer | col_name | formula} [ASC | DESC], ...]
      [HAVING where_definition]
      [ORDER BY {unsigned_integer | col_name | formula} [ASC | DESC] ,...]
      [LIMIT [offset,] rows]
      [PROCEDURE procedure_name]
      [FOR UPDATE | LOCK IN SHARE MODE]]
```

NOTE

In my experience with SQL, the ANSI standard is really more of an ANSI "suggestion." The preceding ANSI SQL syntax will generally work with any SQL engine, but you might find some slight variations. This is because the amount of the ANSI standard that a database implementation must support to be considered compliant is very small compared to the standard as a whole.

You haven't yet had to deal with a complicated syntax diagram. Because many people find syntax diagrams more puzzling than illuminating when learning something new, this book has used simple examples to illustrate particular points. However, we are now at the point where a syntax diagram can help tie the familiar concepts to today's new material.

Don't worry about the exact syntax—it varies slightly from implementation to implementation, anyway. Instead, focus on the relationships. At the top of this statement is SELECT, which you have used many times in the last few lessons. SELECT is followed by FROM, which should appear with every SELECT statement you type. (You learn a new use for FROM in Lesson 6, "Embedding Subqueries in Queries.") WHERE, GROUP BY, HAVING, and ORDER BY all follow. (The other clauses in the diagram—UNION, UNION ALL, INTERSECT, and MINUS—were covered in Lesson 3, "Expressions, Conditions, and Operators.") Each clause plays an important part in selecting and manipulating data.

Specifying Criteria with the WHERE Clause

Using just SELECT and FROM, you are limited to returning every row in a table. For example, using these two key words on the CHECKS table, you get all seven rows:

Input/Output ▼

```
SQL> SELECT *
  2  FROM CHECKS;

  CHECK# PAYEE                  AMOUNT REMARKS
-------- -------------------- -------- --------------------
       1 MA BELL                   150 HAVE SONS NEXT TIME
       2 READING R.R.           245.34 TRAIN TO CHICAGO
       3 MA BELL                200.32 CELLULAR PHONE
       4 LOCAL UTILITIES            98 GAS
       5 JOES STALE $ DENT         150 GROCERIES
      16 CASH                       25 WILD NIGHT OUT
      17 JOANS GAS                25.1 GAS

7 rows selected.
```

With WHERE in your vocabulary, you can be more selective. To find all the checks you wrote with a value of more than 100 dollars, use the following:

Input ▼

```
SQL> SELECT *
  2  FROM CHECKS
  3  WHERE AMOUNT > 100;
```

The WHERE clause returns the four instances in the table that meet the required condition:

Output ▼

```
  CHECK# PAYEE                  AMOUNT REMARKS
-------- -------------------- -------- --------------------
       1 MA BELL                   150 HAVE SONS NEXT TIME
       2 READING R.R.           245.34 TRAIN TO CHICAGO
       3 MA BELL                200.32 CELLULAR PHONE
       5 JOES STALE $ DENT         150 GROCERIES
```

WHERE can also solve other popular puzzles. Given the following table of names and locations, you can ask that popular question, "Where's Waldo?"

Input/Output ▼

```
SQL> SELECT *
  2  FROM PUZZLE;

NAME             LOCATION
---------------  --------------
TYLER            BACKYARD
MAJOR            KITCHEN
SPEEDY           LIVING ROOM
WALDO            GARAGE
LADDIE           UTILITY CLOSET
ARNOLD           TV ROOM

6 rows selected.
SQL> SELECT LOCATION AS "WHERE'S WALDO?"
  2  FROM PUZZLE
  3  WHERE NAME = 'WALDO';

WHERE'S WALDO?
--------------
GARAGE
```

Sorry, we couldn't resist. We promise no more corny queries. Nevertheless, this query shows that the column used in the condition of the WHERE statement does not have to be mentioned in the SELECT clause. In this example, you selected the LOCATION column but used WHERE on the name, which is perfectly legal. Also notice the AS on the SELECT line. AS is an optional assignment operator that assigns the alias WHERE'S WALDO? to LOCATION. You might never see the AS again because it involves extra typing. In most implementations of SQL, you can type

Input ▼

```
SQL> SELECT LOCATION "WHERE'S WALDO?"
  2  FROM PUZZLE
  3  WHERE NAME ='WALDO';
```

and get the same result as the previous query without using the AS keyword, as shown:

Output ▼

```
WHERE'S WALDO?
--------------
GARAGE
```

After SELECT and FROM, WHERE is the third most frequently used SQL term.

Order from Chaos: The ORDER BY Clause

From time to time you will want to present the results of your query in some kind of order. As you know, however, SELECT FROM gives you a listing, and unless you have defined a primary key (see Lesson 15, "Creating Indexes on Tables to Improve Performance"), your query comes out in the order the rows were entered. Consider a beefed-up CHECKS table:

Input/Output ▼

```
SQL> SELECT * FROM CHECKS;

CHECK# PAYEE                    AMOUNT REMARKS
-------- -------------------- --------- --------------------
       1 MA BELL                    150 HAVE SONS NEXT TIME
       2 READING R.R.            245.34 TRAIN TO CHICAGO
       3 MA BELL                 200.32 CELLULAR PHONE
       4 LOCAL UTILITIES             98 GAS
       5 JOES STALE $ DENT          150 GROCERIES
      16 CASH                        25 WILD NIGHT OUT
      17 JOANS GAS                 25.1 GAS
       9 ABES CLEANERS            24.35 X-TRA STARCH
      20 ABES CLEANERS             10.5 ALL DRY CLEAN
       8 CASH                        60 TRIP TO BOSTON
      21 CASH                        34 TRIP TO DAYTON

11 rows selected.
```

The MySQL equivalent is

Input/Output ▼

```
mysql> select * from checks;
+-------+--------------------+--------+--------------------+
| CHECK | PAYEE              | AMOUNT | REMARKS            |
+-------+--------------------+--------+--------------------+
|     3 | MA BELL            | 200.32 | CELLUAR PHONE      |
|     2 | READING R.R.       | 245.34 | TRAIN TO CHICAGO   |
|     3 | MA BELL            | 200.32 | CELLLULAR PHONE    |
|     4 | LOCAL UTILITIES    |  98.00 | GAS                |
|     5 | JOES STALE $ DENT  | 150.00 | GROCERIES          |
|    16 | CASH               |  25.00 | WILD NIGHT OUT     |
|    17 | JOANS GAS          |  25.10 | GAS                |
|     9 | ABES CLEANERS      |  24.35 | X-TRA STARCH       |
|    20 | ABES CLEANERS      |  10.50 | ALL DRY CLEAN      |
|     8 | CASH               |  60.00 | TRIP TO BOSTON     |
|    21 | CASH               |  34.00 | TRIP TO DAYTON     |
+-------+--------------------+--------+--------------------+
11 rows in set (0.00 sec)
```

4

Analysis ▼

You're going to have to trust me on this one, but in most implementations the order of the output is exactly the same as the order in which the data was entered. You will need to check your specific implementation's documentation to see whether it has an assigned default ordering. After you read Lesson 11, "Manipulating Data," and know how to use INSERT to populate tables, you can test how data is ordered by default on your own.

The ORDER BY clause gives you a way of ordering your results. For example, to order the preceding listing by check number, you would use the following ORDER BY clause:

Input/Output ▼

```
SQL> SELECT *
  2  FROM CHECKS
  3  ORDER BY CHECK#;

    CHECK# PAYEE                      AMOUNT REMARKS
 --------- -------------------- --------- --------------------
         1 MA BELL                       150 HAVE SONS NEXT TIME
         2 READING R.R.               245.34 TRAIN TO CHICAGO
         3 MA BELL                    200.32 CELLULAR PHONE
         4 LOCAL UTILITIES                98 GAS
         5 JOES STALE $ DENT             150 GROCERIES
         8 CASH                           60 TRIP TO BOSTON
         9 ABES CLEANERS               24.35 X-TRA STARCH
        16 CASH                           25 WILD NIGHT OUT
        17 JOANS GAS                    25.1 GAS
        20 ABES CLEANERS                10.5 ALL DRY CLEAN
        21 CASH                           34 TRIP TO DAYTON

11 rows selected.
```

The MySQL equivalent is

Input/Output ▼

```
mysql> select * from checks order by `check`;
+-------+--------------------+--------+--------------------+
| check | payee              | amount | remarks            |
+-------+--------------------+--------+--------------------+
|     1 | MA BELL            | 150.00 | HAVE SONS NEXT TIME |
|     2 | READING R.R.       | 245.34 | TRAIN TO CHICAGO   |
|     3 | MA BELL            | 200.32 | CELLULAR PHONE     |
|     4 | LOCAL UTILITIES    |  98.00 | GAS                |
|     5 | JOES STALE $ DENT  | 150.00 | GROCERIES          |
|     8 | CASH               |  60.00 | TRIP TO BOSTON     |
|     9 | ABES CLEANERS      |  24.35 | X-TRA STARCH       |
```

```
¦    16 ¦ CASH             ¦  25.00 ¦ WILD NIGHT OUT      ¦
¦    17 ¦ JOANS GAS        ¦  25.10 ¦ GAS                 ¦
¦    20 ¦ ABES CLEANERS    ¦  10.50 ¦ ALL DRY CLEAN       ¦
¦    21 ¦ CASH             ¦  34.00 ¦ TRIP TO DAYTON      ¦
+-------+------------------+--------+---------------------+
11 rows in set (0.00 sec)
```

Now the data is ordered the way you want it, not the way in which it was entered. As the following example shows, ORDER requires BY; BY is not optional.

Input/Output ▼

```
SQL> SELECT * FROM CHECKS ORDER CHECK#;

SELECT * FROM CHECKS ORDER CHECK#
                           *
ERROR at line 1:
ORA-00924: missing BY keyword
```

What if you want to list the data in reverse order, with the highest number or letter first? You're in luck! The following query generates a list of PAYEEs that begins at the end of the alphabet:

Input/Output ▼

```
SQL> SELECT *
  2  FROM CHECKS
  3  ORDER BY PAYEE DESC;

   CHECK# PAYEE                   AMOUNT REMARKS
--------- -------------------- --------- --------------------
        2 READING R.R.          245.34 TRAIN TO CHICAGO
        1 MA BELL                  150 HAVE SONS NEXT TIME
        3 MA BELL               200.32 CELLULAR PHONE
        4 LOCAL UTILITIES           98 GAS
        5 JOES STALE $ DENT        150 GROCERIES
       17 JOANS GAS               25.1 GAS
       16 CASH                      25 WILD NIGHT OUT
        8 CASH                      60 TRIP TO BOSTON
       21 CASH                      34 TRIP TO DAYTON
        9 ABES CLEANERS          24.35 X-TRA STARCH
       20 ABES CLEANERS           10.5 ALL DRY CLEAN

11 rows selected.
```

The MySQL equivalent is

Input/Output ▼

```
mysql> select * from checks order by payee desc;
+-------+-------------------+--------+--------------------+
| check | payee             | amount | remarks            |
+-------+-------------------+--------+--------------------+
|     2 | READING R.R.      | 245.34 | TRAIN TO CHICAGO   |
|     1 | MA BELL           | 150.00 | HAVE SONS NEXT TIME|
|     3 | MA BELL           | 200.32 | CELLUAR PHONE      |
|     4 | LOCAL UTILITIES   |  98.00 | GAS                |
|     5 | JOES STALE $ DENT | 150.00 | GROCERIES          |
|    17 | JOANS GAS         |  25.10 | GAS                |
|    16 | CASH              |  25.00 | WILD NIGHT OUT     |
|     8 | CASH              |  60.00 | TRIP TO BOSTON     |
|    21 | CASH              |  34.00 | TRIP TO DAYTON     |
|     9 | ABES CLEANERS     |  24.35 | X-TRA STARCH       |
|    20 | ABES CLEANERS     |  10.50 | ALL DRY CLEAN      |
+-------+-------------------+--------+--------------------+
11 rows in set (0.00 sec)
```

The DESC at the end of the ORDER BY clause orders the list in descending order instead of the default (ascending) order. The rarely used optional keyword ASC appears in the following statement:

Input/Output ▼

```
SQL> SELECT PAYEE, AMOUNT
  2  FROM CHECKS
  3  ORDER BY CHECK# ASC;

PAYEE                   AMOUNT
--------------------- ---------
MA BELL                    150
READING R.R.            245.34
MA BELL                 200.32
LOCAL UTILITIES             98
JOES STALE $ DENT          150
CASH                        60
ABES CLEANERS            24.35
CASH                        25
JOANS GAS                 25.1
ABES CLEANERS             10.5
CASH                        34

11 rows selected.
```

The MySQL equivalent is

Input/Output ▼

```
mysql> select payee, amount
    -> from checks
    -> order by check asc;
+-------------------+--------+
| payee             | amount |
+-------------------+--------+
| MA BELL           | 150.00 |
| READING R.R.      | 245.34 |
| MA BELL           | 200.32 |
| LOCAL UTILITIES   |  98.00 |
| JOES STALE $ DENT | 150.00 |
| CASH              |  60.00 |
| ABES CLEANERS     |  24.35 |
| CASH              |  25.00 |
| JOANS GAS         |  25.10 |
| ABES CLEANERS     |  10.50 |
| CASH              |  34.00 |
+-------------------+--------+
11 rows in set (0.00 sec)
```

Analysis ▼

4

The ordering in this list is identical to the ordering of the list at the beginning of the section (without ASC) because ASC is the default. This query also shows that the expression used after the ORDER BY clause does not have to be in the SELECT statement. Although you selected only PAYEE and AMOUNT, you were still able to order the list by CHECK#.

You can also use ORDER BY on more than one field. To order CHECKS by PAYEE and REMARKS, you would query as follows:

Input/Output ▼

```
SQL> SELECT *
  2  FROM CHECKS
  3  ORDER BY PAYEE, REMARKS;

  CHECK# PAYEE                AMOUNT REMARKS
--------- -------------------- --------- --------------------
       20 ABES CLEANERS          10.5 ALL DRY CLEAN
        9 ABES CLEANERS         24.35 X-TRA STARCH
        8 CASH                     60 TRIP TO BOSTON
       21 CASH                     34 TRIP TO DAYTON
       16 CASH                     25 WILD NIGHT OUT
       17 JOANS GAS              25.1 GAS
```

```
          5 JOES STALE $ DENT        150 GROCERIES
          4 LOCAL UTILITIES           98 GAS
          3 MA BELL                200.32 CELLULAR PHONE
          1 MA BELL                   150 HAVE SONS NEXT TIME
          2 READING R.R.           245.34 TRAIN TO CHICAGO
```

The MySQL equivalent is

Input/Output ▼

```
mysql> select *
    -> from checks
    -> order by payee, remarks;
+-------+-------------------+--------+--------------------+
| check | payee             | amount | remarks            |
+-------+-------------------+--------+--------------------+
|    20 | ABES CLEANERS     |  10.50 | ALL DRY CLEAN      |
|     9 | ABES CLEANERS     |  24.35 | X-TRA STARCH       |
|     8 | CASH              |  60.00 | TRIP TO BOSTON     |
|    21 | CASH              |  34.00 | TRIP TO DAYTON     |
|    16 | CASH              |  25.00 | WILD NIGHT OUT     |
|    17 | JOANS GAS         |  25.10 | GAS                |
|     5 | JOES STALE $ DENT | 150.00 | GROCERIES          |
|     4 | LOCAL UTILITIES   |  98.00 | GAS                |
|     3 | MA BELL           | 200.32 | CELLUAR PHONE      |
|     1 | MA BELL           | 150.00 | HAVE SONS NEXT TIME |
|     2 | READING R.R.      | 245.34 | TRAIN TO CHICAGO   |
+-------+-------------------+--------+--------------------+
11 rows in set (0.00 sec)
```

Analysis ▼

Notice the entries for CASH in the PAYEE column. In the previous ORDER BY PAYEE DESC, the CHECK#s were in the order 16, 8, 21. Adding the field REMARKS to the ORDER BY clause puts the entries in alphabetical order according to REMARKS. Does the order of multiple columns in the ORDER BY clause make a difference? Try the same query again, but reverse PAYEE and REMARKS:

Input/Output ▼

```
SQL> SELECT *
  2  FROM CHECKS
  3  ORDER BY REMARKS, PAYEE;

  CHECK# PAYEE                   AMOUNT REMARKS
-------- ------------------- ---------- --------------------
      20 ABES CLEANERS             10.5 ALL DRY CLEAN
       3 MA BELL                 200.32 CELLULAR PHONE
```

```
           17 JOANS GAS                 25.1 GAS
            4 LOCAL UTILITIES            98 GAS
            5 JOES STALE $ DENT          150 GROCERIES
            1 MA BELL                    150 HAVE SONS NEXT TIME
            2 READING R.R.            245.34 TRAIN TO CHICAGO
            8 CASH                       60 TRIP TO BOSTON
           21 CASH                       34 TRIP TO DAYTON
           16 CASH                       25 WILD NIGHT OUT
            9 ABES CLEANERS           24.35 X-TRA STARCH
```

11 rows selected.

The MySQL equivalent is

Input/Output ▼

```
mysql> select *
    -> from checks
    -> order by remarks, payee;
+--------+------------------+--------+---------------------+
| check  | payee            | amount | remarks             |
+--------+------------------+--------+---------------------+
|     20 | ABES CLEANERS    |  10.50 | ALL DRY CLEAN       |
|      3 | MA BELL          | 200.32 | CELLUAR PHONE       |
|     17 | JOANS GAS        |  25.10 | GAS                 |
|      4 | LOCAL UTILITIES  |  98.00 | GAS                 |
|      5 | JOES STALE $ DENT| 150.00 | GROCERIES           |
|      1 | MA BELL          | 150.00 | HAVE SONS NEXT TIME |
|      2 | READING R.R.     | 245.34 | TRAIN TO CHICAGO    |
|      8 | CASH             |  60.00 | TRIP TO BOSTON      |
|     21 | CASH             |  34.00 | TRIP TO DAYTON      |
|     16 | CASH             |  25.00 | WILD NIGHT OUT      |
|      9 | ABES CLEANERS    |  24.35 | X-TRA STARCH        |
+--------+------------------+--------+---------------------+
11 rows in set (0.00 sec)
```

As you probably guessed, the results are completely different. Here's how to list one column in alphabetical order and list the second column in reverse alphabetical order:

Input/Output ▼

```
SQL> SELECT *
  2  FROM CHECKS
  3  ORDER BY PAYEE ASC, REMARKS DESC;

  CHECK# PAYEE                   AMOUNT REMARKS
-------- -------------------- --------- --------------------
       9 ABES CLEANERS            24.35 X-TRA STARCH
      20 ABES CLEANERS             10.5 ALL DRY CLEAN
```

```
16 CASH                    25 WILD NIGHT OUT
21 CASH                    34 TRIP TO DAYTON
 8 CASH                    60 TRIP TO BOSTON
17 JOANS GAS             25.1 GAS
 5 JOES STALE $ DENT      150 GROCERIES
 4 LOCAL UTILITIES         98 GAS
 1 MA BELL                150 HAVE SONS NEXT TIME
 3 MA BELL            200.32 CELLULAR PHONE
 2 READING R.R.       245.34 TRAIN TO CHICAGO
```

11 rows selected.

The MySQL equivalent is

Input/Output ▼

```
mysql> select *
    -> from checks
    -> order by payee asc, remarks desc;
+-------+-------------------+--------+--------------------+
| check | payee             | amount | remarks            |
+-------+-------------------+--------+--------------------+
|     9 | ABES CLEANERS     |  24.35 | X-TRA STARCH       |
|    20 | ABES CLEANERS     |  10.50 | ALL DRY CLEAN      |
|    16 | CASH              |  25.00 | WILD NIGHT OUT     |
|    21 | CASH              |  34.00 | TRIP TO DAYTON     |
|     8 | CASH              |  60.00 | TRIP TO BOSTON     |
|    17 | JOANS GAS         |  25.10 | GAS                |
|     5 | JOES STALE $ DENT | 150.00 | GROCERIES          |
|     4 | LOCAL UTILITIES   |  98.00 | GAS                |
|     1 | MA BELL           | 150.00 | HAVE SONS NEXT TIME|
|     3 | MA BELL           | 200.32 | CELLUAR PHONE      |
|     2 | READING R.R.      | 245.34 | TRAIN TO CHICAGO   |
+-------+-------------------+--------+--------------------+
11 rows in set (0.00 sec)
```

Analysis ▼

In this example, PAYEE is sorted alphabetically, and REMARKS appears in descending order.
Note how the remarks in the three checks with a PAYEE of CASH are sorted. The default
sort order is ascending. Some implementations require only the specification of descending order, whereas other implementations require the sort order to be specified.

TIP

TIP

If you know that a column you want to order your results by is the first column in a table, you can type **ORDER BY 1** in place of spelling out the column name. See the following example.

Input/Output ▼

```
SQL> SELECT *
  2  FROM CHECKS
  3  ORDER BY 1;

    CHECK# PAYEE                    AMOUNT REMARKS
---------- -------------------- ---------- --------------------
         1 MA BELL                     150 HAVE SONS NEXT TIME
         2 READING R.R.             245.34 TRAIN TO CHICAGO
         3 MA BELL                  200.32 CELLULAR PHONE
         4 LOCAL UTILITIES              98 GAS
         5 JOES STALE $ DENT           150 GROCERIES
         8 CASH                         60 TRIP TO BOSTON
         9 ABES CLEANERS             24.35 X-TRA STARCH
        16 CASH                         25 WILD NIGHT OUT
        17 JOANS GAS                  25.1 GAS
        20 ABES CLEANERS              10.5 ALL DRY CLEAN
        21 CASH                         34 TRIP TO DAYTON

11 rows selected.
```

The MySQL equivalent is

Input/Output ▼

```
mysql> select * from checks order by 1;
+-------+--------------------+--------+---------------------+
| check | payee              | amount | remarks             |
+-------+--------------------+--------+---------------------+
|     1 | MA BELL            | 150.00 | HAVE SONS NEXT TIME |
|     2 | READING R.R.       | 245.34 | TRAIN TO CHICAGO    |
|     3 | MA BELL            | 200.32 | CELLUAR PHONE       |
|     4 | LOCAL UTILITIES    |  98.00 | GAS                 |
|     5 | JOES STALE $ DENT  | 150.00 | GROCERIES           |
|     8 | CASH               |  60.00 | TRIP TO BOSTON      |
|     9 | ABES CLEANERS      |  24.35 | X-TRA STARCH        |
|    16 | CASH               |  25.00 | WILD NIGHT OUT      |
|    17 | JOANS GAS          |  25.10 | GAS                 |
|    20 | ABES CLEANERS      |  10.50 | ALL DRY CLEAN       |
|    21 | CASH               |  34.00 | TRIP TO DAYTON      |
+-------+--------------------+--------+---------------------+
11 rows in set (0.00 sec)
```

4

This result is identical to the result produced by the SELECT statement that you used earlier in this lesson when you ordered by check#.

The following is an example of ORDER BY ordering by a column not in the SELECT clause:

Input/Output ▼

```
SQL> SELECT PAYEE, AMOUNT, REMARKS
  2 FROM CHECKS
  3 ORDER BY CHECK#

PAYEE                 AMOUNT REMARKS
--------- -------------------- --------- -------------------
MA BELL                  150 HAVE SONS NEXT TIME
READING R.R.          245.34 TRAIN TO CHICAGO
MA BELL               200.32 CELLULAR PHONE
LOCAL UTILITIES           98 GAS
JOES STALE $ DENT        150 GROCERIES
CASH                      60 TRIP TO BOSTON
ABES CLEANERS          24.35 X-TRA STARCH
CASH                      25 WILD NIGHT OUT
JOANS GAS               25.1 GAS
ABES CLEANERS           10.5 ALL DRY CLEAN
CASH                      34 TRIP TO DAYTON

11 rows selected.
```

The GROUP BY Clause

In Lesson 7, "Molding Data with Built-in Functions," you will learn how to use aggregate functions (COUNT, SUM, AVG, MIN, and MAX). If you wanted to find the total amount of money spent from the modified CHECKS table, you would type

Input ▼

```
SQL> SELECT *
  2 FROM CHECKS;
```

Here's the modified table:

Output ▼

```
CHECKNUM PAYEE              AMOUNT REMARKS
======== =========== =============== ======================
       1 MA BELL                 150 HAVE SONS NEXT TIME
       2 READING R.R.         245.34 TRAIN TO CHICAGO
       3 MA BELL              200.33 CELLULAR PHONE
       4 LOCAL UTILITIES          98 GAS
```

```
 5 JOES STALE $ DENT       150 GROCERIES
16 CASH                     25 WILD NIGHT OUT
17 JOANS GAS              25.1 GAS
 9 ABES CLEANERS         24.35 X-TRA STARCH
20 ABES CLEANERS          10.5 ALL DRY CLEAN
 8 CASH                     60 TRIP TO BOSTON
21 CASH                     34 TRIP TO DAYTON
```

Then you would type

Input/Output ▼

```
SQL> SELECT SUM(AMOUNT)
  2 FROM CHECKS;

         SUM
----------------

     1159.87
```

This statement returns the sum of the column AMOUNT. What if you wanted to find out how much you have spent on each PAYEE? SQL helps you with the GROUP BY clause. To find out whom you have paid and how much, you would query like this:

Input/Output ▼

```
SQL> SELECT PAYEE, SUM(AMOUNT)
  2 FROM CHECKS
  3 GROUP BY PAYEE;

PAYEE                          SUM
==================== ================

ABES CLEANERS          34.849998
CASH                         119
JOANS GAS              40.849998
JOES STALE $ DENT            150
LOCAL UTILITIES            219.5
MA BELL                350.33002
READING R.R.              245.34
```

The MySQL equivalent is

Input/Output ▼

```
mysql> select payee, sum(amount)
    -> from checks
    -> group by payee;
+--------------------+-------------+
| payee              | sum(amount) |
+--------------------+-------------+
```

```
¦ ABES CLEANERS    ¦      34.85 ¦
¦ CASH             ¦     119.00 ¦
¦ JOANS GAS        ¦      40.85 ¦
¦ JOES STALE $ DENT ¦    150.00 ¦
¦ LOCAL UTILITIES  ¦     219.50 ¦
¦ MA BELL          ¦     350.33 ¦
¦ READING R.R.     ¦     245.34 ¦
+------------------+------------+
6 rows in set (0.28 sec)
```

The SELECT clause has a normal column selection, PAYEE, followed by the aggregate function SUM(AMOUNT). If you had tried this query in Oracle y with only the FROM CHECKS that follows, here's what you would see:

Input/Output ▼

```
SQL> SELECT PAYEE, SUM(AMOUNT)
  2 FROM CHECKS;

Dynamic SQL Error
-SQL error code = -104
-invalid column reference
```

SQL is complaining about the combination of the normal column and the aggregate function. This condition requires the GROUP BY clause. GROUP BY runs the aggregate function described in the SELECT statement for each grouping of the column that follows the GROUP BY clause. The table CHECKS returned 14 rows when queried with SELECT * FROM CHECKS. The query on the same table, SELECT PAYEE, SUM(AMOUNT) FROM CHECKS GROUP BY PAYEE, took the 14 rows in the table and made seven groupings, returning the SUM of each grouping.

Suppose you wanted to know how much you gave to whom with how many checks. Can you use more than one aggregate function?

Input/Output ▼

```
SQL> SELECT PAYEE, SUM(AMOUNT), COUNT(PAYEE)
  2 FROM CHECKS
  3 GROUP BY PAYEE;
```

PAYEE	SUM	COUNT
====================	===============	===========
ABES CLEANERS	34.849998	2
CASH	119	3
JOANS GAS	40.849998	2
JOES STALE $ DENT	150	1
LOCAL UTILITIES	219.5	3
MA BELL	350.33002	2
READING R.R.	245.34	1

The MySQL equivalent is

Input/Output ▼

```
mysql> select payee, sum(amount), count(payee)
    -> from checks
    -> group by payee;
+-------------------+-------------+--------------+
| payee             | sum(amount) | count(payee) |
+-------------------+-------------+--------------+
| ABES CLEANERS     |       34.85 |            2 |
| CASH              |      119.00 |            3 |
| JOANS GAS         |       40.85 |            2 |
| JOES STALE $ DENT |      150.00 |            1 |
| LOCAL UTILITIES   |      219.50 |            3 |
| MA BELL           |      350.33 |            2 |
| READING R.R.      |      245.34 |            1 |
+-------------------+-------------+--------------+
6 rows in set (0.00 sec)
```

This SQL is becoming increasingly useful! In the preceding example, you were able to perform group functions on unique groups using the GROUP BY clause. Also notice that the results were ordered by PAYEE. GROUP BY also acts like the ORDER BY clause. What would happen if you tried to group by more than one column? Try this:

4

Input/Output ▼

```
SQL> SELECT PAYEE, SUM(AMOUNT), COUNT(PAYEE)
  2 FROM CHECKS
  3 GROUP BY PAYEE, REMARKS;
```

PAYEE	SUM	COUNT
ABES CLEANERS	10.5	1
ABES CLEANERS	24.35	1
CASH	60	1
CASH	34	1
CASH	25	1
JOANS GAS	40.849998	2
JOES STALE $ DENT	150	1
LOCAL UTILITIES	98	1
LOCAL UTILITIES	34	1
LOCAL UTILITIES	87.5	1
MA BELL	200.33	1
MA BELL	150	1
READING R.R.	245.34	1

The output has gone from 7 groupings of 14 rows to 13 groupings. What is different about the one grouping with more than one check associated with it? Look at the entries for Joans Gas:

Input/Output ▼

```
SQL> SELECT PAYEE, REMARKS
  2 FROM CHECKS
  3 WHERE PAYEE = 'JOANS GAS';

PAYEE                REMARKS
==================== ====================

JOANS GAS            GAS
JOANS GAS            GAS
```

Analysis ▼

You see that the combination of PAYEE and REMARKS creates identical entities, which SQL groups together into one line with the GROUP BY clause. The other rows produce unique combinations of PAYEE and REMARKS and are assigned their own unique groupings.

The next example finds the largest and smallest amounts, grouped by REMARKS:

Input/Output ▼

```
SQL> SELECT MIN(AMOUNT), MAX(AMOUNT)
  2 FROM CHECKS
  3 GROUP BY REMARKS;

            MIN             MAX
=============== ===============

         245.34          245.34
           10.5            10.5
         200.33          200.33
          15.75              98
            150             150
            150             150
             34              34
             60              60
             34              34
           87.5            87.5
             25              25
          24.35           24.35
```

The MySQL equivalent is

Input/Output ▼

```
mysql> select min(amount), max(amount)
    -> from checks
    -> group by remarks;
+-------------+-------------+
| min(amount) | max(amount) |
+-------------+-------------+
|      245.34 |      245.34 |
|       10.50 |       10.50 |
|      200.33 |      200.33 |
|       15.75 |       98.00 |
|      150.00 |      150.00 |
|      150.00 |      150.00 |
|       34.00 |       34.00 |
|       60.00 |       60.00 |
|       34.00 |       34.00 |
|       87.50 |       87.50 |
|       25.00 |       25.00 |
|       24.35 |       24.35 |
+-------------+-------------+
12 rows in set (0.00 sec)
```

Here's what will happen if you try to include in the SELECT statement a column that has several different values within the group formed by GROUP BY:

Input/Output ▼

```
SQL> SELECT PAYEE, MAX(AMOUNT), MIN(AMOUNT)
  2 FROM CHECKS
  3 GROUP BY REMARKS;

Dynamic SQL Error
-SQL error code = -104
-invalid column reference
```

This query tries to group CHECKS by REMARKS. When the query finds two records with the same REMARKS but different PAYEEs, such as the rows that have GAS as a REMARK but have PAYEEs of LOCAL UTILITIES and JOANS GAS, it throws an error.

The rule is, don't use columns in the SELECT statement that are neither aggregated or used in the GROUP BY clause. The reverse is not true. You can use GROUP BY on columns not mentioned in the SELECT statement—for example,

Input/Output ▼

```
SQL> SELECT PAYEE, COUNT(AMOUNT)
  2 FROM CHECKS
  3 GROUP BY PAYEE, AMOUNT;
```

4

```
PAYEE                    COUNT
====================  ===========

ABES CLEANERS               1
ABES CLEANERS               1
CASH                        1
CASH                        1
CASH                        1
JOANS GAS                   1
JOANS GAS                   1
JOES STALE $ DENT           1
LOCAL UTILITIES             1
LOCAL UTILITIES             1
LOCAL UTILITIES             1
MA BELL                     1
MA BELL                     1
READING R.R.                1
```

The MySQL equivalent is

Input/Output ▼

```
mysql> select payee, count(amount)
    -> from checks
    -> group by amount;
+-------------------+---------------+
| payee             | count(amount) |
+-------------------+---------------+
| ABES CLEANERS     |             1 |
| ABES CLEANERS     |             1 |
| CASH              |             1 |
| CASH              |             1 |
| CASH              |             1 |
| JOANS GAS         |             1 |
| JOANS GAS         |             1 |
| JOES STALE $ DENT |             1 |
| LOCAL UTILITIES   |             1 |
| LOCAL UTILITIES   |             1 |
| LOCAL UTILITIES   |             1 |
| MA BELL           |             1 |
| MA BELL           |             1 |
| READING R.R.      |             1 |
+-------------------+---------------+
14 rows in set (0.00 sec)
```

This query shows how many checks you had written for identical amounts to the same
PAYEE. Its real purpose is to show that you can use AMOUNT in the GROUP BY clause, even
though it is not mentioned in the SELECT clause. Try moving AMOUNT out of the GROUP BY
clause and into the SELECT clause, like this:

Input/Output ▼

```
SQL> SELECT PAYEE, AMOUNT, COUNT(AMOUNT)
  2 FROM CHECKS
  3 GROUP BY PAYEE;

Dynamic SQL Error
-SQL error code = -104
-invalid column reference
```

SQL cannot run the query, which makes sense if you play the part of SQL for a moment. Say you had to group the following lines:

Input/Output ▼

```
SQL> SELECT PAYEE, AMOUNT, REMARKS
  2 FROM CHECKS
  3 WHERE PAYEE ='CASH';

PAYEE                     AMOUNT REMARKS
==================== =============== ===============

CASH                          25 WILD NIGHT OUT
CASH                          60 TRIP TO BOSTON
CASH                          34 TRIP TO DAYTON
```

If the user asked you to output all three columns and group by PAYEE only, where would you put the unique remarks? Remember you have only one row per group when you use GROUP BY. SQL can't do two things at once, so it complains:

```
Error #31: Can't do two things at once.
```

The HAVING Clause

How can you qualify the data used in your GROUP BY clause? Use the table ORGCHART and try this:

Input/Output ▼

```
SQL> SELECT * FROM ORGCHART;

NAME             TEAM        SALARY   SICKLEAVE ANNUALLEAVE
=============== ======== =========== =========== ===========

ADAMS            RESEARCH    34000.00          34          12
WILKES           MARKETING   31000.00          40           9
```

4

```
STOKES        MARKETING    36000.00        20        19
MEZA          COLLECTIONS  40000.00        30        27
MERRICK       RESEARCH     45000.00        20        17
RICHARDSON    MARKETING    42000.00        25        18
FURY          COLLECTIONS  35000.00        22        14
PRECOURT      PR           37500.00        24        24
```

The MySQL equivalent is

Input/Output ▼

```
mysql> select * from orgchart;
+------------+-------------+----------+-----------+------------+
| name       | team        | salary   | sickleave | annualleave |
+------------+-------------+----------+-----------+------------+
| ADAMS      | RESEARCH    | 34000.00 |        34 |         12 |
| WILKES     | MARKETING   | 31000.00 |        40 |          9 |
| STOKES     | MARKETING   | 36000.00 |        20 |         19 |
| MEZA       | COLLECTIONS | 40000.00 |        30 |         27 |
| MERRICK    | RESEARCH    | 45000.00 |        20 |         17 |
| RICHARDSON | MARKETING   | 42000.00 |        25 |         18 |
| FURY       | COLLECTIONS | 35000.00 |        22 |         14 |
| PRECOURT   | PR          | 37500.00 |        24 |         24 |
+------------+-------------+----------+-----------+------------+
8 rows in set (0.00 sec)
```

If you wanted to group the output into teams and show the average salary in each team, you would type:

Input/Output ▼

```
SQL> SELECT TEAM, AVG(SALARY)
  2 FROM ORGCHART
  3 GROUP BY TEAM;

TEAM              AVG
=============== ===========

COLLECTIONS       37500.00
MARKETING         36333.33j
PR                37500.00
RESEARCH          39500.00
mysql> select team, avg(salary)
    -> from orgchart
    -> group by team;
+------------+-------------+
| team       | avg(salary) |
+------------+-------------+
```

```
| COLLECTIONS | 37500.000000 |
| MARKETING   | 36333.333333 |
| PR          | 37500.000000 |
| RESEARCH    | 39500.000000 |
+-------------+--------------+
4 rows in set (0.00 sec)
```

The following statement qualifies this query to return only those departments with average salaries under 38000:

Input/Output ▼

```
SQL> SELECT TEAM, AVG(SALARY)
  2 FROM ORGCHART
  3 WHERE AVG(SALARY) < 38000
  4 GROUP BY TEAM;

Dynamic SQL Error
-SQL error code = -104
-Invalid aggregate reference
```

The MySQL equivalent is

Input/Output ▼

```
mysql> select team, avg(salary)
    -> from orgchart
    -> where avg(salary) < 30000
    -> group by team;
ERROR 1111: Invalid use of group function
```

This error occurred because WHERE does not work with aggregate functions. To make this query work, you need something new: the HAVING clause. If you type the following query, you get what you ask for:

Input/Output ▼

```
SQL> SELECT TEAM, AVG(SALARY)
  2 FROM ORGCHART
  3 GROUP BY TEAM
  4 HAVING AVG(SALARY) < 38000;

TEAM                 AVG
=============== ===========

COLLECTIONS     37500.00
MARKETING       36333.33
PR              37500.00
```

The MySQL equivalent is

Input/Output ▼

```
mysql> select team, avg(salary)
    -> from orgchart
    -> group by team
    -> having avg(salary) < 38000;
+-------------+-------------+
¦ team        ¦ avg(salary) ¦
+-------------+-------------+
¦ COLLECTIONS ¦ 37500.000000 ¦
¦ MARKETING   ¦ 36333.333333 ¦
¦ PR          ¦ 37500.000000 ¦
+-------------+-------------+
3 rows in set (0.00 sec)
```

Analysis ▼

HAVING enables you to use aggregate functions in a comparison statement, providing for aggregate functions what WHERE provides for individual rows. Does HAVING work with nonaggregate expressions? Try this:

Input/Output ▼

```
SQL> SELECT TEAM, AVG(SALARY)
  2 FROM ORGCHART
  3 GROUP BY TEAM
  4 HAVING SALARY < 38000;


TEAM                     AVG
=============== ===========

PR              37500.00
```

Analysis ▼

Why is this result different from the last query? The HAVING AVG(SALARY) < 38000 clause evaluated each grouping and returned only those with an average salary of under 38000, just what you expected. HAVING SALARY < 38000, on the other hand, had a different outcome. Take on the role of the SQL engine again. If the user asks you to evaluate and return groups of teams where SALARY < 38000, you would examine each group and reject those where an individual SALARY is greater than or equal to 38000. In each team except PR, you would find at least one salary greater than 38000:

Input/Output ▼

```
SQL> SELECT NAME, TEAM, SALARY
  2 FROM ORGCHART
  3 ORDER BY TEAM;
```

```
NAME              TEAM              SALARY
================  ================  ===========

FURY              COLLECTIONS        35000.00
MEZA              COLLECTIONS        40000.00
WILKES            MARKETING          31000.00
STOKES            MARKETING          36000.00
RICHARDSON        MARKETING          42000.00
PRECOURT          PR                 37500.00
ADAMS             RESEARCH           34000.00
MERRICK           RESEARCH           45000.00
```

Therefore, you would reject all other groups except PR. What you really asked was, select all groups where no individual makes more than 38000. Don't you just hate it when the computer does exactly what you tell it to do?

CAUTION

Some implementations of SQL return an error if you use anything other than an aggregate function in a HAVING clause. Don't bet the farm on using the previous example until you check the implementation of the particular SQL you use.

MySQL, for example, will not evaluate this expression:

Input/Output ▼

```
mysql> select team, avg(salary)
    -> from orgchart
    -> group by team
    -> having salary < 38000;
ERROR 1054: Unknown column 'salary' in 'having clause'
```

To get around this, all you have to do is include the nonaggregate column in your select statement:

Input/Output ▼

```
mysql> select team, salary, avg(salary)
    -> from orgchart
    -> group by team
    -> having salary < 38000;
+-----------+----------+---------------+
| team      | salary   | avg(salary)   |
+-----------+----------+---------------+
| MARKETING | 31000.00 | 36333.333333  |
| PR        | 37500.00 | 37500.000000  |
| RESEARCH  | 34000.00 | 39500.000000  |
+-----------+----------+---------------+
3 rows in set (0.00 sec)
```

4

Can you use more than one condition in your HAVING clause? Try this:

Input ▼

```
SQL> SELECT TEAM, AVG(SICKLEAVE),AVG(ANNUALLEAVE)
  2 FROM ORGCHART
  3 GROUP BY TEAM
  4 HAVING AVG(SICKLEAVE)>25 AND
  5 AVG(ANNUALLEAVE)<20;
```

The following table is grouped by TEAM. It shows all the teams with SICKLEAVE averages above 25 days and ANNUALLEAVE averages below 20 days.

Output ▼

TEAM	AVG	AVG
================	===========	===========
MARKETING	28	15
RESEARCH	27	15

The MySQL equivalent is

Input/Output ▼

```
mysql> select team, avg(sickleave), avg(annualleave)
    -> from orgchart
    -> group by team
    -> having avg(sickleave) > 25 and
    -> avg(annualleave) < 20;
+-----------+----------------+------------------+
| team      | avg(sickleave) | avg(annualleave) |
+-----------+----------------+------------------+
| MARKETING |        28.3333 |          15.3333 |
| RESEARCH  |        27.0000 |          14.5000 |
+-----------+----------------+------------------+
2 rows in set (0.00 sec)
```

In some implementations, you can also use an aggregate function in the HAVING clause that was not in the SELECT statement—for example,

Input/Output ▼

```
SQL> SELECT TEAM, AVG(SICKLEAVE),AVG(ANNUALLEAVE)
  2 FROM ORGCHART
  3 GROUP BY TEAM
  4 HAVING COUNT(TEAM) > 1;
```

```
TEAM                      AVG           AVG
===============   ===========   ===========

COLLECTIONS                26            21
MARKETING                  28            15
RESEARCH                   27            15
```

This query returns the number of TEAMs with more than one member. COUNT(TEAM) is not used in the SELECT statement but still functions as expected in the HAVING clause.

The other logical operators all work well within the HAVING clause. Consider this:

Input/Output ▼

```
SQL> SELECT TEAM,MIN(SALARY),MAX(SALARY)
  2 FROM ORGCHART
  3 GROUP BY TEAM
  4 HAVING AVG(SALARY) > 37000
  5 OR
  6 MIN(SALARY) > 32000;

TEAM                      MIN           MAX
===============   ===========   ===========

COLLECTIONS          35000.00      40000.00
PR                   37500.00      37500.00
RESEARCH             34000.00      45000.00
```

4

The operator IN also works in a HAVING clause, as demonstrated here:

Input/Output ▼

```
SQL> SELECT TEAM,AVG(SALARY)
  2 FROM ORGCHART
  3 GROUP BY TEAM
  4 HAVING TEAM IN ('PR','RESEARCH');

TEAM                      AVG
===============   ===========

PR                   37500.00
RESEARCH             39500.00
```

The syntax in these examples is the same for both Oracle and MySQL.

Combining Clauses

Nothing exists in a vacuum, so this section takes you through some composite examples that demonstrate how combinations of clauses perform together.

Example 4.1

Find all the checks written for CASH and GAS in the CHECKS table and order them by REMARKS.

Input/Output ▼

```
SQL> SELECT PAYEE, REMARKS
   2 FROM CHECKS
   3 WHERE PAYEE = 'CASH'
   4 OR REMARKS LIKE'GA%'
   5 ORDER BY REMARKS;


PAYEE                REMARKS
=================== ====================

JOANS GAS            GAS
JOANS GAS            GAS
LOCAL UTILITIES      GAS
CASH                 TRIP TO BOSTON
CASH                 TRIP TO DAYTON
CASH                 WILD NIGHT OUT
```

Analysis ▼

Note the use of LIKE to find the REMARKS that started with GA. With the use of OR, data was returned if the WHERE clause met either one of the two conditions.

What if you asked for the same information and grouped it by PAYEE? The query would look something like this:

Input ▼

```
SQL> SELECT PAYEE, REMARKS
   2 FROM CHECKS
   3 WHERE PAYEE = 'CASH'
   4 OR REMARKS LIKE'GA%'GROUP BY PAYEE
   5 ORDER BY REMARKS;
```

This query would not work because the SQL engine would not know what to do with the remarks. Remember that whatever columns you put in the SELECT clause must also be in the GROUP BY clause—unless you don't specify any columns in the SELECT clause.

Example 4.2

Using the table ORGCHART, find the salary of everyone with less than 25 days of SICK-LEAVE. Order the results by NAME.

Input/Output ▼

```
SQL> SELECT NAME, SALARY
  2 FROM ORGCHART
  3 WHERE SICKLEAVE < 25
  4 ORDER BY NAME;

NAME              SALARY
=============== ===========

FURY            35000.00
MERRICK         45000.00
PRECOURT        37500.00
STOKES          36000.00
```

This query is straightforward and enables you to use your newfound skills with WHERE and ORDER BY.

Example 4.3

Again, using ORGCHART, display TEAM, AVG(SALARY), AVG(SICKLEAVE), and AVG(ANNUALLEAVE) on each team:

Input/Output ▼

```
SQL> SELECT TEAM,
  2 AVG(SALARY),
  3 AVG(SICKLEAVE),
  4 AVG(ANNUALLEAVE)
  5 FROM ORGCHART
  6 GROUP BY TEAM;

TEAM                   AVG         AVG         AVG
=============== =========== =========== ===========

COLLECTIONS       37500.00          26          21
MARKETING         36333.33          28          15
PR                37500.00          24          24
RESEARCH          39500.00          26          15
```

An interesting variation on this query follows. See whether you can figure out what happened:

Input/Output ▼

```
SQL> SELECT TEAM,
  2 AVG(SALARY),
  3 AVG(SICKLEAVE),
  4 AVG(ANNUALLEAVE)
  5 FROM ORGCHART
  6 GROUP BY TEAM
  7 ORDER BY NAME;
```

TEAM	AVG	AVG	AVG
RESEARCH	39500.00	27	15
COLLECTIONS	37500.00	26	21
PR	37500.00	24	24
MARKETING	36333.33	28	15

A simpler query using ORDER BY might offer a clue:

Input/Output ▼

```
SQL> SELECT NAME, TEAM
  2 FROM ORGCHART
  3 ORDER BY NAME, TEAM;
```

NAME	TEAM
ADAMS	RESEARCH
FURY	COLLECTIONS
MERRICK	RESEARCH
MEZA	COLLECTIONS
PRECOURT	PR
RICHARDSON	MARKETING
STOKES	MARKETING
WILKES	MARKETING

When the SQL engine got around to ordering the results of the query, it used the NAME column (remember, it is perfectly legal to use a column not specified in the SELECT statement), ignored duplicate TEAM entries, and came up with the order RESEARCH, COLLECTIONS, PR, and MARKETING. Including TEAM in the ORDER BY clause is unnecessary because you have unique values in the NAME column. You can get the same result by typing this statement:

Input/Output ▼

```
SQL> SELECT NAME, TEAM
  2 FROM ORGCHART
  3 ORDER BY NAME;

NAME             TEAM
=============== ============

ADAMS            RESEARCH
FURY             COLLECTIONS
MERRICK          RESEARCH
MEZA             COLLECTIONS
PRECOURT         PR
RICHARDSON       MARKETING
STOKES           MARKETING
WILKES           MARKETING
```

While you are looking at variations, don't forget that you can also reverse the order:

Input/Output ▼

```
SQL> SELECT NAME, TEAM
  2 FROM ORGCHART
  3 ORDER BY NAME DESC;

NAME             TEAM
=============== ============

WILKES           MARKETING
STOKES           MARKETING
RICHARDSON       MARKETING
PRECOURT         PR
MEZA             COLLECTIONS
MERRICK          RESEARCH
FURY             COLLECTIONS
ADAMS            RESEARCH
```

4

Example 4.4

Is it possible to use everything you have learned in one query? It is, but the results will be convoluted because in many ways you are working with apples and oranges—or aggregates and nonaggregates. For example, WHERE and ORDER BY are usually found in queries that act on single rows, such as the query shown in this example:

Input/Output ▼

```
SQL> SELECT *
  2  FROM ORGCHART
  3  ORDER BY NAME DESC;
```

NAME	TEAM	SALARY	SICKLEAVE	ANNUALLEAVE
WILKES	MARKETING	31000.00	40	9
STOKES	MARKETING	36000.00	20	19
RICHARDSON	MARKETING	42000.00	25	18
PRECOURT	PR	37500.00	24	24
MEZA	COLLECTIONS	40000.00	30	27
MERRICK	RESEARCH	45000.00	20	17
FURY	COLLECTIONS	35000.00	22	14
ADAMS	RESEARCH	34000.00	34	12

GROUP BY and HAVING are normally seen in the company of aggregates:

Input/Output ▼

```
SQL> SELECT PAYEE,
  2  SUM(AMOUNT) TOTAL,
  3  COUNT(PAYEE) NUMBER_WRITTEN
  4  FROM CHECKS
  5  GROUP BY PAYEE
  6  HAVING SUM(AMOUNT) > 50;
```

PAYEE	TOTAL	NUMBER_WRITTEN
CASH	119	3
JOES STALE $ DENT	150	1
LOCAL UTILITIES	219.5	3
MA BELL	350.33002	2
READING R.R.	245.34	1

You have seen that combining these two groups of clauses can have unexpected results, including the following:

Input/Output ▼

```
SQL> SELECT PAYEE,
  2  SUM(AMOUNT) TOTAL,
  3  COUNT(PAYEE) NUMBER_WRITTEN
  4  FROM CHECKS
  5  WHERE AMOUNT >= 100
  6  GROUP BY PAYEE
  7  HAVING SUM(AMOUNT) > 50;
```

```
PAYEE                     TOTAL NUMBER_WRITTEN
==================== ================ ===============

JOES STALE $ DENT              150               1
MA BELL                  350.33002               2
READING R.R.                245.34               1
```

Compare these two result sets and examine the raw data:

Input/Output ▼

```
SQL> SELECT PAYEE, AMOUNT
  2 FROM CHECKS
  3 ORDER BY PAYEE;

PAYEE                     AMOUNT
==================== ================

ABES CLEANERS               10.5
ABES CLEANERS              24.35
CASH                          25
CASH                          34
CASH                          60
JOANS GAS                  15.75
JOANS GAS                   25.1
JOES STALE $ DENT            150
LOCAL UTILITIES               34
LOCAL UTILITIES             87.5
LOCAL UTILITIES               98
MA BELL                      150
MA BELL                   200.33
READING R.R.              245.34
```

Analysis ▼

You see how the WHERE clause filtered out all the checks less than 100 dollars before the GROUP BY was performed on the query. We are not trying to tell you not to mix these groups—you might have a requirement that this sort of construction will meet. However, you should not casually mix aggregate and nonaggregate functions. The previous examples have been tables with only a handful of rows. (Otherwise, you would need a cart to carry this book.) In the real world, you will be working with thousands and thousands (or billions and billions) of rows, and the subtle changes caused by mixing these clauses might not be so apparent.

Summary

In this lesson, you learned all the clauses you need to exploit the power of a SELECT statement. Remember to be careful what you ask for because you just might get it. Your basic SQL education is complete. You already know enough to work effectively with single tables. In the next lesson (Lesson 5, "Joining Tables"), you will have the opportunity to work with multiple tables.

Q&A

Q Why are we covering the GROUP BY clauses in this lesson before we cover functions such as SUM?

A We are looking at the GROUP BY clause in this lesson because it fits more precisely with the topic of clauses. Now when we investigate built-in functions in Lesson 7, you will already be prepared to deal with aggregate functions within your queries.

Workshop

The Workshop provides quiz questions to help solidify your understanding of the material covered, as well as exercises to provide you with experience in using what you have learned. Try to answer the quiz and exercise questions before checking the answers in Appendix A, "Answers." These statements allow you to create and populate the ORGCHART table.

```
create table orgchart
(name            varchar(15)     not null,
 team            varchar(11)     not null,
 salary          decimal(10,2)   not null,
 sickleave       numeric(10)     not null,
 annualleave     numeric(11)     not null);
insert into orgchart values
('ADAMS', 'RESEARCH', '34000.00', '34', '12');
insert into orgchart values
('WILKES', 'MARKETING', '31000.00', '40', '9');
insert into orgchart values
('STOKES', 'MARKETING', '36000.00', '20', '19');
insert into orgchart values
('MEZA', 'COLLECTIONS', '40000.00', '30', '27');
insert into orgchart values
('MERRICK', 'RESEARCH', '45000.00', '20', '17');
insert into orgchart values
('RICHARDSON', 'MARKETING', '42000.00', '25', '18');
insert into orgchart values
('FURY', 'COLLECTIONS', '35000.00', '22', '14');
```

```
insert into orgchart values
('PRECOURT', 'PR', '37500.00', '24', '24');
```

Quiz

1. When performing aggregate functions (`sum(column_name)`) must you group on all nonaggregate columns in your SELECT statement?

2. What is the function of the GROUP BY clause, and what other clause does it act like?

3. Will this SELECT work?

```
SQL> SELECT NAME, AVG(SALARY), DEPARTMENT
     FROM PAY_TBL
     WHERE DEPARTMENT = 'ACCOUNTING'
     ORDER BY NAME
     GROUP BY DEPARTMENT, SALARY;
```

4. When using the HAVING clause, do you always have to use a GROUP BY also?

5. Can you use ORDER BY on a column that is not one of the columns in the SELECT statement?

6. How is the ordering handled with a GROUP BY statement when there is no corresponding ORDER BY clause?

7. What will the ordering of the following statement be?

```
SQL> SELECT NAME, AVG(SALARY), DEPARTMENT
     FROM PAY_TBL
     WHERE DEPARTMENT = 'ACCOUNTING'
     GROUP BY DEPARTMENT, SALARY
     ORDER BY 2,1;
```

Exercises

1. Using the ORGCHART table, find out how many people on each team have 30 or more days of SICKLEAVE.

2. Using the CHECKS table, write a SELECT that will return the following:

```
CHECK#    PAYEE      AMOUNT
    1     MA BELL       150
```

3. Consider the following SQL code and result set:

```
mysql> select team, sum(sickleave), sum(annualleave)
    -> from orgchart
    -> group by team;
```

```
+--------------+----------------+------------------+
| team         | sum(sickleave) | sum(annualleave) |
+--------------+----------------+------------------+
| COLLECTIONS  |             52 |               41 |
| MARKETING    |             85 |               46 |
| PR           |             24 |               24 |
| RESEARCH     |             54 |               29 |
+--------------+----------------+------------------+
```

Add the correct clause to the previous query so that the smallest amount of SICKLEAVE is listed first.

4. Will this query work?

```
mysql> select team, sum(sickleave), sum(annualleave)
    -> from orgchart
    -> where sickleave > annualleave
    -> group by team
    -> having avg(salary) >= 37500
    -> order by name;
```

5. Will this query work in MySQL?

```
mysql> select team, sum(sickleave), sum(annualleave)
    -> from orgchart
    -> where sickleave > annualleave
    -> group by team
    -> having salary >= 37500
    -> order by name;
```

6. This query orders the result set by the employee that has been gone the least, to the most:

```
mysql> select name, team, (sickleave+annualleave)
    -> from orgchart
    -> order by 3;
```

```
+------------+-------------+-------------------------+
| name       | team        | (sickleave+annualleave) |
+------------+-------------+-------------------------+
| FURY       | COLLECTIONS |                      36 |
| MERRICK    | RESEARCH    |                      37 |
| STOKES     | MARKETING   |                      39 |
| RICHARDSON | MARKETING   |                      43 |
| ADAMS      | RESEARCH    |                      46 |
| PRECOURT   | PR          |                      48 |
| WILKES     | MARKETING   |                      49 |
| MEZA       | COLLECTIONS |                      57 |
+------------+-------------+-------------------------+
```

Rewrite the previous query so that it orders the data by the employee that has taken the most leave.

LESSON 5
Joining Tables

One of the most powerful features of SQL is its capability to gather and manipulate data from across several tables. Without this feature you would have to store all the data elements necessary for each application in one table. Without common tables, you would need to store the same data in several tables. Imagine having to redesign, rebuild, and repopulate your tables and databases every time your user needed a query with a new piece of information. The JOIN statement of SQL enables you to design smaller, more specific tables that are easier to maintain than larger tables. By the end of the lesson, you will understand and be able to do the following:

- Perform an equi-join.

- Perform a non-equi-join.

- Perform an inner join.

- Perform an outer join.

- Join a table to itself.

Joining Multiple Tables in a Single SELECT Statement

Like Dorothy in *The Wizard of Oz* (who had the power to return home all along), you have had the power to join tables since Lesson 2, "Introducing the Query," when you learned about SELECT and FROM. Unlike Dorothy, you don't have to click your heels together three times to perform a join. The two following subsections cover some fundamental material with which you need to begin in order to understand join operations. First, we show you the simplest form of the join, and then how to select a common key between tables through which to perform the join operation. We will use the following two tables, named, cleverly enough, TABLE1 and TABLE2.

Input/Output ▼

```
SQL> SELECT *
  2 FROM TABLE1;

ROW         REMARKS
========== =======

row 1       Table 1
row 2       Table 1
row 3       Table 1
row 4       Table 1
row 5       Table 1
row 6       Table 1

SQL> SELECT *
  2 FROM TABLE2;

ROW         REMARKS
.........   ................

row 1       table 2
row 2       table 2
row 3       table 2
row 4       table 2
row 5       table 2
row 6       table 2
```

Notice also the following tables, FOOTBALL and SOFTBALL, which provide a second example that is a little more realistic.

MySQL example:

Input/Output ▼

```
mysql> select * from football;
+---------+
| name    |
+---------+
| ABLE    |
| BRAVO   |
| CHARLIE |
| DECON   |
| EXITOR  |
| FUBAR   |
| GOOBER  |
+---------+
7 rows in set (0.00 sec)
```

MySQL example:

Input/Output ▼

```
mysql> select * from softball;
+-----------+
¦ name      ¦
+-----------+
¦ ABLE      ¦
¦ BAKER     ¦
¦ CHARLIE   ¦
¦ DEAN      ¦
¦ EXITOR    ¦
¦ FALCONER  ¦
¦ GOOBER    ¦
+-----------+
7 rows in set (0.00 sec)
```

Cross Joining Tables

This section illustrates a cross join of two or more tables, also referred to as a *Cartesian product*. To fully understand the workings of a join operation in SQL, you must first understand a join with no restrictions, or conditions, in the WHERE clause.

To join TABLE1 and TABLE2, type this:

Input/Output ▼

```
SQL> SELECT *
  2 FROM TABLE1,TABLE2;

ROW        REMARKS    ROW        REMARKS
========== ========== ========== ========

row 1      Table 1    row 1      table 2
row 1      Table 1    row 2      table 2
row 1      Table 1    row 3      table 2
row 1      Table 1    row 4      table 2
row 1      Table 1    row 5      table 2
row 1      Table 1    row 6      table 2
row 2      Table 1    row 1      table 2
row 2      Table 1    row 2      table 2
row 2      Table 1    row 3      table 2
row 2      Table 1    row 4      table 2
row 2      Table 1    row 5      table 2
row 2      Table 1    row 6      table 2
row 3      Table 1    row 1      table 2
row 3      Table 1    row 2      table 2
row 3      Table 1    row 3      table 2
row 3      Table 1    row 4      table 2
```

5

```
row 3      Table 1    row 5      table 2
row 3      Table 1    row 6      table 2
row 4      Table 1    row 1      table 2
row 4      Table 1    row 2      table 2
row 4      Table 1    row 3      table 2
row 4      Table 1    row 4      table 2
row 4      Table 1    row 5      table 2
row 4      Table 1    row 6      table 2
row 5      Table 1    row 1      table 2
row 5      Table 1    row 2      table 2
row 5      Table 1    row 3      table 2
row 5      Table 1    row 4      table 2
row 5      Table 1    row 5      table 2
row 5      Table 1    row 6      table 2
row 6      Table 1    row 1      table 2
row 6      Table 1    row 2      table 2
row 6      Table 1    row 3      table 2
row 6      Table 1    row 4      table 2
row 6      Table 1    row 5      table 2
row 6      Table 1    row 6      table 2
```

Thirty-six rows! Where did they come from? And what kind of join is this?

Here is an example of this result using two actual tables and MySQL:

Input/Output ▼

```
mysql> select *
-> from football, softball;

+---------+---------+
¦ name    ¦ name    ¦
+---------+---------+
¦ ABLE    ¦ ABLE    ¦
¦ BRAVO   ¦ ABLE    ¦
¦ CHARLIE ¦ ABLE    ¦
¦ DECON   ¦ ABLE    ¦
¦ EXITOR  ¦ ABLE    ¦
¦ FUBAR   ¦ ABLE    ¦
¦ GOOBER  ¦ ABLE    ¦
¦ ABLE    ¦ BAKER   ¦
¦ BRAVO   ¦ BAKER   ¦
¦ CHARLIE ¦ BAKER   ¦
¦ DECON   ¦ BAKER   ¦
¦ EXITOR  ¦ BAKER   ¦
¦ FUBAR   ¦ BAKER   ¦
¦ GOOBER  ¦ BAKER   ¦
¦ ABLE    ¦ CHARLIE ¦
¦ BRAVO   ¦ CHARLIE ¦
¦ CHARLIE ¦ CHARLIE ¦
```

```
¦ DECON   ¦ CHARLIE  ¦
¦ EXITOR  ¦ CHARLIE  ¦
¦ FUBAR   ¦ CHARLIE  ¦
¦ GOOBER  ¦ CHARLIE  ¦
¦ ABLE    ¦ DEAN     ¦
¦ BRAVO   ¦ DEAN     ¦
¦ CHARLIE ¦ DEAN     ¦
¦ DECON   ¦ DEAN     ¦
¦ EXITOR  ¦ DEAN     ¦
¦ FUBAR   ¦ DEAN     ¦
¦ GOOBER  ¦ DEAN     ¦
¦ ABLE    ¦ EXITOR   ¦
¦ BRAVO   ¦ EXITOR   ¦
¦ CHARLIE ¦ EXITOR   ¦
¦ DECON   ¦ EXITOR   ¦
¦ EXITOR  ¦ EXITOR   ¦
¦ FUBAR   ¦ EXITOR   ¦
¦ GOOBER  ¦ EXITOR   ¦
¦ ABLE    ¦ FALCONER ¦
¦ BRAVO   ¦ FALCONER ¦
¦ CHARLIE ¦ FALCONER ¦
¦ DECON   ¦ FALCONER ¦
¦ EXITOR  ¦ FALCONER ¦
¦ FUBAR   ¦ FALCONER ¦
¦ GOOBER  ¦ FALCONER ¦
¦ ABLE    ¦ GOOBER   ¦
¦ BRAVO   ¦ GOOBER   ¦
¦ CHARLIE ¦ GOOBER   ¦
¦ DECON   ¦ GOOBER   ¦
¦ EXITOR  ¦ GOOBER   ¦
¦ FUBAR   ¦ GOOBER   ¦
¦ GOOBER  ¦ GOOBER   ¦
+---------+----------+
49 rows in set (0.00 sec)
```

Analysis ▼

A close examination of the result of your first JOIN shows that each row from TABLE1
was added to each row from TABLE2. An extract from this JOIN shows what happened:

```
ROW         REMARKS      ROW         REMARKS
=====       ==========   =========   ========

row 1       Table 1      row 1       table 2
row 1       Table 1      row 2       table 2
row 1       Table 1      row 3       table 2
row 1       Table 1      row 4       table 2
row 1       Table 1      row 5       table 2
row 1       Table 1      row 6       table 2
```

5

Notice how each row in TABLE2 was combined with row 1 in TABLE1. Congratulations! You have performed your first JOIN. But what kind of join? An inner join? An outer join? Or what? Well, actually this type of join is called a *cross join*. A cross join is not normally as useful as the other joins covered in this lesson, but this join does illustrate the basic combining property of all joins—joins bring tables together.

TIP

When you select from two or more tables without the use of a WHERE clause, you are performing a Cartesian join, also called a *Cartesian product*. This join combines all rows from all the tables in the FROM clause. If each table has 200 rows, you will end up with 40,000 rows in your results (200×200). Always join your tables in the WHERE clause unless you have a real need to join all the rows of all the selected tables.

Suppose you sold parts to bike shops for a living and wanted a database to track the bike parts. When you designed your database, you built one big table with all the pertinent columns. Every time you had a new requirement, you added a new column or started a new table with all the old data plus the new data required to create a specific query. Eventually, your database would collapse from its own weight—not a pretty sight. An alternative design, based on a relational model, would have you put all related data into one table. Here's how your CUSTOMER table would look:

Input/Output ▼

```
SQL> SELECT *
  2 FROM CUSTOMER;

NAME        ADDRESS     STATE  ZIP         PHONE      REMARKS
==========  ==========  ====== ==========  =========  ==========

TRUE WHEEL  550 HUSKER  NE     58702       555-4545   NONE
BIKE SPEC   CPT SHRIVE  LA     45678       555-1234   NONE
LE SHOPPE   HOMETOWN    KS     54678       555-1278   NONE
AAA BIKE    10 OLDTOWN  NE     56784       555-3421   JOHN-MGR
JACKS BIKE  24 EGLIN    FL     34567       555-2314   NONE
```

This table contains all the information you need to describe your customers. The items you sold would go into another table:

Input/Output ▼

```
SQL> SELECT *
  2 FROM PART;
```

```
PARTNUM DESCRIPTION              PRICE
=========== ==================== ===========

       54 PEDALS                 54.25
       42 SEATS                  24.50
       46 TIRES                  15.25
       23 MOUNTAIN BIKE         350.45
       76 ROAD BIKE             530.00
       10 TANDEM               1200.00
```

And the orders you take would have their own table:

Input/Output ▼

```
SQL> SELECT *
  2 FROM ORDERS;

ORDEREDON NAME         PARTNUM    QUANTITY REMARKS
=========== ========== =========== =========== =======

19-MAY-1996 TRUE WHEEL      76           3 PAID
 2-SEP-1996 TRUE WHEEL      10           1 PAID
30-JUN-1996 TRUE WHEEL      42           8 PAID
30-JUN-1996 BIKE SPEC       54          10 PAID
30-MAY-1996 BIKE SPEC       23           8 PAID
17-JAN-1996 BIKE SPEC       76          11 PAID
17-JAN-1996 LE SHOPPE       76           5 PAID
 1-JUN-1996 LE SHOPPE       10           3 PAID
 1-JUN-1996 AAA BIKE        10           1 PAID
 1-JUL-1996 AAA BIKE        76           4 PAID
 1-JUL-1996 AAA BIKE        46          14 PAID
11-JUL-1996 JACKS BIKE      76          14 PAID
```

We have selected all rows from both tables with no restrictions (no WHERE clause); therefore, we see all the data. We have two tables that are related. This is an example of normalizing your database (breaking down tables), which is covered in Lesson 8, "Database Normalization."

Now join PART and ORDERS:

Input/Output ▼

```
SQL> SELECT  O.ORDEREDON, O.NAME, O.PARTNUM,
  2 P.PARTNUM, P.DESCRIPTION
  3 FROM ORDERS O, PART P;
```

5

```
ORDEREDON NAME          PARTNUM    PARTNUM DESCRIPTION
=========== =========== ===========   ========= ===========
15-MAY-1996 TRUE WHEEL        23         54 PEDALS
19-MAY-1996 TRUE WHEEL        76         54 PEDALS
 2-SEP-1996 TRUE WHEEL        10         54 PEDALS
30-JUN-1996 TRUE WHEEL        42         54 PEDALS
30-JUN-1996 BIKE SPEC         54         54 PEDALS
30-MAY-1996 BIKE SPEC         10         54 PEDALS
30-MAY-1996 BIKE SPEC         23         54 PEDALS
17-JAN-1996 BIKE SPEC         76         54 PEDALS
17-JAN-1996 LE SHOPPE         76         54 PEDALS
 1-JUN-1996 LE SHOPPE         10         54 PEDALS
 1-JUN-1996 AAA BIKE          10         54 PEDALS
 1-JUL-1996 AAA BIKE          76         54 PEDALS
 1-JUL-1996 AAA BIKE          46         54 PEDALS
11-JUL-1996 JACKS BIKE        76         54 PEDALS
...
```

Analysis ▼

The preceding code is just a portion of the result set. The actual set is 14 (number of rows in ORDERS) X 6 (number of rows in PART), or 84 rows. It is similar to the result from joining TABLE1, TABLE2 and SOFTBALL, FOOTBALL shown earlier in this lesson, and it is still one statement shy of being useful. Before we reveal that statement, we need to regress a little and talk about another use for the alias.

Finding the Correct Column

When you joined TABLE1 and TABLE2, you used SELECT *, which returned all the columns in both tables. In joining ORDERS to PARTS, the SELECT statement is a bit more complicated:

Syntax ▼

```
SELECT  O.ORDEREDON, O.NAME, O.PARTNUM,
P.PARTNUM, P.DESCRIPTION
```

SQL is smart enough to know that ORDEREDON and NAME exist only in ORDERS and that DESCRIPTION exists only in PARTS, but what about PARTNUM, which exists in both? If you have a column that has the same name in two tables, you must use an alias in your SELECT clause to specify which column you want to display. A common technique is to assign a single character to each table, as you did in the FROM clause:

Syntax ▼

```
FROM ORDERS O, PARTS P
```

You use that character with each column name, as you did in the preceding SELECT clause. The SELECT clause could also be written like this:

Input ▼

```
SELECT  ORDEREDON, NAME, O.PARTNUM, P.PARTNUM, DESCRIPTION
```

But remember, someday you might have to come *back* and maintain this query. It doesn't hurt to make it more readable. Now back to the missing statement.

Joining Tables Based on Equality

An extract from the PARTS/ORDERS join provides a clue as to what is missing:

```
30-JUN-1996 TRUE WHEEL        42        54 PEDALS
30-JUN-1996 BIKE SPEC         54        54 PEDALS
30-MAY-1996 BIKE SPEC         10        54 PEDALS
```

Notice the PARTNUM fields that are common to both tables. What if you wrote the following?

Input/Output ▼

```
SQL> SELECT  O.ORDEREDON, O.NAME, O.PARTNUM,
  2 P.PARTNUM, P.DESCRIPTION
  3 FROM ORDERS O, PART P
  4 WHERE O.PARTNUM = P.PARTNUM;

   ORDEREDON NAME          PARTNUM      PARTNUM DESCRIPTION
=========== ========== =========== ========= ===============

  1-JUN-1996 AAA BIKE          10        10 TANDEM
30-MAY-1996 BIKE SPEC         10        10 TANDEM
  2-SEP-1996 TRUE WHEEL       10        10 TANDEM
  1-JUN-1996 LE SHOPPE        10        10 TANDEM
30-MAY-1996 BIKE SPEC         23        23 MOUNTAIN BIKE
15-MAY-1996 TRUE WHEEL        23        23 MOUNTAIN BIKE
30-JUN-1996 TRUE WHEEL        42        42 SEATS
  1-JUL-1996 AAA BIKE          46        46 TIRES
30-JUN-1996 BIKE SPEC         54        54 PEDALS
  1-JUL-1996 AAA BIKE          76        76 ROAD BIKE
17-JAN-1996 BIKE SPEC         76        76 ROAD BIKE
19-MAY-1996 TRUE WHEEL        76        76 ROAD BIKE
11-JUL-1996 JACKS BIKE        76        76 ROAD BIKE
17-JAN-1996 LE SHOPPE         76        76 ROAD BIKE
```

5

Using the column PARTNUM that exists in both of the preceding tables, you have just combined the information you had stored in the ORDERS table with information from the PARTS table to show a description of the parts that the bike shops have ordered from you.

The join that was used is called an *equi-join* because the goal is to match the values of a column in one table to the corresponding values in the second table based on some sort of equality.

You can further qualify this query by adding more conditions in the WHERE clause—for example,

Input/Output ▼

```
SQL> SELECT  O.ORDEREDON, O.NAME, O.PARTNUM,
  2 P.PARTNUM, P.DESCRIPTION
  3 FROM ORDERS O, PART P
  4 WHERE O.PARTNUM = P.PARTNUM
  5 AND O.PARTNUM = 76;
```

ORDEREDON	NAME	PARTNUM	PARTNUM	DESCRIPTION
1-JUL-1996	AAA BIKE	76	76	ROAD BIKE
17-JAN-1996	BIKE SPEC	76	76	ROAD BIKE
19-MAY-1996	TRUE WHEEL	76	76	ROAD BIKE
11-JUL-1996	JACKS BIKE	76	76	ROAD BIKE
17-JAN-1996	LE SHOPPE	76	76	ROAD BIKE

MySQL example:

Input/Output ▼

```
mysql> select o.orderedon, o.name, o.partnum,
    -> p.partnum, p.description
    -> from orders o,
    -> part p
    -> where p.partnum = o.partnum
    -> and o.partnum = 76;
+------------+------------+---------+---------+-------------+
| orderedon  | name       | partnum | partnum | description |
+------------+------------+---------+---------+-------------+
| 1996-05-19 | TRUE WHEEL |      76 |      76 | ROAD BIKE   |
| 1996-01-17 | BIKE SPEC  |      76 |      76 | ROAD BIKE   |
| 1996-01-17 | LE SHOPPE  |      76 |      76 | ROAD BIKE   |
| 1996-07-01 | AAA BIKE   |      76 |      76 | ROAD BIKE   |
| 1996-07-11 | JACKS BIKE |      76 |      76 | ROAD BIKE   |
+------------+------------+---------+---------+-------------+
5 rows in set (0.26 sec)
```

The number 76 is not very descriptive, and you wouldn't want your sales people to have to memorize a part number. (We have had the misfortune to see many data information systems in the field that require the end user to know some obscure code for something that had a perfectly good name. Please don't write one of those!) Here's another way to write the query:

Input/Output ▼

```
SQL> SELECT  O.ORDEREDON, O.NAME, O.PARTNUM,
  2 P.PARTNUM, P.DESCRIPTION
  3 FROM ORDERS O, PART P
  4 WHERE O.PARTNUM = P.PARTNUM
  5 AND P.DESCRIPTION = 'ROAD BIKE';

ORDEREDON NAME            PARTNUM     PARTNUM DESCRIPTION
=========== ========== =========== ========== ============

 1-JUL-1996 AAA BIKE            76          76 ROAD BIKE
17-JAN-1996 BIKE SPEC          76          76 ROAD BIKE
19-MAY-1996 TRUE WHEEL         76          76 ROAD BIKE
11-JUL-1996 JACKS BIKE         76          76 ROAD BIKE
17-JAN-1996 LE SHOPPE          76          76 ROAD BIKE
```

MySQL example:

Input/Output ▼

```
mysql> select o.orderedon, o.name, o.partnum,
    -> p.partnum, p.description
    -> from part p,
    -> orders o
    -> where p.partnum = o.partnum
    -> and p.description = 'ROAD BIKE';
+------------+------------+---------+---------+------------+
| orderedon  | name       | partnum | partnum | description |
+------------+------------+---------+---------+------------+
| 1996-05-19 | TRUE WHEEL |      76 |      76 | ROAD BIKE  |
| 1996-01-17 | BIKE SPEC  |      76 |      76 | ROAD BIKE  |
| 1996-01-17 | LE SHOPPE  |      76 |      76 | ROAD BIKE  |
| 1996-07-01 | AAA BIKE   |      76 |      76 | ROAD BIKE  |
| 1996-07-11 | JACKS BIKE |      76 |      76 | ROAD BIKE  |
+------------+------------+---------+---------+------------+
5 rows in set (0.02 sec)
```

5

Along the same line, take a look at two more tables to see how they can be joined. In this example, the employee_id column should obviously be unique. You could have employees with the same name, they could work in the same department, and earn the same salary. However, each employee would have his or her own `employee_id`. To join these two tables, you would use the `employee_id` column.

```
EMPLOYEE_TBL              EMPLOYEE_PAY_TBL
employee_id               employee_id
last_name                 salary
first_name                department
middle_name               supervisor
                          marital_status
```

Input/Output ▼

```
SQL> SELECT E.EMPLOYEE_ID, E.LAST_NAME, EP.SALARY
  2 FROM EMPLOYEE_TBL E,
  3 EMPLOYEE_PAY_TBL EP
  4 WHERE E.EMPLOYEE_ID = EP.EMPLOYEE_ID
  5 AND E.LAST_NAME = 'SMITH';

E.EMPLOYEE_ID  E.LAST_NAME   EP.SALARY
=============  ===========   =========
        13245  SMITH          35000.00
```

Back to the original tables. Now you are ready to use all this information about joins to do something really useful, such as finding out how much money you have made from selling road bikes:

Input/Output ▼

```
SQL> SELECT SUM(O.QUANTITY * P.PRICE) TOTAL
  2 FROM ORDERS O, PART P
  3 WHERE O.PARTNUM = P.PARTNUM
  4 AND P.DESCRIPTION = 'ROAD BIKE';

     TOTAL
===========

  19610.00
```

MySQL example:

Input/Output ▼

```
mysql> select sum(o.quantity * p.price) Total
    -> from orders o,
    -> part p
    -> where p.partnum = o.partnum
    -> and p.description = 'ROAD BIKE';
```

```
+----------+
| Total    |
+----------+
| 19610.00 |
+----------+
1 row in set (0.03 sec)
```

With this setup, the sales people can keep the ORDERS table updated, the production department can keep the PARTS table current, and you can find the bottom line without redesigning your database.

NOTE _____ Notice the consistent use of table and column aliases in the SQL statement examples. You will save many keystrokes by using aliases. They also help to make your statement more readable.

This next example is used to generate information to send out an invoice:

Input/Output ▼

```
SQL> SELECT C.NAME, C.ADDRESS, (O.QUANTITY * P.PRICE) TOTAL
   2 FROM ORDERS O, PART P, CUSTOMER C
   3 WHERE O.PARTNUM = P.PARTNUM
   4 AND O.NAME = C.NAME;

NAME        ADDRESS      TOTAL
==========  ==========  ===========

TRUE WHEEL  550 HUSKER    1200.00
LE SHOPPE   HOMETOWN      3600.00
AAA BIKE    10 OLDTOWN    1200.00
TRUE WHEEL  550 HUSKER    2102.70
BIKE SPEC   CPT SHRIVE    2803.60
TRUE WHEEL  550 HUSKER     196.00
AAA BIKE    10 OLDTOWN     213.50
BIKE SPEC   CPT SHRIVE     542.50
TRUE WHEEL  550 HUSKER    1590.00
BIKE SPEC   CPT SHRIVE    5830.00
JACKS BIKE  24 EGLIN      7420.00
LE SHOPPE   HOMETOWN      2650.00
AAA BIKE    10 OLDTOWN    2120.00
```

5

MySQL example:

Input/Output ▼

```
mysql> SELECT C.NAME, C.ADDRESS, (O.QUANTITY * P.PRICE) TOTAL
    -> FROM ORDERS O, PART P, CUSTOMER C
    -> WHERE O.PARTNUM = P.PARTNUM
    -> AND O.NAME = C.NAME;
+------------+------------+---------+
| NAME       | ADDRESS    | TOTAL   |
+------------+------------+---------+
| TRUE WHEEL | 550 HUSKER |  196.00 |
| TRUE WHEEL | 550 HUSKER | 1590.00 |
| TRUE WHEEL | 550 HUSKER | 1200.00 |
| BIKE SPEC  | CPT SHRIVE |  542.50 |
| BIKE SPEC  | CPT SHRIVE | 2803.60 |
| BIKE SPEC  | CPT SHRIVE | 5830.00 |
| LE SHOPPE  | HOMETOWN   | 2650.00 |
| LE SHOPPE  | HOMETOWN   | 3600.00 |
| AAA BIKE   | 10 OLDTOWN |  213.50 |
| AAA BIKE   | 10 OLDTOWN | 2120.00 |
| AAA BIKE   | 10 OLDTOWN | 1200.00 |
| JACKS BIKE | 24 EGLIN   | 7420.00 |
+------------+------------+---------+
12 rows in set (0.00 sec)
```

You could make the output more readable by writing the statement like this:

Input/Output ▼

```
SQL> SELECT C.NAME, C.ADDRESS,
  2 O.QUANTITY * P.PRICE TOTAL
  3 FROM ORDERS O, PART P, CUSTOMER C
  4 WHERE O.PARTNUM = P.PARTNUM
  5 AND O.NAME = C.NAME
  6 ORDER BY C.NAME;

NAME        ADDRESS         TOTAL
==========  ==========  ===========
AAA BIKE    10 OLDTOWN      213.50
AAA BIKE    10 OLDTOWN     2120.00
AAA BIKE    10 OLDTOWN     1200.00
BIKE SPEC   CPT SHRIVE      542.50
BIKE SPEC   CPT SHRIVE     2803.60
BIKE SPEC   CPT SHRIVE     5830.00
JACKS BIKE  24 EGLIN       7420.00
LE SHOPPE   HOMETOWN       2650.00
LE SHOPPE   HOMETOWN       3600.00
TRUE WHEEL  550 HUSKER      196.00
TRUE WHEEL  550 HUSKER     1590.00
TRUE WHEEL  550 HUSKER     1200.00
```

MySQL example:

Input/Output ▼

```
mysql> SELECT C.NAME, C.ADDRESS,
    -> O.QUANTITY * P.PRICE TOTAL
    -> FROM ORDERS O, PART P, CUSTOMER C
    -> WHERE O.PARTNUM = P.PARTNUM
    -> AND O.NAME = C.NAME
    -> ORDER BY C.NAME;
+------------+------------+---------+
| NAME       | ADDRESS    | TOTAL   |
+------------+------------+---------+
| AAA BIKE   | 10 OLDTOWN |  213.50 |
| AAA BIKE   | 10 OLDTOWN | 2120.00 |
| AAA BIKE   | 10 OLDTOWN | 1200.00 |
| BIKE SPEC  | CPT SHRIVE |  542.50 |
| BIKE SPEC  | CPT SHRIVE | 2803.60 |
| BIKE SPEC  | CPT SHRIVE | 5830.00 |
| JACKS BIKE | 24 EGLIN   | 7420.00 |
| LE SHOPPE  | HOMETOWN   | 3600.00 |
| LE SHOPPE  | HOMETOWN   | 2650.00 |
| LE SHOPPE  | HOMETOWN   | 3600.00 |
| TRUE WHEEL | 550 HUSKER |  196.00 |
| TRUE WHEEL | 550 HUSKER | 1590.00 |
| TRUE WHEEL | 550 HUSKER | 1200.00 |
+------------+------------+---------+
12 rows in set (0.00 sec)
```

NOTE

Notice when joining the three tables (ORDERS, PARTS, and CUSTOMER) that the ORDERS table was used in two joins, and the other tables were used only once. The table that will return the fewest rows with the given conditions is commonly referred to as the *driving table,* or the *base table*. Tables other than the base table in a query are usually joined to the base table for more efficient data retrieval. Consequently, the ORDERS table is the base table in this example.

In most databases a few base tables join (either directly or indirectly) all the other tables. (See Lesson 16, "Streamlining SQL Statements for Improved Performance," for more on base tables.)

You can make the previous query more specific, thus more useful, by adding the DESCRIPTION column as in the following example:

Input/Output ▼

```
SQL> SELECT C.NAME, C.ADDRESS,
  2 O.QUANTITY * P.PRICE TOTAL,
  3 P.DESCRIPTION
  4 FROM ORDERS O, PART P, CUSTOMER C
  5 WHERE O.PARTNUM = P.PARTNUM
  6 AND O.NAME = C.NAME
  7 ORDER BY C.NAME;

NAME        ADDRESS        TOTAL DESCRIPTION
========== ========== =========== ===============

AAA BIKE    10 OLDTOWN     213.50 TIRES
AAA BIKE    10 OLDTOWN    2120.00 ROAD BIKE
AAA BIKE    10 OLDTOWN    1200.00 TANDEM
BIKE SPEC   CPT SHRIVE     542.50 PEDALS
BIKE SPEC   CPT SHRIVE    2803.60 MOUNTAIN BIKE
BIKE SPEC   CPT SHRIVE    5830.00 ROAD BIKE
JACKS BIKE  24 EGLIN      7420.00 ROAD BIKE
LE SHOPPE   HOMETOWN      2650.00 ROAD BIKE
LE SHOPPE   HOMETOWN      3600.00 TANDEM
TRUE WHEEL  550 HUSKER     196.00 SEATS
TRUE WHEEL  550 HUSKER    1590.00 ROAD BIKE
TRUE WHEEL  550 HUSKER    1200.00 TANDEM
```

MySQL example:

Input/Output ▼

```
mysql> SELECT C.NAME, C.ADDRESS,
    -> O.QUANTITY * P.PRICE TOTAL,
    -> P.DESCRIPTION
    -> FROM ORDERS O, PART P, CUSTOMER C
    -> WHERE O.PARTNUM = P.PARTNUM
    -> AND O.NAME = C.NAME
    -> ORDER BY C.NAME;
```

NAME	ADDRESS	TOTAL	DESCRIPTION
AAA BIKE	10 OLDTOWN	2120.00	ROAD BIKE
AAA BIKE	10 OLDTOWN	1200.00	TANDEM
AAA BIKE	10 OLDTOWN	213.50	TIRES
BIKE SPEC	CPT SHRIVE	5830.00	ROAD BIKE
BIKE SPEC	CPT SHRIVE	542.50	PEDALS
BIKE SPEC	CPT SHRIVE	2803.60	MOUNTAIN BIKE
JACKS BIKE	24 EGLIN	7420.00	ROAD BIKE
LE SHOPPE	HOMETOWN	2650.00	ROAD BIKE
LE SHOPPE	HOMETOWN	3600.00	TANDEM
TRUE WHEEL	550 HUSKER	196.00	SEATS

```
¦ TRUE WHEEL ¦ 550 HUSKER ¦ 1590.00 ¦ ROAD BIKE      ¦
¦ TRUE WHEEL ¦ 550 HUSKER ¦ 1200.00 ¦ TANDEM         ¦
+-----------+-----------+---------+---------------+
12 rows in set (0.00 sec)
```

This information is a result of joining three tables. You can now use this information to create an invoice.

NOTE

> In the example at the beginning of this lesson, SQL joined TABLE1 and TABLE2 to create a new table with X (rows in TABLE1) × Y (rows in TABLE2) number of rows. A physical table is not created by the join, but rather in a virtual sense. The join between the two tables produces a new set of data that meets all conditions in the WHERE clause, including the join itself.
>
> Adding a join and a condition to the SELECT statement has reduced the number of rows displayed, but to evaluate the WHERE clause, SQL still creates all the possible rows. The sample tables in the lesson examples have only a handful of rows. Your actual data might have thousands of rows. If you are working on a platform with lots of horsepower, using a multiple-table join might not visibly affect performance. However, if you are working in a slower environment, multiple joins could cause a significant slowdown.
>
> We aren't telling you not to use joins because you have seen the advantages to be gained from a relational design. Just be aware of the platform you are using and your customer's requirements for speed versus reliability.

5

Joining Tables Based on Nonequality

Because SQL supports an equi-join, you might assume that SQL also has a non-equi-join. You would be right! Whereas the equi-join uses an = sign in the WHERE statement, the non-equi-join uses everything but an = sign—for example,

Input/Output ▼

```
SQL> SELECT O.NAME, O.PARTNUM, P.PARTNUM,
  2 O.QUANTITY * P.PRICE TOTAL
  3 FROM ORDERS O, PART P
  4 WHERE O.PARTNUM > P.PARTNUM;
```

```
NAME          PARTNUM     PARTNUM        TOTAL
==========  ===========  ===========  ===========

TRUE WHEEL       76          54          162.75
BIKE SPEC        76          54          596.75
LE SHOPPE        76          54          271.25
AAA BIKE         76          54          217.00
JACKS BIKE       76          54          759.50
TRUE WHEEL       76          42           73.50
BIKE SPEC        54          42          245.00
BIKE SPEC        76          42          269.50
LE SHOPPE        76          42          122.50
AAA BIKE         76          42           98.00
AAA BIKE         46          42          343.00
JACKS BIKE       76          42          343.00
TRUE WHEEL       76          46           45.75
BIKE SPEC        54          46          152.50
BIKE SPEC        76          46          167.75
LE SHOPPE        76          46           76.25
AAA BIKE         76          46           61.00
JACKS BIKE       76          46          213.50
TRUE WHEEL       76          23         1051.35
TRUE WHEEL       42          23         2803.60
...
```

MySQL example:

Input/Output ▼

```
mysql> SELECT O.NAME, O.PARTNUM, P.PARTNUM,
    -> O.QUANTITY * P.PRICE TOTAL
    -> FROM ORDERS O, PART P
    -> WHERE O.PARTNUM > P.PARTNUM;
+------------+---------+---------+---------+
| NAME       | PARTNUM | PARTNUM | TOTAL   |
+------------+---------+---------+---------+
| TRUE WHEEL |      76 |      54 |  162.75 |
| BIKE SPEC  |      76 |      54 |  596.75 |
| LE SHOPPE  |      76 |      54 |  271.25 |
| AAA BIKE   |      76 |      54 |  217.00 |
| JACKS BIKE |      76 |      54 |  759.50 |
| TRUE WHEEL |      76 |      42 |   73.50 |
| BIKE SPEC  |      54 |      42 |  245.00 |
| BIKE SPEC  |      76 |      42 |  269.50 |
| LE SHOPPE  |      76 |      42 |  122.50 |
| AAA BIKE   |      76 |      42 |   98.00 |
| AAA BIKE   |      46 |      42 |  343.00 |
| JACKS BIKE |      76 |      42 |  343.00 |
| TRUE WHEEL |      76 |      46 |   45.75 | ....
```

Analysis ▼

This listing goes on to describe all the rows in the join WHERE O.PARTNUM > P.PARTNUM. In the context of your bicycle shop, this information doesn't have much meaning, and in the real world the equi-join is far more common than the non-equi-join. However, you might encounter an application in which a non-equi-join produces the perfect result.

OUTER JOINs **Versus** INNER JOINs

Just as the non-equi-join balances the equi-join, an OUTER JOIN complements the INNER JOIN. An INNER JOIN is when the rows of the tables are combined with each other, producing a number of new rows equal to the product of the number of rows in each table. Also, the INNER JOIN uses these rows to determine the result of the WHERE clause. An OUTER JOIN groups the two tables in a slightly different way. An OUTER JOIN displays all rows of data from one table even though matching data might not reside in the joined table. For example, you might want to generate a list of all products and their prices, although some products might have no orders. Using the PARTS and ORDERS tables from the previous examples, perform the following INNER JOIN:

Input/Output ▼

```
SQL> SELECT P.PARTNUM, P.DESCRIPTION,P.PRICE,
  2 O.NAME, O.PARTNUM
  3 FROM PART P
  4 JOIN ORDERS O ON O.PARTNUM = 54;
PARTNUM DESCRIPTION             PRICE NAME         PARTNUM
======= =================== =========== ========== ===========

     54 PEDALS                54.25 BIKE SPEC           54
     42 SEATS                 24.50 BIKE SPEC           54
     46 TIRES                 15.25 BIKE SPEC           54
     23 MOUNTAIN BIKE        350.45 BIKE SPEC           54
     76 ROAD BIKE            530.00 BIKE SPEC           54
     10 TANDEM              1200.00 BIKE SPEC           54
```

MySQL example:

Input/Output ▼

```
mysql> SELECT P.PARTNUM, P.DESCRIPTION,P.PRICE,
    -> O.NAME, O.PARTNUM
    -> FROM PART P
    -> INNER JOIN ORDERS O ON O.PARTNUM = 54;
```

5

```
+--------+----------------+--------+-----------+--------+
| PARTNUM | DESCRIPTION   | PRICE  | NAME      | PARTNUM |
+--------+----------------+--------+-----------+--------+
|     54 | PEDALS        |  54.25 | BIKE SPEC |     54 |
|     42 | SEATS         |  24.50 | BIKE SPEC |     54 |
|     46 | TIRES         |  15.25 | BIKE SPEC |     54 |
|     23 | MOUNTAIN BIKE | 350.45 | BIKE SPEC |     54 |
|     76 | ROAD BIKE     | 530.00 | BIKE SPEC |     54 |
|     10 | TANDEM        |1200.00 | BIKE SPEC |     54 |
+--------+----------------+--------+-----------+--------+
6 rows in set (0.00 sec)
```

NOTE

> The syntax you used to get this join—JOIN ON—is not ANSI standard. The implementation you used for these examples has additional syntax. You are using it here to specify an inner join and an outer join. Most implementations of SQL have similar extensions. Notice the absence of the WHERE clause in this type of join.

The result is that all the rows in PARTS are spliced onto specific rows in ORDERS where the column PARTNUM is 54. Here's an OUTER JOIN:

Input/Output ▼

```
SQL> SELECT P.PARTNUM, P.DESCRIPTION,P.PRICE,
  2 O.NAME, O.PARTNUM
  3 FROM PART P
  4 RIGHT OUTER JOIN ORDERS O ON O.PARTNUM = 54;
```

PARTNUM	DESCRIPTION	PRICE	NAME	PARTNUM
<null>	<null>	<null>	TRUE WHEEL	76
<null>	<null>	<null>	TRUE WHEEL	10
<null>	<null>	<null>	TRUE WHEEL	42
54	PEDALS	54.25	BIKE SPEC	54
42	SEATS	24.50	BIKE SPEC	54
46	TIRES	15.25	BIKE SPEC	54
23	MOUNTAIN BIKE	350.45	BIKE SPEC	54
76	ROAD BIKE	530.00	BIKE SPEC	54
10	TANDEM	1200.00	BIKE SPEC	54
<null>	<null>	<null>	BIKE SPEC	23
<null>	<null>	<null>	BIKE SPEC	76
<null>	<null>	<null>	LE SHOPPE	76
<null>	<null>	<null>	LE SHOPPE	10
<null>	<null>	<null>	AAA BIKE	10
<null>	<null>	<null>	AAA BIKE	76
<null>	<null>	<null>	AAA BIKE	46
<null>	<null>	<null>	JACKS BIKE	76

MySQL example:

Input/Output ▼

```
mysql> SELECT P.PARTNUM, P.DESCRIPTION,P.PRICE,
    -> O.NAME, O.PARTNUM
    -> FROM PART P
    -> RIGHT OUTER JOIN ORDERS O ON O.PARTNUM = 54;
+---------+---------------+---------+------------+---------+
| PARTNUM | DESCRIPTION   | PRICE   | NAME       | PARTNUM |
+---------+---------------+---------+------------+---------+
|    NULL | NULL          |    NULL | TRUE WHEEL |      76 |
|    NULL | NULL          |    NULL | TRUE WHEEL |      10 |
|    NULL | NULL          |    NULL | TRUE WHEEL |      42 |
|      54 | PEDALS        |   54.25 | BIKE SPEC  |      54 |
|      42 | SEATS         |   24.50 | BIKE SPEC  |      54 |
|      46 | TIRES         |   15.25 | BIKE SPEC  |      54 |
|      23 | MOUNTAIN BIKE |  350.45 | BIKE SPEC  |      54 |
|      76 | ROAD BIKE     |  530.00 | BIKE SPEC  |      54 |
|      10 | TANDEM        | 1200.00 | BIKE SPEC  |      54 |
|    NULL | NULL          |    NULL | BIKE SPEC  |      23 |
|    NULL | NULL          |    NULL | BIKE SPEC  |      76 |
|    NULL | NULL          |    NULL | LE SHOPPE  |      76 |
|    NULL | NULL          |    NULL | LE SHOPPE  |      10 |
|    NULL | NULL          |    NULL | AAA BIKE   |      10 |
|    NULL | NULL          |    NULL | AAA BIKE   |      76 |
|    NULL | NULL          |    NULL | AAA BIKE   |      46 |
|    NULL | NULL          |    NULL | JACKS BIKE |      76 |
+---------+---------------+---------+------------+---------+
17 rows in set (0.00 sec)
```

This type of query is new. First, you specified a RIGHT OUTER JOIN, which caused SQL to return a full set of data from the right table, ORDERS, and to place NULLs in the fields where O.PARTNUM <> 54. The following is a LEFT OUTER JOIN:

Input/Output ▼

```
SQL> SELECT P.PARTNUM, P.DESCRIPTION,P.PRICE,
  2 O.NAME, O.PARTNUM
  3 FROM PART P
  4 LEFT OUTER JOIN ORDERS O ON O.PARTNUM = 54;

PARTNUM DESCRIPTION          PRICE NAME           PARTNUM
======= ==================== ======= ============== ===========

     54 PEDALS               54.25 BIKE SPEC            54
     42 SEATS                24.50 BIKE SPEC            54
     46 TIRES                15.25 BIKE SPEC            54
     23 MOUNTAIN BIKE       350.45 BIKE SPEC            54
```

5

```
      76 ROAD BIKE              530.00 BIKE SPEC           54
      10 TANDEM                1200.00 BIKE SPEC           54
```

MySQL example:

Input/Output ▼

```
mysql> SELECT P.PARTNUM, P.DESCRIPTION,P.PRICE,
    -> O.NAME, O.PARTNUM
    -> FROM PART P
    -> LEFT OUTER JOIN ORDERS O ON O.PARTNUM = 54
    -> ;
+---------+---------------+---------+-----------+---------+
| PARTNUM | DESCRIPTION   | PRICE   | NAME      | PARTNUM |
+---------+---------------+---------+-----------+---------+
|      54 | PEDALS        |   54.25 | BIKE SPEC |      54 |
|      42 | SEATS         |   24.50 | BIKE SPEC |      54 |
|      46 | TIRES         |   15.25 | BIKE SPEC |      54 |
|      23 | MOUNTAIN BIKE |  350.45 | BIKE SPEC |      54 |
|      76 | ROAD BIKE     |  530.00 | BIKE SPEC |      54 |
|      10 | TANDEM        | 1200.00 | BIKE SPEC |      54 |
+---------+---------------+---------+-----------+---------+
6 rows in set (0.00 sec)
```

Analysis ▼

You get the same six rows as the INNER JOIN. Because you specified LEFT (the LEFT table), PART determined the number of rows you would return. Every part in PART was paired with each order placed for PARTNUM = 54. The maximum number of rows returned by this query depends on the number of rows in PART and the number of rows in ORDERS for PARTNUM = 54. If you look back to the ORDERS table, you will see that only one order has been placed for a PARTNUM of 54. If there had been two orders placed for PARTNUM 54, this query would have matched each part with each order for PARTNUM 54, thereby returning 12 rows instead of 6.

Some users don't worry too much about inner and outer joins, or haven't even heard of inner and outer joins. The reason for this might be that some SQL products determine the optimum join for your query. Some implementations, such as Oracle, require you to understand the concept of an outer join. If you write a query and fail to use an outer join, your query might return incomplete or inaccurate data. For example, if you want to get a list of all customers and the total dollar amount each customer has ordered (using the CUSTOMER and ORDERS tables), you will not get every customer record if every customer has not placed an order. In this case, you would have to use an outer join to return all customers, even if a customer has not placed an order. The next example illustrates this situation using an outer join in Oracle.

Some implementations of SQL use the (+) sign instead of OUTER JOIN. The (+) simply means "Show me everything even if something is missing." Here's an Oracle example:

Input/Output ▼

```
SQL> SELECT C.CUST_NAME, O.PROD_ID, O.QUANTITY
  2 FROM CUST C, ORDERS O
  3 WHERE C.CUST_ID = O.CUST_ID(+);

CUST_NAME              PRO   QUANTITY
--------------------   ---   ----------
TOM DAVIDSON           P18          2
TOM DAVIDSON           P01          6
TERRY HOWELL           P30         12
DUSTIN BOLES           P15          5
DAVID RAIDER           P34          2
BETTY WILLIAMS
DAVE MATHEWS           P20          1
BOB HORNER
DOUGLAS TATE           P07          3
MATTHEW GALE           P04          4
MATTHEW GALE           P12          3
CHRISTINA SCHLUGE
BRICE HOREN            P24          1
```

This statement is joining the CUSTOMER and ORDERS tables. Notice the (+) sign on the o.cust_id column in the WHERE clause. The (+) sign represents an outer join on the ORDERS table. For example, CUST_ID values might be missing from the ORDERS table; that is, all customers may not have placed orders. We created a list of all customers, regardless of whether they have placed orders, using an outer join. The (+) sign is placed next to the table column that might lack matching data with the column to which they are being joined.

5

Joining a Table to Itself: The Self Join

The lesson's final topic is the technique of joining a table to itself, also described as performing a *self join*. The syntax of this operation is similar to joining two tables. For example, to join table TABLE1 to itself, type this:

Input/Output ▼

```
SQL> SELECT *
  2 FROM TABLE1, TABLE1;
```

```
ROW          REMARKS      ROW          REMARKS
==========   ==========   ==========   ========

row 1        Table 1      row 1        Table 1
row 1        Table 1      row 2        Table 1
row 1        Table 1      row 3        Table 1
row 1        Table 1      row 4        Table 1
row 1        Table 1      row 5        Table 1
row 1        Table 1      row 6        Table 1
row 2        Table 1      row 1        Table 1
row 2        Table 1      row 2        Table 1
row 2        Table 1      row 3        Table 1
row 2        Table 1      row 4        Table 1
row 2        Table 1      row 5        Table 1
row 2        Table 1      row 6        Table 1
row 3        Table 1      row 1        Table 1
row 3        Table 1      row 2        Table 1
row 3        Table 1      row 3        Table 1
row 3        Table 1      row 4        Table 1
row 3        Table 1      row 5        Table 1
row 3        Table 1      row 6        Table 1
row 4        Table 1      row 1        Table 1
row 4        Table 1      row 2        Table 1
...
```

In its complete form, this join produces the same number of combinations as joining two six-row tables. Again, this is a Cartesian product, or a cross join. This type of join could be used to check the internal consistency of data. What would happen if someone fell asleep in the production department and entered a new part with a PARTNUM that already existed? That would be bad news for everybody—invoices would be wrong; your application would probably blow up; and in general you would be in for a very bad time. And the cause of all your problems would be the duplicate PARTNUM in the following table:

Input/Output ▼

```
SQL> SELECT * FROM PART;

   PARTNUM DESCRIPTION                PRICE
========== ==================== ===========

        54 PEDALS                     54.25
        42 SEATS                      24.50
        46 TIRES                      15.25
        23 MOUNTAIN BIKE             350.45
        76 ROAD BIKE                 530.00
        10 TANDEM                   1200.00
        76 CLIPLESS SHOE              65.00
```

You saved your company from this bad situation by checking PARTS before anyone used it:

Input/Output ▼

```
SQL> SELECT F.PARTNUM, F.DESCRIPTION,
  2  S.PARTNUM,S.DESCRIPTION
  3  FROM PART F, PART S
  4  WHERE F.PARTNUM = S.PARTNUM
  5  AND F.DESCRIPTION <> S.DESCRIPTION;

PARTNUM DESCRIPTION          PARTNUM DESCRIPTION
======= ==================== ======= ====================

     76 ROAD BIKE                 76 CLIPLESS SHOE
```

Now you are a hero until someone asks why the table has only two entries. You, remembering what you have learned about JOINs, retain your hero status by explaining how the JOIN produced two rows that satisfied the condition WHERE F.PARTNUM = S.PARTNUM AND F.DESCRIPTION <> S.DESCRIPTION. Of course, at some point, the row of data containing the duplicate PARTNUM would have to be corrected.

Another excellent example deals with the EMP table, as follows:

Input/Output ▼

```
SQL> SELECT * FROM EMP;

ID   NAME         MGR_ID
---  -----------  ------
1    JOHN              0
2    MARY              1
3    STEVE             1
4    JACK              2
5    SUE               2
```

Notice that MGR_ID is stored with each employee record, which designates the identification of each employee's manager, and each manager is an employee who has an ID. The problem is that we want to print each employee's name and their manager's name on a report. The best we can do without a self join is what we have done in the preceding example. The following example shows the use of a self join in this situation:

Input/Output ▼

```
SQL> SELECT E1.NAME, E2.NAME
  2  FROM EMP E1, EMP E2
  3  WHERE E1.MGR_ID = E2.ID;

NAME         NAME
-----------  -----------
MARY         JOHN
```

5

```
STEVE      JOHN
JACK       MARY
SUE        MARY
```

Here, we have selected from the EMP table twice. We have two sets of data, or virtual tables. The first virtual table, which we named E1, contains the employee information. The second virtual table, E2, contains manager information. Then we simply join E1 by the MGR_ID column to the ID column in E2. We have joined EMP to itself to tell us the name of the manager for each employee.

Summary

Join operations enable you to query multiple tables at the same time to produce useful output. In this lesson, you learned that a join combines all possible combinations of rows present in the selected tables. These new rows are then available for selection based on the information that you want. We covered several different types of joins, including equi-joins, non-equi-joins, inner joins, outer joins, and self joins. Equi-joins, the most common type of join, test for equality of columns between tables. A non-equi-join, much less common, tests for inequality. An inner join combines the rows of two tables, which produces a number of new rows that equals the product of the number of rows in each table. An outer join is a method for joining two or more tables and displaying all rows from one table, even if there are no matches in the other table. A self join is a join of a table to itself, which is not very common but important to know in certain circumstances. Without the capability to join tables, you are limited to the data you can see in the database.

Congratulations—you have learned almost everything there is to know about the SELECT clause. The one remaining item, subqueries, is covered in Lesson 6, "Embedding Subqueries into Queries."

Q&A

Q How many tables can you join on?

A That depends on the implementation. Some implementations have a 25-table limit, whereas others have no limit. Just remember, the more tables you join on, the slower the response time. To be safe, check your implementation to find out the maximum number of tables allowed in a query.

Q **Would it be fair to say that when tables are joined, they actually become one table?**

A Very simply put, that is just about what happens, although a table is not physically created (more of a virtual table is created by the SQL engine). When you join the tables, you can select from any of the columns in either table.

Workshop

The Workshop provides quiz questions to help solidify your understanding of the material covered, as well as exercises to provide you with experience in using what you have learned. Try to answer the quiz and exercise questions before checking the answers in Appendix A, "Answers." This is the code for the CREATE table and INSERT statements for the PARTS and ORDERS tables, which will be used in this Workshop.

```
create table part
(partnum        numeric(10)     not null,
 description    varchar(20)     not null,
 price          decimal(10,2)   not null);

create table orders
(orderedon      date,
 name           varchar(10)     not null,
 partnum        numeric(10)     not null,
 quantity       numeric(10)     not null,
 remarks        varchar(30)     not null);

insert into part values
('54', 'PEDALS', '54.25');

insert into part values
('42', 'SEATS', '24.50');

insert into part values
('46', 'TIRES', '15.25');

insert into part values
('23', 'MOUNTAIN BIKE', '350.45');

insert into part values
('76', 'ROAD BIKE', '530.00');

insert into part values
('10', 'TANDEM', '1200.00');
```

5

```
insert into orders values
('19-MAY-1996', 'TRUE WHEEL', '76', '3', 'PAID');
insert into orders values
('1996-09-02', 'TRUE WHEEL', '10', '1', 'PAID');
insert into orders values
('1996-06-30', 'TRUE WHEEL', '42', '8', 'PAID');
insert into orders values
('1996-06-30', 'BIKE SPEC', '54', '10', 'PAID');
insert into orders values
('1996-05-30', 'BIKE SPEC', '23', '8', 'PAID');
insert into orders values
('1996-01-17', 'BIKE SPEC', '76', '11', 'PAID');
insert into orders values
('1996-01-17', 'LE SHOPPE', '76', '5', 'PAID');
insert into orders values
('1996-06-01', 'LE SHOPPE', '10', '3', 'PAID');
insert into orders values
('1996-06-01', 'AAA BIKE', '10', '1', 'PAID');
insert into orders values
('1996-07-01', 'AAA BIKE', '76', '4', 'PAID');
insert into orders values
('1996-07-01', 'AAA BIKE', '46', '14', 'PAID');
insert into orders values
('1996-07-11', 'JACKS BIKE', '76', '14', 'PAID');
```

Quiz

1. How many rows would a two-table join produce without a condition in the WHERE clause if one table had 50,000 rows and the other had 100?

2. What type of join appears in the following SELECT statement?

```
select e.name, e.employee_id, ep.salary
from employee_tbl e,
    employee_pay_tbl ep
where e.employee_id = ep.employee_id;
```

3. Will the following SELECT statements work?

   a.
   ```
   select name, employee_id, salary
   from employee_tbl e,
       employee_pay_tbl ep
   where employee_id = employee_id
     and name like '%MITH';
   ```

   b.
   ```
   select e.name, e.employee_id, ep.salary
   from employee_tbl e,
       employee_pay_tbl ep
   where name like '%MITH';
   ```

```
c. select e.name, e.employee_id, ep.salary
   from employee_tbl e,
        employee_pay_tbl ep
   where e.employee_id = ep.employee_id
     and e.name like '%MITH';
```

4. When joining tables, are you limited to one-column joins, or can you join on more than one column?

5. What is the primary difference between inner and outer joins?

6. Which type of join would you want to use to query the rows between Table1 and Table2 and to ensure that all rows from Table 1 are displayed?

Exercises

1. In the section "Joining a Table to Itself: The Self Join," the last example returned two combinations. Rewrite the query so that only one entry comes up for each redundant part number.

2. Rewrite the following query to make it more readable and shorter:

```
select orders.orderedon, orders.name, part.partnum,
       part.price, part.description from orders, part
       where orders.partnum = part.partnum and orders.orderedon
       between '1-SEP-96' and '30-SEP-96'
       order by part.partnum;
```

3. From the PARTS table and the ORDERS table, make up a query that will return the following:

```
ORDEREDON              NAME                PARTNUM    QUANTITY
==================     ==================  =======    ========

2-SEP-96               TRUE WHEEL              10           1
```

5

4. Write a query that will return the following:

```
+---------+--------------+---------+------------+---------+
| PARTNUM | DESCRIPTION  | DUE     | NAME       | PARTNUM |
+---------+--------------+---------+------------+---------+
|      76 | ROAD BIKE    | 1590.00 | TRUE WHEEL |      76 |
|      10 | TANDEM       | 1200.00 | TRUE WHEEL |      10 |
|      42 | SEATS        |  196.00 | TRUE WHEEL |      42 |
|      54 | PEDALS       |  542.50 | BIKE SPEC  |      54 |
|      23 | MOUNTAIN BIKE| 2803.60 | BIKE SPEC  |      23 |
|      76 | ROAD BIKE    | 5830.00 | BIKE SPEC  |      76 |
|      76 | ROAD BIKE    | 2650.00 | LE SHOPPE  |      76 |
```

```
|      10 | TANDEM        |  3600.00 | LE SHOPPE   |      10 |
|      10 | TANDEM        |  1200.00 | AAA BIKE    |      10 |
|      76 | ROAD BIKE     |  2120.00 | AAA BIKE    |      76 |
|      46 | TIRES         |   213.50 | AAA BIKE    |      46 |
|      76 | ROAD BIKE     |  7420.00 | JACKS BIKE  |      76 |
+---------+---------------+----------+-------------+---------+
```

5. What is the result of this query?

```
SELECT P.PARTNUM, P.DESCRIPTION,P.PRICE,
O.NAME, O.PARTNUM
FROM PART P
LEFT OUTER JOIN ORDERS O ON O.PARTNUM = 76
```

LESSON 6
Embedding Subqueries into Queries

A *subquery* is a query whose results are passed as the argument for another query. Subqueries enable you to bind several queries together. By the end of this lesson, you will be able to do the following:

- Build a subquery.

- Use the keywords EXISTS, ANY, and ALL with your subqueries.

- Build and use correlated subqueries.

In this lesson, we will be working with the PART and ORDERS tables. To ensure that you have these tables created and that data has been inserted into them, please do the following in your MySQL database. The database bob in the following example should be substituted with the name of the database you created and into which you have been putting your tables:

Input/Output ▼

```
mysql> use bob;
Database changed
mysql> show tables;
+---------------+
| Tables_in_bob |
+---------------+
| characters    |
| checks        |
| orders        |
| orgchart      |
| part          |
| teamstats     |
+---------------+
6 rows in set (0.00 sec)
```

You will need to have the PART and ORDERS tables to proceed. If you do not have them, here is the code:

Input ▼

```
create table part
(partnum        numeric(10)      not null,
 description    varchar(20)      not null,
 price          decimal(10,2)    not null);
create table orders
(orderedon      date,
 name           varchar(10)      not null,
 partnum        numeric(10)      not null,
 quantity       numeric(10)      not null,
 remarks        varchar(30)      not null);

insert into part values
('54', 'PEDALS', '54.25');

insert into part values
('42', 'SEATS', '24.50');

insert into part values
('46', 'TIRES', '15.25');

insert into part values
('23', 'MOUNTAIN BIKE', '350.45');

insert into part values
('76', 'ROAD BIKE', '530.00');

insert into part values
('10', 'TANDEM', '1200.00');

insert into orders values
('19-MAY-1996', 'TRUE WHEEL', '76', '3', 'PAID');

insert into orders values
('1996-09-02', 'TRUE WHEEL', '10', '1', 'PAID');

insert into orders values
('1996-06-30', 'TRUE WHEEL', '42', '8', 'PAID');

insert into orders values
('1996-06-30', 'BIKE SPEC', '54', '10', 'PAID');

insert into orders values
('1996-05-30', 'BIKE SPEC', '23', '8', 'PAID');

insert into orders values
('1996-01-17', 'BIKE SPEC', '76', '11', 'PAID');
```

```
insert into orders values
('1996-01-17', 'LE SHOPPE', '76', '5', 'PAID');

insert into orders values
('1996-06-01', 'LE SHOPPE', '10', '3', 'PAID');

insert into orders values
('1996-06-01', 'AAA BIKE', '10', '1', 'PAID');

insert into orders values
('1996-07-01', 'AAA BIKE', '76', '4', 'PAID');

insert into orders values
('1996-07-01', 'AAA BIKE', '46', '14', 'PAID');

insert into orders values
('1996-07-11', 'JACKS BIKE', '76', '14', 'PAID');
```

NOTE   The examples for this lesson are shown in MySQL. However, you will need to ensure that you have MySQL 4.1 or greater to have support for subqueries. Subqueries are not supported in versions older than 4.1.

Building a Subquery

Simply put, a subquery lets you tie the result set of one query to another. The general syntax is as follows:

Syntax ▼

```
SELECT *
FROM TABLE1
WHERE TABLE1.SOMECOLUMN =
(SELECT SOMEOTHERCOLUMN
FROM TABLE2
WHERE SOMEOTHERCOLUMN = SOMEVALUE)
```

6

Notice how the second query is nested inside the first. Let's view the current content of the tables that we are using as we start to construct a real-world example:

Input/Output ▼

```
mysql> select * from part;
+---------+---------------+---------+
| partnum | description   | price   |
+---------+---------------+---------+
|      54 | PEDALS        |   54.25 |
|      42 | SEATS         |   24.50 |
|      46 | TIRES         |   15.25 |
|      23 | MOUNTAIN BIKE |  350.45 |
|      76 | ROAD BIKE     |  530.00 |
|      10 | TANDEM        | 1200.00 |
+---------+---------------+---------+
6 rows in set (0.04 sec)

mysql> select * from orders;
+------------+------------+---------+----------+---------+
| orderedon  | name       | partnum | quantity | remarks |
+------------+------------+---------+----------+---------+
| 1996-05-19 | TRUE WHEEL |      76 |        3 | PAID    |
| 1996-09-02 | TRUE WHEEL |      10 |        1 | PAID    |
| 1996-06-30 | TRUE WHEEL |      42 |        8 | PAID    |
| 1996-06-30 | BIKE SPEC  |      54 |       10 | PAID    |
| 1996-05-30 | BIKE SPEC  |      23 |        8 | PAID    |
| 1996-01-17 | BIKE SPEC  |      76 |       11 | PAID    |
| 1996-01-17 | LE SHOPPE  |      76 |        5 | PAID    |
| 1996-06-01 | LE SHOPPE  |      10 |        3 | PAID    |
| 1996-06-01 | AAA BIKE   |      10 |        1 | PAID    |
| 1996-07-01 | AAA BIKE   |      76 |        4 | PAID    |
| 1996-07-01 | AAA BIKE   |      46 |       14 | PAID    |
| 1996-07-11 | JACKS BIKE |      76 |       14 | PAID    |
+------------+------------+---------+----------+---------+
12 rows in set (0.00 sec)
```

The tables share a common field called PARTNUM. Suppose that you didn't know (or didn't want to know) the PARTNUM, but instead wanted to work with the description of the part. Using a subquery, you could type this:

Input/Output ▼

```
mysql> select *
    -> from orders where partnum=
    -> (select partnum
    ->  from part
    ->  where description like 'ROAD%');
```

```
+-----------+-----------+---------+----------+---------+
| orderedon | name      | partnum | quantity | remarks |
+-----------+-----------+---------+----------+---------+
| 0000-00-00| TRUE WHEEL|      76 |        3 | PAID    |
| 1996-01-17| BIKE SPEC |      76 |       11 | PAID    |
| 1996-01-17| LE SHOPPE |      76 |        5 | PAID    |
| 1996-07-01| AAA BIKE  |      76 |        4 | PAID    |
| 1996-07-11| JACKS BIKE|      76 |       14 | PAID    |
+-----------+-----------+---------+----------+---------+
5 rows in set (0.00 sec)
```

Let's break down the subquery concept using the previous example, and also by breaking down the query into its component parts, as shown in the following:

Input/Output ▼

```
mysql> select partnum
    -> from part
    -> where description like 'ROAD%';
+---------+
| partnum |
+---------+
|      76 |
+---------+
1 row in set (0.04 sec)
```

Analysis ▼

What you see in the MySQL example is the resolution of the subquery. Because the sub-query is always enclosed within parentheses, it is resolved first. The result set (76) is then compared to (or tested for equality) against the PARTNUM column in the ORDERS table. Next is an example of the result set from the outer query.

Input/Output ▼

```
mysql> select * from orders
    -> where partnum = 76;
+-----------+-----------+---------+----------+---------+
| orderedon | name      | partnum | quantity | remarks |
+-----------+-----------+---------+----------+---------+
| 1996-05-19| TRUE WHEEL|      76 |        3 | PAID    |
| 1996-01-17| BIKE SPEC |      76 |       11 | PAID    |
| 1996-01-17| LE SHOPPE |      76 |        5 | PAID    |
| 1996-07-01| AAA BIKE  |      76 |        4 | PAID    |
| 1996-07-11| JACKS BIKE|      76 |       14 | PAID    |
+-----------+-----------+---------+----------+---------+
```

6

Here we were able to provide a value for the condition in our WHERE clause. The value was provided for us by the subquery.

When we began, all we knew was that we wanted to see all rows from the ORDERS table WHERE the PART was something like ROAD.

The subquery can allow us a method of gaining data from both tables, without necessarily joining them to gain our output. Here is an example that uses a join to produce the same set of data.

Input/Output ▼

```
mysql> select o.orderedon,
    -> o.name,
    -> o.partnum,
    -> o.quantity,
    -> o.remarks
    -> from orders o, part p
    -> where o.partnum = p.partnum
    -> and p.description like 'ROAD%';
```

```
+------------+------------+---------+----------+---------+
| orderedon  | name       | partnum | quantity | remarks |
+------------+------------+---------+----------+---------+
| 1996-05-19 | TRUE WHEEL |      76 |        3 | PAID    |
| 1996-01-17 | BIKE SPEC  |      76 |       11 | PAID    |
| 1996-01-17 | LE SHOPPE  |      76 |        5 | PAID    |
| 1996-07-01 | AAA BIKE   |      76 |        4 | PAID    |
| 1996-07-11 | JACKS BIKE |      76 |       14 | PAID    |
+------------+------------+---------+----------+---------+
5 rows in set (0.02 sec)
```

Even better, if you use the concepts you learned on Lesson 5, you could enhance the PARTNUM column in the result by including the DESCRIPTION, making PARTNUM clearer for anyone who hasn't memorized it. Try this:

Input/Output ▼

```
mysql> select o.orderedon, o.partnum,
        -> p.description,o.quantity,o.remarks,
        -> from orders o, part p
        -> where o.partnum=p.partnum
        -> and
        -> o.partnum=
        -> (select partnum
        -> from part
        -> where description like 'ROAD%');
```

```
+-------------+----------+-------------+----------+--------+
¦ orderedon   ¦ partnum  ¦ description ¦ quantity ¦ remarks¦
+-------------+----------+-------------+----------+--------+
¦ 0000-00-00  ¦    76    ¦  ROAD BIKE  ¦    3     ¦  PAID  ¦
¦ 1996-01-17  ¦    76    ¦  ROAD BIKE  ¦   11     ¦  PAID  ¦
¦ 1996-01-17  ¦    76    ¦  ROAD BIKE  ¦    5     ¦  PAID  ¦
¦ 1996-07-01  ¦    76    ¦  ROAD BIKE  ¦    4     ¦  PAID  ¦
¦ 1996-07-11  ¦    76    ¦  ROAD BIKE  ¦   14     ¦  PAID  ¦
+-------------+----------+-------------+----------+--------+
5 rows in set (0.02 sec)
```

The first part of the query is very familiar:

```
SELECT O.ORDEREDON, O.PARTNUM,
P.DESCRIPTION, O.QUANTITY, O.REMARKS
FROM ORDERS O, PART P
```

Here you are using the aliases O and P for tables ORDERS and PART to select the five columns you are interested in. In this case, column aliases were not necessary because each of the columns you asked to return is unique. However, it is easier to make a readable query now than to have to figure it out later. The first WHERE clause you encounter

```
WHERE O.PARTNUM = P.PARTNUM
```

is standard language for joining tables PART and ORDERS specified in the FROM clause. If you didn't use this WHERE clause, you would have all the possible row combinations of the two tables. The next section includes the subquery. The statement

```
AND
O.PARTNUM =
(SELECT PARTNUM
FROM PART
WHERE DESCRIPTION LIKE "ROAD%")
```

adds the qualification that O.PARTNUM must be equal to the result of your simple subquery. The subquery is straightforward; it finds all the part numbers that are LIKE "ROAD%". The use of LIKE is somewhat lazy because it saves the keystrokes required to type ROAD BIKE. However, it turns out you were lucky this time. What if someone in the Parts department had added a new part called ROADKILL?

6

The syntax for adding the ROADKILL row to your PART table is as follows:

Input ▼

```
mysql> insert into part values
    -> (77,'ROADKILL',7.99);
Query OK, 1 row affected (0.00 sec)
```

The revised PART table would look like this:

Input/Output ▼

```
mysql> SELECT * FROM PART;
+---------+---------------+---------+
| partnum | description   | price   |
+---------+---------------+---------+
|      54 | PEDALS        |   54.25 |
|      42 | SEATS         |   24.50 |
|      46 | TIRES         |   15.25 |
|      23 | MOUNTAIN BIKE |  350.45 |
|      76 | ROAD BIKE     |  530.00 |
|      10 | TANDEM        | 1200.00 |
|      77 | ROADKILL      |    7.99 |
+---------+---------------+---------+
7 rows in set (0.00 sec)
```

Suppose you are blissfully unaware of this change and try your query after this new product was added. If you enter

Input ▼

```
mysql>select o.orderedon, o.partnum,
    ->p.description, o.quantity, o.remarks
    ->from orders o, part p
    ->where o.partnum = p.partnum
    ->and
    ->o.partnum =
    ->(select partnum
    ->from part
    ->where description like 'ROAD%');
```

the SQL engine complains with

```
ERROR 1242 (21000): Subquery returns more than 1 row
```

and you don't get any results. The response from your SQL engine may vary, but it still complains and returns nothing.

To find out why you get this undesirable result, assume the role of the SQL engine. You will probably evaluate the subquery first. You would return this:

Input/Output ▼

```
Mysql>select partnum
    ->from part
    ->where description like 'ROAD%';where description

+---------+
| partnum |
+---------+
|      76 |
|      77 |
+---------+
2 rows in set (0.00 sec)
```

You would take this result and apply it to O.PARTNUM =, which is the step that causes the problem.

Analysis ▼

How can PARTNUM be equal to both 76 and 77? This must be what the engine meant when it returned the error. When you used the LIKE clause, you opened yourself up for this error. When you combine the results of a relational operator with another relational operator, such as =, <, or >, you need to make sure the result is singular. In the case of the example we have been using, the solution would be to rewrite the query using an = instead of the LIKE, like this:

Input/Output ▼

```
mysql> select o.orderon, o.partnum,
    -> p.description, o.quantity, o.remarks
    -> from orders o, part p
    -> where o.partnum=p.partnum
    -> and
    -> o.partnum=
    -> (select partnum
    -> from part
    -> where description='ROAD BIKE');

+------------+---------+-------------+----------+---------+
| orderedon  | partnum | description | quantity | remarks |
+------------+---------+-------------+----------+---------+
| 0000-00-00 |      76 | ROAD BIKE   |        3 | PAID    |
| 1996-01-17 |      76 | ROAD BIKE   |       11 | PAID    |
| 1996-01-17 |      76 | ROAD BIKE   |        5 | PAID    |
```

6

```
| 1996-07-01 |      76 |   ROAD BIKE |      4 | PAID    |
| 1996-07-11 |      76 |   ROAD BIKE |     14 | PAID    |
+------------+---------+-------------+--------+---------+
5 rows in set (0.02 sec)
```

This subquery returns only one unique result; therefore narrowing your = condition to a single value. How can you be sure the subquery won't return multiple values if you are looking for only one value?

Avoiding the use of LIKE is a start. Another approach is to ensure the uniqueness of the search field during table design. If you are the untrusting type, you could use the method (described in previous lessons) for joining a table to itself to check a given field for uniqueness. If you design the table yourself (see Lesson 9, "Creating and Maintaining Tables") or trust the person who designed the table, you could require the column you are searching to have a unique value. You could also use a part of SQL that returns only one answer: the aggregate function.

Using Aggregate Functions with Subqueries

The aggregate functions SUM, COUNT, MIN, MAX, and AVG all return a single value. To find the average amount of an order, type this:

Input/Output ▼

```
mysql> select avg(o.quantity * p.price)
    -> from orders o, part p
    -> where o.partnum = p.partnum
    -> ;
+---------------------------+
| avg(o.quantity * p.price) |
+---------------------------+
|               2447.133333 |
+---------------------------+
1 row in set (0.03 sec)
```

This statement returns only one value. To find out which orders were above average, use the preceding SELECT statement for your subquery. The complete query and result are as follows:

Input/Output ▼

```
SQL> SELECT O.NAME, O.ORDEREDON,
  2 O.QUANTITY * P.PRICE TOTAL
  3 FROM ORDERS O, PART P
  4 WHERE O.PARTNUM = P.PARTNUM
  5 AND
  6 O.QUANTITY * P.PRICE  >
  7 (SELECT AVG(O.QUANTITY * P.PRICE)
  8 FROM ORDERS O, PART P
  9 WHERE O.PARTNUM = P.PARTNUM);

NAME         ORDEREDON       TOTAL
==========  ===========  ===========

LE SHOPPE    1-JUN-1996    3600.00
BIKE SPEC   30-MAY-1996    2803.60
LE SHOPPE   17-JAN-1996    2650.00
BIKE SPEC   17-JAN-1996    5830.00
JACKS BIKE  11-JUL-1996    7420.00
```

This example contains a rather unremarkable SELECT/FROM/WHERE clause:

```
SELECT O.NAME, O.ORDEREDON,
O.QUANTITY * P.PRICE TOTAL
FROM ORDERS O, PART P
WHERE O.PARTNUM = P.PARTNUM
```

These lines represent the common way of joining these two tables. This join is necessary because the price is in PART, and the quantity is in ORDERS. The WHERE ensures that you examine only the join-formed rows that are related. You then add the following subquery:

```
AND
O.QUANTITY * P.PRICE  >
(SELECT AVG(O.QUANTITY * P.PRICE)
FROM ORDERS O, PART P
WHERE O.PARTNUM = P.PARTNUM)
```

The preceding condition compares the total of each order with the average you computed in the subquery. Note that the join in the subquery is required for the same reasons as in the main SELECT statement. This join is also constructed exactly the same way.

There are no secret handshakes in subqueries; they have exactly the same syntax as a standalone query. In fact, most subqueries start out as standalone queries and are incorporated as subqueries after their results are tested.

6

Nesting Subqueries

Nesting is the act of embedding a subquery within another subquery—for example,

Syntax ▼

```
SELECT * FROM SOMETHING WHERE ( SUBQUERY(SUBQUERY(SUBQUERY)));
```

Subqueries can be nested as deeply as your implementation of SQL allows. For example, to send out special notices to customers who spend more than the average amount of money, you would combine the information in the table CUSTOMER, as follows:

Input/Output ▼

```
SQL> SELECT *
  2 FROM CUSTOMER;

NAME        ADDRESS     STATE  ZIP         PHONE        REMARKS
==========  ==========  ======  ==========  ===========  ==========

TRUE WHEEL  550 HUSKER  NE      58702       555-4545     NONE
BIKE SPEC   CPT SHRIVE  LA      45678       555-1234     NONE
LE SHOPPE   HOMETOWN    KS      54678       555-1278     NONE
AAA BIKE    10 OLDTOWN  NE      56784       555-3421     JOHN-MGR
JACKS BIKE  24 EGLIN    FL      34567       555-2314     NONE
```

with a slightly modified version of the query you used to find the above-average orders:

Input/Output ▼

```
SQL> SELECT ALL C.NAME, C.ADDRESS, C.STATE,C.ZIP
  2 FROM CUSTOMER C
  3 WHERE C.NAME IN
  4 (SELECT O.NAME
  5 FROM ORDERS O, PART P
  6 WHERE O.PARTNUM = P.PARTNUM
  7 AND
  8 O.QUANTITY * P.PRICE  >
  9 (SELECT AVG(O.QUANTITY * P.PRICE)
 10 FROM ORDERS O, PART P
 11 WHERE O.PARTNUM = P.PARTNUM));

NAME        ADDRESS     STATE  ZIP
==========  ==========  ======  ==========

BIKE SPEC   CPT SHRIVE  LA      45678
LE SHOPPE   HOMETOWN    KS      54678
JACKS BIKE  24 EGLIN    FL      34567
```

Here's a look at what you asked for. In the innermost set of parentheses, you find a familiar statement:

```
SELECT AVG(O.QUANTITY * P.PRICE)
FROM ORDERS O, PART P
WHERE O.PARTNUM = P.PARTNUM
```

This result feeds into a slightly modified version of the SELECT clause you used before:

```
SELECT O.NAME
FROM ORDERS O, PART P
WHERE O.PARTNUM = P.PARTNUM
AND
O.QUANTITY * P.PRICE  >
(...)
```

Note that the SELECT clause has been modified to return a single column, NAME, which, not so coincidentally, is common with the table CUSTOMER. Running this statement by itself, you get:

Input/Output ▼

```
SQL> SELECT O.NAME
   2 FROM ORDERS O, PART P
   3 WHERE O.PARTNUM = P.PARTNUM
   4 AND
   5 O.QUANTITY * P.PRICE  >
   6 (SELECT AVG(O.QUANTITY * P.PRICE)
   7 FROM ORDERS O, PART P
   8 WHERE O.PARTNUM = P.PARTNUM);

NAME
==========

LE SHOPPE
BIKE SPEC
LE SHOPPE
BIKE SPEC
JACKS BIKE
```

6

We just spent some time discussing why your subqueries should return just one value. The reason this query was able to return more than one value becomes apparent in a moment.

You bring these results to the statement:

```
SELECT C.NAME, C.ADDRESS, C.STATE,C.ZIP
FROM CUSTOMER C
WHERE C.NAME IN
(...)
```

The first two lines are unremarkable. The third line reintroduces the keyword IN, last seen on Lesson 2, "Introducing the Query." IN enables you to use the multiple-row output of your subquery. IN, as you remember, looks for matches in a set of values enclosed by parentheses. In this case, IN produces the following values:

```
LE SHOPPE
BIKE SPEC
LE SHOPPE
BIKE SPEC
JACKS BIKE
```

This subquery provides the conditions that give you the mailing list:

```
NAME        ADDRESS     STATE  ZIP
=========== =========== ====== ======

BIKE SPEC   CPT SHRIVE  LA     45678
LE SHOPPE   HOMETOWN    KS     54678
JACKS BIKE  24 EGLIN    FL     34567
```

This use of IN is very common in subqueries. Because IN uses a set of values for its comparison, it does not cause the SQL engine to feel conflicted and inadequate.

Subqueries can also be used with GROUP BY and HAVING clauses. Examine the following query:

Input/Output ▼

```
SQL> SELECT NAME, AVG(QUANTITY)
  2 FROM ORDERS
  3 GROUP BY NAME
  4 HAVING AVG(QUANTITY) >
  5 (SELECT AVG(QUANTITY)
  6 FROM ORDERS);

NAME            AVG
=========== ===========

BIKE SPEC         8
JACKS BIKE        14
```

Let's examine this query in the order the SQL engine would. First, look at the subquery:

Input/Output ▼

```
SQL> SELECT AVG(QUANTITY)
  2 FROM ORDERS;

       AVG
===========

         6
```

By itself, the main portion of the query is as follows:

Input/Output ▼

```
SQL> SELECT NAME, AVG(QUANTITY)
  2 FROM ORDERS
  3 GROUP BY NAME;

NAME              AVG
========== ===========

AAA BIKE            6
BIKE SPEC           8
JACKS BIKE         14
LE SHOPPE           4
TRUE WHEEL          5
```

When combined through the HAVING clause, the subquery produces two rows that have above average QUANTITY.

Input/Output ▼

```
HAVING AVG(QUANTITY) >
(SELECT AVG(QUANTITY)
FROM ORDERS)

NAME              AVG
========== ===========

BIKE SPEC           8
JACKS BIKE         14
```

6

Referencing Outside with Correlated Subqueries

The subqueries you have written so far are self-contained. None of them has used a reference from outside the subquery. *Correlated subqueries* enable you to use an outside reference with some strange and wonderful results. Look at the following query:

Input/Output ▼

```
SQL> SELECT *
  2 FROM ORDERS O
  3 WHERE 'ROAD BIKE' =
  4 (SELECT DESCRIPTION
  5 FROM PART P
  6 WHERE P.PARTNUM = O.PARTNUM);
```

ORDEREDON	NAME	PARTNUM	QUANTITY	REMARKS
===========	==========	===========	===========	==========
19-MAY-1996	TRUE WHEEL	76	3	PAID
17-JAN-1996	BIKE SPEC	76	11	PAID
17-JAN-1996	LE SHOPPE	76	5	PAID
1-JUL-1996	AAA BIKE	76	4	PAID
11-JUL-1996	JACKS BIKE	76	14	PAID

This query actually resembles the following join:

Input/Output ▼

```
SQL> SELECT O.ORDEREDON, O.NAME,
  2 O.PARTNUM, O.QUANTITY, O.REMARKS
  3 FROM ORDERS O, PART P
  4 WHERE P.PARTNUM = O.PARTNUM
  5 AND P.DESCRIPTION = 'ROAD BIKE';
```

ORDEREDON	NAME	PARTNUM	QUANTITY	REMARKS
===========	==========	===========	===========	=======
19-MAY-1996	TRUE WHEEL	76	3	PAID
1-JUL-1996	AAA BIKE	76	4	PAID
17-JAN-1996	LE SHOPPE	76	5	PAID
17-JAN-1996	BIKE SPEC	76	11	PAID
11-JUL-1996	JACKS BIKE	76	14	PAID

Analysis ▼

Except for the order, the results are identical. The correlated subquery acts very much like a JOIN. The correlation is established by using an element from the query in the subquery. In this example, the correlation was established by the statement

```
WHERE P.PARTNUM = O.PARTNUM
```

in which you compare P.PARTNUM, from the table inside your subquery, to O.PARTNUM, from the table outside your query. Because O.PARTNUM can have a different value for every row, the correlated subquery is executed for each row in the query. In the next example, each row in the table ORDERS

Input/Output ▼

```
SQL> SELECT *
  2 FROM ORDERS;
```

ORDEREDON	NAME	PARTNUM	QUANTITY	REMARKS
19-MAY-1996	TRUE WHEEL	76	3	PAID
2-SEP-1996	TRUE WHEEL	10	1	PAID
30-JUN-1996	TRUE WHEEL	42	8	PAID
30-JUN-1996	BIKE SPEC	54	10	PAID
30-MAY-1996	BIKE SPEC	23	8	PAID
17-JAN-1996	BIKE SPEC	76	11	PAID
17-JAN-1996	LE SHOPPE	76	5	PAID
1-JUN-1996	LE SHOPPE	10	3	PAID
1-JUN-1996	AAA BIKE	10	1	PAID
1-JUL-1996	AAA BIKE	76	4	PAID
1-JUL-1996	AAA BIKE	46	14	PAID
11-JUL-1996	JACKS BIKE	76	14	PAID

is processed against the subquery criteria:

```
SELECT DESCRIPTION
FROM PART P
WHERE P.PARTNUM = O.PARTNUM
```

6

This operation returns the DESCRIPTION of every row in PART where P.PARTNUM = O.PARTNUM. These descriptions are then compared in the following WHERE clause:

```
WHERE 'ROAD BIKE' =
```

Analysis ▼

Because each row is examined, the subquery in a correlated subquery can have more than one value. However, don't try to return multiple columns or columns that don't make sense in the context of the WHERE clause. The values returned still must match up against the operation specified in the WHERE clause. For example, in the query you just did, if you returned the PRICE and compared it with ROAD BIKE, you would get the following result:

Input/Output ▼

```
SQL> SELECT *
  2 FROM ORDERS O
  3 WHERE 'ROAD BIKE' =
  4 (SELECT PRICE
  5 FROM PART P
  6 WHERE P.PARTNUM = O.PARTNUM)

conversion error from string "ROAD BIKE"
```

Here's another example of something not to do:

```
SELECT *
FROM ORDERS O
WHERE 'ROAD BIKE' =
(SELECT *
FROM PART P
WHERE P.PARTNUM = O.PARTNUM)
```

This SELECT caused a General Protection Fault on my Windows operating system. The SQL engine simply can't correlate all the columns in PART with the operator =.

Correlated subqueries can also be used with the GROUP BY and HAVING clauses. The following query uses a correlated subquery to find the average total order for a particular part, and then applies that average value to filter the total order grouped by PARTNUM:

Input/Output ▼

```
SQL> SELECT O.PARTNUM, SUM(O.QUANTITY*P.PRICE), COUNT(P.PARTNUM)
  2 FROM ORDERS O, PART P
  3 WHERE P.PARTNUM = O.PARTNUM
  4 GROUP BY O.PARTNUM
  5 HAVING SUM(O.QUANTITY*P.PRICE) >
  6 (SELECT AVG(O1.QUANTITY*P1.PRICE)
  7 FROM PART P1, ORDERS O1
  8 WHERE P1.PARTNUM = O1.PARTNUM
  9 AND P1.PARTNUM = O.PARTNUM);
```

PARTNUM	SUM	COUNT
===========	===========	===========
10	8400.00	4
23	4906.30	2
76	19610.00	5

Analysis ▼

The subquery does not just compute one average using AVG(O1.QUANTITY*P1.PRICE). Because of the correlation between the query and the subquery (AND P1.PARTNUM = O.PARTNUM), this average is computed for every group of parts and then compared:

HAVING SUM(O.QUANTITY*P.PRICE) >

TIP ————

> When using correlated subqueries with GROUP BY and HAVING, the columns in the HAVING clause must exist in either the SELECT clause or the GROUP BY clause. Otherwise, you get an error message along the lines of invalid column reference because the subquery is evoked for each group, not each row. You cannot make a valid comparison to something that is not used in forming the group.

Using EXISTS, ANY, and ALL

The uses of the keywords EXISTS, ANY, and ALL are not intuitively obvious to the casual observer. EXISTS takes a subquery as an argument and returns TRUE if the subquery returns anything, and FALSE if the result set is empty. For example

Input/Output ▼

```
SQL> SELECT NAME, ORDEREDON
  2 FROM ORDERS
  3 WHERE EXISTS
  4 (SELECT *
  5 FROM ORDERS
  6 WHERE NAME ='TRUE WHEEL');
```

6

```
NAME        ORDEREDON
========== ===========

TRUE WHEEL 19-MAY-1996
TRUE WHEEL  2-SEP-1996
TRUE WHEEL 30-JUN-1996
BIKE SPEC  30-JUN-1996
BIKE SPEC  30-MAY-1996
BIKE SPEC  17-JAN-1996
LE SHOPPE  17-JAN-1996
LE SHOPPE   1-JUN-1996
AAA BIKE    1-JUN-1996
AAA BIKE    1-JUL-1996
AAA BIKE    1-JUL-1996
JACKS BIKE 11-JUL-1996
```

Not what you might expect. The subquery inside EXISTS is evaluated only once in this uncorrelated example. Because the return from the subquery has at least one row, EXISTS evaluates to TRUE, and all the rows in the query are printed. If you change the subquery as shown next, you don't get any results.

```
SELECT NAME, ORDEREDON
FROM ORDERS
WHERE EXISTS
(SELECT *
FROM ORDERS
WHERE NAME ='MOSTLY HARMLESS')
```

EXISTS evaluates to FALSE. The subquery does not generate a result set because MOSTLY HARMLESS is not one of your names.

NOTE Notice the use of SELECT * in the subquery inside EXISTS. EXISTS does not care how many columns are returned.

You could use EXISTS in this way to check on the existence of certain rows and control the output of your query based on whether they exist.

If you use EXISTS in a correlated subquery, it is evaluated for every case implied by the correlation you set up—for example,

Input/Output ▼

```
SQL> SELECT NAME, ORDEREDON
  2 FROM ORDERS O
  3 WHERE EXISTS
  4 (SELECT *
  5 FROM CUSTOMER C
  6 WHERE STATE ='NE'
  7 AND C.NAME = O.NAME)

NAME          ORDEREDON
==========  ===========

TRUE WHEEL 19-MAY-1996
TRUE WHEEL  2-SEP-1996
TRUE WHEEL 30-JUN-1996
AAA BIKE    1-JUN-1996
AAA BIKE    1-JUL-1996
AAA BIKE    1-JUL-1996
```

This slight modification of your first, uncorrelated query returns all the bike shops from Nebraska that made orders. The following subquery is run for every row in the query correlated on the CUSTOMER name and ORDER name:

```
(SELECT *
FROM CUSTOMER C
WHERE STATE ='NE'
AND C.NAME = O.NAME)
```

EXISTS is TRUE for those rows that have corresponding names in CUSTOMER located in NE. Otherwise, it returns FALSE.

With the EXISTS operator, the subquery does not need to return specific data. If the conditions in the subquery are met, you can simply return a value of your choice. In the following example, we returned the number 1 instead of the * to improve the performance of the subquery:

```
SELECT NAME, ORDEREDON
FROM ORDERS O
WHERE EXISTS
(SELECT 1
FROM CUSTOMER C
WHERE STATE ='NE'
AND C.NAME = O.NAME)
```

6

Closely related to EXISTS are the keywords ANY, ALL, and SOME. ANY and SOME are identical in function. An optimist would say this feature provides the users with a choice. A pessimist would see this condition as one more complication. EXISTS checks to see whether any data is returned by the subquery. ANY, ALL, and SOME are used to compare a column value from the query to the data returned by the subquery. ANY and SOME both check to see whether the column value is found in the data returned by the subquery. ALL is used to check for an exact match between the column value and the value(s) returned by the subquery. Look at this query:

Input/Output ▼

```
SQL> SELECT NAME, ORDEREDON
  2 FROM ORDERS
  3 WHERE NAME = ANY
  4 (SELECT NAME
  5 FROM ORDERS
  6 WHERE NAME ='TRUE WHEEL');

NAME        ORDEREDON
========== ===========

TRUE WHEEL 19-MAY-1996
TRUE WHEEL  2-SEP-1996
TRUE WHEEL 30-JUN-1996
```

ANY compared the output of the following subquery to each row in the query, and returned TRUE for each row of the query that had a result from the subquery.

```
(SELECT NAME
FROM ORDERS
WHERE NAME ='TRUE WHEEL')
```

Replacing ANY with SOME produces an identical result:

Input/Output ▼

```
SQL> SELECT NAME, ORDEREDON
  2 FROM ORDERS
  3 WHERE NAME = SOME
  4 (SELECT NAME
  5 FROM ORDERS
  6 WHERE NAME ='TRUE WHEEL');

NAME        ORDEREDON
========== ===========

TRUE WHEEL 19-MAY-1996
TRUE WHEEL  2-SEP-1996
TRUE WHEEL 30-JUN-1996
```

You might have already noticed the similarity to IN. The same query using IN is as follows:

Input/Output ▼

```
SQL> SELECT NAME, ORDEREDON
  2 FROM ORDERS
  3 WHERE NAME IN
  4 (SELECT NAME
  5 FROM ORDERS
  6 WHERE NAME ='TRUE WHEEL');

NAME           ORDEREDON
========== ===========

TRUE WHEEL 19-MAY-1996
TRUE WHEEL  2-SEP-1996
TRUE WHEEL 30-JUN-1996
```

As you can see, IN returns the same result as ANY and SOME. Has the world gone mad? Not yet. Can IN do this?

Input/Output ▼

```
SQL> SELECT NAME, ORDEREDON
  2 FROM ORDERS
  3 WHERE NAME > ANY
  4 (SELECT NAME
  5 FROM ORDERS
  6 WHERE NAME ='JACKS BIKE')

NAME           ORDEREDON
========== ===========

TRUE WHEEL 19-MAY-1996
TRUE WHEEL  2-SEP-1996
TRUE WHEEL 30-JUN-1996
LE SHOPPE  17-JAN-1996
LE SHOPPE   1-JUN-1996
```

6

The answer is no. IN works like multiple equals. ANY and SOME can be used with other relational operators such as greater than or less than. Add this tool to your toolkit.

ALL returns TRUE only if all the results of a subquery meet the condition. Oddly enough, ALL is used most commonly as a double negative, as in this query:

Input/Output ▼

```
SQL> SELECT NAME, ORDEREDON
  2 FROM ORDERS
  3 WHERE NAME <> ALL
  4 (SELECT NAME
  5 FROM ORDERS
  6 WHERE NAME ='JACKS BIKE')

NAME        ORDEREDON
========== ===========

TRUE WHEEL 19-MAY-1996
TRUE WHEEL  2-SEP-1996
TRUE WHEEL 30-JUN-1996
BIKE SPEC  30-JUN-1996
BIKE SPEC  30-MAY-1996
BIKE SPEC  17-JAN-1996
LE SHOPPE  17-JAN-1996
LE SHOPPE   1-JUN-1996
AAA BIKE    1-JUN-1996
AAA BIKE    1-JUL-1996
AAA BIKE    1-JUL-1996
```

This statement returns everybody except JACKS BIKE. <> ALL evaluates to TRUE only if the result set does not contain what appears to the left of the <>.

Summary

In this lesson, you performed dozens of exercises involving subqueries. By doing this, you have learned how to use one of the most important parts of SQL. The subquery is a method for placing additional conditions on the data returned by your query. A subquery provides great flexibility in defining conditions, especially conditions for which you do not know the exact value. For example, I might want to get a list of all the products priced above average, but I might not know what the overall average price is offhand. I can include a subquery that calculates the average price.

In this lesson, you also tackled one of the most difficult parts of SQL, a correlated subquery. The correlated subquery creates a relationship between the query and the subquery, which is evaluated for every instance of that relationship. Additionally, you learned about the EXISTS, ANY, SOME, and ALL operators, which are used with subqueries. EXISTS checks to see whether data is returned by the subquery based on the conditions in the subquery. ANY and SOME, similar to the IN operator, check to see whether a column value is in the data returned by a subquery. The ALL operator is used to see whether column data is the same as that returned by the subquery. Don't be intimidated by how long the queries have become. You can easily examine them one subquery at a time.

Q&A

Q **In this lesson, I saw that in some cases there are several ways to get the same result. Isn't this flexibility confusing?**

A No, not really. Having so many ways to achieve the same result enables you to create some really neat statements. Flexibility is the virtue of SQL.

Q **What situations might require me to go outside a query to get information?**

A Subqueries enable you to further specify conditions on data that your query will return. Using a subquery, you can place a condition on a query without knowing the exact values you want to use in your comparison.

Q **What is the real benefit of using a correlated subquery instead of a regular subquery?**

A A correlated subquery gives you a bit more flexibility over a standard subquery because you can join tables in the subquery with tables in the main query. Again, the key is greater flexibility for devising queries.

Workshop

The Workshop provides quiz questions to help solidify your understanding of the material covered, as well as exercises to provide you with experience in using what you have learned. Try to answer the quiz and exercise questions before checking the answers in Appendix A, "Answers."

Quiz

1. In the section "Nesting Subqueries," the sample subquery returned several values:
   ```
   LE SHOPPE
   BIKE SPEC
   LE SHOPPE
   BIKE SPEC
   JACKS BIKE
   ```

   Some of these are duplicates. Why aren't these duplicates in the final result set?

2. Are the following statements true or false?

   a. The aggregate functions SUM, COUNT, MIN, MAX, and AVG all return multiple values.

   b. The maximum number of subqueries that can be nested is two.

   c. Correlated subqueries are completely self-contained.

6

3. Will the following subqueries work using the ORDERS table and the PART table?

```
SQL> SELECT *
     FROM PART;

     PARTNUM  DESCRIPTION    PRICE
          54  PEDALS         54.25
          42  SEATS          24.50
          46  TIRES          15.25
          23  MOUNTAIN BIKE  350.45
          76  ROAD BIKE      530.00
          10  TANDEM        1200.00
6 rows selected.
     SQL> SELECT *
          FROM ORDERS;

ORDEREDON NAME             PARTNUM  QUANTITY  REMARKS
   30-JUN-96 TRUE WHEEL         42         8  PAID
   19-MAY-96 TRUE WHEEL         76         3  PAID
    2-SEP-96 TRUE WHEEL         10         1  PAID
   30-JUN-96 BIKE SPEC          54        10  PAID
   30-MAY-96 BIKE SPEC          23         8  PAID
   17-JAN-96 BIKE SPEC          76        11  PAID
   17-JAN-96 LE SHOPPE          76         5  PAID
    1-JUN-96 LE SHOPPE          10         3  PAID
    1-JUN-96 AAA BIKE           10         1  PAID
    1-JUL-96 AAA BIKE           76         4  PAID
    1-JUL-96 AAA BIKE           46        14  PAID
   11-JUL-96 JACKS BIKE         76        14  PAID
13 rows selected.
```

a. `SQL> SELECT * FROM ORDERS`
```
          WHERE PARTNUM =
          SELECT PARTNUM FROM PART
          WHERE DESCRIPTION = 'TRUE WHEEL';
```

b. `SQL> SELECT PARTNUM`
```
          FROM ORDERS
          WHERE PARTNUM =
          (SELECT * FROM PART
          WHERE DESCRIPTION = 'LE SHOPPE');
```

c. SQL> SELECT NAME, PARTNUM
```
FROM ORDERS
WHERE EXISTS
(SELECT * FROM ORDERS
WHERE NAME = 'TRUE WHEEL');
```

Exercises

1. Imagine that MySQL doesn't support subqueries. Write two separate queries that would return the NAMES and ORDEREDON dates from the ORDERS table for those NAMES that would fall after JACKS BIKE.

   The first step would be to determine the query that creates the result set used in the comparison.

2. Write a query that shows the name of the most expensive part.

6

LESSON 7

Molding Data with Built-in Functions

In this lesson we discuss functions. Functions in SQL enable you to perform feats such as determining the sum of a column, or converting all the characters of a string to uppercase. By the end of this lesson, you will understand and be able to use all the following:

- Aggregate functions

- Date and time functions

- Arithmetic functions

- Character functions

- Conversion functions

- Miscellaneous functions

These functions greatly increase your capability to manipulate the information you retrieved using the basic functions of SQL that were described earlier in the book. The first five aggregate functions, COUNT, SUM, AVG, MAX, and MIN, are defined in the ANSI standard. Most implementations of SQL have extensions to these aggregate functions, some of which are covered in this lesson. Some implementations might use different names for these functions. See Lesson 20, "New Objects in the Latest Standard" for the new aggregate functions. Also, at the end of this lesson there is a list of MySQL functions.

Using Aggregate Functions to Summarize Data

These functions are also referred to as *group functions*. They return a value based on the values in a column. (After all, you wouldn't ask for the average of a single field.) The examples in this section use the table TEAMSTATS:

Input/Output ▼

```
SQL> SELECT * FROM TEAMSTATS;

NAME       POS  AB HITS WALKS SINGLES DOUBLES TRIPLES HR SO
-------    ----- --- ---- ----- ------- ------- ------- -- ---
JONES      1B  145  45 34     31        8       1       5 10
DONKNOW    3B  175  65 23     50       10       1       4 15
WORLEY     LF  157  49 15     35        8       3       3 16
DAVID      OF  187  70 24     48        4       0      17 42
HAMHOCKER  3B   50  12 10     10        2       0       0  3
CASEY      DH    1   0  0      0        0       0       0  1

6 rows selected.
```

COUNT

The function COUNT returns the number of rows that satisfy the condition in the WHERE clause. Say you wanted to know how many ball players were hitting under .350. You would type

Input/Output ▼

```
mysql> select count(*)
    -> from teamstats
    -> where hits/ab < .350;
+----------+
| count(*) |
+----------+
|        4 |
+----------+
1 row in set (0.26 sec)
```

Would it make any difference if you tried a column name instead of the asterisk? (Notice the use of parentheses around the column names.) Try this:

Input/Output ▼

```
SQL> SELECT COUNT(NAME) "NUM_BELOW_350"
  2  FROM TEAMSTATS
  3  WHERE HITS/AB < .350;
NUM_BELOW_350
-------------
            4
```

The answer is no. The NAME column that you selected was not involved in the WHERE statement. If you use COUNT without a WHERE clause, it returns the number of records in the table.

Input/Output ▼

```
SQL> SELECT COUNT(*)
  2  FROM TEAMSTATS;

 COUNT(*)
---------
        6
```

SUM

SUM does just that—it returns the sum of all values in a column. To find out how many singles have been hit, type

Input/Output ▼

```
mysql> select sum(singles) from teamstats;
+--------------+
| sum(singles) |
+--------------+
|          174 |
+--------------+
1 row in set (0.00 sec)
```

To get several sums, use

Input/Output ▼

```
mysql> select sum(singles) "Total Singles", sum(doubles) "Total
    Doubles",
    -> sum(triples) "Total Triples", sum(hr) "Total HR"
    -> from teamstats;
```

7

```
+---------------+---------------+---------------+---------+
| Total Singles | Total Doubles | Total Triples | Total HR |
+---------------+---------------+---------------+---------+
|           174 |            32 |             5 |       29 |
+---------------+---------------+---------------+---------+
1 row in set (0.00 sec)
```

To collect similar information on all .300 or better players, type

Input/Output ▼

```
mysql> select sum(singles) "Total Singles", sum(doubles) "Total
       Doubles",
    -> sum(triples) "Total Triples", sum(hr) "Total HR"
    -> from teamstats
    -> where hits/ab >= .300
    -> ;

+---------------+---------------+---------------+---------+
| Total Singles | Total Doubles | Total Triples | Total HR |
+---------------+---------------+---------------+---------+
|           164 |            30 |             5 |       29 |
+---------------+---------------+---------------+---------+
1 row in set (0.00 sec)
```

To compute a team batting average, type

Input/Output ▼

```
mysql> select sum(hits)/sum(ab) "Team Average"
    -> from teamstats
    -> ;
+--------------+
| Team Average |
+--------------+
|       0.3371 |
+--------------+
1 row in set (0.00 sec)
```

AVG

The AVG function computes the average of a column. To find the average number of strikeouts, use this:

Input/Output ▼

```
mysql> select avg(so) "Avg Strike Outs"
    -> from teamstats;
+-----------------+
| Avg Strike Outs |
+-----------------+
| 16.166666666667 |
+-----------------+
1 row in set (0.00 sec)
```

The following example illustrates the difference between SUM and AVG:

Input/Output ▼

```
mysql> select avg(hits/ab) "Team Avg"
    -> from teamstats;
+----------+
| Team Avg |
+----------+
| 0.268034 |
+----------+
1 row in set (0.00 sec)
```

The team was batting over .300 in the previous example! What happened? AVG computed the average of the combined column hits divided by at-bats, whereas the example with SUM divided the total number of hits by the number of at-bats. For example, player A gets 50 hits in 100 at-bats for a .500 average. Player B gets 0 hits in 1 at-bat for a 0.0 average. The average of 0.0 and 0.5 is .250. If you compute the combined average of 50 hits in 101 at-bats, the answer is a respectable .495. The following statement returns the correct batting average:

Input/Output ▼

```
mysql> select avg(hits)/avg(ab) "Team Avg"
    -> from teamstats;
+----------+
| Team Avg |
+----------+
| 0.337063 |
+----------+
1 row in set (0.00 sec)
```

7

Like the SUM function, AVG works only with numbers.

MAX

If you want to find the largest value in a column, use MAX. For example, what is the highest number of hits?

Input/Output ▼

```
SQL> SELECT MAX(HITS)
  2  FROM TEAMSTATS;

MAX(HITS)
---------
       70
```

Can you find out who has the most hits?

Input/Output ▼

```
SQL> SELECT NAME
  2  FROM TEAMSTATS
  3  WHERE HITS = MAX(HITS);

ERROR at line 3:
ORA-00934: group function is not allowed here
```

Unfortunately, you can't—at least not using this method. The error message is a reminder that this group function (remember that aggregate functions are also called group functions) does not work in the WHERE clause.

What happens if you try a nonnumerical column?

Input/Output ▼

```
mysql> select max(name)
    -> from teamstats;
+-----------+
| max(name) |
+-----------+
| WORLEY    |
+-----------+
1 row in set (0.00 sec)
```

Here's something new. MAX returns the highest (closest to Z) string. Finally, a function that works with both characters and numbers.

MIN

MIN does the expected and works like MAX except that it returns the lowest member of a column. To find out the fewest at-bats, type

Input/Output ▼

```
mysql> select min(ab)
    -> from teamstats;
+---------+
| min(ab) |
+---------+
|       1 |
+---------+
1 row in set (0.00 sec)
```

The following statement returns the name closest to the beginning of the alphabet:

Input/Output ▼

```
mysql> select min(name)
    -> from teamstats;
+-----------+
| min(name) |
+-----------+
| CASEY     |
+-----------+
1 row in set (0.00 sec)
```

You can combine MIN with MAX to give a range of values—for example,

Input/Output ▼

```
mysql> select min(ab), max(ab)
    -> from teamstats;
+---------+---------+
| min(ab) | max(ab) |
+---------+---------+
|       1 |     187 |
+---------+---------+
1 row in set (0.00 sec)
```

This sort of information can be useful when using statistical functions.

7

NOTE

> As we mentioned in the introduction of the lesson, the first five aggregate functions are described in the ANSI standard. The remaining aggregate functions have become de facto standards, present in all important implementations of SQL. We use the Oracle names for these functions. Other implementations might use different names.

VARIANCE

VARIANCE produces the square of the standard deviation, a number vital to many statistical calculations. It works like this:

Input/Output ▼

```
SQL> SELECT VARIANCE(HITS)
  2  FROM TEAMSTATS;

VARIANCE(HITS)
--------------
     669.1389
```

If you try a string

Input/Output ▼

```
SQL> SELECT VARIANCE(NAME)
  2  FROM TEAMSTATS;

ERROR:
ORA-01722: invalid number
no rows selected
```

you find that VARIANCE is another function that works exclusively with numbers.

STDDEV

The final group function, STDDEV, finds the standard deviation of a column of numbers, as demonstrated by this example:

Input/Output ▼

```
SQL> SELECT STDDEV(HITS)
  2  FROM TEAMSTATS;

STDDEV(HITS)
------------
     25.8677
```

It also returns an error when confronted by a string:

Input/Output ▼

```
SQL> SELECT STDDEV(NAME)
  2  FROM TEAMSTATS;

ERROR:
ORA-01722: invalid number
no rows selected
```

These aggregate functions can also be used in various combinations:

Input/Output ▼

```
SQL> SELECT COUNT(AB),
  2  AVG(AB),
  3  MIN(AB),
  4  MAX(AB),
  5  STDDEV(AB),
  6  VARIANCE(AB),
  7  SUM(AB)
  8  FROM TEAMSTATS;

COUNT(AB)  AVG(AB)  MIN(AB) MAX(AB) STDDEV(AB)  VARIANCE(AB)  SUM(AB)
---------  -------  ------- ------- ----------  ------------  -------
6          119.167        1     187    68.9986     4760.8056      715
```

The next time you hear a sportscaster use statistics to fill the time between plays, you will know that SQL is at work somewhere behind the scenes.

Using Functions to Format Date and Time Values

We live in a civilization governed by times and dates, and most major implementations of SQL have functions to cope with these concepts. This section uses the table PROJECT to demonstrate the time and date functions.

Input/Output ▼

```
mysql> select * from project;
+--------------+------------+------------+
| task         | startdate  | enddate    |
+--------------+------------+------------+
| KICKOFF MTG  | 1998-04-01 | 1998-04-01 |
| TECH SURVEY  | 1998-04-02 | 1998-05-01 |
| USER MTGS    | 1998-05-15 | 1998-05-30 |
```

```
¦ DESIGN WIDGET ¦ 1998-06-01 ¦ 1998-06-30 ¦
¦ CODE WIDGET   ¦ 1998-07-01 ¦ 1998-09-02 ¦
¦ TESTING       ¦ 1998-09-03 ¦ 1999-01-17 ¦
+---------------+------------+------------+
6 rows in set (0.07 sec)
```

NOTE ⸺ This table used the Date data type. Most implementations of SQL have a Date data type, but the exact syntax may vary.

ADD_MONTHS/ADD_DATE

This function adds a number of months to a specified date. For example, say something extraordinary happened, and the preceding project needed to be adjusted out by two months.

The function that you use in MySQL is ADD_DATE(). Following the Oracle example will be an example of the syntax used to add months to a date in MySQL.

You could make a new schedule by typing

Input/Output ▼

```
SQL> SELECT TASK,
  2  STARTDATE,
  3  ENDDATE ORIGINAL,
  4  ADD_MONTHS(ENDDATE,2)
  5  FROM PROJECT;

TASK             STARTDATE  ORIGINAL   ADD_MONTH
---------------  ---------  ---------  ---------
KICKOFF MTG      01-APR-98  01-APR-98  01-JUN-98
TECH SURVEY      02-APR-98  01-MAY-98  01-JUL-98
USER MTGS        15-MAY-98  30-MAY-98  30-JUL-98
DESIGN WIDGET    01-JUN-98  30-JUN-98  31-AUG-98
CODE WIDGET      01-JUL-98  02-SEP-98  02-NOV-98
TESTING          03-SEP-98  17-JAN-99  17-MAR-99

6 rows selected.
```

The MySQL equivalent is

Input/Output ▼

```
mysql> select task, startdate, enddate Original,
    -> date_add(enddate,interval 2 month) New
    -> from project
    -> ;
+---------------+------------+------------+------------+
| task          | startdate  | Original   | New        |
+---------------+------------+------------+------------+
| KICKOFF MTG   | 1998-04-01 | 1998-04-01 | 1998-06-01 |
| TECH SURVEY   | 1998-04-02 | 1998-05-01 | 1998-07-01 |
| USER MTGS     | 1998-05-15 | 1998-05-30 | 1998-07-30 |
| DESIGN WIDGET | 1998-06-01 | 1998-06-30 | 1998-08-30 |
| CODE WIDGET   | 1998-07-01 | 1998-09-02 | 1998-11-02 |
| TESTING       | 1998-09-03 | 1999-01-17 | 1999-03-17 |
+---------------+------------+------------+------------+
6 rows in set (0.00 sec)
```

Not that a slip like this is possible, but it's nice to have a function that makes it so easy. ADD_MONTHS/ADD_DATE also works outside the SELECT clause. Typing

Input ▼

```
SQL> SELECT TASK "TASKS_SHORTER_THAN_ONE_MONTH"
  2  FROM PROJECT
  3  WHERE ADD_MONTHS(STARTDATE,1) > ENDDATE;
```

produces the following result:

Output ▼

```
TASKS_SHORTER_THAN_ONE_MONTH
----------------
KICKOFF MTG
TECH SURVEY
USER MTGS
DESIGN WIDGET
```

7

The MySQL equivalent is

Input/Output ▼

```
mysql> select task
    -> from project
    -> where date_add(startdate, interval 1 month) > enddate;
+---------------+
¦ task          ¦
+---------------+
¦ KICKOFF MTG   ¦
¦ TECH SURVEY   ¦
¦ USER MTGS     ¦
¦ DESIGN WIDGET ¦
+---------------+
4 rows in set (0.01 sec)
```

You will find that all the functions in this section work in more than one place. However, ADD MONTHS/ADD_DATE does not work with other data types such as Character or Number/ Numeric without the help of the functions TO_CHAR and TO_DATE, which are discussed later in the lesson.

LAST_DAY

LAST_DAY returns the last day of a specified month. It is for those of us who haven't mastered the "Thirty days has September..." rhyme—or at least those of us who have not yet taught it to our computers. If, for example, you need to know what the last day of the month is in the column ENDDATE, you would type

Input ▼

```
SQL> SELECT ENDDATE, LAST_DAY(ENDDATE)
  2   FROM PROJECT;
```

Here's the result:

Output ▼

```
ENDDATE    LAST_DAY(ENDDATE)
--------- ---------
01-APR-98 30-APR-98
01-MAY-98 31-MAY-98
30-MAY-98 31-MAY-98
30-JUN-98 30-JUN-98
02-SEP-98 30-SEP-98
17-JAN-99 31-JAN-99

6 rows selected.
```

How does LAST_DAY handle leap years?

Input/Output ▼

```
SQL> SELECT LAST_DAY('1-FEB-98') NON_LEAP,
  2    LAST_DAY('1-FEB-99') LEAP
  3    FROM PROJECT;

NON_LEAP   LEAP
---------  ---------
28-FEB-98  29-FEB-99
28-FEB-98  29-FEB-99
28-FEB-98  29-FEB-99
28-FEB-98  29-FEB-99
28-FEB-98  29-FEB-99
28-FEB-98  29-FEB-99

6 rows selected.
```

You got the right result, but why were so many rows returned? Because you didn't specify an existing column or any conditions, the SQL engine applied the date functions in the statement to each existing row. Let's get something less redundant by using the DISTINCT clause with the following:

Input/Output ▼

```
SQL> SELECT DISTINCT LAST_DAY('1-FEB-98') NON_LEAP,
  2    LAST_DAY('1-FEB-99') LEAP
  3    FROM PROJECT;
NON_LEAP   LEAP
---------  ---------
28-FEB-98  29-FEB-99
```

As you can see, this function understands which years are leap years. However, you should check your implementations documentation before assuming that it covers this as well.

MONTHS_BETWEEN

If you need to know how many months fall between month *x* and month *y*, and you're working in an Oracle database, use MONTHS_BETWEEN like this:

7

Input/Output ▼

```
SQL> SELECT TASK, STARTDATE, ENDDATE,MONTHS_BETWEEN(STARTDATE,ENDDATE)
     DURATION
  2  FROM PROJECT;

TASK             STARTDATE ENDDATE    DURATION
---------------  --------- ---------  ---------
KICKOFF MTG      01-APR-98 01-APR-98          0
TECH SURVEY      02-APR-98 01-MAY-98  -.9677419
USER MTGS        15-MAY-98 30-MAY-98   -.483871
DESIGN WIDGET    01-JUN-98 30-JUN-98  -.9354839
CODE WIDGET      01-JUL-98 02-SEP-98  -2.032258
TESTING          03-SEP-98 17-JAN-99  -4.451613

6 rows selected.
```

Wait a minute—that doesn't look right. Try this:

Input/Output ▼

```
SQL> SELECT TASK, STARTDATE, ENDDATE,
  2  MONTHS_BETWEEN(ENDDATE,STARTDATE) DURATION
  3  FROM PROJECT;

TASK             STARTDATE ENDDATE    DURATION
---------------  --------- ---------  ---------
KICKOFF MTG      01-APR-98 01-APR-98          0
TECH SURVEY      02-APR-98 01-MAY-98  .96774194
USER MTGS        15-MAY-98 30-MAY-98  .48387097
DESIGN WIDGET    01-JUN-98 30-JUN-98  .93548387
CODE WIDGET      01-JUL-98 02-SEP-98  2.0322581
TESTING          03-SEP-98 17-JAN-99  4.4516129

6 rows selected.
```

That's better. You see that MONTHS_BETWEEN is sensitive to the way you order the months. Negative months might not be bad. For example, you could use a negative result to determine whether one date happened before another. For example, the following statement shows all the tasks that started before May 19, 1998:

Input/Output ▼

```
SQL> SELECT *
  2  FROM PROJECT
  3  WHERE MONTHS_BETWEEN('19-MAY-98', STARTDATE) > 0;
```

```
TASK            STARTDATE ENDDATE
--------------- --------- ---------
KICKOFF MTG     01-APR-98 01-APR-98
TECH SURVEY     02-APR-98 01-MAY-98
USER MTGS       15-MAY-98 30-MAY-98
```

NEXT_DAY

NEXT_DAY finds the name of the first day of the week that is equal to or later than another specified date. For example, to send a report on the Friday following the first day of each event, you would type

Input/Output ▼

```
SQL> SELECT STARTDATE,
  2  NEXT_DAY(STARTDATE, 'FRIDAY')
  3  FROM PROJECT;


STARTDATE NEXT_DAY(
--------- ---------
01-APR-98 07-APR-98
02-APR-98 07-APR-98
15-MAY-98 19-MAY-98
01-JUN-98 02-JUN-98
01-JUL-98 07-JUL-98
03-SEP-98 08-SEP-98

6 rows selected.
```

The output tells you the date of the first Friday that occurs after your STARTDATE.

SYSDATE

SYSDATE returns the system time and date.

NOTE	When selecting the SYSDATE (in an Oracle database), we will use a pseudotable called DUAL, which is used by Oracle. The DUAL table is used mainly for calculations and contains one column, as shown in the following code. Check your implementation for the DUAL table or another table that might exist for the same use. MySQL does not require the reference of a workspace table name such as DUAL for computations.

7

Input/Output ▼

```
SQL> DESCRIBE DUAL
 Name                                Null?    Type
 --------------------------------    -------- ----
 DUMMY                                        VARCHAR2(1)

SQL> SELECT DISTINCT SYSDATE
  2  FROM DUAL;

SYSDATE
---------------
18-JUN-08 1020PM
```

The MySQL equivalent is

Input/Output ▼

```
mysql> select distinct now();
+---------------------+
| now()               |
+---------------------+
| 2008-05-28 17:55:24 |
+---------------------+
1 row in set (0.00 sec)
```

If you wanted to see where you stood today in a certain project, you could type

Input/Output ▼

```
SQL> SELECT *
  2  FROM PROJECT
  3  WHERE STARTDATE > SYSDATE;

TASK             STARTDATE ENDDATE
---------------- --------- ---------
CODE WIDGET      01-JUL-98 02-SEP-98
TESTING          03-SEP-98 17-JAN-99
```

The MySQL equivalent is

Input/Output ▼

```
mysql> select * from project
    -> where startdate > now();
Empty set (0.04 sec)
```

Now you can see what parts of the project start after today. The MySQL example would seem to indicate that all of the projects were due to have started before today (now()).

Using Functions for Arithmetic Operations

Many of the uses you have for the data you retrieve involve mathematics. Most implementations of SQL provide arithmetic functions similar to the functions covered here. The examples in this section use the NUMBERS table:

Input/Output ▼

```
mysql> select * from numbers;
+----------+---------+
| a        | b       |
+----------+---------+
|   3.1415 |  4.0000 |
| -45.0000 |  0.7070 |
|   5.0000 |  9.0000 |
| -57.6670 | 42.0000 |
|  15.0000 | 55.0000 |
|  -7.2000 |  5.3000 |
+----------+---------+
6 rows in set (0.39 sec)
```

ABS

The ABS function returns the absolute value of the number you point to—for example,

Input/Output ▼

```
mysql> select abs(a) "Absolute Value"
    -> from numbers;
+----------------+
| Absolute Value |
+----------------+
|         3.1415 |
|        45.0000 |
|         5.0000 |
|        57.6670 |
|        15.0000 |
|         7.2000 |
+----------------+
6 rows in set (0.00 sec)
```

ABS changes all the negative numbers to positive and leaves positive numbers alone.

7

CEIL **and** FLOOR

CEIL returns the smallest integer greater than or equal to its argument. FLOOR does just the reverse, returning the largest integer equal to or less than its argument—for example,

Input/Output ▼

```
mysql> select b, ceil(b)
    -> from numbers;
+---------+---------+
| b       | ceil(b) |
+---------+---------+
|  4.0000 |       4 |
|  0.7070 |       1 |
|  9.0000 |       9 |
| 42.0000 |      42 |
| 55.0000 |      55 |
|  5.3000 |       6 |
+---------+---------+
6 rows in set (0.00 sec)
```

and

Input/Output ▼

```
mysql> select a, floor(a)
    -> from numbers;
+----------+----------+
| a        | floor(a) |
+----------+----------+
|   3.1415 |        3 |
| -45.0000 |      -45 |
|   5.0000 |        5 |
| -57.6670 |      -58 |
|  15.0000 |       15 |
|  -7.2000 |       -8 |
+----------+----------+
6 rows in set (0.00 sec)
```

EXP

EXP enables you to raise e (e is a mathematical constant used in various formulas) to a power. Here's how EXP raises e by the values in column A:

Input/Output ▼

```
SQL> SELECT A, EXP(A)
  2  FROM NUMBERS;

         A      EXP(A)
--------- ---------
   3.1415   23.138549
      -45   2.863E-20
        5   148.41316
  -57.667   9.027E-26
       15   3269017.4
     -7.2   .00074659

6 rows selected.
```

LN and LOG

These two functions center on logarithms. LN returns the natural logarithm of its argument—for example,

Input/Output ▼

```
SQL> SELECT A, LN(A)
  2  FROM NUMBERS;

ERROR:
ORA-01428: argument '-45' is out of range
```

The MySQL equivalent is

Input/Output ▼

```
mysql> select ln(a)
    -> from numbers;
ERROR 1064: You have an error in your SQL syntax near '(a)
from numbers' at line 1
```

Did we neglect to mention that the argument had to be positive? Write

Input/Output ▼

```
SQL> SELECT A, LN(ABS(A))
  2  FROM NUMBERS;

         A  LN(ABS(A))
--------- ----------
   3.1415   1.1447004
      -45   3.8066625
```

7

```
       5  1.6094379
 -57.667  4.0546851
      15  2.7080502
    -7.2  1.974081
```

6 rows selected.

Notice how you can embed the function ABS inside the LN call. The other logarithmic function, LOG, takes two arguments, returning the logarithm of the first argument in the base of the second. The following query returns the logarithms of column B in base 10.

Input/Output ▼

```
SQL> SELECT B, LOG(B, 10)
  2  FROM NUMBERS;

B          LOG(B,10)
---------- ----------
        4  1.660964
     .707  -6.640962
        9  1.0479516
       42  .61604832
       55  .57459287
      5.3  1.3806894
```

6 rows selected.

MOD

You have encountered MOD before. In Lesson 3, "Expressions, Conditions, and Operators," you saw that the ANSI standard for the modulo operator % is sometimes implemented as the function MOD. Here's a query that returns a table showing the remainder of A divided by B:

Input/Output ▼

```
SQL> SELECT A, B, MOD(A,B)
  2  FROM NUMBERS;

         A          B  MOD(A,B)
---------- ---------- ----------
    3.1415          4     3.1415
       -45       .707      -.459
         5          9          5
   -57.667         42    -15.667
        15         55         15
      -7.2        5.3       -1.9
```

6 rows selected.

POWER

To raise one number to the power of another, use POWER. In this function, the first argument is raised to the power of the second:

Input/Output ▼

```
SQL> SELECT A, B, POWER(A,B)
  2  FROM NUMBERS;

ERROR:
ORA-01428: argument '-45' is out of range
```

At first glance, you are likely to think that the first argument can't be negative. But that impression can't be true because a number like –4 can be raised to a power. Therefore, if the first number in the POWER function is negative, the second must be an integer. You can work around this problem by using CEIL (or FLOOR):

Input/Output ▼

```
SQL> SELECT A, CEIL(B), POWER(A,CEIL(B))
  2  FROM NUMBERS;

         A   CEIL(B) POWER(A,CEIL(B))
---------- --------- ----------------
    3.1415         4          97.3976
       -45         1              -45
         5         9          1953125
   -57.667        42        9.098E+73
        15        55        4.842E+64
      -7.2         6        139314.07

6 rows selected.
```

SIGN

SIGN returns -1 if its argument is less than 0, 0 if its argument is equal to 0, and 1 if its argument is greater than 0, as shown in the following example:

Input/Output ▼

```
SQL> SELECT A, SIGN(A)
  2  FROM NUMBERS;

         A   SIGN(A)
---------- ---------
    3.1415         1
```

7

```
      -45          -1
        5           1
  -57.667          -1
       15           1
     -7.2          -1
```

7 rows selected.

You could also use SIGN in a SELECT WHERE clause like this:

Input/Output ▼

```
SQL> SELECT A
  2  FROM NUMBERS
  3  WHERE SIGN(A) = 1;

       A
---------
    3.1415
        5
       15
```

SQRT

The function SQRT returns the square root of an argument. Because the square root of a negative number is undefined, you cannot use SQRT on negative numbers.

Input/Output ▼

```
SQL> SELECT A, SQRT(A)
  2  FROM NUMBERS;

ERROR:
ORA-01428: argument '-45' is out of range
```

However, you can fix this limitation with ABS:

Input/Output ▼

```
SQL> SELECT ABS(A), SQRT(ABS(A))
  2  FROM NUMBERS;

  ABS(A) SQRT(ABS(A))
--------- ------------
   3.1415    1.7724277
       45    6.7082039
        5     2.236068
```

```
 57.667    7.5938791
     15    3.8729833
    7.2    2.6832816
```

7 rows selected.

Using Functions to Modify the Appearance of Character Values

Many implementations of SQL provide functions to manipulate characters and strings of characters. This section covers the most common character functions. The examples in this section use the table CHARACTERS.

Input/Output ▼

```
mysql> select * from characters;
+-----------+-----------+------+------+
| lastname  | firstname | m    | code |
+-----------+-----------+------+------+
| PURVIS    | KELLY     | A    |   32 |
| TAYLOR    | CHUCK     | J    |   67 |
| CHRISTINE | LAURA     | C    |   65 |
| ADAMS     | FESTER    | M    |   87 |
| COSTALES  | ARMANDO   | A    |   77 |
| KONG      | MAJOR     | G    |   52 |
+-----------+-----------+------+------+
6 rows in set (0.04 sec)
```

CHR

CHR returns the character equivalent of the number it uses as an argument. The character it returns depends on the character set of the database. For this example, the database is set to ASCII. The column CODE includes numbers.

Input/Output ▼

```
SQL> SELECT CODE, CHR(CODE)
  2  FROM CHARACTERS;

      CODE CH
---------- --
        32
        67 C
        65 A
        87 W
```

7

```
77 M
52 4
```

6 rows selected.

The space opposite the 32 shows that 32 is a *space* in the ASCII character set.

CONCAT

You used the equivalent of this function in Lesson 3, when you learned about operators. The ¦¦ symbol splices two strings together, as does CONCAT. It works like this:

Input/Output ▼

```
mysql> select concat(firstname, lastname)
    -> from characters;
+----------------------------+
| concat(firstname, lastname) |
+----------------------------+
| KELLYPURVIS                |
| CHUCKTAYLOR                |
| LAURACHRISTINE             |
| FESTERADAMS                |
| ARMANDOCOSTALES            |
| MAJORKONG                  |
+----------------------------+
6 rows in set (0.00 sec)
```

Consider the following:

Input/Output ▼

```
mysql> select concat(firstname,',',' ',lastname)
    -> from characters;
+-----------------------------------+
| concat(firstname,',',' ',lastname) |
+-----------------------------------+
| KELLY, PURVIS                     |
| CHUCK, TAYLOR                     |
| LAURA, CHRISTINE                  |
| FESTER, ADAMS                     |
| ARMANDO, COSTALES                 |
| MAJOR, KONG                       |
+-----------------------------------+
6 rows in set (0.00 sec)
```

The CONCAT function allows for any number of string expressions to be connected to each other. Here is another way of approaching the concatenation issue in MySQL:

Input/Output ▼

```
mysql> select concat_ws(', ',firstname,lastname) Name
    -> from characters;
+------------------+
| Name             |
+------------------+
| KELLY, PURVIS    |
| CHUCK, TAYLOR    |
| LAURA, CHRISTINE |
| FESTER, ADAMS    |
| ARMANDO, COSTALES |
| MAJOR, KONG      |
+------------------+
6 rows in set (0.00 sec)
```

CONCAT WS() allows you to concatenate columns together, plus it allows you to specify what will separate the columns. In this case we have specified a comma and a space (,).

INITCAP

INITCAP capitalizes the first letter of a word and makes all other characters lowercase in Oracle SQL*Plus.

Input/Output ▼

```
SQL> SELECT FIRSTNAME BEFORE, INITCAP(FIRSTNAME) AFTER
  2  FROM CHARACTERS;

BEFORE          AFTER
--------------- ---------------
KELLY           Kelly
CHUCK           Chuck
LAURA           Laura
FESTER          Fester
ARMANDO         Armando
MAJOR           Major

6 rows selected.
```

LOWER and UPPER

As you might expect, LOWER changes all the characters to lowercase; UPPER does just the reverse.

The following example starts by doing a little magic with the UPDATE function (you learn more about this next week) to change one of the values to lowercase:

7

Input/Output ▼

```
mysql> select * from characters;
+-----------+-----------+------+------+
| lastname  | firstname | m    | code |
+-----------+-----------+------+------+
| PURVIS    | KELLY     | A    |   32 |
| TAYLOR    | CHUCK     | J    |   67 |
| CHRISTINE | LAURA     | C    |   65 |
| ADAMS     | FESTER    | M    |   87 |
| COSTALES  | ARMANDO   | A    |   77 |
| KONG      | MAJOR     | G    |   52 |
+-----------+-----------+------+------+
6 rows in set (0.00 sec)

mysql> update characters
    -> set firstname = 'kelly'
    -> where firstname = 'KELLY';
Query OK, 1 row affected (0.34 sec)
Rows matched: 1  Changed: 1  Warnings: 0

mysql> select firstname
    -> from characters;
+-----------+
| firstname |
+-----------+
| kelly     |
| CHUCK     |
| LAURA     |
| FESTER    |
| ARMANDO   |
| MAJOR     |
+-----------+
6 rows in set (0.00 sec)
```

Then you write

Input/Output ▼

```
mysql> select firstname, upper(firstname), lower(firstname)
    -> from characters;
+-----------+------------------+------------------+
| firstname | upper(firstname) | lower(firstname) |
+-----------+------------------+------------------+
| kelly     | KELLY            | kelly            |
| CHUCK     | CHUCK            | chuck            |
| LAURA     | LAURA            | laura            |
| FESTER    | FESTER           | fester           |
```

```
¦ ARMANDO   ¦ ARMANDO          ¦ armando          ¦
¦ MAJOR     ¦ MAJOR            ¦ major            ¦
+-----------+------------------+------------------+
6 rows in set (0.00 sec)
```

Now you see the desired behavior.

LPAD **and** RPAD

LPAD and RPAD take a minimum of two and a maximum of three arguments. The first argument is the character string to be operated on. The second is the number of characters to pad it with, and the optional third argument is the character to pad it with. The third argument defaults to a blank, or it can be a single character or a character string. The following statement adds five pad characters, assuming that the field LASTNAME is defined as a 15-character field:

Input/Output ▼

```
SQL> SELECT LASTNAME, LPAD(LASTNAME,20,'*')
  2  FROM CHARACTERS;

LASTNAME         LPAD(LASTNAME,20,'*'
---------------  --------------------
PURVIS           *****PURVIS
TAYLOR           *****TAYLOR
CHRISTINE        *****CHRISTINE
ADAMS            *****ADAMS
COSTALES         *****COSTALES
KONG             *****KONG

6 rows selected.
```

Why were only five pad characters added? Remember that the LASTNAME column is 15 characters wide, and that LASTNAME includes the blanks to the right of the characters that make up the name. Some column data types eliminate padding characters if the width of the column value is less than the total width allocated for the column. Check your implementation. Now, try the right side:

Input/Output ▼

```
SQL> SELECT LASTNAME, RPAD(LASTNAME,20,'*')
  2  FROM CHARACTERS;

LASTNAME         RPAD(LASTNAME,20,'*'
---------------  --------------------
PURVIS           PURVIS        *****
TAYLOR           TAYLOR        *****
```

7

```
CHRISTINE        CHRISTINE        *****
ADAMS            ADAMS            *****
COSTALES         COSTALES         *****
KONG             KONG             *****

6 rows selected.
```

Here you see that the blanks are considered part of the field name for these operations. The next two functions come in handy in this type of situation.

LTRIM **and** RTRIM

LTRIM and RTRIM take at most two arguments. The first argument, like LPAD and RPAD, is a character string. The optional second element is either a character or character string, or defaults to a blank. If you use a second argument that is not a blank, the trim functions will trim that character the same way they trim the blanks in the following examples:

Input/Output ▼

```
SQL> SELECT LASTNAME, RTRIM(LASTNAME)
  2  FROM CHARACTERS;

LASTNAME         RTRIM(LASTNAME)
---------------  ---------------
PURVIS           PURVIS
TAYLOR           TAYLOR
CHRISTINE        CHRISTINE
ADAMS            ADAMS
COSTALES         COSTALES
KONG             KONG

6 rows selected.
```

You can make sure that the characters have been trimmed with the following statement:

Input/Output ▼

```
SQL> SELECT LASTNAME, RPAD(RTRIM(LASTNAME),20,'*')
  2  FROM CHARACTERS;

LASTNAME         RPAD(RTRIM(LASTNAME)
---------------  --------------------
PURVIS           PURVIS**************
TAYLOR           TAYLOR**************
CHRISTINE        CHRISTINE***********
```

```
ADAMS          ADAMS**************
COSTALES       COSTALES***********
KONG           KONG***************
```

6 rows selected.

The output proves that trim is working. Now try `LTRIM`:

Input/Output ▼

```
SQL> SELECT LASTNAME, LTRIM(LASTNAME, 'C')
  2  FROM CHARACTERS;

LASTNAME        LTRIM(LASTNAME,
--------------- ---------------
PURVIS          PURVIS
TAYLOR          TAYLOR
CHRISTINE       HRISTINE
ADAMS           ADAMS
COSTALES        OSTALES
KONG            KONG
```

6 rows selected.

Note the missing *C*s in the third and fifth rows. It should be noted that the MySQL implementation only trims blank spaces.

REPLACE

`REPLACE` does just that—it replaces data. Of its three arguments, the first is the string to be searched. The second is the search key. The last is the optional replacement string. If the third argument is left out or `NULL`, each occurrence of the search key on the string to be searched is removed and is not replaced with anything. It is important to know the implementation you're working in. The `REPLACE` function requires that all *three* arguments be present in order for the function to work.

Input/Output ▼

```
mysql> select lastname, replace(lastname,'ST')
    -> from characters;
ERROR 1064: You have an error in your SQL syntax near ')
from characters' at line 1
```

What this error is telling us is that the MySQL parser was expecting another argument near the closing quotation mark and closing parenthesis.

Input/Output ▼

```
mysql> select lastname, replace(lastname,'ST',null)
    -> from characters;
+-----------+-----------------------------+
| lastname  | replace(lastname,'ST',null) |
+-----------+-----------------------------+
| PURVIS    | PURVIS                      |
| TAYLOR    | TAYLOR                      |
| CHRISTINE | NULL                        |
| ADAMS     | ADAMS                       |
| COSTALES  | NULL                        |
| KONG      | KONG                        |
+-----------+-----------------------------+
6 rows in set (0.31 sec)
```

If you have a third argument, it is substituted for each occurrence of the search key in the target string—for example,

Input/Output ▼

```
SQL> SELECT LASTNAME, REPLACE(LASTNAME, 'ST','**') REPLACEMENT
  2  FROM CHARACTERS;

LASTNAME          REPLACEMENT
---------------   -----------
PURVIS            PURVIS
TAYLOR            TAYLOR
CHRISTINE         CHRI**INE
ADAMS             ADAMS
COSTALES          CO**ALES
KONG              KONG

6 rows selected.
```

If the second argument is NULL, the target string is returned with no changes in an Oracle database. You still receive an error in MySQL because MySQL requires all three arguments. If you try to replace an occurrence of NULL with another character, the following happens.

Input/Output ▼

```
mysql> select lastname, replace(lastname,null,'**')
    -> from characters;
+-----------+-----------------------------+
| lastname  | replace(lastname,null,'**') |
+-----------+-----------------------------+
| PURVIS    | NULL                        |
```

```
| TAYLOR    | NULL                          |
| CHRISTINE | NULL                          |
| ADAMS     | NULL                          |
| COSTALES  | NULL                          |
| KONG      | NULL                          |
+-----------+-------------------------------+
```

```
SQL> SELECT LASTNAME, REPLACE(LASTNAME, NULL) REPLACEMENT
  2  FROM CHARACTERS;
```

```
LASTNAME          REPLACEMENT
---------------   ---------------
PURVIS            PURVIS
TAYLOR            TAYLOR
CHRISTINE         CHRISTINE
ADAMS             ADAMS
COSTALES          COSTALES
KONG              KONG
```

```
6 rows selected.
```

SUBSTR

This three-argument function enables you to take a piece out of a target string. The first argument is the target string. The second argument is the position of the first character to be output. The third argument is the number of characters to show.

Input/Output ▼

```
SQL> SELECT FIRSTNAME, SUBSTR(FIRSTNAME,2,3)
  2  FROM CHARACTERS;
```

```
FIRSTNAME         SUB
---------------   ---
kelly             ell
CHUCK             HUC
LAURA             AUR
FESTER            EST
ARMANDO           RMA
MAJOR             AJO
```

```
6 rows selected.
```

7

The MySQL equivalent is

Input/Output ▼

```
mysql> select firstname, mid(firstname,2,3)
    -> from characters;
+----------------------------------+
| firstname | mid(firstname,2,3) |
+-----------+----------------------+
| kelly     | ell                |
| CHUCK     | HUC                |
| LAURA     | AUR                |
| FESTER    | EST                |
| ARMANDO   | RMA                |
| MAJOR     | AJO                |
+-----------+----------------------+
6 rows in set (0.38 sec)
```

The implementation MySQL uses the function MID() or SUBSTRING. MID is a synonym for SUBSTRING and is used in the same manner.

If you use a negative number as the second argument, the starting point is determined by counting backward from the end, like this:

Input/Output ▼

```
SQL> SELECT FIRSTNAME, SUBSTR(FIRSTNAME,-13,2)
  2  FROM CHARACTERS;

FIRSTNAME       SU
--------------- --
kelly           ll
CHUCK           UC
LAURA           UR
FESTER          ST
ARMANDO         MA
MAJOR           JO

6 rows selected.
```

The MySQL equivalent is

Input/Output ▼

```
mysql> select mid(firstname, -13,2)
    -> from characters;
+----------------------+
| mid(firstname, -13,2) |
+----------------------+
|                      |
|                      |
```

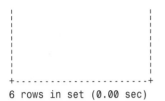

```
6 rows in set (0.00 sec)
```

Remember that the character field FIRSTNAME in this example is 15 characters long. That is why you used a -13 to start at the third character. Counting back from 15 puts you at the start of the third character, not at the start of the second. But this is in our Oracle implementation example. Remember the difference between the output in our two SQL implementations when we explored the CONCAT function? Generally speaking, Oracle accounts for all of the allocated space when using functions, whereas MySQL only performs the function where actual data exists and ignores any unused spaces in the column.

If you don't have a third argument, use the following statement instead:

Input/Output ▼

```
SQL> SELECT FIRSTNAME, SUBSTR(FIRSTNAME,3)
  2  FROM CHARACTERS;

FIRSTNAME       SUBSTR(FIRSTN
--------------- -------------
kelly           lly
CHUCK           UCK
LAURA           URA
FESTER          STER
ARMANDO         MANDO
MAJOR           JOR

6 rows selected.
```

The MySQL equivalent is

Input/Output ▼

```
mysql> select firstname, mid(firstname,3)
    -> from characters;
+-----------+------------------+
| firstname | mid(firstname,3) |
+-----------+------------------+
| kelly     | lly              |
| CHUCK     | UCK              |
| LAURA     | URA              |
| FESTER    | STER             |
```

7

```
| ARMANDO  | MANDO              |
| MAJOR    | JOR                |
+----------+-------------------+
6 rows in set (0.00 sec)
```

The rest of the target string is returned.

Input/Output ▼

```
SQL> SELECT * FROM SSN_TABLE;

SSN_____
300431117
301457111
459789998
3 rows selected.
```

Reading the results of the preceding output is difficult—Social Security numbers usually have dashes. Now try something fancy and see whether you like the results:

Input/Output ▼

```
SQL> SELECT SUBSTR(SSN,1,3)||'-'||SUBSTR(SSN,4,2)||'-'||SUBSTR(SSN,6,4) SSN
  2  FROM SSN_TABLE;

SSN_____
300-43-1117
301-45-7111
459-78-9998
3 rows selected.
```

The MySQL equivalent is

Input/Output ▼

```
mysql> select concat(mid(ssn,1,3),'-',mid(ssn,4,2),'-',mid(ssn,6,4))
    -> from ssn_table;
+-------------------------------------------------------+
| concat(mid(ssn,1,3),'-',mid(ssn,4,2),'-',mid(ssn,6,4)) |
+-------------------------------------------------------+
| 300-43-1117                                           |
| 301-45-7111                                           |
| 459-78-9998                                           |
+-------------------------------------------------------+
3 rows in set (0.00 sec)
```

> **NOTE**
>
> This particular use of the SUBSTR/MID function could come in very handy with large numbers using commas, such as 1,343,178,128, and in area codes and phone numbers using dashes, such as 123-456-7890.

Here is another good use of the SUBSTR/MID function. Suppose you are writing a report and a few columns are more than 50 characters wide. You can use the SUBSTR/MID function to reduce the width of the columns to a more manageable size if you know the nature of the actual data. Consider the following two examples:

Input/Output ▼

```
SQL> SELECT NAME, JOB, DEPARTMENT FROM JOB_TBL;

NAME_____
JOB_____DEPARTMENT_____
ALVIN SMITH
VICEPRESIDENT               MARKETING
1 ROW SELECTED.
```

Notice how the columns wrapped around, which makes reading the results a little too difficult. Now try this SELECT:

Input/Output ▼

```
SQL> SELECT SUBSTR(NAME, 1,15) NAME, SUBSTR(JOB,1,15) JOB, DEPARTMENT
  2  FROM JOB_TBL;
NAME_____JOB_____DEPARTMENT_____
ALVIN SMITH         VICEPRESIDENT      MARKETING
```

Much better!

TRANSLATE

The function TRANSLATE takes three arguments: the target string, the FROM string, and the TO string. Elements of the target string that occur in the FROM string are translated to the corresponding element in the TO string. MySQL does not have a TRANSLATE function.

Input/Output ▼

```
SQL> SELECT FIRSTNAME, TRANSLATE(FIRSTNAME
  2  '0123456789ABCDEFGHIJKLMNOPQRSTUVWXYZ
  3  'NNNNNNNNNNAAAAAAAAAAAAAAAAAAAAAAAAAAAA)
  4  FROM CHARACTERS;
```

7

```
FIRSTNAME       TRANSLATE(FIRST
--------------- ---------------
kelly           kelly
CHUCK           AAAAA
LAURA           AAAAA
FESTER          AAAAAA
ARMANDO         AAAAAAA
MAJOR           AAAAA

6 rows selected.
```

Notice that the function is case sensitive.

INSTR

To find out where in a string a particular pattern occurs, use INSTR. Its first argument is the target string. The second argument is the pattern to match. The third and forth arguments are numbers representing where to start looking and which match to report. INSTR works the same in both Oracle and MySQL. This example returns a number representing the first occurrence of 0 starting with the second character:

Input/Output ▼

```
SQL> SELECT LASTNAME, INSTR(LASTNAME, 'O', 2, 1)
  2  FROM CHARACTERS;

LASTNAME        INSTR(LASTNAME,'O',2,1)
--------------- -----------------------
PURVIS                                0
TAYLOR                                5
CHRISTINE                             0
ADAMS                                 0
COSTALES                              2
KONG                                  2

6 rows selected.
```

The default for the third and fourth arguments is 1. If the third argument is negative, the search starts at a position determined from the end of the string, instead of from the beginning.

LENGTH

LENGTH returns the length of its lone character argument—for example,

Input/Output ▼

```
mysql> select firstname, length(firstname)
    -> from characters;
+-----------+-------------------+
| firstname | length(firstname) |
+-----------+-------------------+
| kelly     |                 5 |
| CHUCK     |                 5 |
| LAURA     |                 5 |
| FESTER    |                 6 |
| ARMANDO   |                 7 |
| MAJOR     |                 5 |
+-----------+-------------------+
6 rows in set (0.00 sec)
```

Conversion Functions

These three conversion functions provide a handy way of converting one type of data to another. These examples use the table CONVERSIONS.

Input/Output ▼

```
SQL> SELECT * FROM CONVERT;

NAME             TESTNUM
--------------- ---------
40                    95
13                    23
74                    68
```

The NAME column is a character string 15 characters wide, and TESTNUM is a number.

TO_CHAR

The primary use of TO_CHAR is to convert a number into a character. Different implementations might also use it to convert other data types, like Date, into a character, or to include different formatting arguments. The next example illustrates the primary use of TO_CHAR:

7

Input/Output ▼

```
SQL> SELECT TESTNUM, TO_CHAR(TESTNUM)
  2  FROM CONVERT;

  TESTNUM TO_CHAR(TESTNUM)
--------- ----------------
       95               95
       23               23
       68               68
```

It is not very exciting, or convincing. Here's how to verify that the function returned a character string:

Input/Output ▼

```
SQL> SELECT TESTNUM, LENGTH(TO_CHAR(TESTNUM))
  2  FROM CONVERT;

  TESTNUM LENGTH(TO_CHAR(TESTNUM))
--------- ------------------------
       95                        2
       23                        2
       68                        2
```

LENGTH of a number would have returned an error. Notice the difference between TO CHAR and the CHR function discussed earlier. CHR would have turned this number into a character or a symbol, depending on the character set.

The MySQL version of TO_CHAR is CHAR. CHAR returns a string made from converting each number to the character corresponding to that ASCII value.

Input/Output ▼

```
mysql> select testnum, char(testnum)
    -> from `convert`;
+---------+---------------+
| testnum | char(testnum) |
+---------+---------------+
|      23 |               |
|      68 | D             |
|      95 | _             |
+---------+---------------+
```

3 rows in set (0.00 sec)

TO_NUMBER

TO_NUMBER is the companion function to TO_CHAR, and of course, it converts a string into a number—for example,

Input/Output ▼

```
SQL> SELECT NAME, TESTNUM, TESTNUM*TO_NUMBER(NAME)
  2 FROM CONVERT;

NAME             TESTNUM TESTNUM*TO_NUMBER(NAME)
--------------- --------- -----------------------
40                    95                    3800
13                    23                     299
74                    68                    5032
```

This test would have returned an error if TO_NUMBER had returned a character.

Miscellaneous Functions

Here are three miscellaneous functions you might find useful.

GREATEST **and** LEAST

These functions find the GREATEST or the LEAST member from a series of expressions—for example,

Input/Output ▼

```
SQL> SELECT GREATEST('ALPHA', 'BRAVO','FOXTROT', 'DELTA')
  2 FROM CONVERT;

GREATEST
-------
FOXTROT
FOXTROT
FOXTROT
```

Notice that GREATEST found the word closest to the end of the alphabet. Notice also a seemingly unnecessary FROM and three occurrences of FOXTROT. If FROM is missing, you will get an error. Every SELECT needs a FROM. The particular table used in the FROM has three rows, so the function in the SELECT clause is performed for each of them.

7

Input/Output ▼

```
SQL> SELECT LEAST(34, 567, 3, 45, 1090)
  2  FROM CONVERT;

LEAST(34,567,3,45,1090)
-----------------------
                      3
                      3
                      3
```

As you can see, GREATEST and LEAST also work with numbers.

USER

USER returns the character name of the current user of the database.

Input/Output ▼

```
SQL> SELECT USER FROM CONVERT;

USER
------------------------------
PERKINS
PERKINS
PERKINS
```

There really is only one of me. Again, there is an echo because of the number of rows in the table. USER is similar to the date functions explained earlier today. Even though USER is not an actual column in the table, it is selected for each row in the table. If you are using MySQL, you can formulate the following SQL SELECT statement to determine who the current user is.

Input/Output ▼

```
mysql> select user();
+----------------+
| user()         |
+----------------+
| ODBC@localhost |
+----------------+
1 row in set (0.12 sec)
```

Supplemental Examples of MySQL Character Functions

This section lists the syntax and examples of MySQL character functions. These functions will be used in the Workshop. Note similarities and differences to ANSI syntax as previously shown in this chapter. MySQL character functions are listed in addition to ANSI SQL functions because character functions tend to vary widely between SQL implementations.

LENGTH

LENGTH(str) returns the length of the string str.

Input/Output ▼

```
mysql> select LENGTH('text');
        -> 4
mysql> select OCTET_LENGTH('text');
        -> 4
```

Note that for CHAR_LENGTH( ), multibyte characters are only counted once.

LOCATE

LOCATE(substr,str) returns the position of the first occurrence of substring substr in string str. It returns 0 if substr is not in str.

Input/Output ▼

```
mysql> select LOCATE('bar', 'foobarbar');
        -> 4
mysql> select LOCATE('xbar', 'foobar');
        -> 0
```

LOCATE(substr,str,pos) returns the position of the first occurrence of substring substr in string str, starting at position pos. It returns 0 if substr is not in str.

Input/Output ▼

```
mysql> select LOCATE('bar', 'foobarbar',5);
        -> 7
```

7

INSTR

INSTR(str,substr) returns the position of the first occurrence of substring substr in string str. This is the same as the two-argument form of LOCATE(), except that the arguments are swapped.

Input/Output ▼

```
mysql> select INSTR('foobarbar', 'bar');
        -> 4
mysql> select INSTR('xbar', 'foobar');
        -> 0
```

LPAD

LPAD(str,len,padstr) returns the string str, left-padded with the string padstr until str is len characters long. If str is longer than len, it will be shortened to len characters.

Input/Output ▼

```
mysql> select LPAD('hi',4,'??');
        -> '??hi'
```

RPAD

RPAD(str,len,padstr) returns the string str, right-padded with the string padstr until str is len characters long. If str is longer than len, it will be shortened to len characters.

Input/Output ▼

```
mysql> select RPAD('hi',5,'?');
        -> 'hi???'
```

LEFT

LEFT(str,len) returns the leftmost len characters from the string str.

Input/Output ▼

```
mysql> select LEFT('foobarbar', 5);
        -> 'fooba'
```

RIGHT

RIGHT(str,len) returns the right-most len characters from the string str.

Input/Output ▼

```
mysql> select RIGHT('foobarbar', 4);
        -> 'rbar'
```

SUBSTRING

Syntax ▼

```
SUBSTRING(str,pos,len)

SUBSTRING(str FROM pos FOR len)
```

This returns a substring len characters long from string str, starting at position pos. The variant form that uses FROM is ANSI SQL92 syntax.

Input/Output ▼

```
mysql> select SUBSTRING('Quadratically',5,6);
        -> 'ratica'

SUBSTRING(str,pos)

SUBSTRING(str FROM pos)
```

This returns a substring from string str starting at position pos.

Input/Output ▼

```
mysql> select SUBSTRING('Quadratically',5);
        -> 'ratically'
mysql> select SUBSTRING('foobarbar' FROM 4);
        -> 'barbar'
```

LTRIM

LTRIM(str) returns the string str with leading space characters removed.

Input/Output ▼

```
mysql> select LTRIM('  barbar');
        -> 'barbar'
```

7

RTRIM

RTRIM(str) returns the string str with trailing space characters removed.

Input/Output ▼

```
mysql> select RTRIM('barbar    ');
        -> 'barbar'
```

This function is multibyte safe.

TRIM

Syntax ▼

```
TRIM([[BOTH ¦ LEADING ¦ TRAILING] [remstr] FROM] str)
```

This returns the string str with all remstr prefixes and/or suffixes removed. If none of the BOTH, LEADING, or TRAILING specifiers are given, BOTH is assumed. If remstr is not specified, spaces are removed.

Input/Output ▼

```
mysql> select TRIM('  bar   ');
        -> 'bar'

mysql> select TRIM(LEADING 'x' FROM 'xxxbarxxx');
        -> 'barxxx'

mysql> select TRIM(BOTH 'x' FROM 'xxxbarxxx');
        -> 'bar'

mysql> select TRIM(TRAILING 'xyz' FROM 'barxxyz');
        -> 'barx'
```

Supplemental Examples of MySQL Date Functions

This section lists the syntax and examples of MySQL date functions. These functions will be used in the Workshop. Note similarities and differences to ANSI syntax as previously shown in this chapter. MySQL date functions are listed in addition to ANSI SQL functions because date functions tend to differ between SQL implementations.

DATE_FORMAT

DATE_FORMAT(*date, format*) formats the date value according to the format string. The following specifiers can be used in the format string:

%M	Month name (January..December)
%W	Weekday name (Sunday..Saturday)
%D	Day of the month with English suffix (1st, 2nd, 3rd, and so on)
%Y	Year, numeric, 4 digits
%y	Year, numeric, 2 digits
%X	Year for the week where Sunday is the first day of the week, numeric, 4 digits, used with %V
%x	Year for the week where Monday is the first day of the week, numeric, 4 digits, used with %v
%a	Abbreviated weekday name (Sun..Sat)
%d	Day of the month, numeric (00..31)
%e	Day of the month, numeric (0..31)
%m	Month, numeric (01..12)
%c	Month, numeric (1..12)
%b	Abbreviated month name (Jan..Dec)
%j	Day of the year (001..366)
%H	Hour (00..23)
%k	Hour (0..23)
%h	Hour (01..12)
%I	Hour (01..12)
%l	Hour (1..12)
%i	Minutes, numeric (00..59)
%r	Time, 12-hour (hh:mm:ss [AP]M)
%T	Time, 24-hour (hh:mm:ss)
%S	Seconds (00..59)
%s	Seconds (00..59)
%p	AM or PM
%w	Day of the week (0=Sunday..6=Saturday)
%U	Week (0..53), where Sunday is the first day of the week
%u	Week (0..53), where Monday is the first day of the week
%V	Week (1..53), where Sunday is the first day of the week used with %X
%v	Week (1..53), where Monday is the first day of the week used with %x
%%	A literal %

7

All other characters are just copied to the result without interpretation.

Input/Output ▼

```
mysql> select DATE_FORMAT('1997-10-04 22:23:00', '%W %M %Y');
        -> 'Saturday October 1997'

mysql> select DATE_FORMAT('1997-10-04 22:23:00', '%H:%i:%s');
        -> '22:23:00'

mysql> select DATE_FORMAT('1997-10-04 22:23:00',
                            '%D %y %a %d %m %b %j');
        -> '4th 97 Sat 04 10 Oct 277'

mysql> select DATE_FORMAT('1997-10-04 22:23:00',
                            '%H %k %I %r %T %S %w');
        -> '22 22 10 10:23:00 PM 22:23:00 00 6'

mysql> select DATE_FORMAT('1999-01-01', '%X %V');
        -> '1998 52'
```

TIME_FORMAT

Syntax ▼

```
TIME_FORMAT(time,format)
```

This is used like the DATE_FORMAT() function mentioned earlier, but the format string can contain only those format specifiers that handle hours, minutes, and seconds. Other specifiers produce a NULL value or 0.

CURDATE

CURDATE() returns today's date as a value in YYYY-MM-DD or YYYYMMDD format, depending on whether the function is used in a string or numeric context.

Input/Output ▼

```
mysql> select CURDATE();
        -> '1997-12-15'

mysql> select CURDATE() + 0;
        -> 19971215
```

CURTIME

`CURTIME()` returns the current time as a value in HH:MM:SS or HHMMSS format, depending on whether the function is used in a string or numeric context.

Input/Output ▼

```
mysql> select CURTIME();
       -> '23:50:26'
mysql> select CURTIME() + 0;
       -> 235026
```

Summary

It has been a long lesson. We covered 47 functions—from aggregates to conversions. You don't have to remember every function—just knowing the general types (aggregate functions, date and time functions, arithmetic functions, character functions, conversion functions, and miscellaneous functions) is enough to point you in the right direction when you build a query that requires a function.

Q&A

Q Why are so few functions defined in the ANSI standard and so many defined by the individual implementations?

A ANSI standards are broad strokes and are not meant to drive companies into bankruptcy by forcing all implementations to have dozens of functions. On the other hand, when Company X adds a statistical package to its SQL and it sells well, you can bet Companies Y and Z will follow suit.

Q I thought you said SQL was simple. Will I really use all of these functions?

A The answer to this question is similar to the answer a trigonometry teacher might give to the question, "Will I ever need to know how to figure the area of an isosceles triangle in real life?" The answer, of course, depends on your profession. The same concept applies with the functions and all the other options available with SQL. How you use functions in SQL depends mostly on you or your company's needs. As long as you understand how functions work as a whole, you can apply the same concepts to your own queries.

7

Workshop

The Workshop provides quiz questions to help solidify your understanding of the material covered, as well as exercises to provide you with experience in using what you have learned. Try to answer the quiz and exercise questions before checking the answers in Appendix A, "Answers." Here are the CREATE TABLE statements and INSERT statements for the following work:

```
create table teamstats
(name        varchar(10)    not null,
 pos         varchar(3)     not null,
 ab          numeric(3)     not null,
 hits        numeric(4)     not null,
 walks       varchar(5)     not null,
 singles     varchar(7)     not null,
 doubles     varchar(7)     not null,
 triples     varchar(7)     not null,
 hr          numeric(2)     not null,
 so          varchar(2)     not null);
create table characters
(lastname    varchar(15)     not null,
 firstname   varchar(15)     not null,
 m           char(1)         null,
 code        numeric(10)     not null);
insert into teamstats values
('JONES', '1B', '145', '45', '34', '31', '8', '1', '5', '10');
insert into teamstats values
('DONKNOW', '3B', '175', '65', '23', '50', '10', '1', '4', '15');
insert into teamstats values
('WORLEY', 'LF', '157', '49', '15', '35', '8', '3', '3', '16');
insert into teamstats values
('DAVID', 'OF', '187', '70', '24', '48', '4', '0', '17', '42');
insert into teamstats values
('HAMHOCKER', '3B', '50', '12', '10', '10', '2', '0', '0', '13');
insert into teamstats values
('CASEY', 'DH', '1', '0', '0', '0', '0', '0', '0', '1');
```

Type the following to ensure that you are in the correct database:

```
mysql> use <database name>
mysql> use bob
Database changed
```

Type **show tables;** to see your growing list of tables.

Quiz

1. Which function capitalizes the first letter of a character string and makes the rest lowercase?

2. Which functions are also known by the name *group functions*?

3. Will this query work?

   ```
   SQL> SELECT COUNT(LASTNAME) FROM CHARACTERS;
   ```

4. How about this one?

   ```
   SQL> SELECT SUM(LASTNAME) FROM CHARACTERS;
   ```

5. Assuming that they are separate columns, which function(s) would splice FIRSTNAME and LASTNAME together?

6. What does the answer 6 mean from the following SELECT?

   ```
   SQL> SELECT COUNT(*) FROM TEAMSTATS;
   ```

7. Will the following statement work?

   ```
   SQL> SELECT SUBSTR LASTNAME,1,5 FROM NAME_TBL;
   ```

Exercises

1. Using this lesson's TEAMSTATS table, write a query to determine who is batting under .250. (For the baseball-challenged reader, batting average is hits/ab [at-bats].)

2. Using today's CHARACTER table, write a query that will return the following:

   ```
   INITIALS_____CODE
   k.A.P.                32

   1 row selected.
   ```

3. Using the TEAMSTATS table, write a query that produces the following result set:

   ```
   +--------------+--------------+
   | max(hits/ab) | min(hits/ab) |
   +--------------+--------------+
   |         0.37 |         0.00 |
   +--------------+--------------+
   1 row in set (0.01 sec)
   ```

4. In the TEAMSTATS table, what is the maximum at-bats?

5. What is the minimum at-bats?

6. Rewrite queries 4 and 5 so that they are represented in one query.

7

7. Using the CHARACTERS table, write a query that produces the following result set:

```
+---------------------------------------------------------+
| concat(lastname,',',' ',firstname,',',' ',m,' ',code) |
+---------------------------------------------------------+
| PURVIS, KELLY, A 32                                      |
| TAYLOR, CHUCK, J 67                                      |
| CHRISTINE, LAURA, C 65                                   |
| ADAMS, FESTER, M 87                                      |
| COSTALES, ARMANDO, A 77                                  |
| KONG, MAJOR, G 52                                        |
+---------------------------------------------------------+
6 rows in set (0.00 sec)
```

8. Select the firstname, lastname, and m from the CHARACTERS table.

9. Rewrite the query in exercise 8 so that the result set is in all lowercase.

10. BONUS: Although MySQL does not have an INITCAP function, the following is a possible workaround:

```
mysql> select concat(upper(mid(firstname,1,1)),lower(mid(firstname,2)))
    -> from characters;
+---------------------------------------------------------+
| concat(upper(mid(firstname,1,1)),lower(mid(firstname,2))) |
+---------------------------------------------------------+
| Kelly                                                   |
| Chuck                                                   |
| Laura                                                   |
| Fester                                                  |
| Armando                                                 |
| Major                                                   |
+---------------------------------------------------------+
```

LESSON 8
Database Normalization

In this lesson you will learn how to break up a raw collection of data into more logical units, or tables, to reduce the occurrence of redundant data in the database. This process of reducing data redundancy is referred to as *normalization*. We will also discuss the advantages and disadvantages of a normalized database versus a normalized database that has been denormalized, as well as data integrity and performance issues that pertain to normalization.

By the end of this lesson, you should understand and be able to apply the following concepts:

- Normalization
- Benefits of normalization
- Denormalization
- Guidelines of normalization
- The three normal forms

Normalizing a Database

Normalization is the process of reducing the repetition and redundancies of data in a database. Didn't we already say that? If we were to normalize the first sentence in this paragraph, it might read, "Normalization is the process of reducing redundant information in a database."

The Raw Database

When you begin designing a database, or migrating a database from one implementation to another, you might find yourself staring at a massive collection of data. All of your data is there, but it is not in a manageable order.

A database that is not normalized might contain data that resides in one or more different tables for no apparent reason. This could be bad for reasons of security, disk space use, speed of queries, efficiency of database updates, and most importantly, data integrity.

A database before normalization is one that has not been broken down logically into smaller, more manageable tables. In our experience, databases can consist of just a couple of tables, each table housing data for hundreds of columns (or fields).

Logical Database Design

Any database should be designed with the end user in mind. Logical database design, also referred to as the *logical model*, is the process of arranging data into logical, organized groups that can easily be maintained and referenced by the end-user community. The logical design of a database should reduce or even go so far as to completely eliminate data repetition. After all, why store the same data twice?

The logical database design is not only the first step in implementing a physical database (see Figure 8.1), but the first step in providing a database environment in which the physical structure and limitations are transparent to the user.

FIGURE 8.1
The physical structure of the database can be transparent when a good logical design is implemented.

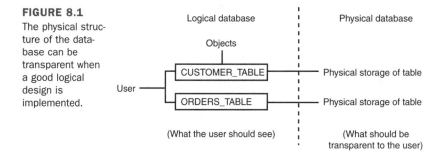

The Needs of the End User

The needs of the end users should be at the top of the list of considerations when designing a database. Remember that the end users are the people that ultimately use the database and input from the end users should be considered to achieve a well-designed database. So put your ego aside and open your ears. There should be ease of use through the users' front-end tool (a program that allows them access to a database), but this along with optimal performance cannot be achieved if the users' needs are not taken into consideration.

Here are some questions you might ask the end users:

- What data should be stored in the database?
- How will the users access the database?
- How should the data be grouped in the database?
- What data is the most commonly accessed?
- How is all data related in the database?
- What measures should be taken to ensure accurate data?

Data Redundancy

Data should not be redundant, meaning that the duplication of data should be kept to a minimum for several reasons. For example, it is not necessary to store an employee's home address in more than one table. With duplicate data, unnecessary space is used, and confusion is always a threat. As in the case of the employee's address, an address for an employee in one table might not match the address of the same employee in another table. Which table is correct? Do you have documentation to verify the employee's current address? Maybe, but maybe not. As if data management is not difficult enough, redundancy of data could prove to be a disaster.

Understanding the Normal Forms

In the next section and following subsections, we discuss the normal forms. The *normal forms* are ways of measuring the levels, or depth, to which a database has been normalized.

The three most common normal forms in the normalization process are

- The first normal form
- The second normal form
- The third normal form

Of the three normal forms, each subsequent normal form depends upon normalization steps taken in the previous normal form. For instance, to normalize a database using the second normal form, the database must already be in the first normal form. For the database to be normalized using the third normal form, the database must already be in the second normal form (which means that, at some point, the database was in the first normal form). See Figure 8.2. The three normal forms are discussed in the following sections.

FIGURE 8.2
Normal forms
must be imple-
mented in sequen-
tial order.

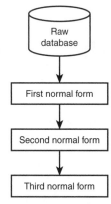

The First Normal Form

The First Normal Form

The objective of the first normal form is to divide the base data into logical units called *tables*. After each table has been designed, a primary key is assigned to most or all tables. A primary key in a table is one or more columns that make every row of data in a table unique. In Lesson 10, "Controlling Data Integrity," we show you how to actually create primary keys on tables. Examine Figure 8.3, which illustrates how a raw database has been redeveloped using the first normal form.

FIGURE 8.3
The first normal
form.

EMPLOYEES	CUSTOMERS
emp_id	cust_id
emp_name	cust_name
address	address
city	city
state	state
zip	zip
phone	phone
position	fax
department	contact
salary	
hire_date	

You can see that to achieve the first normal form, we had to break our data into logical units, each having a primary key, and had to ensure that there are no repeated groups in any of the tables. Instead of one large table, we now have smaller, more manageable tables: EMPLOYEES and CUSTOMERS. The primary keys are normally the first columns you list in a table—in this case, EMP_ID and CUST_ID.

The Second Normal Form

The objective of the second normal form is to take data that is only partly dependent on the primary key and store that data in another table. Figure 8.4 illustrates the second normal form.

8

FIGURE 8.4
The second normal form.

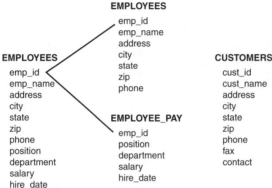

According to Figure 8.4, we derived the second normal form from the first normal form by further breaking two tables into more specific units.

EMPLOYEES was split into two tables, called EMPLOYEES and EMPLOYEE_PAY. Personal employee information is dependent on the primary key, or EMP_ID, so that information remained in EMPLOYEES (EMP_ID, EMP_NAME, ADDRESS, CITY, STATE, ZIP, and PHONE).

On the other hand, the information that is only partly dependent on the EMP_ID (each individual employee) was used to populate EMPLOYEE_PAY (EMP_ID, POSITION, DEPARTMENT, HIRE DATE, and SALARY). Notice that both tables contain the column EMP_ID. This is the primary key of each table and will be used to match up corresponding data between the two tables. The process of merging the data between two tables is called a *join operation*, which was discussed during Lesson 5, "Joining Tables."

NOTE	When normalizing a database, primary key and foreign key constraints are used to manage the integrity of data. These constraints are mentioned later in this lesson and are covered in more detail in Lesson 10.

The Third Normal Form

The objective of the third normal form is to remove data in a table that is not dependent on the primary key. Figure 8.5 illustrates the third normal form.

FIGURE 8.5
The third normal form.

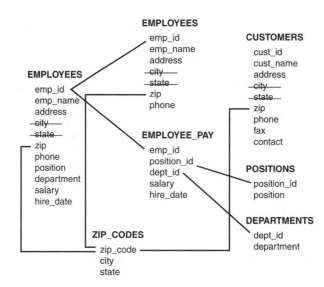

Upon converting our tables to the third normal form, we created additional tables to house more specific data. We took EMPLOYEE_PAY and split it into three tables: one table containing the actual employee pay information (EMPLOYEE_PAY), one containing the position descriptions (POSITIONS), and another containing a list of departments (DEPARTMENTS).

The information in the POSITIONS and DEPARTMENTS tables does not need to be stored with employee pay data because neither of these tables has data dependencies on the primary key, EMP_ID. Each unique position and department will now be stored only once. Only an identification number, or code, for the positions and departments will be duplicated in the database.

NOTE

When normalizing a database, one of the most basic considerations is the use of naming conventions. You should give your tables names that accurately describe the type of information they contain. A companywide naming convention should be set that provides guidance on the naming of not only tables within the database, but also users, filenames, and other related objects. When a company designs and enforces naming conventions, it takes one of the first steps toward a successful database implementation.

Making Normalization Work

Now that you know the basic concepts of normalization, you must learn how to make normalization work in a real database. You need to know when to normalize a database and when to denormalize a database. A good rule of thumb when designing a database is the more time spent upfront in planning and design, the fewer headaches during the implementation and maintenance of a database. The following sections help you understand how to

8

- Use constraints to enforce referential integrity
- Know when to use normalization
- Know when to denormalize a database

Referential Integrity

Referential integrity is the assurance of consistent and accurate data within a database. Referential integrity simply means that the values of one column in a table depend upon the values of a column in another table. For instance, for a customer to have a record in the ORDERS table, there must first be a record for that customer in the CUSTOMERS table. For data to be in the EMPLOYEE_PAY table, there must first be a corresponding personnel record in the EMPLOYEES table.

Integrity constraints can also control values entered by restricting a range of values for a column. The integrity constraint should be created upon the table creation. Referential integrity is typically controlled through the use of primary keys and foreign keys.

A *foreign key* is a key in a table, normally a single field, that directly references one or more fields in another table to enforce referential integrity. Figure 8.6 depicts two examples of a basic primary key/foreign key relationship. The first example shows a one-to-one table relationship between the EMP table and the EMP_PAY table. The EMP_ID in the EMP_PAY table is a foreign key that references the EMP_ID column in the EMP table (which is a primary key). For every employee record, there should be a corresponding pay record. Every EMP_ID value in the EMP_PAY table must be found in the EMP table. The second example in Figure 8.6 illustrates a one-to-many table relationship, meaning that there can be many orders per product. The PROD_ID column in the ORDERS table is a foreign key constraint that references the PROD_ID column in the PRODUCTS table. The PROD_ID column in the PRODUCTS table is a primary key because we should store only one record per unique product. In Lesson 10, we discuss foreign keys and other constraints in much more detail.

FIGURE 8.6

A basic primary key/foreign key relationship.

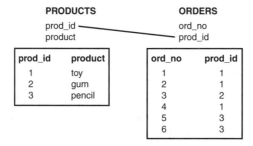

(One-to-one relationship)

EMP			EMP_PAY	
emp_id			emp_id	
name			salary	

emp_id	name		emp_id	salary
1	john		1	32000
2	mary		2	41000
3	steve		3	22000
4	jack		4	18000

(One-to-many relationship)

PRODUCTS			ORDERS	
prod_id			ord_no	
product			prod_id	

prod_id	product		ord_no	prod_id
1	toy		1	1
2	gum		2	1
3	pencil		3	2
			4	1
			5	3
			6	3

NOTE

Although foreign keys do exist in MySQL, they do not operate. Future stable versions of MySQL are planned with more functionality.

Foreign keys are required for many SQL implementations, which is why the syntax and the capability to use them in CREATE TABLE statements exists, but the designers of MySQL decided that fully functioning foreign keys would generally have undesired effects for the MySQL database.

Benefits of Normalization

Normalization provides numerous benefits to a database. Some of the major benefits include

- Greater overall database organization
- The reduction of redundant data
- Data consistency within the database
- A much more flexible database design
- A better handle on database security

Organization is obtained from the normalization process, making everyone's job easier—from the user who accesses tables to the database administrator (DBA) who is responsible for the overall management of every object in the database. Data redundancy is reduced, which simplifies data structures and conserves disk space. Because duplicate data is minimized, the possibility of inconsistent data is greatly reduced. You avoid situations in which one table lists an individual's name as "STEVE SMITH" and another table lists the name as "STEPHEN R. SMITH."

Because the database has been normalized and broken into smaller tables, you have more flexibility when modifying existing structures. It is much easier to modify a small table with little data than to modify one big table containing all of the vital data in the database. Security is also provided in the sense that the DBA has better control over access permissions. Security is easier to control once normalization has occurred. Most importantly, the integrity of the data is not violated. By normalizing a database, you make it easier to maintain accurate data, thus making everyone's job easier and keeping the end user happy.

Drawbacks of Normalization

Although most successful databases are normalized at least to some degree, there is one substantial drawback to a normalized database: reduced database performance. The acceptance of reduced performance requires the knowledge that when a query or transaction request is sent to the database, there are factors involved such as CPU use, memory use, and input/output (I/O).

A normalized database requires much more CPU, memory, and I/O to process transactions and database queries than does a denormalized database. This is because it must locate the requested tables, and then join the data from the tables to get the requested information or to process the desired data.

Denormalizing a Database

Denormalization is the process of taking a normalized database and modifying table structures to allow controlled redundancy for increased database performance. Why would you want to denormalize a database? The only reason to ever denormalize a database is to improve performance. A denormalized database is different than a database that has not been normalized.

Denormalizing a database is the process of taking the level of normalization within the database down a notch or two. Remember, normalization might actually slow performance because table join operations will frequently occur. Denormalization might involve recombining separate tables, or creating duplicate data within tables to reduce the number of tables that need to be joined when retrieving data. Doing so will result in less I/O and CPU time, thus increasing performance.

There are, however, costs to denormalization. In a denormalized database, where columns that were once split into separate tables are once again combined, data redundancy is increased. When a normalized database has been denormalized to a given extent, you wind up with related data in one larger table (versus several smaller tables); thus the queries on the larger table run faster because the data is all stored together. A denormalized database can improve performance, but more extraneous efforts are required to keep track of the location of related data. For example, the customer's name can be stored in two separate tables, as opposed to being consolidated in a single table. If a customer's name is updated, it must be updated in both tables. Otherwise, you have conflicting data. Application coding (end-user forms, programs, queries, and so on) can render more complications because the data redundancy is increased (as in the case of the customer's name that is stored in two tables).

Also, referential integrity will be more of a chore because related data has been divided among a number of tables. There is a happy medium in both normalization and denormalization, but both require a thorough knowledge of the actual data and the specific business requirements of the pertinent company.

Summary

As you have learned, a preliminary decision about normalization has to be made during the design phase of a database. In this lesson, we covered the three most common normal forms, concepts behind the normalization process, and the integrity of data. The normalization process involves many steps, most optional, that are vital to the functionality and performance of your database. Regardless of how deep you decide to normalize, there will most always be a trade-off—either between simple maintenance and questionable performance, or complicated maintenance and better performance. In the end, the individual or team of individuals designing the database must decide, and those individuals will be responsible.

Q&A

Q Why should I be so concerned with the end users' needs when designing the database?

A The end users are the real experts on the data and are the people who will be using the database, and in that respect, should be the main focus of any database design effort. The database designer only helps to organize the data.

Q **It seems to me that normalization is more advantageous than denormalization. Do you agree?**

A Well, yes, it can be more advantageous; however, denormalization to a point can be more advantageous. Remember, there are many factors that help determine which way to go, as discussed in this lesson. You will probably normalize your database to reduce repetition, but might turn around and denormalize to a certain extent to improve performance.

Workshop

The Workshop provides quiz questions to help solidify your understanding of the material covered, as well as exercises to provide you with experience in using what you have learned. Try to answer the quiz and exercise questions before checking the answers in Appendix A, "Answers."

Quiz

1. True or false: Normalization is the process of grouping data into logically related groups.

2. True or false: Having no duplicate or redundant data in a database and having a completely normalized database is always the best way to go.

3. True or false: If data is in the third normal form, it is automatically in the first and second normal forms.

4. What is a major advantage of a denormalized database?

5. What is the main disadvantage of denormalization?

6. What effect do foreign keys have on a MySQL database?

Exercises

1. Normalize the following data as much as possible. This data contains information about different types of services provided to customers.

```
EMPLOYEE DATA     CUSTOMER DATA     SERVICE DATA
emp_id            cust_id           service_id
emp_name          cust_name         service_type
emp_address       cust_address      service_date
emp_city          cust_city         service_comments
emp_state         cust_state        service_cost
emp_phone         cust_zip          service_hours
emp_pay           cust_phone        amt_due
emp_pay_date      cust_fax          date_due
```

```
emp_hire_date
emp_dob
emp_sex
emp_dependents
emp_withholding
emp_education_level
emp_position
emp_department
emp_cust_assigned
```

2. Designate primary and foreign keys on the tables that you normalized in the first exercise. Do not worry about creating statements to designate these keys. The commands used to create keys on tables will be covered in Lesson 10.

LESSON 9
Creating and Maintaining Tables

This lesson covers the CREATE DATABASE, CREATE TABLE, ALTER TABLE, DROP TABLE, and DROP DATABASE statements, which are collectively known as *data definition statements*. In contrast, the SELECT, UPDATE, INSERT, and DELETE statements are often described as *data manipulation statements*. By the end of this lesson, you will understand and be able to do the following:

- Create key fields.

- Create a database with its associated tables.

- Create, alter, and drop a table.

- Drop databases.

You now know much of the SQL vocabulary and have examined the SQL query in some detail, beginning with its basic syntax. In Lesson 2, "Introducing the Query," you learned how to select data from the database. Later in Lesson 11, "Manipulating Data," you will learn how to insert, update, and delete data from the database. Along the way we have presented CREATE TABLE and INSERT statements so that you are able to see the mechanisms of storing data. By executing these commands in each chapter, you have begun to have the ability to interact with a database using SQL. For the sake of brevity, we have also presented the MySQL CREATE DATABASE command and have shown how to move from one database to another in MySQL. Now we will go into a detailed discussion and demonstration of creating and maintaining tables.

The syntax of the CREATE statements can range from the extremely simple to the complex, depending on the options your database management system (DBMS) supports and how detailed you want to be when building a database.

| NOTE | The examples used in this lesson were generated using Oracle Personal Edition and MySQL. Please see the documentation of your specific SQL implementation for any minor differences in syntax. |

Beginning with the CREATE DATABASE Statement

The first logical step in any database project is to create the database. Many of today's modern systems allow you to use a graphical interface to simplify this task. However, it is useful to know the underlying syntax that is used so you can create a SQL script for the database creation from scratch. You will see the value in using scripts during development as you continue to make changes to the database structure that would otherwise become time-consuming to re-create using the graphical tools.

The syntax for the typical CREATE DATABASE statement looks like this:

Syntax ▼

```
CREATE DATABASE database_name
```

Remember earlier when we demonstrated how to CREATE a database in MySQL? This statement is probably the most straightforward for accomplishing the task. Because the syntax varies so widely from system to system, we will not expand on the CREATE DATABASE statement's syntax. Instead of focusing on its syntax, we will spend some time discussing the options to consider when creating a database.

When you first log into MySQL, there are two databases that automatically are created for you: MYSQL and TEST. You can see all databases by issuing this command:

Input/Output ▼

```
mysql> show databases;
+----------+
| Database |
+----------+
| BOB      |
| matt     |
| mysql    |
| test     |
+----------+
3 rows in set (0.00 sec)
```

As you can see, an additional database MATT has been created.

CREATE DATABASE **Options**

The syntax for the CREATE DATABASE statement can vary widely. Many SQL texts skip over the CREATE DATABASE statement and move directly to the CREATE TABLE statement. Because you must create a database before you can build a table, this section focuses on some of the concepts a developer must consider when building a database. The first consideration is your level of permission. If you are using an RDBMS that supports user permissions, you must make sure that either you have system administrator-level permission settings, or that the system administrator has granted you CREATE DATABASE permission. Refer to your RDBMS documentation for more information on this.

9

Most RDBMSs also allow you to specify a default database size, usually in terms of hard disk space (such as megabytes). You will need to understand how your database system stores and locates data on the disk to accurately estimate the size you need. The responsibility for managing this space falls primarily on system administrators, and possibly at your location, a database administrator will build you a test database.

Don't let the CREATE DATABASE statement intimidate you. At its simplest, you can create a database named PAYMENTS with the following statement:

Input ▼

```
SQL> create database PAYMENTS;
```

Here's the MySQL example:

Input ▼

```
mysql> create database payments;
Query OK, 1 row affected (0.00 sec)
```

To use a specified database, you issue the MySQL command

Input ▼

```
mysql> use payments;
Database changed
```

NOTE

> Again, be sure to consult your database management system's documentation to learn the specifics of building a database, as the CREATE DATABASE statement can and does vary for the different implementations. Each implementation also has some unique options.

Database Design

Designing a database properly is extremely important to the success of your application. See Lesson 8, "Database Normalization," which covers the topics of relational database theory and database normalization.

Normalization is the process of breaking your data into separate components to reduce the repetition. Each level of normalization reduces the repetition of data. Normalizing your data can be an extremely complex process, and numerous database design tools enable you to plan this process in a logical fashion.

Many factors can influence the design of your database, including the following:

- Security
- Disk space available
- Speed of database searches and retrievals
- Speed of database updates
- Speed of multiple-table joins to retrieve data
- RDBMS support for temporary tables

Disk space is always an important factor. Although you might not think that disk space is a major concern in an age of terabyte storage medium, remember that the bigger your database is, the longer it takes to retrieve records. If you have done a poor job of designing your table structure, chances are that you have needlessly repeated much of your data.

Often the opposite problem can occur. You might have sought to completely normalize your tables' design with the database and in doing so created many tables. Although in theory you might have approached database design nirvana, the truth is that any query operations done against this kind of database might take a very long time to execute.

Databases designed in this manner are sometimes difficult to maintain because the table structure might obscure the designer's intent. This problem underlines the importance of always documenting your code or design so that others can come in after you (or work with you) and have some idea of what you were thinking at the time you created your database structure. In database designer's terms, this documentation is known as a *data dictionary* or *system catalog*. All references to the system catalog in this book call it the data dictionary.

Creating a Data Dictionary (System Catalog)

A data dictionary is the database designer's most important form of documentation. It performs the following functions:

- Describes the purpose of the database and who will be using it.

- Documents the specifics behind the database itself: what device it was created on, the database's default size, or the size of the log file (used to store database operations information in some RDBMSs).

- Contains SQL source code for any database install or uninstall scripts, including documentation on the use of import/export tools, which are discussed in Lesson 11.

- Provides a detailed description of each table within the database and explains each table's purpose in business process terminology.

- Documents the internal structure of each table, including all fields and their data types with comments, all indexes, and all views. (See Lesson 13, "Creating Views," and Lesson 15, "Creating Indexes on Tables to Improve Performance.")

- Contains SQL source code for all stored procedures and triggers.

- Describes database constraints such as the use of unique values or NOT NULL values. The documentation should also mention whether these constraints are enforced at the RDBMS level or whether the database programmer is expected to check for these constraints within the source code.

Many computer-aided software engineering (CASE) tools aid the database designer in the creation of this data dictionary. For instance, Microsoft Access comes prepackaged with a database documenting tool that prints out a detailed description of every object in the database. See Lesson 21, "Using SQL to Generate SQL Statements," for more details on the data dictionary.

NOTE

Most of the major RDBMS packages come with either the data dictionary installed or scripts to install it.

The data dictionary is one of the most important pieces of documentation that is available to you after the database has been created. A supplement to the data dictionary can be created that includes a complete description of all objects in the database: tables, fields, views, indexes, stored procedures, triggers, and so on. A complete data dictionary also contains a brief comment explaining the purpose behind each item in the database. You should update the data dictionary supplement whenever you make changes to the database.

Creating Key Fields

Along with documenting your database design, the most important design goal you should have is to create your table structure so that each table has a primary key and a foreign key. The primary key should meet the following goals:

- Each record is unique within a table. (No other record within the table has all of its columns equal to any other.)

- For a record to be unique, all the columns are necessary; that is, data in one column should not be repeated anywhere else in the table.

Regarding the second goal, the column that has completely unique data throughout the table is known as the *primary key field*. The primary key can consist of one column or a combination of columns, as long as the combination of columns is unique for each row of data in the table. A *foreign key field* is a field that links one table to another table's primary or foreign key. The following example should clarify this situation.

Assume you have three tables: BILLS, BANK_ACCOUNTS, and COMPANY. Table 9.1 shows the fields contained in these three tables.

TABLE 9.1   Table Structure for the PAYMENTS Database

BILLS	BANK_ACCOUNTS	COMPANY
NAME, CHAR(30)	ACCOUNT_ID, NUMBER	NAME, CHAR(30)
AMOUNT, NUMBER	TYPE, CHAR(30)	ADDRESS, CHAR(50)
ACCOUNT_ID, NUMBER	BALANCE, NUMBERCITY, CHAR(20)	
	BANK, CHAR(30)	STATE, CHAR(2)

Take a moment to examine these tables. Which fields do you think are the primary keys? Which are the foreign keys?

The primary key in the BILLS table is the NAME field. This field should not be duplicated because you have only one bill with this value. (In reality, you would probably have a check number or a date to make this record truly unique, but assume for now that the NAME field works.) The ACCOUNT_ID field in the BANK_ACCOUNTS table is the primary key for that table. The NAME field is the primary key for the COMPANY table.

The foreign keys in this example are probably easy to spot also. The ACCOUNT_ID field in the BILLS table joins the BILLS table with the BANK_ACCOUNTS table. The NAME field in the BILLS table joins the BILLS table with the COMPANY table. If this were a full-fledged database design, you would have many more tables and data breakdowns. For instance, the BANK field in the BANK_ACCOUNTS table could point to a BANK table containing bank information, such as addresses and phone numbers. The COMPANY table could be linked with another table (or database for that matter) containing information about the company and its products.

Breaking Down Your Data

Let's take a moment to examine an incorrect database design using the same information contained in the BILLS, BANK_ACCOUNTS, and COMPANY tables. A mistake many beginning users make is not breaking down their data into as many logical groups as possible. For instance, one poorly designed BILLS table might look like this:

Column Names	Comments
NAME, CHAR(30)	Name of the company that the bill is owed to
AMOUNT, NUMBER	Amount of the bill in dollars
ACCOUNT_ID, NUMBER	Bank account number of the bill (linked to BANK_ACCOUNTS table)
ADDRESS, CHAR(30)	Address of the company that the bill is owed to
CITY, CHAR(15)	City of the company that the bill is owed to
STATE, CHAR(2)	State of the company that the bill is owed to

The results might look correct, but take a moment to really look at the data here. If over several months you wrote several bills to the company in the NAME field, each time a new record was added for a bill, the company's ADDRESS, CITY, and STATE information would be duplicated. Now multiply that duplication over several hundred or thousand records and then multiply that figure by 10, 20, or 30 tables. You can begin to see the importance of a properly normalized database.

Before you actually fill these tables with data, you will need to know how to create a table.

Defining Tables with the CREATE TABLE Statement

The process of creating a table is far more standardized than the CREATE DATABASE statement. Here's the basic syntax for the CREATE TABLE statement:

Syntax ▼

```
CREATE TABLE table_name
(      field1 datatype [ NOT NULL ],
       field2 datatype [ NOT NULL ],
       field3 datatype [ NOT NULL ]...)
```

A simple example of a CREATE TABLE statement follows:

Input ▼

```
SQL>  CREATE TABLE BILLS_TEST (
  2     NAME CHAR(30),
  3     AMOUNT NUMBER,
  4     ACCOUNT_ID NUMBER);

Table created.
```

MySQL example:

Input ▼

```
mysql> create table bills_test
    -> (name        char(30),
    -> amount       numeric,
    -> account_id   numeric);
Query OK, 0 rows affected (0.07 sec)
```

Analysis ▼

This statement creates a table named BILLS. Within the BILLS table are three fields: NAME, AMOUNT, and ACCOUNT_ID. The NAME field has a data type of Character and can store strings up to 30 characters long. The AMOUNT and ACCOUNT_ID fields can contain number values only. Remember that different SQL implementations can have similar data types, but they might not always be used interchangeably, as in Number and Numeric.

The following section examines components of the CREATE TABLE command.

The Table Name

When creating a table using Oracle Personal Edition, several constraints apply when naming the table. First, the table name can be no more than 30 characters long. Because Oracle is not case sensitive, you can use either uppercase or lowercase for the individual characters. However, the first character of the name must be a letter between A and Z. The remaining characters can be letters or the symbols _, #, $, and @. Of course, the table name must be unique within its schema. The name also cannot be one of the Oracle or SQL reserved words (such as SELECT).

MySQL table names may be up to 64 characters except for the / and . characters. Column names also may contain up to 64 characters. Column aliases can be up to 255 characters long.

> **NOTE**
>
> You can have duplicate table names as long as the owner, schema, or database is different. Table names in the same schema must be unique.

The Field Name

The same constraints that apply to the table name also apply to the field name. However, a field name can be duplicated within the database. The restriction is that the field name must be unique within its table. For instance, assume that you have two tables in your database: TABLE1 and TABLE2. Both of these tables could have fields called ID. You cannot, however, have two fields within TABLE1 called ID, even if they are of different data types.

The Field's Data Type

If you have ever programmed in any language, you are familiar with the concept of data types, or the type of data that is to be stored in a specific field. For instance, a Character data type constitutes a field that stores only character string data. Table 9.2 shows the data types supported by Oracle.

TABLE 9.2   Data Types Supported by Oracle

Data Type	Comments
CHAR(size)	Alphanumeric data with a length between 1 and 255 characters.
	Be aware when using this data type that spaces are padded to the right of the value to supplement the total allocated length of the column. The (size) is the total length allowed for a value in a column defined as CHAR. For example, CHAR(10) allows for a character value up to 10 characters in length.
DATE	Included as part of the date are century, year, month, day, hour, minute, and second.
LONG	Variable-length alphanumeric strings up to 2 gigabytes. (See the following Note.)
LONG RAW	Binary data up to 2 gigabytes. (See the following Note.)
NUMBER	Numeric 0, positive or negative fixed or floating-point data.
	NUMBER(SIZE) NUMBER COLUMN specifies size.
	NUMBER(SIZE,D) NUMBER COLUMN specifies size with digits.
SMALLINT	Same as NUMBER.
RAW(size)	Binary data up to 255 bytes.
RAW MLSLABEL	Binary format for a secure operating system label.

TABLE 9.2 Continued

Data Type	Comments
ROWID	Hexadecimal string representing the unique address of a row in a table. (See the following Note.)
VARCHAR2(size)	Alphanumeric data that is variable length; this field must be between 1 and 2,000 characters long.
VARCHAR	Same as VARCHAR2; might not be supported in the future.
INTEGER	Same as NUMBER. Does not accept decimal digits.
INTEGER(n)	Specifies size of an integer (n) digits wide.
LONG VARCHAR	Same as LONG.
MLSLABEL	A secure operating system label, 4 bytes.
BLOB	A binary large object with a limit of 4GB in length.
CLOB	A character large object with a limit of 4GB in length.
NCLOB	The same as CLOB, but uses multibyte character sets.

NOTE

The LONG data type is often called a MEMO data type in other database management systems. It is primarily used to store large amounts of text for retrieval at some later time.

The LONG RAW data type is often called a binary large object (BLOB) in other database management systems. It is typically used to store graphics, sound, or video data. Although relational database management systems were not originally designed to serve this type of data, many multimedia systems today store their data in LONG RAW or BLOB fields.

The ROWID field type is used to give each record within your table a unique, nonduplicating value. Many other database systems support this concept with a COUNTER field (Microsoft Access) or with an IDENTITY field (SQL Server).

Check your implementation for supported data types, as they may vary.

The NULL Value

SQL also enables you to identify what can be stored within a column. A NULL value is almost an oxymoron because having a field with a value of NULL means that the field actually has no value stored in it.

When building a table, most database systems enable you to denote a column with the NOT NULL keywords. NOT NULL means the column cannot contain any NULL values for any records in the table. NOT NULL means that every record must have an actual value in this column. The following example illustrates the use of the NOT NULL keywords.

Input ▼

```
SQL>  CREATE TABLE BILLS (
 2      NAME CHAR(30) NOT NULL,
 3      AMOUNT NUMBER,
 4      ACCOUNT_ID NOT NULL);
```

MySQL example:

Input ▼

```
mysql> CREATE TABLE BILLS (
    -> NAME            CHAR(30)      NOT NULL,
    -> AMOUNT          NUMERIC,
    -> ACCOUNT_ID      NUMERIC       NOT NULL);
Query OK, 0 rows affected (0.28 sec)
```

Analysis ▼

In this table you want to save the name of the company you owe the money to, along with the bill's amount. If the NAME field and/or the ACCOUNT_ID were not stored, the record would be meaningless. You would end up with a record containing a bill, but you would have no idea whom you should pay.

The first statement in the next example inserts a valid record containing data for a bill to be sent to Joe's Computer Service for $25.

Input ▼

```
SQL> INSERT INTO BILLS VALUES("JOE'S COMPUTER SERVICE", 25, 1);

1 row inserted.
```

MySQL example:

Input ▼

```
mysql> INSERT INTO BILLS VALUES("JOE'S COMPUTER SERVICE", 25, 1);
Query OK, 1 row affected (0.29 sec)
```

9

Now another Oracle example:

Input ▼

```
SQL> INSERT INTO BILLS VALUES(NULL, 25000, 1);

INSERT INTO BILLS VALUES(NULL, 25000, 1)
            *
ERROR at line 1:
ORA-01400: cannot insert NULL into ("RYAN"."BILLS"."NAME")
```

Analysis ▼

Notice that the second record in the preceding example does not contain a NAME value. We are attempting to insert a NULL value into the NAME column. (You might think that missing the payee is a good thing because the bill is $25,000, but we won't consider that.) Because the table was created with a NOT NULL value for the NAME field, the second insert raised an error.

A good rule of thumb is that the primary key field and all foreign key fields should never contain NULL values.

Unique Fields

One of your design goals should be to have one unique column within each table. This column or field is a primary key field. Some database management systems allow you to set a field as unique. Other database management systems, such as Oracle and SQL Server, allow you to create a unique index on a field (see Lesson 15). This feature keeps you from inserting duplicate key field values into the database.

You should notice several things when choosing a key field. As we mentioned, Oracle provides a ROWID field that is incremented for each row that is added, which makes this field by default always a unique key. ROWID fields make excellent key fields for several reasons. First, it is much faster to join on an integer value than on an 80-character string. Such joins result in smaller database sizes over time if you store an integer value in every primary and foreign key as opposed to a long CHAR value.

Now you can create the tables you used earlier in this lesson. See Tables 9.3–9.5 for sample table data.

Input/Output ▼

```
SQL>  create database PAYMENTS;

Statement processed.

SQL>  create table BILLS (
```

```
  2   NAME CHAR(30) NOT NULL,
  3   AMOUNT NUMBER,
  4   ACCOUNT_ID NUMBER NOT NULL);

Table created.

SQL>  create table BANK_ACCOUNTS (
  2   ACCOUNT_ID NUMBER NOT NULL,
  3   TYPE CHAR(30),
  4   BALANCE NUMBER,
  5   BANK CHAR(30));

Table created.

SQL>  create table COMPANY (
  2   NAME CHAR(30) NOT NULL,
  3   ADDRESS CHAR(50),
  4   CITY CHAR(30),
  5   STATE CHAR(2));

Table created.
```

9

Study the following sequence of MySQL commands:

Input ▼

```
create database PAYMENTS;

use database PAYMENTS;

create table BILLS (
NAME CHAR(30) NOT NULL,
AMOUNT NUMERIC,
ACCOUNT_ID NUMERIC NOT NULL);

create table BANK_ACCOUNTS (
ACCOUNT_ID NUMERIC NOT NULL,
TYPE CHAR(30),
BALANCE NUMERIC,
BANK CHAR(30));
create table COMPANY (
NAME CHAR(30) NOT NULL,
ADDRESS CHAR(50),
CITY CHAR(30),
STATE CHAR(2));
```

| NOTE | The preceding is an example of how to CREATE a database in MySQL and how to tell MySQL that you would like to work within that database, followed by three CREATE TABLE statements. These tables will be within the newly created database. |

TABLE 9.3 Sample Data for the BILLS Table

NAME	AMOUNT	ACCOUNT_ID
Phone Company	125	1
Power Company	75	1
Record Club	25	2
Software Company	250	1
Cable TV Company	35	3

TABLE 9.4 Sample Data for the BANK_ACCOUNTS Table

ACCOUNT_ID	TYPE	BALANCE	BANK
1	Checking	500	First Federal
2	Money market	1200	First Investor
3	Checking	90	Credit Union

TABLE 9.5 Sample Data for the COMPANY Table

NAME	ADDRESS	CITY	STATE
Phone Company	111 1st Street	Atlanta	GA
Power Company	222 2nd Street	Jacksonville	FL
Record Club	333 3rd Avenue	Los Angeles	CA
Software Company	444 4th Drive	San Francisco	CA
Cable TV Company	555 5th Drive	Austin	TX

Table Storage and Sizing

Most major RDBMSs have default settings for table sizes and table locations. If you do not specify table size and location, the table will take the defaults. The defaults might be very undesirable, especially for large tables. The default sizes and locations will vary among the implementations. Here is an example of a CREATE TABLE statement with a storage clause (from Oracle):

Input ▼

```
SQL>    CREATE TABLE TABLENAME
   2      (COLUMN1    CHAR    NOT NULL,
   3       COLUMN2    NUMBER,
   4       COLUMN3    DATE)
   5      TABLESPACE TABLESPACE NAME
```

```
 6      STORAGE
 7      INITIAL SIZE,
 8      NEXT SIZE,
 9      MINEXTENTS value,
10      MAXEXTENTS value,
11      PCTINCREASE value);
```

```
Table created.
```

In Oracle, you can specify a tablespace in which you want the table to reside. A decision is usually made according to the space available, often by the database administrator (DBA). INITIAL SIZE is the size for the initial extent of the table (the initial allocated space). NEXT SIZE is the value for any additional extents the table might take through growth. MINEXTENTS and MAXEXTENTS identify the minimum and maximum extents allowed for the table, and PCTINCREASE identifies the percentage by which the next extent will be increased each time the table grows, or takes another extent.

Creating a Table from an Existing Table

The most common way to create a table is with the CREATE TABLE command. However, some database management systems provide an alternative method of creating tables, using the format and data of an existing table. This method is useful when you want to select the data out of a table for temporary modification. It can also be useful when you have to create a table similar to the existing table and fill it with similar data. (You won't have to reenter all this information.) The syntax for Oracle follows:

Syntax ▼

```
CREATE TABLE NEW_TABLE(FIELD1, FIELD2, FIELD3)
AS (SELECT FIELD1, FIELD2, FIELD3
    FROM OLD_TABLE <WHERE...>
```

This syntax allows you to create a new table with the same data types as those of the fields that are selected from the old table. It also allows you to rename the fields in the new table by giving them new names.

Input ▼

```
SQL>  CREATE TABLE NEW_BILLS(NAME, AMOUNT, ACCOUNT_ID)
  2   AS (SELECT * FROM BILLS WHERE AMOUNT < 50);
```

```
Table created.
```

The preceding statement creates a new table (NEW_BILLS) with all the records from the BILLS table that have an AMOUNT less than 50. Here are a couple of CREATE TABLE statements in MySQL using tables from previous exercises in this book.

Input/Output ▼

```
mysql> show databases;
+----------+
| Database |
+----------+
| BOB      |
| matt     |
| mysql    |
| test     |
+----------+
```

After you have started MySQL, you can see your database by issuing the SHOW DATABASES command. To work within the BOB database, issue the following:

Input ▼

```
mysql> use bob;
Database changed
```

To see a list of your tables:

Input/Output ▼

```
mysql> show tables;
+---------------+
| Tables_in_bob |
+---------------+
| characters    |
| checks        |
| orders        |
| orgchart      |
| part          |
| teamstats     |
+---------------+
6 rows in set (0.01 sec)
mysql> create table max_hits
    -> as select * from teamstats
    -> where hits > 51;
Query OK, 2 rows affected (0.06 sec)
Records: 2  Duplicates: 0  Warnings: 0
mysql> select * from max_hits;
```

```
+---------+-----+-----+------+-------+---------+---------+---------+----+----+
| name    | pos | ab  | hits | walks | singles | doubles | triples | hr | so |
+---------+-----+-----+------+-------+---------+---------+---------+----+----+
| DONKNOW | 3B  | 175 |   65 | 23    | 50      | 10      | 1       |  4 | 15 |
| DAVID   | OF  | 187 |   70 | 24    | 48      | 4       | 0       | 17 | 42 |
+---------+-----+-----+------+-------+---------+---------+---------+----+----+
2 rows in set (0.03 sec)
```

This example created a table from an existing table. Notice again that all the column names are the same, but that the new table only contains two rows. These rows meet the conditions specified in the WHERE CLAUSE.

9

Some database systems also allow you to use the following syntax to insert data into one table based on data from another table:

Syntax ▼

```
INSERT NEW_TABLE
SELECT <field1, field2... | *> from OLD_TABLE
<WHERE...>
```

An example of this concept in Oracle is as follows:

Input ▼

```
INSERT INTO NEW_BILLS
SELECT * FROM BILLS WHERE AMOUNT < 50;
```

Modifying Table Structures with the ALTER TABLE Statement

Many times your database design does not account for everything it should. Also, requirements for applications and databases are always subject to change. The ALTER TABLE statement enables the database administrator or designer to change the structure of a table after it has been created.

The ALTER TABLE command is a powerful feature in SQL that enables you to modify the structure of a table after it has been created. Without the ALTER TABLE command, you would have to drop a table and re-create it every time you wanted to make a change to its structure. This section discusses two of the main features of the ALTER TABLE command:

- Adding a column to an existing table
- Modifying an existing column

The syntax for the ALTER TABLE statement is as follows:

Syntax ▼

```
ALTER TABLE table_name
  <ADD column_name data_type; |
  MODIFY column_name data_type;>
```

The following command changes the NAME field of the newly created MAX_HITS table to hold 40 characters:

Input ▼

```
mysql> alter table max_hits
    -> modify name char(40);
Query OK, 2 rows affected (0.12 sec)
Records: 2  Duplicates: 0  Warnings: 0
```

NOTE

> You can increase or decrease the length of columns; however, you cannot decrease a column's length if the current size of one of its values is greater than the value you want to assign to the column length.

Here is an example of the error you receive when you attempt to modify a column to a length that is shorter than the largest current value in the column.

Input ▼

```
mysql> alter table max_hits
    -> modify name(3);
ERROR 1064: You have an error in your SQL syntax near '(3)' at line 2
```

Here's a statement that adds a new column to the MAX_HITS table:

Input ▼

```
mysql> alter table max_hits
    -> add column food char(40);
Query OK, 2 rows affected (0.08 sec)
Records: 2  Duplicates: 0  Warnings: 0
```

This statement would add a new column named FOOD capable of holding 40 characters. The field would be added to the right, or end, of all the existing fields.

In several implementations of SQL, restrictions apply to using the ALTER TABLE statement. You cannot use it to add or delete fields from a database. It can change a column from NOT NULL to NULL, but not necessarily the other way around. A column specification can be changed from NULL to NOT NULL only if the column does not contain any NULL values. To change a column from NOT NULL to NULL, use the following syntax:

Syntax ▼

```
ALTER TABLE table_name  MODIFY (column_name data_type NULL);
```

MySQL, on the other hand, does allow you to add, delete, and rename columns. MySQL includes an option with the ALTER TABLE statement called CHANGE.

When using the CHANGE option as part of your MySQL ALTER TABLE statement, it is important to remember that MySQL will first want to know what you want to change your column name to. If you don't want to change the name of the column, all you have to do is provide the current name of the column, and the name will stay intact.

MySQL will also require that you re-input column definitions, even if there is no change. With this said, keep in mind that it is important to put time into planning your database before building it to avoid the hassle of having to modify table structures more than necessary. Unfortunately, it is difficult to design a perfect database that will never need modification.

Here is the MySQL ALTER TABLE syntax using the CHANGE option:

Syntax ▼

```
ALTER TABLE table_name CHANGE old_column_name new_column_name
column_definitions;
```

In this example we are going to change the NAME in the MAX_HITS table from a NOT NULL column to a NULL column. Additionally, we will change the type to char(9). The word NULL will be the only change from what exists in the table.

Input ▼

```
mysql> alter table max_hits
    -> change name name char(9) null;
Query OK, 2 rows affected (0.05 sec)
Records: 2  Duplicates: 0  Warnings: 0
```

In the next example we will change the name of the column and leave the data type alone, but make the column bigger and cause the column to no longer accept NULL values.

Input ▼

```
mysql> alter table max_hits
    -> change name pizza char(20) not null;
Query OK, 2 rows affected (0.06 sec)
Records: 2  Duplicates: 0  Warnings: 0
```

NOTE ____ | In MySQL, you also have the option of dropping a column.

The following ALTER TABLE statement adds the column PIZZA (we really like pizza) to the ORGCHART table:

Input ▼

```
mysql> alter table orgchart
    -> add column pizza char(20) not null;
Query OK, 8 rows affected (0.06 sec)
Records: 8  Duplicates: 0  Warnings: 0
```

Upon reflection, however, we have decided that not everyone likes pizza, so in the interest of harmony, we will drop the PIZZA column from our table.

Input ▼

```
mysql> alter table orgchart
    -> drop column pizza;
Query OK, 8 rows affected (0.09 sec)
Records: 8  Duplicates: 0  Warnings: 0
```

Analysis ▼

To change a column from NULL to NOT NULL, in some implementations, you might have to take several steps:

1. Determine whether the column has any NULL values.
2. Deal with any NULL values that you find. (Delete those records, update the column's value, and so on.)
3. Issue the ALTER TABLE command.

> **NOTE**
>
> Some database management systems allow the use of the MODIFY clause; others do not. Still others have added other clauses to the ALTER TABLE statement. In Oracle, you can even alter the table's storage parameters. Check the documentation of the system you are using to determine the implementation of the ALTER TABLE statement.

The DROP TABLE Statement

SQL provides a command to completely remove a table from a database. The DROP TABLE command deletes a table along with all its associated constraints and indexes. After this command has been issued, there is no turning back. The most common use of the DROP TABLE statement is when you have created a table for temporary use. When you have completed all operations on the table that you planned to do, issue the DROP TABLE statement the following syntax:

Syntax ▼

```
DROP TABLE table_name;
```

Here's how to drop the MAX_HITS table:

Input ▼

```
SQL> DROP TABLE MAX_HITS;

Table dropped.
mysql> drop table max_hits;
Query OK, 0 rows affected (0.00 sec)
```

Analysis ▼

Don't be thrown by the 0 rows affected comment in the MySQL example. The table is gone. To test this, you could try to execute a SELECT from the table that you just tried to drop. If there are no rows, you know the table is gone.

Also, notice the absence of system prompts. This command did not ask Are you sure? (Y/N). After the DROP TABLE command is issued, the table is permanently deleted.

CAUTION

> If you issue
>
> ```
> SQL> DROP TABLE  MAX_HITS;
> ```
>
> you could be dropping the incorrect table. When dropping tables, you should *always* use the owner or schema name. The recommended syntax is
>
> ```
> SQL> DROP TABLE OWNER.MAX_HITS;
> or
> mysql>DROP TABLE BOB.MAX_HITS;
> ```
>
> We are stressing this syntax because we once had to repair a production database from which the wrong table had been dropped. The table was not properly identified with the schema name. Restoring the database was an eight-hour job, and we had to work until well past midnight.

The DROP DATABASE **Statement**

Some database management systems also provide the DROP DATABASE statement, which is identical in usage to the DROP TABLE statement. The syntax for this statement is as follows:

Syntax ▼

```
DROP DATABASE database_name
```

NOTE

> The various relational database implementations require you to take different steps to drop a database. After the database is dropped, you will need to clean up the operating system files that compose the database.

Working with DROP TABLE **and** DROP DATABASE

Create a database with one table in it. Issue the DROP TABLE command and then issue the DROP DATABASE command. Does your database system allow you to do this? Single-file–based systems, such as Microsoft Access, do not support this command. The database is contained in a single file. An Oracle database, although composed of many files, does not support the DROP DATABASE command. To create a database, you must use the menu options provided in the product itself. To delete a database, simply delete the file from the hard drive.

Summary

In this lesson, you learned five new statements: CREATE DATABASE, CREATE TABLE, ALTER TABLE, DROP TABLE, and DROP DATABASE. This lesson also discussed the importance of creating a good database design.

You learned that the CREATE DATABASE statement is not a standard element within database systems. This variation is primarily due to the many different ways vendors store their databases on disk. Each implementation enables a different set of features and options, which results in a completely different CREATE DATABASE statement. Simply issuing CREATE DATABASE <database_name> creates a default database with a default size on most systems. The DROP DATABASE statement permanently removes that database.

The CREATE TABLE statement is used to create a new table. With this command, you can create the fields you need and identify their data types. Some database management systems also allow you to specify other attributes for the field, such as whether it can allow NULL values or whether that field should be unique throughout the table. The ALTER TABLE statement can alter the structure of an existing table. The DROP TABLE statement can delete a table from a database.

Q&A

Q Why does the CREATE DATABASE statement vary so much from one system to another?

A CREATE DATABASE varies because the actual process of creating a database varies from one database system to another. Small PC-based databases usually rely on files that are created within some type of application program. To distribute the database on a large server, related database files are simply distributed over several disk drives. When your code accesses these databases, there is no database process running on the computer, just your application accessing the files directly. More powerful database systems must take into account disk space management, as well as support features such as security, transaction control, and stored procedures embedded within the database itself. When your application program accesses a database, a database server manages your requests (along with many others' requests) and returns data to you through a sometimes complex layer of middle-ware. These topics are discussed toward the end of this book. For now, learn all you can about how your particular database management system creates and man-ages databases.

Q Can I create a table temporarily and then automatically drop it when I am done with it?

A Yes. Many database management systems support the concept of a temporary table. This type of table is created for temporary use and is automatically deleted when your user's process ends or when you issue the DROP TABLE command.

Q Can I remove columns with the ALTER TABLE statement?

A In some implementations, yes. In some implementations, the ALTER TABLE com-mand can be used only to add or modify columns within a table. To remove columns, you would have to create a new table with the desired format and then select the records from the old table into the new table. However, some implemen-tations do allow you to remove columns with the ALTER TABLE statement.

Workshop

The Workshop provides quiz questions to help solidify your understanding of the mater-ial covered, as well as exercises to provide you with experience in using what you have learned. Try to answer the quiz and exercise questions before checking the answers in Appendix A, "Answers." For this lesson's exercises we will create an entirely new data-base and tables, and insert some rows into the tables by following the information pro-vided. We will then realize that our table structure is in error, so we will take corrective action. The tables will be based upon other tables and drop tables. We will also do some SELECT statements.

Quiz

1. True or false: The ALTER DATABASE statement is often used to modify an existing table's structure.

2. True or false: The DROP TABLE command is functionally equivalent to the DELETE FROM <table_name> command.

3. True or false: To add a new table to a database, use the CREATE TABLE command.

4. What is wrong with the following statement?
```
CREATE TABLE new_table (
ID number,
FIELD1 char(40),
FIELD2 char(80),
ID char(40);
```

5. What is wrong with the following statement?

```
ALTER DATABASE BILLS (
COMPANY char(80));
```

6. When a table is created, who is the owner?

7. If data in a character column has varying lengths, what would be the best choice for the data type?

8. Can you have duplicate table names?

9. Can you alter a column with a NULL constraint to not allow NULLs, and vice versa?

9

Exercises

1. Create a table to hold data that pertains to movie rentals. Here are the statements:

```
create table stock
(stock_id    numeric(10)    not null,
title        varchar(80)    not null,
amount       numeric(10)    not null);
insert into stock values
(1,'SAHARA',3);
insert into stock values
(2,'CASABLANCA',3);
insert into stock values
(3,'TO HAVE AND HAVE NOT',1);
insert into stock values
(4,'THE MALTESE FALCON',5);
insert into stock values
(5,'THE BIG SLEEP',4);
insert into stock values
(6,'SAVING PRIVATE RYAN',7);
create table media
(media_id    numeric(10)    not null,
description  varchar(5)     not null);
insert into media values
(1,'DVD');
insert into media values
(2,'VIDEO');
```

2. Create a table to hold data that pertains to customers who rent movies. Here are the statements:

```
CREATE TABLE CUST
(CUST_ID     NUMERIC(5)     NOT NULL,
STOCK_ID     NUMERIC(5)     NOT NULL,
MEDIA_ID     NUMERIC(1)     NOT NULL,
FNAME        VARCHAR(10)    NOT NULL,
LNAME        VARCHAR(10)    NOT NULL,
DOB          DATE           NOT NULL,
```

```
DT_RENT     DATE        NULL,
DAYS_RENT   NUMERIC(1)  NOT NULL,
DT_RT       DATE        NULL);
INSERT INTO CUST VALUES
(11122,3,1,'TULL','JETHRO','1980-05-02','2002-04-14',5,NULL);
INSERT INTO CUST VALUES
(11122,4,1,'TULL','JETHRO','1980-05-02','2002-05-01',5,'2002-05-04');
INSERT INTO CUST VALUES
(22233,5,1,'SMITH','MISTER','1962-09-03','2002-06-01',1,NULL);
INSERT INTO CUST VALUES
(21243,6,2,'KAYLEIGH','YVONNE','1986-05-01','2002-06-10',5,NULL);
INSERT INTO CUST VALUES
(34213,2,2,'JUSTESS','HEATHER','1985-12-31','2002-06-02',3,'2002-06-05');
```

3. Perform a DESCRIBE command on the CUST table:

   `desc cust;`

   Change the data type for CUST_ID from NUMERIC(DECIMAL(5,0)) to VARCHAR(5).

4. Perform another DESCRIBE on the three tables you just made. CREATE a table that contains the following data:

   FNAME, TITLE, and MEDIA DESCRIPTION

   Call the table VIEW.

5. Create a table that contains the full name of the customer, the title of the movies they have rented, the rating of the movie, and the customer's age in years. Call this table AGE.

6. Add a column to your AGE table to hold information on what type of junk food the customer buys when he rents movies. Call the column JUNK_FOOD.

7. Wait a minute, I was just kidding when I said to call the column JUNK_FOOD. Make it something that sounds a bit more professional. And why did you make it a NOT NULL column? Not everybody is going to buy this stuff.

8. Take one last look at your tables. Make some tables of your own using the data provided or create new tables of your own. When you are done, DROP the AGE table.

LESSON 10
Controlling Data Integrity

In this lesson, you will learn about table constraints and how they allow you to control the data that is inserted into your database. You will also get plenty of practice creating tables, dropping tables, and re-creating them with constraints. By the end of the lesson, you should understand the following things about constraints:

- What they are and how they are used
- The different types of constraints
- How to create constraints using SQL
- The difference between data integrity and referential integrity
- How to manage constraints

Introducing Constraints

A *constraint* is an object in a relational database that places rules on data inserted into a column of a table. This lesson covers the several types of constraints in SQL and gives examples of their use to maintain a high level of data integrity in your database. First, you must understand data integrity and the concepts behind the use of constraints.

Data Integrity

Constraints are used to ensure accuracy and consistency of data in a relational database. Data integrity is this assurance of accurate and consistent data in the database. Data integrity is handled in a relational database through the use of constraints on tables. Any time humans are entering data into a database (the data has to get there somehow), mistakes are made that might violate the accuracy.

Data integrity involves making sure data is entered consistently and stored consistently in the database. You don't want one data entry clerk to enter somebody's phone number as

1234567890

and another to enter the phone number as

(123) 456-7890

Data must be accurate and stored consistently in the database to allow for it to be accurately retrieved, and for accurate comparisons to be made between data.

Why Use Constraints?

To answer that question, let's look at the basic components of data integrity (data accuracy and consistency) and how you would enforce data integrity in a database through the use of constraints.

Accuracy of data involves placing rules (constraints) on table columns so that the database only allows certain types of data to be inserted into these columns. For example, you might want only numeric data inserted into a column containing employee pay rates. You want to make sure that the NAME column of a table accepts alphanumeric values. You might want to make sure that the STATE_ABBREV_CODE column contains values that consist of only two characters.

There are different ways to ensure that data is entered correctly. The first thing you want to do is place constraints on your table columns that allow only certain types of data and lengths of data to be entered. In a column such as SSN or PHONE_NUMBER, only the value itself should be stored, and not the dashes.

The data can be extracted in a way to include dashes and other characters, thus making the output of a query more readable. The front-end application should have edits that control the types of values inserted into a table, or that make a user select a value from a list. Database constraints and front-end edits should work in conjunction with one another to provide the best possible data integrity. However, as a database administrator (DBA), you cannot trust that every front-end application or access point will follow the proper rules of data integrity. Therefore, it will fall upon you to ensure that your database exerts enough control to maintain data integrity. In short, trust no one.

Database normalization can also help provide data consistency because the occurrence of redundant data is being reduced in the database (covered in Lesson 8, "Database Normalization"). Later in the lesson, you'll see how the implementation of referential integrity constraints (foreign keys) will help maintain consistent data in a normalized database.

NOTE

> Without the use of constraints, data management can be a very complicated and nearly impossible task, especially when dealing with databases containing thousands or millions of rows. The more time spent planning a database and creating constraints, the less time spent in the overall management of data.

Exploring Types of Constraints

Now you'll study the different types of constraints that can be created on database tables. The following is a list of those constraints:

- NOT NULL
- Primary key
- Unique
- Foreign key
- Check

10

Each of these constraints has its own function. The functions and syntax of each of these constraints are discussed in the following subsections, as well as their place in a relational database.

NOT NULL Constraints

When you initially create a table, you must assign a data type to each column in the table. The data type assigned to a column tells the database what kind of data can be inserted into that column in a table. The different types of data mainly include Character data, Numeric data, and Date and Time data.

A basic CREATE TABLE statement might look like this:

Input/Output ▼

```
CREATE TABLE EMP
(EMP_ID        VARCHAR2(9),
 EMP_NAME      VARCHAR2(30),
 ADDRESS       VARCHAR2(30),
 CITY          VARCHAR2(30),
 STATE         VARCHAR2(2),
 ZIP           VARCHAR2(5),
 PHONE         VARCHAR2(10));

Table created.
```

MySQL does not support the VARCHAR2 data type. However, VARCHAR will work.

Input/Output ▼

```
mysql> CREATE TABLE EMP
    -> (EMP_ID          VARCHAR(9),
    ->  EMP_NAME        VARCHAR(30),
    ->  ADDRESS         VARCHAR(30),
    ->  CITY            VARCHAR(30),
    ->  STATE           VARCHAR(2),
    ->  ZIP             VARCHAR(5),
    ->  PHONE           VARCHAR(10));
Query OK, 0 rows affected (0.35 sec)
```

After a column has been created, a NOT NULL constraint can be placed on the column. NULL equates to a missing or unknown value. If you do not insert a value into a column when you insert a row of data into a table, the value of the column is NULL. If you specify a column as NOT NULL, that means that NULL values are not allowed in the column. NOT NULL means that the column is required.

The following example depicts how you specify a column as NOT NULL:

Input/Output ▼

```
CREATE TABLE EMP
(EMP_ID          VARCHAR2(9)      NOT NULL,
 EMP_NAME        VARCHAR2(30)     NOT NULL,
 ADDRESS         VARCHAR2(30)     NOT NULL,
 CITY            VARCHAR2(30)     NOT NULL,
 STATE           VARCHAR2(2)      NOT NULL,
 ZIP             VARCHAR2(5)      NOT NULL,
 PHONE           VARCHAR2(10));

Table created.

mysql> CREATE TABLE EMP
    -> (EMP_ID          VARCHAR(9)       NOT NULL,
    ->  EMP_NAME        VARCHAR(30)      NOT NULL,
    ->  ADDRESS         VARCHAR(30)      NOT NULL,
    ->  CITY            VARCHAR(30)      NOT NULL,
    ->  STATE           VARCHAR(2)       NOT NULL,
    ->  ZIP             VARCHAR(5)       NOT NULL,
    ->  PHONE           VARCHAR(10));
Query OK, 0 rows affected (0.06 sec)
```

Analysis ▼

If a column is not defined as NOT NULL, NULL values are allowed in the column. In this example, the PHONE column is optional when inserting a new row of data into the EMP table.

Primary Key Constraints

A *primary key* is the term that is used to identify one or more columns in a table that make a row of data unique. Although the primary key typically consists of one column in a table, more than one column can comprise the primary key. For example, the logical primary key for an employee table would be the employee's Social Security number, or an assigned employee identification number.

The objective is for every record to have a unique primary key, or value, for the employee's identification number. Because there is probably no need to have more than one record for each employee in an employee table, the employee identification number makes a logical primary key. The primary key is assigned upon table creation.

10

In the following example, we have identified the EMP_ID column as the primary key for the EMP table.

Input/Output ▼

```
CREATE TABLE EMP
(EMP_ID          CHAR(9)         NOT NULL PRIMARY KEY,
 EMP_NAME        VARCHAR2(40)    NOT NULL,
 ADDRESS         VARCHAR2(20)    NOT NULL,
 CITY            VARCHAR2(15)    NOT NULL,
 STATE           CHAR(2)         NOT NULL,
 ZIP             NUMBER(5)       NOT NULL,
 PHONE           NUMBER(10)      NULL);

Table created.

mysql> CREATE TABLE EMP
    -> (EMP_ID          VARCHAR(9)      not null        primary key,
    ->  EMP_NAME        VARCHAR(30)     not null,
    ->  ADDRESS         VARCHAR(30)     not null,
    ->  CITY            VARCHAR(30)     not null,
    ->  STATE           VARCHAR(2)      not null,
    ->  ZIP             VARCHAR(5)      not null,
    ->  PHONE           VARCHAR(10));
Query OK, 0 rows affected (0.02 sec)
```

This method of defining a primary key is accomplished during table creation. The primary key in this case is an implied constraint.

NOTE

If you would like to re-create the EMP table as in the following example, you must first be sure to DROP the table, and then re-create it.

You can also specify a primary key explicitly as a constraint when setting up a table, as follows:

```
mysql> drop table emp;
```

Input/Output ▼

```
CREATE TABLE EMP
(EMP_ID        CHAR(9)        NOT NULL,
 EMP_NAME      VARCHAR2(40)   NOT NULL,
 ADDRESS       VARCHAR2(20)   NOT NULL,
 CITY          VARCHAR2(15)   NOT NULL,
 STATE         CHAR(2)        NOT NULL,
 ZIP           NUMBER(5)      NOT NULL,
 PHONE         NUMBER(10)     NULL,
 PRIMARY KEY (EMP_ID));

Table created.

mysql> CREATE TABLE EMP
    -> (EMP_ID          VARCHAR(9)      not null,
    ->  EMP_NAME        VARCHAR(30)     not null,
    ->  ADDRESS         VARCHAR(30)     not null,
    ->  CITY            VARCHAR(30)     not null,
    ->  STATE           VARCHAR(2)      not null,
    ->  ZIP             VARCHAR(5)      not null,
    ->  PHONE           VARCHAR(10)         NULL,
    ->  PRIMARY KEY (EMP_ID));
Query OK, 0 rows affected (0.04 sec)
```

Notice that in this example, the primary key constraint is defined after the column list in the CREATE TABLE statement.

You can also use the ALTER TABLE statement to specify a primary key on a table after the table has been created, as follows:

Syntax ▼

```
ALTER TABLE EMP ADD CONSTRAINT EMP_PK PRIMARY KEY (EMP_ID);

Table altered.

mysql> ALTER TABLE EMP ADD PRIMARY KEY (EMP_ID);
Query OK, 0 rows affected (0.05 sec)
Records: 0  Duplicates: 0  Warnings: 0
```

In this example, we assume that the EMP table has already been created. You can always add constraints to a table after the table has been created. We have altered the EMP table by adding a primary key constraint and specifying the column EMP_ID as the primary key.

Unique Constraints

A unique constraint is similar to a primary key in the sense that every value in that column must be unique. Although a primary key constraint is placed on one column, you can place a unique constraint on another column, even though it is not actually used as the primary key.

10

Study the following example:

Input/Output ▼

```
CREATE TABLE EMP
(EMP_ID         CHAR(9)         NOT NULL    PRIMARY KEY,
 EMP_NAME       VARCHAR2(40)    NOT NULL,
 ADDRESS        VARCHAR2(20)    NOT NULL,
 CITY           VARCHAR2(15)    NOT NULL,
 STATE          CHAR(2)         NOT NULL,
 ZIP            NUMBER(5)       NOT NULL,
 PHONE          NUMBER(10)      NULL        UNIQUE);

Table created.

mysql> CREATE TABLE EMP
    -> (EMP_ID         CHAR(9)         NOT NULL    PRIMARY KEY,
    -> EMP_NAME        VARCHAR(40)     NOT NULL,
    -> ADDRESS         VARCHAR(20)     NOT NULL,
    -> CITY            VARCHAR(15)     NOT NULL,
    -> STATE           CHAR(2)         NOT NULL,
    -> ZIP             NUMERIC(5)      NOT NULL,
    -> PHONE           NUMERIC(10)     NULL        UNIQUE);
Query OK, 0 rows affected (0.32 sec)
```

In this example, the primary key is `EMP_ID`, meaning that the employee identification number is the column that ensures that every record in the table is unique. The primary key is a column that is normally referenced in queries, particularly to join tables, as you will learn later. The column `PHONE` has been designated as a `UNIQUE` value, meaning that no two employees may have the same telephone number. There is not a lot of difference between the two values, except that the primary key provides order to data in a table and is normally used to join tables in a query.

Foreign Key Constraints

A *foreign key* is a column in a child table that references a column in the parent table. A foreign key constraint is the main feature of the relational database that is used to enforce referential integrity between tables. A column defined as a foreign key is used to reference a column defined as a primary key in another table. In other words, a foreign key is a column that is tied back to a column in another table, ensuring that corresponding data exists in both tables.

The following is an example of the specification of a foreign key constraint in the `EMP_PAY` table:

Input/Output ▼

```
CREATE TABLE EMP_PAY
(EMP_ID            CHAR(9)       NOT NULL,
 POSITION          VARCHAR2(15)  NOT NULL,
 PAY_RATE          NUMBER(4,2)   NOT NULL,
 FOREIGN KEY EMP_ID_FK (EMP_ID) REFERENCES EMP (EMP_ID));

Table created.

mysql> CREATE TABLE EMP_PAY
    -> (EMP_ID           CHAR(9)       NOT NULL,
    -> POSITION          VARCHAR(15)   NOT NULL,
    -> PAY_RATE          DECIMAL(4,2)  NOT NULL,
    -> FOREIGN KEY EMP_ID_FK (EMP_ID) REFERENCES EMP (EMP_ID));
Query OK, 0 rows affected (0.29 sec)
```

Analysis ▼

In this example, the `EMP_ID` column has been designated as the foreign key for the `EMP_PAY` table. This foreign key, as you can see, references the `EMP_ID` column in the `EMP` table. This foreign key ensures that for every `EMP_ID` in the `EMP_PAY`, there is a corresponding `EMP_ID` in the `EMP`.

Parent/Child Table Relationships

The EMP table and the EMP_PAY table are in a parent/child relationship. The parent table is the EMP table, and the child table is the EMP_PAY table. Study Figure 10.1 for a better understanding of the parent/child table relationship.

In Figure 10.1, the EMP_ID column in the child table references the EMP_ID column in the parent table. For a value to be inserted into EMP_ID in the child table, a value in EMP_ID must first exist in the parent table. Likewise, for a value to be removed from EMP_ID in the parent table, all corresponding values of EMP_ID must first be removed from the child table. This is how referential integrity works.

FIGURE 10.1
The parent/child table relationship.

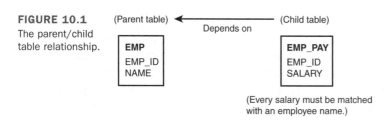

As with primary keys, a foreign key can be added to a table using the ALTER TABLE command.

Syntax ▼

```
ALTER TABLE EMP_PAY
ADD CONSTRAINT EMP_ID_FK FOREIGN KEY (EMP_ID)
REFERENCES EMP (EMP_ID);
```

Analysis ▼

In this example, we are altering the structural definition of the EMP_PAY table by adding a foreign key constraint called EMP_ID_FK, where the EMP_ID column in the EMP_PAY table references the EMP_ID column in the EMP table. A row of data for an employee cannot be inserted into the EMP_PAY table without there first being a record with a matching EMP_ID in the EMP table (see Figure 10.2).

NOTE

The syntax and options of the ALTER TABLE command might differ among different vendors' implementations of SQL, particularly when dealing with constraints. Also, the actual use and definitions of constraints might vary, but the concept of referential integrity is the same with all relational databases that are ANSI-compliant.

10

FIGURE 10.2
The foreign key constraint.

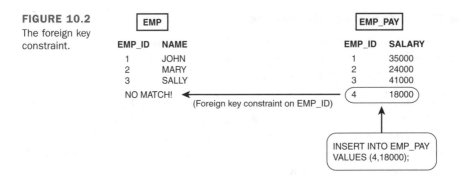

(Foreign key constraint on EMP_ID)

Check Constraints

Check constraints can be utilized to check the validity of data entered into particular columns of a table. Check constraints also are used to provide back-end database edits, although edits are commonly found in the front-end application as well. General edits restrict values that can be entered into columns or objects, whether within the database itself or on a window application. The check constraint is a way of providing another protective layer for the data. As with the FOREIGN KEY constraint, the CHECK CONSTRAINT is not a functioning part of the MySQL implementation unless you use the InnoDB option for your database. The syntax works, but only to make the CREATE TABLE syntax compatible with other vendors of SQL.

The following example illustrates the use of a check constraint:

Input/Output ▼

```
CREATE TABLE EMP
(EMP_ID          CHAR(9)          NOT NULL     PRIMARY KEY,
 EMP_NAME        VARCHAR2(40)     NOT NULL,
 ADDRESS         VARCHAR2(20)     NOT NULL,
 CITY            VARCHAR2(15)     NOT NULL,
 STATE           CHAR(2)          NOT NULL,
 ZIP             NUMBER(5)        NOT NULL,
 PHONE           NUMBER(10),
 CONSTRAINT CHK_EMP_ZIP CHECK ( ZIP = '46234'));
Table created.

mysql> CREATE TABLE EMP
    -> (EMP_ID          CHAR(9)          NOT NULL     PRIMARY KEY,
    -> EMP_NAME         VARCHAR(40)      NOT NULL,
    -> ADDRESS          VARCHAR(20)      NOT NULL,
    -> CITY             VARCHAR(15)      NOT NULL,
    -> STATE            CHAR(2)          NOT NULL,
    -> ZIP              NUMERIC(5)       NOT NULL,
    -> PHONE            NUMERIC(10),
    -> CONSTRAINT CHK_EMP_ZIP CHECK ( ZIP = '46234'));
Query OK, 0 rows affected (0.05 sec)
```

The check constraint in this table has been placed on the ZIP column, ensuring that all employees entered into this table have a ZIP Code of 46234. All right, perhaps that is a little restricting, but nevertheless, you can see how it works.

If you wanted to use a check constraint to verify that the ZIP Code is within a list of values, your constraint definition could look like this:

Syntax ▼

```
CONSTRAINT CHK_EMP_ZIP CHECK (ZIP in ('46234','46227','46745') );
```

If there is a minimum pay rate that can be designated for an employee, you could have a constraint that looks like this:

Input/Output ▼

```
CREATE TABLE EMP_PAY
(EMP_ID          CHAR(9)         NOT NULL,
 POSITION        VARCHAR2(15)    NOT NULL,
 PAY_RATE        NUMBER(4,2)     NOT NULL,
 FOREIGN KEY EMP_ID_FK (EMP_ID) REFERENCES EMP (EMP_ID),
 CONSTRAINT CHK_PAY CHECK ( PAY_RATE> 12.50 ) );

Table created.
```

10

In this example, any employee entered into this table must be paid more than $12.50 an hour. You can use just about any condition in a check constraint, as you can with a SQL query.

Managing Constraints

How do you manage constraints in a database? First, you must understand the relationship between tables in your database. What are the dependencies? What columns depend on other columns? Can a column contain a NULL value, or must it contain data? Is there a list of allowed values for each column? How are the tables accessed by an application?

You should spend a lot of time upfront in the design phase of your database to ensure that you have a good, sound structure. After you have created your database, you must understand how the tables are related and know what constraints are in the database. If you do not know what all of the constraints are in your database (and you probably won't if your database is very big), you can always find that information in the database's system catalog.

Later in this section, we show you a couple of reports that mine information from Oracle's data dictionary to present a nice report showing primary key/foreign key constraints and their relationships with one another.

Using the Right Order

When you create tables with constraints using the CREATE TABLE command or add constraints to tables with the ALTER TABLE command, referential integrity constraints must be specified in the correct order. For example, you must define a primary key before you can define a foreign key that references that primary key.

Likewise, when you drop a table using the DROP TABLE command or drop a constraint using the ALTER TABLE DROP command, you must remove constraints in the appropriate order. Some implementations, such as Oracle, allow you to drop a table and all related constraints using the command DROP TABLE table_name CASCADE CONSTRAINTS. You cannot drop a primary key constraint from a table if that primary key is being referenced by some foreign key. You must drop all associated foreign key constraints before dropping a primary key on a table. Likewise, you cannot drop a table that has a primary key referenced by a foreign key in another table.

The same concept applies to data. You cannot create a child record unless there is a parent record. You cannot delete a parent record unless all child records are deleted first. Study Figure 10.3.

FIGURE 10.3
Deleting records that are part of a parent/child relationship.

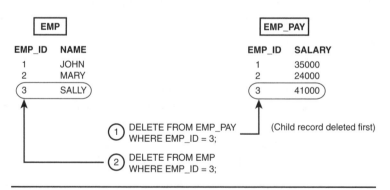

Figure 10.3 shows two things: the order in which parent/child records must be deleted, and what would happen if there was no foreign key constraint, and thus general employee data was deleted before employee pay data. Notice, in the bottom part of the figure, that there would be no name associated with the salary of employee number 3.

Different Approaches to Creating Constraints

There are basically two ways to create and drop constraints on your tables. One way is to specify constraint definitions in the CREATE TABLE statement; the other way is to specify a constraint definition on a table using the ALTER TABLE command. Both methods are fine; some users just prefer one over the other.

We normally stick all constraint definitions in the CREATE TABLE statement, particularly for small databases. Sometimes for large databases, we create the table first, and then add the constraints to tables using the ALTER TABLE command. It really doesn't matter; just try to be consistent with each database.

10

NOTE It is always a good idea to maintain the scripts that were used to create your tables, constraints, indexes, and all other database objects. These scripts often come in handy if you need to re-create the database, or replicate the database in another environment. (Although the code can be reverse-engineered from the database's system catalog, this can be a time-consuming process.)

Example Oracle Referential Integrity Reports

In this section, we show how you might use a SQL query to derive information from the database about your table relationships according to *referential integrity* (primary keys and foreign keys that you have set up in your database). The two reports listed contain the same information, but one report is grouped by parent tables, whereas the other report is grouped by child tables.

These queries were written using Oracle's SQL*Plus. Note that some of the commands used in this code might not be available in some implementations of SQL, such as the SET, COL, and BREAK ON commands. The query itself should be basically the same in any other implementation (SELECT, FROM, WHERE, and so on).

Referential Integrity Report by Child Table

The following code is an Oracle SQL*Plus script that reports referential integrity constraints by a child table. The child table is listed first, followed by a listing of all the
tables that each child table references.

Input/Output ▼

```
set linesize 110
tti 'REFERENTIAL INTEGRITY REPORT BY TABLE'
col table_name head 'CHILD TABLE' for a20
col column_name head 'FOREIGN KEY' for a20
col constraint_name head 'CONSTRAINT' for a20
col rtbl head 'PARENT TABLE' for a20
col rcol head 'PRIMARY KEY' for a20
break on report on table_name skip 1
spool test.lst
select c.table_name, cc.column_name, c.constraint_name,
       r.table_name rtbl, r.column_name rcol
from user_constraints c,
     user_cons_columns cc,
     user_cons_columns r
where c.constraint_name = cc.constraint_name
  and c.r_constraint_name = r.constraint_name
  and c.constraint_type = 'R'
order by 1,2
/
spool off
```

```
REFERENTIAL INTEGRITY REPORT BY TABLE

CHILD TABLE      FOREIGN KEY      CONSTRAINT           PARENT TABLE      PRIMARY KEY
---------------  ---------------  -------------------  ----------------  ------------
ACCT_PAY         PROD_ID          AP_PROD_ID_FK        PRODUCTS          PROD_ID
                 VEND_ID          AP_VEND_ID_FK        VENDORS           VEND_ID

ACCT_REC         ORD_NO           AR_ORD_NO_FK         ORDERS            ORD_NO

CUST_PROFILE     CUST_ID          CP_CUST_ID_FK        CUST              CUST_ID
                 EDUC_ID          CP_EDUC_ID_FK        EDUCATION_CODES   EDUC_ID

EMP_PAY          DEPT_ID          EPAY_DEPT_ID_FK      DEPARTMENTS       DEPT_ID
                 EDUC_ID          EPAY_EDUC_ID_FK      EDUCATION_CODES   EDUC_ID
                 EID              EPAY_EID_FK          EMP               EID
                 MGR_ID           EPAY_MGR_ID_FK       EMP               EID
                 POSITION_ID      EPAY_POS_ID_FK       POSITIONS         POSITION_ID

INVENTORY        PROD_ID          INV_PROD_ID_FK       PRODUCTS          PROD_ID

ORDERS           CUST_ID          ORDERS_CUST_ID_FK    CUST              CUST_ID
                 PROD_ID          ORDERS_PROD_ID_FK    PRODUCTS          PROD_ID
```

PRODUCTS	VEND_ID	VEND_ID_FK	VENDORS	VEND_ID
RETURNS	CUST_ID	RETURNS_CUST_ID_FK	CUST	CUST_ID
	ORD_NO	RETURNS_ORD_NO_FK	ORDERS	ORD_NO
STOCK_INV	PROD_ID	STOCK_PROD_ID_FK	PRODUCTS	PROD_ID

Analysis ▼

In the output from this query, notice that the leftmost column is the child table. Each child table should have one or more foreign key constraints. The foreign keys for each child table reference a primary key in a parent table. For example, look at the row where the child table is the PRODUCTS table. The column defined as the foreign key in the PRODUCTS table is the VEND_ID column. The name of the foreign key constraint is VEND_ID_FK. (Remember that constraints are objects that are stored in the database, as are tables.)

The parent table is the VENDORS table. The parent column in the parent table is the VEND_ID column. This means that the VEND_ID in the PRODUCTS table references the VEND_ID column in the VENDORS table. In other words, in order for a product to be assigned to a particular vendor in the PRODUCTS table, there must first be a record for that vendor in the VENDORS table.

10

Referential Integrity Report by Parent Table

The following code is an Oracle SQL*Plus script that reports referential integrity constraints by parent table. The parent table is listed first, followed by a listing of all the tables that reference the parent table.

Input/Output ▼

```
set linesize 110
tti 'REFERENTIAL INTEGRITY REPORT BY TABLE'
col rtbl head 'PARENT TABLE' for a20
col rcol head 'PRIMARY KEY' for a20
col table_name head 'CHILD TABLE' for a20
col column_name head 'FOREIGN KEY' for a20
col constraint_name head 'CONSTRAINT' for a20
break on report on rtbl skip 1
spool test.lst
select r.table_name rtbl, r.column_name rcol,
       c.table_name, c.column_name, c.constraint_name
from user_constraints c,
    user_cons_columns cc,
    user_cons_columns r
```

```
where c.constraint_name = cc.constraint_name
  and c.r_constraint_name = r.constraint_name
  and c.constraint_type = 'R'
order by 1,2
/
spool off
```

REFERENTIAL INTEGRITY REPORT BY TABLE

PARENT TABLE	PRIMARY KEY	CHILD TABLE	FOREIGN KEY	CONSTRAINT
CUST	CUST_ID	CUST_PROFILE	CUST_ID	CP_CUST_ID_FK
	CUST_ID	ORDERS	CUST_ID	ORDERS_CUST_ID_FK
	CUST_ID	RETURNS	CUST_ID	RETURNS_CUST_ID_FK
DEPARTMENTS	DEPT_ID	EMP_PAY	DEPT_ID	EPAY_DEPT_ID_FK
EDUCATION_CODES	EDUC_ID	CUST_PROFILE	EDUC_ID	CP_EDUC_ID_FK
	EDUC_ID	EMP_PAY	EDUC_ID	EPAY_EDUC_ID_FK
EMP	EID	EMP_PAY	EID	EPAY_EID_FK
	EID	EMP_PAY	MGR_ID	EPAY_MGR_ID_FK
ORDERS	ORD_NO	ACCT_REC	ORD_NO	AR_ORD_NO_FK
	ORD_NO	RETURNS	ORD_NO	RETURNS_ORD_NO_FK
POSITIONS	POSITION_ID	EMP_PAY	POSITION_ID	EPAY_POS_ID_FK
PRODUCTS	PROD_ID	ACCT_PAY	PROD_ID	AP_PROD_ID_FK
PRODUCTS	PROD_ID	INVENTORY	PROD_ID	INV_PROD_ID_FK
	PROD_ID	ORDERS	PROD_ID	ORDERS_PROD_ID_FK
	PROD_ID	STOCK_INV	PROD_ID	STOCK_PROD_ID_FK
VENDORS	VEND_ID	ACCT_PAY	VEND_ID	AP_VEND_ID_FK
	VEND_ID	PRODUCTS	VEND_ID	VEND_ID_FK

Analysis ▼

This report is basically the same as the previous report, except we show the parent table first, and the report is grouped by the parent table information. This report is useful if you want to see all of the tables having columns (foreign keys) that depend on the parent table column (primary key). For example, if you find the row in the output for the PRODUCTS table in the leftmost column, you will see that there are four different tables that have columns dependent on the PROD_ID column in the PRODUCTS table. Before an order can be placed on a product, the product must first exist. Before we keep inventory on a product, a record in the PRODUCTS table must first exist. We think you get the point.

Summary

In this lesson we talked about creating and managing constraints in a relational database. A constraint is an object created in the database that places rules on data stored in columns, and enforces these rules to protect your data. For example, if you try to insert data into a table column and the data does not follow the rules specified by the constraint, the database will not allow the violating data to be stored in the column.

We also talked about several different types of constraints. One was the primary key, which is a combination of one or more columns that make every row of data in a table unique. The unique constraint also ensures uniqueness of data in a table just like the primary key constraint. You can only have one primary key constraint on a table (remember that a primary key can be defined by more than one column), but may have many unique constraints.

A foreign key constraint is a constraint that references a primary key constraint in another table. The foreign key constraint makes sure that data exists in the referenced primary key column before data is allowed in the column with the foreign key constraint. A NOT NULL constraint simply disallows the existence of NULL values in a table column. Finally, a check constraint makes sure that the data entered into a column is found in a list specified in the check constraint definition.

10

NOTE

> Normally, a foreign key is a column that references a primary key in another table. However, a foreign key constraint might also reference a column in the same table.

Q&A

Q **Can constraints cause problems when importing data into a database?**

A Yes, constraints are often violated when trying to import data, say, from one database into another. You might want to disable constraints before the import and then enable the constraints after the import. Keep in mind, though, that if there is data in a table that violates a disabled constraint, the constraint cannot be enabled. You have to fix the data, remove duplicate records, or whatever is required first, and then enable the constraint.

Q **Can you have more than one column in a table that makes up a primary key?**

A Yes, multiple columns can be used to define the primary key for a table. The combination of the columns that define the primary key must be a unique value for every row of data in the table.

Q **Do constraints and referential concepts apply to MySQL?**

A Yes and no. Later versions of MySQL have the capability to accept referential integrity constraints. For instance, with newer versions of MySQL you can use the InnoDB type of database in order to fully implement referential integrity within your system. You need to check your particular version's documentation to see what is supported.

Workshop

The Workshop provides quiz questions to help solidify your understanding of the material covered, as well as exercises to provide you with experience in using what you have learned. Try to answer the quiz and exercise questions before checking the answers in Appendix A, "Answers."

Quiz

1. Is there a limit to the number of columns in a table that can be defined as unique?
2. What does a check constraint do?
3. When inserting data into the database, which record must be inserted first, the parent or the child?
4. When deleting data from the database, which record must be deleted first, the parent or the child?

Exercises

1. You created the CUST, STOCK, and MEDIA tables in the previous lesson. Perform the DESCRIBE command on each of these tables. Next, determine which columns should be a primary key and which should be a foreign key in each table.
2. Using the ALTER TABLE statement, create a primary key on the appropriate columns you have identified as requiring one.
3. Alter the CUST table by adding a foreign key constraint on the STOCK_ID column. Have the constraint reference the appropriate column in the appropriate table.
4. Create a check constraint for the following table that will accept only the values M for male and F for female.
   ```
   SEX_CODES
   sex  char(1)
   ```

LESSON 11
Manipulating Data

In this lesson, we discuss data manipulation. By the end of this lesson, you should understand

- How to manipulate data using the INSERT, UPDATE, and DELETE commands

- The importance of using the WHERE clause when you are manipulating data

- The basics of importing and exporting data from foreign data sources

Introducing Data-Manipulation Statements

Up to this point, you have learned how to retrieve data from a database using every selection criterion imaginable. After this data is retrieved, you can use it in an application program or edit it. Part 1 focused on retrieving data. However, you might have wondered how to enter data into the database in the first place. You might also be wondering what to do with data that has been edited. In this lesson, we discuss three SQL statements that enable you to manipulate the data within a database's table. The three statements are as follows:

- INSERT
- UPDATE
- DELETE

You might have used a PC-based product such as Access, dBASE IV, or FoxPro to enter your data in the past. These products come packaged with excellent tools to enter, edit, and delete records from databases. One reason that SQL provides data-manipulation statements is that it is primarily used within application programs that enable the user to edit the data using the application's own tools. The SQL programmer needs to be able to return the data to the database using SQL. In addition, most large-scale database systems are not designed with the database designer or programmer in mind. Because these systems are designed to be used in high-volume, multiuser environments, the primary design emphasis is placed on the query optimizer and data retrieval engines.

Most commercial relational database systems also provide tools for importing and exporting data. This data is traditionally stored in a delimited text file format. Often a format file is stored that contains information about the table being imported. Tools such as Oracle's SQL*Loader, SQL Server's BCP (bulk copy), and Microsoft Access Import/Export are covered at the end of the lesson. Microsoft SQL Server 2005 has a tool called SQL Server Integration Services (SSIS), which provides a graphical interface to perform this kind of functionality.

Entering Data with the `INSERT` Statement

The `INSERT` statement enables you to enter data into the database. It can be broken down into two statements:

Syntax ▼

```
INSERT...VALUES
```

and

```
INSERT...SELECT
```

Entering One Record with the `INSERT...VALUES` Statement

The `INSERT...VALUES` statement enters data into a table one record at a time. It is useful for small operations that deal with just a few records. The syntax of this statement is as follows:

Syntax ▼

```
INSERT INTO table_name
(col1, col2...)
VALUES(value1, value2...)
```

The basic format of the INSERT...VALUES statement adds a record to a table using the columns you give it and the corresponding values you instruct it to add. You must follow three rules when inserting data into a table with the INSERT...VALUES statement:

- The values used must be the same data type as the fields to which they are being added.
- The data's size must be within the column's size. For instance, an 80-character string cannot be added to a 40-character column.
- The data's location in the VALUES list must correspond to the location in the column list of the column to which it is being added (that is, the first value must be entered into the first column, the second value into the second column, and so on).

Example 11.1

Assume you have a COLLECTION table that lists all the important stuff you have collected. Better yet, let's actually create the table.

Input ▼

```
SQLSQLSQLSlsls> CREATE TABLE COLLECTION
  2 (ITEM VARCHAR(20) UNIQUE,
  3 WORTH DECIMAL(5,2) NOT NULL,
  4 REMARKS VARCHAR(30));

SQL> INSERT INTO COLLECTION VALUES
  2 ('NBA ALL STAR CARDS',300,'SOME STILL IN BIKE SPOKES');

SQL> INSERT INTO COLLECTION VALUES
  2('MALIBU BARBIE',150,'TAN STILL NEEDS WORK');

SQL> INSERT INTO COLLECTION VALUES
  2 ('STAR WARS GLASS',5.5,'HANDLE CHIPPED');

SQL> INSERT INTO COLLECTION VALUES
  2('LOCK OF EX-SPOUSES HAIR',1,'HASN\'T NOTICED BALD SPOT YET');
```

11

CAUTION — Notice in the last insert statement how the quote is prefixed with the \ character. This is known as an escape character. Remember that if you need to use a quote in one of your data values that you need to prefix it with the escape character.

You can display the table's contents by writing

Input ▼

```
SQL> SELECT * FROM COLLECTION;
```

which would yield this:

Output ▼

```
ITEM                    WORTH REMARKS
--------------------    ------  ----------------------------
NBA ALL STAR CARDS        300 SOME STILL IN BIKE SPOKES
MALIBU BARBIE             150 TAN NEEDS WORK
STAR WARS GLASS          5.5 HANDLE CHIPPED
LOCK OF EX-SPOUSES HAIR    1 HASN'T NOTICED BALD SPOT YET
```

If you wanted to add a new record to this table, you would write the following:

Input ▼

```
SQL> INSERT INTO COLLECTION
  2  (ITEM, WORTH, REMARKS)
  3  VALUES('SUPERMANS CAPE', 250.00, 'TUGGED ON IT');

1 row created.
```

The preceding INSERT statement entered one row of data into the COLLECTION table. To convince yourself that this statement worked, you can execute a simple SELECT statement to verify the insertion:

Input/Output ▼

```
SQL> SELECT * FROM COLLECTION;

ITEM                    WORTH REMARKS
--------------------    ------  ----------------------------
NBA ALL STAR CARDS        300 SOME STILL IN BIKE SPOKES
MALIBU BARBIE             150 TAN NEEDS WORK
STAR WARS GLASS          5.5 HANDLE CHIPPED
LOCK OF SPOUSES HAIR       1 HASN'T NOTICED BALD SPOT YET
SUPERMANS CAPE           250 TUGGED ON IT
```

The INSERT statement does not require column names. If the column names are not entered, SQL lines up the values with their corresponding column numbers. In other words, SQL inserts the first value into the first column, the second value into the second column, and so on.

Example 11.2

The following statement inserts the values into the table from Example 11.1:

Input/Output ▼

```
SQL> INSERT INTO COLLECTION VALUES
  2  ('STRING',1000.00,'SOME DAY IT WILL BE VALUABLE');

1 row created.
```

By issuing the same SELECT statement as you did in Example 11.1, you can verify that the insertion worked as expected:

Input/Output ▼

```
SQL> SELECT * FROM COLLECTION;

ITEM                    WORTH REMARKS
-------------------- --------- -----------------------------
NBA ALL STAR CARDS        300 SOME STILL IN BIKE SPOKES
MALIBU BARBIE             150 TAN NEEDS WORK
STAR WARS GLASS          5.5  HANDLE CHIPPED
LOCK OF SPOUSES HAIR        1 HASN'T NOTICED BALD SPOT YET
SUPERMANS CAPE           250 TUGGED ON IT
STRING                  1000 SOME DAY IT WILL BE VALUABLE

6 rows selected.
```

11

Inserting NULL Values

In Lesson 9, "Creating and Maintaining Tables," you learned how to create tables using the SQL CREATE TABLE statement. Recall that when a column is created, it can have several different limitations placed upon it. One of these limitations is that the column should (or should not) be allowed to contain NULL values. A NULL value means that the value is empty. It is neither a zero, in the case of an integer, nor a space, in the case of a string. Instead, no data at all exists for that record's column. If a column is defined as NOT NULL (that column is not allowed to contain a NULL value), you *must* insert a value for that column when using the INSERT statement. The INSERT is canceled if this rule is broken, and you should receive a descriptive error message concerning your error.

| CAUTION | You could insert spaces for a null column, but these spaces will be treated as a value. NULL simply means nothing is there. |

Input/Output ▼

```
SQL> insert into collection values
  2  ('SPORES MILDEW FUNGUS', 50.00, ' ');

1 row inserted.
```

Using `' '` instead of NULL inserted a space in the COLLECTION table. You then can select the space.

Input/Output ▼

```
SQL> select * from collection
  2  where remarks = ' ';

ITEM                    WORTH    REMARKS
SPORES MILDEW FUNGUS    50.00

1 row selected.
```

The resulting answer comes back as if a NULL is there. With the output of character fields, it is impossible to tell the difference between a null value and a mere space.

Assume the column REMARKS in the preceding table has been defined as NOT NULL. Typing

Input/Output ▼

```
SQL> INSERT INTO COLLECTION
  2  VALUES('SPORES MILDEW FUNGUS',50.00,NULL);
```

produces the following error:

Output ▼

```
INSERT INTO COLLECTION
          *
ERROR at line 1:
ORA-01400: mandatory (NOT NULL) column is missing or NULL during insert
```

NOTE

> Notice the syntax. Number data types do not require quotes; NULL does not require quotes; Character data types do require quotes.

Inserting Unique Values

Many database management systems also allow you to create a UNIQUE column attribute. This attribute means that within the current table, the values within this column must be completely unique and cannot appear more than once. This limitation can cause problems when inserting or updating values into an existing table, as the following exchange demonstrates:

Input/Output ▼

```
SQL> INSERT INTO COLLECTION VALUES('STRING', 50, 'MORE STRING');

INSERT INTO COLLECTION VALUES('STRING', 50, 'MORE STRING')
              *
ERROR at line 1:
ORA-00001: unique constraint (PERKINS.UNQ_COLLECTION_ITEM) violated
```

In this example you tried to insert another ITEM called STRING into the COLLECTION table. Because this table was created with ITEM as a unique value, it returned the appropriate error. ANSI SQL does not offer a solution to this problem, but several commercial implementations include extensions that would allow you to use something like the following:

Syntax ▼

```
if not exists (select * from COLLECTION WHERE NAME = 'STRING')

INSERT INTO COLLECTION VALUES('STRING', 50, 'MORE STRING');
```

This particular example is supported in the Sybase system.

A properly normalized table should have a unique, or *key*, field. This field is useful for joining data between tables, and it often improves the speed of your queries when using indexes. (See Lesson 15, "Creating Indexes on Tables to Improve Performance.")

11

> **NOTE**
>
> Here's an example of an INSERT statement that inserts a new employee into a table:
>
> ### Input ▼
>
> ```
> SQL> insert into employee_tbl values
>       ('300500177', 'SMITHH', 'JOHN');
>
> 1 row inserted.
> ```

After pressing Enter, you notice that you misspelled SMITH. Not to fret! It can be corrected. In some implementations, all you have to do is issue the ROLLBACK command and the row will not be inserted. See Lesson 14, "Controlling Transactions," for more on the ROLLBACK command.

Entering Multiple Records with the INSERT...SELECT Statement

The INSERT...VALUES statement is useful when adding single records to a database table, but it obviously has limitations. Would you like to use it to add 25,000 records to a table? In situations like this, the INSERT...SELECT statement is more beneficial, as it enables the programmer to copy information from a table or group of tables into another table. You will want to use this statement in several situations. *Lookup tables* are often created for performance gains and can contain data that is spread out across multiple tables in multiple databases. Because multiple-table joins are slower to process than simple queries, it is much quicker to execute a SELECT query against a lookup table than to execute a long, complicated joined query. Lookup tables are often stored on the client machines in client/server environments to reduce network traffic.

Many database systems also support *temporary tables*. Temporary tables exist for the life of your database connection and are deleted when your connection is terminated. The INSERT...SELECT statement can take the output of a SELECT statement and insert these values into a temporary table.

Here is an example in Oracle:

Input/Output ▼

```
SQL> CREATE TEMP TABLE TMP_TBL(COL1 VARCHAR(50));

SQL> INSERT INTO TMP_TBL
  2  SELECT * FROM TABLE;

19,999 rows inserted.
```

You are selecting all the rows in a table and then inserting them into tmp_tbl.

NOTE Not all database management systems support temporary tables. Check the documentation of the specific system you are using to determine whether this feature is supported.

The syntax of the `INSERT...SELECT` statement is as follows:

Syntax ▼

```
INSERT INTO table_name
(col1, col2...)
SELECT col1, col2...
FROM tablename
WHERE search_condition
```

Essentially, the output of a standard `SELECT` query is then input into a database table. The same rules that applied to the `INSERT...VALUES` statement apply to the `INSERT...SELECT` statement. To copy the contents of the `COLLECTION` table into a new table called `INVENTORY`, execute the set of statements in Example 11.3.

Example 11.3

This example creates the new table `INVENTORY`:

Input/Output ▼

```
SQL> CREATE TABLE INVENTORY
  2  (ITEM CHAR(20),
  3  COST NUMBER,
  4  ROOM CHAR(20),
  5  REMARKS CHAR(40));

Table created.
```

11

The following `INSERT` fills the new `INVENTORY` table with data from `COLLECTION`.

Input/Output ▼

```
SQL> INSERT INTO INVENTORY (ITEM, COST, REMARKS)
  2  SELECT ITEM, WORTH, REMARKS
  3  FROM COLLECTION;

6 rows created.
```

You can verify that the `INSERT` works with this `SELECT` statement:

Input/Output ▼

```
SQL> SELECT * FROM INVENTORY;

ITEM                 COST ROOM     REMARKS
-------------------- -------- -------- ----------------------------
NBA ALL STAR CARDS        300          SOME STILL IN BIKE SPOKES
MALIBU BARBIE             150          TAN NEEDS WORK
```

```
STAR WARS GLASS          5.5      HANDLE CHIPPED
LOCK OF SPOUSES HAIR       1      HASN'T NOTICED BALD SPOT YET
SUPERMANS CAPE           250      TUGGED ON IT
STRING                  1000      SOME DAY IT WILL BE VALUABLE

6 rows selected.
```

NOTE

The data appears to be in the table; however, the transaction is not finalized until a COMMIT is issued. The transaction can be committed either by issuing the COMMIT command or by simply exiting. This, however, is not true for all databases. MySQL, for example, is auto-committing, as is SQL Server by default. Please check your specific implementation's documentation for details. See Lesson 14 for more on the COMMIT command.

You have successfully, and somewhat painlessly, moved the data from the COLLECTION table to the new INVENTORY table!

The INSERT...SELECT statement requires you to follow several new rules:

- The SELECT statement cannot select rows from the table into which it is being inserted.

- The number of columns in the INSERT INTO statement must equal the number of columns returned from the SELECT statement.

- The data types of the columns in the INSERT INTO statement must be the same as the data types of the columns returned from the SELECT statement.

Another use of the INSERT...SELECT statement is to back up a table that you are going to drop, truncate, or rebuild. The process requires you to create a table and temporarily insert data that is contained in your original table into the temporary table by selecting everything from the original table. The syntax is

Syntax ▼

```
SQL> insert into copy_table
  2  select * from original_table;
```

Now you can make changes to the original table with a clear conscience.

<table>
<tr>
<td>NOTE</td>
<td>Later in this lesson, you learn how to input data into a table using data from another database format. Nearly all businesses use a variety of database formats to store data for their organizations. The applications programmer is often expected to convert these formats, and you will learn some common methods for doing just that.</td>
</tr>
</table>

Modifying Existing Data with the UPDATE Statement

The purpose of the UPDATE statement is to change the values of existing records. The syntax is

Syntax ▼

```
UPDATE table_name
SET columnname1 = value1
[, columnname2 = value2]...
WHERE search_condition
```

11

This statement checks the WHERE clause first. For all records in the given table in which the WHERE clause evaluates to TRUE, the corresponding value is updated.

Example 11.4

This example illustrates the use of the UPDATE statement:

Input/Output ▼

```
SQL> UPDATE COLLECTION
  2   SET WORTH = 900
  3   WHERE ITEM = 'STRING';

1 row updated.
```

To confirm the change, the query

Input/Output ▼

```
SQL> SELECT * FROM COLLECTION
  2   WHERE ITEM = 'STRING';
```

yields

```
ITEM                    WORTH REMARKS
--------------------    --------- -----------------------------
STRING                        900 SOME DAY IT WILL BE VALUABLE
```

Here is a multiple-column update:

Input/Output ▼

```
SQL> update collection
  2   set worth = 900, item = 'ball'
  3   where item = 'STRING';

1 row updated.
```

> **NOTE**
>
> Your implementation might use a different syntax for multiple-row updates.
>
> Notice in the set that 900 does not have quotes because it is a Numeric data type. On the other hand, STRING is a Character data type, so it requires the quotes.

Example 11.5

If the WHERE clause is omitted, every record in the COLLECTION table is updated with the value given.

Input/Output ▼

```
SQL> UPDATE COLLECTION
  2   SET WORTH = 555;

6 rows updated.
```

Performing a SELECT query shows that every record in the database was updated with that value:

Input/Output ▼

```
SQL> SELECT * FROM COLLECTION;

ITEM                    WORTH REMARKS
--------------------    --------- -----------------------------
NBA ALL STAR CARDS            555 SOME STILL IN BIKE SPOKES
MALIBU BARBIE                 555 TAN NEEDS WORK
```

```
STAR WARS GLASS              555 HANDLE CHIPPED
LOCK OF SPOUSES HAIR         555 HASN'T NOTICED BALD SPOT YET
SUPERMANS CAPE               555 TUGGED ON IT
STRING                       555 SOME DAY IT WILL BE VALUABLE

6 rows selected.
```

You, of course, should check whether the column you are updating allows for unique values only.

Some database systems provide an extension to the standard UPDATE syntax. SQL Server's Transact-SQL language, for instance, enables programmers to update the contents of a table based on the contents of several other tables using a FROM clause. The extended syntax looks like this:

Syntax ▼

```
UPDATE table_name
SET columnname1 = value1
[, columname2 = value2]...
FROM table_list
WHERE search_condition
```

Example 11.6

Here's an example of the extension:

Input ▼

```
SQL> UPDATE COLLECTION
  2   SET WORTH = WORTH * 0.05
  3   FROM INVENTORY
  4   WHERE COST = 300;
```

This changes the table to the following:

Input/Output ▼

```
SQL> SELECT * FROM COLLECTION;

ITEM                 WORTH REMARKS
-------------------- --------- -----------------------------
NBA ALL STAR CARDS   2.775 SOME STILL IN BIKE SPOKES
MALIBU BARBIE         555 TAN NEEDS WORK
STAR WARS GLASS       555 HANDLE CHIPPED
LOCK OF SPOUSES HAIR  555 HASN'T NOTICED BALD SPOT YET
SUPERMANS CAPE        555 TUGGED ON IT
STRING                555 SOME DAY IT WILL BE VALUABLE
```

11

Notice that the worth of NBA ALL STAR CARDS has changed to 2.775.

This syntax is useful when the contents of one table need to be updated following the manipulation of the contents of several other tables. Keep in mind that this syntax is non-standard and that you need to consult the documentation for your particular database management system before you use it.

The UPDATE statement can also update columns based on the result of an arithmetic expression. When using this technique, remember that the data type of the result must be the same as the data type of the field being modified. Also, the size of the value must fit within the size of the field that is being modified.

Two problems can result from the use of calculated values: truncation and overflow. *Truncation* results when the database system converts a fractional number to an integer, for instance. *Overflow* happens when the resulting value is larger than the capacity of the modified column, which will cause an error to be returned by your database system.

NOTE	Some database systems handle the overflow problem for you. Oracle 11 converts the number to exponential notation and presents the number that way. You should keep this potential error in mind when using Number data types.

TIP	If you update a column(s) and notice an error after you run the update, issue the ROLLBACK command, if it's supported, (as you would for an incorrect INSERT statement) to void the update. See Lesson 14 for more on the ROLLBACK command.

Removing Information with the DELETE Statement

In addition to adding data to a database, you will also need to delete data from a database. The syntax for the DELETE statement is

Syntax ▼

```
DELETE FROM tablename
WHERE condition
```

The first thing you will probably notice about the DELETE command is that it doesn't have a confirmation prompt. Users are accustomed to being prompted for assurance when, for instance, a directory or file is deleted at the operating system level. Are you sure? (Y/N) is a common question asked before the operation is performed. Using SQL, when you instruct the database management system (DBMS) to delete a group of records from a table, it obeys your command without asking. That is, when you tell SQL to delete a group of records, it will really do it!

In Lesson 14, you will learn about transaction control. Transactions are database operations that enable programmers to either COMMIT or ROLLBACK changes to the database. These operations are very useful with online transaction-processing applications in which you want to execute a batch of modifications to the database in one logical execution. Data integrity problems will occur if operations are performed while other users are modifying the data at the same time. For now, assume that no transactions are being undertaken.

NOTE In some implementations, for example, Oracle, a COMMIT command is automatically issued when you exit SQL. In others, such as MySQL, a COMMIT is automatically issued unless a command is specifically wrapped in a transaction.

11

Depending on the use of the DELETE statement's WHERE clause, SQL can do the following:

- Delete single rows
- Delete multiple rows
- Delete all rows
- Delete no rows

Here are several points to remember when using the DELETE statement:

- The DELETE statement cannot delete an individual field's values (use UPDATE instead). The DELETE statement deletes entire records from a single table.
- Like INSERT and UPDATE, deleting records from one table can cause referential integrity problems within other tables. Keep this potential problem area in mind when modifying data within a database.
- Using the DELETE statement deletes only records, not the table itself. Use the DROP TABLE statement (see Lesson 9) to remove an entire table.

Example 11.7

This example shows you how to delete all the records from COLLECTION where WORTH is less than 275:

Input/Output ▼

```
SQL> DELETE FROM COLLECTION
  2  WHERE WORTH < 275;

4 rows deleted.
```

The result is a table that looks like this:

Input/Output ▼

```
SQL> SELECT * FROM COLLECTION;

ITEM                   WORTH REMARKS
-------------------- --------- ----------------------------
MALIBU BARBIE            555 TAN NEEDS WORK
STAR WARS GLASS          555 HANDLE CHIPPED
LOCK OF SPOUSES HAIR     555 HASN'T NOTICED BALD SPOT YET
SUPERMANS CAPE           555 TUGGED ON IT
STRING                   555 SOME DAY IT WILL BE VALUABLE
```

> **CAUTION**
>
> Like the UPDATE statement, if you omit a WHERE clause from the DELETE statement, all rows in that particular table will be deleted.

Example 11.8 uses all three data-manipulation statements to perform a set of database operations.

Example 11.8

This example inserts some new rows into the COLLECTION table you used earlier in this lesson:

Input/Output ▼

```
SQL> INSERT INTO COLLECTION
  2  VALUES('CHIA PET', 5,'WEDDING GIFT');

1 row created.
SQL> INSERT INTO COLLECTION
  2  VALUES('TRS MODEL III', 50, 'FIRST COMPUTER');

1 row created.
```

Now create a new table and copy this data to it:

Input/Output ▼

```
SQL> CREATE TABLE TEMP
  2    (NAME CHAR(20),
  3    VALUE NUMBER,
  4    REMARKS CHAR(40));

Table created.
SQL> INSERT INTO TEMP(NAME, VALUE, REMARKS)
  2    SELECT ITEM, WORTH, REMARKS
  3    FROM COLLECTION;

4 rows created.

SQL> SELECT * FROM TEMP;

NAME                    VALUE REMARKS
-------------------- --------- --------------------------------
ITEM                    WORTH REMARKS
-------------------- --------- --------------------------------
MALIBU BARBIE             555 TAN NEEDS WORK
STAR WARS GLASS           555 HANDLE CHIPPED
LOCK OF SPOUSES HAIR      555 HASN'T NOTICED BALD SPOT YET
SUPERMANS CAPE            555 TUGGED ON IT
STRING                    555 SOME DAY IT WILL BE VALUABLE


CHIA PET                    5 WEDDING GIFT
TRS MODEL III              50 FIRST COMPUTER
```

Now change some values:

Input/Output ▼

```
SQL> UPDATE TEMP
  2    SET VALUE = 100
  3    WHERE NAME = 'TRS MODEL III';

1 row updated.
SQL> UPDATE TEMP
  2    SET VALUE = 8
  3    WHERE NAME = 'CHIA PET';

1 row updated.

SQL> SELECT * FROM TEMP;
```

11

```
NAME                      VALUE REMARKS
------------------- --------- ----------------------------
NBA ALL STAR CARDS          300 SOME STILL IN BIKE SPOKES
STRING                     1000 SOME DAY IT WILL BE VALUABLE
CHIA PET                      8 WEDDING GIFT
TRS MODEL III               100 FIRST COMPUTER
```

And update these values back to the original table. The first step is to delete the four rows in the COLLECTION table, and then do the INSERT into the COLLECTION table:

Input/Output ▼

```
SQL> DELETE FROM COLLECTION;

4 rows deleted.
SQL> INSERT INTO COLLECTION
  2 SELECT * FROM TEMP;
SQL> DROP TABLE TEMP;
```

The DROP TABLE and CREATE TABLE statements are discussed on Lesson 9. Recall that CREATE TABLE builds a new table with the format you give it, and DROP TABLE deletes the table. Keep in mind that DROP TABLE permanently removes a table, whereas DELETE FROM *tablename* removes only the records from a table.

To check what you have done, select the records from the COLLECTION table. You will see that the changes you made now exist in the COLLECTION table.

Input/Output ▼

```
SQL>SELECT * FROM COLLECTION;

NAME                      VALUE REMARKS
------------------- --------- ----------------------------
NBA ALL STAR CARDS          300 SOME STILL IN BIKE SPOKES
STRING                     1000 SOME DAY IT WILL BE VALUABLE
CHIA PET                      8 WEDDING GIFT
TRS MODEL III               100 FIRST COMPUTER
```

The previous example used all three data-manipulation commands—INSERT, UPDATE, and DELETE—to perform a set of operations on a table. The DELETE statement is the easiest of the three to use.

CAUTION

Always keep in mind that any modifications can affect the referential integrity of your database. Think through all your database-editing steps to make sure that you have updated all the tables correctly.

Importing and Exporting Data from Foreign Sources

The INSERT, UPDATE, and DELETE statements are extremely useful from within a database program. They are used with the SELECT statement to provide the foundation for all other database operations you will perform. However, SQL as a language does not have a way to import or export data from foreign data sources.

For example, assume that your office might have been using a dBASE application for several years that has outgrown itself. Now your manager wants to convert this application to a client/server application using the Oracle relational DBMS (RDBMS). Unfortunately for you, these dBASE files contain thousands of records that must be converted to an Oracle database. Obviously, the INSERT, UPDATE, and DELETE commands will help you after your Oracle database has been populated, but you would rather quit than retype 300,000 records. Fortunately, Oracle and other manufacturers provide tools that can assist you in this task.

Nearly all database systems allow you to import and export data using ASCII text file formats. Although the SQL language does not include this feature, SQL will not do you (or your boss) much good when you have an empty database. We will examine the import/export tools available in the following products: Microsoft Access, Microsoft and Sybase SQL Server, and Personal Oracle.

11

Microsoft Access

Microsoft Access is a PC-only database product that contains many of the features of an RDBMS. Access also includes powerful reporting tools, a macro language similar to Visual Basic, and the capability to import and export data from various database and text file formats. This section examines this last feature, particularly the capability to export to delimited text files. *Delimited* means that each field is separated, or delimited, by some special character. This character is often a tab, comma, quotation mark, or space.

Access allows you to import and export various database formats, including dBASE, FoxPro, and SQL Database. The SQL Database option is actually an Open Database Connectivity (ODBC) data source connection.

After opening an Access database (with File, Open), select the table or view, right-click, select Export, then select a Destination type such as Microsoft Excel. A Destination dialog box (for Exporting) is displayed. Enter in the destination file location in the top most textbox. The boxes below the textbox allow you to select several options such as preserving the formatting or opening the export file once the process has completed. The Import/Export Setup dialog box is shown in Figure 11.1.

FIGURE 11.1
The Import/Export
Setup dialog box.

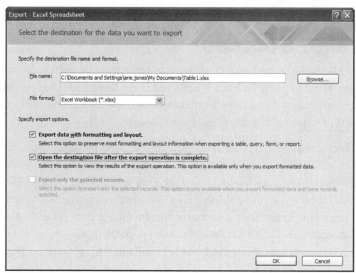

Notice that in this dialog box, you can select the Text Delimiter and the Field Separator for your export file. As a final step, save the specification for use later. This specification is stored internally within the database.

Microsoft SQL Server

Microsoft and Sybase have jointly developed a powerful database system that is very popular in client/server application development. The name of this system is SQL Server. Microsoft has agreed to develop versions of the RDBMS for some platforms, and Sybase has developed its version for all the other platforms. Although the arrangement has ended, we mention this agreement here to help you avoid confusion when you begin examining the various database systems available on the market today.

SQL Server provides file import/export capabilities with the BCP tool. BCP is short for *bulk copy*. The basic concept behind BCP is the same as that behind Microsoft Access. Unfortunately, the BCP tool is not graphical in nature. You must issue commands from the operating system command prompt, instead of through dialog boxes or windows.

BCP imports and exports fixed-width text files. It is possible to export a file using the Microsoft Access method described earlier and then import that same file directly into a SQL Server table using BCP. BCP uses format files (usually with an .FMT extension) to store the import specification. This specification tells BCP the column names, field widths, and field delimiters. You can run BCP from within a SQL database build script to completely import data after the database has been built.

Microsoft SQL Server also provides a graphical interface for doing import/export routines named SQL Server Integration Services (SSIS). This platform provides wizards for most import/export scenarios, as well as a development platform to create more extensive ETL processes.

Oracle

Oracle allows you to import and export data from ASCII text files containing delimited or fixed-length records. The tool you use is SQL*Loader. This graphical tool uses a control file (with the .CTL extension). This file is similar to SQL Server's format (FMT) file. The information contained in this file tells SQL*Loader what it needs to know to load the data from the file.

The SQL*Loader dialog box appears in Figure 11.2.

FIGURE 11.2
The SQL*Loader
dialog box.

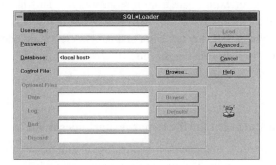

11

MySQL

Like many other SQL implementations, MySQL allows you to import and export data from and to ASCII text files containing delimited or fixed-length records. There is a MySQL tool called mysqlimport that allows data to be read from a text file and loaded into database tables. Data can be exported using the MySQL tool called mysqldump. Data can also be exported into a text file using the SELECT statement to generate data based on a query.

Summary

SQL provides three statements that you can use to manipulate data within a database.

The INSERT statement has two variations. The INSERT...VALUES statement inserts a set of values into one record. The INSERT...SELECT statement is used in combination with a SELECT statement to insert multiple records into a table based on the contents of one or more tables. The SELECT statement can join multiple tables, and the results of this join can be added to another table.

The UPDATE statement changes the values of one or more columns and should be based on some condition. Otherwise you might update all rows when you only intended to update specific rows. The updated value can also be the result of an expression or calculation.

The DELETE statement is the simplest of the three statements. It deletes all rows from a table based on the result of an optional WHERE clause. If the WHERE clause is omitted, all records from the table are deleted. It is important to remember that some SQL implementations, such as Oracle, have the capability to undo or ROLLBACK your data manipulation in case of errors.

Modern database systems supply various tools for data manipulation. Some of these tools enable developers to import or export data from foreign sources. This feature is particularly useful when a database is upsized or downsized to a different system. Microsoft Access, Microsoft and Sybase SQL Server, and Personal Oracle 11 include many options that support the migration of data between systems.

Q&A

Q Does SQL have a statement for file import/export operations?

A No. Import and export are implementation-specific operations. In other words, the ANSI committee allows individual manufacturers to create whatever features or enhancements they feel are necessary.

Q Can I copy data from a table into itself using the INSERT command? I would like to make duplicate copies of all the existing records and change the value of one field.

A No. You cannot insert data into the same table that you selected from. However, you can select the original data into a temporary table, modify the data in this temporary table, and then select back into the original table. (True temporary tables are discussed in Lesson 19.) Make sure that you watch out for unique fields you might have already created.

Q I know you have stressed caution when using INSERT, UPDATE, and DELETE, but simple fixes seem to effectively correct whatever I did wrong. Is that a fair statement?

A Yes. For example, a simple way to fix a misspelled name is to issue a ROLLBACK command and redo the INSERT. But this will not work in some implementations of SQL. Another fix would be to do an update to fix the name. Or you could delete the row and redo the INSERT with the corrected spelling of the name.

But suppose you inserted a million rows into a table and didn't notice that you had misspelled a name when you issued the COMMIT command. A few weeks later, someone notices some bad data. You have had two weeks' worth of database activity. You would more than likely have to issue individual updates to make individual corrections, instead of making any type of global change. In most cases, you probably will not know what to change. You better hope your boss is understanding because you might have to perform a restore of the database.

Workshop

The Workshop provides quiz questions to help solidify your understanding of the material covered, as well as exercises to provide you with experience in using what you have learned. Try to answer the quiz and exercise questions before checking the answers in Appendix A, "Answers."

Quiz

1. What is wrong with the following statement?

```
DELETE COLLECTION;
```

2. What is wrong with the following statement?

```
INSERT INTO COLLECTION
SELECT * FROM TABLE_2;
```

11

3. What is wrong with the following statement?

```
UPDATE COLLECTION ('HONUS WAGNER CARD',
25000, 'FOUND IT');
```

4. What would happen if you issued the following statement?

```
SQL> DELETE * FROM COLLECTION;
```

5. What would happen if you issued the following statement?

```
SQL> DELETE FROM COLLECTION;
```

6. What would happen if you issued the following statement?

```
SQL> UPDATE COLLECTION
SET WORTH = 555
SET REMARKS = 'UP FROM 525';
```

7. Will the following SQL statement work?

```
SQL> INSERT INTO COLLECTION
SET VALUE = 900
WHERE ITEM = 'STRING';
```

8. Will the following SQL statement work?
```
SQL> UPDATE COLLECTION
SET VALUE = 900
WHERE ITEM = 'STRING';
```

Exercises

1. Use the DESCRIBE command to view the structure of the CHECKS table. Insert a row into the table that contains the following information:

    ```
    (0,'JETHRO TULL','225','MUSIC LESSONS')
    ```

    Now do a SELECT from the CHECKS table and view the data.

2. After viewing the data in the CHECKS table, you notice that there is a mistake in one of the entries. You decide that the REMARKS column for check number 6 might not be appropriate, so do an UPDATE to the table to correct the situation:

    ```
    (6,'CASH',25.00,'CHOIR DUES')
    ```

3. There, that should be better, shouldn't it? Just to be sure, perhaps you should do another SELECT from the CHECKS table.

4. After careful study of the CHECKS table you notice that several entries need to be corrected.

    There are two rows with check number 6. Get rid of the one you do not want.

    Your study of SQL and databases has taught you that the storage of periods (.) or other forms of punctuation in your tables is not a practical use of space. Correct this situation for check number 2.

    There is a check number listed as 0. After some research you discover that it in fact should have been check number 10. Make the correction.

    The data in the CHECKS table now seems to be okay, but you've noticed that three check numbers seem to have been skipped. After much frantic searching, you find the receipts and can now put the data into the table.

    ```
    (7,'WE B CATS',,13.42,'SCOOPER')
    (8,'JOES STALE & DENT',,4.32,'AIR FRESHENER')
    (9,'BLOOMBURGS',7.14,'CAT TOYS')
    ```

5. Check number 9 has been voided. DELETE the data associated with check number 9 from the CHECKS table.

LESSON 12
Dates and Time in SQL

In this lesson, you will learn about the nature of dates and time in SQL and how they are stored and used in a relational database. Not only will we discuss the DATETIME data type in more detail; we will show how some implementations utilize dates, explain some of the common rules, and show how to extract the date and time in a desired format. By the end of this lesson, you should understand the following about dates and time in SQL:

- How the date and time are stored

- Typical date and time formats

- How to use date functions

- How to perform date conversions

NOTE

As you know by now, there are many different implementations of SQL. In this book we use the ANSI standard and the most common nonstandard functions, commands, and operators. We are using Oracle and MySQL for most of our examples. Even in Oracle, the date can be stored in different formats. So, you must check your particular implementation for the date storage. No matter how the date and time are stored, your implementation should have functions that will convert date formats.

How Are Date and Time Values Stored?

Date and time values are stored in table columns like any other data. Dates can be stored as either a character string, or stored internally by the database in the available DATE data type format. Each implementation has a default storage format for the date and time. The default format often varies among different implementations, as do other data types for each implementation. In the following subsections, we study the standard format of the DATETIME data type and its elements. Later, we show you the data types for date and time in some popular implementations of SQL, including Oracle, Sybase, MySQL, and Microsoft SQL Server.

ANSI Standard Data Types for Date and Time

There are three standard SQL data types for date and time (DATETIME) storage, although the use of these might differ in each implementation of SQL:

- DATE
- TIME
- TIMESTAMP

Data Type	Usage
DATE	Stores date literals
TIME	Stores time literals
TIMESTAMP	Stores date and time literals

The format and range of valid values for each data type follow.

DATE

Format: YYYY-MM-DD

Range: 0001-01-01 to 9999-12-31

> YYYY = four-digit year
>
> MM = two-digit month
>
> DD = two-digit day

TIME

Format: HH:MI:SS.*nn*...

Range: 00:00:00... to 23:59:61.999...

> HH = two-digit hours
>
> MI = two-digit minutes of an hour
>
> SS = two-digit seconds of a minute

NOTE You are probably wondering why ANSI allows 61.999 seconds in a minute. The range value of seconds accounts for the possibility of leap seconds. Keep in mind that this range of date elements in particular might vary among different implementations of SQL.

TIMESTAMP

Format: YYYY-MM-DD HH:MI:SS.*nn*...

Range: 0001-01-01 00:00:00... to 9999-12-31 23:59:61.999...

DATETIME Elements

DATETIME elements are date and time elements that are included as part of a DATETIME definition. We have listed the constrained DATETIME elements and a valid range of values for each element:

YEAR	0001 to 9999
MONTH	01 to 12
DAY	01 to 31
HOUR	00 to 23
MINUTE	00 to 59
SECOND	00.000... to 61.999...

12

Notice that seconds can be represented in decimal format, allowing the expression of tenths of a second, hundredths of a second, milliseconds, and so on. These elements are self explanatory and are standard elements of time.

Implementation of Specific Data Types

As with other data types, each implementation provides its own representation and syntax. In this subsection, we show how four products (Oracle, Sybase, MySQL, and SQLBase) have implemented the date and time data types.

Product	Data Type	Use
Oracle	DATE	Stores both date and time information.
Sybase	DATETIME	Stores both date and time information.
	SMALLDATETIME	Stores both date and time information, but includes a smaller date range than DATETIME.
MySQL	DATE	Stores date information.
	DATETIME	Stores both date and time information.
	TIME	Stores time value.
	TIMESTAMP	Presents the current date and time as a string value.
	YEAR	Stores the year value.
SQLBase	DATETIME	Stores both date and time information.
	TIMESTAMP	Stores both date and time information.
	DATE	Stores a date value.
	TIME	Stores a time value.

NOTE

Each implementation has its own specific data type(s) for date and time information. However, most implementations comply with the ANSI standard because all elements of the date and time are included in their associated data types. The way the date is internally stored is specific to each implementation of SQL.

Applying Date Functions to the Query

Date functions are available in SQL, varying on each specific implementation. The syntax might vary, but the overall concept and functionality are the same. Date functions, similar to character string functions, are used to manipulate the representation of date and time data. Date functions are often used to format the output of dates and time in a more presentable format, to compare date values with one another, to compute intervals between dates, and so on.

The Current Date

You might have already wondered how you get the current date from the database. The need to retrieve the current date from the database might originate from several situations, but the current date is normally returned either to compare to a stored date, or simply to return the value of the current date as some sort of a timestamp. You might want to include the current date in a report that you generate with a SQL query, for example.

The current date is ultimately stored in the host operating system environment for the database, and is called the *system date*. The database, which interfaces with the appropriate operating system, has the capability to retrieve the system date for various uses, such as to resolve database queries.

Let us take a look at a couple of methods for deriving the system date based on commands from three different implementations (Sybase, MySQL, and Oracle).

Sybase uses a function called GETDATE() to return the system date. This function is used in a query as follows:

Syntax ▼

```
SELECT GETDATE()
```

This query would return

```
Dec 31, 1997
```

if today's date were New Year's Eve before 1998.

In MySQL you would select the current date.

Input ▼

```
mysql> select current_date;
```

12

To return

Output ▼

```
+--------------+
¦ current_date ¦
+--------------+
¦ 2002-06-09   ¦
+--------------+
1 row in set (0.00 sec)
```

Most options discussed in this book for Sybase's and Microsoft's implementations are applicable to both implementations because both use SQL Server as their database server. Both implementations also use an extension to standard SQL known as Transact-SQL, which is discussed later in the book (see Lesson 27, "An Introduction to Transact-SQL").

Oracle also has a function to derive the current date, called SYSDATE. SYSDATE is also referred to as a *pseudocolumn* because the SYSDATE can be selected from any table in the database. SYSDATE acts as any other column in a table, and thus can be selected from any table in the database, although it is not actually part of the table's definition.

To return the system date in Oracle, use the following statement:

Input ▼

```
SQL> SELECT SYSDATE FROM DUAL;
```

NOTE   In this example, we used a table in Oracle called DUAL. The DUAL table is a dummy table in Oracle that has one record. When we select the SYSDATE from DUAL, we get one row back because the DUAL table has only one row of data. You can also select SYSDATE from any other valid table.

This statement would return

Output ▼

```
SYSDATE
--------
31-DEC-98
```

if today were New Year's Eve before 1999.

Time Zones

The use of time zones might be a factor when dealing with date and time information. For instance, a time of 6:00 p.m. in the central United States does not equate to the same time in Australia, although the actual point in time is the same. Some of us who live within the daylight savings time zones are used to adjusting our clocks twice a year. If time zones are considerations when maintaining data in your case, you might find it necessary to consider time zones and perform time conversions if they are available in your SQL implementation.

The following are some common time zones and their abbreviations:

Abbreviation	Definition
AST, ADT	Atlantic standard, daylight time
BST, BDT	Bering standard, daylight time
CST, CDT	Central standard, daylight time
EST, EDT	Eastern standard, daylight time
GMT	Greenwich mean time
HST, HDT	Alaska/Hawaii standard, daylight time
MST, MDT	Mountain standard, daylight time
NST	Newfoundland standard, daylight time
PST, PDT	Pacific standard, daylight time
YST, YDT	Yukon standard, daylight time

12

NOTE Some implementations have functions that allow you to deal with different time zones; however, not all implementations might support the use of time zones. Be sure to verify the use of time zones in your particular implementation, if applicable.

Adding Time to Dates

Days, months, and other parts of time can be added to dates for the purpose of comparing one date to another, or to provide more specific conditions in the WHERE clause of a query.

Intervals can be used to add periods of time to a DATETIME value. As defined by the standard, intervals are used to manipulate the value of a DATETIME value. See the following examples:

DATE '1998-12-31' + INTERVAL '1' DAY yields '1999-01-01'

DATE '1998-12-31' + INTERVAL '1' MONTH yields '1999-01-31'

The following example shows the use of the SQL Server/MySQL function
DATEADD/DATE_ADD:

Input/Output ▼

```
SQL> SELECT DATE_HIRE, DATEADD(MONTH, 1, DATE_HIRE) ADD_MONTH
  2 FROM EMPPAY

DATE_HIRE ADD_MONTH
--------- ---------
23-MAY-89 23-JUN-89
17-JUN-90 17-JUL-90
14-AUG-94 14-SEP-94
28-JUN-97 28-JUL-97
22-JUL-96 22-AUG-96
14-JAN-91 14-FEB-91

6 rows affected.
```

In this example, we have selected the DATE_HIRE for each employee. We have also used
the function DATEADD to add one month to the DATE_HIRE for each employee.

Here is the DATE_ADD function in MySQL. Note the differences and similarities in the
syntax.

Input/Output ▼

```
mysql> select startdate, date_add(startdate, interval 1 month) "Add Month"
    -> from project;
+------------+------------+
| startdate  | Add Month  |
+------------+------------+
| 1998-04-01 | 1998-05-01 |
| 1998-04-02 | 1998-05-02 |
| 1998-05-15 | 1998-06-15 |
| 1998-06-01 | 1998-07-01 |
| 1998-07-01 | 1998-08-01 |
| 1998-09-03 | 1998-10-03 |
+------------+------------+
6 rows in set (0.00 sec)
```

Note that in the MySQL example the word INTERVAL must be stated in order for the
function to work.

NOTE	You can also use negative values to subtract an interval of time in these various ADD functions.

Input/Output ▼

```
mysql> select startdate,
    -> date_add(startdate, interval 1 month) "Add Month",
    -> date_add(startdate, interval -1 month) "Sub Month"
    -> from project;
+------------+------------+------------+
| startdate  | Add Month  | Sub Month  |
+------------+------------+------------+
| 1998-04-01 | 1998-05-01 | 1998-03-01 |
| 1998-04-02 | 1998-05-02 | 1998-03-02 |
| 1998-05-15 | 1998-06-15 | 1998-04-15 |
| 1998-06-01 | 1998-07-01 | 1998-05-01 |
| 1998-07-01 | 1998-08-01 | 1998-06-01 |
| 1998-09-03 | 1998-10-03 | 1998-08-03 |
+------------+------------+------------+
6 rows in set (0.00 sec)
```

The following example uses the Oracle function ADD_MONTHS:

Input/Output ▼

```
SELECT DATE_HIRE, ADD_MONTHS(DATE_HIRE,1) ADD_MONTH
FROM EMPPAY;

DATE_HIRE ADD_MONTH
--------- ---------
23-MAY-89 23-JUN-89
17-JUN-90 17-JUL-90
14-AUG-94 14-SEP-94
28-JUN-97 28-JUL-97
22-JUL-96 22-AUG-96
14-JAN-91 14-FEB-91

6 rows selected.
```

12

Adding one day to a date in Oracle produces this:

Input/Output ▼

```
SQL> SELECT DATE_HIRE, DATE_HIRE + 1
  2 FROM EMPLOYEE_PAY_TBL
  3 WHERE EMP_ID = '311549902';

DATE_HIRE DATE_HIRE
--------- ---------
23-MAY-89 24-MAY-89

1 row selected.
```

Here, we have selected the DATE_HIRE and added 1 (one day) to it. Notice that only one row was returned by this query. This is because we included a WHERE clause that selected a particular EMP_ID.

Notice that these examples in MySQL and Oracle, although they differ syntactically from the ANSI examples, derive their results based on the same concept described by the SQL standard.

Subtracting Dates

Dates can be subtracted from other dates to report the time period between the two dates. When a date is subtracted from another date, the number of days between the two dates is returned in decimal format. The decimal value represents part of a whole day, including hours, minutes, and seconds.

For example, study the following Oracle examples, which determine an individual's age based on the date of birth:

Input/Output ▼

```
SQL> SELECT NAME, DOB
  2 FROM BIRTH_DAYS;

NAME                            DOB
------------------------------- -----------
DANIEL                          26-JAN-1999
JACK                            15-MAR-1970
```

In this first query, we have selected the individual's name and date of birth from the BIRTH_DAYS table. Note that the SYSDATE in these examples is 01-AUG-1999.

Input/Output ▼

```
SQL> SELECT NAME, SYSDATE - DOB "DAYS OLD"
  2 FROM BIRTH_DAYS;

NAME                                 DAYS OLD
------------------------------       ----------
DANIEL                               187.587928
JACK                                 10731.5879
```

Here, we have subtracted the DOB column from SYSDATE to derive the number of days an individual has lived. Unfortunately, the number of days is not too useful to most of us. Note that the number of days is in decimal format, which accounts for the precise number of days down to the minutes and seconds.

Input/Output ▼

```
SQL> SELECT NAME, (SYSDATE - DOB)/365 "YEARS OLD"
  2  FROM BIRTH_DAYS;

NAME                                 YEARS OLD
------------------------------       ----------
DANIEL                               .513943937
JACK                                 29.4016152
```

Here, we have divided the difference between the two dates by 365 (the number of days in a year) to derive the individual's age. This query is more useful because it's now in a format familiar to us.

Input/Output ▼

```
SQL> SELECT NAME, TRUNC((SYSDATE - DOB)/365) "YEARS OLD"
  2 FROM BIRTH_DAYS;

NAME                                 YEARS OLD
------------------------------       ----------
DANIEL                                       0
JACK                                        29
```

In this example, we have used the TRUNC function to truncate the decimal value of the individual's age. Notice that Daniel is less than one year old; therefore, a zero is printed. You could also write a query to determine the number of months old if the age is less than one, as shown in the next example.

12

Input/Output ▼

```
SQL> SELECT NAME, (SYSDATE - DOB)/365 * 12 "MONTHS OLD"
   2 FROM BIRTH_DAYS
   3 WHERE (SYSDATE - DOB)/365 < 1;

NAME                            MONTHS OLD
------------------------------- ----------
DANIEL                          6.16780327
```

In this example, if anyone is less than one year old, the decimal value representing the number of years is multiplied by 12 to determine the number of months.

 NOTE   An individual's age is rarely stored in a database because the value of an individual's age is constantly changing with every day, hour, minute, and second. You should store the individual's date of birth, which remains constant. The age can always be derived based on the comparison of the date of birth and the current date.

Comparing Dates and Time Periods

A powerful standard SQL conditional operator for DATETIME values is OVERLAPS. The OVERLAPS operator is used to compare two time frames and return a Boolean value of either TRUE or FALSE, depending on whether the two time frames overlap one another.

For example, the following comparison returns the value TRUE.

```
(TIME '01:00:00' , TIME '05:59:00')
OVERLAPS
(TIME '05:00:00' , TIME '07:00:00')
```

The following returns FALSE:

```
(TIME '01:00:00' , TIME '05:59:00')
OVERLAPS
(TIME '06:00:00 , TIME '07:00:00')
```

Other Miscellaneous Date Functions

The following are some additional powerful date functions that exist in the implementations for SQL Server, MySQL, and Oracle.

SQL Server

DATEPART	Returns the integer value of a date part for a date.
DATENAME	Returns the text value of a date part for a date.
GETDATE()	Returns the system date.
DATEDIFF	Returns the difference between two dates for specified date parts, such as days, minutes, seconds, and so on.

MySQL

DATE_FORMAT	Returns the specified date in a specified format.
DAYNAME	Returns the name of the day of the week for a specified date.
QUARTER	Returns the number of the quarter of the given date.
PERIOD_DIFF	Returns the number of months between two dates that are in YYMM or YYYYMM format.

Oracle

NEXT_DAY	Returns the next day of the week as specified (for example, FRIDAY) since a given date.
MONTHS_BETWEEN	Returns the number of months between two given dates.

Converting Date Formats

12

The conversion of dates takes place for any number of reasons. Conversions are mainly used to alter the data type of values defined as DATETIME values.

Typical reasons for date conversions are

- To compare date values of different data types
- To format a date value as a character string
- To convert a character string into a date format

The ANSI CAST operator is used to convert data types into other data types. The basic syntax is

Syntax ▼

```
CAST ( EXPRESSION AS NEW_DATA_TYPE )
```

Individual implementations of SQL might use another function instead of CAST. For example, in Oracle, the TO_DATE function is used to convert a character string to a date format, and the TO_CHAR function is used to convert a value stored in a date format to a character string of your choice.

In the following subsections, we provide some implementation-specific examples of

- Date pictures
- Conversions of dates to character strings
- Conversions of character strings to dates

Date Pictures

A *date picture* is composed of formatting elements that are used to extract date and time information from the database in a desired format. Date pictures might not be available in all implementations of SQL.

Without the use of a date picture and some type of conversion function, the date and time information will be retrieved from the database in a default format, such as

```
2002-05-31
31-MAY-02
2002-05-31 23:59:01.11
...
```

If you wanted the date displayed as

```
May 31, 2002
```

you would have to convert the date from a DATETIME format into a character string format. This is accomplished by implementing specific functions for this purpose, which are further illustrated in the following parts of this section. Table 13.1 lists the common MySQL, and Oracle date pictures.

TABLE 13.1 Common MySQL and Oracle Date Pictures

Date Picture	Description
	MySQL Date Pictures
%a	Short weekday name (Sun, Mon, and so on)
%b	Short month name (Jan, Feb, and so on)
%D	Day of the month with ordinal suffix (1st, 2nd, and so on)
%d	Day of the month
%H	24-hour (always two digits; for example, 01)
%h/%I	12-hour (always two digits; for example, 09)
%i	Minutes
%j	Day of the year
%k	24-hour (one or two digits; for example, 1)
%l	12-hour (one or two digits; for example, 9)
%M	Name of the Month
%m	Number of the month (January is 1)
%p	a.m. or p.m.
%r	12-hour total time (including a.m./p.m.)
%S	Seconds (always two digits; for example, 04)
%s	Seconds (one or two digit; for example, 4)
%T	24-total time
%U	Week of the year (new weeks begin on Sunday)
%W	Name of the weekday
%w	Number of the weekday (0 is Sunday)
%Y	4-digit year
%y	2-digit year
	Oracle Date Pictures
AD	Anno Domini (in the year of our Lord)
AM	Ante Meridiem
BC	Before Christ
CC	Century
D	Number of the day in the week
DD	Number of the day in the month
DDD	Number of the day in the year

12

TABLE 13.1 Continued

Date Picture	Description
	Oracle Date Pictures
DAY	The day spelled out (MONDAY)
Day	The day spelled out (Monday)
day	The day spelled out (monday)
DY	The three-letter abbreviation of the day (MON)
Dy	The three-letter abbreviation of the day (Mon)
dy	The three-letter abbreviation of the day (mon)
HH	Hour of the day
HH12	Hour of the day
HH24	Hour of the day for a 24-hour clock
J	Julian days since 12-31-4713 BC
MI	Minute of the hour
MM	Number of the month
MON	Three-letter abbreviation of the month (JAN)
Mon	Three-letter abbreviation of the month (Jan)
mon	Three-letter abbreviation of the month (jan)
MONTH	Month spelled out (JANUARY)
Month	Month spelled out (January)
month	Month spelled out (january)
PM	Post Meridiem
Q	Number of the quarter
RM	Roman numeral for the month
RR	Two digits of the year
SS	Second of a minute
SSSSS	Seconds since midnight
SYYYY	Signed year, if BC 500, then BC = −500
W	Number of the week in a month
WW	Number of the week in a year
Y	Last digit of the year
YY	Last two digits of the year
YYY	Last three digits of the year
YYYY	Year
YEAR	Year spelled out (NINETEEN-NINETY-NINE)
Year	Year spelled out (Nineteen-Ninety-Nine)
year	Year spelled out (nineteen-ninety-nine)

Converting Dates to Character Strings

DATETIME values are converted to character strings to alter the appearance of output from a query. A conversion function is used to achieve this. The following examples convert date and time data into a character string as designated by a query.

A SQL Server date conversion using the DATENAME function follows:

Input/Output ▼

```
SELECT DATE_HIRE = DATENAME(MONTH, DATE_HIRE)
FROM EMPPAY

DATE_HIRE
----------
May
June
August
June
July
Jan

6 rows affected.
```

In this SQL Server example, we have selected only the month name from the value of the DATE_HIRE column using the DATENAME function.

An Oracle date conversion using the TO_CHAR function follows:

Input/Output ▼

```
SQL> SELECT DATE_HIRE, TO_CHAR(DATE_HIRE,'Month dd, yyyy') "HIRE DATE"
  2 FROM EMP_PAY;

DATE_HIRE HIRE DATE
--------- --------------------
23-MAY-89 May 23, 1989
17-JUN-90 June 17, 1990
14-AUG-94 August 14, 1994
28-JUN-97 June 28, 1997
22-JUL-96 July 22, 1996
14-JAN-91 January 14, 1991

6 rows selected.
```

Here, we have reformatted the HIRE_DATE column with Oracle's TO_CHAR function in the format of Month dd, yyyy. Refer back to Table 13.1.

12

Converting Character Strings to Dates

The following example illustrates a method from one implementation of converting a character string into a date format. After the conversion is complete, the data can be stored in a column defined as having some form of a DATETIME data type.

Input/Output ▼

```
SQL> SELECT TO_DATE('JANUARY 01 1998','MONTH DD YYYY')
  2 FROM EMP_PAY;

TO_DATE('
---------
01-JAN-98
01-JAN-98
01-JAN-98
01-JAN-98
01-JAN-98
01-JAN-98

6 rows selected.
```

In this example, we have used Oracle's TO_DATE function to convert a character string with an apparent date-like value to an internal Oracle date format. Again, we have used an Oracle date picture to tell Oracle how to store the different parts of the character string as a date.

You might be wondering why six rows were selected from this query when only one date value was provided. The reason is because the conversion of the literal string was selected from the EMPPAY, which has six rows of data; therefore, the conversion of the literal string was selected against each record in the table.

NOTE Be aware of how your implementation of SQL stores the date. Does the default date format include the four-digit year, or is it a two-digit year? By default, Oracle displays the year of a date with a two-digit format, and accepts values for a year in a two-digit format. Oracle also allows you to change the default date format of the database. In most cases, it is always better to store the date with a four-digit year format to avoid any problems with the rollover into the next millennium.

Summary

In this lesson, we have provided you with an understanding of DATETIME values based on the ANSI-provided standard. However, as with many elements of SQL, most implementations have deviated from the exact functions and syntax of standard SQL commands. The concepts, however, will always remain the same as far as the basic representation and manipulation of date and time information. In Lesson 14, "Controlling Transactions," you'll learn how functions greatly vary depending upon each implementation. In this lesson, you have seen some of the differences between Date and Time data types, functions, and operators. Keep in mind that not all examples discussed in this lesson will work with your particular implementation, but the concepts of dates and times are the same and can be applied to any implementation.

Q&A

Q Why do implementations choose to deviate from a standard set of data types and functions?

A Implementations differ as far as the representation of data types and functions mainly because of the way each vendor has chosen to internally store data and provide the most efficient means of data retrieval. However, you will find that all implementations should provide the same means for the storage of date and time values based on the required elements prescribed by ANSI, such as the year, month, day, hour, minute, second, and so on.

Q What if I want to store date and time information differently from the default date format in my implementation?

A Dates can be stored in nearly any type of format if you choose to define the column for a date as a variable length character. The main issue to remember is that when comparing date values to one another, you must first convert the character string representation of the date to a valid DATETIME format for your implementation.

12

Workshop

The Workshop provides quiz questions to help solidify your understanding of the material covered, as well as exercises to provide you with experience in using what you have learned. Try to answer the quiz and exercise questions before checking the answers in Appendix A, "Answers."

Quiz

1. From where is the system date and time for a relational database normally derived?
2. List the standard internal elements of a DATETIME value.
3. What could be a major factor concerning the representation and comparison of date and time values if your company is an international organization?
4. Why is it not a good idea to store an individual's age in a database?
5. Given a table STUDENTS that contains the columns NAME and DOB (for date of birth), how would you use Oracle to write the query to get everyone's age?
6. What operator in SQL is used to determine whether a set of time periods overlap one another?
7. In general, what is the result when subtracting two date values?

Exercises

Exercises 1–3 are intended for use with Oracle's implementation of SQL. Exercises 4–9 are specific to MySQL.

Provide SQL code for the exercises, given the following information:

- Use SYSDATE to represent the current date and time.
- Use the TO_CHAR function to convert dates to character strings, with the syntax TO_CHAR('EXPRESSION','DATE_PICTURE').
- Use the TO_DATE function to convert character strings to dates, with the syntax TO_DATE('EXPRESSION','DATE_PICTURE').

Date picture information:

Date Picture	Meaning
MONTH	Month spelled out
DAY	Day spelled out
DD	Day of the month, number
MM	Month of the year, number
YY	Two-digit year
YYYY	Four-digit year
MI	Minutes of the hour
SS	Seconds of the minute

1. Assuming today is 1998-12-31, convert the current date to the format December 31 1998.

2. Convert the following string to DATE format:
   'DECEMBER 31 1997'

3. Write the code to return the day of the week that New Year's Eve of 1999 fell upon. Assume that the date is stored in the format 31-DEC-98, which is a valid DATETIME data type.

4. Using MySQL, select the current DATETIME.

5. Assuming that today is 2002-07-08, determine what day of the week it is.

6. Using the MySQL function DATE_FORMAT(), present the current date in the following format:
   Tuesday, July 9th, 2002

7. What day of the week did these dates fall on?
   1990-09-27, 1992-09-07, 1962-09-03

8. 1999-12-31 23:59:59 is a valid DATETIME picture in MySQL. Using the DATE_ADD function, change this date to the new year.

9. Add 10 years to 1991-06-21 and double check your results with the current date.

12

LESSON 13
Creating Views

In this lesson we begin to cover a topic that might be new even to programmers or database users who have already had some exposure to SQL. Lessons 1 through 8 covered nearly all the introductory material you need to get started using SQL and relational databases. Lesson 9, "Creating and Maintaining Tables," was devoted to a discussion of database design, table creation, and other data-manipulation commands. The common feature of the objects discussed so far—databases, tables, records, and fields—is that they are all physical objects that are ultimately located in a data file on a hard disk. In this lesson, the focus shifts to a feature of SQL that provides you with more flexibility as a programmer. This feature is the *view*. By the end of this lesson, you will know how to do the following:

- Create views

- Modify data using views

- Use views to summarize data

- Use views to implement security

- Drop an existing view

Introducing Views

A view is often referred to as a *virtual table*, which means that a view looks like a table and is referenced like a table. However, views do not contain data like tables do. The only storage required for a view is the storage to maintain the definition of the view. A view is defined by a query on one or more database tables. A view is nothing more than a predefined query.

Views are created by using the CREATE VIEW statement. After the view has been created, you can use the following SQL commands to refer to that view:

- SELECT
- INSERT
- UPDATE
- DELETE

NOTE

> We used Oracle to generate this lesson's examples, but most modern implementations, including MySQL, support views. Please refer to your particular implementation's documentation for information as to what is and is not currently supported.

Using Views

You can use views, or virtual tables, to encapsulate complex queries. After a view on a set of data has been created, you can treat that view as another table. However, special restrictions are placed on modifying the data within views. When data in a table changes, what you see when you query the view also changes. Remember that views do not take up physical space in the database as tables do.

The syntax for the CREATE VIEW statement is

Syntax ▼

```
CREATE VIEW <view_name> [(column1, column2...)] AS
SELECT <table_name column_names>
FROM <table_name>
```

NOTE

> In some implementations, such as in Oracle, there are special types of views called "Materialized Views" that do actually consume space on the database because they contain a snapshot of the data at a point in time. Although these specific cases are not covered in this book, you might want to check your specific implementation documentation to see the full set of options that are available to you.

As usual, this syntax might not be clear at first glance, but this lesson's material contains many examples that illustrate the uses and advantages of views. This command tells SQL to create a view (with the name of your choice) composed of columns in parentheses (with the names of your choice, if you like). A SQL SELECT statement determines the fields in these columns and their data types. Yes, this is the same SELECT statement that you have used repeatedly for the last several lessons.

Before you can do anything useful with views, you need to create some tables and populate those tables with data.

Input/Output ▼

```
SQL>  create table BILLS (
  2    NAME CHAR(30) NOT NULL,
  3    AMOUNT NUMBER,
  4    ACCOUNT_ID NUMBER NOT NULL);

Table created.

SQL>  create table BANK_ACCOUNTS (
  2    ACCOUNT_ID NUMBER NOT NULL,
  3    TYPE CHAR(30),
  4    BALANCE NUMBER,
  5    BANK CHAR(30));

Table created.

SQL>  create table COMPANY (
  2    NAME CHAR(30) NOT NULL,
  3    ADDRESS CHAR(50),
  4    CITY CHAR(30),
  5    STATE CHAR(2));

Table created.
```

You would use the INSERT statement to populate the previously created tables with data (see Tables 13.1 through 13.3).

13

TABLE 13.1   Sample Data for the BILLS Table

NAME	AMOUNT	ACCOUNT_ID
Phone Company	125	1
Power Company	75	1
Record Club	25	2
Software Company	250	1
Cable TV Company	35	3
Joe's Car Palace	350	5
S.C. Student Loan	200	6
Florida Water Company	20	1
U-O-Us Insurance Company	125	5
Debtor's Credit Card	35	4

TABLE 13.2   Sample Data for the BANK_ACCOUNTS Table

ACCOUNT_ID	TYPE	BALANCE	BANK
1	Checking	500	First Federal
2	Money market	1200	First Investor
3	Checking	90	Credit Union
4	Savings	400	First Federal
5	Checking	2500	Second Mutual
6	Business	4500	Fidelity

TABLE 13.3   Sample Data for the COMPANY Table

NAME	ADDRESS	CITY	STATE
Phone Company	111 1st Street	Atlanta	GA
Power Company	222 2nd Street	Jacksonville	FL
Record Club	333 3rd Avenue	Los Angeles	CA
Software Company	444 4th Drive	San Francisco	CA
Cable TV Company	555 5th Drive	Austin	TX
Joe's Car Palace	1000 Govt. Blvd	Miami	FL
S.C. Student Loan	25 College Blvd	Columbia	SC
Florida Water Company	1883 Hwy 87	Navarre	FL
U-O-Us Insurance Company	295 Beltline Hwy	Macon	GA
Debtor's Credit Card	115 2nd Avenue	Newark	NJ

Now that you have successfully used the CREATE TABLE and INSERT commands to input all this information, you are ready for an in-depth discussion of the view.

Exploring a Simple View

Let's begin with the simplest of all views. Suppose, for some unknown reason, you want to make a view on the BILLS table that looks identical to the table but has a different name. (We call it DEBTS.) Here's the statement:

Input ▼

```
SQL> CREATE VIEW DEBTS AS
     SELECT * FROM BILLS;
```

To confirm that this operation did what it should, you can treat the view just like a table:

Input/Output ▼

```
SQL> SELECT * FROM DEBTS;

NAME                    AMOUNT  ACCOUNT_ID
Phone Company              125           1
Power Company               75           1
Record Club                 25           2
Software Company           250           1
Cable TV Company            35           3
Joe's Car Palace           350           5
S.C. Student Loan          200           6
Florida Water Company       20           1
U-O-Us Insurance Company   125           5
Debtor's Credit Card        35           4

10 rows selected.
```

In this example, we have created a view called DEBTS that is based on the BILLS table. Notice that we did not specify a column list directly after the CREATE VIEW statement (before the AS keyword). Because we did not specify a column list, the column names in the view inherit the same names as the columns selected from the base table.

Using the previous syntax, the view is created in our users' default schema. What if we wanted to create the view in a specific schema so that other users could access it easily? Well, we would just need to prepend the correct schema to the name in the form <SCHEMA>.<VIEW NAME>. The following example shows our previous view being created in the BILLING schema.

13

Input ▼

```
SQL> CREATE VIEW BILLING.DEBTS AS
     SELECT * FROM BILLS;
```

You can even create new views from existing views. Be careful when creating views of views. Although this practice is acceptable, it complicates maintenance. Suppose you have a view three levels down from a table, such as a view of a view of a view of a table. What do you think will happen if the first view on the table is dropped? The other two views will still exist, but they will be useless because they get part of their information from the first view. Remember, after the view has been created, it functions as a virtual table.

Input/Output ▼

```
SQL>  CREATE VIEW CREDITCARD_DEBTS AS
  2     SELECT * FROM DEBTS
  3     WHERE ACCOUNT_ID = 4;
SQL>  SELECT * FROM CREDITCARD_DEBTS;
```

NAME	AMOUNT	ACCOUNT_ID
Debtor's Credit Card	35	4

```
1 row selected.
```

In this example, we are filtering the data the users see with a view. We do not want the view to contain all records from the DEBTS table; we want the view to include information only about account number 4.

The CREATE VIEW also enables you to select individual columns from a table and place them in a view. The following example selects the NAME and STATE fields from the COMPANY table.

Input ▼

```
SQL>  CREATE VIEW COMPANY_INFO (NAME, STATE) AS
  2     SELECT NAME, STATE FROM COMPANY;
```

The following statement is the same as the previous one:

```
SQL>  CREATE VIEW COMPANY_INFO AS
  2     SELECT NAME, STATE FROM COMPANY;
```

In the second example, we did not specify a column list; therefore, the column names in the view will be the same as those in the base table.

Now, let's select data from our view:

Input/Output ▼

```
SQL> SELECT * FROM COMPANY_INFO;

NAME                       STATE
Phone Company                GA
Power Company                FL
Record Club                  CA
Software Company             CA
Cable TV Company             TX
Joe's Car Palace             FL
S.C. Student Loan            SC
Florida Water Company        FL
U-O-Us Insurance Company     GA
Debtor's Credit Card         NJ

10 rows selected.
```

NOTE

> Users may create views to query specific data. Say you have a table with 50 columns and hundreds of thousands of rows, but you need to see data in only 2 columns. You can create a view on these two columns, and then by querying from the view, you should see a remarkable difference in the amount of time it takes for your query results to be returned.

Renaming Columns

Views simplify the representation of data. In addition to naming the view, the SQL syntax for the CREATE VIEW statement enables you to rename selected columns. Consider the preceding example a little more closely. What if you wanted to combine the ADDRESS, CITY, and STATE fields from the COMPANY table to print them on an envelope? The following example illustrates this. This example uses the SQL || (concatenation) operator to combine the address fields into one long address by combining spaces and commas with the character data.

13

Input/Output ▼

```
SQL>  CREATE VIEW ENVELOPE (COMPANY, MAILING_ADDRESS) AS
   2    SELECT NAME, ADDRESS || ` ` || CITY || `, ` || STATE
   3    FROM COMPANY;
SQL> SELECT * FROM ENVELOPE;
```

```
COMPANY                      MAILING_ADDRESS
Phone Company                111 1st Street Atlanta, GA
Power Company                222 2nd Street Jacksonville, FL
Record Club                  333 3rd Avenue Los Angeles, CA
Software Company             444 4th Drive San Francisco, CA
Cable TV Company             555 5th Drive Austin, TX
Joe's Car Palace             1000 Govt. Blvd Miami, FL
S.C. Student Loan            25 College Blvd. Columbia, SC
Florida Water Company        1883 Hwy. 87 Navarre, FL
U-O-Us Insurance Company     295 Beltline Hwy. Macon, GA
Debtor's Credit Card         115 2nd Avenue Newark, NJ

10 rows selected.
```

The SQL syntax requires you to supply a virtual field name whenever the view's virtual field is created using a calculation or SQL function. This procedure makes sense because you wouldn't want a view's column name to be COUNT(*) or AVG(PAYMENT).

NOTE   Check your implementation for the use of the || operator.

Examining SQL View Processing

Views can represent data within tables in a more convenient fashion than what actually exists in the database's table structure. Views can also be extremely convenient when performing several complex queries in a series (such as within a stored procedure or application program). To solidify your understanding of the view and the SELECT statement, the next section examines the way in which SQL processes a query against a view. Suppose you have a query that occurs often; for example, you routinely join the BILLS table with the BANK_ACCOUNTS table to retrieve information on your payments, as follows:

Input/Output ▼

```
SQL> SELECT BILLS.NAME, BILLS.AMOUNT, BANK_ACCOUNTS.BALANCE,
  2  BANK_ACCOUNTS.BANK FROM BILLS, BANK_ACCOUNTS
  3  WHERE BILLS.ACCOUNT_ID = BANK_ACCOUNTS.ACCOUNT_ID;

NAME                     AMOUNT        BALANCE          BANK
Phone Company            125           500              First Federal
Power Company            75            500              First Federal
Record Club              25            1200             First Investor
Software Company         250           500              First Federal
Cable TV Company         35            90               Credit Union
Joe's Car Palace         350           2500             Second Mutual
```

```
S.C. Student Loan          200      4500        Fidelity
Florida Water Company       20       500        First Federal
U-O-Us Insurance Company   125      2500        Second Mutual
Debtor's Credit Card        35       400        First Federal
10 rows selected.
```

You could convert this process into a view using the following statement:

Input/Output ▼

```
SQL> CREATE VIEW BILLS_DUE (NAME, AMOUNT, ACCT_BALANCE, BANK) AS
  2   SELECT BILLS.NAME, BILLS.AMOUNT, BANK_ACCOUNTS.BALANCE,
  3   BANK_ACCOUNTS.BANK FROM BILLS, BANK_ACCOUNTS
  4   WHERE BILLS.ACCOUNT_ID = BANK_ACCOUNTS.ACCOUNT_ID;

View created.
```

If you queried the BILLS_DUE view using some condition, the statement would look like this:

Input/Output ▼

```
SQL> SELECT * FROM BILLS_DUE
  2   WHERE ACCT_BALANCE > 500;

NAME                          AMOUNT    ACCT_BALANCE   BANK
Record Club                       25            1200   First Investor
Joe's Car Palace                 350            2500   Second Mutual
S.C. Student Loan                200            4500   Fidelity
U-O-Us Insurance Company         125            2500   Second Mutual

4 rows selected.
```

SQL uses several steps to process the preceding statement. Because BILLS_DUE is a view, not an actual table, SQL first looks for a table named BILLS_DUE and finds nothing. The SQL processor will probably (depending on what database system you are using) find out from a system table that BILLS_DUE is a view. It will then use the view's plan to construct the following query:

13

Input/Output ▼

```
SQL> SELECT BILLS.NAME, BILLS.AMOUNT, BANK_ACCOUNTS.BALANCE,
  2   BANK_ACCOUNTS.BANK FROM BILLS, BANK_ACCOUNTS
  3   WHERE BILLS.ACCOUNT_ID = BANK_ACCOUNTS.ACCOUNT_ID
  4   AND BANK_ACCOUNTS.BALANCE > 500;
```

```
NAME                     AMOUNT BALANCE BANK
------------------------ ------ ------- ---------------
Record Club                  25    1200 First Investor
Joe's Car Palace            350    2500 Second Mutual
U-O-Us Insurance Company    125    2500 Second Mutual
S.C. Student Loan           200    4500 Fidelity
```

Example 13.1

Construct a view that shows all states to which the bills are being sent. Also display the total amount of money and the total number of bills being sent to each state.

First of all, you know that the CREATE VIEW part of the statement will look like this:

Syntax ▼

```
CREATE VIEW EXAMPLE (STATE, TOTAL_BILLS, TOTAL_AMOUNT) AS...
```

Now you must determine what the SELECT query will look like. You know that you want to select the STATE field first using the SELECT DISTINCT syntax based on the requirement of showing the states to which bills are being sent—for example,

Input/Output ▼

```
SQL> SELECT DISTINCT STATE FROM COMPANY;

STATE
GA
FL
CA
TX
SC
NJ

6 rows selected.
```

In addition to selecting the STATE field, you need to total the number of payments sent to that STATE. Therefore, you need to join the BILLS table and the COMPANY table.

Input/Output ▼

```
SQL> SELECT DISTINCT COMPANY.STATE, COUNT(BILLS.*) FROM BILLS, COMPANY
  2  WHERE BILLS.NAME = COMPANY.NAME
  3  GROUP BY COMPANY.STATE;

STATE      COUNT(BILLS.*)
GA                      2
FL                      3
```

```
CA                  2
TX                  1
SC                  1
NJ                  1
```

6 rows selected.

Now that you have successfully returned two-thirds of the desired result, you can add the final required return value. Use the SUM function to total the amount of money sent to each state.

Input/Output ▼

```
SQL> SELECT DISTINCT COMPANY.STATE, COUNT(BILLS.NAME), SUM(BILLS.AMOUNT)
  2  FROM BILLS, COMPANY
  3  WHERE BILLS.NAME = COMPANY.NAME
  4  GROUP BY COMPANY.STATE;
```

```
STATE     COUNT(BILLS.NAME)    SUM(BILLS.AMOUNT)
GA                2                    250
FL                3                    445
CA                2                    275
TX                1                     35
SC                1                    200
NJ                1                     35
```

6 rows selected.

As the final step, you can combine this SELECT statement with the CREATE VIEW statement you created at the beginning of this project:

Input/Output ▼

```
SQL> CREATE VIEW EXAMPLE (STATE, TOTAL_BILLS, TOTAL_AMOUNT) AS
  2  SELECT DISTINCT COMPANY.STATE, COUNT(BILLS.NAME), SUM(BILLS.AMOUNT)
  3  FROM BILLS, COMPANY
  4  HAVING BILLS.NAME = COMPANY.NAME
  5  GROUP BY COMPANY.STATE;
View created.
```

13

Input/Output ▼

```
SQL> SELECT * FROM EXAMPLE;
```

```
STATE     TOTAL_BILLS      TOTAL_AMOUNT
GA              2               250
FL              3               445
```

CA	2	275
TX	1	35
SC	1	200
NJ	1	35

```
6 rows selected.
```

The preceding example shows you how to plan the CREATE VIEW statement and the SELECT statements. This code tests the SELECT statements to see whether they will generate the proper results and then combines the statements to create the view.

Example 13.2

Assume that your creditors charge a 10% service charge for all late payments, and unfortunately you are late on everything this month. You want to see this late charge along with the type of accounts the payments are coming from.

This join is straightforward. (You don't need to use anything like COUNT or SUM.) However, you will discover one of the primary benefits of using views. You can add the 10% service charge and present it as a field within the view. From that point on, you can select records from the view and already have the total amount calculated for you. The statement would look like this:

Input/Output ▼

```
SQL>  CREATE VIEW LATE_PAYMENT (NAME, NEW_TOTAL, ACCOUNT_TYPE) AS
   2    SELECT BILLS.NAME, BILLS.AMOUNT * 1.10, BANK_ACCOUNTS.TYPE
   3    FROM BILLS, BANK_ACCOUNTS
   4    WHERE BILLS.ACCOUNT_ID = BANK_ACCOUNTS.ACCOUNT_ID;

View created.

SQL> SELECT * FROM LATE_PAYMENT;
```

NAME	NEW_TOTAL	ACCOUNT_TYPE
Phone Company	137.50	Checking
Power Company	82.50	Checking
Record Club	27.50	Money Market
Software Company	275	Checking
Cable TV Company	38.50	Checking
Joe's Car Palace	385	Checking
S.C. Student Loan	220	Business
Florida Water Company	22	Checking
U-O-Us Insurance Company	137.50	Business
Debtor's Credit Card	38.50	Savings

```
10 rows selected.
```

Restrictions on Using SELECT

SQL places certain restrictions on using the SELECT statement to formulate a view. The following two rules apply when using the SELECT statement:

- You cannot use the UNION operator.
- You cannot use the ORDER BY clause. However, you can use the GROUP BY clause in a view to perform the same functions as the ORDER BY clause.

Modifying Data in a View

As you have learned, by creating a view on one or more physical tables within a database, you can create a virtual table for use throughout a SQL script or a database application. After the view has been created using the CREATE VIEW...SELECT statement, you can update, insert, or delete view data using the UPDATE, INSERT, and DELETE commands you learned about on Lesson 11, "Manipulating Data."

We discuss the limitations on modifying a view's data in greater detail later. The next group of examples illustrates how to manipulate data that is in a view.

To continue on the work you did in Example 13.2, update the BILLS table to reflect that unfortunate 10% late charge.

Input/Output ▼

```
SQL>  ALTER VIEW LATE_PAYMENT AS
  2    SELECT * FROM BILLS;

View created.

SQL>  UPDATE LATE_PAYMENT
  2    SET AMOUNT = AMOUNT * 1.10;

10 row(s) updated.

SQL>  SELECT * FROM LATE_PAYMENT;
```

NAME	AMOUNT	ACCOUNT_ID
Phone Company	137.50	1
Power Company	82.50	1
Record Club	27.50	2
Software Company	275	1
Cable TV Company	38.50	3
Joe's Car Palace	385	5
S.C. Student Loan	220	6
Florida Water Company	22	1

13

```
U-O-Us Insurance Company        137.50                  5
Debtor's Credit Card             38.50                  4

10 rows selected.
```

To verify that the UPDATE actually updated the underlying table BILLS, query the BILLS table.

Input/Output ▼

```
SQL> SELECT * FROM BILLS;

NAME                            AMOUNT      ACCOUNT_ID
Phone Company                   137.50              1
Power Company                    82.50              1
Record Club                      27.50              2
Software Company                   275              1
Cable TV Company                 38.50              3
Joe's Car Palace                   385              5
S.C. Student Loan                  220              6
Florida Water Company               22              1
U-O-Us Insurance Company        137.50              5
Debtor's Credit Card             38.50              4

10 rows selected.
```

Now delete a row from the view:

Input/Output ▼

```
SQL>  DELETE FROM LATE_PAYMENT
  2   WHERE ACCOUNT_ID = 4;

1 row deleted.

SQL> SELECT * FROM LATE_PAYMENT;

NAME                            AMOUNT      ACCOUNT_ID
Phone Company                   137.50              1
Power Company                    82.50              1
Record Club                      27.50              2
Software Company                   275              1
Cable TV Company                 38.50              3
Joe's Car Palace                   385              5
S.C. Student Loan                  220              6
Florida Water Company               22              1
U-O-Us Insurance Company        137.50              5

9 rows selected.
```

The final step is to test the UPDATE function. For all bills that have an AMOUNT greater than 100, add an additional 10.

Input/Output ▼

```
SQL> UPDATE LATE_PAYMENT
  2    SET AMOUNT = AMOUNT + 10
  3    WHERE AMOUNT > 100;

9 rows updated.

SQL> SELECT * FROM LATE_PAYMENT;
```

NAME	AMOUNT	ACCOUNT_ID
Phone Company	147.50	1
Power Company	82.50	1
Record Club	27.50	2
Software Company	285	1
Cable TV Company	38.50	3
Joe's Car Palace	395	5
S.C. Student Loan	230	6
Florida Water Company	22	1
U-O-Us Insurance Company	147.50	5

```
9 rows selected.
```

Notice the changes in the preceding output. All values in the NEW_TOTAL column greater than $100 have $10 added to them.

Problems with Modifying Data Using Views

Because what you see through a view can be some set of a group of tables, modifying the data in the underlying tables is not always as straightforward as the previous examples. The following is a list of the most common restrictions you will encounter while working with views:

- You cannot use DELETE statements on multiple table views.
- You cannot use the INSERT statement unless all NOT NULL columns used in the underlying table are included in the view. This restriction applies because the SQL processor does not know which values to insert into the NOT NULL columns.
- If you do insert or update records through a join view, all records that are updated must belong to the same physical table.
- If you use the DISTINCT clause to create a view, you cannot update or insert records within that view.
- You cannot update a *virtual column* (a column that is the result of an expression or function).

13

Common Applications of Views

Here are a few of the tasks that views can perform:

- Providing user security functions
- Converting between units
- Simplifying the construction of complex queries
- Summarizing data from multiple tables

Providing Security with Views

Although a complete discussion of database security appears in Lesson 17, "Database Security," we briefly touch on the topic now to explain how you can use views in performing security functions.

All relational database systems in use today include a full suite of built-in security features. Users of the database system are generally divided into groups based on the way they use the database. Common group types are database administrators, database developers, data entry personnel, and public users. These groups of users have varying degrees of privileges when using the database. The database administrator will probably have complete control of the system, including UPDATE, INSERT, DELETE, and ALTER database privileges. The public group may be granted only SELECT privileges—and perhaps may be allowed to SELECT only from certain tables within certain databases.

Views are commonly used in this situation to control the information that the database user has access to. For instance, if you wanted users to have access only to the NAME field of the BILLS table, you could simply create a view called BILLS_NAME:

Input/Output ▼

```
SQL>  CREATE VIEW BILLS_NAME AS
  2   SELECT NAME FROM BILLS;

View created.
```

The owner of the view could grant the public group SELECT privileges on the BILLS_NAME view. This group would not have any privileges on the underlying BILLS table. As you might guess, SQL has provided data security statements for your use also. Keep in mind that views are very useful for implementing database security.

Using Views to Convert Units

Views are also useful in situations in which you need to present the user with data that is different from the data that actually exists within the database. For instance, if the

AMOUNT field is actually stored in U.S. dollars and you don't want Canadian users to have to continually do mental calculations to see the AMOUNT total in Canadian dollars, you could create a simple view called CANADIAN_BILLS:

Input/Output ▼

```
SQL>  CREATE VIEW CANADIAN_BILLS (NAME, CAN_AMOUNT) AS
   2    SELECT NAME, AMOUNT / 1.10
   3    FROM BILLS;

View Created.

SQL> SELECT * FROM CANADIAN_BILLS;

NAME                         CAN_AMOUNT
Phone Company                    134.09
Power Company                        75
Record Club                          25
Software Company                 259.09
Cable TV Company                     35
Joe's Car Palace                 359.09
S.C. Student Loan                209.09
Florida Water Company                20
U-O-Us Insurance Company         134.09

9 rows selected.
```

When converting units like this, keep in mind the possible problems inherent in modifying the underlying data in a table when a calculation (such as the preceding example) was used to create one of the columns of the view. As always, you should consult your database system's documentation to determine exactly how the system implements the CREATE VIEW command.

Simplifying Complex Queries Using Views

Views are also useful in situations that require you to perform a sequence of queries to arrive at a result. The following example illustrates the use of a view in this situation.

To give the name of all banks that sent bills to the state of Texas with an amount less than $50, you would break the problem into two separate parts:

- Retrieve all bills that were sent to Texas.
- Retrieve all bills less than $50.

Let's solve this problem using two separate views: BILLS1 and BILLS2.

13

Input/Output ▼

```
SQL>   CREATE VIEW BILLS1 AS
  2    SELECT * FROM BILLS
  3    WHERE AMOUNT < 50;

View created.

SQL>   CREATE VIEW BILLS2 (NAME, AMOUNT, ACCOUNT_ID) AS
  2    SELECT BILLS.* FROM BILLS, COMPANY
  3    WHERE BILLS.NAME = COMPANY.NAME AND COMPANY.STATE = `TX`;
View created.
```

Because you want to find all bills sent to Texas *and* all bills that were less than $50, you can now use the SQL IN clause to find which bills in BILLS1 were sent to Texas. Use this information to create a new view called BILLS3:

Input/Output ▼

```
SQL>   CREATE VIEW BILLS3 AS
  2    SELECT * FROM BILLS2 WHERE NAME IN
  3    (SELECT NAME FROM BILLS1);
View created.
```

Now combine the preceding query with the BANK_ACCOUNTS table to satisfy the original requirements of this example:

Input/Output ▼

```
SQL>   CREATE VIEW BANKS_IN_TEXAS (BANK) AS
  2    SELECT BANK_ACCOUNTS.BANK
  3    FROM BANK_ACCOUNTS, BILLS3
  4    WHERE BILLS3.ACCOUNT_ID = BANK_ACCOUNTS.ACCOUNT_ID;
View created.

SQL> SELECT * FROM BANKS_IN_TEXAS;

BANK
Credit Union

1 row selected.
```

As you can see, after the queries were broken down into separate views, the final query was rather simple. Also, you can reuse the individual views as often as necessary.

Summarizing Data from Multiple Tables

Views can be used to summarize data from one or many tables. By summarizing data in a view, you can simplify many of the queries that take place against the tables that make up the view.

For example, take a look at the following tables:

```
PRODUCTS          ORDERS
product_id        ord_no
product_name      prod_id
product_cost      qty
```

The PRODUCTS table has general product information, and the ORDERS table maintains information about orders that have been placed for a particular product.

```
create view prod_sum as
select p.prod_id, p.prod_name, sum(o.qty) sum_qty,
       max(o.qty) max_qty, min(o.qty) min_qty, avg(o.qty) avg_qty
from products p,
     orders o
where p.prod_id = o.prod_id
group by p.prod_id, p.prod_name;
```

In this view definition, we have essentially selected all product names and summarized information about each product, such as the total quantity ordered for a product, the minimum and maximum quantity of a product in an order, and the average quantity of a product per order. The table join occurs in the WHERE clause of the SELECT statement.

> **NOTE**
> Notice that we are using aggregate functions in the SELECT statement that defines the view. Whenever using functions in a view definition, you must provide a column alias because each item selected becomes a virtual column in a virtual table. A column in a table or view cannot use the syntax of a function.

13

Now we can simply issue the following query to return summarized information about each product:

```
select * from prod_sum;
```

You can join as many tables as you want to define a view. In this example, we used two tables. Remember that a view definition is simply a SELECT statement.

Removing Views with the DROP VIEW Statement

In common with every other SQL CREATE command, CREATE VIEW has a corresponding DROP command. The DROP VIEW command simply drops the VIEW from the database. The table or tables the VIEW was created from are not affected by dropping the VIEW. The syntax is as follows:

Syntax ▼

```
DROP VIEW view_name;
```

The only thing to remember when using the DROP VIEW command is that all other views that reference that view are now invalid. Some database systems even drop all views that used the view you dropped. Using Personal Oracle, if you drop the view BILLS1, the final query would produce the following error:

Input/Output ▼

```
SQL> DROP VIEW BILLS1;

View dropped.

SQL> SELECT * FROM BANKS_IN_TEXAS;
*
ERROR at line 1:
ORA-04063: view "PERKINS.BANKS_IN_TEXAS" has errors
```

NOTE — A view can be dropped without any of the actual tables being modified, which explains why we often refer to views as virtual tables. (The same logic can be applied to the technology of virtual reality.)

Summary

Views can be thought of as virtual tables and are simply a way of presenting data in a format that is different from the way it actually exists in the database. The syntax of the CREATE VIEW statement uses a standard SELECT statement to create the view (with some exceptions). You can treat a view as a regular table and perform inserts, updates, deletes, and selects on it. We briefly discussed the use of database security and how views are commonly used to implement this security. Database security is covered in greater detail in Lesson 17.

The basic syntax used to create a view is

Syntax ▼

```
CREATE VIEW view_name AS
SELECT field_name(s) FROM table_name(s);
```

Here are the most common uses of views:

- To perform user security functions
- To convert units
- To create a new virtual table format
- To simplify the construction of complex queries

Q&A

Q How can a view contain data but require no physical storage?

A Actually, a view does not contain data at all. A view is a virtual table or a predefined query. The only space required for a view is for the view definition. Remember that a view is defined by a SELECT statement.

Q What happens to a view if a table on which a view is dependent is dropped?

A The view will become invalid because the underlying data that defines the view no longer exists.

Workshop

The Workshop provides quiz questions to help solidify your understanding of the material covered, as well as exercises to provide you with experience in using what you have learned. Try to answer the quiz and exercise questions before checking the answers in Appendix A, "Answers."

13

Quiz

1. Can a row of data be deleted from a view that was created from multiple tables?
2. When creating a table, the owner is automatically granted all privileges on the table. Is this true when a view is created?
3. What clause can be used to sort data in a CREATE VIEW statement?

4. Is the following CREATE statement correct?

```
SQL> create view credit_debts as
     (select * from debts
     where account_id = 4);
```

5. Is the following CREATE statement correct?

```
SQL> create unique view debts as
     select * from debts_tbl;
```

6. Is the following DROP statement correct?

```
SQL> drop * from view debts;
```

7. How would you create the following view in the ACCOUNTANT schema?

```
SQL> create view credit_debts as
     (select * from debts
     where account_id = 4);
```

Exercises

1. Examine the database system you are using. Does it support views? What options are you allowed to use when creating a view? Write a simple SQL statement that will create a view using the appropriate syntax. Perform some traditional operations such as SELECT or DELETE and then DROP the view.

2. Use the Oracle syntax as shown in this chapter for the remaining exercises.

   Write a simple SQL statement that will create a view called TEST using the appropriate syntax. Now issue the SQL statement SELECT * FROM TEST;.

3. Create a view called TEST1 from the view TEST that you created in exercise 2. Then drop the TEST view that you created in exercise 2. After dropping the TEST view, issue a SELECT from the view TEST1 created in this step. What do you think the results of your query will be?

LESSON 14

Controlling Transactions

You have spent the last 13 lessons learning virtually everything that you can do with data within a relational database. For example, you know how to use the SQL SELECT statement to retrieve data from one or more tables based on a number of conditions supplied by the user. You have also had a chance to use data-modification statements such as INSERT, UPDATE, and DELETE. At this point, you have become an intermediate level SQL and database user. If required, you could build a database with its associated tables, each of which would contain several fields of different data types. Using proper design techniques, you could leverage the information contained within this database into a powerful application.

If you are a casual user of SQL who occasionally needs to retrieve data from a database, the topics of the first 13 lessons provide most of the information you will need. However, if you intend to (or are currently required to) develop a professional application using any type of relational database, the advanced topics covered over the next lessons—transaction control, performance, security, embedded SQL programming, and database procedures will help you a great deal. We begin with transaction control. By the end of this lesson, you will know the following:

- The basics of transaction control

- How to finalize and/or cancel a transaction

- Some of the differences between SQL Server, MySQL, and Oracle transactions

NOTE
We used both Oracle and SQL Server to generate this lesson's examples. Please see the documentation of your specific SQL implementation for any minor differences in syntax. For instance, MySQL are only supported when using certain storage engines such as InnoDB.

Transaction Management

Transaction control, or transaction management, refers to the capability of a relational database management system to perform database transactions. Transactions are units of work that must be done in a logical order and successfully as a group or not at all. The term *unit of work* means that a transaction has a beginning and an end. If anything goes wrong during the transaction, the entire unit of work can be canceled if desired. If everything looks good, the entire unit of work can be saved to the database.

In the coming months or years, you will probably be implementing applications for multiple users to use across a network. Client/server environments are designed specifically for this purpose. Traditionally, a server (in this case, a database server) supports multiple network connections to it. As often happens with technology, this newfound flexibility adds a new degree of complexity to the environment. Consider the banking application described in the next few paragraphs.

The Banking Application

You are employed by First Federal Financial Bank to set up an application that handles checking account transactions consisting of debits and credits to customers' checking accounts. You have set up a nice database, which has been tested and verified. After calling up your application, you verify that when you take $20 out of the account, $20 actually disappears from the database. When you add $50.25 to the checking account, this deposit shows up as expected. You proudly announce to your bosses that the system is ready to go, and several computers are set up in a local branch to begin work.

Within minutes, you notice a situation that you did not anticipate: As one teller is depositing a check, another teller is withdrawing money from the same account. Soon, many depositors' balances are incorrect because multiple users are updating tables simultaneously. Unfortunately, these multiple updates are overwriting each other. Shortly thereafter, your application is pulled offline for an overhaul. We will work through this problem with a database called CHECKING. Within this database are two tables, shown in Tables 14.1 and 14.2.

TABLE 14.1 The CUSTOMERS Table

Name	Address	City	State	Zip	Customer_IDs
Bill Turner	725 N. Deal Parkway	Washington	DC	20085	1
John Keith	1220 Via De Luna Dr.	Jacksonville	FL	33581	2
Mary Rosenberg	482 Wannamaker Avenue	Williamsburg	VA	23478	3
David Blanken	405 N. Davis Highway	Greenville	SC	29652	4
Rebecca Little	7753 Woods Lane	Houston	TX	38764	5

TABLE 14.2 The BALANCES Table

Average_Bal	Curr_Bal	Account_ID
1298.53	854.22	1
5427.22	6015.96	2
211.25	190.01	3
73.79	25.87	4
1285.90	1473.75	5
1234.56	1543.67	6
345.25	348.03	7

Assume now that your application program performs a SELECT operation and retrieves the following data for Bill Turner:

```
NAME:  Bill Turner
ADDRESS:  725 N. Deal Parkway
CITY:  Washington
STATE:  DC
ZIP:  20085
CUSTOMER_ID:  1
```

While this information is being retrieved, another user with a connection to this database updates Bill Turner's address information:

Input ▼

```
SQL> UPDATE CUSTOMERS SET Address = "11741 Kingstowne Road"
     WHERE Name = "Bill Turner";
```

14

As you can see, the information you retrieved earlier could be invalid if the update occurred during the middle of your SELECT. If your application fired off a letter to be sent to Mr. Bill Turner, the address it used would be wrong. Obviously, if the letter has already been sent, you won't be able to change the address. However, if you had used a transaction, this data change could have been detected, and all your other operations could have been rolled back.

Beginning a Transaction

Transactions are quite simple to implement. You will examine the SQL syntax used to perform transactions with the Sybase SQL Server and the Oracle relational database management system (RDBMS).

All database systems that support transactions must have a way to explicitly tell the system that a transaction is beginning. (Remember that a transaction is a logical grouping of work that has a beginning and an end.) Using Personal Oracle, the syntax looks like this:

Syntax ▼

```
SET TRANSACTION {READ ONLY | USE ROLLBACK SEGMENT segment};
```

The SQL standard specifies that each database's SQL implementation must support statement-level read consistency; that is, data must stay consistent while one statement is executing. However, in many situations data must remain valid across a single unit of work, not just within a single statement. Oracle enables the user to specify when the transaction will begin by using the SET TRANSACTION statement. If you wanted to examine Bill Turner's information and make sure that the data was not changed, you could do the following:

Input/Output ▼

```
SQL> SET TRANSACTION READ ONLY;
SQL> SELECT * FROM CUSTOMERS
     WHERE NAME = 'Bill Turner';

---Do Other Operations---

SQL> COMMIT;
```

We discuss the COMMIT statement later in this lesson. The SET TRANSACTION READ ONLY option enables you to effectively lock a set of records until the transaction ends. You can use the READ ONLY option with the following commands:

- SELECT
- LOCK TABLE
- SET ROLE

- ALTER SESSION
- ALTER SYSTEM

The option USE ROLLBACK SEGMENT tells Oracle which database segment to use for rollback storage space. This option is an Oracle extension to the standard SQL syntax. Consult your Oracle documentation for more information on using segments to maintain your database.

SQL Server's Transact-SQL language implements the BEGIN TRANSACTION command with the following syntax:

Syntax ▼

```
begin {transaction | tran} [transaction_name]
```

This implementation is a little different from the Oracle implementation. Sybase does not allow you to specify the READ ONLY option. However, Sybase does allow you to give a transaction a name, as long as that transaction is the outermost of a set of nested transactions.

MySQL has limited support for transactions and mainly only supports the ability to start, rollback, or commit a transaction. MySQL begins a transaction with the following syntax:

Syntax ▼

```
start transaction
```

Notice how we do not have the ability to name the transaction as we did in the previous Sybase SQL Server example. This would prevent us from using many important features like nested transactions. Considering this limitation we will proceed with using examples from the Sybase SQL Server syntax in order to demonstrate the full usage of transactions within a RDBMS system.

The following group of statements illustrates the use of nested transactions using SQL Server:

Input ▼

```
1> begin transaction new_account
2> insert CUSTOMERS values
3> ("Izetta Parsons", "1285 Pineapple Highway",  "Greenville", "AL",32854, 6)
4> if exists(select * from CUSTOMERS where Name = "Izetta Parsons")
5> begin
```

14

```
6> begin transaction
7> insert BALANCES values(1250.76, 1431.26, 8)
8> end
9> else
10> rollback transaction
11> if exists(select * from BALANCES where Account_ID = 8)
12> begin
13> begin transaction
14> insert ACCOUNTS values(8, 6)
15> end
16> else
17> rollback transaction
18> if exists (select * from ACCOUNTS where Account_ID = 8 and Customer_ID = 6)
19> commit transaction
20> else
21> rollback transaction;
```

For now, don't worry about the ROLLBACK TRANSACTION and COMMIT TRANSACTION state-ments. The important aspect of this example is the nested transaction—or a transaction within a transaction.

Analysis ▼

Notice that the original transaction (new_account) begins on line 1. After the first INSERT, you check to make sure the INSERT was executed properly. Another transaction begins on line 5. This transaction within a transaction is termed a *nested transaction*.

Other databases support the AUTOCOMMIT option. This option can be used with the SET command—for example,

Syntax ▼

```
SET AUTOCOMMIT [ON | OFF]
```

By default, in SQL Server the SET AUTOCOMMIT ON command is executed at startup. It tells SQL to automatically commit all statements you execute. If you do not want these commands to be automatically executed, set the AUTOCOMMIT option to off:

Syntax ▼

```
SET AUTOCOMMIT OFF
```

NOTE

Check your database system's documentation to determine how you would begin a transaction.

Finishing a Transaction

The Oracle syntax to end a transaction is as follows:

Syntax ▼

```
COMMIT [WORK]
[ COMMENT 'text'
| FORCE 'text' [, integer] ] ;
```

Here is the same command using MySQL syntax:

Syntax ▼

```
COMMIT [WORK] [AND [NO] CHAIN] [[NO] RELEASE]
```

The COMMIT command saves all changes made during a transaction. Executing a COMMIT statement before beginning a transaction ensures that no errors were made and no previous transactions are left hanging.

The following example verifies that the COMMIT command can be used by itself without receiving an error from the database system.

Input ▼

```
SQL> COMMIT;
SQL> SET TRANSACTION READ ONLY;
SQL> SELECT * FROM CUSTOMERS
     WHERE NAME = 'Bill Turner';
---Do Other Operations---

SQL> COMMIT;
```

An Oracle SQL use of the COMMIT statement would look like this:

Input/Output ▼

```
SQL> SET TRANSACTION READ WRITE;
SQL> INSERT INTO CUSTOMERS VALUES
     ("John MacDowell", "2000 Lake Lunge Road", "Chicago", "IL", 42854, 7);
SQL> COMMIT;
SQL> SELECT * FROM CUSTOMERS;
Name               Address              City           State   Zip     Customer_ID
Bill Turner        725 N. Deal Parkway  Washington     DC      20085   1
John Keith         1220 Via De Luna Dr. Jacksonville   FL      33581   2
Mary Rosenberg     482 Wannamaker Avenue Williamsburg  VA      23478   3
David Blanken      405 N. Davis Highway Greenville     SC      29652   4
```

14

```
Rebecca Little   7753 Woods Lane           Houston      TX    38764  5
Izetta Parsons   1285 Pineapple Highway    Greenville   AL    32854  6
John MacDowell   2000 Lake Lunge Road      Chicago      IL    42854  7
```

A Sybase SQL Server use of the COMMIT statement would look like this:

Input/Output ▼

```
1> begin transaction
2> insert into CUSTOMERS values
   ("John MacDowell", "2000 Lake Lunge Road", "Chicago", "IL", 42854, 7)
3> commit transaction;
4> select * from CUSTOMERS;
```

```
Name            Address                 City          State  Zip    Customer_ID
Bill Turner     725 N. Deal Parkway     Washington    DC     20085  1
John Keith      1220 Via De Luna Dr.    Jacksonville  FL     33581  2
Mary Rosenberg  482 Wannamaker Avenue   Williamsburg  VA     23478  3
David Blanken   405 N. Davis Highway    Greenville    SC     29652  4
Rebecca Little  7753 Woods Lane         Houston       TX     38764  5
Izetta Parsons  1285 Pineapple Highway  Greenville    AL     32854  6
John MacDowell  2000 Lake Lunge Road    Chicago       IL     42854  7
```

Analysis ▼

The preceding statements accomplish the same thing as they do using the Oracle syntax. However, by putting the COMMIT command soon after the transaction begins, you ensure that the new transaction will execute correctly.

NOTE	The COMMIT WORK command performs the same operation as the COMMIT command. It is provided simply to comply with ANSI SQL syntax.

Remember that every COMMIT command must correspond with an earlier executed SET TRANSACTION or BEGIN TRANSACTION command. Note the errors you receive with the following statements.

Oracle SQL:

Input ▼

```
SQL> INSERT INTO BALANCES values (18765.42, 19073.06, 8);
SQL> COMMIT WORK;
```

Sybase SQL Server:

Input ▼

```
1> insert into balances values (18765.42, 19073.06, 8);
2> commit work;
```

Canceling the Transaction

While a transaction is in progress, some type of error checking is usually performed to determine whether it is executing successfully. You can undo your transaction even after successful completion by issuing the ROLLBACK statement, but it must be issued before a COMMIT. The ROLLBACK statement must be executed from within a transaction. The ROLLBACK statement rolls the transaction back to its beginning; in other words, the state of the database is returned to what it was at the transaction's beginning. The syntax for this command using Oracle is the following:

Syntax ▼

```
ROLLBACK [WORK]
[ TO [SAVEPOINT] savepoint
| FORCE 'text' ];
```

As you can see, this command makes use of a transaction savepoint. We discuss this technique later in the section, "Using Transaction Savepoints."

An Oracle SQL sequence of commands might look like this:

Input ▼

```
SQL> SET TRANSACTION READ WRITE;

SQL> INSERT INTO CUSTOMERS VALUES
     ("Bubba MacDowell", "2222 Blue Lake Way", "Austin", "TX", 39874, 8);

SQL> ROLLBACK;
SQL> SELECT * FROM CUSTOMERS;
```

The following table shows what the output of the previous Oracle SQL commands would be.

14

Output ▼

```
Name             Address                  City           State   Zip     Customer_ID
Bill Turner      725 N. Deal Parkway      Washington     DC      20085   1
John Keith       1220 Via De Luna Dr.     Jacksonville   FL      33581   2
Mary Rosenberg   482 Wannamaker Avenue    Williamsburg   VA      23478   3
David Blanken    405 N. Davis Highway     Greenville     SC      29652   4
Rebecca Little   7753 Woods Lane          Houston        TX      38764   5
Izetta Parsons   1285 Pineapple Highway   Greenville     AL      32854   6
John MacDowell   2000 Lake Lunge Road     Chicago        IL      42854   7
```

As you can see, the new record was not added because the ROLLBACK statement rolled the INSERT back.

Suppose you are writing an application for a graphical user interface (GUI), such as Microsoft Windows. You have a dialog box that queries a database and allows the user to change values. If the user selects OK, the database saves the changes. If the user selects Cancel, the changes are canceled. Obviously, this situation gives you an opportunity to use a transaction.

When the dialog box is loaded, these SQL statements are executed:

Input ▼

```
SQL> SET TRANSACTION READ WRITE;

SQL> SELECT CUSTOMERS.NAME, BALANCES.CURR_BAL, BALANCES.ACCOUNT_ID
  2  FROM CUSTOMERS, BALANCES
  3  WHERE CUSTOMERS.NAME = "Rebecca Little"
  4  AND CUSTOMERS.CUSTOMER_ID = BALANCES.ACCOUNT_ID;
```

The dialog box allows the user to change the current account balance, so you need to store this value back to the database.

When the user selects OK, the update will run.

Input ▼

```
SQL> UPDATE BALANCES SET CURR_BAL = 'new-value' WHERE ACCOUNT_ID = 5;
SQL> COMMIT;
```

When the user selects Cancel, the ROLLBACK statement is issued.

Input ▼

```
SQL> ROLLBACK;
```

When the dialog box is loaded using Sybase SQL Server, these SQL statements are executed:

Input ▼

```
1> begin transaction
2> select customers.name, balances.curr_bal, balances.account_id
3> from customers, balances
4> where customers.name = "Rebecca Little"
5> and customers.customer_id = balances.account_id;
```

The dialog box allows the user to change the current account balance, so you can store this value back to the database.

Here again, when the OK button is selected, the update will run.

Input ▼

```
1> update BALANCES set Curr_BAL = 'new-value' WHERE Account_ID = 5;
2> commit transaction;
```

When the user selects Cancel, the ROLLBACK statement is issued.

Input ▼

```
1> rollback transaction;
```

Analysis ▼

The ROLLBACK statement cancels the entire transaction. When you are nesting transactions, the ROLLBACK statement completely cancels all the transactions, rolling them back to the beginning of the outermost transaction.

If no transaction is currently active, issuing the ROLLBACK statement or the COMMIT command has no effect on the database system (think of them as dead commands with no purpose).

After the COMMIT statement has been executed, all actions with the transaction are executed. At this point, it is too late to roll back the transaction.

Using Transaction Savepoints

Rolling back a transaction cancels the entire transaction. But suppose you want to "semi-commit" your transaction midway through its statements. Both MySQL and Oracle SQL allow you to save the transaction with a *savepoint*. From that point on, if a ROLLBACK is

14

issued, the transaction is rolled back to the savepoint. All statements that were executed up to the point of the savepoint are saved. The syntax for creating a savepoint using Oracle SQL or MySQL is as follows:

Syntax ▼

```
SAVEPOINT savepoint_name;
```

The following is the Sybase SQL Server syntax to create a savepoint:

Syntax ▼

```
SAVE TRAN[SACTION]_name
```

This following example uses Oracle SQL syntax.

Input/Output ▼

```
SQL> SET TRANSACTION READ WRITE;
SQL> UPDATE BALANCES SET CURR_BAL = 25000 WHERE ACCOUNT_ID = 5;
SQL> SAVEPOINT save_it;
SQL> DELETE FROM BALANCES WHERE ACCOUNT_ID = 5;
SQL> ROLLBACK TO SAVEPOINT save_it;
SQL> COMMIT;
SQL> SELECT * FROM BALANCES;
```

Average_Bal	Curr_Bal	Account_ID
1298.53	854.22	1
5427.22	6015.96	2
211.25	190.01	3
73.79	25.87	4
1285.90	25000.00	5
1234.56	1543.67	6
345.25	348.03	7
1250.76	1431.26	8

This example uses Sybase SQL Server syntax:

Input/Output ▼

```
1> begin transaction;
2> update BALANCES set Curr_Bal = 25000 where Account_ID = 5;
3> save transaction save_it;
4> delete from BALANCES where Account_ID = 5;
5> rollback transaction save_it;
6> commit transaction;

1> select * from BALANCES;
```

```
Average_Bal    Curr_Bal        Account_ID
1298.53        854.22          1
5427.22        6015.96         2
211.25         190.01          3
73.79          25.87           4
1285.90        25000.00        5
1234.56        1543.67         6
345.25         348.03          7
1250.76        1431.26         8
```

Analysis ▼

The previous examples created a savepoint called SAVE_IT. An update was made to the database that changed the value of the CURR_BAL column of the BALANCES table. You then saved this change as a savepoint. Following this save, you executed a DELETE statement, but you rolled the transaction back to the savepoint immediately thereafter. Then you executed COMMIT TRANSACTION, which committed all commands up to the savepoint. Had you executed a ROLLBACK TRANSACTION after the ROLLBACK TRANSACTION *savepoint_name* command, the entire transaction would have been rolled back, and no changes would have been made.

This example uses Oracle SQL syntax:

Input/Output ▼

```
SQL> SET TRANSACTION READ WRTIE;
SQL> UPDATE BALANCES SET CURR_BAL = 25000 WHERE ACCOUNT_ID = 5;
SQL> SAVEPOINT save_it;
SQL> DELETE FROM BALANCES WHERE ACCOUNT_ID = 5;
SQL> ROLLBACK TO SAVEPOINT save_it;
SQL> ROLLBACK;
SQL> SELECT * FROM BALANCES;
```

```
Average_Bal    Curr_Bal        Account_ID
1298.53        854.22          1
5427.22        6015.96         2
211.25         190.01          3
73.79          25.87           4
1285.90        1473.75         5
1234.56        1543.67         6
345.25         348.03          7
1250.76        1431.26         8
```

14

This example uses Sybase SQL Server syntax:

Input/Output ▼

```
1> begin transaction;
2> update BALANCES set Curr_Bal = 25000 where Account_ID = 5;
3> save transaction save_it;
4> delete from BALANCES where Account_ID = 5;
5> rollback transaction save_it;
6> rollback transaction;

1> select * from BALANCES
```

Average_Bal	Curr_Bal	Account_ID
1298.53	854.22	1
5427.22	6015.96	2
211.25	190.01	3
73.79	25.87	4
1285.90	1473.75	5
1234.56	1543.67	6
345.25	348.03	7
1250.76	1431.26	8

Summary

A transaction can be defined as an organized unit of work. The work done during a transaction is usually a series of operations that depends on previously executed operations. If one of these operations is not executed properly or if data is changed for some reason, the rest of the work in a transaction should be canceled. Otherwise, if all statements are executed correctly, the transaction's work should be saved.

The process of canceling a transaction is called a *rollback*. The process of saving the work of a correctly executed transaction is called a *commit*. SQL syntax supports these two processes through syntax similar to the following two statements:

Syntax ▼

```
BEGIN TRANSACTION;
    statement 1;
    statement 2;
    statement 3;
ROLLBACK TRANSACTION;
```

or

```
BEGIN TRANSACTION;
    statement 1;
```

```
    statement 2;
    statement 3;
COMMIT TRANSACTION;
```

Q&A

Q **If I have a group of transactions and one transaction is unsuccessful, will the rest of the transactions process?**

A No. The entire group must run successfully.

Q **After issuing the COMMIT command, I discovered that I made a mistake. How can I correct the error?**

A Use the DELETE, INSERT, and UPDATE commands.

Q **Must I issue the COMMIT command after every transaction?**

A No. But it is safer to do so to ensure that no errors were made and no previous transactions are left hanging.

Workshop

The Workshop provides quiz questions to help solidify your understanding of the material covered, as well as exercises to provide you with experience in using what you have learned. Try to answer the quiz and exercise questions before checking the answers in Appendix A, "Answers."

Quiz

1. When nesting transactions, does issuing a ROLLBACK TRANSACTION command cancel the current transaction and roll back the batch of statements into the upper-level transaction? Why or why not?

2. Can savepoints be used to "save off" portions of a transaction? Why or why not?

3. Can a COMMIT command be used by itself, or must it be embedded?

4. If you issue the COMMIT command and then discover a mistake, can you still use the ROLLBACK command?

5. Will using a savepoint in the middle of a transaction save all that happened before it automatically?

14

Exercises

1. Using Oracle syntax, correct the syntax (if necessary) for the following:

```
SQL> START TRANSACTION
SQL> INSERT INTO CUSTOMERS VALUES
SQL> ('SMITH', 'JOHN')
SQL> COMMIT;
```

2. Using Oracle syntax, correct the syntax (if necessary) for the following:

```
SQL> SET TRANSACTION READ WRITE;
SQL> UPDATE BALANCES SET CURR_BAL = 25000;
SQL> COMMIT;
```

3. Using Oracle syntax, correct the syntax (if necessary) for the following:

```
SQL> SET TRANSACTION READ WRITE;
SQL> INSERT INTO BALANCES VALUES
   > ('567.34', '230.00', '8');
SQL> ROLLBACK;
```

LESSON 15
Creating Indexes on Tables to Improve Performance

In this lesson, we talk about indexes, which provide you with a shorter route to your data. So far, you have learned how to create tables, populate tables with data, and select data from tables. Now, how can we get to data faster? By using indexes, which are objects based on data in tables. Unlike views, which we discussed during Lesson 13, indexes do indeed require physical storage. By the end of this lesson, you will understand the following:

- How to create indexes
- How to create composite indexes
- What indexes do
- When indexes should be used
- When it is better not to use an index

An *index* is a way of presenting data differently than the way it appears on the disk. Special types of indexes reorder the record's physical location within a table. Indexes can be created on a column within a table or on a combination of columns within a table. When an index is used, the data is presented to the user in a sorted order, which you can control with the CREATE INDEX statement. You can usually gain substantial performance improvements by indexing on the correct fields, particularly fields that are being joined between tables.

Indexes are used in a SQL database for three primary reasons:

- To enforce referential integrity constraints by using the UNIQUE or PRIMARY KEY keywords
- To facilitate the ordering of data based on the contents of the index's field or fields
- To optimize the execution speed of queries

What Are Indexes?

Data can be retrieved from a database using two methods. The first method, often called the *sequential access method*, requires SQL to go through each record looking for a match. This search method is inefficient, but it is the only way for SQL to locate the correct record. Think back to the days when libraries had massive card catalog filing systems. Suppose the librarian removed the alphabetical index cards, tossed the cards into the air, and then placed them back into the filing cabinets.

When you wanted to look up this book's shelf location, you would probably start at the very beginning and then go through one card at a time until you found the information you wanted. (Chances are, you would stop searching as soon as you found any book on this topic!)

Now suppose the librarian sorted the book titles alphabetically. You could quickly access this book's information by using your knowledge of the alphabet to move through the catalog.

Imagine the flexibility if the librarian was diligent enough to not only sort the books by title, but also create another catalog sorted by author's name and another sorted by topic. This process would provide you, the library user, with a great deal of flexibility in retrieving information. Also, you would be able to retrieve your information in a fraction of the time it originally would have taken.

Adding indexes to your database enables SQL to use the *direct access method*. SQL uses a tree-like structure to store and retrieve the index's data. Pointers to a group of data are stored at the top of the tree. These groups are called *nodes*. Each node contains pointers to other nodes. The nodes pointing to the left contain values that are less than its parent node. The pointers to the right point to values greater than the parent node. Oracle and MySQL call this type of index a *B-tree* index. Figure 15.1 illustrates the structure of a tree-like index.

FIGURE 15.1
A sample layout of a tree structure index.

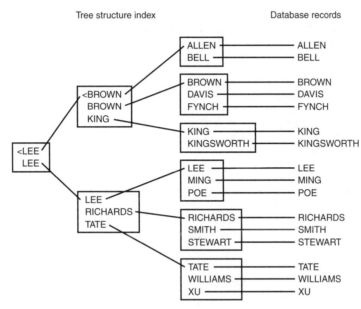

The database system starts its search at the top node and simply follows the pointers until it is successful.

NOTE

> The result of a query against the unindexed table is commonly referred to as a *full-table scan*. A full-table scan is the process used by the database server to search every row of a table until all rows are returned with the given condition(s). This operation is comparable to searching for a book in the library by starting at the first book on the first shelf and scanning every book until you find the one you want. On the other hand, to find the book quickly, you would probably look in the (computerized) card catalog. Similarly, an index enables the database server to point to specific rows of data quickly within a table.

Fortunately you are not required to actually implement the tree structure yourself, just as you are not required to write the implementation for saving and reading in tables or databases. The basic SQL syntax to create an index is as follows:

Syntax ▼

```
SQL>   CREATE INDEX index_name
  2      ON table_name(column_name1, [column_name2], ...);
```

As you have seen many times before, the syntax for CREATE INDEX can vary widely among database systems. For instance, the basic CREATE INDEX statement using Oracle looks like this:

Syntax ▼

```
CREATE INDEX [schema.]index
ON { [schema.]table (column [!!under!!ASC|DESC]
     [, column [!!under!!ASC|DESC]] ...)
   | CLUSTER [schema.]cluster }
[INITRANS integer] [MAXTRANS integer]
[TABLESPACE tablespace]
[STORAGE storage_clause]
[PCTFREE integer]
[NOSORT]
```

The syntax for CREATE INDEX using MicrosoftMicrosof SQL Server is as follows:

Syntax ▼

```
create [unique] [clustered | nonclustered]
       index index_name
on [[database.]owner.]table_name (column_name
   [, column_name]...)
[with {fillfactor = x, ignore_dup_key, pad_index,
     drop_existing , statistics_norecompute}]
[on filegroup]
```

The syntax in MySQL is as follows:

Syntax ▼

```
CREATE [UNIQUE|FULLTEXT|SPATIAL] INDEX index_name
[USING {BTREE|HASH|RTREE}]
ON tbl_name (col_name[(length)][ASC|DESC],...)
[KEY_BLOCK_SIZE = value]|[index_type]|[WITH PARSER parser_name]|
[COMMENT 'string']
```

Notice that all these implementations have several points in common, starting with this basic statement:

Syntax ▼

```
CREATE INDEX index_name ON table_name (column_name, ...)
```

SQL Server and Oracle allow you to create a clustered index, which is discussed later. Oracle, MySQL, and SQL Server also allow you to designate whether the column name should be sorted in ascending or descending order. We hate to sound like a broken record, but, once again, you should definitely consult your database management system's documentation when using the CREATE INDEX command.

> **NOTE**
>
> Prior to MySQL version 3.22, the CREATE INDEX statement did not actually do anything in the MySQL database. The syntax was allowed to make MySQL statements portable across different implementations of SQL. Starting with version 3.22, the CREATE INDEX statement is actually tied to the ALTER TABLE command in MySQL.
>
> We will be using the same tables and data that we used in Lesson 13, "Creating Views."

Example 15.1

For instance, to create an index on the ACCOUNT_ID field of the BILLS table, the CREATE INDEX statement would look like this:

Input/Output ▼

```
SQL> SELECT * FROM BILLS;
```

NAME	AMOUNT	ACCOUNT_ID
Phone Company	125	1
Power Company	75	1
Record Club	25	2
Software Company	250	1
Cable TV Company	35	3
Joe's Car Palace	350	5
S.C. Student Loan	200	6
Florida Water Company	20	1
U-O-Us Insurance Company	125	5
Debtor's Credit Card	35	4

```
10 rows selected.
mysql> select * from bills;
+-------------------------+--------+------------+
| name                    | amount | account_id |
+-------------------------+--------+------------+
| Phone Company           |    125 |          1 |
| Power Company           |     75 |          1 |
| Record Club             |     25 |          2 |
| Software Company        |    250 |          1 |
| Cable TV Company        |     35 |          3 |
| Joe's Car Palace        |    350 |          5 |
| S.C. Student Loan       |    200 |          6 |
| Florida Water Company   |     20 |          1 |
| U-O-Us Insurance Company|    125 |          5 |
| Debtor's Credit Card    |     35 |          4 |
+-------------------------+--------+------------+
10 rows in set (0.09 sec)
```

SQL> **CREATE INDEX ID_INDEX ON BILLS(ACCOUNT_ID);**

```
Index created.
mysql> create index ID_INDEX on BILLS (account_id);
Query OK, 10 rows affected (0.40 sec)
Records: 10  Duplicates: 0  Warnings: 0
```

In the MySQL example, note that you receive a message that tells you, among other things, that all 10 rows were affected by the index.

Input/Output ▼

SQL> **SELECT * FROM BILLS;**

```
NAME                      AMOUNT    ACCOUNT_ID
Phone Company             125                1
Power Company             75                 1
Software Company          250                1
Florida Water Company     20                 1
Record Club               25                 2
Cable TV Company          35                 3
Debtor's Credit Card      35                 4
Joe's Car Palace          350                5
U-O-Us Insurance Company  125                5
S.C. Student Loan         200                6

10 rows selected.
```

```
mysql> select * from bills;
+---------------------------+--------+------------+
| name                      | amount | account_id |
+---------------------------+--------+------------+
| Phone Company             |    125 |          1 |
| Power Company             |     75 |          1 |
| Record Club               |     25 |          2 |
| Software Company          |     50 |          1 |
| Cable TV Company          |     35 |          3 |
| Joe's Car Palace          |    350 |          5 |
| S.C. Student Loan         |    200 |          6 |
| Florida Water Company     |     20 |          1 |
| U-O-Us Insurance Company  |    125 |          5 |
| Debtor's Credit Card      |     35 |          4 |
+---------------------------+--------+------------+
10 rows in set (0.00 sec)
```

Here is a good illustration of what we mean when we say that you should have a good understanding of the SQL implementation that you are working with. In the Oracle example, the BILLS table is sorted by the ACCOUNT_ID field until the index is dropped using the DROP INDEX statement. However, this does not occur in MySQL. If you select the indexed column by name, you can see that the data in the column has in fact been sorted.

Input/Output ▼

```
mysql> select account_id from bills;
+------------+
| account_id |
+------------+
|          1 |
|          1 |
|          1 |
|          1 |
|          2 |
|          3 |
|          4 |
|          5 |
|          5 |
|          6 |
+------------+
10 rows in set (0.00 sec)
```

The DROP INDEX statement removes an INDEX from the database. As usual, the DROP INDEX statement is very straightforward:

Input ▼

```
SQL> DROP INDEX index_name;
```

Here's what happens when the index is dropped:

Input/Output ▼

```
SQL> DROP INDEX ID_INDEX;

Index dropped.
```

In MySQL, it would read

Input/Output ▼

```
Mysql> drop index id_index on bills;

SQL> SELECT * FROM BILLS;

NAME                        AMOUNT      ACCOUNT_ID
Phone Company                  125               1
Power Company                   75               1
Record Club                     25               2
Software Company               250               1
Cable TV Company                35               3
Joe's Car Palace               350               5
S.C. Student Loan              200               6
Florida Water Company           20               1
U-O-Us Insurance Company       125               5
Debtor's Credit Card            35               4

10 rows selected.

mysql> select account_id from bills;
+------------+
| account_id |
+------------+
|          1 |
|          1 |
|          2 |
|          1 |
|          3 |
|          5 |
|          6 |
|          1 |
|          5 |
|          4 |
+------------+
```

Now the BILLS table is in its original form. Using the simplest form of the CREATE INDEX statement did not physically change the way the table was stored.

You might be wondering why database systems even provide indexes if they also enable you to use the ORDER BY clause.

15

Input/Output ▼

```
SQL> SELECT * FROM BILLS ORDER BY ACCOUNT_ID;
```

NAME	AMOUNT	ACCOUNT_ID
Phone Company	125	1
Power Company	75	1
Software Company	250	1
Florida Water Company	20	1
Record Club	25	2
Cable TV Company	35	3
Debtor's Credit Card	35	4
Joe's Car Palace	350	5
U-O-Us Insurance Company	125	5
S.C. Student Loan	200	6

```
10 rows selected.
```

This SELECT statement and the ID_INDEX on the BILLS table generate the same result. The difference is that an ORDER BY clause re-sorts and orders the data each time you execute the corresponding SQL statement. When using an index, the database system creates a physical index object (using the tree structure explained earlier) and reuses the same index each time you query the table.

> **CAUTION** When a table is dropped, all indexes associated with the table are dropped as well.

Example 15.2

Create an index on the BILLS table that will sort the AMOUNT field in descending order. The following example is from Oracle:

Input/Output ▼

```
SQL> CREATE INDEX DESC_AMOUNT
    ON  BILLS(AMOUNT DESC);

Index created.
```

This is the first time you have used the DESC operator, which tells SQL to sort the index in descending order. (By default, a number field is sorted in ascending order.) Now you can examine your handiwork:

Input/Output ▼

```
SQL> SELECT * FROM BILLS;
```

NAME	AMOUNT	ACCOUNT_ID
Joe's Car Palace	350	5
Software Company	250	1
S.C. Student Loan	200	6
Phone Company	125	1
U-O-Us Insurance Company	125	5
Power Company	75	1
Cable TV Company	35	3
Debtor's Credit Card	35	4
Record Club	25	2
Florida Water Company	20	1

```
10 rows selected.
```

This example created an index using the DESC operator on the column amount. Notice in the output that the amount is ordered from largest to smallest.

Indexing Tips

Listed here are several tips to keep in mind when using indexes:

- For small tables, the use of indexes does not result in any performance improvement.

- Indexes produce the greatest improvement when the columns you have indexed contain a wide variety of data. This is often referred to as *cardinality*.

- Indexes can optimize your queries when those queries are returning a small amount of data. (A good rule of thumb is less than 25% of the data.) If you are returning a large amount of data most of the time, indexes simply add overhead.

- Indexes can improve the speed of data retrieval. However, they slow data updates. Keep this in mind when doing many inserts, deletes, or updates in a row with an index. For very large inserts, deletes, or updates, you might consider dropping the index before you perform the update. When the insert, delete, or update is complete, simply rebuild your index. On one particular update, we were able to save the programmers 18 hours by dropping the index and re-creating it after the data load.

- Indexes take up space within your database. If you are using a database management system that enables you to manage the disk space taken up by your database, factor in the size of indexes when planning your database's size.

- Always index on fields that are used in joins between tables. This technique can greatly increase the speed of a join.

- Most database systems do not allow you to create an index on a view. If your database system allows it, use the GROUP BY clause with the SELECT statement that builds the view to order the data within the view. (Unfortunately, many systems don't enable the ORDER BY clause with the CREATE VIEW statement either.)

- Do not index on fields that are updated or modified regularly. The overhead required to constantly update the index will offset any performance gain you hope to acquire.

- Do not store indexes and tables on the same physical drive. Separating these objects will eliminate drive contention and result in faster queries.

- Indexes should not be used on columns that contain a high number of NULL values.

Indexing on More Than One Field

SQL also enables you to index on more than one field. This type of index is a *composite index*, or a *covering index*. The following code illustrates a simple composite index. Note that even though two fields are being combined, only one physical index is created (called ID_CMPD_INDEX).

Input/Output ▼

```
SQL> CREATE INDEX ID_CMPD_INDEX ON BILLS( ACCOUNT_ID, AMOUNT );

Index created.
mysql> create index cmpd_index on bills(account_id,amount);
Query OK, 10 rows affected (0.29 sec)
Records: 10  Duplicates: 0  Warnings: 0

SQL> SELECT * FROM BILLS;
```

NAME	AMOUNT	ACCOUNT_ID
Florida Water Company	20	1
Power Company	75	1
Phone Company	125	1
Software Company	250	1
Record Club	25	2
Cable TV Company	35	3
Debtor's Credit Card	35	4

```
U-O-Us Insurance Company       125              5
Joe's Car Palace               350              5
S.C. Student Loan              200              6

10 rows selected.

mysql> select account_id,amount
    -> from bills;
+------------+--------+
| account_id | amount |
+------------+--------+
|          1 |     20 |
|          1 |     75 |
|          1 |    125 |
|          1 |    250 |
|          2 |     25 |
|          3 |     35 |
|          4 |     35 |
|          5 |    125 |
|          5 |    350 |
|          6 |    200 |
+------------+--------+
10 rows in set (0.00 sec)

SQL> DROP INDEX ID_CMPD_INDEX;
mysql> drop index cmpd_index on bills;
Query OK, 10 rows affected (0.07 sec)
Records: 10  Duplicates: 0  Warnings: 0

Index dropped.
```

You can achieve performance gains by selecting the column with the most unique values. For instance, every value in the NAME field of the BILLS table is unique. When using a compound index, place the most selective field first in the column list. That is, place the field that you expect to select most often at the beginning of the list. (The order in which the column names appear in the CREATE INDEX statement does not have to be the same as their order within the table.) Assume you are routinely using a statement such as the following:

Input ▼

```
SQL> SELECT * FROM BILLS WHERE NAME = `Cable TV Company`;
```

To achieve performance gains, you must create an index using the NAME field as the leading column. Here are two examples:

```
SQL> CREATE INDEX NAME_INDEX ON BILLS(NAME, AMOUNT);
```

or

```
SQL> CREATE INDEX NAME_INDEX ON BILLS(NAME);
```

The NAME field is the leftmost column for both of these indexes, so the preceding query would be optimized to search on the NAME field.

Composite indexes are also used to combine two or more columns that, by themselves, may have low selectivity. For an example of *selectivity*, examine the BANK_ACCOUNTS table:

```
ACCOUNT_ID    TYPE            BALANCE    BANK
         1    Checking            500    First Federal
         2    Money Market       1200    First Investor
         3    Checking             90    Credit Union
         4    Savings             400    First Federal
         5    Checking           2500    Second Mutual
         6    Business           4500    Fidelity
```

Notice that out of six records, the value Checking appears in three of them. This column has a lower selectivity than the ACCOUNT_ID field. Notice that every value of the ACCOUNT_ID field is unique. To improve the selectivity of your index, you could combine the TYPE and ACCOUNT_ID fields in a new index. This step would create a unique index value (which, of course, is the highest selectivity you can get).

NOTE

An index containing multiple columns is often referred to as a composite index. Performance issues might sway your decision on whether to use a single-column or composite index. For example, you might decide to use a single-column index if most of your queries involve one particular column as part of a condition; on the other hand, you would probably create a composite index if the columns in that index are often used together as conditions for a query. Check your specific implementation for guidance when creating multiple-column indexes.

Using the UNIQUE Keyword with
CREATE INDEX

Composite indexes are often used with the UNIQUE keyword to prevent multiple records from appearing with the same data. Suppose you wanted to force the BILLS table to have the following built-in rule: Each bill paid to a company must come from a different bank account. You would create a UNIQUE index on the NAME and ACCOUNT_ID fields. The following example demonstrates the UNIQUE keyword with CREATE INDEX using Oracle.

```
SQL> CREATE UNIQUE INDEX UNIQUE_ID_NAME
   2 ON BILLS(ACCOUNT_ID, NAME);
Index created.

SQL > SELECT * FROM BILLS;
```

NAME	AMOUNT	ACCOUNT_ID
Florida Water Company	20	1
Power Company	75	1
Phone Company	125	1
Software Company	250	1
Record Club	25	2
Cable TV Company	35	3
Debtor's Credit Card	35	4
U-O-Us Insurance Company	125	5
Joe's Car Palace	350	5
S.C. Student Loan	200	6

Now try to insert a record into the BILLS table that duplicates data.

```
1>insert into BILLS (NAME, AMOUNT, ACCOUNT_ID)
2>values("Power Company", 125, 1)
3>go
```

You should have received an error message telling you that the INSERT command was not allowed. This type of error message can be trapped within an application program, and a message could tell the users that they inserted invalid data.

> **NOTE**
> Indexes are implicitly created by the database if a primary key is specified for a table because every value in a primary key must be unique. Primary key and unique constraints both cause system-generated indexes.

Indexes and Joins

When using complicated joins in queries, your SELECT statement can take a long time. With large tables, this amount of time can approach several seconds (as compared to the milliseconds you are used to waiting). This type of performance in a client/server environment with many users becomes extremely frustrating to the users of your application.

Creating an index on fields that are frequently used in joins can optimize the performance of your query considerably. However, if too many indexes are created, they can slow down the performance of your system, rather than speed it up. We recommend that you experiment with using indexes on several large tables (on the order of thousands of records). This type of experimentation leads to a better understanding of optimizing SQL statements.

15

> **NOTE** Most implementations have a mechanism for gathering the elapsed time of a query; Oracle refers to this feature as *timing*. Check your implementation for specific information.

The following example creates an index on the ACCOUNT_ID fields in the BILLS and BANK_ACCOUNTS tables:

Input/Output ▼

```
SQL> CREATE INDEX BILLS_INDEX ON BILLS(ACCOUNT_ID);

Index created.

SQL> CREATE INDEX BILLS_INDEX2 ON BANK_ACCOUNTS(ACCOUNT_ID);

Index created.

SQL> SELECT BILLS.NAME NAME, BILLS.AMOUNT AMOUNT, BANK_ACCOUNTS.BALANCE
  2    ACCOUNT_BALANCE
  3  FROM BILLS, BANK_ACCOUNTS
  4  WHERE BILLS.ACCOUNT_ID = BANK_ACCOUNTS.ACCOUNT_ID;

NAME                         AMOUNT     ACCOUNT_BALANCE
Phone Company                   125                 500
Power Company                    75                 500
Software Company                250                 500
Florida Water Company            20                 500
Record Club                      25                1200
Cable TV Company                 35                  90
Debtor's Credit Card             35                 400
Joe's Car Palace                350                2500
U-O-Us Insurance Company        125                2500
S.C. Student Loan               200                4500

10 rows selected.
```

This example first created an index for the ACCOUNT_ID on both tables in the associated query. By creating indexes for ACCOUNT_ID on each table, the join can more quickly access specific rows of data. As a rule, you should index the column(s) of a table that are unique or that you plan to join tables with in queries.

Using Clustered Indexes

Although we originally said that indexes can be used to present a view of a table that is different from the existing physical arrangement, this statement is not entirely accurate. A special type of index supported by many database systems allows the database manager or developer to *cluster* data. When tables are clustered, the data is stored in the same data blocks as the index, allowing fewer database block reads and resulting in quicker performance. When a clustered index is used, the physical arrangement of the data within a table is modified. Using a clustered index usually results in faster data retrieval than using a traditional, nonclustered index. However, many database systems (such as Sybase SQL Server) allow only one clustered index per table.

The field used to create the clustered index is usually the primary key field. Using Sybase Transact-SQL, you could create a clustered, unique index on the ACCOUNT_ID field of the BANK_ACCOUNTS table using the following syntax:

```
create unique clustered index id_index
on BANK_ACCOUNTS(ACCOUNT_ID)
 go
```

Oracle treats the concept of clusters differently. When using the Oracle relational database, a cluster is a database object like a database or table. A cluster is used to store tables with common fields so that their access speed is improved.

Here is the syntax to create a cluster using Oracle:

Syntax ▼

```
CREATE CLUSTER [schema.]cluster
(column datatype [,column datatype] ... )
[PCTUSED integer] [PCTFREE integer]
[SIZE integer [K|M] ]
[INITRANS integer] [MAXTRANS integer]
[TABLESPACE tablespace]
[STORAGE storage_clause]
[[!!under!!INDEX
| [HASH IS column] HASHKEYS integer]
```

You should then create an index within the cluster based on the tables that will be added to it. Then you can add the tables. You should add tables only to clusters that are frequently joined. Do not add tables to clusters that are accessed individually through a simple SELECT statement.

Clusters are a vendor-specific feature of SQL. We will not go into more detail here on their use or on the syntax that creates them. However, consult the documentation to determine whether your database management system supports these useful objects.

Summary

Indexes are physical database objects stored by your database management system that can be used to retrieve data already sorted from the database. In addition, thanks to the way indexes are mapped out, using indexes and properly formed queries can yield significant performance improvements.

The basic syntax used to create an index looks like this:

Syntax ▼

```
CREATE INDEX index_name
ON table_name(field_name(s));
```

Q&A

Q If the data within my table is already in sorted order, why should I use an index on that table?

A An index still gives you a performance benefit by looking quickly through key values in a tree. The index can locate records faster than a direct access search through each record within your database. Remember—the SQL query processor doesn't necessarily know that your data is in sorted order.

Q Can I create an index that contains fields from multiple tables?

A No, you cannot. However, Oracle, for instance, allows you to create a cluster. You can place tables within a cluster and create cluster indexes on fields that are common to the tables. This implementation is the exception, not the rule, so be sure to study your documentation on this topic.

Q If I drop an index in order for a batch job to complete faster, how long does it normally take to rebuild the index?

A Many factors are involved, such as the size of the base table for the index, CPU use, disk contention and I/O, and other concurrent processes running on the machine.

Workshop

The Workshop provides quiz questions to help solidify your understanding of the material covered, as well as exercises to provide you with experience in using what you have learned. Try to answer the quiz and exercise questions before checking the answers in Appendix A, "Answers."

Quiz

1. What will happen if a unique index is created on a non-unique field?
2. Are the following statements true or false?

   a. Indexes take up space in the database and therefore must be factored in the planning of the database size.

   b. If you have the disk space and you really want to get your queries smoking, the more indexes the better.

   c. An index is implicitly created when a primary key is specified for a table.

3. Is the following `CREATE` statement correct?
   ```
   SQL> create index id_index on bills
        (account_id);
   ```

4. What are some major disadvantages to using indexes?
5. Should a column with a large number of `NULL` values be indexed?
6. Where is the index stored in relation to the data when using a clustered index?
7. If you are loading large amounts of data into a table that contains several indexes, what is one of the techniques you can use to help speed up the execution of the data load?

Exercises

1. For the following situations, decide whether an index should be used, and if so, what type of index should be used.

   a. Several columns, but a rather small table.

   b. Medium-sized table; no duplicates should be allowed.

   c. Several columns; very large table; several columns used as filters in the `WHERE` clause.

   d. Large table; many columns; much data manipulation.

2. Examine the database system you are using to determine how it supports indexes. You will undoubtedly have a wide range of options. Try out some of these options on a table that exists within your database. In particular, determine whether you are allowed to create UNIQUE or CLUSTERED indexes on a table within your database.

3. If possible, locate a table that has several thousand records. Use a stopwatch or clock to time various operations against the database. Add some indexes and see whether you can notice a performance improvement. Try to follow the tips given to you in this lesson.

15

LESSON 16

Streamlining SQL Statements for Improved Performance

Streamlining SQL statements is as much a part of application performance as database designing and tuning. No matter how fine-tuned the database or how sound the database structure, you will not receive timely query results that are acceptable to you, or even worse, acceptable to the customer, if you don't follow some basic guidelines. Trust us, if the customer is not satisfied, you can bet your boss won't be satisfied either.

You already know about the major components of the relational database language of SQL and how to communicate with the database; now it's time to apply your knowledge to real-life performance concerns. The objective of today is to recommend methods for improving the performance of, or streamlining, a SQL statement. By the end of this lesson, you should

- Understand the concept of streamlining your SQL code

- Understand the differences between batch loads and transactional processing and their effects on database performance

- Be able to manipulate the conditions in your query to expedite data retrieval

- Be familiar with some underlying elements that affect the tuning of the entire database

Here's an example to help you understand the phrase "streamline a SQL statement": The objective of competitive swimmers is to complete an event in as little time as possible without being disqualified. The swimmers must have an acceptable technique, be able to torpedo themselves through the water, and use all their physical resources as effectively as possible. With each stroke and breath they take, competitive swimmers remain streamlined and move through the water with very little resistance.

Look at your SQL query the same way. You should always know exactly what you want to accomplish and then strive to follow the path of least resistance. The more time you spend planning, the less time you'll have to spend revising later. Your goal should always be to retrieve accurate data and to do so in as little time as possible. An end user waiting on a slow query is like a hungry diner impatiently awaiting a tardy meal. Although you can write most queries in several ways, the arrangement of the components within the query is the factor that makes the difference of seconds, minutes, and sometimes hours when you execute the query. In some instances, such as in the banking industry, your queries might be required to run within a certain time period or risk failure. Think of how frustrating it would be if a query that was responsible for posting ATM withdrawals was not optimized to perform within the time limit and denied individuals from withdrawing funds from their accounts. *Streamlining SQL* is the process of finding the optimal arrangement of the elements within your query.

In addition to streamlining your SQL statement, you should also consider several other factors when trying to improve general database performance—for example, concurrent user transactions that occur within a database, indexing of tables, and deep-down database tuning.

NOTE

> Many of this lesson's examples use Oracle Express Edition and tools that are available with the Oracle relational database management system (RDBMS). The concepts discussed in this lesson are not restricted to Oracle; they may be applied to other RDBMSs.

Making Your SQL Statements Readable

Even though readability doesn't affect the actual performance of SQL statements, good programming practice calls for readable code. Readability is especially important if you have multiple conditions in the WHERE clause. Anyone reading the clause should be able to determine whether the tables are being joined properly and should be able to understand the order of the conditions.

Try to read this statement:

Syntax ▼

```
SQL> SELECT EMPLOYEE_TBL.EMPLOYEE_ID, EMPLOYEE_TBL.NAME,
        EMPLOYEE_PAY_TBL.SALARY,EMPLOYEE_PAY_TBL.HIRE_DATE
   2  FROM EMPLOYEE_TBL, EMPLOYEE_PAY_TBL
   3  WHERE EMPLOYEE_TBL.EMPLOYEE_ID = EMPLOYEE_PAY_TBL.EMPLOYEE_ID AND
   4  EMPLOYEE_PAY_TBL.SALARY > 30000 OR (EMPLOYEE_PAY_TBL.SALARY BETWEEN 25000
   5  AND 30000 AND EMPLOYEE_PAY_TBL.HIRE_DATE < SYSDATE - 365);
```

Here's the same query reformatted to enhance readability:

Syntax ▼

```
SQL> SELECT E.EMPLOYEE_ID, E.NAME, P.SALARY, P.HIRE_DATE
   2  FROM EMPLOYEE_TBL E,
   3  EMPLOYEE_PAY_TBL P
   4  WHERE E.EMPLOYEE_ID = P.EMPLOYEE_ID
   5    AND P.SALARY > 30000
   6     OR (P.SALARY BETWEEN 25000 AND 30000
   7    AND P.HIRE_DATE < SYSDATE - 365);
```

NOTE

Notice the use of table aliases in the preceding query. EMPLOYEE_TBL in line 2 has been assigned the alias E, and EMPLOYEE_PAY_TBL in line 3 has been assigned the alias P. You can see that in lines 4, 5, 6, and 7, the E and P stand for the full table names. Aliases require less typing than when spelling out the full table name, and even more important, queries that use aliases are better organized and easier to read than queries cluttered with full table names.

The two queries are identical, but the second one is obviously much easier to read. It is very *structured*; that is, the logical components of the query have been separated by carriage returns and consistent spacing. You can quickly see what is being selected (the SELECT clause), what tables are being accessed (the FROM clause), and what conditions need to be met (the WHERE clause).

Avoiding the Full-Table Scan

A *full-table scan* occurs when the database server reads every record in a table to execute a SQL statement. Full-table scans are normally an issue when dealing with queries or the SELECT statement. However, a full-table scan can also come into play when dealing with updates and deletes. A full-table scan occurs when the columns in the WHERE clause do not have an index associated with them. A full-table scan is like reading a book from cover to cover and trying to find a keyword. Most often, you will opt to use the index in order to zero in on exactly where the keyword is reference in the book. You also can utilize indexes on the columns used by the WHERE clause of an UPDATE statement.

You can avoid a full-table scan by creating an index on columns that are used as conditions in the WHERE clause of a SQL statement. Indexes provide a direct path to the data the same way an index in a book refers the reader to a page number. Adding an index speeds up data access. (See Lesson 15, "Creating Indexes on Tables to Improve Performance.")

Although programmers usually frown upon full-table scans, they are sometimes appropriate. For example, use full-tables scans when

- You are selecting most of the rows from a table.
- You are updating every row in a table.
- The tables are small.

In the first two cases, an index would be inefficient because the database server would have to refer to the index, read the table, refer to the index again, read the table again, and so on. On the other hand, indexes are most efficient when the data you are accessing is a small percentage, usually no more than 25% of the total data contained within the table.

In addition, indexes are best used on large tables. You should always consider table size when you are designing tables and indexes. Properly indexing tables involves familiarity with the data and knowing which columns will be referenced most. This might also require experimentation to see which indexes work best.

NOTE   When speaking of a large table, *large* is a relative term. A table that is extremely large to one individual might be minute to another. The size of a table is relative to the size of other tables in the database, to the disk space available, and to the number of disks available and is based on simple common sense. Obviously, a 2GB table is large, whereas a 16KB table is small. In a database environment where the average table size is 100MB, a 500MB table might be considered massive.

Adding a New Index

You will often find yourself in situations in which a SQL statement is running for an unreasonable amount of time, although the performance of other statements seems to be acceptable—for example, when conditions for data retrieval change or when table structures change.

This type of slowdown also occurs when a new screen or window has been added to a front-end application. One of the first things to do when you begin to troubleshoot is to find out whether the target table has an index. In most of the cases, the target table has an index, but one of the new conditions in the WHERE clause might lack an index. Look at the WHERE clause of the SQL statement and ask, "Should I add another index?" The answer might be yes if

16

- The most restrictive condition(s) returns less than 25% of the rows in a table.
- The most restrictive condition(s) will be used often in a SQL statement.
- The condition(s) on columns with an index will return unique values.
- Columns are often referenced in the ORDER BY and GROUP BY clauses.

The term *most restrictive condition* refers to a condition in the WHERE clause that will return the fewest records or rows of data.

Composite indexes may also be used. A *composite index* is an index on two or more columns in a table. These indexes can be more efficient than single-column indexes if the indexed columns are often used together as conditions in the WHERE clause of a SQL statement. If the indexed columns are used separately as well as together, especially in other queries, single-column indexes might be more appropriate. Use your judgment and run tests on your data to see which type of index best suits your database (see Lesson 15).

Arranging Elements in a Query

The best arrangement of elements within your query, particularly in the WHERE clause, really depends on the order of the processing steps in a specific implementation. The arrangement of conditions depends on the columns that are indexed, as well as on which condition will retrieve the fewest records.

You do not have to use a column that is indexed in the WHERE clause, but it is obviously more beneficial to do so. Try to narrow down the results of the SQL statement by using an index that returns the fewest number of rows. If you recall, the condition that returns the fewest records in a table is said to be the most restrictive condition. As a general statement, you should place the most restrictive conditions last in the WHERE clause. (Oracle's query optimizer reads a WHERE clause from the bottom up, so in a sense, you would be placing the most restrictive condition first.)

When the optimizer reads the most restrictive condition first, it is able to narrow down the first set of results before proceeding to the next condition. The next condition, instead of looking at the whole table, should look at the subset that was selected by the most restrictive condition. Ultimately, data is retrieved faster. The most restrictive condition might be unclear in complex queries with multiple conditions, subqueries, calculations, and several combinations of AND, OR, and LIKE.

TIP

> Always check your database documentation to see how SQL statements are processed in your implementation.

The following test is one of many we have run to measure the difference of elapsed time between two uniquely arranged queries with the same content. These examples use the Oracle RDBMS. Remember, the optimizer in this implementation reads the WHERE clause from the bottom up.

Before creating the SELECT statement, we selected distinct row counts on each condition that we planned to use. Here are the values selected for each condition:

Condition	Distinct Values
calc_ytd = '-2109490.8'	13,000 +
dt_stmp = '01-SEP-96'	15
output_cd = '001'	13
activity_cd = 'IN'	10
status_cd = 'A'	4
function_cd = '060'	6

NOTE

> The most restrictive condition is also the condition with the most distinct values.

The next example places the most restrictive conditions first in the WHERE clause:

Input/Output ▼

```
SQL> SET TIMING ON
  2  SELECT COUNT(*)
  3  FROM FACT_TABLE
  4  WHERE CALC_YTD = '-2109490.8'
  5    AND DT_STMP = '01-SEP-96'
  6    AND OUTPUT_CD = '001'
  7    AND ACTIVITY_CD = 'IN'
  8    AND STATUS_CD = 'A'
  9    AND FUNCTION_CD = '060';

COUNT(*)
--------
       8
1 row selected.
Elapsed:  00:00:15.37
```

This example places the most restrictive conditions last in the WHERE clause:

Input/Output ▼

```
SQL> SET TIMING ON
  2  SELECT COUNT(*)
  3  FROM FACT_TABLE
  4  WHERE FUNCTION_CD = '060'
  5    AND STATUS_CD = 'A'
  6    AND ACTIVITY_CD = 'IN'
  7    AND OUTPUT_CD = '001'
  8    AND DT_STMP = '01-SEP-96'
  9    AND CALC_YTD = '-2109490.8';

COUNT(*)
--------
       8
1 row selected.
Elapsed:  00:00:01.80
```

Notice the difference in elapsed time. Simply by changing the order of conditions according to the given table statistics, the second query ran almost 14 seconds faster than the first one. Imagine the difference on a poorly structured query that runs for three hours!

Procedures

For queries that are executed on a regular basis, try to use procedures. A *procedure* is a potentially large group of SQL statements.

Procedures are compiled by the database engine and then executed. Unlike a SQL statement, procedures do not need to be optimized by the database engine before they are executed. Procedures, as opposed to numerous individual queries, might be easier for the user to maintain and more efficient for the database. Additionally, in most RDBMS systems, a special cache is used to hold the query plans of recently executed procedures. You will need to check with your specific system's documentation to find out what benefits are in place for using procedures.

Avoiding OR

Avoid using the logical operator OR in a query if possible. OR inevitably slows down nearly any query made against a substantially large table. We find that IN is generally much quicker than OR. This advice certainly doesn't agree with documentation stating that optimizers convert IN arguments to OR conditions. Nevertheless, here is an example of a query using multiple ORs:

Input ▼

```
SQL> SELECT *
  2  FROM FACT_TABLE
  3  WHERE STATUS_CD = 'A'
  4      OR STATUS_CD = 'B'
  5      OR STATUS_CD = 'C'
  6      OR STATUS_CD = 'D'
  7      OR STATUS_CD = 'E'
  8      OR STATUS_CD = 'F'
  9  ORDER BY STATUS_CD;
```

Here is the same query using SUBSTR and IN:

Input ▼

```
SQL> SELECT *
  2  FROM FACT_TABLE
  3  WHERE SUBSTR(STATUS_CD, 1, 1) IN ('A','B','C','D','E','F')
  4  ORDER BY STATUS_CD;
```

Try testing something similar yourself. Although books are excellent sources for standards and direction, you will find it is often useful to come to your own conclusions on certain issues, such as performance.

Here is another example using SUBSTR and IN. Notice that the first query combines LIKE with OR.

Input ▼

```
SQL> SELECT *
  2  FROM FACT_TABLE
  3  WHERE PROD_CD LIKE 'AB%'
  4     OR PROD_CD LIKE 'AC%'
  5     OR PROD_CD LIKE 'BB%'
  6     OR PROD_CD LIKE 'BC%'
  7     OR PROD_CD LIKE 'CC%'
  8  ORDER BY PROD_CD;
```

Input ▼

```
SQL> SELECT *
  2  FROM FACT_TABLE
  3  WHERE SUBSTR(PROD_CD,1,2) IN ('AB','AC','BB','BC','CC')
  4  ORDER BY PROD_CD;
```

The second example not only avoids the OR but also eliminates the combination of the OR and LIKE operators. You might want to try this example to see what the real-time performance difference is for your data.

OLAP Versus OLTP

When tuning a database, you must first determine what the database is being used for. An *online analytical processing (OLAP)* database is a system that functions to provide query capabilities to the end user for statistical and general informational purposes. The data retrieved in this type of environment is often used for statistical reports that aid in corporate decision-making processes. These types of systems are also referred to as *decision support systems (DSSs)*.

An *online transactional processing (OLTP)* database is a system the main function of which is to provide an environment for end-user input, and may also involve queries against day-to-day information. OLTP systems are used to manipulate information within the database on a daily basis. Data warehouses and DSSs get their data from online transactional databases, and sometimes from other OLAP systems.

Tuning an OLTP System

A transactional database is a delicate system that is heavily accessed in the form of transactions and queries against day-to-day information. However, an OLTP does not usually require a vast sort area, at least not to the extent to which it is required in an OLAP environment. Most OLTP transactions require quick input and do not involve much sorting.

One of the biggest issues in a transactional database is the rollback of data. The amount and size of rollback segments heavily depend on how many users are concurrently accessing the database, as well as the amount of work in each transaction. The best approach is to have several rollback segments in a transactional environment.

Another concern in a transactional environment is the integrity of the *transaction logs,* which are written to after each transaction. These logs exist for the sole purpose of recovery. Therefore, each SQL implementation needs a way to back up the logs for use in a point-in-time recovery. SQL Server uses backup devices; Oracle uses a database mode known as `ARCHIVELOG` mode. Transaction logs also involve a performance consideration because backing up logs requires additional overhead.

Tuning an OLAP System

Tuning OLAP systems, such as a data warehouse or decision support system, is much different from tuning a transactional database. Normally, more space is needed for sorting.

Because the purpose of this type of system is to retrieve useful decision-making data, you can expect many complex queries, which normally involve the grouping and sorting of data. Compared to a transactional database, OLAP systems typically take more space for the sort area, but less space for the rollback area.

Most transactions in an OLAP system take place as part of a batch process. Instead of having several rollback areas for user input, you might resort to one large rollback area for the loads, which can be taken offline during daily activity to reduce overhead.

Additionally, the OLAP databases tend to be less normalized (see Lesson 8, "Database Normalization,") than their OLTP counterparts. The denormalization of the data normally is used to allow for faster and easier reporting.

Batch Loads Versus Transactional Processing

A major factor in the performance of a database and SQL statements is the type of processing that takes place within a database. One type of processing is OLTP, discussed earlier in this lesson. When we talk about transactional processing, we are going to refer to two types: user input and batch loads.

Regular user input usually consists of SQL statements such as INSERT, UPDATE, and DELETE. These types of transactions are often performed by the end user, or the customer. End users are normally using a front-end application such as PowerBuilder to interface with the database, and therefore they seldom issue visible SQL statements. The end users use applications built with tools such as PowerBuilder, Visual Basic, and Oracle's Designer and Developer.

Your main focus when optimizing the performance of a database should be the end-user transactions. After all, no customer equates to no database, which in turn means that you are out of a job. Always try to keep your customers happy, even though their expectations of system/database performance might sometimes be unreasonable. One consideration with end-user input is the number of concurrent users. The more concurrent database users you have, the greater the possibilities of performance degradation.

16

A *batch load* occurs when heaps of transactions are being performed against the database at once. For example, suppose you are archiving last year's data into a massive history table. You might need to insert thousands, or even millions, of rows of data into your history table. You probably wouldn't want to do this task manually, so you are likely to create a batch job or script to automate the process. (Numerous techniques are available for loading data in a batch.)

Batch loads are notorious for taxing system and database resources. These database resources might include table access, data dictionary access, the database rollback segment, and sort area space; system resources might include available CPU and shared memory. Many other factors are involved, depending on your operating system and database server.

Both end-user transactions and batch loads are necessary for most databases to be successful, but your system could experience serious performance problems if these two types of processing lock horns. Therefore, you should know the difference between them and keep them segregated as much as possible. For example, you would not want to load massive amounts of data into the database when user activity is high. The database response might already be slow because of the number of concurrent users. Always try to run batch loads when user activity is at a minimum. Many shops reserve times in the evenings or early morning to load data in batch to avoid interfering with daily processing.

You should always plan the timing for massive batch loads and be careful to avoid scheduling them when the database is expected to be available for normal use. Figure 16.1 depicts heavy batch updates running concurrently with several user processes, all of which are contending for system resources.

FIGURE 16.1
System resource
contention.

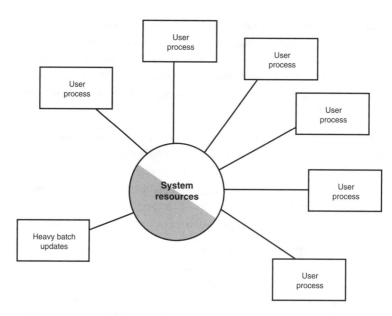

As you can see, many processes are contending for system resources. The heavy batch updates that are being done throw a monkey wrench into the equation. Instead of the system resources being dispersed somewhat evenly among the users, the batch updates appear to be hogging them. This situation is just the beginning of resource contention. As the batch transactions proceed, the user processes might eventually be forced out of the picture. This condition is not a good way of doing business. Even if the system has only one user, significant contention for that user could occur.

Another problem with batch processes is that the process may hold locks on a table that a user is trying to access. If there is a lock on a table, the user will be refused access until the lock is freed by the batch process, which could be hours. Batch processes should take place when system resources are at their best if possible. Don't make the users' transactions compete with batch updates. Nobody wins that game.

Optimizing Data Loads by Dropping Indexes

One way to expedite batch updates is by dropping indexes. Imagine the history table with many thousands of rows. That history table is also likely to have one or more indexes. When you think of an index, you normally think of faster table access, but in the case of batch loads, you can benefit by dropping the index(es) (see Lesson 15).

When you load data into a table with an index, you can usually expect a great deal of index use, especially if you are updating a high percentage of rows in the table. Look at it this way: If you are studying a book and highlighting key points for future reference, you might find it quicker to browse through the book from beginning to end rather than using the index to locate your key points. (Using the index would be efficient if you were highlighting only a small portion of the book.)

To maximize the efficiency of batch loads/updates that affect a high percentage of rows in a table, you can take these three basic steps to disable an index:

1. Drop the appropriate index(es).
2. Load/update the table's data.
3. Rebuild the table's index.

16

COMMIT Statement

When performing batch transactions, you must know how often to perform a COMMIT statement. As you learned in Lesson 14, "Controlling Transactions," a COMMIT statement finalizes a transaction. A COMMIT saves a transaction or writes any changes to the applicable table(s). Behind the scenes, however, much more is going on. Some areas in the database are reserved to store completed transactions before the changes are actually written to the target table. Oracle calls these areas *rollback segments*. When you issue a COMMIT statement, transactions associated with your SQL session in the rollback segment are updated in the target table. After the update takes place, the contents of the rollback segment are removed. A ROLLBACK command, on the other hand, clears the contents of the rollback segment without updating the target table.

As you can guess, if you never issue a COMMIT or ROLLBACK command, transactions keep building within the rollback segments. Subsequently, if the data you are loading is greater in size than the available space in the rollback segments, the database will essentially come to a halt and ban further transactional activity. Not issuing COMMIT commands is a common programming pitfall; regular COMMITs help to ensure stable performance of the entire database system.

NOTE — The designers of MySQL looked at the potential cost in terms of performance and made the choice not to make use of rollback segments. An automatic COMMIT occurs for all table types in MySQL. However, you can use COMMIT and ROLLBACK if you specifically define a TRANSACTION object.

The management of rollback segments is a complex and vital database administrator (DBA) responsibility because transactions dynamically affect the rollback segments, and in turn affect the overall performance of the database, as well as individual SQL statements. So when you are loading large amounts of data, be sure to issue the COMMIT command on a regular basis. Bulk-loading routines often take advantage of this scenario by sending batches of commands followed by a COMMIT command to ensure that the data does not overwhelm the rollback segments. Check with your DBA for advice on how often to use COMMIT during batch transactions (see Figure 16.2).

FIGURE 16.2
The rollback area.

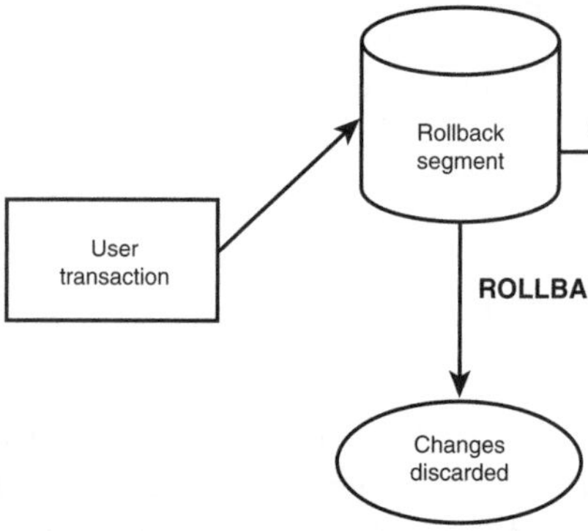

As you can see in Figure 16.2, when a user performs a transaction, the changes are retained in the rollback area.

Rebuilding Tables and Indexes in a Dynamic Environment

The term *dynamic database environment* refers to a large database that is in a constant state of change. The changes that we are referring to are frequent batch updates and continual daily transactional processing. Dynamic databases usually entail heavy OLTP systems, but can also refer to DSSs or data warehouses, depending upon the volume and frequency of data loads.

The result of constant high-volume changes to a database is growth, which in turn yields fragmentation. Fragmentation can easily get out of hand if growth is not managed properly. Oracle allocates an initial extent to tables when they are created. When data is loaded and fills the table's initial extent, the next extent, which is also allocated when the table is created, is taken.

Sizing tables and indexes is essentially a DBA function and can drastically affect SQL statement performance. The first step in growth management is to be proactive. Allow room for tables to grow from day one, within reason. Also plan to defragment the database on a regular basis, even if doing so means developing a weekly routine. Here are the basic conceptual steps involved in defragmenting tables and indexes in an RDBMS:

1. Get a good backup of the table(s) and/or index(es).
2. Drop the table(s) and/or index(es).
3. Rebuild the table(s) and/or index(es) with new space allocation.
4. Restore the data into the newly built table(s).
5. Re-create the index(es) if necessary.
6. Reestablish user/role permissions on the table if necessary.
7. Save the backup of your table until you are absolutely sure that the new table was built successfully. If you choose to discard the backup of the original table, you should first make a backup of the new table after the data has been fully restored.

16

> **CAUTION** Never get rid of the backup of your table until you are sure that the new table was built successfully.

The following example demonstrates a practical use of a mailing list table in an Oracle database environment:

Input/Output ▼

```
SQL> CREATE TABLE MAILING_TBL_BKUP AS
  2 SELECT * FROM MAILING_TBL;

Table Created.

SQL> DROP TABLE MAILING_TBL;

Table Dropped.

SQL> CREATE TABLE MAILING_TBL
  2 (
  3 INDIVIDUAL_ID       VARCHAR2(12)     NOT NULL,
  4 INDIVIDUAL_NAME     VARCHAR2(30)    NOT NULL,
  5 ADDRESS             VARCHAR(40)     NOT NULL,
  6 CITY                VARCHAR(25)     NOT NULL,
  7 STATE               VARCHAR(2)      NOT NULL,
  8 ZIP_CODE            VARCHAR(9)      NOT NULL,
```

```
 9 )
10  TABLESPACE TABLESPACE_NAME
11  STORAGE    (    INITIAL       NEW_SIZE,
12         NEXT       NEW_SIZE    );
```

Table created.

```
SQL> INSERT INTO MAILING_TBL
  2 SELECT * FROM MAILING_TBL_BKUP;
```

93,451 rows inserted.

```
SQL> CREATE INDEX MAILING_IDX ON MAILING TABLE
  2 (
  3 INDIVIDUAL_ID
  4 )
  5 TABLESPACE TABLESPACE_NAME
  6 STORAGE    (    INITIAL       NEW_SIZE,
  7         NEXT       NEW_SIZE    );
```

Index Created.

```
SQL> GRANT SELECT ON MAILING_TBL TO PUBLIC;
```

Grant Succeeded.

```
SQL> DROP TABLE MAILING_TBL_BKUP;
```

Table Dropped.

Rebuilding tables and indexes that have grown enables you to optimize storage, which improves overall performance. Remember to drop the backup table only after you have verified that the new table has been created successfully. Also keep in mind that you can achieve the same results with other methods. Check the options that are available to you in your database documentation.

NOTE

Some RDBMS systems such as Microsoft's SQL Server contain maintenance commands that allow the DBA to defragment data and indexes while the database is online. You should check your specific implementation's documentation to determine what options are available to you and fit in best with your environment.

Tuning the Database

Tuning a database includes fine-tuning the database server's performance. As a newcomer to SQL, you probably will not be exposed to database tuning unless you are a new DBA, or a DBA moving into a relational database environment. Whether you will be managing a database or using SQL in applications or programming, you will benefit from knowing something about the database-tuning process. The key to the success of any database is for all parties to work together as one entity. Some general tips for tuning a database follow:

16

- Minimize the overall size required for the database—It's good to allow room for growth when designing a database, but don't go overboard. Don't tie up resources that you might need to accommodate database growth.

- Experiment with the user process's time-slice variable—This variable controls the amount of time the database server's scheduler allocates to each user's process.

- Optimize the network packet size used by applications—The larger the amount of data sent over the network, the larger the network packet size should be. Consult your database and network documentation for more details.

- Store transaction logs on separate hard disks—For each transaction that takes place, the server must write the changes to the transaction logs. If you store these log files on the same disk on which you store data, you could create a performance bottleneck (see Figure 16.3).

FIGURE 16.3
Using available disks to enhance performance.

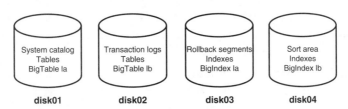

System catalog	Transaction logs	Rollback segments	Sort area
Tables	Tables	Indexes	Indexes
BigTable la	BigTable lb	BigIndex la	BigIndex lb

disk01   **disk02**   **disk03**   **disk04**

- Spread extremely large tables across multiple disks—If concurrent users are accessing a large table that is spread over multiple disks, there is much less chance of having to wait for system resources (refer to Figure 16.3).

- Store database sort, data dictionary, and rollback areas on separate hard disks—These are all areas in the database that most users access frequently. By spreading these areas over multiple disk drives, you are maximizing the use of system resources (refer to Figure 16.3).

- Add CPUs—This system administrator (SA) function can drastically improve database performance. Adding CPUs can speed up data processing for obvious reasons. If you have multiple CPUs on a machine, you might be able to implement parallel processing strategies. See your database documentation for more information on parallel processing, if it is available with your implementation.

- Add memory—Generally, the more the better.

- Store tables and indexes on separate hard disks—You should store indexes and their related tables on separate disk drives whenever possible. This arrangement enables the table to be read at the same time the index is being referenced on another disk. The capability to store objects on multiple disks might depend on how many disks are connected to a controller (refer to Figure 16.3).

Figure 16.3 shows a simple example of how you might segregate the major areas of your database.

The scenario in Figure 16.3 uses four devices: disk01 through disk04. The objective when spreading your heavy database areas and objects is to keep areas of high use away from each other.

- disk01—The data dictionary stores information about tables, indexes, users, statistics, database files, sizing, growth, and other pertinent data that is often accessed by a high percentage of transactions.

- disk02—Transaction logs are updated every time a change is made to a table (INSERT, UPDATE, or DELETE). Transaction logs are an important factor in an online transactional database. They are not of great concern in a read-only environment, such as a data warehouse or DSS.

- disk03—Rollback segments are also significant in a transactional environment. However, if there is little transactional activity (INSERT, UPDATE, or DELETE), rollback segments will not be heavily used.

- disk04—The database's sort area, on the other hand, is used as a temporary area for SQL statement processing when sorting data, as in a GROUP BY or ORDER BY clause. Sort areas are typically an issue in a data warehouse or DSS. However, the use of sort areas should also be considered in a transactional environment.

TIP

Also note how the application tables and indexes have been placed on each disk. Tables and indexes should be spread out as much as possible.

Notice that in Figure 16.3 the tables and indexes are stored on different devices.

You can also see how a big table or index may be *striped* across two or more devices. This technique splits the table into smaller segments that can be accessed simultaneously. Striping a table or index across multiple devices is a way to control fragmentation. In this scenario, tables may be read while their corresponding indexes are being referenced, which increases the speed of overall data access.

This example is really quite simple. Depending on the function, size, and system-related issues of your database, you might find a similar method for optimizing system resources that works better. In a perfect world where money is no obstacle, the best configuration is to have a separate disk for each major database entity, including large tables and indexes.

16

NOTE   The DBA and SA should work together to balance database space allocation and optimize the memory that is available on the server. Without the proper system resources available to the database system, no amount of tuning is going to help the performance of the database.

Tuning a database very much depends on the specific database system you are using. Obviously, tuning a database entails much more than just preparing queries and letting them fly. On the other hand, you won't get much reward for tuning a database when the application SQL is not fine tuned itself. Professionals who tune databases for a living often specialize on one database product and learn as much as they possibly can about its features and idiosyncrasies. Although database tuning is often looked upon as a painful task, it can provide very lucrative employment for the people who truly understand it.

Identifying Performance Obstacles

We have already mentioned some of the countless possible pitfalls that can hinder the general performance of a database. These are typically general bottlenecks that involve system-level maintenance, database maintenance, and management of SQL statement processing.

This section summarizes the most common obstacles in system performance and database response time:

- Not making use of available devices on the server—A company purchases multiple disk drives for a reason. If you do not use them accordingly by spreading apart the vital database components, you are limiting the performance capabilities. Maximizing the use of system resources is just as important as maximizing the use of the database server capabilities.

- Not performing frequent COMMITs—Failing to use periodic COMMITs or ROLLBACKs during heavy batch loads will ultimately result in database bottlenecks.

- Allowing batch loads to interfere with daily processing—Running batch loads during times when the database is expected to be available will cause problems for everybody. The batch process will be in a perpetual battle with end users for system resources.

- Being careless when creating SQL statements—Carelessly creating complex SQL statements will more than likely contribute to substandard response time.

TIP

You can use various methods to optimize the structure of a SQL statement, depending upon the steps taken by the database server during SQL statement processing.

- Running batch loads with table indexes—You could end up with a batch load that runs all day and all night, as opposed to a batch load that finishes within a few hours. Indexes slow down batch loads that are accessing a high percentage of the rows in a table.

- Having too many concurrent users for allocated memory—As the number of concurrent database and system users grows, you might need to allocate more memory for the shared process. See your SA.

- Creating indexes on columns with few unique values—Indexing on a column such as gender, which has only two unique values, is not very efficient. Instead, try to index columns that will return a low percentage of rows in a query.

- Creating indexes on small tables—By the time the index is referenced and the data read, a full-table scan could have been accomplished.

- Not managing system resources efficiently—Poor management of system resources can result from wasted space during database initialization, table creation, uncontrolled fragmentation, and irregular system/database maintenance.

- Not sizing tables and indexes properly—Poor estimates for tables and indexes that grow tremendously in a large database environment can lead to serious fragmentation problems, which if not tended to, will snowball into more serious problems.

Using Built-in Tuning Tools

Check with your DBA or database vendor to determine what tools are available to you for performance measuring and tuning. You can use performance-tuning tools to identify deficiencies in the data access path; in addition, these tools can sometimes suggest changes to improve the performance of a particular SQL statement.

Oracle has two popular tools for managing SQL statement performance. These tools are EXPLAIN PLAN and TKPROF. The EXPLAIN PLAN tool identifies the access path that will be taken when the SQL statement is executed. TKPROF measures the performance by time elapsed during each phase of SQL statement processing. Oracle Corporation also provides other tools that help with SQL statement and database analysis, but the two mentioned here are the most popular. If you want to simply measure the elapsed time of a query in Oracle, you can use the SQL*Plus command SET TIMING ON.

SET TIMING ON and other SET commands are covered in more depth on Lesson 25, "Using Oracle SQL*Plus to Satisfy Reporting Needs."

Microsoft's SQL Server has diagnostic tools for SQL statements. These options are in the form of SET commands that you can add to your SQL statements. (These commands are similar to Oracle's SET commands). Some common commands are SET SHOWPLAN ON, SET STATISTIC IO ON, and SET STATISTICS TIME ON. These SET commands display output concerning the steps performed in a query, the number of reads and writes required to perform the query, and general statement-parsing information. SQL Server SET commands are covered on Lesson 27, "An Introduction to Transact-SQL."

16

Summary

Two major elements of streamlining, or tuning, directly affect the performance of SQL statements: application tuning and database tuning. Each has its own role, but one cannot be optimally tuned without the other. The first step toward success is for the technical team and system engineers to work together to balance resources and take full advantage of the database features that aid in improving performance. Many of these features are built into the database software provided by the vendor.

Application developers must know the data. The key to an optimal database design is thorough knowledge of the application's data. Developers and production programmers must know when to use indexes, when to add another index, and when to allow batch jobs to run. Always plan batch loads and keep batch processing separate from daily transactional processing.

Databases can be tuned to improve the performance of individual applications that access them. DBAs must be concerned with the daily operation and performance of the database. In addition to the meticulous tuning that occurs behind the scenes, the DBA can usually offer creative suggestions for accessing data more efficiently, such as manipulating indexes or reconstructing a SQL statement. The DBA should also be familiar with the tools that are readily available with the database software to measure performance and provide suggestions for statement tweaking.

Q&A

Q If I streamline my SQL statement, how much of a gain in performance should I expect?

A Performance gain depends on the size of your tables, whether columns in the table are indexed, and other relative factors. In a very large database, a complex query that runs for hours can sometimes be cut to minutes. In the case of transactional processing, streamlining a SQL statement can save important seconds for the end user.

Q How do I coordinate my batch loads or updates?

A Check with the database administrator and, of course, with management when scheduling a batch load or update. If you are a system engineer, you probably will not know everything that is going on within the database.

Q How often should I commit my batch transactions?

A Check with the DBA for advice. The DBA will need to know approximately how much data you are inserting, updating, or deleting. The frequency of COMMIT statements should also take into account other batch loads occurring simultaneously with other database activities.

Q Should I stripe all my tables?

A Striping offers performance benefits only for large tables and/or for tables that are heavily accessed on a regular basis.

Workshop

The Workshop provides quiz questions to help solidify your understanding of the material covered, as well as exercises to provide you with experience in using what you have learned. Try to answer the quiz and exercise questions before checking the answers in Appendix A, "Answers."

Quiz

1. What does it mean to streamline a SQL statement?
2. Should tables and their corresponding indexes reside on the same disk?
3. Why is the arrangement of conditions in a SQL statement important?
4. What happens during a full-table scan?
5. How can you avoid a full-table scan?
6. What are some common hindrances of general performance?
7. What would you generally structure an OLAP system for? What about an OLTP system?
8. What is one method of defragmenting the data within a table?

16

Exercises

1. Make the following SQL statement more readable:

```
SELECT EMPLOYEE.LAST_NAME, EMPLOYEE.FIRST_NAME, EMPLOYEE.MIDDLE_NAME,
EMPLOYEE.ADDRESS, EMPLOYEE.PHONE_NUMBER, PAYROLL.SALARY, PAYROLL.POSITION,
EMPLOYEE.SSN, PAYROLL.START_DATE FROM EMPLOYEE, PAYROLL WHERE
EMPLOYEE.SSN = PAYROLL.SSN AND EMPLOYEE.LAST_NAME LIKE 'S%' AND
PAYROLL.SALARY > 20000;
```

2. Rearrange the conditions in the following query to optimize data retrieval time. Use the following statistics (on the tables in their entirety) to determine the order of the conditions:

    593 individuals have the last name of SMITH.

    712 individuals live in INDIANAPOLIS.

    3,492 individuals are MALES.

    1,233 individuals earn a salary >= 30,000.

    5,009 individuals are SINGLE.

    Individual_id is the primary key for both tables.

```
SELECT M.INDIVIDUAL_NAME, M.ADDRESS, M.CITY, M.STATE, M.ZIP_CODE,
       S.SEX, S.MARITAL_STATUS, S.SALARY
FROM MAILING_TBL M,
     INDIVIDUAL_STAT_TBL S
WHERE M.NAME LIKE 'SMITH%'
  AND M.CITY = 'INDIANAPOLIS'
  AND S.SEX = 'MALE'
  AND S.SALARY >= 30000
  AND S.MARITAL_STATUS = 'S'

  AND M.INDIVIDUAL_ID = S.INDIVIDUAL_ID;
```

LESSON 17
Database Security

In this lesson, we discuss database security. We specifically look at various SQL statements and constructs that enable you to administer and effectively manage a relational database. Like many other topics you have studied thus far, how a database management system (DBMS) implements security varies widely among products. We focus on the popular database products, Oracle and MySQL, to introduce this topic. By the end of the lesson, you will be able to do the following:

- Create users
- Change passwords
- Create roles
- Use views for security purposes
- Use synonyms in place of views

Security's Role in Database Administration

Security is an often overlooked aspect of database design. Most computer professionals enter the computer world with some knowledge of computer programming or hardware, and they tend to concentrate on those areas. For instance, if your boss asked you to work on a brand-new project that obviously required some type of relational database design, what would be your first step? After choosing some type of hardware and software baseline, you would probably begin by designing the basic database for the project. This phase would gradually be split up among several people—one of them a graphical user interface (GUI) designer, another a low-level component builder. Perhaps you, after reading this book, might be asked to code the SQL queries to provide the guts of the application. Along with this task comes the responsibility of actually administering and maintaining the database.

Many times, little thought or planning goes into the actual production phase of the application. What happens when many users are allowed to use the application across a wide area network (WAN)? With today's powerful personal computer software and with technologies such as Microsoft's Open Database Connectivity (ODBC), any user with access to your network can find a way to get at your database. (We won't even bring up the complexities involved when your company decides to hook your local area network [LAN] up to the Internet or some other wide-ranging computer network!) Are you prepared to face this situation?

Fortunately for you, software manufacturers provide most of the tools you need to handle this security problem. Every new release of a network operating system faces more stringent security requirements than its predecessors. In addition, most major database vendors build some degree of security into their products, which exists independently of your operating system or network security. Implementation of these security features varies widely from product to product.

Popular Database Products and Security

As you know by now, many relational database systems are vying for your business. Every vendor wants you for short- and long-term reasons. During the development phase of a project, you might purchase a small number of product licenses for testing, development, and so forth. However, the total number of licenses required for your production database can reach the hundreds or even thousands. In addition, when you decide to use a particular database product, the chances are good that you will stay with that product for years to come. Here are some points to keep in mind when you examine these products:

- Microsoft FoxPro DBMS is a powerful database system that is used primarily in single-user environments. FoxPro uses a limited subset of SQL. No security measures are provided with the system. It also uses an Xbase file format, with each file containing one table. Indexes are stored in separate files.

- Microsoft Access relational DBMS implements more of SQL. Access is still intended for use on the PC platform, although it does contain a rudimentary security system. The product enables you to build queries and store them within the database. In addition, the entire database and all its objects exist within one file.

- Oracle RDBMS supports nearly the full SQL standard. In addition, Oracle has added its own extension to SQL, called PL/SQL. It contains full security features, including the capability to create roles as well as assign permissions and privileges on objects in the database.

■ Microsoft SQL Server is similar in power and features to the Oracle product. SQL Server also provides a wide range of security features and has its own extensions to the SQL language, called Transact-SQL.

■ MySQL server is an RDBMS that has been designed for speed, flexibility, and dependability. Many of its capabilities are a direct result of automatic commits on inserts, updates, and deletes. This eliminates the need for rollback segments and other tuning mechanisms found in other SQL implementations. Equipped with various security tools, it is able to assign permissions and privileges.

The purpose behind describing these products is to illustrate that not all software is suitable for every application. If you are in a business environment, your options may be limited. Factors such as cost and performance are extremely important. However, without adequate security measures, any savings your database creates can be easily offset by security problems.

17

Up to this point you haven't worried much about the security of the databases you have created. Has it occurred to you that you might not want other users to come in and tamper with the database information you have so carefully entered? What would your reaction be if you logged on to the server one morning and discovered that the database you had slaved over had been dropped (remember how silent the DROP DATABASE command is)? We examine in some detail how two popular database management systems (Oracle Express and MySQL) enable you to set up a secure database. You will be able to apply most of this information to other DBMSs, so make sure you read this information even if Oracle or MySQL are not your systems of choice.

TIP

Keep the following questions in mind as you plan your security system:

■ Who gets the database administrator (DBA) role?

■ How many users will need access to the database?

■ Which users will need which privileges and which roles?

■ How will you remove users who no longer need access to the database?

Oracle Express and MySQL Security

Oracle implements security by using three basic constructs:

- Users
- Roles
- Privileges

MySQL utilizes Users and Privileges.

Creating Users

Users are account names that are allowed to log on to the Oracle database. The Oracle SQL syntax used to create a new user is as follows:

Syntax ▼

```
CREATE USER user
IDENTIFIED {BY password | EXTERNALLY}
[DEFAULT TABLESPACE tablespace]
[TEMPORARY TABLESPACE tablespace]
[QUOTA {integer [K|M] | UNLIMITED} ON tablespace]
[PROFILE profile]
```

If the BY password option is chosen, the system prompts the user to enter a password each time he or she logs on. As an example, create a username for yourself:

Input/Output ▼

```
SQL> CREATE USER Bryan IDENTIFIED BY CUTIGER;

User created.
```

Analysis ▼

Each time I log on with my username Bryan, I am prompted to enter my password: CUTIGER.

If the EXTERNALLY option was chosen, Oracle relies on your computer system logon name and password. When you log on to your system, you have essentially logged on to Oracle.

Some implementations allow users to keep the external, or operating system, password as a default when using SQL (IDENTIFIED externally). However, we recommend that you force users to enter a password by utilizing the IDENTIFIED BY clause (IDENTIFIED BY password).

As you can see from looking at the rest of the CREATE USER syntax, Oracle also allows you to set up default tablespaces and quotas. You can learn more about these topics by examining the Oracle documentation.

MySQL approached the CREATE USER situation differently than Oracle. In the MySQL environment there are two databases that come as part of the server package: MYSQL and TEST. If you were to log in to MySQL and switch to the MYSQL database, then show all tables within the MYSQL database, you would get the following result:

17

Input/Output ▼

```
mysql> use mysql;
Database changed
mysql> show tables;
+-----------------+
| Tables_in_mysql |
+-----------------+
| columns_priv    |
| db              |
| func            |
| host            |
| tables_priv     |
| user            |
+-----------------+
6 rows in set (0.01 sec)
```

This is where MySQL stores system information. By issuing an INSERT statement into the USER table, a new user can be created. Note the structure of the USER table.

Input/Output ▼

```
mysql> desc user;
```

Field	Type	Null	Key	Default	Extra
Host	char(60) binary		PRI		
User	char(16) binary		PRI		
Password	char(16) binary				
Select_priv	enum('N','Y')			N	

```
| Insert_priv     | enum('N','Y')  |     |     | N        |        |
| Update_priv     | enum('N','Y')  |     |     | N        |        |
| Delete_priv     | enum('N','Y')  |     |     | N        |        |
| Create_priv     | enum('N','Y')  |     |     | N        |        |
| Drop_priv       | enum('N','Y')  |     |     | N        |        |
| Reload_priv     | enum('N','Y')  |     |     | N        |        |
| Shutdown_priv   | enum('N','Y')  |     |     | N        |        |
| Process_priv    | enum('N','Y')  |     |     | N        |        |
| File_priv       | enum('N','Y')  |     |     | N        |        |
| Grant_priv      | enum('N','Y')  |     |     | N        |        |
| References_priv | enum('N','Y')  |     |     | N        |        |
| Index_priv      | enum('N','Y')  |     |     | N        |        |
| Alter_priv      | enum('N','Y')  |     |     | N        |        |
+-----------------+----------------+-----+-----+----------+--------+
17 rows in set (0.02 sec)
```

The following INSERT statement could create a new user in the user table.

Input ▼

```
mysql> insert into user
    > (host, user, password, select_priv, insert_priv)
    > values
    > ('localhost','bob','bob','Y','Y');
```

The user bob has been created with only the SELECT and INSERT privileges. Subsequently, you may also use the UPDATE and DELETE commands to change a user's information or to delete the user from the database.

As with every other CREATE command you have learned about in this book, there is also an ALTER USER command. An example in Oracle looks like this:

Syntax ▼

```
ALTER USER user
[IDENTIFIED {BY password | EXTERNALLY}]
[DEFAULT TABLESPACE tablespace]
[TEMPORARY TABLESPACE tablespace]
[QUOTA {integer [K|M] | UNLIMITED} ON tablespace]
[PROFILE profile]
[DEFAULT ROLE { role [, role] ...
   | ALL [EXCEPT role [, role] ...] | NONE}]
```

You can use this command to change all the user's options, including the password and profile. For example, to change the user Bryan's password, you type this:

Input/Output ▼

```
SQL> ALTER USER Bryan
  2  IDENTIFIED BY ROSEBUD;

User altered.
```

To change the default tablespace, type this:

Input/Output ▼

```
SQL> ALTER USER RON
  2  DEFAULT TABLESPACE USERS;

User altered.
```

To remove a user, simply issue the DROP USER command, which removes the user's entry in the system database. Here's the syntax for the Oracle version of this command:

Syntax ▼

```
DROP USER user_name [CASCADE];
```

If the CASCADE option is used, all objects owned by the user are dropped along with the user's account. If CASCADE is not used, and the user denoted by user_name still owns objects, that user is not dropped. This feature is somewhat confusing, but it is useful if you are ever required to drop users.

NOTE

Some implementations, such as Microsoft SQL Server, have a different meaning for *user*. In their system, a person is given an *login* to access the database server instance, and then a *user* is an account created within a database to grant access. You will need to check with your implementation's documentation to ensure you understand the manner in which security is implemented.

Creating Roles

A *role* is a privilege or set of privileges that allows a user to perform certain functions in the database. To grant a role to an Oracle user, use the following syntax:

Syntax ▼

```
GRANT role TO user [WITH ADMIN OPTION];
```

If `WITH ADMIN OPTION` is used, that user can then grant roles to other users. Isn't power exhilarating?

To remove a role in Oracle, use the `REVOKE` command:

Syntax ▼

```
REVOKE role FROM user;
```

When you log on to the system using the account you created earlier, you have exhausted the limits of your permissions. You can log on, but that is about all you can do. Oracle lets you register as one of three roles:

- Connect
- Resource
- DBA

These three roles have varying degrees of privileges.

NOTE — If you have the appropriate privileges, you can create your own role, grant privileges to your role, and then grant your role to a user for further security.

The Connect Role

The Connect role can be thought of as the entry-level role. Users who have been granted Connect role access can be granted various privileges that allow them to do something with a database.

Input/Output ▼

```
SQL> GRANT CONNECT TO Bryan;

Grant succeeded.
```

The Connect role enables users to select, insert, update, and delete records from tables belonging to other users (after the appropriate permissions have been granted). These users can also create tables, views, sequences, clusters, and synonyms.

The Resource Role

The Resource role gives the users more access to Oracle databases. In addition to the permissions that can be granted to the Connect role, Resource roles can also be granted permission to create procedures, triggers, and indexes.

Input/Output ▼

```
SQL> GRANT RESOURCE TO Bryan;

Grant succeeded.
```

The DBA Role

The DBA role includes all privileges. Users with this role are able to do essentially anything they want to the database system. You should keep the number of users with this role to a minimum to ensure system integrity.

Input/Output ▼

```
SQL> GRANT DBA TO Bryan;

Grant succeeded.
```

After the three preceding steps, user Bryan was granted the Connect, Resource, and DBA roles. This is somewhat redundant because the DBA role encompasses the other two roles, so you can drop them now, using the REVOKE command.

Input/Output ▼

```
SQL> REVOKE CONNECT FROM Bryan;

Revoke succeeded.

SQL> REVOKE RESOURCE FROM Bryan;

Revoke succeeded.
```

Bryan can do everything he needs to do with the DBA role.

User Privileges

After you decide which roles to grant your users, your next step is deciding which permissions these users will have on database objects. (Oracle calls these permissions *privileges*.) The types of privileges vary depending on what role you have been granted. If you actually create an object, you can grant privileges on that object to other users as long as their role permits access to that privilege. Oracle defines two types of privileges that can be granted to users: system privileges and object privileges

System privileges apply system wide. The syntax used to grant a system privilege is as follows:

Syntax ▼

```
GRANT system_privilege TO {user_name | role | PUBLIC}
[WITH ADMIN OPTION];
```

WITH ADMIN OPTION enables the grantee to grant this privilege to someone else.

User Access to Views

The following command permits all users of the system to have CREATE VIEW access within their own schema:

Input/Output ▼

```
SQL> GRANT CREATE VIEW
  2  TO PUBLIC;

Grant succeeded.
```

Analysis ▼

The PUBLIC keyword means that everyone has CREATE VIEW privileges. Obviously, these system privileges enable the grantee to have a lot of access to nearly all the system settings. System privileges should be granted only to special users or to users who have a real need to use these privileges. Table 17.1 shows the system privileges you will find in the help files included with Personal Oracle.

CAUTIOUS | Use caution when granting privileges to PUBLIC. Granting privileges to PUBLIC gives all users with access to the database privileges you might not want them to have.

TABLE 17.1   The More Commonly Used System Privileges in Oracle

System Privilege	Operations Permitted
ALTER ANY INDEX	Allows the grantees to alter any index in any schema.
ALTER ANY PROCEDURE	Allows the grantees to alter any stored procedure, function, or package in any schema.
ALTER ANY ROLE	Allows the grantees to alter any role in the database.
ALTER ANY TABLE	Allows the grantees to alter any table or view in the schema.
ALTER ANY TRIGGER	Allows the grantees to enable, disable, or compile any database trigger in any schema.
ALTER DATABASE	Allows the grantees to alter the database.
ALTER USER	Allows the grantees to alter any user. This privilege authorizes the grantee to change another user's password or authentication method, assign quotas on any tablespace, set default and temporary tablespaces, and assign a profile and default roles.
ALTER ANY CLUSTER	Allows the grantees to alter any cluster.
ALTER ANY SEQUENCE	Allows the grantees to alter any sequence.
ALTER ANY SNAPSHOT	Allows the grantees to alter any snapshot.
ALTER ANY TYPE	Allows the grantees to alter any type.
CREATE ANY INDEX	Allows the grantees to create an index on any table in any schema.
CREATE ANY PROCEDURE	Allows the grantees to create stored procedures, functions, and packages in any schema.
CREATE ANY TABLE	Allows the grantees to create tables in any schema. The owner of the schema containing the table must have space quota on the tablespace to contain the table.
CREATE ANY TRIGGER	Allows the grantees to create a database trigger in any schema associated with a table in any schema.
CREATE ANY VIEW	Allows the grantees to create views in any schema.
CREATE PROCEDURE	Allows the grantees to create stored procedures, functions, and packages in their own schema.
CREATE PROFILE	Allows the grantees to create profiles.
CREATE ROLE	Allows the grantees to create roles.
CREATE SYNONYM	Allows the grantees to create synonyms in their own schemas.
CREATE TABLE	Allows the grantees to create tables in their own schemas. To create a table, the grantees must also have space quota on the tablespace to contain the table.

17

TABLE 17.1 Continued

System Privilege	Operations Permitted
CREATE TRIGGER	Allows the grantees to create a database trigger in their own schemas.
CREATE USER	Allows the grantees to create users. This privilege also allows the creator to assign quotas on any tablespace, set default and temporary tablespaces, and assign a profile as part of a CREATE USER statement.
CREATE VIEW	Allows the grantees to create views in their own schemas.
CREATE SESSION	Allows the grantees to connect to a specified database.
DELETE ANY TABLE	Allows the grantees to delete rows from tables or views in any schema, or truncate tables in any schema.
DROP ANY INDEX	Allows the grantees to drop indexes in any schema.
DROP ANY PROCEDURE	Allows the grantees to drop stored procedures, functions, or packages in any schema.
DROP ANY ROLE	Allows the grantees to drop roles.
DROP ANY SYNONYM	Allows the grantees to drop private synonyms in any schema.
DROP ANY TABLE	Allows the grantees to drop tables in any schema.
DROP ANY TRIGGER	Allows the grantees to drop database triggers in any schema.
DROP ANY VIEW	Allows the grantees to drop views in any schema.
DROP USER	Allows the grantees to drop users.
EXECUTE ANY PROCEDURE	Allows the grantees to execute procedures or functions (standalone or packaged) or reference public package variables in any schema.
GRANT ANY PRIVILEGE	Allows the grantees to grant any system privilege.
GRANT ANY ROLE	Allows the grantees to grant any role in the database.
INSERT ANY TABLE	Allows the grantees to insert rows into tables and views in any schema.
LOCK ANY TABLE	Allows the grantees to lock tables and views in any schema.
SELECT ANY SEQUENCE	Allows the grantees to reference sequences in any schema.
SELECT ANY TABLE	Allows the grantees to query tables, views, or snapshots in any schema.
UPDATE ANY TABLE	Allows the grantees to update rows in tables.

Object privileges are privileges that can be used against specific database objects. Table 17.2 lists the object privileges in Oracle.

TABLE 17.2 Object Privileges Enabled Under Oracle

Privilege
ALL
ALTER
DELETE
EXECUTE
INDEX
INSERT
REFERENCES
SELECT
UPDATE
READ

You can use the following form of the GRANT statement to give other users access to your tables:

Syntax ▼

```
GRANT {object_priv | ALL [PRIVILEGES]} [ (column
[, column]...) ]
[, {object_priv | ALL [PRIVILEGES]} [ (column
[, column] ...) ] ] ...
ON [schema.]object
TO {user | role | PUBLIC} [, {user | role | PUBLIC}] ...
[WITH GRANT OPTION]
```

To remove the object privileges you have granted to someone, use the REVOKE command with the following syntax:

Syntax ▼

```
 REVOKE {object_priv | ALL [PRIVILEGES]}
[, {object_priv | ALL [PRIVILEGES]} ]
ON [schema.]object
FROM {user | role | PUBLIC} [, {user | role | PUBLIC}]
[CASCADE CONSTRAINTS]
```

From Creating a Table to Granting Roles

Create a table named SALARIES with the following structure:

```
NAME, CHAR(30)
SALARY, NUMBER
AGE, NUMBER
```

Input/Output ▼

```
SQL> CREATE TABLE SALARIES (
  2   NAME CHAR(30),
  3   SALARY NUMBER,
  4   AGE NUMBER);

Table created.
```

Now, create two users—Jack and Jill:

Input/Output ▼

```
SQL> create user Jack identified by Jack;

User created.

SQL> create user Jill identified by Jill;

User created.

SQL> grant connect to Jack;

Grant succeeded.

SQL> grant resource to Jill;

Grant succeeded.
```

So far, you have created two users and granted each a different role. Therefore, they will have different capabilities when working with the database. First create the SALARIES table with the following information:

Input/Output ▼

```
SQL> SELECT * FROM SALARIES;

NAME                             SALARY       AGE
------------------------------  --------  --------
JACK                              35000        29
JILL                              48000        42
JOHN                              61000        55
```

Analysis ▼

You could then grant various privileges to this table based on some arbitrary reasons for this example. We are assuming that you currently have DBA privileges and can grant any system privilege. Even if you do not have DBA privileges, you can still grant object privileges on the SALARIES table because you own it (assuming you just created it).

Because Jack belongs only to the Connect role, you want him to have only SELECT privileges.

Input/Output ▼

```
SQL> GRANT SELECT ON SALARIES TO JACK;

Grant succeeded.
```

Because Jill belongs to the Resource role, you allow her to select and insert some data into the table. To liven things up a bit, allow Jill to update values only in the SALARY field of the SALARIES table.

Input/Output ▼

17

```
SQL> GRANT SELECT, UPDATE(SALARY) ON SALARIES TO Jill;

Grant succeeded.
```

Now that this table and these users have been created, you need to look at how a user accesses a table created by another user. Both Jack and Jill have been granted SELECT access on the SALARIES table. However, if Jack tries to access the SALARIES table, he will be told that it does not exist because Oracle requires the username or schema that owns the table to precede the table name.

Qualifying a Table

Make a note of the username you used to create the SALARIES table (mine was Bryan). For Jack to select data out of the SALARIES table, he must address the SALARIES table with that username.

Input/Output ▼

```
SQL> SELECT * FROM SALARIES;
SELECT * FROM SALARIES
              *

ERROR at line 1:
ORA-00942: table or view does not exist
```

Here Jack was warned that the table did not exist. Now use the owner's username to identify the table:

Input/Output ▼

```
SQL> SELECT *
  2  FROM Bryan.SALARIES;

NAME                          SALARY      AGE
------------------------------ ---------- ----------
JACK                           35000       29
JILL                           48000       42
JOHN                           61000       55
```

You can see that now the query worked. Now test out Jill's access privileges. First log out of Jack's logon and log on again as Jill (using the password `Jill`).

Input/Output ▼

```
SQL> SELECT *
  2  FROM Bryan.SALARIES;

NAME                          SALARY      AGE
------------------------------ ---------- ----------
JACK                           35000       29
JILL                           48000       42
JOHN                           61000       55
```

That worked just fine. Now try to insert a new record into the table.

Input/Output ▼

```
SQL> INSERT INTO Bryan.SALARIES
  2    VALUES('JOE',85000,38);
INSERT INTO Bryan.SALARIES
                   *
ERROR at line 1:
ORA-01031: insufficient privileges
```

This operation did not work because Jill does not have INSERT privileges on the SALARIES table.

Input/Output ▼

```
SQL> UPDATE Bryan.SALARIES
  2    SET AGE = 42
  3    WHERE NAME = 'JOHN';
UPDATE Bryan.SALARIES
              *
ERROR at line 1:
ORA-01031: insufficient privileges
```

Once again, Jill tried to go around the privileges that she had been given. Naturally, Oracle caught this error and corrected her quickly.

Input/Output ▼

```
SQL> UPDATE Bryan.SALARIES
  2  SET SALARY = 35000
  3  WHERE NAME = 'JOHN';

1 row updated.

SQL> SELECT *
  2  FROM Bryan.SALARIES;
```

NAME	SALARY	AGE
JACK	35000	29
JILL	48000	42
JOHN	35000	55

You can see now that the update works as long as Jill abides by the privileges she has been given.

Using Views for Security Purposes

As mentioned in Lesson 13, "Creating Views," views are virtual tables that you can use to present a view of data that is different from the way it physically exists in the database. Later in this lesson you will learn more about how to use views to implement security measures. First, however, we explain how views can simplify SQL statements.

Earlier you learned that when a user must access a table or database object that another user owns, that object must be referenced with a username. As you can imagine, this procedure can get wordy if you have to write several SQL queries in a row. More importantly, novice users would be required to determine the owner of a table before they could select the contents of a table, which is not something you want all your users to do.

Assume that you are logged on as Jack, your friend from earlier examples. You learned that for Jack to look at the contents of the SALARIES table, he must use the following statement:

Input/Output ▼

```
SQL> SELECT *
  2  FROM Bryan.SALARIES;
```

```
NAME                            SALARY      AGE
------------------------------- ---------   ---------
JACK                             35000       29
JILL                             48000       42
JOHN                             35000       55
```

If you were to create a view named SALARY_VIEW, a user could simply select from that view.

Input/Output ▼

```
SQL> CREATE VIEW SALARY_VIEW
  2  AS SELECT *
  3  FROM Bryan.SALARIES;

View created.

SQL> SELECT * FROM SALARY_VIEW;

NAME                            SALARY      AGE
------------------------------- ---------   ---------
JACK                             35000       29
JILL                             48000       42
JOHN                             35000       55
```

The preceding query returned the same values as the records returned from Bryan.SALARIES.

Using Synonyms in Place of Views

SQL also provides an object known as a *synonym*. A synonym provides an alias for a table to simplify or minimize keystrokes when using a table in a SQL statement. There are two types of synonyms: private and public. Any user with the resource role can create a *private synonym*. On the other hand, only users with the DBA role can create *public synonyms*.

The syntax for a public synonym follows:

Syntax ▼

```
CREATE [PUBLIC] SYNONYM [schema.]synonym
FOR [schema.]object[@dblink]
```

In the preceding example, you could have issued the following command to achieve the same results:

Input/Output ▼

```
SQL> CREATE PUBLIC SYNONYM SALARY FOR SALARIES
```

```
Synonym created.
```

Then log back on to Jack and type this:

Input/Output ▼

```
SQL> SELECT * FROM SALARY;
```

```
NAME                             SALARY      AGE
-------------------------------- --------- ---------
JACK                              35000      29
JILL                              48000      42
JOHN                              35000      55
```

Using Views to Solve Security Problems

Suppose you changed your mind about Jack and Jill and decided that neither of them should be able to look at the SALARIES table completely. You can use views to change this situation and allow them to examine only their own information.

Input/Output ▼

```
SQL> CREATE VIEW JACK_SALARY AS
  2  SELECT * FROM BRYAN.SALARIES
  3  WHERE NAME = 'JACK';
```

```
View created.
```

```
SQL> CREATE VIEW JILL_SALARY AS
  2  SELECT * FROM BRYAN.SALARIES
  3  WHERE NAME = 'JILL';
```

```
View created.
```

```
SQL> GRANT SELECT ON JACK_SALARY
  2  TO JACK;
```

```
Grant succeeded.
```

```
SQL> GRANT SELECT ON JILL_SALARY
  2  TO JILL;
```

```
Grant succeeded.
```

```
SQL> REVOKE SELECT ON SALARIES FROM JACK;

Revoke succeeded.

SQL> REVOKE SELECT ON SALARIES FROM JILL;

Revoke succeeded.
```

Now log on as Jack and test out the view you created for him:

Input/Output ▼

```
SQL> SELECT * FROM Bryan.JACK_SALARY;

NAME        SALARY      AGE
----------- ----------- ----
Jack        35000        29

SQL> SELECT * FROM Bryan.SALARIES;
SELECT * FROM BRYAN.SALARIES
                    *
ERROR at line 1:
ORA-00942: table or view does not exist
```

Log out of Jack's account and test Jill's:

Input/Output ▼

```
SQL> SELECT * FROM Bryan.JILL_SALARY;

NAME                SALARY          AGE
------------------- --------------- ---
Jill                          48000  42
```

Analysis ▼

You can see that access to the SALARIES table was completely controlled using views. SQL enables you to create these views as you like and then assign permissions to other users. This technique allows a great deal of flexibility.

The syntax to drop a synonym is

Syntax ▼

```
SQL> drop [public] synonym synonym_name;
```

NOTE
> By now, you should understand the importance of keeping to a minimum the number of people with DBA roles. A user with this access level can have complete access to all commands and operations within the database.

Using the WITH GRANT OPTION Clause

What do you think would happen if Jill attempted to pass her UPDATE privilege to Jack? At first glance you might think that Jill, because she was entrusted with the UPDATE privilege, should be able to pass it to other users who are allowed that privilege. However, using the GRANT statement as you did earlier, Jill cannot pass her privileges to others:

Input ▼

```
SQL> GRANT SELECT, UPDATE(SALARY) ON Bryan.SALARIES TO Jill;
```

Here is the syntax for the GRANT statement that was introduced earlier this lesson:

Syntax ▼

```
GRANT {object_priv | ALL [PRIVILEGES]} [ (column
[, column]...) ]
[, {object_priv | ALL [PRIVILEGES]} [ (column
[, column] ...) ] ] ...
ON [schema.]object
TO {user | role | PUBLIC} [, {user | role | PUBLIC}] ...
[WITH GRANT OPTION]
```

What you are looking for is the WITH GRANT OPTION clause at the end of the GRANT statement. When object privileges are granted and WITH GRANT OPTION is used, these privileges can be passed to others. So, if you want to allow Jill to pass this privilege to Jack, you would do the following:

Input/Output ▼

```
SQL> GRANT SELECT, UPDATE(SALARY)
  2  ON Bryan.SALARIES TO JILL
  3  WITH GRANT OPTION;

Grant succeeded.
```

Jill could then log on and issue the following command:

Input/Output ▼

```
SQL> GRANT SELECT, UPDATE(SALARY)
  2  ON Bryan.SALARIES TO JACK;

Grant succeeded.
```

Summary

Security is an often overlooked topic that can cause many problems if not properly thought out and administered. Fortunately, SQL provides several useful commands for implementing security on a database.

Users are originally created using the CREATE USER command, which sets up a username and password for the user. After the user account has been set up, this user must be assigned to a role to accomplish any work.

The GRANT command gives a permission or privilege to a user. The REVOKE command can take that permission or privilege away from the user. The two types of privileges are system privileges and object privileges. System privileges should be monitored closely and should not be granted to inexperienced users. Giving inexperienced users access to commands allows them to perhaps inadvertently destroy data or databases you have painstakingly set up. Object privileges give users access to individual objects existing in the owner's database schema.

All these techniques and SQL statements provide the SQL user with a broad range of tools to use when setting up system security. Although we focused on the security features of Oracle, you can apply much of this information to the database system at your site. Just remember that no matter what product you are using, it is important to enforce some level of database security.

Q&A

Q I understand the need for security, but doesn't Oracle carry it a bit too far?

A No, especially in larger applications where there are multiple users. Because different users will be doing different types of work in the database, you'll want to limit what users can and can't do. Users should have only the necessary roles and privileges they need to do their work.

Q **It appears that there is a security problem when the DBA that created my ID also knows the password. Is this true?**

A Yes, it is true. The DBA creates the IDs and passwords. Therefore, users should use the ALTER USER command to change their ID and password immediately after receiving them.

Workshop

The Workshop provides quiz questions to help solidify your understanding of the material covered, as well as exercises to provide you with experience in using what you have learned. Try to answer the quiz and exercise questions before checking the answers in Appendix A, "Answers."

Quiz

17

1. What is wrong with the following statement?

   ```
   SQL> GRANT CONNECTION TO DAVID;
   ```

2. True or false (and why): Dropping a user will cause all objects owned by that user to be dropped as well.

3. What would happen if you created a table and granted SELECT privileges on the table to PUBLIC?

4. Is the following SQL statement correct?

   ```
   SQL> create user RON
   identified by RON;
   ```

5. Is the following SQL statement correct?

   ```
   SQL> alter RON
   identified by RON;
   ```

6. Is the following SQL statement correct?

   ```
   SQL> grant connect, resource to RON;
   ```

7. If you own a table, who can select from that table?

8. Does MySQL have role-based security?

Exercises

1. Go the MYSQL database, find the USER table, and do a describe on that table. Now do a SELECT statement that selects only the HOST, USER, and PASSWORD columns.

2. Make a note of the value in the HOST column. It should be something such as 'localhost'.

3. Create a new user in the user table. Only insert values into the first three columns ('localhost','betty','betty').

4. Select all rows from USER where the user = betty. Notice that all of the privileges are N. Update the table so that user betty has all available privileges. Do another SELECT from the table to see what you have changed.

5. Use the USE DATABASE_NAME command to go to another database that you have created that contains tables. Grant INSERT, UPDATE, and DELETE privileges to betty.

6. View the results of this in the mysql.tables_priv table.

7. Add the ALTER_PRIV and the DROP_PRIV on the emp_tbl to betty and then revoke the UPDATE_PRIV.

8. Experiment with your database system's security by creating a table and then creating a user. Give this user various privileges and then take them away.

LESSON 18

Exploring the Data Dictionary (System Catalog)

In this lesson, we discuss the data dictionary, also known as the system catalog. By the end of this lesson, you should have a solid understanding of the following:

- The definition of the data dictionary

- The type of information the data dictionary contains

- Different types of tables within the data dictionary

- Effective ways to retrieve useful information from the data dictionary

An Introduction to the Data Dictionary

Every relational database has some form of data dictionary, or system catalog. (We use both terms in this lesson's presentation.) A *data dictionary* is a system area within a database environment that contains information about the ingredients of a database. Data dictionaries include information such as database design, stored SQL code, user statistics, database processes, database growth, and database performance statistics.

The data dictionary has tables that contain database design information, which are populated upon the creation of the database and the execution of Data Definition Language (DDL) commands such as CREATE TABLE. This part of the data dictionary stores information about a table's columns and attributes, table-sizing information, table privileges, and table growth. Other objects that are stored within the data dictionary include indexes, triggers, procedures, packages, and views.

User statistics tables report the status of items such as database connectivity information and privileges for individual users. These privileges are divided into two major components: system-level privileges and object-level privileges. The authority to create another user is a system-level privilege, whereas the capability to access a table is an object-level privilege. Roles are also used to enforce security within a database. This information, which you learned about in Lesson 17, "Database Security," is stored here as well.

This lesson extends what you learned in Lesson 16, "Streamlining SQL Statements for Improved Performance." Data retrieved from the data dictionary can be used to monitor database performance and to modify database parameters that will improve database and SQL statement performance.

The data dictionary is one of the most useful tools available in a database. It's a way of keeping a database organized, much like an inventory file in a retail store. It's also a mechanism that ensures the integrity of the database. For instance, when you create a table, how does the database server know whether a table with the same name exists? When you create a query to select data from a table, how can it be verified that you have been given the proper privileges to access the table? The data dictionary is the heart of a database, so you need to know how to use it.

Identifying Data Dictionary Users

End users, system engineers, and database administrators all use the data dictionary, whether they realize it or not. Their access to it can be either direct or indirect.

End users, often the customers for whom the database was created, access the data dictionary indirectly. When a user attempts to log on to the database, the data dictionary is referenced to verify that user's username, password, and privileges to connect to the database. The database is also referenced to see whether the user has the appropriate privileges to access certain data. The most common method for an end user to access the data dictionary is through a front-end application. Many graphical user interface (GUI) tools, which allow a user to easily construct a SQL statement, have been developed. When logging on to the database, the front-end application might immediately perform a SELECT against the data dictionary to define the tables to which the user has access. The front-end application might then build a "local" data dictionary for the individual user based on the data retrieved from the data dictionary. The customers can use the local catalog to select the specific tables they want to query.

System engineers are database users who are responsible for tasks such as database modeling and design, application development, and application management. (Some companies use other titles, such as programmers, programmer analysts, and data modelers, to refer to their system engineers.) System engineers use the data dictionary directly to manage the development process as well as to maintain existing projects. Access may also be achieved through front-end applications, development tools, and computer assisted software engineering (CASE) tools.

Common areas of the data dictionary for these users are queries against objects under groups of schemas, queries against application roles and privileges, and queries to gather statistics on schema growth. System engineers might also use the data dictionary to reverse engineer database objects in a specified schema.

Database administrators (DBAs) are most definitely the largest percentage of direct users of the data dictionary. Unlike the other two groups of users, who occasionally use the data dictionary directly, DBAs must explicitly include the use of the data dictionary as part of their daily routine. Access is usually through a SQL query but can also be through administration tools such as Oracle's Server Manager or web-based management system. A DBA uses data dictionary information to manage users and resources and ultimately to achieve a well-tuned database.

As you can see, all the database users need to use the data dictionary. Even more important, a relational database cannot exist without some form of a data dictionary.

18

Exploring the Contents of the Data Dictionary

This section examines the data dictionaries of our main RDBMS vendors, Oracle and MySQL. Although the implementations have unique specifications for their data dictionaries, they serve the same function. Don't concern yourself with the different names of the system tables; simply focus on the concept of a data dictionary and the data it contains.

Oracle's Data Dictionary

Because every table must have an owner, the owner of the system tables in an Oracle data dictionary is SYS. Oracle's data dictionary tables are divided into three basic categories: user-accessible views, DBA views, and dynamic performance tables, which also appear as views. User-accessible views allow the user to query the data dictionary for information about the individual database account, such as privileges or a catalog of created tables.

The DBA views aid in the everyday duties of a database administrator, allowing the DBA to manage users and objects within the database. The DBA also uses the dynamic performance tables in Oracle to provide a more in-depth look at monitoring the performance of a database. These views provide information such as statistics on processes, the dynamic use of rollback segments, memory use, and so on. The dynamic performance tables are all prefixed with V$.

MySQL Data Dictionary

There is a database called mysql that is part of the MySQL set-up. Within mysql is a short set of tables that provide useful information concerning tables and various privileges accessed via the SHOW command. Additionally, as of MySQL 5.0, MySQL provides a virtual database known as the INFORMATION_SCHEMA, which conforms more thoroughly with the SQL:2003 standard.

The MySQL package also includes an executable called MySQL Administrator. This administrative GUI tool<$I~tools;GUI (Graphical User is used in much the same way as traditional data dictionary tables. Through the use of various SHOW commands, you can view statistical data at the command line. Additionally, the package contains a tool called MySQL Query Browser, which can be used to enter in commands much like Oracle's web administration tool.

> **NOTE**
> MySQL Administrator is an administrative tool and is not made to modify the data. Instead, use the INSERT, UPDATE, and DELETE commands to modify data, and use the ALTER TABLE command to modify data types through the MySQL Query Browser tool.

A Look Inside Oracle's Data Dictionary

The examples in this section show you how to retrieve information from the data dictionary and are applicable to most relational database users (system engineer, end user, or DBA). Oracle's data dictionary has a vast array of system tables and views for all types of database users, which is why we have chosen to explore Oracle's data dictionary in more depth. The examples that follow are representative of the type of data that you will see in your data dictionary but will vary from your results in order to keep them readable.

User Views

User views are data dictionary views that are common to all database users. The only privilege a user needs to query against a user view is the CREATE SESSION system privilege, which should be common to all users.

Who Are You?

Before venturing into the seemingly endless knowledge contained within a database, you should know exactly who you are (in terms of the database) and what you can do. The following two examples show SELECT statements from two tables: one to find out who you are, and the other to see who else shares the database.

Input/Output ▼

```
SQL> SELECT USERNAME, USER_ID, DEFAULT_TABLESPACE, TEMPORARY_TABLESPACE, CREATED
  2  FROM USER_USERS;
```

USERNAME	USER_ID	DEFAULT_TABLESPACE	TEMPORARY TABLESPACE	CREATED
JSMITH	29	USERS	TEMP	14-MAR-97

```
1 row selected.
```

Analysis ▼

The USER_USERS view allows you to view how and when your Oracle ID was set up, and it also shows other user-specific vital statistics. The default tablespace and the temporary tablespace are also shown. The default tablespace, USERS, is the tablespace that objects will be created under as that user. The temporary tablespace is the designated tablespace to be used during large sorts and group functions for JSMITH.

Input/Output ▼

```
SQL> SELECT *
  2  FROM ALL_USERS;
```

USERNAME	USER_ID	CREATED
SYS	0	01-JAN-97
SYSTEM	5	01-JAN-97
SCOTT	8	01-JAN-97
JSMITH	10	14-MAR-97
TJONES	11	15-MAR-97
VJOHNSON	12	15-MAR-97

Analysis ▼

As you can see in the results of the preceding query, you can view all users that exist in the database by using the ALL_USERS view. However, the ALL_USERS view does not provide the same specific information that the previous view (USER_USERS) provided because there is no need for this information at the user level. More specific information may be required at the system level.

18

What Are Your Privileges?

Now that you know who you are, it would be nice to know what you can do. Several views are collectively able to give you that information. The USER_SYS_PRIVS view and the USER_ROLE_PRIVS view will give you (as the user) a good idea of what authority you have.

You can use the USER_SYS_PRIVS view to examine your system privileges. Remember, system privileges are privileges that allow you to do certain things within the database as a whole. These privileges are not specific to any one object or set of objects.

Input/Output ▼

```
SQL> SELECT *
  2  FROM USER_SYS_PRIVS;

USERNAME          PRIVILEGE             ADM
------------      --------------------  ---
JSMITH            UNLIMITED TABLESPACE  NO
JSMITH            CREATE SESSION        NO

2 rows selected.
```

Analysis ▼

JSMITH has been granted two system-level privileges outside of any granted roles. Notice the second privilege, CREATE SESSION. CREATE SESSION is also contained within an Oracle standard role, CONNECT, which is covered in the next example.

You can use the USER_ROLE_PRIVS view to view information about roles you have been granted within the database. Database roles are very similar to system-level privileges. A role is created much like a user and then granted privileges. After the role has been granted privileges, the role can be granted to a user. Remember that object-level privileges may also be contained within a role.

Input/Output ▼

```
SQL> SELECT *
  2  FROM USER_ROLE_PRIVS;

USERNAME          GRANTED_ROLE          ADM   DEF   OS_
------------      --------------------  ---   ---   ---
JSMITH            CONNECT               NO    YES   NO
JSMITH            RESOURCE              NO    YES   NO

2 rows selected.
```

Analysis ▼

The USER_ROLE_PRIVS view enables you to see the roles that have been granted to you. As mentioned earlier, CONNECT contains the system privilege CREATE SESSION, as well as other privileges. RESOURCE has a few privileges of its own. You can see that both roles have been granted as the user's default role; the user cannot grant these roles to other users, as noted by the Admin option (ADM); and the roles have not been granted by the operating system (OS) (refer to Lesson 17).

What Do You Have Access To?

Now you might ask, "What do I have access to? I know who I am, I know my privileges, but where can I get my data?" You can answer these questions by looking at various available user views in the data dictionary. This section identifies a few helpful views.

Probably the most basic user view is USER_CATALOG, which is simply a catalog of the tables, views, synonyms, and sequences owned by the current user.

Input/Output ▼

```
SQL> SELECT *
  2  FROM USER_CATALOG;

TABLE_NAME                         TABLE_TYPE
-----------------------------      ----------
MAGAZINE_TBL                       TABLE
MAG_COUNTER                        SEQUENCE
MAG_VIEW                           VIEW
SPORTS                             TABLE

4 rows selected.
```

18

Analysis ▼

This example provides a quick list of tables and related objects that you own. You can also use a public synonym for USER_CATALOG for simplicity's sake: CAT (that is, try SELECT * FROM CAT;).

Another useful view is ALL_CATALOG, which enables you to see tables owned by other individuals.

Input/Output ▼

```
SQL> SELECT *
  2  FROM ALL_CATALOG;

OWNER                        TABLE_NAME              TABLE_TYPE
--------------------         --------------------    -----------
SYS                          DUAL                    TABLE
PUBLIC                       DUAL                    SYNONYM
JSMITH                       MAGAZINE_TBL            TABLE
JSMITH                       MAG_COUNTER             SEQUENCE
JSMITH                       MAG_VIEW                VIEW
JSMITH                       SPORTS                  TABLE
VJOHNSON                     TEST1                   TABLE
VJOHNSON                     HOBBIES                 TABLE
VJOHNSON                     CLASSES                 TABLE
VJOHNSON                     STUDENTS                VIEW

10 rows selected.
```

Analysis ▼

More objects than appear in the preceding list will be accessible to you as a user. (The SYSTEM tables alone will add many tables.) We have simply shortened the list. The ALL_CATALOG view is the same as the USER_CATALOG view, but it shows you all tables, views, sequences, and synonyms to which you have access (not just the ones you own).

Input/Output ▼

```
SQL> SELECT SUBSTR(OBJECT_TYPE,1,15) OBJECT_TYPE,
  2         SUBSTR(OBJECT_NAME,1,30) OBJECT_NAME,
  3         CREATED,
  4         STATUS
  5  FROM USER_OBJECTS
  6  ORDER BY 1;

OBJECT_TYPE         OBJECT_NAME              CREATED       STATUS
---------------     --------------------     ------------  ------
INDEX               MAGAZINE_INX             14-MAR-97     VALID
INDEX               SPORTS_INX               14-MAR-97     VALID
INDEX               HOBBY_INX                14-MAR-97     VALID
TABLE               MAGAZINE_TBL             01-MAR-97     VALID
TABLE               SPORTS                   14-MAR-97     VALID
TABLE               HOBBY_TBL                16-MAR-97     VALID

6 rows selected.
```

Analysis ▼

You can use the USER_OBJECTS view to select general information about a user's owned objects, such as the name, type, date created, date modified, and the status of the object. In the previous query, you are checking the data created and validation of each owned object.

Input/Output ▼

```
SQL> SELECT TABLE_NAME, INITIAL_EXTENT, NEXT_EXTENT
  2  FROM USER_TABLES;

TABLE_NAME                      INITIAL_EXTENT    NEXT EXTENT
-----------------------------   --------------    -----------
MAGAZINE_TBL                           1048576         540672
SPORTS                                  114688         114688

2 rows selected.
```

Analysis ▼

Much more data is available when selecting from the USER_TABLES view, depending upon what you want to see. Most data consists of storage information.

18

NOTE

> Notice in the output that the values for the initial and next extents are in bytes. In some implementations, you can use column formatting to make your output more readable by adding commas. See Lesson 25, "Using Oracle SQL*Plus to Satisfy Reporting Needs," and Lesson 27, "An Introduction to Transact-SQL," for information specific to these implementations.

The ALL_TABLES view is to USER_TABLES as the ALL_CATALOG view is to USER_CATALOG. In other words, ALL_TABLES allows you to see all the tables to which you have access, instead of just the tables you own. The ALL_TABLES view may include tables that exist in another user's catalog.

Input/Output ▼

```
SQL> SELECT SUBSTR(OWNER,1,15) OWNER,
  2         SUBSTR(TABLE_NAME,1,25) TABLE_NAME,
  3         SUBSTR(TABLESPACE_NAME,1,13) TABLESPACE
  4  FROM ALL_TABLES;
```

OWNER	TABLE_NAME	TABLESPACE
SYS	DUAL	SYSTEM
JSMITH	MAGAZINE_TBL	USERS
SMITH	SPORTS	USERS
VJOHNSON	TEST1	USERS
VJOHNSON	HOBBIES	USERS
VJOHNSON	CLASSES	USERS

6 rows selected.

Analysis ▼

Again, you have selected only the desired information. Many additional columns in
ALL_TABLES may also contain useful information.

As a database user, you can monitor the growth of tables and indexes in your catalog by
querying the USER_SEGMENTS view. As the name suggests, USER_SEGMENTS gives you
information about each segment, such as storage information and extents taken. A segment may consist of a table, index, cluster rollback, or cache. The following example
shows how you might retrieve selected information from the USER_SEGMENTS view:

Input/Output ▼

```
SQL> SELECT SUBSTR(SEGMENT_NAME,1,30) SEGMENT_NAME,
  2        SUBSTR(SEGMENT_TYPE,1,8) SEG_TYPE,
  3        SUBSTR(TABLESPACE_NAME,1,25) TABLESPACE_NAME,
  4        BYTES, EXTENTS
  5        FROM USER_SEGMENTS
  6        ORDER BY EXTENTS DESC;
```

SEGMENT_NAME	SEG_TYPE	TABLESPACE_NAME	BYTES	EXTENTS
MAGAZINE_TBL	TABLE	USERS	4292608	7
SPORTS_INX	INDEX	USERS	573440	4
SPORTS	TABLE	USERS	344064	2
MAGAZINE_INX	INDEX	USERS	1589248	1

4 rows selected.

Analysis ▼

The output in the preceding query was sorted by extents in descending order; the segments with the most growth (most extents taken) appear first in the results.

Now that you know which tables you have access to, you will want to find out what you can do to each table. For example, are you limited to query only, or can you update a table? The ALL_TAB_PRIVS view lists all privileges that you have as a database user on each table available to you.

Input/Output ▼

```
SQL> SELECT SUBSTR(TABLE_SCHEMA,1,10) OWNER,
  2         SUBSTR(TABLE_NAME,1,25) TABLE_NAME,
  3         PRIVILEGE
  4         FROM ALL_TAB_PRIVS;
```

OWNER	TABLE_NAME	PRIVILEGE
SYS	DUAL	SELECT
JSMITH	MAGAZINE_TBL	SELECT
JSMITH	MAGAZINE_TBL	INSERT
JSMITH	MAGAZINE_TBL	UPDATE
JSMITH	MAGAZINE_TBL	DELETE
JSMITH	SPORTS	SELECT
JSMITH	SPORTS	INSERT
JSMITH	SPORTS	UPDATE
JSMITH	SPORTS	DELETE
VJOHNSON	TEST1	SELECT
VJOHNSON	TEST1	INSERT
VJOHNSON	TEST1	UPDATE
VJOHNSON	TEST1	DELETE
VJOHNSON	HOBBIES	SELECT
VJOHNSON	CLASSES	SELECT

```
15 rows selected.
```

18

Analysis ▼

As you can see, you can manipulate the data in some tables, whereas you have read-only access (SELECT only) to others.

When you create objects, you usually need to know where to place them in the database unless you allow your target destination to take the default. An Oracle database is broken up into tablespaces, each of which are capable of storing objects. Each tablespace is allocated a certain amount of disk space according to what is available on the system. Disk space is usually acquired through the system administrator (SA).

The following query is from a view called USER_TABLESPACES, which lists the tablespaces that you have access to, the default initial and next sizes of objects created within them, and their status.

Input/Output ▼

```
SQL> SELECT SUBSTR(TABLESPACE_NAME,1,30) TABLESPACE_NAME,
  2  INITIAL_EXTENT,
  3  NEXT_EXTENT,
  4  PCT_INCREASE,
  5  STATUS
  6  FROM USER_TABLESPACES;
```

TABLESPACE_NAME	INITIAL_EXTENT	NEXT_EXTENT	PCT_INCREASE	STATUS
SYSTEM	32768	16384	1	ONLINE
RBS	2097152	2097152	1	ONLINE
TEMP	114688	114688	1	ONLINE
TOOLS	32768	16384	1	ONLINE
USERS	32768	16384	1	ONLINE

```
5 rows selected.
```

Analysis ▼

This type of query is very useful when you are creating objects that will require storage, such as tables and indexes. When a table or index is created, if the initial and next storage parameters are not specified in the DDL, the table or index will take the tablespace's default values.

The same concept applies to PCT INCREASE, which is an Oracle parameter specifying the percentage of allocated space an object should take when it grows. If a value for PCT_INCREASE is not specified when the table or index is created, the database server will allocate the default value that is specified for the corresponding tablespace. Seeing the default values enables you to determine whether you need to use a storage clause in the CREATE statement.

Sometimes, however, you need to know more than which tablespaces you may access (that is, build tables under). For example, you might need to know what your limits are within the tablespaces so that you can better manage the creation and sizing of your objects. The USER_TS_QUOTAS view provides the necessary information. The next query displays a user's space limits for creating objects in the database.

Input/Output ▼

```
SQL> SELECT SUBSTR(TABLESPACE_NAME,1,30) TABLESPACE_NAME,
  2  BYTES, MAX_BYTES
  3  FROM USER_TS_QUOTAS;
```

```
TABLESPACE_NAME                    BYTES  MAX_BYTES
-------------------------------   --------  ---------
SYSTEM                                  0          0
TOOLS                             5242880      16384
USERS                              573440         -1
3 rows selected.
```

Analysis ▼

The preceding output is typical of output from an Oracle data dictionary. BYTES identifies the total number of bytes in that tablespace that are associated with the user. MAX BYTES identifies the maximum bytes allotted to the user, or the user's quota, on the tablespace. The first two values in this column are self-explanatory. The -1 in the third row means the quota is unlimited—that is, no limits are placed on the user for that tablespace.

These examples all show how an ordinary database user can extract information from the data dictionary. These views are just a few of the many that exist in Oracle's data dictionary. It's important to check your database implementation to see what is available to you in your data dictionary. Remember, you should use the data dictionary to manage your database activities. Although data dictionaries will differ by implementation, you need only to understand the concept and know how to retrieve data necessary to supplement your job.

18

System DBA Views

The DBA views that reside within an Oracle data dictionary are usually the primary, or most common, views that a DBA would access. These views are invaluable to the productivity of any DBA. Taking these tables away from a DBA would be like depriving a carpenter of a hammer.

As you might expect, you must have the SELECT_ANY_TABLE system privilege, which is contained in the DBA role, to access the DBA tables. For example, suppose you are JSMITH, who does not have the required privilege to select from the DBA tables.

Input/Output ▼

```
SQL> SELECT *
  2  FROM USER_ROLE_PRIVS;

USERNAME              GRANTED_ROLE           ADM   DEF   OS_
-----------------     --------------------   ---   ---   ---
JSMITH                CONNECT                NO    YES   NO
JSMITH                RESOURCE               NO    YES   NO
2 rows selected.
```

```
SQL> SELECT *
2  FROM SYS.DBA_ROLES;

FROM SYS.DBA_ROLES;
     *

ERROR at line 2:
ORA-00942: table or view does not exist
```

Analysis ▼

When you try to access a table to which you do not have the appropriate privileges, an error is returned stating that the table does not exist. This message can be a little misleading. Virtually, the table does not exist because the user cannot "see" the table. A solution to this problem would be to grant the role DBA to JSMITH. This role would have to be granted by a DBA, of course.

Database User Information

The USER_USERS and ALL_USERS views give you minimal information about the users. The DBA view called DBA_USERS (owned by SYS) gives you information on all users if you have the DBA role or SELECT_ANY_TABLE privilege, as shown in the next example.

Input/Output ▼

```
SQL> SELECT USERNAME,USER_ID,PASSWORD,DEFAULT_TABLESPACE,
2  TEMPORARY_TABLESPACE,CREATED,PROFILE
3  FROM SYS.DBA_USERS;

USERNAME                            USER_ID PASSWORD
-------------------------------     ------- -------------------------------
DEFAULT_TABLESPACE                  TEMPORARY_TABLESPACE          CREATED
-------------------------------     -------------------------------  ---------
PROFILE
-------------------------------
SYS                                 0 4012DA490794C16B
SYSTEM                              TEMP                          06-JUN-96
DEFAULT

JSMITH                              5 A4A94B17405C10B7
USERS                               TEMP                          06-JUN-96
DEFAULT
2 rows selected.
```

Analysis ▼

When you select all from the DBA_USERS view, you can see the vital information on each user. Notice that the password is encrypted. DBA_USERS is the primary view used by a DBA to manage users.

Database Security

Three basic data dictionary views deal with security, although these views can be tied together with other related views for more complete information. These three views deal with database roles, roles granted to users, and system privileges granted to users. The three views introduced in this section are DBA_ROLES, DBA_ROLE_PRIVS, and DBA_SYS_PRIVS. The following sample queries show how to obtain information pertinent to database security.

Input/Output ▼

```
SQL> SELECT *
  2  FROM SYS.DBA_ROLE_PRIVS
  3  WHERE GRANTEE='SYS'
  4  AND ROWNUM<=10;
```

GRANTEE	GRANTED_ROLE	ADM	DEF
SYS	DBA	YES	YES
SYS	CTXAPP	YES	YES
SYS	CONNECT	YES	YES
SYS	RESOURCE	YES	YES
SYS	XDBADMIN	YES	YES
SYS	PLUSTRACE	YES	YES
SYS	OEM_ADVISOR	YES	YES
SYS	OEM_MONITOR	YES	YES
SYS	AQ_USER_ROLE	YES	YES
SYS	HS_ADMIN_ROLE	YES	YES

```
10 rows selected.
```

18

Analysis ▼

The DBA_ROLE_PRIVS view provides information about database roles that have been granted to users. The first column is the grantee, or user. The second column displays the granted role. Notice that every role granted to the user corresponds to a record in the table. ADM identifies whether the role was granted with the Admin option, meaning that the user is able to grant the matching role to other users. The last column is DEFAULT, stating whether the matching role is a default role for the user.

Input/Output ▼

```
SQL> SELECT *
  2  FROM SYS.DBA_SYS_PRIVS
  3  WHERE GRANTEE = 'RJENNINGS';

GRANTEE                            PRIVILEGE                             ADM
--------------------------------   ------------------------------------  ---
RJENNINGS                          CREATE SESSION                        NO
RJENNINGS                          UNLIMITED TABLESPACE                  NO

2 rows selected.
```

Analysis ▼

The DBA_SYS_PRIVS view lists all system-level privileges that have been granted to the user. This view is similar to DBA_ROLE_PRIVS. You can include these system privileges in a role by granting system privileges to a role, as you would to a user.

Database Objects

Database objects are another major focus for a DBA. Several views within the data dictionary provide information about objects, such as tables and indexes. These views can contain general information, or they can contain detailed information about the objects that reside within the database.

Input/Output ▼

```
SQL> SELECT *
  2  FROM SYS.DBA_CATALOG
  3  WHERE ROWNUM < 5;

OWNER                    TABLE_NAME                    TABLE_TYPE
---------------------    --------------------------    ----------
SYS                      CDEF$                         TABLE
SYS                      TAB$                          TABLE
SYS                      IND$                          TABLE
SYS                      CLU$                          TABLE

4 rows selected.
```

Analysis ▼

The DBA_CATALOG is the same thing as the USER_CATALOG, except the owner of the table is included. In contrast, the USER_CATALOG view deals solely with tables that belong to the current user. DBA_CATALOG is a view that the DBA can use to take a quick look at all tables.

The following query shows you what type of objects exist in a particular database.

Input/Output ▼

```
SQL> SELECT DISTINCT(OBJECT_TYPE)
  2  FROM SYS.DBA_OBJECTS;

OBJECT_TYPE
-------------
CLUSTER
DATABASE LINK
FUNCTION
INDEX
PACKAGE
PACKAGE BODY
PROCEDURE
SEQUENCE
SYNONYM
TABLE
TRIGGER
VIEW

12 rows selected.
```

18

Analysis ▼

The DISTINCT function in the preceding query lists all unique object types that exist in the database. This query is a good way to find out what types of objects the database designers and developers are using.

The DBA_TABLES view gives specific information about database tables, mostly concerning storage.

Input/Output ▼

```
SQL> SELECT SUBSTR(OWNER,1,8) OWNER,
  2  SUBSTR(TABLE_NAME,1,25) TABLE_NAME,
  3  SUBSTR(TABLESPACE_NAME,1,30) TABLESPACE_NAME
  4  FROM SYS.DBA_TABLES
  5  WHERE OWNER = 'JSMITH';
```

```
OWNER      TABLE_NAME           TABLESPACE_NAME
--------   ------------------   --------------------------------
JSMITH     MAGAZINE_TBL         USERS
JSMITH     HOBBY_TBL            USERS
JSMITH     ADDRESS_TBL          SYSTEM
JSMITH     CUSTOMER_TBL         USERS

4 rows selected.
```

Analysis ▼

All tables are in the USERS tablespace except for ADDRESS_TBL, which is in the SYSTEM tablespace. Because the only table you should ever store in the SYSTEM tablespace is the SYSTEM table, the DBA needs to be aware of this situation. It's a good thing you ran this query.

JSMITH should immediately be asked to move his table into another eligible tablespace.

Now suppose that you want to get a list of all tables and their indexes that belong to JSMITH. You would write a query similar to the following, using DBA_INDEXES.

Input/Output ▼

```
SQL> SELECT SUBSTR(TABLE_OWNER,1,10) TBL_OWNER,
  2    SUBSTR(TABLE_NAME,1,30) TABLE_NAME,
  3    SUBSTR(INDEX_NAME,1,30) INDEX_NAME
  4    FROM SYS.DBA_INDEXES
  5    WHERE OWNER = 'JSMITH'
  6    AND ROWNUM < 5
  7    ORDER BY TABLE_NAME;

TBL_OWNER   TABLE_NAME                       INDEX_NAME
----------  -------------------------------  ------------
JSMITH      ADDRESS_TBL                      ADDR_INX
JSMITH      CUSTOMER_TBL                     CUST_INX
JSMITH      HOBBY_TBL                        HOBBY_PK
JSMITH      MAGAZINE_TBL                     MAGAZINE_INX

4 rows selected.
```

Analysis ▼

A query such as the previous one is an easy way to list all indexes that belong to a schema and match them up with their corresponding tables.

Input/Output ▼

```
SQL> SELECT SUBSTR(TABLE_NAME,1,15) TABLE_NAME,
  2  SUBSTR(INDEX_NAME,1,30) INDEX_NAME,
  3  SUBSTR(COLUMN_NAME,1,15) COLUMN_NAME,
  4  COLUMN_POSITION
  5  FROM SYS.DBA_IND_COLUMNS
  6  WHERE TABLE_OWNER = 'JSMITH'
  7  AND ROWNUM < 10
  8  ORDER BY 1,2,3;
```

TABLE_NAME	INDEX_NAME	COLUMN_NAME	COLUMN_POSITION
ADDRESS_TBL	ADDR_INX	PERS_ID	1
ADDRESS_TBL	ADDR_INX	NAME	2
ADDRESS_TBL	ADDR_INX	CITY	3
CUSTOMER_TBL	CUST_INX	CUST_ID	1
CUSTOMER_TBL	CUST_INX	CUST_NAME	2
CUSTOMER_TBL	CUST_INX	CUST_ZIP	3
HOBBY_TBL	HOBBY_PK	SAKEY	1
MAGAZINE_TBL	MAGAZINE_INX	ISSUE_NUM	1
MAGAZINE_TBL	MAGAZINE_INX	EDITOR	2

```
9 rows selected.
```

Analysis ▼

Now you have selected each column that is indexed in each table and ordered the results by the order the column appears in the index. You have learned about tables, but what holds tables? Tablespaces are on a higher level than objects such as tables, indexes, and so on. Tablespaces are Oracle's mechanism for allocating space to the database. To allocate space, you must know what tablespaces are currently available. You can perform a SELECT from DBA_TABLESPACES to see a list of all tablespaces and their status, as shown in the next example.

Input/Output ▼

```
SQL> SELECT TABLESPACE_NAME, STATUS
  2  FROM SYS.DBA_TABLESPACES;
```

TABLESPACE_NAME	STATUS
SYSTEM	ONLINE
RBS	ONLINE
TEMP	ONLINE
TOOLS	ONLINE

18

```
USERS                        ONLINE
DATA_TS                      ONLINE
INDEX_TS                     ONLINE

7 rows selected.
```

Analysis ▼

The preceding output tells you that all tablespaces are online, which means that they are available for use. If a tablespace is offline, the database objects within it (that is, the tables) are not accessible.

What is JSMITH's quota on all tablespaces to which he has access? In other words, how much room is available for JSMITH's database objects?

Input/Output ▼

```
SQL> SELECT TABLESPACE_NAME,
  2    BYTES,
  3    MAX_BYTES
  4    FROM SYS.DBA_TS_QUOTAS
  5    WHERE USERNAME = 'JSMITH';

TABLESPACE_NAME                 BYTES  MAX_BYTES
------------------------------  ----------  ----------
DATA_TS                      134111232         -1
INDEX_TS                     474390528         -1

2 rows selected.
```

Analysis ▼

JSMITH has an unlimited quota on both tablespaces to which he has access. In this case, the total number of bytes available in the tablespace is available on a first-come first-served basis. For instance, if JSMITH uses all the free space in DATA_TS, no one else can create objects there.

Database Growth

This section looks at two views that aid in the measurement of database growth: DBA_SEGMENTS and DBA_EXTENTS. The DBA_SEGMENTS view provides information about each *segment*, or object in the database, such as storage allocation, space used, and extents. Each time a table or index grows and must grab more space as identified by the NEXT_EXTENT, the table takes another extent. A table usually becomes fragmented when it grows this way. DBA_EXTENTS provides information about each extent of a segment.

Input/Output ▼

```
SQL> SELECT SUBSTR(SEGMENT_NAME,1,30) SEGMENT_NAME,
  2    SUBSTR(SEGMENT_TYPE,1,12) SEGMENT_TYPE,
  3    BYTES,
  4    EXTENTS
  5    FROM SYS.DBA_SEGMENTS
  6    WHERE OWNER = 'TWILLIAMS'
  7    AND ROWNUM < 5;
```

SEGMENT_NAME	SEGMENT_TYPE	BYTES	EXTENTS
INVOICE_TBL	TABLE	163840	10
COMPLAINT_TBL	TABLE	4763783	3
HISTORY_TBL	TABLE	547474996	27
HISTORY_INX	INDEX	787244534	31

```
4 rows selected.
```

Analysis ▼

By looking at the output from DBA_SEGMENTS and referring to the number of extents, you can easily identify which tables are experiencing the most growth. Both HISTORY_TBL and HISTORY_INX have grown much more than the other two tables.

Space Allocated

Oracle allocates space to the database by using *data files*. Space logically exists within a tablespace, but data files are the physical entities of tablespaces. In other implementations, data is also ultimately contained in data files, although these data files may be referenced by another name. The view called DBA_DATA_FILES enables you to see what is actually allocated to a tablespace.

Input/Output ▼

```
SQL> SELECT SUBSTR(TABLESPACE_NAME,1,25) TABLESPACE_NAME,
  2    SUBSTR(FILE_NAME,1,40) FILE_NAME,
  3    BYTES
  4    FROM SYS.DBA_DATA_FILES;
```

TABLESPACE_NAME	FILE_NAME	BYTES
SYSTEM	/disk01/system0.dbf	41943040
RBS	/disk02/rbs0.dbf	524288000
TEMP	/disk03/temp0.dbf	524288000
TOOLS	/disk04/tools0.dbf	20971520
USERS	/disk05/users0.dbf	20971520
DATA_TS	/disk06/data0.dbf	524288000
INDEX_TS	/disk07/index0.dbf	524288000

```
7 rows selected.
```

18

Analysis ▼

You can now see how much space has been allocated for each tablespace that exists in the database. Notice that the names of the data files correspond to the tablespace to which they belong.

Dynamic Performance Views

Oracle DBAs frequently access dynamic performance views because they provide greater detail about the internal performance measures than many of the other data dictionary views. (The DBA views contain some of the same information.)

These views involve extensive details that are implementation-specific. This section simply provides an overview of the type of information that a given data dictionary contains.

Session Information

A DESCRIBE command of the V$SESSION view follows. (DESCRIBE is a SQL*Plus command and will be covered in Lesson 25.) You can see the detail that is contained in the view.

Input/Output ▼

```
SQL> DESCRIBE V$SESSION;

Name                              Null?     Type
------------------------------    --------  ----
SADDR                                       RAW(4)
SID                                         NUMBER
SERIAL#                                     NUMBER
AUDSID                                      NUMBER
PADDR                                       RAW(4)
USER#                                       NUMBER
USERNAME                                    VARCHAR2(30)
COMMAND                                     NUMBER
TADDR                                       VARCHAR2(8)
LOCKWAIT                                    VARCHAR2(8)
STATUS                                      VARCHAR2(8)
SERVER                                      VARCHAR2(9)
SCHEMA#                                     NUMBER
SCHEMANAME                                  VARCHAR2(30)
OSUSER                                      VARCHAR2(15)
PROCESS                                     VARCHAR2(9)
MACHINE                                     VARCHAR2(64)
TERMINAL                                    VARCHAR2(10)
PROGRAM                                     VARCHAR2(48)
TYPE                                        VARCHAR2(10)
SQL_ADDRESS                                 RAW(4)
SQL_HASH_VALUE                              NUMBER
```

```
PREV_SQL_ADDR                    RAW(4)
PREV_HASH_VALUE                  NUMBER
MODULE                           VARCHAR2(48)
MODULE_HASH                      NUMBER
ACTION                           VARCHAR2(32)
ACTION_HASH                      NUMBER
CLIENT_INFO                      VARCHAR2(64)
FIXED_TABLE_SEQUENCE             NUMBER
ROW_WAIT_OBJ#                    NUMBER
ROW_WAIT_FILE#                   NUMBER
ROW_WAIT_BLOCK#                  NUMBER
ROW_WAIT_ROW#                    NUMBER
LOGON_TIME                       DATE
LAST_CALL_ET                     NUMBER
```

To get information about current database sessions, you can write a SELECT statement similar to the one that follows from V$SESSION.

Input/Output ▼

```
SQL> SELECT USERNAME, COMMAND, STATUS
  2  FROM V$SESSION
  3  WHERE USERNAME IS NOT NULL;

USERNAME                         COMMAND STATUS
-------------------------------- ------- --------
TWILLIAMS                              3 ACTIVE
JSMITH                                 0 INACTIVE

2 rows selected.
```

Analysis ▼

TWILLIAMS is logged on to the database and is performing a SELECT from the database, which is represented by command 3.

JSMITH is merely logged on to the database. His session is inactive, and he is not performing any type of commands. Refer to your database documentation to find out how the commands are identified in the data dictionary. Commands include SELECT, INSERT, UPDATE, DELETE, CREATE TABLE, and DROP TABLE.

A Look Inside MySQL's Data Dictionary

The examples in this section show you how to retrieve information from MySQL's data dictionary. Because MySQL closely conforms to the SQL:2003 standard by providing an

INFORMATION_SCHEMA database, it will provide a basis to work with other systems that support it, such as Microsoft's SQL Server.

Showing Table Commands Within MySQL

Although MySQL does not contain a series of data dictionary tables as Oracle does, you do have the capability to view and manipulate the data contained in the MySQL database (which is a part of the server package). Also, there are a series of SHOW commands that you can issue from the command line to view statistical data.

Here is a list of various SHOW commands:

Syntax ▼

```
SHOW DATABASES [LIKE wildcard]
SHOW [OPEN] TABLES [FROM db_name] [LIKE wildcard]
SHOW [FULL] COLUMNS FROM tbl_name [FROM db_name] [LIKE wildcard]
SHOW INDEX FROM tbl_name [FROM db_name]
SHOW TABLE STATUS [FROM db_name] [LIKE wildcard]
SHOW STATUS [LIKE wildcard]
SHOW VARIABLES [LIKE wildcard]
SHOW LOGS
SHOW [FULL] PROCESSLIST
SHOW GRANTS FOR user
SHOW CREATE TABLE table_name
SHOW MASTER STATUS
SHOW MASTER LOGS
SHOW SLAVE STATUS
SHOW PROCESSLIST
```

In essence, these commands behave much like a SELECT * statement.

Before you can issue the SHOW command, you first must tell MySQL what database you want to work from.

Input/Output ▼

```
mysql> use mysql;
mysql> show processlist;
+----+------+-----------+-------+---------+------+-------+------------------+
| Id | User | Host      | db    | Command | Time | State | Info             |
+----+------+-----------+-------+---------+------+-------+------------------+
| 17 | ODBC | localhost | NULL  | Sleep   | 1743 |       | NULL             |
| 20 | ODBC | localhost | mysql | Query   | 0    | NULL  | show processlist |
+----+------+-----------+-------+---------+------+-------+------------------+
```

In this example we have retrieved information on processes that are currently running.

As previously indicated, the MySQL database contains tables that provide information on privileges. Users can perform actions upon these tables just like any other table, as long as they have been granted the corresponding privilege.

Using INFORMATION_SCHEMA

MySQL 5.0 comes complete with a virtual database by the name of INFORMATION_SCHEMA. This database is created and populated by the MySQL instance, and it is not possible to change the information held within by means of any INSERT, UPDATE, or DELETE commands. Your only possible action is to use the SELECT command to access the information.

Table Information

The INFORMATION_SCHEMA database contains a table by the name of TABLES that contains information on all the tables within the MySQL instance. For example, if we wanted to know all of the tables contained within our database named 'Bob', we could execute the following query:

Input/Output ▼

```
mysql> select table_schema,table_name
    > from information_schema.tables
    > where table_schema='Bob';
```

18

```
+--------------+------------+
| table_schema | table_name |
+--------------+------------+
| Bob          | bikes      |
| Bob          | bills      |
| Bob          | characters |
| Bob          | checks     |
| Bob          | convert    |
| Bob          | customer   |
| Bob          | deposits   |
| Bob          | football   |
| Bob          | friends    |
| Bob          | hilow      |
| Bob          | job_tbl    |
| Bob          | numbers    |
| Bob          | orders     |
| Bob          | orgchart   |
| Bob          | part       |
| Bob          | parts      |
| Bob          | precedence |
| Bob          | price      |
| Bob          | products   |
| Bob          | project    |
```

```
¦ Bob          ¦ puzzle      ¦
¦ Bob          ¦ remains     ¦
¦ Bob          ¦ salaries    ¦
¦ Bob          ¦ softball    ¦
¦ Bob          ¦ ssn_table   ¦
¦ Bob          ¦ teamstats   ¦
¦ Bob          ¦ vacation    ¦
+-------------+-----------+
27 rows in set (0.00 sec)
```

User Privileges

You can also find out about user privileges in the INFORMATION_SCHEMA database in much
the same way that you did with Oracle by utilizing the USER_PRIVILEGES table. To see all
of the privilege types available to be granted, you could view the privileges assigned to
the user root, which is the database administrator account within MySQL. To do this you
would use the following command:

Input/Output ▼

```
mysql> select grantee,privilege_type
    > from information_schema.user_privileges
    > where grantee like '%root%localhost%';
+-------------------+------------------------+
¦ grantee           ¦ privilege_type         ¦
+-------------------+------------------------+
¦ 'root'@'localhost' ¦ SELECT                 ¦
¦ 'root'@'localhost' ¦ INSERT                 ¦
¦ 'root'@'localhost' ¦ UPDATE                 ¦
¦ 'root'@'localhost' ¦ DELETE                 ¦
¦ 'root'@'localhost' ¦ CREATE                 ¦
¦ 'root'@'localhost' ¦ DROP                   ¦
¦ 'root'@'localhost' ¦ RELOAD                 ¦
¦ 'root'@'localhost' ¦ SHUTDOWN               ¦
¦ 'root'@'localhost' ¦ PROCESS                ¦
¦ 'root'@'localhost' ¦ FILE                   ¦
¦ 'root'@'localhost' ¦ REFERENCES             ¦
¦ 'root'@'localhost' ¦ INDEX                  ¦
¦ 'root'@'localhost' ¦ ALTER                  ¦
¦ 'root'@'localhost' ¦ SHOW DATABASES         ¦
¦ 'root'@'localhost' ¦ SUPER                  ¦
¦ 'root'@'localhost' ¦ CREATE TEMPORARY TABLES ¦
¦ 'root'@'localhost' ¦ LOCK TABLES            ¦
¦ 'root'@'localhost' ¦ EXECUTE                ¦
¦ 'root'@'localhost' ¦ REPLICATION SLAVE      ¦
¦ 'root'@'localhost' ¦ REPLICATION CLIENT     ¦
¦ 'root'@'localhost' ¦ CREATE VIEW            ¦
¦ 'root'@'localhost' ¦ SHOW VIEW              ¦
¦ 'root'@'localhost' ¦ CREATE ROUTINE         ¦
```

```
¦ 'root'@'localhost' ¦ ALTER ROUTINE          ¦
¦ 'root'@'localhost' ¦ CREATE USER            ¦
+--------------------+------------------------+
25 rows in set (0.00 sec)
```

Now that you have seen how easy it is to gather information from the INFORMATION_
SCHEMA database, you can investigate on your own the other types of data that you can
gather from it and put it to good use.

Summary

The data dictionary is a DBA's best friend. You do not have to memorize the data dictionary; however, you must be very familiar with it because it is used frequently. Although
the details of the data dictionary vary from one implementation to another, the content
remains conceptually the same in all relational databases. You must follow the syntax
and rules of your database management system, but this lesson's examples should give
you the confidence to query your data dictionary and to be creative when doing so.

TIP	You can save queries that you might use on a regular basis. This saves you the time it would take to rewrite the queries.
	Exploring the data dictionary is an adventure, and you will need to explore to learn to use it effectively.

18

Q&A

Q Why should I use the views and tables in the data dictionary?

A Using the views in the data dictionary is the most accurate way to discover the
nature of your database. The tables can tell you what you have access to and what
your privileges are. They can also help you monitor various other database events
such as user processes and database performance.

Q How is the data dictionary created?

A The data dictionary is created when the database is initialized. Oracle provides several scripts to run when creating each database. These scripts create all necessary
tables and views for that particular database's data dictionary.

Q How is the data dictionary updated?

A The data dictionary is updated internally by the RDBMS during daily operations. When you change the structure of a table, the appropriate changes are made to the data dictionary internally. You should *never* attempt to update any tables in the data dictionary yourself. Doing so may cause a corrupt database.

Q How can I find out who did what in a database?

A Normally, tables or views in a data dictionary allow you to audit user activity.

Workshop

The Workshop provides quiz questions to help solidify your understanding of the material covered, as well as exercises to provide you with experience in using what you have learned. Try to answer the quiz and exercise questions before checking the answers in Appendix A, "Answers."

Quiz

1. In Oracle, how can you find out what tables and views you own?

2. What types of information are stored in the data dictionary?

3. How can you use performance statistics?

4. What are some database objects?

5. What is the name of the virtual database that MySQL uses for its data dictionary?

6. What is one advantage of MySQL using the INFORMATION_SCHEMA implementation?

Exercises

Questions 1, 2, and 3 are based upon the MySQL implementation of SQL.

1. MySQL has a database that is part of the server package that contains tables holding data pertaining to privileges. What is the name of the database?

2. Although you didn't create the USER table in the MYSQL database, you have the capability to view the SQL code that did. Type the following at the MySQL prompt:

```
mysql>show create table user;
```

3. If you want to view the table privileges (hint: use the table `TABLE_PRIVILEGES`) that a user has been granted, which command against the information_schema might you use? Issue the command.

4. Create another query, this time using the Oracle syntax, that will give you information on grants related to a user (hint: use the table `TABLES_PRIV`). Only provide the username, the table name, the grantor, and the privilege granted.

5. Using the `TABLES_PRIV` table again, show which tables users have been granted access to by selecting the user, the table name, and the timestamp.

6. The format for the timestamp seems difficult to read. Redo the previous query so that the timestamp column is in the following format: *day name, month name date, year hh:mm:ss*. Use the following syntax:

```
SELECT USER, TABLE_NAME,
DATE_FORMAT(TIMESTAMP, "%W, %M %D, %Y %T")
FROM ALL_TABLES_PRIV;
```

7. This portion of the exercises is written with Oracle SQL in mind. Refer to the examples from this lesson. Suppose you are managing a small- to medium-sized database. Your job responsibilities include developing and managing the database. Another individual is inserting large amounts of data into a table and receives an error indicating a lack of space. You must determine the cause of the problem. Does the user's tablespace quota need to be increased, or do you need to allocate more space to the tablespace? Prepare a step-by-step list that explains how you will gather the necessary information from the data dictionary. You do not need to list specific table or view names.

18

LESSON 19

Temporary Tables, Stored Procedures, Triggers, and Cursors

Over the course of the past 18 lessons, you have examined every major topic used to write powerful queries to retrieve data from a database. You have also briefly explored aspects of database design and database security. This lesson's objective is to cover advanced SQL topics, which include the following:

- Temporary tables

- Cursors

- Stored procedures

- Triggers

- Embedded SQL

NOTE

This lesson's examples use MySQL, Oracle, and Microsoft SQL Server's Transact-SQL implementations. We made an effort to give examples using both flavors of SQL wherever possible. You do not need to own a copy of the SQL Server database product. Feel free to choose your database product based on your requirements. (If you are reading this to gain enough knowledge to begin a project for your job, chances are you won't have a choice.) We have tried to provide both sets of examples to broaden your exposure to different platforms.

Creating Temporary Tables

The first advanced topic we discuss is the use of temporary tables, which are simply tables that exist temporarily within a database and are automatically dropped when users log out or their database connection ends. Transact-SQL creates these temporary tables in the TEMPDB database. This database is created when you install a SQL server. Two types of syntax are used to create a temporary table, as follows:

Syntax ▼

```
create table #table_name (
field1 datatype,
.
.
.
fieldn datatype)
```

The syntax above creates a temporary table. A temporary table is available only to its creator. Additionally, MySQL has the following syntax:

Syntax ▼

```
create temporary table table_name (
field1 datatype,
.
.
.
fieldn datatype)
```

Fifty users could simultaneously issue the following commands:

```
mysql> create temporary table albums (
mysql> artist char(30),
mysql> album_name char(50),
mysql> media_type int);
```

The temporary identifier before the table command is the identifier that MySQL uses to flag a temporary table. Each of the 50 users would essentially receive a private table for his or her own use. Each user could update, insert, and delete records from this table without worrying about other users invalidating the table's data. This table could be dropped as usual by issuing the following command:

```
mysql>drop temporary table albums;
```

The table could also be dropped automatically when the user who created it logs out of the MySQL instance. If you created this statement using some type of dynamic SQL connection (such as ODBC), the table will be deleted when that dynamic SQL connection is closed.

Example 19.1 illustrates that temporary tables are indeed temporary, using the two different forms of syntax. Following these two forms, Example 19.2 illustrates a common usage of temporary tables: to temporarily store data returned from a query. This data can then be used with other queries.

You need to create a database to use these examples. The database MUSIC is created with the following tables:

- ARTISTS
- MEDIA
- RECORDINGS

Use the following SQL statements to create these tables:

Input ▼

```
mysql> create table artists (
    > name char(30),
    > homebase char(40),
    > style char(20),
    > artist_id int);

mysql> create table media (
    > media_type int,
    > description char(30),
    > price float);

mysql> create table recordings (
    > artist_id int,
    > media_type int,
    > title char(50),
    > year int);
```

19

Tables 19.1, 19.2, and 19.3 show some sample data for these tables.

Table 19.1   The ARTISTS Table

NAME	HOMEBASE	STYLE	ARTIST_ID
Soul Asylum	Minneapolis	Rock	1
Maurice Ravel	France	Classical	2
Dave Matthews Band	Charlottesville	Rock	3
Vince Gill	Nashville	Country	4
Oingo Boingo	Los Angeles	Pop	5
Crowded House	New Zealand	Pop	6
Mary Chapin-Carpenter	Nashville	Country	7
Edward MacDowell	U.S.A.	Classical	8

Table 19.2   The MEDIA Table

MEDIA_TYPE	DESCRIPTION	PRICE
1	Record	4.99
2	Tape	9.99
3	CD	13.99
4	CD-ROM	29.99
5	DAT	19.99

Table 19.3   The RECORDINGS Table

ARTIST_ID	MEDIA_TYPE	TITLE	YEAR
1	2	Hang Time	1988
1	3	Made to Be Broken	1986
2	3	Bolero	1990
3	5	Under the Table and Dreaming	1994
4	3	When Love Finds You	1994
5	2	Boingo	1987
5	1	Dead Man's Party	1984
6	2	Woodface	1990
6	3	Together Alone	1993
7	5	Come On, Come On	1992
7	3	Stones in the Road	1994
8	5	Second Piano Concerto	1985

Example 19.1

You can create a temporary table in the MUSIC database. After inserting a dummy record into this table, log out. After logging back into the MySQL database, try to select the dummy record out of the temporary table. Note the results:

Input ▼

```
mysql> CREATE TEMPORARY TABLE ALBUMS (
    > ARTIST CHAR(30),
    > ALBUM_NAME CHAR(50),
    > MEDIA_TYPE INT);

Query OK, 0 rows affected (0.13 sec)

mysql> INSERT INTO ALBUMS VALUES (`THE REPLACEMENTS`, `PLEASED TO MEET ME`, 1);

Query OK, 1 rows affected (0.13 sec)
```

Now log out of the MySQL connection using the EXIT command. After logging back in and switching to the database you last used, try the following command:

Input ▼

```
mysql> SELECT * FROM ALBUMS;
ERROR 1146 (42S02): Table 'music.albums' doesn't exist
```

This table does not exist in the current database.

Example 19.2

This example shows a common use of temporary tables in MySQL: to store the results of complex queries for use in later queries.

Input ▼

```
mysql> CREATE TEMPORARY TABLE TEMP_INFO (
    > NAME CHAR(30),
    > HOMEBASE CHAR(40),
    > STYLE CHAR(20),
    > ARTIST_ID INT);

mysql> INSERT INTO TEMP_INFO
    > SELECT * FROM ARTISTS WHERE HOMEBASE = "NASHVILLE";

mysql> SELECT RECORDINGS.* FROM RECORDINGS, TEMP_INFO
WHERE RECORDINGS.ARTIST_ID = TEMP_INFO.ARTIST_ID;
```

19

The preceding batch of commands selects the recording information for all the artists whose HOMEBASE is NASHVILLE.

The following command is another way to write the set of SQL statements used in Example 19.2:

Input ▼

```
mysql> SELECT RECORDINGS.* FROM ARTISTS, RECORDINGS WHERE
    >RECORDINGS.ARTIST_ID = ARTISTS.ARTIST_ID
    > AND ARTISTS.HOMEBASE = `Nashville`;
```

Using Cursors

A database cursor is similar to the cursor on a word processor screen. As you press the Down Arrow key, the cursor scrolls down through the text one line at a time. Pressing the Up Arrow key scrolls your cursor up one line at a time. Pressing other keys such as Page Up and Page Down results in a leap of several lines in either direction. Database cursors operate in the same way.

Database cursors enable you to select a group of data, scroll through the group of records (often called a *recordset*), and examine each individual line of data as the cursor points to it. You can use a combination of local variables and a cursor to individually examine each record and perform any external operations needed before moving on to the next record.

One other common use of cursors is to save a query's results for later use. A cursor's result set is created from the result set of a SELECT query. If your application or procedure requires the repeated use of a set of records, it is faster to create a cursor once and reuse it several times than to repeatedly query the database. (You also have the added advantage of being able to scroll through the query's result set with a cursor.)

Follow these steps to create, use, and close a database cursor:

1. Create the cursor.
2. Open the cursor for use within the procedure or application.
3. Fetch a record's data one row at a time until you have reached the end of the cursor's records.
4. Close the cursor when you are finished with it.
5. Deallocate the cursor to completely discard it (only in some implementations).

Creating a Cursor

To create a cursor using MySQL, issue the following syntax:

Syntax ▼

```
DECLARE CURSOR_NAME CURSOR
    FOR SELECT_STATEMENT
```

The Oracle SQL syntax used to create a cursor looks like this:

Syntax ▼

```
DECLARE CURSOR_NAME CURSOR
    FOR {SELECT COMMAND | STATEMENT_NAME | BLOCK_NAME}
```

By executing the DECLARE cursor_name CURSOR statement, you have defined the cursor result set that will be used for all your cursor operations. A cursor has two important parts: the cursor result set and the cursor position.

The following statement creates a cursor based on the ARTISTS table:

Input ▼

```
mysql> declare artists_cursor cursor
for select * from artists;
```

You now have a simple cursor object named ARTISTS_CURSOR that contains all the records in the ARTISTS table, but first you must open the cursor.

Opening a Cursor

The simple command to open a cursor for use is

Syntax ▼

```
OPEN CURSOR_NAME
```

Executing the following statement opens ARTISTS_CURSOR for use:

```
mysql> open artist_cursor;
```

Now you can use the cursor to scroll through the result set.

Scrolling a Cursor

To scroll through the cursor's result set, MySQL provides the following FETCH command:

19

Syntax ▼

```
FETCH CURSOR_NAME [INTO FETCH_TARGET_LIST]
```

Oracle SQL provides the following syntax:

Syntax ▼

```
FETCH CURSOR_NAME {INTO : HOST_VARIABLE
    [[INDICATOR] : INDICATOR_VARIABLE]
      [,   : HOST_VARIABLE
      [[INDICATOR] : INDICATOR_VARIABLE] ]...
    | USING DESCRIPTOR DESCRIPTOR }
```

Each time the FETCH command is executed, the cursor pointer advances through the result set one row at a time. If desired, data from each row can be fetched into the FETCH_target_list or HOST_VARIABLE variables.

The following statements fetch the data from the artists_cursor result set and return the data to the program variables:

Input ▼

```
1> DECLARE @NAME CHAR(30)
2> DECLARE @HOMEBASE CHAR(40)
3> DECLARE @STYLE CHAR(20)
4> DECLARE @ARTIST_ID INT
5> FETCH ARTISTS_CURSOR INTO @NAME, @HOMEBASE, @STYLE, @ARTIST_ID
6> PRINT @NAME
7> PRINT @HOMEBASE
8> PRINT @STYLE
9> PRINT CHAR(@ARTIST_ID)
10> GO
```

You can use the WHILE loop (see Lesson 26, "An Introduction to Oracle PL/SQL") to loop through the entire result set. But how do you know when you have reached the end of the records?

Testing a Cursor's Status

MySQL provides a way to determine whether you have reached the end of a cursor. This is typically done by the use of a CONTINUE HANDLER. This is used in conjunction with a looping command such as REPEAT, as in the following pseudocode:

Syntax ▼

```
DECLARE DONE INT DEFAULT 0;
DECLARE ARTIST CHAR(30);
CREATE TEMPORARY TABLE MYARTISTS(NAME CHAR(30));
DECLARE ARTIST_CURSOR CURSOR FOR SELECT NAME FROM MUSIC.ARTISTS;
DECLARE CONTINUE HANDLER FOR NOT FOUND SET DONE=1;
OPEN ARTIST_CURSOR

REPEAT
    FETCH ARTIST_CURSOR INTO ARTIST;
    IF NOT DONE THEN
            INSERT INTO MYARTIST VALUES(ARTIST);
    END IF;
UNTIL DONE END REPEAT;

SELECT * FROM MYARTISTS;
```

Now you have a fully functioning cursor! The only step left is to close the cursor.

Closing a Cursor

Closing a cursor is a very simple matter. The statement to close a cursor is as follows:

Syntax ▼

```
close cursor_name
```

In some implementations, such as Oracle or SQL Server, this cursor still exists; however, it must not be reopened. Closing a cursor essentially closes out its result set, not its entire existence. When you are completely finished with a cursor, the DEALLOCATE command frees the memory associated with a cursor and frees the cursor name for reuse. The DEALLOCATE statement syntax is as follows:

Syntax ▼

```
DEALLOCATE CURSOR CURSOR_NAME
```

The Scope of Cursors

Unlike tables, indexes, and other objects such as triggers and stored procedures, cursors do not exist as database objects after they are created. Instead, cursors have a limited scope of use.

19

CAUTION

> Remember that memory remains allocated for the cursor, even though its name may no longer exist. Before going outside the cursor's scope, the cursor should always be closed and deallocated.

A cursor can be created within three regions:

- Session—A session begins when a user logs on. If the user logs on to a SQL server and then creates a cursor, cursor_name exists until the user logs off. The user will not be able to reuse cursor_name during the current session.

- Stored procedure—A cursor created inside a stored procedure is good only during the execution of the stored procedure. As soon as the stored procedure exits, cursor_name is no longer valid.

- Trigger—A cursor created inside a trigger has the same restrictions as one created inside a stored procedure.

Creating and Using Stored Procedures

The concept of stored procedures is an important one for the professional database programmer to master. *Stored procedures* are functions that contain potentially large groupings of SQL statements. These functions are called and executed just as a C, FORTRAN, or Visual Basic function is called. A stored procedure should encapsulate a logical set of commands that are often executed (such as a complex set of queries, updates, or inserts). Stored procedures enable the programmer to simply call the stored procedure as a function instead of repeatedly executing the statements inside the stored procedure. However, stored procedures have additional advantages.

Sybase, Inc. pioneered stored procedures with its SQL Server product in the late 1980s. These procedures are created and then stored as part of a database, just as tables and indexes are stored inside a database. Transact-SQL permits both input and output parameters to stored procedure calls. This mechanism enables you to create the stored procedures in a generic fashion so that variables can be passed to them.

One of the biggest advantages to stored procedures lies in the design of their execution. When executing a large batch of SQL statements to a database server over a network, your application is in constant communication with the server, which can quickly create an extremely heavy load on the network. As multiple users become engaged in this communication, the performance of the network and the database server becomes increasingly slower. The use of stored procedures enables the programmer to greatly reduce this communication load.

After the stored procedure is executed, the SQL statements run sequentially on the database server. Some message or data is returned to the user's computer only when the procedure is finished. This approach improves performance and offers other benefits as well. Stored procedures are actually compiled by database engines the first time they are used. The compiled map is stored on the server with the procedure. Therefore, you do not have to optimize the SQL statements each time you execute them, which also improves performance.

Use the following syntax to create a stored procedure using MySQL:

Syntax ▼

```
CREATE PROCEDURE PROCEDURE_NAME
    [[(]@PARAMETER_NAME
        DATATYPE [(LENGTH) | (PRECISION [, SCALE])
    [, @PARAMETER_NAME
        DATATYPE [(LENGTH) | (PRECISION [, SCALE])
    AS SQL_STATEMENTS
```

This CALL command executes the procedure:

Syntax ▼

```
CALL PROCEDURE_NAME
    [[@PARAMETER_NAME =] VALUE |
        [@PARAMETER_NAME =] @VARIABLE...]]
```

Example 19.3

This example creates a simple procedure. Notice how we use the delimeter command so that the line does not execute on the semi-colon. The delimeter command is used in order to change the delimeter that tells MySQL to execute the command. In this instance we use the single pipe for our delimiter.

Input ▼

```
mysql> delimiter |
    >create procedure print_artist_name (inout a_name char(30))
    > begin
    > set a_name =  concat('Hello, ', a_name,'!') ;
    > end
    > |
    > end delimiter
```

You can now execute the print_artist_name procedure using the EXECUTE statement:

19

Input ▼

```
mysql> CALL print_artist_name(@a_name) ;

mysql > SELECT @a_name
```

Example 19.3 was a small stored procedure; however, a stored procedure can contain many statements, which means that you do not have to execute each statement individually.

Removing a Stored Procedure

By now, you can probably make an educated guess as to how to get rid of a stored procedure. If you guessed the DROP command, you are absolutely correct. The following statement removes a stored procedure from a database:

Syntax ▼

```
DROP PROCEDURE PROCEDURE_NAME
```

The DROP command is used frequently: Before a stored procedure can be re-created, the old procedure with its name must be dropped. From personal experience, we can tell you that there are few instances in which a procedure is created and then never modified. Many times, in fact, errors occur somewhere within the statements that make up the procedure. We recommend that you create your stored procedures using a SQL script file containing all your statements. You can run this script file through your database server to execute your desired statements and rebuild your procedures. This technique enables you to use common text editors such as vi or Windows Notepad to create and save your SQL scripts. When running these scripts, however, you need to remember to always drop the procedure, table, and so forth from the database before creating a new one. If you forget the DROP command, errors will result because the procedure will already exist.

The following syntax is often used in MySQL script files before creating a database object:

Syntax ▼

```
DROP PROCEDURE IF EXISTS(`SCHEMA`.`PROCEDURE_NAME`);
CREATE PROCEDURE PROCEDURE_NAME
 .
 .
 .
```

These commands check to see whether the object exists. If it does, it is dropped before the new one is created. Creating script files and following these steps saves you a large amount of time (and many potential errors) in the long run.

Designing and Using Triggers

A *trigger* is essentially a special type of stored procedure that can be executed in response to one of three conditions:

- UPDATE
- INSERT
- DELETE

The MySQL syntax to create a trigger looks like this:

Syntax ▼

```
CREATE TRIGGER TRIGGER_NAME
   TRIGGER_TIME TRIGGER_EVENT
   ON TABLE_NAME
   FOR EACH ROW
   AS SQL_STATEMENTS
```

The Oracle SQL syntax used to create a trigger follows:

Syntax ▼

```
CREATE [OR REPLACE] TRIGGER [SCHEMA.]TRIGGER_NAME
  {BEFORE | AFTER | INSTEAD OF}
  {DELETE | INSERT | UPDATE [OF COLUMN[, COLUMN]...]}
[OR {DELETE | INSERT | UPDATE [OF COLUMN [, COLUMN] ...]}]...
   ON [SCHEMA.](TABLE | VIEW)
[[REFERENCING { OLD [AS] OLD [NEW [AS] NEW]
      | NEW [AS] NEW [OLD [AS] OLD]}]
FOR EACH ROW
[WHEN (CONDITION)] ]
PL/SQL STATEMENTS...
```

19

Triggers are most useful for enforcing referential integrity, as mentioned in Lesson 9, "Creating and Maintaining Tables," when you learned how to create tables. Referential integrity enforces rules used to ensure that data remains valid across multiple tables. Suppose a user entered the following command:

Input ▼

```
mysql> insert RECORDINGS values (12, "The Cross of Changes", 3, 1994);
```

Analysis ▼

This perfectly valid SQL statement inserts a new record in the RECORDINGS table. However, a quick check of the ARTISTS table shows that there is no artist_id = 12. A user with INSERT privileges in the RECORDINGS table can completely destroy your referential integrity.

> **NOTE**
>
> Although many database systems can enforce referential integrity through the use of constraints in the CREATE TABLE statement, triggers provide a great deal more flexibility. Constraints return system error messages to the users, and (as you probably know by now) these error messages are not always helpful. On the other hand, triggers can print error messages, call other stored procedures, or try to rectify a problem if necessary. Triggers might also cause problems if you are not aware that they exist, especially during batch transactions. Triggers are often disabled before batch transactions and enabled after batch transactions complete to improve database performance.

Triggers and Transactions

The actions executed within a trigger are implicitly executed as part of a transaction. Here's the broad sequence of events:

1. A BEGIN TRANSACTION statement is implicitly issued (for tables with triggers).
2. The INSERT, UPDATE, or DELETE operation occurs.
3. The trigger is called, and its statements are executed.
4. The trigger either rolls back the transaction or the transaction is implicitly committed.

Example 19.4

This example illustrates the solution to the RECORDINGS table update problem mentioned earlier.

Input ▼

```
mysql> delimiter |
    >CREATE TRIGGER CHECK_ARTISTS
    >BEFORE INSERT
    > ON RECORDINGS FOR EACH ROW BEGIN
    >        IF NOT EXISTS (SELECT * FROM ARTISTS, RECORDINGS
    >        WHERE ARTISTS.ARTIST_ID = RECORDINGS.ARTIST_ID)
    >        BEGIN
    >          ROLLBACK TRANSACTION;
    >        END
    > END;
    > |
    > end delimiter
```

Restrictions on Using Triggers

The trigger is a powerful feature of the relational database that promotes flexibility and maximized control of data processing. However, triggers do have their limitations. You must observe the following restrictions when you use triggers:

- Triggers cannot be created on temporary tables.

- Triggers must be created on tables in the current database.

- Triggers cannot be created on views.

- When a table is dropped, all triggers associated with that table are automatically dropped with it.

Nested Triggers

19

Triggers can also be nested. Say that you have created a trigger to fire on a DELETE, for instance. If this trigger itself then deletes a record, the database server can be set to fire another trigger. This approach would, of course, result in a loop, ending only when all the records in the table were deleted (or some internal trigger conditions were met). Nesting behavior is not the default, however. The environment must be set to enable this type of functionality. Consult your database server's documentation for more information on this topic.

Using Embedded SQL

This book uses the term *embedded SQL* to refer to the larger topic of writing actual program code using SQL—that is, writing stored procedures embedded in the database that can be called by an application program to perform some task. Some database systems come with complete toolkits that enable you to build simple screens and menu objects using a combination of a proprietary programming language and SQL. The SQL code is embedded within this code.

On the other hand, embedded SQL commonly refers to what is technically known as Static SQL.

Static and Dynamic SQL

Static SQL means embedding SQL statements directly within programming code. This code cannot be modified at runtime. In fact, most implementations of static SQL require the use of a precompiler that fixes your SQL statement at runtime. Both Oracle and MySQL have developed Static SQL packages for their database systems. These products contain precompilers for use with several languages, including the following:

- C++
- Pascal
- Ada
- COBOL
- FORTRAN

Some advantages of static SQL are

- Improved runtime speed
- Compile-time error checking

The disadvantages of static SQL are that

- It is inflexible.
- It requires more code (because queries cannot be formulated at runtime).
- Static SQL code is not portable to other database systems (a factor that you should always consider).

If you print a copy of static SQL code, the SQL statements appear next to the C language code (or whatever language you are using). Program variables are bound to database fields using a precompiler command. See Example 19.5 for a simple example of static SQL code.

Dynamic SQL, on the other hand, enables the programmer to build a SQL statement at runtime and pass this statement to the database engine. The engine then returns data in program variables, which are also bound at runtime. This topic is discussed thoroughly in Lesson 24, "Embedding SQL in Application Programming."

Example 19.5

This example illustrates the use of static SQL in a C function. Please note that the syntax used here does not comply with the ANSI standard. This static SQL syntax does not actually comply with any commercial product, although the syntax used is similar to that of most commercial products.

Input ▼

```
BOOL PRINT_EMPLOYEE_INFO (VOID)
{
INT AGE = 0;
CHAR NAME[41] = "\0";
CHAR ADDRESS[81] = "\0";
/* NOW BIND EACH FIELD WE WILL SELECT TO A PROGRAM VARIABLE */
#SQL BIND(AGE, AGE)
#SQL BIND(NAME, NAME);
#SQL BIND(ADDRESS, ADDRESS);
/* THE ABOVE STATEMENTS "BIND" FIELDS FROM THE DATABASE TO VARIABLES
   FROM THE PROGRAM.  AFTER WE QUERY THE DATABASE, WE WILL SCROLL
   THE RECORDS RETURNED AND THEN PRINT THEM TO THE SCREEN */

#SQL SELECT AGE, NAME, ADDRESS FROM EMPLOYEES;

#SQL FIRST_RECORD
IF (AGE == NULL)
{
    RETURN FALSE;
}
WHILE (AGE != NULL)
{
    PRINTF("AGE = %D\N, AGE);
    PRINTF("NAME = %S\N, NAME);
    PRINTF("ADDRESS = %S\N", ADDRESS);
    #SQL NEXT_RECORD
}
RETURN TRUE;
}
```

19

Analysis ▼

After you type in your code and save the file, the code usually runs through some type of precompiler. This precompiler converts the lines that begin with the #SQL precompiler directive to actual C code, which is then compiled with the rest of your program to accomplish the task at hand.

If you have never seen or written a C program, don't worry about the syntax used in Example 19.5. (As was stated earlier, the static SQL syntax is only pseudocode. Consult the static SQL documentation for your product's actual syntax.)

Summary

The popularity of programming environments such as Visual Basic, Delphi, and PowerBuilder gives database programmers many tools that are great for executing queries and updating data with a database. However, as you become increasingly involved with databases, you will discover the advantages of using the tools and topics discussed in this lesson. Unfortunately, concepts such as cursors, triggers, and stored procedures are recent database innovations and have a low degree of standardization across products. However, the basic theory of use behind all these features remains the same regardless of the database management system.

Temporary tables are tables that exist during a user's session. These tables typically exist in a special database or location and are often identified with a unique date-time stamp along with their name. Temporary tables can store a result set from a query for later use by other queries.

Cursors can store a result set to scroll through this result set one record at a time (or several records at a time, if desired). The FETCH statement is used with a cursor to retrieve an individual record's data and also to scroll the cursor to the next record. Various system variables can be monitored to determine whether the end of the records has been reached.

Stored procedures are database objects that can combine multiple SQL statements into one function. Stored procedures can accept and return parameter values, as well as call other stored procedures. These procedures are executed on the database server and are stored in compiled form in the database. Using stored procedures, rather than executing standalone queries, improves performance.

Triggers are special stored procedures that are executed when a table undergoes an INSERT, a DELETE, or an UPDATE operation. Triggers often enforce referential integrity and can also call other stored procedures.

Embedded SQL is the use of SQL in the code of an actual program. Embedded SQL consists of both static and dynamic SQL statements. Static SQL statements cannot be modified at runtime; dynamic SQL statements are subject to change.

Q&A

Q If I create a temporary table, can any other users use my table?

A No, the temporary table is available only to its creator.

Q Why must I close and deallocate a cursor?

A Because memory is still allocated for the cursor, even though its name might no longer exist.

Q Are triggers, stored procedures, and embedded SQL ANSI SQL?

A Yes.

Q Do triggers respond only to INSERTs, UPDATEs, and DELETEs?

A Yes, triggers are a special type of stored procedure that are executed in response to an INSERT, UPDATE, or DELETE.

Workshop

The Workshop provides quiz questions to help solidify your understanding of the material covered, as well as exercises to provide you with experience in using what you have learned. Try to answer the quiz and exercise questions before checking the answers in Appendix A, "Answers."

Quiz

1. True or false: Triggers can be fired upon SELECT, INSERT, and UPDATE statements.
2. True or false: A cursor is automatically opened upon creation.
3. True or false: Dynamic SQL requires the use of a precompiler.
4. What identifier is used to designate a table as temporary in the create table statement for MySQL?
5. What must be done after closing a cursor to return memory in MySQL?
6. Are triggers used with the SELECT statement?
7. If you have a trigger on a table and the table is dropped, does the trigger still exist?

19

Exercises

For the following exercises, suppose that you work for a company that distributes various products. Your company has a need for a database that stores information about products in inventory, such as quantity and prices. The database also needs to keep track of orders placed by customers and must update inventory data based on orders placed. No code will be entered into MySQL for these exercises.

1. List the tables, columns, and data types that you would create to store basic product information.

2. Stored procedures store the code and business rules that control how data is modified. What stored procedures would you define to control data processing for customer orders?

3. Triggers are blocks of code that are executed when an event takes place in the database. What triggers would you define to manage inventory information when customer orders are placed?

LESSON 20
New Objects in the Latest Standard

In this lesson, you learn some of the features and concepts that were added recently to the SQL standard. Although there are many enhancements to the general SQL syntax, this lesson discusses only the more predominant enhancements.

By the end of this lesson, you should have an understanding of the following:

- New features in the SQL standard

- Basic syntax of the new features

- Basic concepts of the new features

TIP

The new features mentioned in this lesson have already been introduced in most relational database management systems (RDBMSs). Some of these topics have been discussed in previous lessons. This lesson has been added to clarify major additions to the objects in the SQL standard. There are likely to be differences between the proposed standard and what is actually implemented in the new SQL standard. It is easy to comprehend the need for the new SQL standard based on concepts already adopted by major RDBMS vendors today.

Exploring the CREATE ROLE Statement

The SQL standard has adopted roles as a smarter way of managing many users and their privileges. (The CREATE ROLE statement was also discussed in Lesson 17, "Database Security.") The documentation in this lesson concentrates specifically on the introduction of these new objects to the SQL standard.

A *role* is a single element (object) that contains group-like privileges. Roles offers many benefits to managing security, including the following:

- It can reduce security maintenance by not having to grant explicit privileges directly to a user.

- Group privilege management is easier to change. A role's privileges can be changed, and such a change is transparent to the user.

- It allows for dynamic role granting. If a user needs SELECT and UPDATE table privileges on a table at a specified time within an application, a role with those privileges can temporarily be assigned until the transaction is complete.

When a role is first created, it has no real value other than being a role within a database. It can be granted to users or other roles. Let's say that a schema named RECOWN grants the SELECT table privilege to the RECORDS_CLERK role on the table RECOWN.MASTER_RECS. Any user or role granted the RECORDS_CLERK role now would have SELECT privileges on the RECOWN.MASTER_RECS table.

Likewise, if RECOWN revoked the SELECT table privilege from the RECORDS_CLERK role on the table RECOWN.MASTER_REC, any user or role granted the RECORDS_CLERK role would no longer have SELECT privileges on that table. This concept is illustrated in Figure 20.1. The manager in Figure 20.1 has the privileges necessary to execute both portions of the application, whereas the clerks only have the privileges needed to execute the clerks' portions of the application.

The syntax to create and drop a role is as follows:

Syntax ▼

```
CREATE ROLE < Role name > [ WITH ADMIN < grantor > ]
< grantor > ::= CURRENT_USER | CURRENT_ROLE
DROP ROLE < Role name >
```

Granting privileges to roles is the same as granting privileges to a user.

FIGURE 20.1
Managing security
with roles.

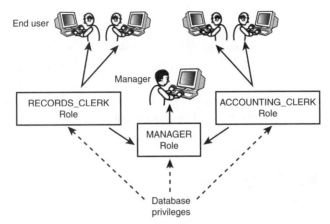

We have used Oracle to derive most of the examples in this lesson and have annotated where MySQL may be used. Some of
these options might not yet be available on your implementation
of the RDBMS. If your implementation has the capability to create
the objects discussed in this lesson, the exact syntax will probably
be slightly different.

Example 20.1

Input/Output ▼

```
create role records_clerk;

Role created.

grant select, insert on RECOWN.MASTER_REC to records_clerk;

Grant succeeded.

grant records_clerk to user1 with grant option;

Grant succeeded.

grant records_clerk to user2;

Grant succeeded.

revoke records_clerk from user2;

Revoke succeeded.
```

20

Analysis ▼

In Example 20.1, we first created a role called RECORDS_CLERK. After this role is created, it has no functionality until privileges are granted to the role. We then granted the SELECT and INSERT privileges on the table RECOWN.MASTER_REC to the role as the owner of the table. Now, through the use of the role, we can easily grant and revoke the privileges contained in the role to users in the database or to another role. Finally, we revoked the role from user2.

Creating Triggers

A *trigger* is a PROCEDURE that is invoked when an event occurs on a specified table. Trigger events can perform database manipulation language (DML) commands (such as INSERT, UPDATE, and DELETE) on the specified database tables. The action that occurs is based on the PL/SQL code used when the trigger was created. Triggers are fired implicitly by the database server when an event occurs on the trigger table, regardless of who the user is. Some of the uses for triggers are as follows:

- Data manipulation
- Referential integrity enforcement
- Database auditing and monitoring
- Business rules enforcement

Figure 20.2 illustrates a trigger. First, the user issues a transaction to the database. Because the trigger is a *before* trigger, the trigger is fired before the trigger table (EMP) is updated. The trigger causes the EMP_PAY table to be updated before the EMP table. Events that fire off a trigger are INSERTs, UPDATEs, and DELETEs.

There are three basic parts that make up a trigger:

- The executing statement
- The trigger restrictions (WHEN clause)
- The trigger action

FIGURE 20.2
The order in which a before event trigger fires.

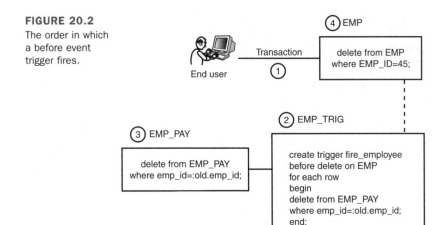

Syntax for the CREATE TRIGGER and DROP TRIGGER statements are as follows:

Syntax ▼

```
CREATE TRIGGER < Trigger Name >
{ BEFORE | AFTER } < trigger event >  ON < Table_name >
[ REFERENCING < old or new values alias list > ]
< trigger action >

< trigger event > ::=
INSERT |
DELETE |
UPDATE [ OF < trigger Column list > ]
< trigger Column list > ::= < Column name > [ { , < Column name > } …]
< old or new values alias list > ::=
< old or new values alias > …
< old or new values alias > ::=
OLD [ ROW ] [ AS ] old values < Correlation name > |
NEW [ ROW ] [ AS ] new values < Correlation name > |
OLD TABLE [ AS ] < old values Table alias > |
NEW TABLE [ AS ] < new values Table alias >
< old values Table alias > ::= < identifier >
< new values Table alias> ::= < identifier >|
DROP TRIGGER < Trigger name >
```

20

Here is an example of a trigger:

Input/Output ▼

```
SQL> CREATE TRIGGER FIRE_EMPLOYEE
  > BEFORE DELETE ON EMP
  > FOR EACH ROW
  > BEGIN
  > DELETE FROM EMP_PAY
  > WHERE SSN=:OLD.SSN;
  > END;
  > .
  > RUN

Trigger created.

SQL> DROP TRIGGER FIRE_EMPLOYEE;

Trigger dropped.
```

Analysis ▼

In this example, if the DELETE action is used on the EMP, the corresponding record(s) in the EMP_PAY will be deleted first. A trigger is not accessed or executed by a user, but rather by the database. A trigger is automatically invoked by the database when an event specified in the CREATE TRIGGER statement occurs on the trigger table (on the EMP in this example). For more information on triggers, refer to Lesson 19, "Temporary Tables, Stored Procedures, Triggers, and Cursors" and Lesson 26, "An Introduction to Oracle PL/SQL."

Using the CREATE TYPE Statement

SQL was developed as the standard for relational databases. Within the past several years, technology has advanced, and object-oriented languages such as .NET and Java have emerged. Therefore, object orientation is now introduced in the new SQL standard. It is possible that object-oriented concepts could eventually supersede the SQL standard. A large amount of time and energy has been invested to achieve the level of today's ANSI SQL. Therefore, ANSI SQL offers object orientation to preserve the language.

This technology is still fairly new, especially in a relational database environment. The concept of object orientation can be difficult to grasp unless you have studied an object-oriented language in the past. For that reason, we will cover the concept only lightly and with minimal syntax options.

NOTE

> For more information on DBMS object orientation, consult the developer's guidance documentation specific to your version of the RDBMS.

The CREATE TYPE statement in SQL applies to the object/relational concept. There are several pieces that can be applied to characterize a *user-defined type (UDT)*. Prior to SQL3, all data types, such as CHAR and NUMBER, were predefined. UDTs allow you to create your own customized data types. Some of the options available in the CREATE TYPE statement include

- Comparison operators can be used with the UDT definition to tell whether one value is greater than another.
- Built-in arithmetic operators can be used in a UDT definition.
- Cast operations allow one data type to be converted to another.

NOTE

> UDTs are not currently supported by MySQL.

The full ANSI SQL syntax for the CREATE TYPE, ALTER TYPE, and DROP TYPE statements is as follows:

Syntax ▼

```
CREATE TYPE < UDT name >
[ UNDER  < supertype UDT name > ]
[ AS { < predefined type > | < Attribute definition list > } ]
[ { INSTATIABLE | NOT INSTATIABLE } ]
{ FINAL | NOT FINAL }
[ < reference type specification > ]
[ < cast option > ]
[ < method specification > [ { , < method specification > } … ] ]

< Attribute definition list > ::=
( < Attribute definition > [ { , < Attribute definition > } … ])
< Attribute definition > ::=
< Attribute name > { < data type > | < Domain name > }
[ REFERENCES ARE [ NOT ] CHECKED [ ON DELETE
{ NO ACTION | CASCADE | RESTRICT | SET NULL | SET DEFAULT } ] ]
[ DEFAULT default value ]
[ COLLATE < Collation name > ]
```

20

```
< reference type specification > ::=
REF USING < predefined type > [ < ref cast option > ] |
REF < Attributed name > [ { , < Attribute name > } … ] |
REF IS SYSTEM GENERATED
< ref cast option > ::=
[ CAST ( SOURCE AS REF ) WITH < cast-to-ref identifier > ]
[ CAST ( REF AS SOURCE ) WITH < cast-to-type identifier > ]
< cast option > ::=
[ CAST ( SOURCE AS DISTINCT ) WITH < cast to distinct identifier > ]
[ CAST ( DISTINCT AS SOURCE ) WITH < cast to source identifier > ]
< method specification > ::=
< original method specification > |
OVERRIDING [ INSTANCE | STATIC ] < partial method specification >
< original method specification > ::=
[ INSTANCE | STATIC ]  < partial method specification >
[ SELF AS RESULT ] [ SELF AS LOCATOR ]
[ LANGUAGE { ADA | C | COBOL | FORTRAN | MUMPS | PASCAL | PLI | SQL } ]
[ PARAMETER STYLE { SQL | GENERAL } ]
[ [ NOT ] DETERMINISTIC ]
[ { NO SQL | CONTAINS SQL | READS SQL DATA | MODIFIES SQL DATA } ]
[ { RETURN NULL ON NULL INPUT | CALL ON NULL INPUT } ]

< partial method specification > ::=
METHOD < routine name >
( SQL parameter declaration list )
RETURNS < data type >

ALTER TYPE < UDT name > < alter type action >

        < alter type action > ::=
        ADD ATTRIBUTE < Attribute definition > |
        DROP ATTRIBUTE < Attribute name >

DROP TYPE < UDT name > { CASCADE | RESTRICT }
```

We do not expect you to understand every piece of the syntax introduced here. However, you should try to understand the basic concepts of UDTs, and we have provided the following example using Oracle's RDBMS to help you along.

First, we create our own UDT:

Input ▼

```
SQL> CREATE TYPE PERSON AS OBJECT
   > (NAME          CHAR(30),
   > SSN           NUMBER(9));
   > .
   > RUN
Type created.
```

Next, we use the DESCRIBE command in Oracle to show the attributes of our UDT:

Input/Output ▼

```
DESCRIBE PERSON;

Name                                     Null?    Type
----------------------------------       -------- ---------------------
NAME                                              CHAR(30)
SSN                                               NUMBER(9)
```

Here, a UDT was created as an object type with the attributes NAME and SSN.

Now we create a table and use our UDT to define a column in the table:

Input ▼

```
SQL> CREATE PAY_TBL
   > (EMPLOYEE        PERSON,
   > SALARY          NUMBER(10,2),
   > DEPT_NO         NUMBER(6),
   > HIRE_DT         DATE);

   Table created.
```

Analysis ▼

Notice that the data type assigned to the EMPLOYEE column in the PAY_TBL table is PERSON, which was defined by the previous CREATE TYPE statement. Within the EMPLOYEE column, we have two subcolumns, which are defined by our UDT called PERSON (subcolumns include NAME and SSN).

Input/Output ▼

```
SQL> DESCRIBE PAY_TBL;

Name                                     Null?    Type
----------------------------------       -------- ---------------------
EMPLOYEE                                          PERSON
SALARY                                            NUMBER(10,2)
DEPT_NO                                           NUMBER(6)
HIRE_DT                                           DATE
```

20

A table was created using the type PERSON for the column EMPLOYEE. The EMPLOYEE column in the PAY_TBL corresponds to the attributes NAME and SSN from the PERSON type.

Input ▼

```
SQL> INSERT INTO PAY_TBL
   > (PERSON('CLARK KENT', 344801726), 45900.00, 849, '3-MAR-96');

1 row inserted.
```

To insert records into the PAY_TBL, the attribute PERSON must be specified. The PERSON attribute is used to resolve which values are UDTs and which values are predefined table data types.

Here is what our output looks like if we select data from our table with a UDT:

Input/Output ▼

```
SQL> SELECT EMPLOYEE FROM PAY_TBL;

EMPLOYEE(NAME, SSN)
------------------------------------------------------------------------
PERSON('CLARK KENT', 344801726)
```

Analysis ▼

Notice the appearance of the output. EMPLOYEE is a column in the PAY_TBL table whose data type is user-defined and called PERSON. The PERSON data type is allocated for two values, one containing the individual's name and the other containing the individual's Social Security number.

The next example shows you how to select columns individually from within a column with a UDT.

Input/Output ▼

```
SQL> SELECT P..EMPLOYEE.NAME,P.EMPLOYEE.SSN,P.SALARY,P.DEPT_NO,P.HIRE_DT
   > FROM PAY_TBL P;

EMPLOYEE.NAME                   EMPLOYEE.SSN    SALARY   DEPT_NO     HIRE_DT
------------------------------- ------------ --------- --------- - --------
CLARK KENT                        344801726     45900       849  03-MAR-96
```

To retrieve the data with a SELECT statement, an alias for the PAY_TBL is used (the alias we chose was p). In Oracle, an error is returned if a table alias is not used. The table alias (p) prefixes the UDT column name. When a TYPE is created, a function is also implicitly created. The function is used to relate the attributes of the TYPE with the UDT of the table.

Regular Expressions

Regular expressions are a pattern-matching reference that can be used to implement complex search features in your SQL statements. We have already studied the operator LIKE in previous lessons, and although it is extremely useful in doing simple searches such as the following:

```
SELECT * FROM tbl_Employees WHERE Name Like '%Jones%'
```

it does not do so well with more complex searches within strings. For example, what if we had to make a match based on a proper phone number format, such as 111-1111? Although it would be difficult using the LIKE operator, we could accomplish it easily with the regex operators.

MySQL has two operators that can be used interchangeably to accomplish this: REGEXP and RLIKE. RLIKE is merely a synonym for REGEXP, so there is no real difference whatsoever. The REGEXP operator is used in much the same way as the LIKE operator:

Syntax ▼

```
SELECT column1,column2,…  FROM tablename WHERE REGEXP '<pattern>'
```

For the example of the phone number match, let's use a simple REGEXP statement on our Customer table to verify that all of our entries are in the proper format:

Input/Output ▼

```
mysql>select * from customer
    ->where phone regexp '[0-9][0-9][0-9]-[0-9][0-9][0-9][0-9]';
+------------+-------------+-------+-------+----------+----------+
¦ name       ¦ address     ¦ state ¦ zip   ¦ phone    ¦ remarks  ¦
+------------+-------------+-------+-------+----------+----------+
¦ TRUE WHEEL ¦ 550 HUSKER  ¦ NE    ¦ 58702 ¦ 555-4545 ¦ NONE     ¦
¦ BIKE SPEC  ¦ CPT SHRIVE  ¦ LA    ¦ 45678 ¦ 555-1234 ¦ NONE     ¦
¦ LE SHOPPE  ¦ HOMETOWN    ¦ KS    ¦ 54678 ¦ 555-1278 ¦ NONE     ¦
¦ AAA BIKE   ¦ 10 OLDTOWN  ¦ NE    ¦ 56784 ¦ 555-3421 ¦ JOHN-MGR ¦
¦ JACKS BIKE ¦ 24 EGLIN    ¦ FL    ¦ 34567 ¦ 555-2314 ¦ NONE     ¦
+------------+-------------+-------+-------+----------+----------+
5 rows in set (0.00 sec)
```

Excellent! All of our data is in working order. In the same fashion, it might be easier for us to check on the reverse, or return only those rows that did not conform. Let's update one of the rows and then make the reverse check:

20

Input/Output ▼

```
mysql> update customer set phone='55-4545' where phone='555-4545';
Query OK, 1 row affected (0.03 sec)
Rows matched: 1  Changed: 1  Warnings: 0

mysql>select * from customer
->where phone not regexp '[0-9][0-9][0-9]-[0-9][0-9][0-9][0-9]';
+------------+------------+-------+-------+----------+---------+
¦ name       ¦ address    ¦ state ¦ zip   ¦ phone    ¦ remarks ¦
+------------+------------+-------+-------+----------+---------+
¦ TRUE WHEEL ¦ 550 HUSKER ¦ NE    ¦ 58702 ¦ 55-4545  ¦ NONE    ¦
+------------+------------+-------+-------+----------+---------+
1 row in set (0.00 sec)
```

Analysis ▼

Although this was a simple example, the regex library has a very extensive and compli-cated list of matching criteria to work with. If you begin to use the regular expressions functions extensively, you will want to check with your implementation's documentation to get the details on the regular expression-matching syntax.

Working with BLOB Data Types

A *BLOB data type* is a very large variable-length, binary object that is normally used to store data of a binary nature, such as electronic files or pictures.

For example, we could easily decide that we need to store an electronic version of a customer registration form with our customer data. To do this, we would need a table within the database to store it, and the following would be an example of the syntax we would use:

Syntax ▼

```
CREATE TABLE CustomerRegistration(
Customer_Name   VARCHAR(10),
File_Size INT,
File_BLOB    BLOB);
```

You can treat the BLOB column in the preceding table as a type of VARBINARY value. Normally, BLOB data types interact through some sort of higher-level programming lan-guage such as VB.NET to write and consume their values into something meaningful. In the preceding example, we could write a small VB.NET application to handle the uploading and downloading of the documents to our table. Please check with your vendor-specific documentation for its implementation of the BLOB data type, as well as the size limitations that need to be considered when working with them.

A Short XML Example

The Extensible Markup Language (XML) is a specification that is used for defining custom markup elements. The main purpose of XML is to present a uniform and highly structured environment for the sharing of data. An example of a simple XML fragment is shown here:

Syntax ▼

```
<?xml version"1.0" encoding="UTF-8"?>
<catalog>
    <book>
        <title>Learn SQL in 1 Hour a Day</title>
        <author>Ryan Stephens</author>
        <description>A book to learn the SQL language.</description>
    </book>
</catalog>
```

You might be sharing the same kinds of data using what are commonly referred to as *flat files*. These are files that normally contain one record per line, and data is either formatted in fixed width columns or separated by a delimiter. So what is the difference? Why should you consider using XML?

There are two main characteristics of XML that you need to consider: validation and accessibility. XML contains a variety of methods to apply what is known as a *schema* against an XML document. The schema is much the same as a database schema and merely spells out what the format of the XML document should look like. If we have a schema for an XML document, we can quite readily ask the system to check our incoming XML to see whether it is in the proper format. Trying to do something similar within the context of a flat file would be a pain. You will need to check with your specific implementation's documentation to understand how it implements XML and what built-in functions are available to validate XML against a schema.

20

XML is also more accessible than most flat file counterparts because of a querying tool known as XPATH (XML Path Language) that allows the user to query the XML markup for certain data. If the preceding short XML example with the book catalog were a flat file, how would you go about querying the file to determine what authors you had listed? With XML, it is rather easy:

Input/Output ▼

```
mysql> select ExtractValue('<catalog>
    ->        <book>
    ->            <title>Learn SQL in 1 Hour a Day</title>
    ->            <author>Ryan Stephens</author>
    ->            <description>A book to learn the SQL language.</description>
    ->        </book>
    -> </catalog>','/catalog/book/author') as val1;
+---------------+
| val1          |
+---------------+
| Ryan Stephens |
+---------------+
1 row in set (0.00 sec)
```

Analysis ▼

As you can see, it becomes fairly easy to extract only what you need from the XML file. Again, be sure to check your particular implementation's documentation so that you fully understand what features and limitations you have to work with.

Summary

The addition of roles, triggers, UDTs, regular expressions, BLOB data types, and XML to the SQL standard provides SQL with many times more flexibility than it once had. Although most of the new features are optional to implement, many of the new features have already been adopted by most RDBMS vendors.

These features offer greater control and efficiency for today's business models. These concepts should be considered during new development phases in RDBMS applications. The future in SQL will continue to grow toward an object-relational–oriented RDBMS because of its overwhelming success.

Q&A

Q I have actually used roles and triggers before. Were they not a part of the standard before?

A Some implementations have used roles and triggers; however, they were not fully realized in the SQL standard until SQL3. Even now, they are not required for an implementation to be considered SQL-compliant.

Q What value does the CREATE TYPE statement add to the SQL standard?

A The CREATE TYPE statement offers the availability of object-relational technology. You can define and use your own UDTs. These UDTs allow you more flexibility when defining the structure of your database, and when organizing the data.

Q I understand about views being difficult to manage; would you consider the use of roles difficult to manage?

A The management of roles could become as difficult as views. The number of roles used, the combinations of privileges assigned to each role, and what roles to assign to users or other roles all add to the difficulty.

Workshop

The Workshop provides quiz questions to help solidify your understanding of the material covered, as well as exercises to provide you with experience in using what you have learned. Try to answer the quiz and exercise questions before checking the answers in Appendix A, "Answers."

Quiz

1. What are the three basic components of a trigger?
2. What are the three events that can cause a trigger to fire?
3. What is the advantage of implementing role security?
4. Name four uses for a trigger.
5. What does the abbreviation UDT stand for?
6. What equivalent data type can be used to describe a BLOB?
7. What function is used within MySQL to get values from an XML fragment?
8. What are the two main benefits of XML?
9. What two operators are used for regular expressions with MySQL? What is the difference between them?

20

Exercises

1. Use the Oracle syntax as shown in this lesson for this exercise. Write out the code to create a role and assign the SELECT privilege to that role. Then grant the role to a user.
2. Use the Oracle syntax as shown in this lesson to create a UDT, and then create a table using the newly created UDT. Insert a row of data into your table. Issue a query selecting all data from your table.

LESSON 21

Using SQL to Generate SQL Statements

In this lesson, you learn the concepts behind generating one or more SQL statements from a query. By the end of this lesson you should understand the following:

- The benefits of generating SQL statements from a query
- How to make the output from a query appear in the form of another SQL statement
- How to use the data dictionary, database tables, or both to form SQL statements

Understanding the Power of SQL Statement Generation

Generating SQL from another SQL statement simply means writing a SQL statement whose output forms another SQL statement or command. Until now, all the SQL statements that you have learned to write either do something, such as manipulate the data in a table one row at a time, or produce some kind of report from a query. In this lesson, you learn how to write a query whose output forms another query or SQL statement.

Why would you ever need to produce a SQL statement from a query? Initially, it is a matter of simplicity and efficiency. You might never *need* to produce a SQL statement, but without ever doing so you would be ignoring one of SQL's most powerful features, one that too many people do not realize exists.

Generating SQL statements is rarely mandatory because you can manually create and issue all SQL statements, although the process can be tedious in certain situations. On the same note, generating SQL statements might be necessary when you have a tight deadline. For example, suppose your boss wants to grant access on a new table to all 90 users in the marketing department (and you want to get home for dinner). Because some users of this database do not work in marketing, you cannot simply grant access on the table to the public. When you have multiple groups of users with different types of access, you might want to enforce role security, which is a built-in method for controlling user access to data. In this situation, you can create a SQL statement that generates GRANT statements to all individuals in the marketing department; that is, it grants each individual the appropriate role(s).

You will find many situations in which it is advantageous to produce a SQL statement as output to another statement. For example, you might need to execute many similar SQL statements as a group, or you might need to regenerate DDL from the data dictionary. When producing SQL as output from another statement, you will always get the data for your output from either the data dictionary or the schema tables in the database. Figure 21.1 illustrates this procedure.

FIGURE 21.1
The process of generating SQL from the database.

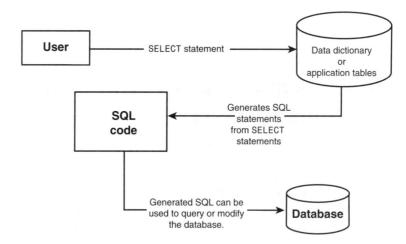

As you can see in Figure 21.1, a SELECT statement can be issued to the database; it draws its output results either from the data dictionary or from application tables in the database. Your statement can arrange the retrieved data into one or more SQL statements. For instance, if one row is returned, you will have generated one SQL statement. If 100 rows are returned from your statement, you will have generated 100 SQL statements. When you successfully generate SQL code from the database, you can run that code against the database, which may perform a series of queries or database actions.

The remainder of this lesson is devoted to examples that show you how to produce output in the form of SQL statements. Most of your information will come from the data dictionary covered in Lesson 18, "Exploring the Data Dictionary (System Catalog)."

NOTE　　This lesson's examples use Personal Oracle. As always, you should apply the concepts discussed in this lesson to the syntax of your specific database implementation.

CAUTION　　Until you completely understand the concepts presented in this lesson, use caution when generating SQL statements that will modify existing data or database structures.

Miscellaneous SQL*Plus Commands

This lesson's examples use a few new commands. These commands, known as SQL*Plus commands, are specific to Personal Oracle and control the format of your output results (see Lesson 25, "Using Oracle SQL*Plus to Satisfy Reporting Needs"). SQL*Plus commands are issued at the SQL> prompt, or they can be used in a file.

NOTE　　Although these commands are specific to Oracle, similar commands are available in other implementations, such as Transact-SQL (see Lesson 27, "An Introduction to Transact-SQL").

SET ECHO ON/OFF

When you use SET ECHO ON, you will see your SQL statements as they execute. SET ECHO OFF means that you do not want to see your SQL statements as they execute—you just want to see the output.

Syntax ▼

```
SET ECHO [ ON | OFF ]
```

21

SET FEEDBACK ON/OFF

Feedback is the row count of your output. For instance, if you executed a SELECT statement that returned 30 rows of data, your feedback would be

```
30 rows selected.
```

SET FEEDBACK ON displays the row count; SET FEEDBACK OFF eliminates the row count from your output.

Syntax ▼

```
SET FEEDBACK [ ON | OFF ]
```

SET HEADING ON/OFF

The headings being referred to here are the column headings in the output of a SELECT statement, such as LAST_NAME or CUSTOMER_ID. SET HEADING ON, which is the default, displays the column headings of your data as a part of the output. SET HEADING OFF, of course, eliminates the column headings from your output.

Syntax ▼

```
SET HEADING [ ON | OFF ]
```

SPOOL FILENAME/OFF

Spooling is the process of directing the results of your query to a file. To open a spool file, you enter

```
SPOOL FILENAME
```

To close your spool file, you would type

Syntax ▼

```
SPOOL OFF
```

START FILENAME

Most SQL commands that we have covered so far have been issued at the SQL> prompt. Another method for issuing SQL statements is to create and then execute a file. In SQL*Plus, the command to execute a SQL file is START FILENAME.

Syntax ▼

```
START FILENAME
```

EDIT FILENAME

EDIT is a Personal Oracle command that opens a file (an existing one or a new one) and uses the shorthand syntax ED for the fullname. When you open a file with ED, you are using a full-screen editor, which is often easier than trying to type a lengthy SQL statement at the SQL> prompt. You will use this command to modify the contents of your spool file. You will find that you use this command often when generating SQL script because you might have to modify the contents of the file for customization. However, you can achieve most customization through SQL*Plus commands.

Syntax ▼

```
ED FILENAME
```

Counting the Rows in All Tables

The first example shows you how to edit your spool file to remove irrelevant lines in your generated code, thus allowing your SQL statement to run without being tarnished with syntax errors.

NOTE

Take note of the editing technique used in this example because we will not show the step in the rest of the examples in this lesson. We assume that you know the basic syntax of SQL statements by now. In addition, you may choose to edit your spool file in various ways.

Start by recalling the function to count all rows in a table: COUNT(*). You already know how to select a count on all rows in a single table—for example,

Input/Output ▼

```
SQL> SELECT COUNT(*)
  > FROM TBL1;

COUNT(*)
--------
      29
1 rows selected.
```

21

That technique is handy, but suppose you want to get a row count on all tables that you own or that are in your schema. For example, here's a list of the tables you own:

Input/Output ▼

```
SQL> SELECT * FROM CAT;

TABLE_NAME                        TABLE_TYPE
--------------------------------  -----------
ACCT_PAY                          TABLE
ACCT_REC                          TABLE
CUSTOMERS                         TABLE
EMPLOYEES                         TABLE
HISTORY                           TABLE
INVOICES                          TABLE
ORDERS                            TABLE
PRODUCTS                          TABLE
PROJECTS                          TABLE
VENDORS                           TABLE

10 rows selected.
```

Analysis ▼

If you want to get a row count on all your tables, you could manually issue the COUNT(*) statement on each table. The feedback would be

```
10 rows selected.
```

The following SELECT statement creates more SELECT statements to obtain a row count on all the preceding tables:

Input/Output ▼

```
SQL> SET ECHO OFF
SQL> SET FEEDBACK OFF
SQL> SET HEADING OFF
SQL> SPOOL CNT.SQL
SQL> SELECT 'SELECT COUNT(*) FROM ' || TABLE_NAME || ';'
  2  FROM CAT
  3  /

SELECT COUNT(*) FROM ACCT_PAY;
SELECT COUNT(*) FROM ACCT_REC;
SELECT COUNT(*) FROM CUSTOMERS;
SELECT COUNT(*) FROM EMPLOYEES;
SELECT COUNT(*) FROM HISTORY;
SELECT COUNT(*) FROM INVOICES;
```

```
SELECT COUNT(*) FROM ORDERS;
SELECT COUNT(*) FROM PRODUCTS;
SELECT COUNT(*) FROM PROJECTS;
SELECT COUNT(*) FROM VENDORS;
```

Analysis ▼

The first action in the preceding example is to use some SQL*Plus commands. Setting ECHO OFF, FEEDBACK OFF, and HEADING OFF condenses the output to what is actually being selected. Remember, the output is not being used as a report, but rather as a SQL statement that is ready to be executed. The next step is to use the SPOOL command to direct the output to a file, which is specified as cnt.sql. The final step is to issue the SELECT statement, which will produce output in the form of another statement. Notice the use of single quotation marks to select a literal string. The combination of single quotation marks and the concatenation (||) character allows you to combine actual data and literal strings to form another SQL statement. This example selects its data from the data dictionary.

TIP

> Always edit your output file before running it to eliminate syntax discrepancies and to further customize the file that you have created.

Input ▼

```
SQL> SPOOL OFF
SQL> ED CNT.SQL
```

Analysis ▼

The command SPOOL OFF closes the spool file, and then the ED command edits the file. At this point you are inside the file that you created. You should remove unnecessary lines from the file, such as the SELECT statement, which was used to achieve the results, and the SPOOL OFF at the end of the file.

Here is how your file should look after the edit. Notice that each line is a valid SQL statement.

21

```
SELECT COUNT(*) FROM ACCT_PAY;
SELECT COUNT(*) FROM ACCT_REC;
SELECT COUNT(*) FROM CUSTOMERS;
SELECT COUNT(*) FROM EMPLOYEES;
```

```
SELECT COUNT(*) FROM HISTORY;
SELECT COUNT(*) FROM INVOICES;
SELECT COUNT(*) FROM ORDERS;
SELECT COUNT(*) FROM PRODUCTS;
SELECT COUNT(*) FROM PROJECTS;
SELECT COUNT(*) FROM VENDORS;
```

Now, execute the file:

Input/Output ▼

```
SQL> SET ECHO ON
SQL> SET HEADING ON
SQL> START CNT.SQL

SQL> SELECT COUNT(*) FROM ACCT_PAY;

 COUNT(*)
---------
        7
SQL> SELECT COUNT(*) FROM ACCT_REC;

 COUNT(*)
---------
        9
SQL> SELECT COUNT(*) FROM CUSTOMERS;

 COUNT(*)
---------
        5
SQL> SELECT COUNT(*) FROM EMPLOYEES;

 COUNT(*)
---------
       10

SQL> SELECT COUNT(*) FROM HISTORY;

 COUNT(*)
---------
       26
SQL> SELECT COUNT(*) FROM INVOICES;

 COUNT(*)
---------
        0
SQL> SELECT COUNT(*) FROM ORDERS;

 COUNT(*)
---------
        0
```

```
SQL> SELECT COUNT(*) FROM PRODUCTS;

 COUNT(*)
---------
       10
SQL> SELECT COUNT(*) FROM PROJECTS;

 COUNT(*)
---------
       16
SQL> SELECT COUNT(*) FROM VENDORS;

 COUNT(*)
---------
       22
SQL>
```

Analysis ▼

SET ECHO ON enables you to see each statement that was executed. SET HEADING ON displays the column heading COUNT(*) for each SELECT statement. If you had included

SET FEEDBACK ON

then

```
1 row selected.
```

would have been displayed after each count. This example executed the SQL script by using the SQL*Plus START command. However, what if you were dealing with 50 tables instead of just 10?

NOTE

The proper use of single quotation marks when generating a SQL script is vital. Use these quotations generously and make sure that you are including all elements that will make your generated statement complete. In this example, single quotation marks enclose the components of your generated statement (output) that cannot be selected from a table—for example, 'SELECT COUNT(*) FROM' and ';'.

21

Granting System Privileges to Multiple Users

As a database administrator or an individual responsible for maintaining users, you will often receive requests for user IDs. In addition to having to grant privileges to users that allow them proper database access, you also have to modify users' privileges to accommodate their changing needs. You can get the database to generate the GRANT statements to grant system privileges or roles to many users.

Input/Output ▼

```
SQL> SET ECHO OFF
SQL> SET HEADING OFF
SQL> SET FEEDBACK OFF
SQL> SPOOL GRANTS.SQL
SQL> SELECT 'GRANT CONNECT, RESOURCE TO ' || USERNAME || ';'
  2  FROM SYS.DBA_USERS
  3  WHERE USERNAME NOT IN ('SYS','SYSTEM','SCOTT','RYAN','PO7','DEMO')
  4  /

GRANT CONNECT, RESOURCE TO KEVIN;
GRANT CONNECT, RESOURCE TO JOHN;
GRANT CONNECT, RESOURCE TO JUDITH;
GRANT CONNECT, RESOURCE TO STEVE;
GRANT CONNECT, RESOURCE TO RON;
GRANT CONNECT, RESOURCE TO MARY;
GRANT CONNECT, RESOURCE TO DEBRA;
GRANT CONNECT, RESOURCE TO CHRIS;
GRANT CONNECT, RESOURCE TO CAROL;
GRANT CONNECT, RESOURCE TO EDWARD;
GRANT CONNECT, RESOURCE TO BRANDON;
GRANT CONNECT, RESOURCE TO JACOB;
```

Input/Output ▼

```
SQL> SPOOL OFF

SQL> START GRANTS.SQL


SQL> GRANT CONNECT, RESOURCE TO KEVIN;

Grant succeeded.

SQL> GRANT CONNECT, RESOURCE TO JOHN;

Grant succeeded.
```

```
SQL> GRANT CONNECT, RESOURCE TO JUDITH;

Grant succeeded.

SQL> GRANT CONNECT, RESOURCE TO STEVE;

Grant succeeded.

SQL> GRANT CONNECT, RESOURCE TO RON;

Grant succeeded.

SQL> GRANT CONNECT, RESOURCE TO MARY;

Grant succeeded.

SQL> GRANT CONNECT, RESOURCE TO DEBRA;

Grant succeeded.

SQL> GRANT CONNECT, RESOURCE TO CHRIS;

Grant succeeded.

SQL> GRANT CONNECT, RESOURCE TO CAROL;

Grant succeeded.

SQL> GRANT CONNECT, RESOURCE TO EDWARD;

Grant succeeded.

SQL> GRANT CONNECT, RESOURCE TO BRANDON;

Grant succeeded.

SQL> GRANT CONNECT, RESOURCE TO JACOB;

Grant succeeded.
```

Analysis ▼

In this example, you saved many tedious keystrokes by generating GRANT statements using a simple SQL statement, rather than typing each one manually.

21

NOTE	The following examples omit the step in which you edit your output file. You can assume that the files are already edited.

Granting Privileges on Your Tables to Another User

Granting privileges on a table to another user is quite simple, as is selecting a row count on a table. But if you have multiple tables to which you wish to grant access to a role or user, you can make SQL generate a script for you—unless you just love to type.

First, review a simple GRANT to one table:

Input/Output ▼

```
SQL> GRANT SELECT ON HISTORY TO BRANDON;

Grant succeeded.
```

Are you ready for some action? The next statement creates a GRANT statement for each of the 10 tables in your schema.

Input/Output ▼

```
SQL> SET ECHO OFF
SQL> SET FEEDBACK OFF
SQL> SET HEADING OFF
SQL> SPOOL GRANTS.SQL
SQL> SELECT 'GRANT SELECT ON ' || TABLE_NAME || ' TO BRANDON;'
  2  FROM CAT
  3  /

GRANT SELECT ON ACCT_PAY TO BRANDON;
GRANT SELECT ON ACCT_REC TO BRANDON;
GRANT SELECT ON CUSTOMERS TO BRANDON;
GRANT SELECT ON EMPLOYEES TO BRANDON;
GRANT SELECT ON HISTORY TO BRANDON;
GRANT SELECT ON INVOICES TO BRANDON;
GRANT SELECT ON ORDERS TO BRANDON;
GRANT SELECT ON PRODUCTS TO BRANDON;
GRANT SELECT ON PROJECTS TO BRANDON;
GRANT SELECT ON VENDORS TO BRANDON;
```

Analysis ▼

A GRANT statement has been automatically prepared for each table. BRANDON is to have SELECT access on each table.

Now close the output file with the SPOOL command, and assuming that the file has been edited, the file is ready to run.

Input/Output ▼

```
SQL> SPOOL OFF

SQL> SET ECHO ON
SQL> SET FEEDBACK ON
SQL> START GRANTS.SQL

SQL> GRANT SELECT ON ACCT_PAY TO BRANDON;

Grant succeeded.

SQL> GRANT SELECT ON ACCT_REC TO BRANDON;

Grant succeeded.

SQL> GRANT SELECT ON CUSTOMERS TO BRANDON;

Grant succeeded.

SQL> GRANT SELECT ON EMPLOYEES TO BRANDON;

Grant succeeded.

SQL> GRANT SELECT ON HISTORY TO BRANDON;

Grant succeeded.

SQL> GRANT SELECT ON INVOICES TO BRANDON;

Grant succeeded.

SQL> GRANT SELECT ON ORDERS TO BRANDON;

Grant succeeded.

SQL> GRANT SELECT ON PRODUCTS TO BRANDON;

Grant succeeded.

SQL> GRANT SELECT ON PROJECTS TO BRANDON;

Grant succeeded.

SQL> GRANT SELECT ON VENDORS TO BRANDON;

Grant succeeded.
```

Analysis ▼

The echo and feedback were turned on. Turning feedback on displayed the statement
Grant succeeded. The SELECT privilege has been granted to BRANDON on all 10 tables
with very little effort. Again, keep in mind that you will often be dealing with many
more than 10 tables.

Disabling Table Constraints to Load Data

When loading data into tables, you will sometimes have to disable the constraints on
your tables. Suppose that you have truncated your tables and you are loading data into
your tables from scratch. More than likely, your tables will have referential integrity constraints, such as foreign keys. Because the database will not let you insert a row of data
into a table that references another table (if the referenced column does not exist in the
other table), you might have to disable constraints to initially load your data. Of course,
after the load is successful, you would want to enable the constraints.

Input/Output ▼

```
SQL> SET ECHO OFF
SQL> SET FEEDBACK OFF
SQL> SET HEADING OFF
SQL> SPOOL DISABLE.SQL
SQL> SELECT 'ALTER TABLE ' || TABLE_NAME ||
  2         'DISABLE CONSTRAINT ' || CONSTRAINT_NAME || ';'
  3  FROM SYS.DBA_CONSTRAINTS
  4  WHERE OWNER = 'RYAN'
  5  /

ALTER TABLE ACCT_PAY DISABLE CONSTRAINT FK_ACCT_PAY_ID;
ALTER TABLE ACCT_REC DISABLE CONSTRAINT FK_ACCT_REC_ID;
ALTER TABLE CUSTOMERS DISABLE CONSTRAINT FK_CUSTOMER_ID;
ALTER TABLE HISTORY DISABLE CONSTRAINT FK_ACCT_HIST_ID;
ALTER TABLE INVOICES DISABLE CONSTRAINT FK_ACCT_INV_ID;
ALTER TABLE ORDERS DISABLE CONSTRAINT FK_ACCT_ORD_ID;
```

Analysis ▼

The objective is to generate a series of ALTER TABLE statements that will disable the constraints on all tables owned by RYAN. The semicolon concatenated to the end of the
selected code completes each SQL statement.

Input/Output ▼

```
SQL> SPOOL OFF

SQL> SET ECHO OFF
```

```
SQL> SET FEEDBACK ON
SQL> START DISABLE.SQL
Constraint Disabled.

Constraint Disabled.

Constraint Disabled.

Constraint Disabled.

Constraint Disabled.

Constraint Disabled.
```

Analysis ▼

Notice that echo is off, which means that you will not see the individual statements. Because the feedback is on, you can see the results:

```
Constraint Disabled.
```

If both echo and feedback were off, nothing would be displayed. There would simply be a pause for as long as it would take to execute the ALTER TABLE statements, and then a SQL> prompt would be returned.

Now you can load your data without worrying about receiving errors caused by your constraints. Constraints are good, but they can be barriers during data loads. You may use the same idea to enable the table constraints.

Creating Numerous Synonyms in a Single Bound

Another tedious and exhausting task is creating numerous synonyms, whether they are public or private. Only a DBA or a user who has the CREATE PUBLIC SYNONYM privilege can create public synonyms, but any user can create private synonyms.

The following example creates public synonyms for all tables owned by RYAN:

Input/Output ▼

```
SQL> SET ECHO OFF
SQL> SET FEEDBACK OFF
SQL> SET HEADING OFF
SQL> SPOOL PUB_SYN.SQL
SQL> SELECT 'CREATE PUBLIC SYNONYM ' || TABLE_NAME || ' FOR ' ||
```

21

```
2               OWNER || '.' || TABLE_NAME || ';'
3  FROM SYS.DBA_TABLES
4  WHERE OWNER = 'RYAN'
5  /

CREATE PUBLIC SYNONYM ACCT_PAY FOR RYAN.ACCT_PAY;
CREATE PUBLIC SYNONYM ACCT_REC FOR RYAN.ACCT_REC;
CREATE PUBLIC SYNONYM CUSTOMERS FOR RYAN.CUSTOMERS;
CREATE PUBLIC SYNONYM EMPLOYEES FOR RYAN.EMPLOYEES;
CREATE PUBLIC SYNONYM HISTORY FOR RYAN.HISTORY;
CREATE PUBLIC SYNONYM INVOICES FOR RYAN.INVOICES;
CREATE PUBLIC SYNONYM ORDERS FOR RYAN.ORDERS;
CREATE PUBLIC SYNONYM PRODUCTS FOR RYAN.PRODUCTS;
CREATE PUBLIC SYNONYM PROJECTS FOR RYAN.PROJECTS;
CREATE PUBLIC SYNONYM VENDORS FOR RYAN.VENDORS;
```

Now run the file.

Input/Output ▼

```
SQL> SPOOL OFF
SQL> ED PUB_SYN.SQL
SQL> SET ECHO ON
SQL> SET FEEDBACK ON
SQL> START PUB_SYN.SQL

SQL> CREATE PUBLIC SYNONYM ACCT_PAY FOR RYAN.ACCT_PAY;

Synonym created.

SQL> CREATE PUBLIC SYNONYM ACCT_REC FOR RYAN.ACCT_REC;

Synonym created.

SQL> CREATE PUBLIC SYNONYM CUSTOMERS FOR RYAN.CUSTOMERS;

Synonym created.

SQL> CREATE PUBLIC SYNONYM EMPLOYEES FOR RYAN.EMPLOYEES;

Synonym created.

SQL> CREATE PUBLIC SYNONYM HISTORY FOR RYAN.HISTORY;

Synonym created.

SQL> CREATE PUBLIC SYNONYM INVOICES FOR RYAN.INVOICES;

Synonym created.
```

```
SQL> CREATE PUBLIC SYNONYM ORDERS FOR RYAN.ORDERS;

Synonym created.

SQL> CREATE PUBLIC SYNONYM PRODUCTS FOR RYAN.PRODUCTS;

Synonym created.

SQL> CREATE PUBLIC SYNONYM PROJECTS FOR RYAN.PROJECTS;

Synonym created.

SQL> CREATE PUBLIC SYNONYM VENDORS FOR RYAN.VENDORS;

Synonym created.
```

Analysis ▼

Almost instantly, all database users have access to a public synonym for all tables that RYAN owns. Now a user does not need to qualify the table when performing a SELECT operation. (Qualifying means identifying the table owner, as in RYAN.VENDORS.)

What if public synonyms do not exist? Suppose that BRANDON has SELECT access to all tables owned by RYAN and wants to create private synonyms.

Input/Output ▼

```
SQL> CONNECT BRANDON
ENTER PASSWORD: *******
CONNECTED.

SQL> SET ECHO OFF
SQL> SET FEEDBACK OFF
SQL> SET HEADING OFF
SQL> SPOOL PRIV_SYN.SQL
SQL> SELECT 'CREATE SYNONYM ' || TABLE_NAME || ' FOR ' ||
  2         OWNER || '.' || TABLE_NAME || ';'
  3  FROM ALL_TABLES
  4  /

CREATE SYNONYM DUAL FOR SYS.DUAL;
CREATE SYNONYM AUDIT_ACTIONS FOR SYS.AUDIT_ACTIONS;
CREATE SYNONYM USER_PROFILE FOR SYSTEM.USER_PROFILE;
CREATE SYNONYM CUSTOMERS FOR RYAN.CUSTOMERS;
CREATE SYNONYM ORDERS FOR RYAN.ORDERS;
CREATE SYNONYM PRODUCTS FOR RYAN.PRODUCTS;
CREATE SYNONYM INVOICES FOR RYAN.INVOICES;
CREATE SYNONYM ACCT_REC FOR RYAN.ACCT_REC;
CREATE SYNONYM ACCT_PAY FOR RYAN.ACCT_PAY;
```

21

```
CREATE SYNONYM VENDORS FOR RYAN.VENDORS;
CREATE SYNONYM EMPLOYEES FOR RYAN.EMPLOYEES;
CREATE SYNONYM PROJECTS FOR RYAN.PROJECTS;
CREATE SYNONYM HISTORY FOR RYAN.HISTORY;

SQL> SPOOL OFF

SQL> SET ECHO OFF
SQL> SET FEEDBACK ON
SQL> START PRIV_SYN.SQL
Synonym created.

Synonym created.

Synonym created.

Synonym created.

Synonym created.

Synonym created.

Synonym created.

Synonym created.

Synonym created.

Synonym created.

Synonym created.

Synonym created.

Synonym created.
```

Analysis ▼

With hardly any effort, BRANDON has synonyms for all tables owned by RYAN and no longer needs to qualify the table names.

Creating Views on Your Tables

If you want to create views on a group of tables, you could try something similar to the following example:

Input/Output ▼

```
SQL> SET ECHO OFF
SQL> SET FEEDBACK OFF
SQL> SET HEADING OFF
SQL> SPOOL VIEWS.SQL
SQL> SELECT 'CREATE VIEW ' || TABLE_NAME || '_VIEW AS SELECT * FROM ' ||
  2         TABLE_NAME || ';'
  3  FROM CAT
  4  /

CREATE VIEW ACCT_PAY_VIEW AS SELECT * FROM ACCT_PAY;
CREATE VIEW ACCT_REC_VIEW AS SELECT * FROM ACCT_REC;
CREATE VIEW CUSTOMERS_VIEW AS SELECT * FROM CUSTOMERS;
CREATE VIEW EMPLOYEES_VIEW AS SELECT * FROM EMPLOYEES;
CREATE VIEW HISTORY_VIEW AS SELECT * FROM HISTORY;
CREATE VIEW INVOICES_VIEW AS SELECT * FROM INVOICES;
CREATE VIEW ORDERS_VIEW AS SELECT * FROM ORDERS;
CREATE VIEW PRODUCTS_VIEW AS SELECT * FROM PRODUCTS;
CREATE VIEW PROJECTS_VIEW AS SELECT * FROM PROJECTS;
CREATE VIEW VENDORS_VIEW AS SELECT * FROM VENDORS;
```

Input/Output ▼

```
SQL> SPOOL OFF
SQL> SET ECHO OFF
SQL> SET FEEDBACK ON
SQL> START VIEWS.SQL
View Created.

View Created.

View Created.

View Created.

View Created.

View Created.

View Created.

View Created.

View Created.

View Created.
```

21

Analysis ▼

The file `views.sql` was generated by the previous SQL statement. This output file has become another SQL statement file and contains statements to create views on all specified tables. After running `views.sql`, you can see that the views have been created.

Truncating All Tables in a Schema

Truncating tables is an event that occurs in a development environment. To effectively develop and test data load routines and SQL statement performance, data is reloaded frequently. This process identifies and exterminates bugs, and the application being developed or tested is moved into a production environment.

The following example truncates all tables in a specified schema:

Input/Output ▼

```
SQL> SET ECHO OFF
SQL> SET FEEDBACK OFF
SQL> SET HEADING OFF
SQL> SPOOL TRUNC.SQL
SQL> SELECT 'TRUNCATE TABLE ' || TABLE_NAME || ';'
  2  FROM ALL_TABLES
  3  WHERE OWNER = 'RYAN'
  4  /

TRUNCATE TABLE ACCT_PAY;
TRUNCATE TABLE ACCT_REC;
TRUNCATE TABLE CUSTOMERS;
TRUNCATE TABLE EMPLOYEES;
TRUNCATE TABLE HISTORY;
TRUNCATE TABLE INVOICES;
TRUNCATE TABLE ORDERS;
TRUNCATE TABLE PRODUCTS;
TRUNCATE TABLE PROJECTS;
TRUNCATE TABLE VENDORS;
```

Go ahead and run your script if you dare.

```
SQL> SPOOL OFF
SQL> SET FEEDBACK ON
SQL> START TRUNC.SQL

Table Truncated.

Table Truncated.
```

```
Table Truncated.

Table Truncated.

Table Truncated.

Table Truncated.

Table Truncated.

Table Truncated.

Table Truncated.

Table Truncated.
```

Analysis ▼

Truncating all tables owned by RYAN removes all the data from those tables. Table truncation is easy. You can use this technique if you plan to repopulate your tables with new data.

TIP	Before performing an operation such as truncating tables in a schema, you should always have a good backup of the tables you plan to truncate, even if you are sure that you will never need the data again. (You will need it—somebody is sure to ask you to restore the old data.)

Using SQL to Generate Shell Scripts

You can also use SQL to generate other forms of scripts, such as shell scripts. For example, an Oracle RDBMS server might be running in a UNIX environment, which is typically much larger than a PC operating system environment. Therefore, UNIX requires a more organized approach to file management. You can use SQL to easily manage the database files by creating shell scripts.

The following scenario drops tablespaces in a database. Although tablespaces can be dropped using SQL, the actual data files associated with these tablespaces must be removed from the operating system separately.

The first step is to generate a SQL script to drop the tablespaces.

21

Input/Output ▼

```
SQL> SET ECHO OFF
SQL> SET FEEDBACK OFF
SQL> SET HEADING OFF
SQL> SPOOL DROP_TS.SQL
SQL> SELECT 'DROP TABLESPACE ' || TABLESPACE_NAME || ' INCLUDING CONTENTS;'
  2  FROM SYS.DBA_TABLESPACES
  3  /

DROP TABLESPACE SYSTEM INCLUDING CONTENTS;
DROP TABLESPACE RBS INCLUDING CONTENTS;
DROP TABLESPACE TEMP INCLUDING CONTENTS;
DROP TABLESPACE TOOLS INCLUDING CONTENTS;
DROP TABLESPACE USERS INCLUDING CONTENTS;
```

Next you need to generate a shell script to remove the data files from the operating system after the tablespaces have been dropped.

Input/Output ▼

```
SQL> SPOOL OFF
SQL> SPOOL RM_FILES.SH
SQL> SELECT 'rm -f ' || FILE_NAME
  2  FROM SYS.DBA_DATA_FILES
  3  /

rm -f /disk01/orasys/db01/system0.dbf
rm -f /disk02/orasys/db01/rbs0.dbf
rm -f /disk03/orasys/db01/temp0.dbf
rm -f /disk04/orasys/db01/tools0.dbf
rm -f /disk05/orasys/db01/users0.dbf
SQL> SPOOL OFF
```

Analysis ▼

Now that you have generated both scripts, you may run the script to drop the tablespaces and then execute the operating system shell script to remove the appropriate data files. You will also find many other ways to manage files and generate non-SQL scripts using SQL.

Applying SQL Generation and Other Concepts to the Real World

The generation of SQL commands using SQL is one of the first steps in applying ingenuity to solve real-world problems encountered on the job. Depending on your specific job, you might encounter situations in which you have to create a lot of SQL code. If the process of creating the code is more tedious than logical, you might ask yourself if there is an easier way to create the code. If the information needed to create the code is already stored in the database, why re-create it manually?

Thinking problems out fully before attempting a solution is always the best policy when coding SQL, or writing any computer program for that matter. You can ask yourself the following questions when coding SQL to maximize your time usage and render better solutions in the end:

- What is the problem?
- What seems to be the obvious solution?
- If the coding requires logic, have all angles been studied?
- Are there any chances of returning incomplete or inaccurate data?
- Does a similar SQL program exist that can be used as a template?
- Is the coding process tedious? If so, can any of the process be automated? Consider generating the SQL code.
- Are you creating many SQL statements with the same syntax, but different data? If so, consider generating the SQL.
- Does the data you need for your query already exist in the database? If so, consider generating the SQL.
- Have you tested your query and spot-checked the results for accuracy? This could save embarrassment for you and/or the person to whom you are providing the SQL report.

Remember that there are almost always multiple solutions to a single problem. Also remember that there might be many angles to a seemingly simple problem. Study all angles and consider all possible solutions. SQL is an extremely powerful language. Although some individual SQL commands seem to have limitations, particularly depending on the implementation, SQL as a whole has everything you need to process data in a relational database. In all the years we have dealt with SQL, we have always been able to find solutions to problems. Sometimes, you simply must be creative.

Summary

21

Generating statements directly from the database spares you the often tedious job of coding SQL statements. Regardless of your job scope, using SQL statement-generation techniques frees you to work on other phases of your projects.

What you have learned in this lesson is basic, and although these examples use the Oracle database, you can apply the concepts to any relational database. Be sure to check your specific implementation for variations in syntax and data dictionary structure. If you keep an open mind, you will continually find ways to generate SQL scripts, from simple statements to complex high-level system management.

Q&A

Q How do I decide when to issue statements manually and when to write SQL to generate SQL?

A Ask yourself these questions:

- How often will I be issuing the statements in question?
- Will it take me longer to write the "parent" statement than it would to issue each statement manually?

Q From which tables may I select to generate SQL statements?

A You may select from any tables to which you have access, whether they are tables that you own, or tables that reside in the data dictionary. Also keep in mind that you can select from any valid object in your database, such as views or snapshots.

Q Are there any limits to the statements that I can generate with SQL?

A For the most part, any statement that you can write manually can be generated somehow using SQL. Check your implementation for specific options for spooling output to a file and formatting the output the way you want it. Remember that you can always modify the generated statements later because the output is spooled to a file.

Q I know that you can modify the generated SQL statements, but why would you want to?

A It is a good idea to modify, or edit, the generated file for several reasons: You might want to create a spool file for it, set feedback and echo back on, and check for any errors before executing the generated file.

Q This concept of using SQL to generate SQL seems to be a good thing. What can go wrong, or what should I watch out for?

A A couple of things that can go wrong are the following: You could be wasting time writing SQL to generate SQL when it would be faster to issue the command manually, and when writing a SQL statement to generate drops, truncates, deletes, or anything else that modifies the data or structure of the database, you could be asking for trouble.

Workshop

The Workshop provides quiz questions to help solidify your understanding of the material covered, as well as exercises to provide you with experience in using what you have learned. Try to answer the quiz and exercise questions before checking the answers in Appendix A, "Answers."

Quiz

The following quiz questions refer to the Oracle examples shown in this lesson.

1. From which two sources can you generate SQL scripts?

2. Will the following SQL statement work? Will the generated output work?

```
SQL> SET ECHO OFF
SQL> SET FEEDBACK OFF
SQL> SPOOL CNT.SQL
SQL> SELECT 'COUNT(*) FROM  ' || TABLE_NAME || ';'
  2  FROM CAT
  3  /
```

3. Will the following SQL statement work? Will the generated output work?

```
SQL> SET ECHO OFF
SQL> SET FEEDBACK OFF
SQL> SPOOL GRANT.SQL
SQL> SELECT 'GRANT CONNECT DBA TO ' || USERNAME || ';'
  2  FROM SYS.DBA_USERS
  3  WHERE USERNAME NOT IN ('SYS','SYSTEM','SCOTT')
  4  /
```

4. Will the following SQL statement work? Will the generated output work?

```
SQL> SET ECHO OFF
SQL> SET FEEDBACK OFF
SQL> SELECT 'GRANT CONNECT, DBA TO ' || USERNAME || ';'
  2  FROM SYS.DBA_USERS
  3  WHERE USERNAME NOT IN ('SYS','SYSTEM','SCOTT)
  4  /
```

5. True or false: It is best to turn on the feedback feature when generating SQL.

6. True or false: When generating SQL from SQL, always spool to a list or log file for a record of what happened.

7. True or false: Before generating SQL to truncate tables, you should always make sure that you have a good backup of the tables.

8. What is the ED command?

9. What does the SPOOL OFF command do?

21

Exercises

1. Using the SYS.DBA_USERS view (Oracle), write (use Oracle if available to you) a SQL statement that will generate a series of GRANT statements to five new users: John, Kevin, Ryan, Ron, and Chris. Use the column called USERNAME. Grant them SELECT access to history_tbl.

2. Using the examples in this lesson as guidelines, write some SQL statements that will generate SQL that you can use.

3. Enter the following SELECT statement into MySQL to generate a list of DESCRIBE commands for all tables in your MySQL database:

```
SELECT CONCAT('DESCRIBE ',TABLE_NAME,';') FROM TABLES_PRIV;
```

4. Using MySQL, enter the following SELECT statement to generate the SQL code to count all rows in each of your tables. (Hint: This is similar to exercise 1.)

```
SELECT CONCAT('SELECT COUNT(*) FROM ',TABLE_NAME,';') FROM TABLES_PRIV;
```

LESSON 22
Creating Complex SQL Queries

This lesson discusses, mostly by example, complex queries. Complex queries are an everyday part of life for the SQL programmer. Many of this lesson's examples may prove to be useful to you, as many are real examples that we have actually used. By the end of the lesson, you should understand

- How SQL commands interact with each other

- How functions, expressions, and operators can be used together

- How to use complex arithmetic combinations in the SELECT clause

- How to formulate complex queries on your own

NOTE

> We have used Personal Oracle for this lesson's examples. Although most of the examples are ANSI standard syntax, take note of the different options in your implementation of SQL if they differ from Oracle.
>
> MySQL examples are mixed in with the Oracle examples to give you a feel for how errors appear if you are using MySQL.

CREATE TABLE statements

For the examples in this lesson, we have used several of Oracle's data dictionary (system catalog) views and several tables that we created ourselves. The following are the CREATE TABLE statements for the tables that we have defined for this lesson.

Input ▼

```
CREATE TABLE EMP_TBL
(EMP_ID              CHAR(9)          NOT NULL,
LAST_NAME            VARCHAR(15)      NOT NULL,
FIRST_NAME           VARCHAR(15)      NOT NULL,
MIDDLE_NAME          VARCHAR(15)      NULL,
ST_ADD               VARCHAR(20)      NOT NULL,
CITY                 VARCHAR(20)      NOT NULL,
ST                   CHAR(2)          NOT NULL,
ZIP                  VARCHAR(5)       NOT NULL,
HOME_PH              VARCHAR(10)      NULL,
EMER_CONT            VARCHAR(30)      NULL,
EMER_PH              VARCHAR(10)      NULL,
CONSTRAINT EMP_PK PRIMARY KEY (EMP_ID));

CREATE TABLE EMP_PAY_TBL
(EMP_ID              CHAR(9)          NOT NULL,
DT_START             DATE             NOT NULL,
POSITION             VARCHAR(15)      NOT NULL,
SALARY               DECIMAL(8,2)     NULL,
HR_PAY               DECIMAL(4,2)     NULL,
COUNTY               VARCHAR(15)      NOT NULL,
DEPARTMENT           VARCHAR(15)      NOT NULL,
CONSTRAINT EMP_PAY_PK PRIMARY KEY (EMP_ID));

CREATE TABLE MEMBER_TBL
(MEM_NO              VARCHAR(30)      NOT NULL,
MEM_LAST_NAME        VARCHAR(20)      NOT NULL,
MEM_FIRST_NAME       VARCHAR(20)      NOT NULL,
MEM_MID_NAME         VARCHAR(20)      NULL,
MEM_ST_ADD           VARCHAR(20)      NOT NULL,
MEM_CITY             VARCHAR(15)      NOT NULL,
MEM_ST               CHAR(2)          NOT NULL,
MEM_ZIP              VARCHAR(5)       NOT NULL,
DT_LAST_ORDER        DATE,
PREFERENCE           VARCHAR(8)       NULL,
MUSIC_STY_1          VARCHAR(15)      NULL,
MUSIC_STY_2          VARCHAR(15)      NULL,
MUSIC_STY_3          VARCHAR(15)      NULL,
CONSTRAINT MEM_PK PRIMARY KEY (MEM_NO));

CREATE TABLE FORMER_MEM_TBL
(FMEM_NO             VARCHAR(30)      NOT NULL,
FMEM_LAST_NAME       VARCHAR(20)      NOT NULL,
FMEM_FIRST_NAME      VARCHAR(20)      NOT NULL,
FMEM_MID_NAME        VARCHAR(20)      NULL,
FMEM_ST_ADD          VARCHAR(20)      NOT NULL,
FMEM_CITY            VARCHAR(20)      NOT NULL,
FMEM_ST              CHAR(2)          NOT NULL,
FMEM_ZIP             VARCHAR(5)       NOT NULL,
```

```
FDT_LAST_ORDER     DATE,
FPREFERENCE        VARCHAR(8)     NULL,
FMUSIC_STY_1       VARCHAR(15)    NULL,
FMUSIC_STY_2       VARCHAR(15)    NULL,
FMUSIC_STY_3       VARCHAR(15)    NULL,
REASON_TERM        VARCHAR(50)    NULL,
CONSTRAINT FMEM_PK PRIMARY KEY (FMEM_NO));

CREATE TABLE MEM_PROFILE_TBL
(MEM_NO            VARCHAR(30)    NOT NULL,
REGION             VARCHAR(10)    NOT NULL,
SEX                VARCHAR(6)     NULL,
DOB                DATE,
INCOME             DECIMAL(8,2)   NULL,
CONSTRAINT MEM_PRO_PK PRIMARY KEY (MEM_NO));

CREATE TABLE PROD_PROFILE_TBL
(PROD_NO           VARCHAR(15)    NOT NULL,
VEND_NO            VARCHAR(20)    NOT NULL,
ARTIST             VARCHAR(30)    NOT NULL,
TITLE              VARCHAR(30)    NOT NULL,
COST               DECIMAL(4,2)   NOT NULL,
STYLE              VARCHAR(15)    NULL,
FORMAT             VARCHAR(8),
CONSTRAINT PROD_PRO_PK PRIMARY KEY (PROD_NO));

CREATE TABLE INVENTORY_TBL
(PROD_NO           VARCHAR(15)    NOT NULL,
FORMAT             VARCHAR(8)     NOT NULL,
QTN                DECIMAL(20)    NOT NULL,
ON_ORDER           DECIMAL(20)    NULL,
DATE_ORDERED       DATE,
DELIVERY_DATE      DATE,
CONSTRAINT INV_PK PRIMARY KEY (PROD_NO));

CREATE TABLE RETURNS_TBL
(PROD_NO           VARCHAR(15)    NOT NULL,
MEM_NO             VARCHAR(30)    NOT NULL,
QTN                DECIMAL(20)    NOT NULL,
STYLE              VARCHAR(15)    NOT NULL,
FORMAT             VARCHAR(8)     NOT NULL,
DISTRIBUTOR        VARCHAR(20)    NULL,
REASON_RT          VARCHAR(50)    NULL,
CONSTRAINT RTNS_PK PRIMARY KEY (PROD_NO, MEM_NO));

CREATE TABLE VENDOR_TBL
(VEND_NO           VARCHAR(15)    NOT NULL,
VEND_NAME          VARCHAR(25)    NOT NULL,
VEND_ST_ADD        VARCHAR(20)    NOT NULL,
VEND_CITY          VARCHAR(15)    NOT NULL,
VEND_ST            CHAR(2)        NOT NULL,
```

22

```
VEND_ZIP            VARCHAR(5)      NOT NULL,
VEND_PH             VARCHAR(10)     NOT NULL,
VEND_FAX_PH         VARCHAR(10)     NULL,
CONTACT             VARCHAR(25)     NULL,
TYPE_PROD           VARCHAR(20)     NOT NULL,
CONSTRAINT VEND_PK PRIMARY KEY (VEND_NO));

CREATE TABLE MEM_ORDER_TBL
(MEM_NO             VARCHAR(30)     NOT NULL,
PROD_NO             VARCHAR(25)     NOT NULL,
DATE_ORD            DATE,
STYLE               VARCHAR(15)     NOT NULL,
FORMAT              VARCHAR(8)      NOT NULL,
QTN                 DECIMAL(20)      NOT NULL,
SHIP_COST           DECIMAL(5,2)     NOT NULL,
CONSTRAINT MEM_ORD_PK PRIMARY KEY (MEM_NO, PROD_NO));
CREATE TABLE EMP_HIGH_PAY_CITY_TBL AS SELECT * FROM EMP_TBL;
```

NOTE	The syntax for these CREATE TABLE statements is valid in both Oracle and MySQL. Although we encourage you to create complex queries using MySQL, you will find that some of these queries will not work in MySQL. In some cases, MySQL syntax has been included with examples to provide you with a base for complex queries.

Analysis ▼

The last CREATE TABLE statement creates a table called EMP_HIGH_PAY_CITY_TBL based on the EMP_TBL table. The new table will look just like the original table, and it will contain the same columns and same data types for those columns. In addition to the table structure being created, the data is also populated in the new table with this command.

Examples of Complex Queries

This section focuses on complex queries. We have included example SQL queries, sample output, and explanations of each example. As we go through each example, you might want to review the first three parts of this book that talks about each command, operator, and function.

Computing Age from Date of Birth

It is generally rare that you would store an individual's age in a database. The age is a dynamic value that changes every day. Conversely, you would store a more static value, such as the date of birth. By comparing the date of birth with the current date, you can easily determine an individual's age. The following query will determine an individual's age in years:

Input/Output ▼

```
SQL> SELECT ((SYSDATE - DOB)/365) AGE
  2 FROM MEM_PROFILE_TBL;

        AGE
----------------
     59.1381147
     27.7874298
     44.4394846
```

Here is the equivalent MySQL syntax:

Input ▼

```
mysql> select ((curdate() - dob) / 365) age
    > from mem_profile_tbl;
```

Analysis ▼

Notice that the date of birth is carried out to seven decimals. In our society, no one is 59.1381147 years old. (The decimal value represents a fraction of a day in hours, minutes, and seconds.) A person is 59 years old until his next birthday. Although the answers are correct, they are not practical. Now let's try using the TRUNC command to remove the decimal value:

Input/Output ▼

```
SQL> SELECT TRUNC((SYSDATE - DOB)/365) AGE
    > FROM MEM_PROFILE_TBL;

          AGE
------------------------
           59
           27
           44
```

Breaking a Fraction of a Day into Hours, Minutes, and Seconds

Suppose you have a value that represents the number of days in a decimal format—for example:

```
9.67 days
```

The number of whole days is 9, and we also have a fraction of a day (.67). You might say 9 and 67/100 days. To understand how we are going to design a query that converts the fraction of the day in hours, minutes, and seconds, we must first perform the conversion manually:

```
9.67 days
```

The number of days is 9.

Now, we must determine the number of hours that .67 represents. We must multiply .67 by 24 because there are 24 hours in a day.

```
Hours = .67 * 24 = 16.08
```

Now we have another decimal value. The .08 represents the number of minutes in the output. We must multiply .08 by 60 because there are 60 minutes in an hour.

```
Minutes = .08 * 60 = 4.8
```

We have one last decimal value (.8), which represents the number of seconds in the left-over minute. We must multiply .8 by 60 because there are 60 seconds in a minute.

```
Seconds = .8 * 60 = 48
```

The following three solutions yield exactly the same output. These solutions definitely show that there are different ways to achieve the same results. The examples will use pseudo code SQL examples using a ficticious table named 'days' that contains a single column 'day' to show you the process of paring down a very large query into something much more readable.

Sample Solution 1

Input/Output ▼

```
select trunc(day) days,
 trunc(substr(day,instr(day,'.',1,1)) * 24) hours,
 trunc(substr(substr(day,instr(day,'.',1,1)) * 24,
  instr(substr(day,instr(day,'.',1,1)) * 24,'.',1,1)) * 60) minutes,
 trunc(substr(substr(substr(day,instr(day,'.',1,1)) * 24,
   instr(substr(day,instr(day,'.',1,1)) * 24, '.',1,1)) *60,
  instr(substr(substr(day,instr(day,'.',1,1)) * 24,
   instr(substr(day,
       instr(day,'.',1,1)) * 24,'.',1,1)) * 60,'.',1,1)) * 60) seconds
from days;
```

DAYS	HOURS	MINUTES	SECONDS
9	16	4	48

Analysis ▼

This first example is probably a little more complicated than it needs to be. Instead of relying on arithmetic functions, we are utilizing the SUBSTR and INSTR functions, which are used primarily for character strings.

Sample Solution 2

Input/Output ▼

```
select trunc(day) days,
       trunc((day - trunc(day)) * 24) hours,
        trunc((((day - trunc(day)) * 24 -
         trunc((day - trunc(day)) * 24)) * 60) minutes,
        trunc(((((day - trunc(day)) * 24 -
         trunc((day - trunc(day)) * 24)) * 60) -
        trunc(((day - trunc(day)) * 24 -
         trunc((day - trunc(day)) * 24)) * 60)) * 60) seconds
from days;
```

DAYS	HOURS	MINUTES	SECONDS
9	16	4	48

Analysis ▼

In this example, we used only the TRUNC function, which is much simpler, compared to the previous example. However, it is still a little confusing because we have to subtract a value from a truncated version of the value to get the decimal (part of an hour, minute, and second). The next example solves this problem.

Sample Solution 3

Input/Output ▼

```
select floor(day) days,
       floor(mod(day,1) * 24) hours,
       floor(mod(mod(day,1) * 24, 1) * 60) minutes,
       floor(mod(mod(mod(day,1) * 24, 1) * 60, 1) * 60) seconds
from days;
```

DAYS	HOURS	MINUTES	SECONDS
9	16	4	48

This is probably the easiest method for achieving the desired results. No subtraction is required to get the decimal value (part of an hour, minute, and second) because we are using the MOD function. Here, we also used the FLOOR function in place of the TRUNC function. Both functions do the same thing in this case—they remove the decimal value from a number.

Converting Bytes to Kilobytes to Megabytes

Our next example might prove handy to you: It will convert bytes into megabytes by dividing bytes by 1024 twice. (There are 1024 bytes in a kilobyte, 1024 kilobytes in a megabyte, and so on.) We are using an Oracle data dictionary view to get our results. First we show you the results in bytes and then in megabytes.

Input/Output ▼

```
select name, bytes
from v$datafile;
```

```
NAME                                              BYTES
-------------------------------------------------

/disk3/oradata/pti1/users_0.dbf         104857600
```

Analysis ▼

As you can see, it might be difficult to determine at a glance how many bytes (or megabytes) 104,857,600 is equivalent to. You actually have to count over six places to the left to get a rough estimate of the number of megabytes, or you can manually do the division. Why not have the database do the work for you?

Input/Output ▼

```
SQL> SELECT NAME,BYTES/1024/1024 MEG
  2 FROM V$DATAFILE
  3 ORDER BY NAME;
```

```
NAME                                              Meg
------------------------------------------------

/disk3/oradata/pti1/users_0.dbf         100
```

As you can see, the output is 100MB. The bytes were divided by 1024, and that answer was divided by 1024. This simple equation changed bytes into megabytes.

Database Fragmentation Report

The next example is a query that produces a fragmentation report based on the number of extents an object has in an Oracle database. We are selecting the sum of bytes for a segment, the sum of blocks used, and a count of the number of extents. We want to show only those segments that have more than three extents. Once again, we are using an Oracle data dictionary view.

Input/Output ▼

```
SQL> SELECT OWNER,SEGMENT_NAME,SEGMENT_TYPE,
  2 SUM(BYTES),SUM(BLOCKS),COUNT(*)
  3 FROM DBA_EXTENTS
  4 HAVING COUNT(*)>3
  5 GROUP BY OWNER,SEGMENT_NAME,SEGMENT_TYPE
  6 ORDER BY OWNER,SEGMENT_NAME,SEGMENT_TYPE;
```

OWNER	SEGMENT NAME	SEGMENT TYPE	SUM(BYTES)	SUM(BLOCKS)	COUNT(*)
SYS	VIEW$	TABLE	630784	77	6

Subqueries in DML

In this next example, we combine the INSERT with the SELECT and a subquery. We are attempting to insert all rows from the emp_tbl into the emp_high_pay_city_tbl. We want all salaries that are greater than $25,000 for employees who are paid a salary. For employees paid an hourly rate, we want the hourly pay rate to be greater than $12.50 per hour.

Input ▼

```
SQL> INSERT INTO EMP_HIGH_PAY_CITY_TBL
  2 SELECT * FROM EMP_TBL
  3 WHERE CITY IN (SELECT E.CITY
  4                FROM EMP_PAY_TBL P,
  5                EMP_TBL E
  6                WHERE P.EMP_ID=E.EMP_ID
  7                AND (P.SALARY>25000
  8                OR P.HR_PAY>12.50));
11 rows inserted
```

<table>
<tr>
<td>**NOTE**</td>
<td>Take note that we used the IN operator instead of the = operator to compare the values in the city column with the value(s) returned by the subquery. If more than one row is returned by a subquery, the = operator will cause an error. Notice the neatness and readability of the previous SQL statement due to indentation. We recommend that you be neat and consistent when writing your SQL statements.</td>
</tr>
</table>

Formatting Your Dates

Let's try a date conversion with the RPAD function and concatenation. Refer back to Lesson 12, "Dates and Time in SQL," for a review of date conversions and date pictures.

Input/Output ▼

```
SQL> SELECT RPAD(M.MEM_FIRST_NAME || ',' ||M.MEM_LAST_NAME, 30, '.') ||
  2      ' HAS A DATE OF BIRTH OF: ' ||
  3      TO_CHAR(MP.DOB, 'MONTH DD, YYYY') "BIRTHDAYS"
  4  FROM MEM_PROFILE_TBL MP,
  5  MEMBER_TBL
  6  WHERE MP.MEM_NO = M.MEM_NO;
BIRTHDAYS
------------------------------------------------------------------------
KEITH,MOORE.................. has a date of birth of: November  20, 1950
DAVID,RICHARDS............... has a date of birth of:
LARRY,THOMAS................. has a date of birth of:
PAUL,BAKER................... has a date of birth of: January   17, 1980
BEVERLY,STONE................ has a date of birth of: January   02, 1960
JEREMY,WYATT................. has a date of birth of:
JOHNATHAN,ELLIS.............. has a date of birth of: June      15, 1970
JAMES,STEWART................ has a date of birth of: July      06, 1940
```

Analysis ▼

Take notice of the missing dates of birth. Someone reading this report would probably question why some dates of birth are missing.

Any confusion as to missing date of birth values can be cleared by using the NVL function in the SQL statement. This is an Oracle-specific function that allows us to substitute one value if the first value is NULL. So in our example we will swap ***NO DOB ENTERED*** for every instance of a NULL date of birth.

Input/Output ▼

```
SQL> SELECT RPAD(M.MEM_FIRST_NAME || ',' ||M.MEM_LAST_NAME, 30, '.') ||
  2    ' HAS A DATE OF BIRTH OF: ' ||
  3    NVL(TO_CHAR(MP.DOB, 'MONTH DD, YYYY'), '***NO DOB ENTERED***')
  4  "BIRTHDAYS"
  5  FROM MEM_PROFILE_TBL MP,
  6  MEMBER_TBL M
  7  WHERE MP.MEM_NO = M.MEM_NO;

BIRTHDAYS
------------------------------------------------------------------------
KEITH,MOORE.................. has a date of birth of: November  20, 1950
DAVID,RICHARDS.............. has a date of birth of: ***NO DOB ENTERED***
LARRY,THOMAS................ has a date of birth of: ***NO DOB ENTERED***
PAUL,BAKER.................. has a date of birth of: January   17, 1980
BEVERLY,STONE............... has a date of birth of: January   02, 1960
JEREMY,WYATT................ has a date of birth of: ***NO DOB ENTERED***
JOHNATHAN,ELLIS............. has a date of birth of: June      15, 1970
JAMES,STEWART............... has a date of birth of: July      06, 1940
```

22

Analysis ▼

Basically what we did here was cover ourselves by passing the buck to the data entry department for the missing dates of birth by printing ***NO DOB ENTERED***.

The previous two examples are not compatible with MySQL syntax.

Subquery Involving a Maximum Value

Here is a SQL statement that will determine, by name of the employee, who has the greatest salary in the company. We use concatenation, the MAX function, and a subquery to obtain the results.

Input/Output ▼

```
SQL> SELECT E.LAST_NAME || ', ' || E.FIRST_NAME  FULL_NAME
  2  FROM EMP_TBL E,
  3  EMP_PAY_TBL EP
  4  WHERE E.EMP_ID = EP.EMP_ID
  5  AND EP.SALARY = (SELECT MAX(SALARY)
  6                   FROM EMP_PAY_TBL);
FULL_NAME
--------------------------------
SMITH, HENRY
```

Analysis ▼

Because the subquery contains a single-group function (MAX is being performed on all records and will return one value), we can use the = sign. It is always safe, however, to use the IN operator in place of the = sign.

The MySQL equivalent to the previous example is as follows. (Remember that in the current version of MySQL, 5.1, subqueries are now supported.)

Input/Output ▼

```
mysql> select CONCAT(e.last_name ,', ' , e.first_name)  name
    > from emp_tbl e,
    > emp_pay_tbl ep
    > where e.emp_id = ep.emp_id
    > and ep.salary = (select max(salary)
    >                 from emp_pay_tbl);

+-------------+
¦ name        ¦
+-------------+
¦ SMITH,HENRY ¦
+-------------+
1 row in set (0.11 sec)
```

Multiple Subqueries

Here is a SQL statement that uses two subqueries. We want to know how many employees are paid above the average salary and/or hourly rate. Some employees are paid a salary, and some an hourly rate. We want to consider employees with both pay types in this query.

Input/Output ▼

```
SQL> SELECT COUNT(*)
  2 FROM EMP_PAY_TBL
  3 WHERE HR_PAY> (SELECT AVG(HR_PAY)
  4                FROM EMP_PAY_TBL)
  5 OR SALARY> (SELECT AVG(SALARY)
  6                FROM EMP_PAY_TBL);
COUNT(*)
----------
       7
```

Analysis ▼

We did not want to see individual records, just a count of all employees who meet our criteria in the WHERE clause. We have two conditions in the WHERE clause, separated by the

OR operator. When the OR operator is used, only one of the conditions must be true for data to be returned. One condition checks to see whether HR_PAY is greater than the average HR_PAY of all rows from the table, whereas the other condition does the same thing for SALARY.

The previous example is also compatible with MySQL.

22

<table>
<tr><td>NOTE</td><td>Remember that NULL values are not considered when aggregate functions such as AVG are used. Because NULL values are not considered, we did not have to add the condition to the first sub-query WHERE HR_PAY IS NOT NULL and the condition WHERE SALARY IS NOT NULL to the second subquery.</td></tr>
</table>

Using Dashes and Parentheses to Format Numeric Values

The next example is an employee listing by name, Social Security number, and phone number. Notice that there is a comma after the last name, dashes are in the Social Security number, a dash is used in the phone number, and () are used around the area code. Now how did we accomplish this?

Input/Output ▼

```
SQL> SELECT INITCAP(LAST_NAME || ', ' || FIRST_NAME) "NAME",
  2    SUBSTR(EMP_ID, 1, 3) || '-' ||
  3    SUBSTR(EMP_ID, 4, 2) || '-' ||
  4    SUBSTR(EMP_ID, 6, 4) "SSN",
  5    '(' || SUBSTR(HOME_PH, 1, 3) || ')' ||
  6    SUBSTR(HOME_PH, 4, 3) || '-' ||
  7    SUBSTR(HOME_PH, 7, 4) "PHONE"
  8 FROM EMP_TBL;
```

NAME	SSN	PHONE
Mercer, Richard	324-54-0787	(317)823-4528
Pierce, Thomas	313-21-9830	(317)546-2918
Reynolds, William	435-66-3121	(317)792-6529
Taylor, Virginia	412-33-1221	(317)987-2335

Analysis ▼

We used the INITCAP, concatenation, and SUBSTR in combination. The INITCAP capitalized the first letter in the last and first names. One point of interest here is how we placed the parentheses around the area code. This is done simply by using single quotes around each parenthesis to select a literal value and by using concatenation.

Increasing a Numeric Value by a Given Percent

Here is an update statement that will increase the hourly pay rate of the employee with the employee ID of 435663121 by 20%. The hourly pay rate is currently $9.00.

Input ▼

```
SQL> UPDATE EMP_PAY_TBL
  2 SET HR_PAY = HR_PAY * 1.2
  3 WHERE EMP_ID = '435663121';

1 row updated
```

If we did a SELECT from EMP_PAY_TBL, we would see that the hourly pay rate is now $10.80.

Input/Output ▼

```
SQL> SELECT EMP_ID, HR_PAY
  2 FROM EMP_PAY_TBL
  3 WHERE EMP_ID = '435663121';

EMP_ID      HR_PAY
---------  ----------
435663121    10.80
```

The previous two examples are both compatible with the MySQL syntax.

Finding the Next Highest Numeric Value in a Column

Now we need to find out the next product number to assign to our newest product. We will use MAX, TO_NUMBER, and the addition arithmetic operator (+). The SQL statement will first convert the PROD_NO to a number, and then get the highest number and add 1 to it. From the results, 8893 was the highest number.

Input/Output ▼

```
SQL> SELECT MAX(TO_NUMBER(PROD_NO) + 1)
  2 FROM PROD_PROFILE_TBL;

MAX(TO_NUMBER(PROD_NO)+1)
-------------------------
                     8894
```

The preceding example wasn't too difficult, but what if your product numbers were in the format of P01, P02, and so on? How do you think you would go about incrementing the highest product number by 1 to find the next product number?

Well, if the highest product number is P20, without a lot of thought, you would figure the next product number to be P21. Take a look at the first example and try to increment the highest value by 1.

22

Input/Output ▼

```
SQL> SELECT PROD_ID FROM PROD;

PRO
---
P1
P2
P3
```

The greatest value of PROD_ID in this table is P3. You would expect the next greater value for PROD_ID to be P4. However, you will not always know the highest value, so you want to write a query that will retrieve the information you need.

Input/Output ▼

```
SQL> SELECT MAX(PROD_ID) FROM PROD;

MAX
---
P3
```

In this example, we have selected the maximum value for PROD_ID using the MAX aggregate function.

Input/Output ▼

```
SQL> SELECT MAX(PROD_ID) +1 FROM PROD;
SELECT MAX(PROD_ID) +1 FROM PROD
           *
ERROR at line 1:
ORA-01722: invalid number
```

In this example, we have attempted to add 1 to the maximum value of PROD_ID. The problem is that PROD_ID is a character value. You cannot perform arithmetic operations on a character value.

Input/Output ▼

```
SQL> SELECT SUBSTR(MAX(PROD_ID),2) + 1 FROM PROD;
sdfsdfsd
SUBSTR(MAX(PROD_ID),2)+1
- - - - - - - - - - - - - - - - - - - - - -
                        4
```

Here, we have extracted just the numeric piece of the PROD_ID using the SUBSTR command, and then have added the value of 1. Our result is 4, which should be the next highest value for PROD_ID.

Input/Output ▼

```
SQL> SELECT 'P' || TO_CHAR(SUBSTR(MAX(PROD_ID),2) + 1) "NEXT PROD ID"
  2 FROM PROD;

NEXT PROD ID
- - - - - - - - - - - - - - - - - - - - - - - - - - - - - - - - - - - - - - - -
P4
```

Finally, we converted the numeric value back to a character value using the TO_CHAR function, and then concatenated the value (4 in this case) with the literal value of P. You must convert the numeric value of 4 back to a character data type before concatenating it with the value P.

Dealing with NULL Values

Now, for some strange reason, the boss wants a listing of vendor names, phone numbers, fax numbers, and the point of contact. He wants the listing formatted as follows: parentheses () around the area code for the phone number, a dash in the phone number, two dashes in the fax number, and the first letter in the contact's name capitalized. (And as she's telling you this, you're thinking, isn't it time to go home?)

Input/Output ▼

```
SQL> SELECT VEND_NAME VENDOR, '(' || SUBSTR(VEND_PH, 1, 3) || ')' ||
  2                    SUBSTR(VEND_PH, 4, 3) || '-' ||
  3                    SUBSTR(VEND_PH, 7, 4) PHONE,
  4     SUBSTR(VEND_FAX_PH, 1, 3) || '-' ||
  5     SUBSTR(VEND_FAX_PH, 4, 3) || '-' ||
  6     SUBSTR(VEND_FAX_PH, 7, 4) FAX,
  7     INITCAP(CONTACT) POC
  8 FROM VENDOR_TBL;
```

```
VENDOR                      PHONE          FAX           POC
------------------------    -------------  ------------  -------------------------
SONY                        (813)545-1007  813-545-1002  Robert Mcelroy
CAPITOL PACKING             (212)703-5888  212-703-6790  Betsy Conway
OFFICE DEPOT                (317)552-7007  --
UPS                         (317)898-2301  --
APPLE RECORDS               (213)221-5009  213-221-5020  Cindy Roberts
COLUMBIA RECORDING          (517)299-6013  --
```

Here is the similar MySQL syntax for the previous example:

Input ▼

```
mysql> select vend_name vendor, concat('(' , substring(vend_ph, 1, 3) , ')' ,
    >                  substring(vend_ph, 4, 3) , '-' ,
    >                  substring(vend_ph, 7, 4)) phone,
    > concat(substring(vend_fax_ph, 1, 3) , '-' ,
    > substring(vend_fax_ph, 4, 3) , '-' ,
    > substring(vend_fax_ph, 7, 4)) fax,
    > initcap(contact) poc      > from vendor_tbl;
```

Great—however, what are the dashes in the fax column doing there? And what about the missing names in the POC? Well, let's fix these! The following are two possible solutions:

Input/Output ▼

```
SQL> SELECT VEND_NAME VENDOR, '(' || SUBSTR(VEND_PH, 1, 3) || ')' ||
  2                  SUBSTR(VEND_PH, 4, 3) || '-' ||
  3                  SUBSTR(VEND_PH, 7, 4) PHONE,
  4    SUBSTR(VEND_FAX_PH, 1, 3) || '-' ||
  5    SUBSTR(VEND_FAX_PH, 4, 3) || '-' ||
  6    SUBSTR(VEND_FAX_PH, 7, 4) FAX,
  7    INITCAP(CONTACT) POC
  8 FROM VENDOR_TBL
  9 WHERE VEND_FAX_PH IS NOT NULL
 10 UNION
 11 SELECT VEND_NAME VENDOR, '(' || SUBSTR(VEND_PH, 1, 3) || ')' ||
 12    SUBSTR(VEND_PH, 4, 3) || '-' ||
 13    SUBSTR(VEND_PH, 7, 4) PHONE,
 14    NVL(VEND_FAX_PH, 'UNKNOWN') FAX,
 15    NVL(INITCAP(CONTACT), 'UNKNOWN') POC
 16 FROM VENDOR_TBL
 17 WHERE VEND_FAX_PH IS NULL;
```

```
VENDOR                    PHONE         FAX          POC
- - - - - - - - - - - - - - - - - - -  - - - - - - - - - - - -  - - - - - - - - - - - -  - - - - - - - - - - - - - - - - - - - - - - -
APPLE RECORDS             (213)221-5009 213-221-5020 Cindy Roberts
CAPITOL PACKING           (212)703-5888 212-703-6790 Betsy Conway
COLUMBIA RECORDING        (517)299-6013 UNKNOWN      UNKNOWN
OFFICE DEPOT              (317)552-7007 UNKNOWN      UNKNOWN
SONY                      (813)545-1007 813-545-1002 Robert Mcelroy
UPS                       (317)898-2301 UNKNOWN      UNKNOWN


SQL> SELECT VEND_NAME VENDOR, '(' || SUBSTR(VEND_PH, 1, 3) || ')' ||
  2                     SUBSTR(VEND_PH, 4, 3) || '-' ||
  3                     SUBSTR(VEND_PH, 7, 4) PHONE,
  4     SUBSTR(VEND_FAX_PH, 1, 3) || '-' ||
  5     SUBSTR(VEND_FAX_PH, 4, 3) || '-' ||
  6     NVL(SUBSTR(VEND_FAX_PH, 7, 4),'UNKNOWN') FAX,
  7     NVL(INITCAP(CONTACT),'UNKNOWN') POC
  8 FROM VENDOR_TBL;


VENDOR                    PHONE         FAX          POC
- - - - - - - - - - - - - - - - - - -  - - - - - - - - - - - -  - - - - - - - - - - - -  - - - - - - - - - - - - - - - - - - - - - - -
APPLE RECORDS             (213)221-5009 213-221-5020 Cindy Roberts
CAPITOL PACKING           (212)703-5888 212-703-6790 Betsy Conway
COLUMBIA RECORDING        (517)299-6013 UNKNOWN      UNKNOWN
OFFICE DEPOT              (317)552-7007 UNKNOWN      UNKNOWN
SONY                      (813)545-1007 813-545-1002 Robert Mcelroy
UPS                       (317)898-2301 UNKNOWN      UNKNOWN
```

Analysis ▼

We used the UNION operator in this last example to allow the use of two SELECT statements in the query. The first SELECT statement gets all records where the fax number is not NULL; the second SELECT statement gets all records where the fax number is NULL. We used this logic to control the printing of the fax number if it is NULL. (Refer to the previous example, where a double dash (- -) was printed if the fax number was NULL.)

The syntax of the previous two examples is not compatible with MySQL because of the use of the NVL function.

Tips for Building Complex Queries

The following are tips that might help you out when you come across problems requiring complex queries:

- If a request for a query comes to you in the form of hard copy, discreetly place it on your coworker's desk. (Just kidding!)

- Understand what the requester is asking for.
- Identify the tables that should be used to resolve the query.
- Study the relationships between your tables. Know what data to expect from queries.
- Describe the tables to determine the exact column names. You should show only pertinent information on the report.
- Sometimes it is helpful to construct a rough draft of the query on paper before you attempt to type it into a file and run it.
- Code one piece at a time. If the report is complicated, make sure you are able to get the most basic information first. Then, add the various functions, union operators, formatting commands, or whatever is necessary to complete the report.
- If you are dealing with embedded functions, remember that the innermost function is always resolved first. To visualize what you are doing, sometimes it is easier to run the query with a single function, and then after a successful run, begin embedding functions.
- Save your query to a script file, even if you do not think you will ever need it again. Whenever you get rid of a file, it seems like you need it the next day. You can easily run it later.
- Document your scripts for readability, modifications, and debugging.
- Have somebody else review the data in your output for accuracy. Sometimes, a condition in your query might cause incomplete or inaccurate data to be returned, which might not be very noticeable to the requester.
- Always test your queries thoroughly. When initially testing a query that will return a high number of rows, add a condition to your WHERE clause so that only one or a few rows will be returned. It usually takes only one or two rows of data to verify that you are getting the correct results from your query. You can limit the rows returned by using ROWNUM in the WHERE clause. The following is an example that returns five rows of data, assuming that there are at least five rows of data in the table. Check your implementation for the existence of ROWNUM. (Your implementation might have another name for ROWNUM.)

Summary

As you have seen in this lesson, functions, expressions, DML, DDL, views, conditions, and operators can be used in many combinations to obtain data from the database. We have attempted to show you several examples, which hopefully will open your mind to quicker and better ways of obtaining and manipulating data.

Keep in mind that there are many ways to perform tasks in SQL, as well as any other language. You could possibly write a SQL statement that has several lines of code, and then someone else might come up with a combination that only uses a couple of lines of code, yet you both get the same results. The bottom line is that reading, practice, experience, and experimentation will help you become a SQL expert.

Q&A

Q **Is it true that all implementations have extensions to SQL, and if so, wouldn't this make SQL more difficult?**

A Most implementations, if not all, have their own extensions or enhancements to ANSI SQL. For example, Oracle has PL/SQL (see Lesson 26, "An Introduction to Oracle PL/SQL") and SQL*Plus (see Lesson 25, "Using Oracle SQL*Plus to Satisfy Reporting Needs"); another is Microsoft's Transact-SQL (see Lesson 27, "An Introduction to Transact-SQL"). The major implementations are ANSI-compliant. After you learn ANSI SQL, you should be able to easily migrate from one implementation to another.

Q **What sort of conventions/styles should I think about using?**

A There is not one convention written in stone that you should use when designing queries. Every programmer has an individual style. You should, however, select a style and stick to it. Consistency in programming is as important as consistency when raising a child.

Q **What are the chances of two people coming up with the same code for a complex query?**

A The chances are good for simple queries, but slim for more complex queries, such as the ones shown in this lesson. Everyone thinks differently, and there are many commands and options available in SQL that can be used to derive the same outcome.

Workshop

The Workshop provides quiz questions to help solidify your understanding of the material covered, as well as exercises to provide you with experience in using what you have learned. Try to answer the quiz and exercise questions before checking the answers in Appendix A, "Answers."

Quiz

1. With embedded functions, which function is resolved first, the innermost function or the outermost function?

2. Are NULL values considered when an average of values in a column is calculated?

3. When you convert bytes to megabytes, why do you divide by 1,024 twice?

4. What must you do to a value in a `character` format before using the value in a calculation?

Exercises

1. Using the `emp_tbl` table, write a SQL statement using MySQL that will return the following results:

```
RESIDENCE
- - - - - - - - - - - - - - - - - - - - - - - - - - - - - - - - - - - - - - - - - - - - - - - - - - - - - - - - - -
WILLIAM REYNOLDS LIVES AT 1231 FARNSWORTH BLVD IN CARMEL, IN.

HENRY SMITH LIVES AT 33 BEACON CT IN INDIANAPOLIS, IN.

VIRGINIA TAYLOR LIVES AT 1390 DAYTON ST IN NOBLESVILLE, IN.
```

2. Write a query, using Oracle syntax as shown in this lesson, that lists all members that have placed orders and the total amount spent per customer with the following criteria:

    a. An order amount greater than the average order amount for all customers.

    b. Consider only orders placed in July 1997.

    c. Make sure that the member considered has not returned any items.

LESSON 23
Debugging Your SQL Statements

In this lesson, you will see various common errors that everyone—from novice to professional users—makes when using SQL. You will never be able to avoid all errors and/or mistakes, but being familiar with a wide range of errors will help you resolve them in as short a time as possible. By the end of this lesson, you will be familiar with the following:

- Several typical errors and their resolutions
- Common logical shortcomings of SQL users
- Ways to prevent daily setbacks caused by errors

Keep in mind that some mistakes will actually yield error messages, whereas others might just be inadequacies in logic that will inevitably cause more significant errors or problems down the road. With a strict attention to detail, you can avoid most problems, although you will always find yourself stumbling upon errors.

Exploring Common SQL Errors

This section describes many common errors that you will receive while executing all types of SQL statements. Most are simple and make you want to kick yourself on the hind side, whereas other seemingly obvious errors are misleading.

Table or View that Does Not Exist

When you receive an error stating that the table you are trying to access does not exist, it seems obvious—for example:

Input/Output ▼

```
SQL> spool tables.lst
SQL> set echo on
SQL> set feedback on
SQL> set pagesize 1000
SQL> select owner|| '.' || table_name
  2  from sys.dba_table
  3  where owner = 'SYSTEM'
  4  order by table_name
  5  /
     from sys.dba_table
        *
ERROR at line 2:
ORA-00942: table or view does not exist
 SQL> spool off
 SQL>

mysql> select * from jobs
    -> ;
ERROR 1146: Table 'mysql.jobs' doesn't exist
```

Analysis ▼

Notice the asterisk below the word table in the Oracle example. The correct table name is sys.dba_tables. An *s* was omitted from the table name.

The MySQL example is a much simpler SQL statement, however. The error specifies the database in question, mysql, followed by a period, and then the table name, jobs.

But what if you know the table exists and you still receive this error? Sometimes when you receive this error, there might be a security problem; that is, the table exists, but you do not have access to it. This error can also be the database server's way of saying nicely, "You don't have permission to access this table!"

TIP

> Before you allow panic to set in, immediately verify whether the table exists using a DBA account, if available, or the schema account. You will often find that the table does exist and that the user lacks the appropriate privileges to access it.

Invalid Username or Password

The following example covers the invalid username or password error. This error is caused either by entering the incorrect username or the incorrect password. Try again. If unsuccessful, have your password reset. If you are sure that you typed the correct user-name and password, make sure that you are attempting to connect to the correct database, if you have access to more than one.

Input/Output ▼

```
SQL*Plus: Release 10.2.0.1.0 - Production on Sun Mar 29 12:10:01 2009
Copyright (c) 1982, 2005, Oracle.  All rights reserved.
Enter user-name: rplew
Enter password:

ERROR: ORA-01017: invalid username/password; logon denied
Enter user-name:
```

23

FROM Keyword Not Specified

The following error can be misleading. The keyword FROM is there, but you are missing a left parenthesis between substr and file_name on line 2. This error can also be caused by a missing comma between column names in the SELECT. If a column in the SELECT is not followed by a comma, the query processor automatically looks for the FROM keyword.

Input/Output ▼

```
SQL> spool tblspc.lst
SQL> set echo on
SQL> set feedback on
SQL> set pagesize 1000
SQL> select substr(tablespace_name,1,15) a,
  2          substrfile_name, 1,45) c, bytes
  3  from sys.dba_data_files
  4  order by tablespace_name;
    substrfile_name, 1,45) c, bytes
    *
ERROR at line 2:
ORA-00923: FROM keyword not found where expected
SQL> spool off
SQL>
```

The previous statement has been corrected as follows:

Input ▼

```
SQL> select substr(tablespace_name,1,15) a,
  2          substr(file_name,1,45) c, bytes
  3  from sys.dba_data_files
  4  order by tablespace_name;
```

Notice that in the MySQL attempt to create the same error, a different and possibly just as misleading error is generated:

Input/Output ▼

```
mysql> select substring(payee,1,10),
    -> substringremarks,1,10)
    -> from checks;
ERROR 1064: You have an error in your SQL syntax near ')
from checks' at line 2
```

Analysis ▼

A lot of the errors you will encounter will require you to look around the area of the error, as the error code will most likely be ambiguous.

Group Function Not Allowed

The following example shows an error that is raised by an invalid value in the GROUP BY clause of a query.

Input/Output ▼

```
SQL> select count(last_name), first_name, home_ph
  2  from emp_tbl
  3  group by count(last_name), first_name, home_ph
  4  /

    group by count(last_name), first_name, home_ph
           *
ERROR at line 3:
ORA-00934: group function is not allowed here
SQL>
```

A similar error is generated using MySQL:

Input/Output ▼

```
mysql> select count(quantity), name, orderedon
    -> from orders
    -> group by count(quantity), name, orderedon;
ERROR 1111: Invalid use of group function
```

As with any group function, COUNT may not be used in the GROUP BY clause. You can list only column and nongroup functions, such as SUBSTR, in the GROUP BY clause. Review Lesson 4, "Clauses in SQL Queries," for more on the GROUP BY clause.

23

The previous statement has been corrected using the proper syntax:

Input ▼

```
SQL> select count(last_name), first_name, home_ph
    2  from emp_tbl
    3  group by last_name, first_name, phome_ph;
```

Invalid Column Name

The following example shows an error that is raised by an invalid column name specified in the SELECT clause of a query. Column names used in queries must be specified exactly as they appear in their appropriate table definitions.

Input/Output ▼

```
SQL> spool tables.lst
SQL> set echo on
SQL> set feedback on
SQL> set pagesize 1000
SQL> select owner|| '.' || tablename
  2  from sys.dba_tables
  3  where owner = 'SYSTEM'
  4  order by table_name
  5  /
    select owner|| '.' || tablename
                  *
ERROR at line 1:
ORA-00904: invalid column name
SQL> spool off
SQL>
```

Analysis ▼

In line 1, the column `tablename` is incorrect. The correct column name is `table_name`. The underscore was omitted. To see the correct columns, use the `DESCRIBE` command. This error can also occur when you are trying to qualify a column in the `SELECT` by the wrong table name.

Missing Keyword

In the following example, the syntax is incorrect. This error occurs when you omit a mandatory word with any given command syntax. If you are using an optional part of the command, that option might require a certain keyword. The missing keyword in this example is `AS`.

Input/Output ▼

```
SQL> create view emp_view
  2 select * from emp_tbl
  3 /

    select * from emp_tbl
    *
ERROR at line 2:
ORA-00905: missing keyword
SQL>
```

The statement should look like this:

Input ▼

```
SQL> create view emp_view as
        2 select * from emp_tbl
        3 /
```

Missing Left Parenthesis

On line 2 of the following query, a parenthesis does not appear before the Social Security number. The parentheses are mandatory components of `INSERT` as it is used here. Remember that the values being inserted are enclosed by parentheses.

Input/Output ▼

```
SQL> insert into emp_tbl values
  2 '303785523', 'SMITH', 'JOHN', 'JAY', '1 3RD ST', 'CAMBY', 'IN', '46113')
  3 /
    '303785523', 'SMITH', 'JOHN', 'JAY', '1 3RD ST', 'CAMBY', 'IN', '46113')
```

```
       *
  ERROR at line 2:
  ORA-00906: missing left parenthesis
SQL>
```

The correct syntax should look like this:

Input ▼

```
SQL> insert into emp_tbl values
  2 ('303785523', 'SMITH', 'JOHN', 'JAY', '1 3RD ST', 'CAMBY', 'IN', '46113')
  3 /
```

23

A similar error is generated using MySQL:

Input/Output ▼

```
mysql> insert into teams values '1','HACKERS');
ERROR 1064: You have an error in your SQL syntax near ''1','HACKERS')' at line 2
```

Missing Right Parenthesis

On line 1 of the following query, the right parenthesis is missing from the SUBSTR function:

Input/Output ▼

```
SQL> spool tblspc.lst
SQL> set echo on
SQL> set feedback on
SQL> set pagesize 1000
SQL> select substr(tablespace_name,1,15 a,
  2         substr(file_name, 1,45) c, bytes
  3 from sys.dba_data_files
  4 order by tablespace_name;
    select substr(tablespace_name,1,15 a,
                     *
ERROR at line 1:
ORA-00907: missing right parenthesis
SQL> spool off
SQL>
```

The correct syntax should look like this:

Input ▼

```
SQL> select substr(tablespace_name,1,15) a,
  2          substr(file_name,1,45) c, bytes
  3  from sys.dba_data_files
  4  order by tablespace_name;
```

Missing Comma

In the following example, a comma is missing on line 2 between the Social Security number and SMITH:

Input/Output ▼

```
SQL> spool ezinsert.lst
SQL> set echo on
SQL> set feedback on
SQL> set pagesize 1000
SQL> insert into office_tbl values
  2  ('303785523' 'SMITH', 'OFFICE OF THE STATE OF INDIANA, ADJUTANT
GENERAL')
  3  /
    ('303785523' 'SMITH', 'OFFICE OF THE STATE OF INDIANA, ADJUTANT
[GENERAL')
        *
ERROR at line 2:
ORA-00917: missing comma
SQL> spool off
SQL>
```

Column Ambiguously Defined

In the following example, on line 1, the column name has not been defined. The tables have been given aliases of e and p. Decide which table to pull the name from and define it with the table alias.

Input/Output ▼

```
SQL> spool employee.lst
SQL> set echo on
SQL> set feedback on
SQL> set pagesize 1000

SQL> select emp_id, e.last_name, e.address, e.phone
  2  from emp_tbl e,
  3  emp_pay_tbl p
```

```
    4  where e.emp_id =p.emp_id;
       select p.emp_id, e.last_name, e.address, e.phone
                  *
ERROR at line 1:
ORA-00918: column ambiguously defined
SQL> spool off
SQL>
```

SQL Command Not Properly Ended

In the following example, the SQL engine complains that the command has not been
properly ended. This leads you to believe that something is missing.

Input/Output ▼

```
SQL> create view employee_tbl as
  2  select * from emp_tbl
  3  order by last_name
  4  /

     order by name
       *
ERROR at line 3:
ORA-00933: SQL command not properly ended
SQL>
```

Analysis ▼

Why is the command not properly ended? You know you can use a / to end a SQL statement. Another fooler—an ORDER BY cannot be used in a CREATE VIEW statement. Use a
GROUP BY instead. Here the query processor is looking for a terminator (semicolon or forward slash) before the ORDER BY clause because the processor assumes the ORDER BY is
not part of the CREATE VIEW statement. Because the terminator is not found before the
ORDER BY, this error is returned instead of an error pointing to the ORDER BY.

Missing Expression

Notice the comma after table on the first line of the following example; the query processor is looking for another column in the SELECT clause. At this point, the processor is not
expecting the FROM clause.

Input/Output ▼

```
SQL> spool tables.lst
SQL> set echo on
SQL> set feedback on
```

```
SQL> set pagesize 1000
SQL> select owner|| '.' || table,
  2  from sys.dba_tables
  3  where owner = 'SYSTEM'
  4  order by table_name
  5  /
     from sys.dba_tables
     *
ERROR at line 2:
ORA-00936: missing expression
SQL> spool off
SQL>
```

Not Enough Arguments for Function

In the following example, there aren't enough arguments for the DECODE function. An argument is missing. We did not list what we were searching for, nor did we list what to decode it to. See Lesson 25, "Using Oracle SQL*Plus to Satisfy Reporting Needs," for more information about the DECODE function. Check your implementation for the proper syntax.

Input/Output ▼

```
SQL> spool tblspc.lst
SQL> set echo on
SQL> set feedback on
SQL> set pagesize 1000
SQL> select substr(tablespace_name,1,15) a,
  2        decode(substr(file_name,1,45)) c, bytes
  3  from sys.dba_data_files
  4  order by tablespace_name;
     decode(substr(file_name,1,45)) c, bytes
          *
ERROR at line 2:
ORA-00938: not enough arguments for function
SQL> spool off
SQL>
```

Not Enough Values

In the following example, a column value is missing. Perform a DESCRIBE command on the table to find the missing column.

Input/Output ▼

```
SQL> spool ezinsert.lst
SQL> set echo on
SQL> set feedback on
```

```
SQL> set pagesize 1000

SQL> insert into emp_tbl values
  2  ('303785523', 'SMITH', 'JOHN', 'JAY', '1 3RD ST', 'CAMBY', 'IN', '46113')
  3  /
     insert into emp_tbl values

            *
ERROR at line 1:
ORA-00947: not enough values
SQL> spool off
SQL>
```

You can insert the specified data only if you list the columns that will hold the inserted data, as shown in the next example:

Input ▼

```
SQL> spool ezinsert.lst
SQL> set echo on
SQL> set feedback on
SQL> set pagesize 1000
SQL> insert into emp_tbl (emp_id, last_name, first_name, mid_name, sex)
  2  values ('303785523', 'SMITH', 'JOHN', 'JAY', '1 3RD ST', 'CAMBY', 'IN',
➥'46113')
  3  /

SQL> spool off
SQL>
```

Integrity Constraint Violated—Parent Key Not Found

The following error was caused by attempting to insert nonexistent data into a child table. Check the parent table for correct data. If missing, you must insert the data into the parent table before attempting to insert data into the child table.

Input/Output ▼

```
SQL> insert into emp_pay_tbl values
  2  ('111111111','1/1/2009','CLERK','20000.00',NULL,'HENDRICKS','ACCOUNTING')
  3  /

     insert into payroll_tbl values
                 *
ERROR at line 1:
ORA-02291: integrity constraint (employee_cons) violated - parent
key not found
SQL>
```

Oracle Not Available

In the following example, the user was trying to connect to the database using Oracle's SQL*Plus. The database is probably down. Check the status of the database. Also, make sure that you are trying to connect to the correct database if you have access to multiple databases.

Input/Output ▼

```
(sun_su3)/home> sqlplus
SQL*Plus: Release 10.2.0.1.0 - Production on Sun Mar 29 12:10:01 2009
Copyright (c) 1982, 2005, Oracle.  All rights reserved.
Enter user-name: rplew
Enter password:

ERROR: ORA-01034: ORACLE not available
ORA-07318: smsget: open error when opening sgadef.dbf file.
```

Inserted Value Too Large for Column

In the following example, one of the values being inserted is too large for the column. Use the DESCRIBE command on the table for the correct data length. If necessary, you can perform an ALTER TABLE command on the table to expand the column width.

Input/Output ▼

```
SQL> spool ezinsert.lst
SQL> set echo on
SQL> set feedback on
SQL> set pagesize 1000

SQL> insert into office_tbl values
  2 ('303785523', 'SMITH', 'OFFICE OF THE STATE OF INDIANA, ADJUTANT
➥GENERAL')
  3 /
    insert into office_tbl values
            *
ERROR at line 1:
ORA-01401: inserted value too large for column
SQL> spool off
SQL>
```

In MySQL, no error is returned. However, after review of the inserted data, you can see that the data has been truncated to fit into the column as defined. In the following example, you can see that the team name has been truncated to 10 characters, which happens to be the maximum number of characters allowed for a team name in this particular table.

Input/Output ▼

```
mysql> insert into teams values ('1','THE HACKERS');
Query OK, 1 row affected (0.05 sec)

mysql> select * from teams;
|---------------------|
| team_id | team_name |
|---------------------|
| 1       | THE HACKER |
|---------------------|
1 row in set (0.06 sec)
```

23

TNS: Listener Could Not Resolve SID Given in Connect Descriptor

The following error is very common in Oracle databases. The listener referred to is the process that allows requests from a client to communicate with the database on a remote server. Here, you were attempting to connect to the database. Either the incorrect database name was typed or the listener is down. Check the database name and try again. If unsuccessful, notify the database administrator of the problem.

Input/Output ▼

```
SQLDBA> connect rplew/xxxx@database1

ORA-12505: TNS:listener could not resolve SID given in connect descriptor
SQLDBA> disconnect
Disconnected.
SQLDBA>
```

Insufficient Privileges During Grants

The following error occurs if you are trying to grant privileges on another user's table and you do not have the proper privilege to do so. You must own the table to be able to grant privileges on it to other users. In Oracle, you may be granted a privilege with the Admin option, which means that you can grant the specified privilege on one user's table to another user. Check your implementation for the particular privileges you need to grant a privilege.

Input/Output ▼

```
SQL> grant select on emp_tbl to ron;

grant select on emp_tbl to ron
                  *
```

```
ERROR at line 1:
ORA-01749: you may not GRANT/REVOKE privileges to/from yourself
SQL>

SQL> grant select on demo.emp_tbl to ron;

grant select on demo.emp_tbl to ron
                      *
ERROR at line 1:
ORA-01031: insufficient privileges
SQL>
```

Escape Character in Your Statement—Invalid Character

Escape characters are very frustrating when trying to debug a broken SQL statement. This situation can occur if you use the backspace key while you are entering your SQL statement in the buffer or a file. Sometimes the backspace key puts an invalid character in the statement depending upon how your keys are mapped, even though you might not be able to see the character.

Cannot Create Operating System File

This error has a number of causes. The most common causes are that the associated disk is full or incorrect permissions have been set on the file system. If the disk is full, you must remove unwanted files. If permissions are incorrect, change them to the correct settings. This error is more of an operating system error, so you might need to get advice from your system administrator.

Exploring Common Logical Mistakes

So far in this lesson, we have covered faults in SQL statements that generate actual error messages. Most of these errors are obvious, and their resolutions leave little to the imagination. The next few mistakes are more or less logical, and they might cause problems later—if not immediately.

Using Reserved Words in Your SQL Statement

In the following example, the query processor is not expecting the word DATE because it is a reserved word:

Input/Output ▼

```
SQL> select sysdate DATE
  2  from dual;

select sysdate DATE
              *
ERROR at line 1:
ORA-00923: FROM keyword not found where expected
```

Analysis ▼

There is no comma after the pseudocolumn SYSDATE; therefore, the next element expected is the FROM clause.

A *reserved word* in an implementation is a word that is used as a command, operator, or function. The reserved word cannot be used in any other manner than what the implementation has reserved it for. Check your implementation for a listing of reserved words.

Input/Output ▼

```
SQL> select sysdate "DATE"
  2  from dual;

DATE
- - - - - - - - - -
15-MAY-97
```

Notice how the reserved word problem is alleviated by enclosing the word DATE with double quotation marks. Double quotations allow you to display the literal string DATE as a column alias.

> **CAUTION**
>
> Be sure to check your specific database documentation to get a list of reserved words, as these reserved words will vary among different implementations.

You may or may not have to use double quotation marks when naming a column alias. In the following example, you do not have to use double quotation marks because TODAY is not a reserved word. To be sure, check your specific implementation.

Input/Output ▼

```
SQL> select sysdate TODAY
  2  from dual;

TODAY
---------
15-MAY-97
SQL>
```

The Use of DISTINCT When Selecting Multiple Columns

You cannot use DISTINCT multiple times in a query.

Input/Output ▼

```
SQL> select distinct(city), distinct(zip)
  2  from address_tbl;

select distinct(city), distinct(zip)
                          *
ERROR at line 1:
ORA-00936: missing expression
SQL>
```

A similar error is generated using MySQL:

Input/Output ▼

```
mysql> select distinct(team_id), distinct(team_name) from teams;
ERROR 1064: You have an error in your SQL syntax near 'distinct(team_name) from
➥teams' at line 1
```

Analysis ▼

A city can have more than one zip code. As a rule, you should use the DISTINCT command on only one selected column. See Lesson 2, "Introducing the Query," for more on the DISTINCT command.

Dropping an Unqualified Table

When dropping a table, always use the owner or schema. You can have duplicate table names in the database, so users Bob and Ron might both have a table named emp_tbl. If you don't use the owner/schema name, the wrong table could be dropped.

The risky syntax for dropping a table is

Input ▼

```
SQL> drop table emp_tbl;
```

The next statement is much safer because it specifies the owner of the table you want
to drop:

Input ▼

```
SQL> drop table ron.pemp_tbl;
```

23

> **CAUTION** Qualifying the table when dropping it is always a safe practice,
> although sometimes this step might be unnecessary. Never issue
> the DROP TABLE command without first verifying the user ID by
> which you are connected to the database.

The Use of Public Synonyms in a Multischema Database

Synonyms make life easier for users; however, public synonyms open tables that you
might not want all users to see. Use caution when granting public synonyms, especially
in a multischema environment.

The Dreaded Cartesian Product

The following situation is caused when you do not join the tables in the WHERE clause.
This is called a *Cartesian product*. Although this is not technically an error, it is definitely a problem in most cases.

Input/Output ▼

```
SQL> SELECT A.SSN, P.LAST_NAME
  2  FROM ADDRESS_TBL A,
  3       EMP_TBL P;

SSN       LAST_NAME
--------- ---------------
303785523 SMITH
313507927 SMITH
490552223 SMITH
312667771 SMITH
```

```
420001690 SMITH
303785523 JONES
313507927 JONES
490552223 JONES
312667771 JONES
420001690 JONES
303785523 OSBORN
313507927 OSBORN
490552223 OSBORN
312667771 OSBORN
420001690 OSBORN
303785523 JONES
313507927 JONES
490552223 JONES
312667771 JONES
420001690 JONES
16 rows selected.
```

Analysis ▼

Notice how many rows were selected. Both of the preceding tables have 4 rows; therefore, we wanted 4 rows returned instead of the 16 rows that we received. Without the use
of a join in the WHERE clause, each row in the first table is matched up with each row in
the second. To calculate the total number of rows returned, you would multiply 4 rows
by 4 rows, which yields 16. Unfortunately, most of your tables will contain more than
4 rows of data, with some possibly exceeding thousands or millions of rows. In these
cases, don't bother doing the multiplication, for your query will without a doubt become
a runaway query.

Failure to Enforce Input Standards

Assuring that input standards are adhered to is commonly known as *quality assurance
(QA)*. Without frequent checks on the data entered by data entry clerks, you run a very
high risk of hosting trash in your database. A good way to keep a handle on QA is to
create several QA reports using SQL, run them on a timely basis, and present their output to the data entry manager for appropriate action to correct errors or data inconsisten-
cies.

Failure to Enforce File System Structure Conventions

You can waste a lot of time when you work with file systems that are not standardized.
Check your implementation for recommended file system structures.

Allowing Large Tables to Take Default Storage Parameters

Default storage parameters will vary with implementations, but they are usually rather small. When a large or dynamic table is created and forced to take the default storage, serious table fragmentation can occur, which can severely hinder database performance. Good planning before table creation will help to avoid this hazard. The following example uses Oracle's storage parameter options:

Input ▼

```
SQL> CREATE TABLE TEST_TBL
  2  (SSN   NUMBER(9) NOT NULL,
  3  NAME  VARCHAR2(30) NOT NULL)
  4  STORAGE
  5  (INITIAL 100M
  6   NEXT 20M
  7   MINEXTENTS 1
  8   MAXEXTENTS 121
  9   PCTINCREASE 0);
```

23

Analysis ▼

The TEST_TBL was created with an initial size of 100MB. Should that space be filled, the next extent or chunk of space would be 20MB. We set a minimum of one extent and a maximum of 121 extents, which means that the table can grow to 2500MB. pctincrease was set to 0. This means that each of the 121 extents allowed will all be limited to 20MB.

Placing Objects in the System Tablespace

The following statement shows a table being created in the SYSTEM tablespace. Although this statement will not return an error, it is likely to cause future problems.

Input ▼

```
SQL> CREATE TABLE TEST_TBL
  2  (SSN   NUMBER(9) NOT NULL,
  3  NAME  VARCHAR2(30) NOT NULL)
  4  TABLESPACE SYSTEM
  5  STORAGE
  6  (INITIAL 100M
  7  NEXT 20M
  8  MINEXTENTS 1
  9  MAXEXTENTS 121
 10  PCTINCREASE 0);
```

The next example corrects this so-called problem:

Input ▼

```
SQL> CREATE TABLE TEST_TBL
  2  (SSN   NUMBER(9) NOT NULL,
  3  NAME  VARCHAR2(30) NOT NULL)
  4  TABLESPACE LINDA_TS
  5  (INITIAL 100M
  6   NEXT 20M
  7  MINEXTENTS 1
  8  MAXEXTENTS 121
  9  PCTINCREASE 0);
```

Analysis ▼

In Oracle, the SYSTEM tablespace is typically used to store SYSTEM-owned objects, such as those composing the data dictionary. If you happen to place dynamic tables in this tablespace and they grow, you run the risk of corrupting or at least filling up the free space, which in turn will probably cause the database to crash. In this event, the database might be forced into an unrecoverable state. Always store application and user tables in separately designated tablespaces.

Failure to Compress Large Backup Files

If you do large exports and do not compress the files, you will probably run out of disk space to store the files. Always compress the export files. If you are storing archived log files on hard disk instead of on tape, these files can be and probably should be compressed to save space. Most modern database systems also have cleanup file tasks associated with the backup files that will allow you to specify how long to retain backup files. However, realize that this can be a bit misleading because the maintenance plan will wait until the current backup has completed and is verified before it will attempt to clean up the old backup files. So, if you have a 200GB database, you might very well need in excess of 400GB to store a single day's backup file.

Failure to Budget System Resources

You should always budget your system resources before you create your database. The result of not budgeting system resources could be a poorly performing database. You should know what the database is going to be used for, whether it will be transactional, warehousing, or query only. The database's function will affect the number and size of rollback segments. The number of database users will inevitably affect the size of the USERS and TEMP tablespaces. Do you have enough space to stripe your larger tables?

Tables and indexes should be stored on separate devices to reduce disk contention. You should also keep the redo logs and the data tablespaces on separate devices to alleviate disk contention. These are just a few of the issues to address when considering system resources.

Preventing Problems with Your Data

Your data processing center should have a backup system set up. If your database is small to medium-sized, you can take the extra precaution of using EXPORT to ensure that your data is backed up. You should make a backup of the export file and keep it in another location for further safety. Remember that these files can be large and will require a great deal of space.

23

If your database is perfectly planned, you should not have a problem with duplicate records. You can avoid duplicate records by using constraints, foreign keys, and unique indexes, as discussed in Lesson 10, "Controlling Data Integrity."

Summary

Many different types of errors—literally hundreds—can stand in the way of you and your data. Luckily, most errors/mistakes are not disasters and are easy to remedy. However, some errors/mistakes that happen are very serious. You need to be careful whenever you try to correct an error/mistake, as the error can multiply if you do not dig out the root of the problem. When you do make mistakes, as you definitely will, use them as learning experiences.

NOTE

We prefer to document everything related to database errors, especially uncommon errors that we happen to stumble upon. A file of errors is an invaluable troubleshooting reference.

This lesson provides you with a sample of some of the most common errors you might receive when using Oracle and MySQL. For a complete list of errors and suggested resolutions, remember to refer to your database documentation.

Q&A

Q You make it sound as if every error has a remedy, so why worry?

A Yes, most errors/mistakes are easy to remedy, but suppose you drop a table in a production environment. You might need hours or days to do a database recovery. The database will be down during this time, and your company will be paying overtime to several people to complete the fix. The boss will not be happy.

Q Any advice on how to avoid errors/mistakes?

A Being human, you will never avoid all errors/mistakes; however, you can avoid many of them through training, concentration, self-confidence, good attitude, and a stress-free work environment.

Q I noticed in many of the error examples that the actual error was different than what the error message returned as the error. Is there a way of just knowing what the error is from the error message?

A Through many years of experience, we have learned what to look for. It is true that the error message does not tell you exactly what is incorrect, but if it did, wouldn't it be too simple?

Q Is there written or online documentation for the different errors?

A Yes, Oracle and MySQL have both online and written documentation on errors. Check your implementation.

Workshop

The Workshop provides quiz questions to help solidify your understanding of the material covered and exercises to help put what you've learned into practice. Try to answer the quiz and exercise questions before checking the answers in Appendix A, "Answers."

Quiz

1. A user calls and says, "I can't sign on to the database, but everything was working fine yesterday. The error says invalid user/password. Can you help me?" What steps should you take?

2. Why should tables have storage clauses and a tablespace destination?

3. Will this SQL statement work (according to the Oracle syntax shown in this lesson)?

```
SQL> select sysdate Today
     from dual;
```

4. True or false: The error message will tell you exactly what is in error.

5. True or false: If you create tables in the Oracle system tablespace, you will get an error.

Exercises

1. Suppose you are logged on to an Oracle database as SYSTEM, and you want to drop a table called HISTORY from your schema. Your regular user ID is JSMITH. What is the correct syntax to drop this table?

2. Correct the following syntax and execute the statement using MySQL. (The following exercise depends on this one.)

```
CREATE TABLE MYTEAMS
TEAM_ID      VARCHAR(2)    NOT NULL
TEAM_NAME    VAROHAR(10)   NOT NULL;
```

3. Correct the following syntax and execute in MySQL:

```
INSERT INTO TABLE MYTEAMS
('HA', 'HACKERS');
```

4. Correct the following syntax and execute in MySQL:

```
SELECT * MYTEAMS;
```

5. Correct the following syntax and execute in MySQL:

```
SELECT TEAM_ID, TEAM_NAMES
FROM MYTEAMS
WHERE TEAM_ID = HA;
```

23

LESSON 24

Embedding SQL in Application Programming

This lesson covers, in very broad strokes, practical applications of SQL. We focus on examples showing embedded SQL in applications in the Microsoft Windows environment and the Java environment. All of the principles involved are just as applicable to other software platforms. You will learn the following:

- How various commercial products—Personal Oracle, Open Database Connectivity (ODBC), Java Database Connectivity (JDBC), and Microsoft's .NET—relate to SQL

- How to set up your environment for SQL

- How to create a database using Oracle

- How to use SQL inside applications written in Visual Basic .NET and Java

After reading this material, you will know where to start applying your new SQL skills.

A Quick Trip Through Some Application Development Tools

This section examines several commercial products in the context of the Microsoft Windows operating system and briefly describes how they relate to SQL. The principles, if not the products themselves, apply across various software platforms.

ODBC

One of the underlying technologies in the Windows operating system is ODBC, which enables Windows-based programs to access a database through a driver. Rather than having a custom interface to each database, something you might very well have to write yourself, you can connect to the database of your choice through a driver. The concept of ODBC is very similar to the concept of Windows printer drivers, which enable you to write your program without regard for the printer. Individual differences, which DOS programming forced you to address, are conveniently handled by the printer driver. The result is that you spend your programming time on the tasks specific to your program, not writing printer drivers.

ODBC applies this idea to databases. The visual part of ODBC resides in the Control Panel in Windows XP and Vista, and in its own program group in Windows 2003 Server.

We cover ODBC in more detail when we discuss creating the database later in this lesson.

Oracle Express

Oracle Express is the popular database's latest incursion into the personal PC market. Don't be put off by the number of programs that Oracle installs; we built all the examples used in the first several lessons using only the Oracle Database Manager and SQL*Plus. SQL*Plus is shown in Figure 24.1.

FIGURE 24.1
Oracle's SQL*Plus.

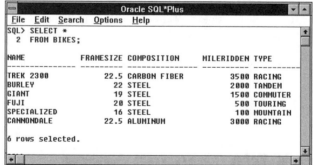

SQL in Java with JDBC

Java is an object-oriented, multiplatform language that has applications on web servers, personal computers, mobile telephones, and embedded devices, among other things. Java has excellent development capacity for graphical user interface (GUI) programming, web application programming, network programming, and database programming. Later in this lesson, we explain how SQL can be used from Java to interact with a database.

SQL in .NET with OleDB

Microsoft's object-oriented .NET programming language is a robust counterpart to Java that runs mainly on Windows operating systems. It has a world-class development suite, as well as several free versions for people to use for their own personal use, such as Visual Studio Express and Visual Web Developer. Later in this lesson, we explain how to write a simple .NET web application to interact with a database.

Getting Set Up for Oracle

Enough with the introductions—let's get to work. After you install your SQL engine or your ODBC-compatible compiler, you must do a certain amount of stage-setting before the stars can do their stuff. With Oracle Express, you created an account for the SYS user during the installation. Initially, you will need to log onto this account to get things started.

After logging on and creating an account, you are ready to get started creating the database.

Creating the Database

This step is where all your SQL training starts to pay off. First, make sure your database is started by clicking Start, All Programs, Oracle 10g Express Edition. From here, a listing allows you to do things such as start and stop your database. Make sure that the database is running and then continue on, either through the command line by using the Run SQL Command Line option, or by using the web-based GUI with the Go To Web Homepage option.

At this point, you can create your tables and enter your data using the CREATE and INSERT keywords. Another common way of creating tables and entering data is with a script file. A script file is usually a text file with the SQL commands typed out in the proper order. Look at this excerpt from a script file delivered with Oracle:

Input ▼

```
-------------------------------------------------------------
-- Script to build seed database for Personal Oracle
-------------------------------------------------------------
-- NTES
     Called from buildall.sql
```

24

```
-- MODIFICATIONS
--   rs  12/04/94 - Comment, clean up, resize, for production

------------------------------------------------------------
startup nomount pfile=%rdbms71%\init.ora
-- Create database for Windows RDBMS
create database oracle
    controlfile reuse
    logfile '%oracle_home%\dbs\wdblog1.ora' size 400K reuse,
            '%oracle_home%\dbs\wdblog2.ora' size 400K reuse
    datafile '%oracle_home%\dbs\wdbsys.ora' size 10M reuse
    character set WE8ISO8859P1;
```

The syntax varies slightly with the implementation of SQL and database you are using, so be sure to check your documentation.

The following excerpt is from one of the files to insert data:

Input ▼

```
/*
 *  Add countries.
 */
INSERT INTO country (country, currency) VALUES ('USA',         'Dollar');
INSERT INTO country (country, currency) VALUES ('England',     'Pound');
INSERT INTO country (country, currency) VALUES ('Canada',      'CdnDlr');
INSERT INTO country (country, currency) VALUES ('Switzerland', 'SFranc');
INSERT INTO country (country, currency) VALUES ('Japan',       'Yen');
INSERT INTO country (country, currency) VALUES ('Italy',       'Lira');
INSERT INTO country (country, currency) VALUES ('France',      'FFranc');
INSERT INTO country (country, currency) VALUES ('Germany',     'D-Mark');
INSERT INTO country (country, currency) VALUES ('Australia',   'ADollar');
INSERT INTO country (country, currency) VALUES ('Hong Kong',   'HKDollar');
INSERT INTO country (country, currency) VALUES ('Netherlands', 'Guilder');
INSERT INTO country (country, currency) VALUES ('Belgium',     'BFranc');
INSERT INTO country (country, currency) VALUES ('Austria',     'Schilling');
INSERT INTO country (country, currency) VALUES ('Fiji',        'fdollar');
```

This example inserts a country name and the type of currency used in that country into the COUNTRY table. (Refer to Lesson 11, "Manipulating Data," for an introduction to the INSERT command.)

There is no magic here. Programmers always find ways to save keystrokes. If you are playing along at home, enter the following tables:

Input ▼

```
/* Table: CUSTOMER*/
CREATE TABLE CUSTOMER (NAME CHAR(10),
        ADDRESS CHAR(10),
        STATE CHAR(2),
        ZIP CHAR(10),
        PHONE CHAR(11),
        REMARKS CHAR(10));

/* Table: ORDERS */
CREATE TABLE ORDERS (ORDEREDON DATE,
        NAME CHAR(10),
        PARTNUM INTEGER,
        QUANTITY INTEGER,
        REMARKS CHAR(10));

/* Table: PART */
CREATE TABLE PART (PARTNUM INTEGER,
        DESCRIPTION CHAR(20),
        PRICE NUMERIC(9, 2));
```

24

Now fill these tables with the following data:

Input/Output ▼

SELECT * FROM CUSTOMER

NAME	ADDRESS	STATE	ZIP	PHONE	REMARKS
TRUE WHEEL	550 HUSKER	NE	58702	555-4545	NONE
BIKE SPEC	CPT SHRIVE	LA	45678	555-1234	NONE
LE SHOPPE	HOMETOWN	KS	54678	555-1278	NONE
AAA BIKE	10 OLDTOWN	NE	56784	555-3421	JOHN-MGR
JACKS BIKE	24 EGLIN	FL	34567	555-2314	NONE

5 rows selected.

SELECT * FROM ORDERS

ORDEREDON	NAME	PARTNUM	QUANTITY	REMARKS
15-MAY-1996	TRUE WHEEL	23	6	PAID
19-MAY-1996	TRUE WHEEL	76	3	PAID
2-SEP-1996	TRUE WHEEL	10	1	PAID
30-JUN-1996	TRUE WHEEL	42	8	PAID
30-JUN-1996	BIKE SPEC	54	10	PAID
30-MAY-1996	BIKE SPEC	10	2	PAID
30-MAY-1996	BIKE SPEC	23	8	PAID

```
17-JAN-1996 BIKE SPEC          76        11 PAID
17-JAN-1996 LE SHOPPE          76         5 PAID
 1-JUN-1996 LE SHOPPE          10         3 PAID
 1-JUN-1996 AAA BIKE           10         1 PAID
 1-JUL-1996 AAA BIKE           76         4 PAID
 1-JUL-1996 AAA BIKE           46        14 PAID
11-JUL-1996 JACKS BIKE         76        14 PAID
15 rows selected.
```

SELECT * FROM PART

```
    PARTNUM DESCRIPTION              PRICE
=========== ==================== ===========

         54 PEDALS                     54.25
         42 SEATS                      24.50
         46 TIRES                      15.25
         23 MOUNTAIN BIKE             350.45
         76 ROAD BIKE                 530.00
         10 TANDEM                   1200.00
```

```
6 rows selected.
```

After you enter this data, the next step is to create an ODBC connection. Open the Control Panel (if you are using Windows) and double-click the Data Sources (ODBC) icon. The initial ODBC screen is shown in Figure 24.2.

FIGURE 24.2
ODBC's Data
Sources selection.

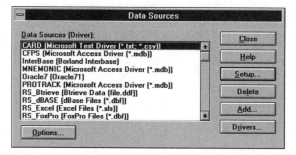

You will want to create a new ODBC connection for the Oracle Express database you have set up. The local Oracle instance is named XE by default. You can leave it like this, or you can use your own name or something short and easy to type, depending on the account you set up for yourself. Those of you coming from a PC or small database background will have to get used to some odd-looking pathnames. These pathnames tell the SQL engine where to look for the database in the galaxy of computers that could be connected via LANs.

Using Java and SQL

A discussion of database tools would not be complete without mentioning JDBC. Java was designed with the philosophy that a programming language should provide seamless portability. It is possible, then, to take a Java program from a UNIX machine and successfully execute the program in the Windows or Macintosh environments. This same philosophy applies to database connectivity.

Following the Java philosophy, the most desirable situation is to connect with many different kinds of databases using the same code, with the fewest number of modifications. JDBC does a good job of making this possible. As long as the database vendor has a JDBC driver for the database management system, the database can be accessed from Java using JDBC.

To access a database from Java, you will need a valid user account, a JDBC driver for the database, and the URL of the database (including the port number).

There are four main parts involved with using SQL to access a database from Java using JDBC:

1. The database driver for the database management system is loaded and registered.
2. A connection to the database is established.
3. Queries or updates are sent to the database.
4. Result sets are returned from the database.

The driver for the database management system is loaded and registered in one step by calling the method:

Input ▼

```
Class.forName()
```

If the JDBC driver is called

Input ▼

```
oracle.jdbc.driver
```

then the following method call should be made to register and load this JDBC driver.

Input ▼

```
Class.forName("oracle.jdbc.driver.OracleDriver");
```

24

After the driver is loaded and registered, a connection needs to be established. To establish a connection to the database, you will need the full URL, username, and password for the database. The database URL should be constructed as follows:

Input ▼

```
"jdbc:oracle:thin:@ip address:1521:dbname"
```

The connection is established as follows:

Input ▼

```
Connection C = null;
String dburl, username, password = null;
C = DriverManager.getConnection(dburl, username, password);
```

Now that the connection is established, SQL can be sent to the database. SQL commands are sent to the database with the `execute()`, `executeUpdate()`, or `executeQuery()` methods of the `Statement` class. Here's how to select the last names and employee numbers of all members of the `CUSTOMER` table:

Input ▼

```
Statement S = C.createStatement(); // C is the Connection Object
S.execute("SELECT * from customer order by name");
```

The final step in SQL execution is to view the results of the query. When a database is queried, a `ResultSet` object is needed to hold the results of the query. The contents of the query executed in the preceding code could be printed to the command line by parsing through the `ResultSet` line by line (using the `ResultSet` `next()` method) as follows:

Input ▼

```
ResultSet R = S.getResultSet(); // S is the Statement Object
while (R.next()) {
        String name = R.getLong("NAME");
        String state = R.getString("STATE");
        String phone = R.getString("PHONE");              System.out.println(name +
➥" " + state + " " + phone);
}
```

Often, we need to use SQL to store data within a database. The procedure for storing or updating data in a database is similar to the preceding except that there will be no `ResultSet` object involved. Instead, there will be a count of the number of rows of data that were affected. The following example demonstrates how to search for an customer with the name of TRUE WHEEL and update their phone number to 555-5454.

Input ▼

```
Statement S = C.createStatement(); // Not needed if already done
S.execute("UPDATE CUSTOMER SET PHONE='555-5454' WHERE NAME='TRUE WHEEL'");
Int lines = s.getUpdateCount();
System.out.println(lines + " rows were modified.");
```

Using .NET and SQL

The .NET framework of languages from Microsoft is another popular application development platform. The .NET framework is an interesting programming platform because it processes all of the code into what is known as an *intermediary language (IL)*. This allows application developers to write code in any number of plug-in front-end languages, such as C#, Visual Basic .NET, J#, NetCobol, and so on. For our examples in this lesson, we will be using Visual Basic .NET because it is similar to a very popular predecessor, VB6.

24

To begin, you need much the same types of things that you needed in the Java example: a database, a connection, and a statement. Let's start by creating our connection.

Input ▼

```
Dim orclConnection As New OracleClient.OracleConnection("Data Source=XE;User
➥ID=test;Password=redshift;Unicode=True")
```

Now we create a SQL statement, open the connection, and execute the command. If the command does not return any values, such as the following UPDATE statement, we use the ExecuteNonQuery function.

Input ▼

```
Dim SQLCommand As String = "UPDATE PART SET PRICE=PRICE*2"
Dim orclCommand As
New OracleClient.OracleCommand(SQLCommand, orclConnection)
orclConnection.Open()
orclCommand.ExecuteNonQuery()
orclConnection.Close()
```

Notice how we must open and close the connection before and after we execute our query. Also notice how the SQL statement does not contain an ending semicolon. If you try to add it, you will receive an error from the Oracle client.

If instead we wanted to write a statement that would return rows, we would use a very different object. In this case, we would use what is known as a *data reader*. The following code sample shows you how you can use the reader to iterate through the rows of the PART table.

Input ▼

```
Dim SQLCommand As String = "SELECT * FROM PART"
Dim orclCommand As New OracleClient.OracleCommand(SQLCommand, orclConnection)
orclConnection.Open()
Dim orclReader As OracleClient.OracleDataReader = orclCommand.ExecuteReader
While orclReader.Read

PrintLine("PARTNUM:" & orclReader.Item(0) & "  DESCRIPTION" & orclReader.Item(1)
➥ & "  PRICE:" & orclReader.Item(2))

End While
orclConnection.Close()
```

As you can see, the basic syntax for dealing with SQL within the framework of an application is very similar, even between different programming languages. After you learn the basic principles, it should be easy enough to transfer your skills to other programming languages and platforms.

Summary

In this lesson, you learned where to start applying SQL using the ordinary, everyday stuff you find lying about your hard drive. We covered examples using Java and .NET—all popular front-end development tools. Many other tools are available on the market today, but what we have shown here should give you an idea of how applications can be developed using these tools to access a relational database with SQL. The best way to build on what you have learned is to go out, query, and practice using SQL as much as you can.

Q&A

Q **What is the difference between the ODBC API and the Oracle APIs?**

A Oracle's API is created specifically to deal with the Oracle database platform. ODBC's API is more generic (it isn't specific to any database). If you need to do something specific to a database or tune the performance of a specific database, you might consider using that database's API library in your code.

Q With all the available products, how do I know what to use?

A In a business environment, product selection is usually a compromise between management and "techies." Management looks at the cost of a product; techies look at the features and how the product can make their lives easier. In the best of all programming worlds, this compromise should help you do your job quickly and efficiently.

Workshop

The Workshop provides quiz questions to help solidify your understanding of the material covered, as well as exercises to provide you with experience in using what you have learned. Try to answer the quiz and exercise questions before checking the answers in Appendix A, "Answers."

24

Quiz

1. Which object does Microsoft Visual Basic .NET use to execute its SQL statements?

2. In which object does Java place its SQL statements?

3. What is ODBC?

4. What driver is required for Java programs with embedded SQL to communicate with a relational database?

Exercise

Write a set of pseudocode in VisualBasic.NET that will connect to the oracle database and update all of the prices in the PART table to ½ off of their original values.

LESSON 25

Using Oracle SQL*Plus to Satisfy Reporting Needs

In this lesson, you learn about SQL*Plus, the SQL interface for Oracle's relational database management system (RDBMS). By the end of the lesson, you will understand the following elements of SQL*Plus:

- How to use the SQL*Plus buffer
- How to attractively format reports
- How to manipulate dates
- How to make interactive queries
- How to construct advanced reports
- How to use the powerful DECODE function

An Introduction to SQL*Plus

We are presenting SQL*Plus in this lesson because of Oracle's dominance in the relational database market and because of the power and flexibility SQL*Plus offers to the database user. SQL*Plus resembles Transact-SQL (see Lesson 27, "An Introduction to Transact-SQL") in many ways. Both implementations comply with the ANSI SQL standard for the most part, which is still the skeleton of any implementation.

SQL*Plus commands can enhance a SQL session and improve the format of queries from the database. SQL*Plus can also format reports, much like a dedicated report writer. SQL*Plus supplements both standard SQL and PL/SQL and helps relational database programmers gather data in a desirable format.

NOTE	The syntax shown in this lesson is not supported by MySQL. This syntax can be used with all versions of Oracle.

The SQL*Plus Buffer

The SQL*Plus buffer is an area that stores commands that are specific to your particular SQL session. These commands include the most recently executed SQL statement and commands that you have used to customize your SQL session, such as formatting commands and variable assignments. This buffer is like a short-term memory. Here are some of the most common SQL buffer commands:

- LIST *line_number*—Lists a line from the statement in the buffer and designates it as the current line.
- CHANGE/*old_value*/*new_value*—Changes *old_value* to *new_value* on the current line in the buffer.
- APPEND *text*—Appends *text* to the current line in the buffer.
- DEL—Deletes the current line in the buffer.
- SAVE *newfile*—Saves the SQL statement in the buffer to a file.
- GET *filename*—Gets a SQL file and places it in the buffer.
- /—Executes the SQL statement in the buffer.

We begin with a simple SQL statement:

Input/Output ▼

```
SQL> SELECT *
  >  FROM PRODUCTS
  >  WHERE UNIT_COST > 25;
PRO PRODUCT_NAME                     UNIT_COST
--- ------------------------------   ---------
P01 MICKEY MOUSE LAMP                    29.95
P06 SQL COMMAND REFERENCE                29.99
P07 BLACK LEATHER BRIEFCASE              99.99
```

The LIST command lists the most recently executed SQL statement in the buffer. The output will simply be the displayed statement.

Input/Output ▼

```
SQL> list

  1   SELECT *
  2   FROM PRODUCTS
  3*  WHERE UNIT_COST > 25
```

Analysis ▼

Notice that each line is numbered. Line numbers are important in the buffer; they act as pointers that enable you to modify specific lines of your statement using the SQL*Plus buffer. The SQL*Plus buffer is not a full-screen editor; after you press Enter, you cannot use the cursor to move up a line, to say line 3 to edit the UNIT_COST constraint, as shown in the following example:

Input ▼

```
SQL> SELECT *
  2   FROM PRODUCTS
  3   WHERE UNIT_COST > 25
  4   /
```

> **NOTE**
> As with standard SQL commands, you may issue SQL*Plus commands in either uppercase or lowercase.

> **TIP**
> You can abbreviate most SQL*Plus commands; for example, LIST can be abbreviated as l.

You can move to a specific line from the buffer by placing a line number after the l:

Input ▼

```
SQL> l3

  3*  WHERE UNIT_COST > 25
```

25

Analysis ▼

Notice the asterisk after the line number 3. This asterisk denotes the current line number. Pay close attention to the placement of the asterisk in this lesson's examples. Whenever a line is marked with an asterisk, you can make changes to that line.

Because you know that your current line is 3, you are free to make changes. The syntax for the CHANGE command is as follows:

Syntax ▼

```
CHANGE/old_value/new_value        or
C/old_value/new_value
```

Here is an example of using the command:

Input/Output ▼

```
SQL> C/>/<

  3* WHERE UNIT_COST < 25

SQL> l
  1   SELECT *
  2   FROM PRODUCTS
  3* WHERE UNIT_COST < 25
```

The greater than sign (>) has been changed to less than (<) on line 3. Notice after the change was made that the newly modified line was displayed. If you issue the LIST command or l, you can see the full statement. Now execute the statement:

Input/Output ▼

```
SQL> /
```

PRO	PRODUCT_NAME	UNIT_COST
P02	NO 2 PENCILS - 20 PACK	1.99
P03	COFFEE MUG	6.95
P04	FAR SIDE CALENDAR	10.5
P05	NATURE CALENDAR	12.99

The forward slash at the SQL> prompt executes any statement that is in the buffer.

Input/Output ▼

```
SQL> L

  1  SELECT *
  2  FROM PRODUCTS
  3* WHERE UNIT_COST < 25
```

Now you can add a line to your statement by typing a new line number at the SQL> prompt and entering text. After you make the addition, you get a full statement listing. Here's an example:

Input/Output ▼

```
SQL> 4 ORDER BY UNIT_COST
SQL> L

  1  select *
  2  from products
  3  where unit_cost < 25
  4* order by unit_cost
```

Deleting a line is easier than adding a line. Simply type DEL 4 at the SQL> prompt to delete line 4. Now get another statement listing to verify that the line is gone.

Input/Output ▼

```
SQL> DEL 4
SQL> L

  1  SELECT *
  2  FROM PRODUCTS
  3* WHERE UNIT_COST < 25
```

Another way to add one or more lines to your statement is to use the INPUT command. As you can see in the preceding list, the current line number is 3. At the prompt, type input and then press Enter. Now you can begin typing text. Each time you press Enter, another line will be created. If you press Enter twice, you will obtain another SQL> prompt. Now if you display a statement listing, as in the following example, you can see that line 4 has been added.

25

Input/Output ▼

```
SQL> INPUT
  4I    AND PRODUCT_ID = 'P01'
  5I    ORDER BY UNIT_COST
SQL> L
  1   SELECT *
  2   FROM PRODUCTS
  3   WHERE UNIT_COST < 25
  4     AND PRODUCT_ID = 'P01'
  5* ORDER BY UNIT_COST
```

To append text to the current line, issue the APPEND command followed by the text. Compare the output in the preceding example—the current line number is 5—to the following example.

Input/Output ▼

```
SQL> APPEND   DESC

  5* ORDER BY UNIT_COST DESC
```

Now get a full listing of your statement:

Input/Output ▼

```
SQL> L

  1   SELECT *
  2   FROM PRODUCTS
  3   WHERE UNIT_COST < 25
  4     AND PRODUCT_ID = 'P01'
  5* ORDER BY UNIT_COST DESC
```

Suppose you want to wipe the slate clean. You can clear the contents of the SQL*Plus buffer by issuing the command CLEAR BUFFER. As you will see later, you can also use the CLEAR command to clear specific settings from the buffer, such as column formatting information and computes on a report.

Input/Output ▼

```
SQL> CLEAR BUFFER

buffer cleared

SQL> L

No lines in SQL buffer.
```

Obviously, you won't be able to retrieve anything from an empty buffer. You aren't a master yet, but you should be able to maneuver with ease by manipulating your commands in the buffer.

Viewing Table Structure with the DESCRIBE Command

The handy DESCRIBE command enables you to view the structure of a table quickly without having to create a query against the data dictionary.

Syntax ▼

```
DESC[RIBE] table_name
```

Take a look at the two tables you will be using throughout the lesson:

Input/Output ▼

```
SQL> DESCRIBE ORDERS

Name                             Null?     Type
-------------------------------- --------  ----
ORDEREDON                                  DATE
NAME                                       CHAR(10)
PARTNUM                                    NUMBER(38)
QUANTITY                                   NUMBER(38)
REMARKS                                    CHAR(10)
```

The following statement uses the abbreviation DESC instead of DESCRIBE:

Input/Output ▼

```
SQL> DESC PART;

Name                             Null?     Type
-------------------------------- --------  ----
PARTNUM                                    NUMBER(38)
DESCRIPTION                                CHAR(20)
PRICE                                      NUMBER(9,2)
```

Analysis ▼

DESC displays each column name, which columns must contain data (NULL/NOT NULL), and the data type for each column. If you are writing many queries, you will find that

25

few days go by without using this command. Over a long time, this command can save you many hours of programming time. Without DESCRIBE, you would have to search through project documentation or even database manuals containing lists of data dictionary tables to get this information.

Displaying Settings with the SHOW Command

The SHOW command displays the session's current settings, from formatting commands to who you are. SHOW ALL displays all settings. This discussion covers some of the most common settings.

Input/Output ▼

```
SQL> SHOW ALL

appinfo is ON and set to "SQL*Plus"
arraysize 15
autocommit OFF
autoprint OFF
autotrace OFF
blockterminator "." (hex 2e)
.
.
.
.
```

The SHOW command displays a specific setting entered by the user. Suppose you have access to multiple database user IDs and you want to see whom you are logged on as. You can issue the following command:

Input/Output ▼

```
SQL> SHOW USER

USER is "AJ"
```

If you wanted to see the current line size of output, you would type

Input/Output ▼

```
SQL> SHOW LINESIZE

linesize 100
```

If you have an error with PROCEDURE, PACKAGE, TRIGGER, or FUNCTION, SHOW ERROR comes in very handy by showing you the error involved.

Input/Output ▼

```
SQL> SHOW ERROR

No errors.
```

Manipulating Files with File Commands

Various commands enable you to manipulate files in SQL*Plus. These commands include creating a file, editing the file using a full-screen editor (as opposed to using the SQL*Plus buffer), and redirecting output to a file. You also need to know how to execute a SQL file after it is created.

The SAVE, GET, and EDIT Commands

The SAVE command saves the contents of the SQL statement in the buffer to a file whose name you specify—for example:

Input/Output ▼

```
SQL> SELECT *
  2  FROM PRODUCTS
  3  WHERE UNIT_COST < 25

SQL> SAVE QUERY1.SQL

Created file query1.sql
```

After a file has been saved, you can use the GET command to list the file. GET is very similar to the LIST command. Just remember that GET deals with statements that have been saved to files, whereas LIST deals with the statement that is stored in the buffer.

Input/Output ▼

```
SQL> GET QUERY1

  1  SELECT *
  2  FROM PRODUCTS
  3* WHERE UNIT_COST < 25
```

You can use the EDIT command either to create a new file or to edit an existing file. When issuing this command, you are taken into a full-screen editor, more than likely

25

Notepad in Windows. You will find that it is usually easier to modify a file with EDIT than through the buffer, particularly if you are dealing with a large or complex statement. Figure 25.1 shows an example of the EDIT command.

Input ▼

```
SQL> EDIT QUERY1.SQL
```

FIGURE 25.1
Editing a file in
SQL*Plus.

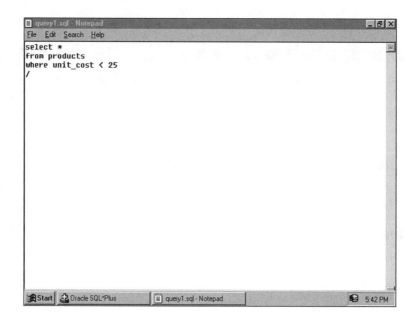

Starting a File

Now that you know how to create and edit a SQL file, the command to execute it is simple. It can take one of the following forms:

Syntax ▼

```
START filename
```

or

Syntax ▼

```
STA filename
```

or

Syntax ▼

```
@filename
```

Notice how some commands like START can be abbreviated with STA. Oracle allows these shortened versions of commands as long as the command is not ambiguous. For example, the EDIT command, which we used previously, can be abbreviated using ED.

> **NOTE** Commands are not case sensitive.

Input/Output ▼

```
SQL> START QUERY1.SQL

PRO PRODUCT_NAME                  UNIT_COST
--- ----------------------------- ---------

P02 NO 2 PENCILS - 20 PACK             1.99
P03 COFFEE MUG                         6.95
P04 FAR SIDE CALENDAR                  10.5
P05 NATURE CALENDAR                   12.99
```

25

> **NOTE** You do not have to specify the file extension .sql to start a file from SQL*Plus. The database assumes that the file you are executing has this extension. Similarly, when you are creating a file from the SQL> prompt or use SAVE, GET, or EDIT, you do not have to include the extension if it is .sql.

Input/Output ▼

```
SQL> @QUERY1

PRO PRODUCT_NAME                  UNIT_COST
--- ----------------------------- ---------

P02 NO 2 PENCILS - 20 PACK             1.99
P03 COFFEE MUG                         6.95
P04 FAR SIDE CALENDAR                  10.5
P05 NATURE CALENDAR                   12.99

SQL> RUN QUERY1
```

```
1  SELECT *
2  FROM PRODUCTS
3* WHERE UNIT_COST < 25

PRO PRODUCT_NAME                   UNIT_COST
--- ----------------------------   ---------
P02 NO 2 PENCILS - 20 PACK              1.99
P03 COFFEE MUG                          6.95
P04 FAR SIDE CALENDAR                  10.5
P05 NATURE CALENDAR                    12.99
```

Analysis ▼

Notice that when you use RUN to execute a query, the statement is echoed, or displayed on the screen. This feature was built into the RUN command. The START command will display only the output.

Spooling Query Output

Viewing the output of your query on the screen is very convenient, but what if you want to save the results for future reference or you want to print the file? The SPOOL command allows you to send your output to a specified file. If the file does not exist, it will be created. If the file exists, it will be overwritten, as shown in Figure 25.2.

Input/Output ▼

```
SQL> SPOOL PROD.LST
SQL> SELECT *
  2  FROM PRODUCTS;

PRO PRODUCT_NAME                   UNIT_COST
--- ----------------------------   ---------
P01 MICKEY MOUSE LAMP                  29.95
P02 NO 2 PENCILS - 20 PACK              1.99
P03 COFFEE MUG                          6.95
P04 FAR SIDE CALENDAR                  10.5
P05 NATURE CALENDAR                    12.99
P06 SQL COMMAND REFERENCE              29.99
P07 BLACK LEATHER BRIEFCASE            99.99

7 rows selected.
```

Analysis ▼

The first command is to create a spool file called PROD.LST. Then we select all rows from the products table. The spool file in this case contains the SQL statement and the returned rows. The SQL statement shows up in the spool file because the echo was turned on. Had echo been turned off, only the rows of data would have been in the spool file.

FIGURE 25.2
Spooling your output to a file.

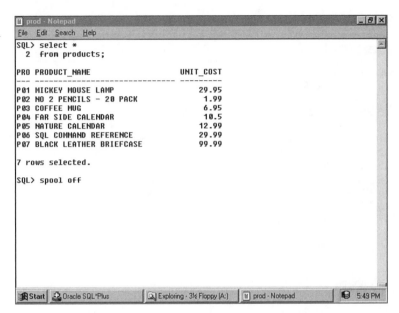

After your output has been returned, you should turn off spooling; otherwise, everything that you do will be in your spooled file until spooling is turned off. To stop spooling, issue the command SPOOL OFF, as in the following example. To read the spooled file, issue the command EDIT PROD.LST. This opens the file.

Input ▼

```
SQL> SPOOL OFF
SQL> EDIT PROD.LIST
```

The output in Figure 25.2 is a SQL*Plus file. You must use the SPOOL OFF command to stop spooling to a file. When you exit SQL*Plus, SPOOL OFF is automatic. But if you do not exit and you continue to work in SQL*Plus, everything you do will be spooled to your file until you issue the command SPOOL OFF.

Customizing the Work Environment with SET Commands

SET commands in Oracle change SQL*Plus session settings. By using these commands, you can customize your SQL working environment and invoke options to make your output results more presentable. You can control many of the SET commands by turning an option on or off.

25

To see how the SET commands work, perform a simple SELECT:

Input/Output ▼

```
SQL> SELECT *
  2  FROM PRODUCTS;

PRO PRODUCT_NAME                    UNIT_COST
--- ---------------------------- ----------
P01 MICKEY MOUSE LAMP                 29.95
P02 NO 2 PENCILS - 20 PACK             1.99
P03 COFFEE MUG                         6.95
P04 FAR SIDE CALENDAR                  10.5
P05 NATURE CALENDAR                   12.99
P06 SQL COMMAND REFERENCE             29.99
P07 BLACK LEATHER BRIEFCASE           99.99

7 rows selected.
```

Analysis ▼

The last line of output

```
7 rows selected.
```

is called *feedback*, which is a SQL setting that can be modified. These settings have defaults, and in this case the default for FEEDBACK is on. If you wanted to, you could type

Input ▼

```
SET FEEDBACK ON
```

before issuing your SELECT statement. Now suppose that you do not want to see the feedback, as happens to be the case with some reports, particularly summarized reports with computations.

Input/Output ▼

```
SQL> SET FEEDBACK OFF
SQL> SELECT *
  2  FROM PRODUCTS;

PRO PRODUCT_NAME                    UNIT_COST
--- ---------------------------- ----------
P01 MICKEY MOUSE LAMP                 29.95
P02 NO 2 PENCILS - 20 PACK             1.99
P03 COFFEE MUG                         6.95
P04 FAR SIDE CALENDAR                  10.5
```

```
P05 NATURE CALENDAR                    12.99
P06 SQL COMMAND REFERENCE              29.99
P07 BLACK LEATHER BRIEFCASE            99.99
```

SET FEEDBACK OFF turns off the feedback display.

In some cases, you might want to suppress the column headings from being displayed on a report. This setting is called HEADING, which can also be set ON or OFF.

Input/Output ▼

```
SQL> SET HEADING OFF
SQL> /
P01 MICKEY MOUSE LAMP                  29.95
P02 NO 2 PENCILS - 20 PACK              1.99
P03 COFFEE MUG                          6.95
P04 FAR SIDE CALENDAR                  10.5
P05 NATURE CALENDAR                    12.99
P06 SQL COMMAND REFERENCE              29.99
P07 BLACK LEATHER BRIEFCASE            99.99
```

The column headings have been eliminated from the output. Only the actual data is displayed. Also notice our use of the / command. In this context it is not used as a terminator as it had been in previous lessons. Here it is used to rerun the contents of the buffer. So we are in effect setting the column heading off and then rerunning the commands in our buffer.

You can change a wide array of settings to manipulate how your output is displayed. One option, LINESIZE, allows you to specify the length of each line of your output. A small line size will more than likely cause your output to wrap; increasing the line size might be necessary to suppress wrapping of a line that exceeds the default of 80 characters. Unless you are using wide computer paper (11×14), you might want to print your report in landscape orientation if you are using a line size greater than 80. The following example shows the use of LINESIZE:

Input/Output ▼

```
SQL> SET LINESIZE 40
SQL> /

P01 MICKEY MOUSE LAMP
    29.95

P02 NO 2 PENCILS - 20 PACK
    1.99
```

25

```
P03 COFFEE MUG
    6.95

P04 FAR SIDE CALENDAR
    10.5

P05 NATURE CALENDAR
    12.99

P06 SQL COMMAND REFERENCE
    29.99

P07 BLACK LEATHER BRIEFCASE
    99.99
```

You can also adjust the size of each page of your output by using the setting PAGESIZE. If you are simply viewing your output onscreen, the best setting for PAGESIZE is 23, which eliminates multiple page breaks per screen. In the following example, PAGESIZE is set to a low number to show you what happens on each page break:

Input/Output ▼

```
SQL> SET LINESIZE 80
SQL> SET HEADING ON
SQL> SET PAGESIZE 7
SQL> /

PRO PRODUCT_NAME                    UNIT_COST
--- ------------------------------  ---------
P01 MICKEY MOUSE LAMP                   29.95
P02 NO 2 PENCILS - 20 PACK               1.99
P03 COFFEE MUG                           6.95
P04 FAR SIDE CALENDAR                    10.5

PRO PRODUCT_NAME                    UNIT_COST
--- ------------------------------  ---------
P05 NATURE CALENDAR                     12.99
P06 SQL COMMAND REFERENCE               29.99
P07 BLACK LEATHER BRIEFCASE             99.99
```

Using the setting of PAGESIZE 7, the maximum number of lines that may appear on a single page is seven. New column headings will print automatically at the start of each new page.

The TIME setting displays the current time as part of your SQL> prompt.

Input/Output ▼

```
SQL> SET TIME ON

08:52:02 SQL>
```

These were just a few of the SET options, but they are all manipulated in basically the same way. As you saw from the vast list of SET commands in the earlier output from the SHOW ALL statement, you have many options when customizing your SQL*Plus session. Experiment with each option and see what you like best. You will probably keep the default settings for many options, but you might find yourself changing other options frequently based on different scenarios.

Removing Settings with the CLEAR Command

In SQL*Plus, settings are cleared by logging off, or by exiting SQL*Plus. Some of your settings may also be cleared by using the CLEAR command, as shown in the following examples:

Input/Output ▼

```
SQL> CLEAR COL

columns cleared

SQL> CLEAR BREAK

breaks cleared

SQL> CLEAR COMPUTE

computes cleared
```

Formatting Your Output

SQL*Plus also has commands that enable you to arrange your output in almost any format. This section covers the basic formatting commands for creating report titles, column headings, and formats, and for giving a column a new value.

25

TTITLE **and** BTITLE

TTITLE and BTITLE enable you to create titles on your reports. Previous lessons covered queries and output, but with SQL*Plus, you can convert simple output into presentable reports. The TTITLE command places a title at the top of each page of your output or report. BTITLE places a title at the bottom of each page. Many options are available with each of these commands, but this lesson's presentation covers the essentials.

Here is the basic syntax of TTITLE and BTITLE:

Syntax ▼

```
TTITLE [center|left¦right] 'text' [&variable] [skip n]
BTITLE [center|left¦right] 'text' [&variable] [skip n]
```

Here are some examples using TTTILE and BTITLE:

Input/Output ▼

```
SQL> TTITLE 'A LIST OF PRODUCTS'
SQL> BTITLE 'THAT IS ALL'
SQL> SET PAGESIZE 15
SQL> /

Wed May 07
page     1
                             A LIST OF PRODUCTS

PRO PRODUCT_NAME                      UNIT_COST
--- ----------------------------- ---------
P01 MICKEY MOUSE LAMP                    29.95
P02 NO 2 PENCILS - 20 PACK                1.99
P03 COFFEE MUG                            6.95
P04 FAR SIDE CALENDAR                    10.5
P05 NATURE CALENDAR                      12.99
P06 SQL COMMAND REFERENCE                29.99
P07 BLACK LEATHER BRIEFCASE              99.99

                             THAT IS ALL

7 rows selected
```

Analysis ▼

A title appears at the top of the page and at the bottom. Many people use the bottom title for signature blocks to verify or make changes to data on the report. Also, in the top title, the date and page number are part of the title.

Formatting Columns (COLUMN, HEADING, FORMAT)

Formatting columns refers to the columns that are to be displayed or the columns that are listed after the SELECT in a SQL statement. The COLUMN, HEADING, and FORMAT commands rename column headings and control the way the data appears on the report.

The COL[UMN] command is normally used with either the HEADING command or the FORMAT command. COLUMN defines the column that you want to format. The column that you are defining must appear exactly as it is typed in the SELECT statement. You may use a column alias instead of the full column name to identify a column with this command.

When using the HEADING command, you must use the COLUMN command to identify the column on which to place the heading.

When using the FORMAT command, you must use the COLUMN command to identify the column you want to format.

The basic syntax for using all three commands follows. Note that the HEADING and FOR-MAT commands are optional. In the FORMAT syntax, you must use an a if the data has a character format or use 0s and 9s to specify number data types. Decimals may also be used with numeric values. The number to the right of the a is the total width that you want to allow for the specified column.

25

Syntax ▼

```
COL[UMN] column_name HEA[DING] "new_heading" FOR[MAT] [a1|99.99]
```

The simple SELECT statement that follows shows the formatting of a column. The specified column is of NUMBER data type, and we want to display the number in a decimal format with a dollar sign.

Input/Output ▼

```
SQL> COLUMN UNIT_COST HEADING "PRICE" FORMAT $99.99
SQL> SELECT PRODUCT_NAME, UNIT_COST
  2  FROM PRODUCTS;


PRODUCT_NAME                    PRICE
------------------------------- -------
MICKEY MOUSE LAMP               $29.95
NO 2 PENCILS - 20 PACK           $1.99
COFFEE MUG                       $6.95
FAR SIDE CALENDAR               $10.50
NATURE CALENDAR                 $12.99
SQL COMMAND REFERENCE           $29.99
BLACK LEATHER BRIEFCASE         $99.99

7 rows selected.
```

Analysis ▼

Because we used the format 99.99, the maximum number that will be displayed is 99.99.

Now try abbreviating the commands. Here's something neat you can do with the HEADING command:

Input/Output ▼

```
SQL> COL UNIT_COST HEA "UNIT|COST" FOR $09.99
SQL> SELECT PRODUCT_NAME, UNIT_COST
  2  FROM PRODUCTS;

                                    UNIT
PRODUCT_NAME                        COST
------------------------------  ---------
MICKEY MOUSE LAMP                  $29.95
NO 2 PENCILS - 20 PACK             $01.99
COFFEE MUG                         $06.95
FAR SIDE CALENDAR                  $10.50
NATURE CALENDAR                    $12.99
SQL COMMAND REFERENCE              $29.99
BLACK LEATHER BRIEFCASE            $99.99

7 rows selected.
```

Analysis ▼

The pipe sign (|) in the HEADING command forces the following text of the column heading to be printed on the next line. You may use multiple pipe signs. The technique is handy when the width of your report starts to push the limits of the maximum available line size. The format of the unit cost column is now 09.99. The maximum number displayed remains 99.99, but now a 0 will precede all numbers less than 10. You may prefer this format because it makes the dollar amounts appear uniform.

Creating Report and Group Summaries

What would a report be without summaries and computations? Let's just say that you would have one frustrated programmer. Certain commands in SQL*Plus allow you to break your report into one or more types of groups and perform summaries or computations on each group. BREAK is a little different from SQL's standard group functions, such as COUNT() and SUM(). These functions are used with report and group summaries to provide a more complete report.

BREAK ON

The BREAK ON command breaks returned rows of data from a SQL statement into one or more groups. If you BREAK ON a customer's name, by default the customer's name will be printed only the first time it is returned, and then left blank with each row of data with the corresponding name.

Here is the very basic syntax of the BREAK ON command:

Syntax ▼

```
BRE[AK] [ON column1 ON column2...][SKIP n|PAGE][DUP|NODUP]
```

You may also BREAK ON REPORT and ROW. Breaking on REPORT performs computations on the report as a whole, whereas breaking on ROW performs computations on each group of rows.

The SKIP option allows you to skip a number of lines or a page on each group. DUP or NODUP determines whether you want duplicates to be printed in each group. The default is NODUP.

Here is an example:

Input/Output ▼

```
SQL> COL UNIT_COST HEAD 'UNIT|COST' FOR $09.99
SQL> BREAK ON CUSTOMER
SQL> SELECT O.CUSTOMER, P.PRODUCT_NAME, P.UNIT_COST
  2  FROM ORDERS O,
  3       PRODUCTS P
  4  WHERE O.PRODUCT_ID = P.PRODUCT_ID
  5  ORDER BY CUSTOMER;

CUSTOMER                      PRODUCT_NAME                  UNIT COST
----------------------------  ----------------------------  ---------
JONES and SONS                MICKEY MOUSE LAMP               $29.95
                              NO 2 PENCILS - 20 PACK          $01.99
                              COFFEE MUG                      $06.95
PARAKEET CONSULTING GROUP     MICKEY MOUSE LAMP               $29.95
                              NO 2 PENCILS - 20 PACK          $01.99
                              SQL COMMAND REFERENCE           $29.99
                              BLACK LEATHER BRIEFCASE         $99.99
                              FAR SIDE CALENDAR               $10.50
PLEWSKY MOBILE CARWASH        MICKEY MOUSE LAMP               $29.95
                              BLACK LEATHER BRIEFCASE         $99.99
                              BLACK LEATHER BRIEFCASE         $99.99
                              NO 2 PENCILS - 20 PACK          $01.99
                              NO 2 PENCILS - 20 PACK          $01.99

13 rows selected.
```

25

Analysis ▼

Each unique customer is printed only once. This report is much easier to read than one in which duplicate customer names are printed. You must order your results in the same order as the column(s) on which you are breaking for the BREAK command to work.

COMPUTE

The COMPUTE command is used with the BREAK ON command. COMPUTE allows you to perform various computations on each group of data and/or on the entire report.

Syntax ▼

```
COMP[UTE] function  OF column_or_alias  ON column_or_row_or_report
```

Some of the more popular functions are

- AVG—Computes the average value on each group.
- COUNT—Computes a count of values on each group.
- SUM—Computes a sum of values on each group.

Suppose you want to create a report that lists the information from the PRODUCTS table and computes the average product cost on the report.

Input/Output ▼

```
SQL> BREAK ON REPORT
SQL> COMPUTE AVG OF UNIT_COST ON REPORT
SQL> SELECT *
  2  FROM PRODUCTS;

PRO PRODUCT_NAME                  UNIT_COST
--- ----------------------------- ---------
P01 MICKEY MOUSE LAMP                 29.95
P02 NO 2 PENCILS - 20 PACK             1.99
P03 COFFEE MUG                         6.95
P04 FAR SIDE CALENDAR                  10.5
P05 NATURE CALENDAR                   12.99
P06 SQL COMMAND REFERENCE             29.99
P07 BLACK LEATHER BRIEFCASE           99.99
                                  ---------
avg                                   27.48
```

You can obtain the information you want by breaking on REPORT and then computing the AVG of the unit_cost on REPORT.

Remember the CLEAR command? Now clear the last compute from the buffer and start again—but this time you want to compute the amount of money spent by each customer. You should also clear the computes because you do not want to see the average any longer.

Input/Output ▼

```
SQL> CLEAR COMPUTE

computes cleared
```

Now clear the last BREAK. (You don't really have to clear the BREAK in this case because you still intend to use the BREAK ON command for the report.)

Input/Output ▼

```
SQL> CLEAR BREAK

breaks cleared
```

The next step is to reenter the breaks and computes the way you want them. You will also have to reformat the column UNIT_COST to accommodate a larger number because you are computing a sum of the UNIT_COST on the report. You need to allow room for the grand total that uses the same format as the column on which it is being calculated, so you need to add another place to the left of the decimal.

Input ▼

```
SQL> COL UNIT_COST HEA 'UNIT|COST' FOR $099.99
SQL> BREAK ON REPORT ON CUSTOMER SKIP 1
SQL> COMPUTE SUM OF UNIT_COST ON CUSTOMER
SQL> COMPUTE SUM OF UNIT_COST ON REPORT
```

Now list the last SQL statement from the buffer:

Input/Output ▼

```
SQL> l

  1  SELECT O.CUSTOMER, P.PRODUCT_NAME, P.UNIT_COST
  2  FROM ORDERS O,
  3       PRODUCTS P
  4  WHERE O.PRODUCT_ID = P.PRODUCT_ID
  5* ORDER BY CUSTOMER
```

25

Now that you have verified that this statement is the one you want, you can execute it:

Input/Output ▼

```
SQL> /

                                                          UNIT
CUSTOMER                      PRODUCT_NAME                COST
- - - - - - - - - - - - - -   - - - - - - - - - - - - -   - - - - -
JONES and SONS                MICKEY MOUSE LAMP           $029.95
                              NO 2 PENCILS - 20 PACK      $001.99
                              COFFEE MUG                  $006.95
*****************************                             - - - - -
sum                                                       $038.89

PARAKEET CONSULTING GROUP     MICKEY MOUSE LAMP           $029.95
                              NO 2 PENCILS - 20 PACK      $001.99
                              SQL COMMAND REFERENCE       $029.99
                              BLACK LEATHER BRIEFCASE     $099.99
                              FAR SIDE CALENDAR           $010.50
*****************************                             - - - - -
sum                                                       $172.42

PLEWSKY MOBILE CARWASH        MICKEY MOUSE LAMP           $029.95
                              BLACK LEATHER BRIEFCASE     $099.99
                              BLACK LEATHER BRIEFCASE     $099.99
                              NO 2 PENCILS - 20 PACK      $001.99
                              NO 2 PENCILS - 20 PACK      $001.99
*****************************                             - - - - -

                                                          UNIT
CUSTOMER                      PRODUCT_NAME                COST
- - - - - - - - - - - - - -   - - - - - - - - - - - - -   - - - - -
sum                                                       $233.91


                                                          - - - - -
sum                                                       $445.22
13 rows selected.
```

This example computed the total amount that each customer spent and also calculated a grand total for all customers.

By now you should understand the basics of formatting columns, grouping data on the report, and performing computations on each group.

Using Variables in SQL*Plus

Without actually getting into a procedural language, you can still define variables in your SQL statement. You can use special options in SQL*Plus (covered in this section) to accept input from the user to pass parameters into your SQL program.

Substitution Variables (&)

An ampersand (&) is the character that calls a value for a variable within a SQL script. If the variable has not previously been defined, the user is prompted to enter a value.

Input/Output ▼

```
SQL> SELECT *
  2  FROM &TBL
  3  ;

Enter value for tbl: products

The user entered the value "products."

old   2: FROM &TBL
new   2: FROM PRODUCTS

PRO PRODUCT_NAME                    UNIT_COST
--- ------------------------------  ---------
P01 MICKEY MOUSE LAMP                   29.95
P02 NO 2 PENCILS - 20 PACK               1.99
P03 COFFEE MUG                           6.95
P04 FAR SIDE CALENDAR                    10.5
P05 NATURE CALENDAR                     12.99
P06 SQL COMMAND REFERENCE               29.99
P07 BLACK LEATHER BRIEFCASE             99.99

7 rows selected.
```

The value products was substituted in the place of &TBL in this interactive query.

DEFINE

You can use DEFINE to assign values to variables within a SQL script file. If you define your variables within the script, users are not prompted to enter a value for the variable at runtime, as they are when you use the ampersand (&). The next example issues the same SELECT statement as the preceding example, but this time the value of TBL is defined within the script.

Input/Output ▼

```
SQL> DEFINE TBL=PRODUCTS
SQL> SELECT *
  2  FROM &TBL;

old   2: FROM &TBL
new   2: FROM PRODUCTS
```

25

```
PRO PRODUCT_NAME                    UNIT_COST
--- ------------------------------  ----------
P01 MICKEY MOUSE LAMP                   29.95
P02 NO 2 PENCILS - 20 PACK               1.99
P03 COFFEE MUG                           6.95
P04 FAR SIDE CALENDAR                    10.5
P05 NATURE CALENDAR                     12.99
P06 SQL COMMAND REFERENCE               29.99
P07 BLACK LEATHER BRIEFCASE             99.99

7 rows selected.
```

Both queries achieved the same result. The next section describes another way to prompt users for script parameters.

ACCEPT

ACCEPT enables the user to enter a value to fill a variable at script runtime. ACCEPT does the same thing as the & with no DEFINE, but is a little more controlled. ACCEPT also allows you to issue user-friendly prompts.

The next example starts by clearing the buffer:

Input/Output ▼

```
SQL> CLEAR BUFFER

buffer cleared
```

Then it uses an INPUT command to enter the new SQL statement into the buffer. If you started to type your statement without issuing the INPUT command first, you would be prompted to enter the value for newtitle first. Alternatively, you could go straight into a new file and write your statement as follows:

Input/Output ▼

```
SQL> INPUT
  1  ACCEPT NEWTITLE PROMPT 'ENTER TITLE FOR REPORT: '
  2  TTITLE CENTER NEWTITLE
  3  SELECT *
  4  FROM PRODUCTS
  5 /
SQL> SAVE PROD

File "prod.sql" already exists.
Use another name or "SAVE filename REPLACE".
```

Whoops...the file `prod.sql` already exists. Let's say that you do not need the old `prod.sql`. You will have to use the replace option to save the statement in the buffer to `prod.sql`. Notice the use of PROMPT in the preceding statement. PROMPT displays text to the screen that tells the user exactly what to enter.

Input/Output ▼

```
SQL> SAVE PROD REPLACE

Wrote file prod
```

Now you can use the START command to execute the file:

Input/Output ▼

```
SQL> START PROD

Enter Title for Report: A LIST OF PRODUCTS

                    A LIST OF PRODUCTS

PRO PRODUCT_NAME                    UNIT_COST
--- ----------------------------- ----------
P01 MICKEY MOUSE LAMP                  29.95
P02 NO 2 PENCILS - 20 PACK              1.99
P03 COFFEE MUG                          6.95
P04 FAR SIDE CALENDAR                   10.5
P05 NATURE CALENDAR                    12.99
P06 SQL COMMAND REFERENCE              29.99
P07 BLACK LEATHER BRIEFCASE            99.99

7 rows selected.
```

The text that you entered becomes the current title of the report.

The next example shows how you can use substitution variables anywhere in a statement:

Input/Output ▼

```
SQL> INPUT
  1  ACCEPT PROD_ID PROMPT 'ENTER PRODUCT ID TO SEARCH FOR: '
  2  SELECT *
  3  FROM PRODUCTS
  4  WHERE PRODUCT_ID = '&PROD_ID'
  5  /
SQL> SAVE PROD1

Created file prod1
```

25

```
SQL> START PROD1

Enter PRODUCT ID to Search for: P01

old   3: WHERE PRODUCT_ID = '&PROD_ID'
new   3: WHERE PRODUCT_ID = 'P01'

PRO PRODUCT_NAME                     UNIT_COST
--- -------------------------------- ---------
P01 MICKEY MOUSE LAMP                    29.95
```

Analysis ▼

You can use variables to meet many needs—for example, to name the file to which to spool your output or to specify an expression in the ORDER BY clause. One of the ways to use substitution variables is to enter reporting dates in the WHERE clause for transactional quality assurance reports. If your query is designed to retrieve information on one particular individual at a time, you might want to add a substitution variable to be compared with the SSN column of a table.

NEW_VALUE

The NEW_VALUE command passes the value of a selected column into an undefined variable of your choice. The syntax is as follows:

Syntax ▼

```
COL[UMN] column_name NEW_VALUE new_name
```

You call the values of variables by using the & character—for example:

Syntax ▼

```
&new_name
```

The COLUMN command must be used with NEW_VALUE.

Notice how the & and COLUMN command are used together in the next SQL*Plus file. The GET command gets the file.

Input/Output ▼

```
SQL> GET PROD1

line 5 truncated.
  1   TTITLE LEFT 'REPORT FOR PRODUCT:   &PROD_TITLE' SKIP 2
  2   COL PRODUCT_NAME NEW_VALUE PROD_TITLE
```

```
   3  SELECT PRODUCT_NAME, UNIT_COST
   4  FROM PRODUCTS
   5* WHERE PRODUCT_NAME = 'COFFEE MUG'
   6  /
SQL> @PROD1

Report for Product:    COFFEE MUG

PRODUCT_NAME                      UNIT_COST
------------------------------   ----------
COFFEE MUG                             6.95

1 row selected.
```

Analysis ▼

The value for the column PRODUCT_NAME was passed into the variable prod_title by means of new_value. The value of the variable prod_title was then called in the TTITLE.

For more information on variables in SQL, see Lesson 26, "An Introduction to Oracle PL/SQL."

25

Using the DUAL Table

The DUAL table is a dummy table that exists in every Oracle database. This table is composed of one column called DUMMY, whose only row of data is the value X. The DUAL table is available to all database users and can be used for general purposes, such as performing arithmetic (where it can serve as a calculator) or manipulating the format of the SYSDATE.

Input/Output ▼

```
SQL> DESC DUAL;

Name                             Null?    Type
------------------------------   -------- ----
DUMMY                                     VARCHAR2(1)


SQL> SELECT *
  2  FROM DUAL;

D
-
X
1 row selected.
```

Take a look at a couple of examples using the DUAL table:

Input/Output ▼

```
SQL> SELECT SYSDATE
  2  FROM DUAL;

SYSDATE
----------
08-DEC-08
1 row selected.

SQL> SELECT 2 * 2
  2  FROM DUAL;

     2*2
----------
       4
1 row selected.
```

Pretty simple. The first statement selects SYSDATE from the DUAL table and gets today's date. The second example shows how to multiply in the DUAL table. Our answer for 2*2 is 4.

Exploring the DECODE Function

The DECODE function is one of the most powerful commands in SQL*Plus—perhaps the most powerful. The standard language of SQL lacks procedural functions that are contained in languages such as COBOL and C.

The DECODE function is similar to an IF...THEN statement in a procedural programming language. Where flexibility is required for complex reporting needs, DECODE is often able to fill the gap between SQL and the functions of a procedural language. The DECODE function simply says to look in a column for a value and, if found, change the value to another value.

Syntax ▼

```
DECODE(column1, value1, output1, value2, output2, output3)
```

The syntax example performs the DECODE function on column1. If column1 has a value of value1, display output1 instead of the column's current value. If column1 has a value of value2, display output2 instead of the column's current value. If column1 has a value of anything other than value1 or value2, display output3 instead of the column's current value.

How about some examples? First, perform a simple SELECT on a new table:

Input/Output ▼

```
SQL> SELECT * FROM STATES;

ST
--
IN
FL
KY
IL
OH
CA
NY

7 rows selected.
```

Now use the DECODE command:

Input/Output ▼

```
SQL> SELECT DECODE(STATE,'IN','INDIANA','OTHER') STATE
  2  FROM STATES;

STATE
-------
INDIANA
OTHER
OTHER
OTHER
OTHER
OTHER
OTHER

7 rows selected.
```

25

Analysis ▼

Only one row met the condition where the value of state was IN, so only that row was displayed as INDIANA. The other states took the default and therefore were displayed as OTHER.

The next example provides output strings for each value in the table. Just in case your table has states that are not in your DECODE list, you should still enter a default value of OTHER.

Input/Output ▼

```
SQL> SELECT DECODE(STATE,'IN','INDIANA',
  2                       'FL','FLORIDA',
  3                       'KY','KENTUCKY',
  4                       'IL','ILLINOIS',
  5                       'OH','OHIO',
  6                       'CA','CALIFORNIA',
  7                       'NY','NEW YORK','OTHER')
  8  FROM STATES;

DECODE(STA
----------
INDIANA
FLORIDA
KENTUCKY
ILLINOIS
OHIO
CALIFORNIA
NEW YORK

7 rows selected.
```

That was too easy. The next example introduces the PAY table. This table shows more of the power contained within DECODE:

Input/Output ▼

```
SQL> COL HOUR_RATE HEA "HOURLY|RATE" FOR 99.00
SQL> COL DATE_LAST_RAISE HEA "LAST|RAISE"
SQL> SELECT NAME, HOUR_RATE, DATE_LAST_RAISE
  2  FROM PAY;

                     HOURLY LAST
NAME                   RATE RAISE
-------------------- ------ ---------
JOHN                  12.60 01-JAN-96
JEFF                   8.50 17-MAR-97
RON                    9.35 01-OCT-96
RYAN                   7.00 15-MAY-96
BRYAN                 11.00 01-JUN-96
MARY                  17.50 01-JAN-96
ELAINE                14.20 01-FEB-97

7 rows selected.
```

Are you ready? It's time to give every individual in the PAY table a pay raise. If the year of an individual's last raise is 1998, calculate a 20% increase. If the year of the individual's last raise is 1999, calculate a 10% increase. In addition, display the percent raise for each individual in either situation.

Input/Output ▼

```
SQL> COL NEW_PAY HEA 'NEW PAY' FOR 99.00
SQL> COL HOUR_RATE HEA 'HOURLY¦RATE' FOR 99.00
SQL> COL DATE_LAST_RAISE HEA 'LAST¦RAISE'
SQL> SELECT NAME, HOUR_RATE, DATE_LAST_RAISE,
  2          DECODE(SUBSTR(DATE_LAST_RAISE,8,2),'98',HOUR_RATE * 1.2,
  3                                              '99',HOUR_RATE * 1.1)
➡NEW_PAY,
  4          DECODE(SUBSTR(DATE_LAST_RAISE,8,2),'98','20%',
  5                                              '99','10%',NULL) INCREASE
  6  FROM PAY;
                   HOURLY LAST
NAME                 RATE RAISE     NEW PAY INC
-------------------- ------ --------- ------- ---
JOHN                12.60 01-JAN-98   15.12 20%
JEFF                 8.50 17-MAR-99    9.35 10%
RON                  9.35 01-OCT-98   11.22 20%
RYAN                 7.00 15-MAY-98    8.40 20%
BRYAN               11.00 01-JUN-98   13.20 20%
MARY                17.50 01-JAN-98   21.00 20%
ELAINE              14.20 01-FEB-99   15.62 10%

7 rows selected.
```

According to the output, everyone will be receiving a 20% pay increase except for Jeff and Elaine, who have already received one raise in 1999.

DATE **Conversions**

If you want to add a touch of class to the way dates are displayed, you can use the TO_CHAR function to change the date picture. This example starts by obtaining today's date:

Input/Output ▼

```
SQL> SELECT SYSDATE
  2  FROM DUAL;

SYSDATE
---------
08-DEC-08
1 row selected.
```

When converting a date to a character string, you use the TO_CHAR function with the following syntax:

25

Syntax ▼

```
TO_CHAR(sysdate,'date picture')
```

date picture is how you want the date to look. Some of the most common parts of the date picture are as follows:

Month	The current month spelled out
Mon	The current month abbreviated
Day	The current day of the week
mm	The number of the current month
yy	The last two numbers of the current year
dd	The current day of the month
yyyy	The current year
ddd	The current day of the year since January 1
hh	The current hour of the day
mi	The current minute of the hour
ss	The current second of the minute
a.m.	Displays a.m. or p.m.

The date picture may also contain commas and literal strings, as long as the string is enclosed by double quotation marks (" ").

Input/Output ▼

```
SQL> COL TODAY FOR A20
SQL> SELECT TO_CHAR(SYSDATE,'MON DD, YYYY') TODAY
  2  FROM DUAL;
TODAY
--------------------
May 08, 1999
1 row selected.
```

Notice how we used the COLUMN command on the alias in this lesson.

Input/Output ▼

```
SQL> COL TODAY HEA 'TODAYS JULIAN DATE' FOR A20
SQL> SELECT TO_CHAR(SYSDATE,'DDD') TODAY
  2  FROM DUAL;

TODAYs JULIAN DATE
--------------------
128
1 row selected.
```

Analysis ▼

Some companies prefer to express the Julian date with the two-digit year preceding the three-digit day. Your date picture could also look like this: yyddd.

Assume that you wrote a little script and saved it as day. The next example gets the file, looks at it, and executes it to retrieve various pieces of converted date information.

Input/Output ▼

```
SQL> GET DAY

line 10 truncated.
  1   SET ECHO ON
  2   COL DAY FOR A10
  3   COL TODAY FOR A25
  4   COL YEAR FOR A25
  5   COL TIME FOR A15
  6   SELECT TO_CHAR(SYSDATE,'DAY') DAY,
  7          TO_CHAR(SYSDATE,'MON DD, YYYY') TODAY,
  8          TO_CHAR(SYSDATE,'YEAR') YEAR,
  9          TO_CHAR(SYSDATE,'HH:MI:SS A.M.') TIME
 10* FROM DUAL
```

Now you can run the script:

Input/Output ▼

```
SQL> @DAY

SQL> SET ECHO ON
SQL> COL DAY FOR A10
SQL> COL TODAY FOR A25
SQL> COL YEAR FOR A25
SQL> COL TIME FOR A15
SQL> SELECT TO_CHAR(SYSDATE,'DAY') DAY,
  2          TO_CHAR(SYSDATE,'MON DD, YYYY') TODAY,
  3          TO_CHAR(SYSDATE,'YEAR') YEAR,
  4          TO_CHAR(SYSDATE,'HH:MI:SS A.M.') TIME
  5   FROM DUAL;
DAY        TODAY                     YEAR                      TIME
---------- ------------------------- ------------------------- ---------------
Thursday   May 08, 1999              Nineteen Ninety-Seven     04:10:43 p.m.
1 row selected.
```

25

Analysis ▼

In this example, the entire statement was shown before it ran because ECHO was set to ON. In addition, SYSDATE was broken into four columns, and the date was converted into four formats.

The TO_DATE function enables you to convert text into a date format. The syntax is basically the same as TO_CHAR.

Syntax ▼

```
TO_DATE(expression,'date_picture')
```

Try a couple of examples:

Input/Output ▼

```
SQL> SELECT TO_DATE('19970501','YYYYMMDD') "NEW DATE"
  2  FROM DUAL;

NEW DATE
---------
01-MAY-97
1 row selected.

SQL> SELECT TO_DATE('05/01/97','MM"/"DD"/"YY') "NEW DATE"
  2  FROM DUAL;

NEW DATE
---------
01/MAY/97
1 row selected.
```

Notice the use of double quotation marks to represent a literal string.

Running a Series of SQL Files

A SQL script file can include anything that you can type into the SQL buffer at the SQL> prompt, even commands that execute another SQL script. Yes, you can start a SQL script from within another SQL script. Figure 25.3 shows a script file that was created using the EDIT command. The file contains multiple SQL statements, as well as commands to run other SQL scripts.

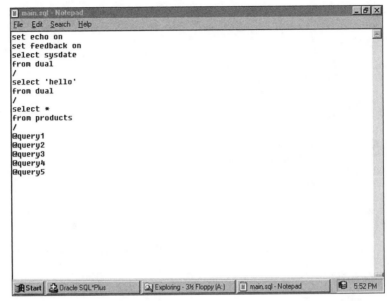

FIGURE 25.3
Running SQL scripts from within a SQL script.

Input ▼

25

```
SQL> EDIT MAIN.SQL

SQL> @MAIN
```

Analysis ▼

By starting main.sql, you will be executing each SQL command that is contained within the script. query1 through query5 will also be executed, in that order, as shown in Figure 25.3.

Adding Comments to Your SQL Script

SQL*Plus gives you three ways to place comments in your file:

- -- places a comment on one line at a time.
- REMARK also places a comment on one line at a time.
- /* */ places a comment(s) on one or more lines.

Study the following example:

Input ▼

```
SQL> INPUT
  1  REMARK THIS IS A COMMENT
  2  - THIS IS A COMMENT TOO
  3  REM
  4  - SET COMMANDS
  5  SET ECHO ON
  6  SET FEEDBACK ON
  7  - SQL STATEMENT
  8  SELECT *
  9  FROM PRODUCTS
 10  /
SQL>
```

To see how comments look in a SQL script file, type the following:

Input ▼

```
SQL> edit
```

Creating Advanced Reports

Now let's have some fun. By taking the concepts that you have learned in this lesson, as well as what you learned earlier, you can now create some fancy reports. Suppose that you have a script named report1.sql. Start it, sit back, and observe.

Input/Output ▼

```
SQL> SET ECHO ON
SQL> SET PAGESIZE 50
SQL> SET FEEDBACK OFF
SQL> SET NEWPAGE 0
SQL> COL PRODUCT_NAME HEA 'PRODUCT|NAME' FOR A20 TRUNC
SQL> COL UNIT_COST HEA 'UNIT|COST' FOR $99.99
SQL> COL PRODUCT_QTY HEA 'QTY' FOR 999
SQL> COL TOTAL FOR $99,999.99
SQL> SPOOL REPORT
SQL> COMPUTE SUM OF TOTAL ON CUSTOMER
SQL> COMPUTE SUM OF TOTAL ON REPORT
SQL> BREAK ON REPORT ON CUSTOMER SKIP 1
SQL> SELECT O.CUSTOMER, P.PRODUCT_NAME, P.UNIT_COST,
  2         O.PRODUCT_QTY, (P.UNIT_COST * O.PRODUCT_QTY) TOTAL
  3  FROM ORDERS O,
  4       PRODUCTS P
```

```
   5  WHERE O.PRODUCT_ID = P.PRODUCT_ID
   6  ORDER BY CUSTOMER
   7  /
                                   PRODUCT                UNIT
   CUSTOMER                        NAME                   COST  QTY       TOTAL
   ------------------------------  --------------------  ------ ----  ----------
   JONES and SONS                  MICKEY MOUSE LAMP     $29.95   50  $1,497.50
                                   NO 2 PENCILS - 20 PA   $1.99   10     $19.90
                                   COFFEE MUG             $6.95   10     $69.50
   ******************************                              ----------
   sum                                                              $1,586.90

   PARAKEET CONSULTING GROUP       MICKEY MOUSE LAMP     $29.95    5    $149.75
                                   NO 2 PENCILS - 20 PA   $1.99   15     $29.85
                                   SQL COMMAND REFERENC  $29.99   10    $299.90
                                   BLACK LEATHER BRIEFC  $99.99    1     $99.99
                                   FAR SIDE CALENDAR     $10.50   22    $231.00
   ******************************                              ----------
   sum                                                                $810.49

   PLEWSKY MOBILE CARWASH          MICKEY MOUSE LAMP     $29.95    1     $29.95
                                   BLACK LEATHER BRIEFC  $99.99    5    $499.95
                                   BLACK LEATHER BRIEFC  $99.99    1     $99.99
                                   NO 2 PENCILS - 20 PA   $1.99   10     $19.90
                                   NO 2 PENCILS - 20 PA   $1.99   10     $19.90
   ******************************                              ----------
   sum                                                                $669.69

                                                              ----------
   sum                                                              $3,067.08
   Input truncated to 9 characters
   SQL> SPOOL OFF
```

Analysis ▼

Several things are taking place in this script. If you look at the actual SQL statement, you can see that it is selecting data from two tables and performing an arithmetic function on that data. The statement joins the two tables in the WHERE clause and is ordered by the customer's name. Those are the basics. In addition, SQL*Plus commands format the data the way we want to see it. These commands break the report into groups by making computations on each group and by making a computation on the report as a whole.

Summary

This lesson explains Oracle's extension to the standard language of SQL. These commands are only a fraction of what is available to you in SQL*Plus. If you use Oracle's products, check your database documentation, take the knowledge that you have learned here, and explore the endless possibilities that lie before you. You will find that you can accomplish almost any reporting task using SQL*Plus rather than by resorting to a procedural programming language.

If you are not using Oracle products, use what you have learned in this lesson to improve the ways you retrieve data in your implementation. Most major implementations have extensions, or enhancements, to the accepted standard language of SQL.

Q&A

Q **Why should I spend valuable time learning SQL*Plus when I can achieve the same results using standard SQL?**

A If your requirements for reports are simple, standard SQL is fine, but you can reduce the time you spend on reports by using SQL*Plus. You can be sure that the people needing your reports will always want more information.

Q **How can I select SYSDATE from the DUAL table if it is not a column?**

A You can select SYSDATE from DUAL or any other valid table because SYSDATE is a pseudocolumn.

Q **When using the DECODE command, can I use a DECODE within another DECODE?**

A Yes, you can DECODE within a DECODE. In SQL, you can perform functions on other functions to achieve the desired results.

Workshop

The Workshop provides quiz questions to help solidify your understanding of the material covered, as well as exercises to provide you with experience in using what you have learned. Try to answer the quiz and exercise questions before checking the answers in Appendix A, "Answers."

Quiz

1. Which commands can modify your preferences for a SQL session?

2. Can your SQL script prompt a user for a parameter and execute the SQL statement using the entered parameter?

3. If you are creating a summarized report on entries in a CUSTOMER table, how would you group your data for your report?

4. Are there any limitations to what you can have in your LOGIN.SQL file?

5. True or false: The DECODE function is the equivalent of a loop in a procedural programming language.

6. True or false: If you spool the output of your query to an existing file, your output will be appended to that file.

Exercises

1. Using the PRODUCTS table at the beginning of this lesson, write a query (use Oracle SQL*Plus syntax as shown earlier this lesson) that selects all data and computes a count of the records returned on the report without using the SET FEEDBACK ON command.

2. Suppose today is Monday, May 12, 2008. Write a query that produces the following output:

```
Today is Monday, May 12 2008
```

3. Use the following SQL statement for this exercise:

```
1  select *
2  from orders
3  where customer_id = '001'
4* order by customer_id;
```

Without retyping the statement in the SQL buffer, change the table in the FROM clause to the CUSTOMER table.

Now append DESC to the ORDER BY clause.

25

LESSON 26
An Introduction to Oracle PL/SQL

PL/SQL is the Oracle technology that enables SQL to act like a procedural language. By the end of this lesson, you should

- Have a basic understanding of PL/SQL

- Understand the features that distinguish PL/SQL from standard SQL

- Have an understanding of the basic elements of a PL/SQL program

- Be able to write a simple PL/SQL program

- Understand how errors are handled in PL/SQL programs

- Be aware of how PL/SQL is used in the real world

Introducing PL/SQL

One way to introduce PL/SQL is to begin by describing standard Structured Query Language, or SQL. SQL is the language that enables relational database users to communicate with the database in a straightforward manner. You can use SQL commands to query the database and modify tables within the database. When you write a SQL statement, you are telling the database what you want to do, not how to do it. The query optimizer decides the most efficient way to execute your statement. If you send a series of SQL statements to the server in standard SQL, the server executes them one at a time in chronological order.

PL/SQL is Oracle's *procedural language;* it comprises the standard language of SQL and a wide array of commands that enable you to control the execution of SQL statements according to different conditions. PL/SQL can also handle runtime errors. Options such as loops and IF...THEN statements give PL/SQL the power of third-generation programming languages. PL/SQL allows you to write interactive, user-friendly programs that can pass values into variables. You can also use several predefined packages, one of which can display messages to the user.

This lesson covers these key features of PL/SQL:

- Programmers can declare variables to be used during statement processing.

- Programmers can use error-handling routines to prevent programs from aborting unexpectedly.

- Programmers can write interactive programs that accept input from the user.

- Programmers can divide functions into logical blocks of code. Modular programming techniques support flexibility during the application development.

- SQL statements can be processed simultaneously for better overall performance.

NOTE

> The syntax shown in this lesson is not supported by MySQL but can be used with all versions of Oracle. If you want to evaluate Oracle Express, you can download or order an evaluation copy. If you are considering a purchase of any version of Oracle, entering the syntax in this lesson is an excellent way of evaluating the software, and for enhancing your knowledge of SQL.

NOTE

> PL/SQL is primarily used to create database objects such as stored procedures and triggers.

The Structure of a PL/SQL Block

PL/SQL is a block-structured language, meaning that PL/SQL programs are divided and written in logical blocks of code. Within a PL/SQL block of code, processes such as data manipulation or queries can occur. The following parts of a PL/SQL block are discussed in this section:

- The DECLARE section contains the definitions of variables and other objects such as constants and cursors. This section is an optional part of a PL/SQL block.

- The PROCEDURE section contains conditional commands and SQL statements and is where the block is controlled. This section is the only mandatory part of a PL/SQL block.

- The EXCEPTION section tells the PL/SQL block how to handle specified errors and user-defined exceptions. This section is an optional part of a PL/SQL block.

NOTE
> A block is a logical unit of PL/SQL code and contains at the least a PROCEDURE section and optionally the DECLARE and EXCEPTION sections.

Here is the basic structure of a PL/SQL block:

Syntax ▼

```
BEGIN        -- optional, denotes beginning of block
  DECLARE    -- optional, variable definitions
  BEGIN      -- mandatory, denotes beginning of procedure section
  EXCEPTION  -- optional, denotes beginning of exception section
  END        -- mandatory, denotes ending of procedure section
END          -- optional, denotes ending of block
```

Analysis ▼

Notice that the only mandatory parts of a PL/SQL block are the second BEGIN and the first END, which make up the PROCEDURE section. Of course, you will have statements in between. If you use the first BEGIN, you must use the second END, and vice versa.

26

NOTE
> PL/SQL directly supports Data Manipulation Language (DML) commands and database queries. However, it does not support Data Dictionary Language (DDL) commands. You can generally use PL/SQL to manipulate the data within database structures, but not to manipulate those structures.

The DECLARE Section

The DECLARE section of a block of PL/SQL code consists of variables, constants, cursor definitions, and special data types. As a PL/SQL programmer, you can declare all types of variables within your blocks of code. However, you must assign a data type to every variable that you define, and that data type must conform to Oracle's data type rules. Variables must also conform to Oracle's object naming standards.

Variable Assignment

Variables are values that are subject to change within a PL/SQL block. PL/SQL variables must be assigned a valid data type upon declaration and can be initialized if necessary. The following example defines a set of variables in the DECLARE portion of a block:

Input ▼

```
DECLARE
  owner char(10);
  tablename char(30);
  bytes number(10);
  today date;
```

Analysis ▼

The DECLARE portion of a block cannot be executed by itself. The DECLARE section starts with the DECLARE statement. Individual variables are then defined on separate lines. Notice that each variable declaration ends with a semicolon.

Variables may also be initialized in the DECLARE section—for example,

Input ▼

```
DECLARE
  customer char(30);
  fiscal_year number(2) := '97';
```

Analysis ▼

You can use the symbol := to initialize, or assign an initial value to variables in the DECLARE section. You must initialize a variable that is defined as NOT NULL.

Input ▼

```
DECLARE
  customer char(30);
  fiscal_year number(2) NOT NULL := '97';
```

Analysis ▼

The NOT NULL clause in the definition of fiscal_year resembles a column definition in a CREATE TABLE statement.

Constant Assignment

Constants are defined the same way as variables, but constant values are static; they do not change. In the previous example, fiscal_year is probably a constant.

> **CAUTION** You must end each constant declaration with a semicolon.

Cursor Definitions

A cursor is another type of variable in PL/SQL. Usually when you think of a variable, a single value comes to mind. A cursor is a variable that points to a row of data from the results of a query. In a multiple-row result set, you need a way to scroll through each record to analyze the data. A cursor does just that. When the PL/SQL block looks at the results of a query within the block, it uses a cursor to point to each returned row. Here is an example of a cursor being defined in a PL/SQL block:

Input ▼

```
DECLARE
 CURSOR EMPLOYEE_CURSOR IS
    SELECT * FROM EMP_TBL;
```

Analysis ▼

A cursor is similar to a view. With the use of a loop in the PROCEDURE section, you can scroll a cursor. This technique is covered shortly. In this example, a cursor is defined with all records from the EMP_TBL table. A cursor is always defined by a query.

The %TYPE Attribute

%TYPE is a variable attribute that returns the value of a given column of a table. Instead of hard-coding the data type into your PL/SQL block, you can use %TYPE to maintain data type consistency within your blocks of code.

26

Input ▼

```
DECLARE
  CURSOR EMPLOYEE_CURSOR IS
    SELECT EMP_ID, LAST_NAME FROM EMP_TBL;
  ID_NUM EMP_TBL.EMP_ID%TYPE;
  NAME EMP_TBL.LAST_NAME%TYPE;
```

Analysis ▼

The variable id_num is declared to have the same data type as emp_id in the EMP_TBL table. %TYPE declares the variable name to have the same data type as the column last_name in the EMP_TBL table.

The %ROWTYPE Attribute

Variables are not limited to single values. If you declare a variable that is associated with a defined cursor, you can use the %ROWTYPE attribute to declare the data type of that variable to be the same as each column in one entire row of data from the cursor. In Oracle's lexicon, the %ROWTYPE attribute creates a record variable.

Input ▼

```
DECLARE
  CURSOR EMPLOYEE_CURSOR IS
    SELECT EMP_ID, LAST_NAME FROM EMP_TBL;
  EMPLOYEE_RECORD EMPLOYEE_CURSOR%ROWTYPE;
```

Analysis ▼

This example declares a variable called employee_record. The %ROWTYPE attribute defines this variable as having the same data type as an entire row of data in the employee_cursor. Variables declared using the %ROWTYPE attribute are called aggregate variables.

The %ROWCOUNT Attribute

The PL/SQL %ROWCOUNT attribute maintains a count of rows that the SQL statements in the particular block have accessed in a cursor.

Input ▼

```
DECLARE
  CURSOR EMPLOYEE_CURSOR IS
    SELECT EMP_ID, LAST_NAME FROM EMP_TBL;
  RECORDS_PROCESSED := EMPLOYEE_CURSOR%ROWCOUNT;
```

Analysis ▼

In this example, the variable `records_processed` represents the current number of rows that the PL/SQL block has accessed in the `employee_cursor`.

CAUTION	Beware of naming conflicts with table names when declaring variables. For instance, if you declare a variable that has the same name as a table that you are trying to access with the PL/SQL code, the local variable will take precedence over the table name.

The PROCEDURE Section

The PROCEDURE section is the only mandatory part of a PL/SQL block. This part of the block calls variables and uses cursors to manipulate data in the database. The PROCEDURE section is the main part of a block; it contains conditional statements and SQL commands.

BEGIN...END

In a block, the BEGIN statement denotes the beginning of a procedure. Similarly, the END statement marks the end of a procedure. The following example shows the basic structure of the PROCEDURE section:

Syntax ▼

```
BEGIN
  open a cursor;
  condition1;
    statement1;
  condition2;
    statement2;
  condition3;
    statement3;
  .
  .
  .
  close the cursor;
END
```

26

Cursor Control Commands

Now that you have learned how to define cursors in a PL/SQL block, you need to know how to access the defined cursors. This section explains the basic cursor control commands: DECLARE, OPEN, FETCH, and CLOSE.

DECLARE

Earlier in this lesson, you learned how to define a cursor in the DECLARE section of a block. The DECLARE statement belongs in the list of cursor control commands.

OPEN

Now that you have defined your cursor, how do you use it? You cannot use this book unless you open it. Likewise, you cannot use a cursor until you have opened it with the OPEN command—for example:

Syntax ▼

```
BEGIN
  open employee_cursor;
  statement1;
  statement2;
  .
  .
  .
END
```

FETCH

FETCH populates a variable with values from a cursor. Here are two examples using FETCH—one populates an aggregate variable, and the other populates individual variables.

Input ▼

```
DECLARE
  CURSOR EMPLOYEE_CURSOR IS
    SELECT EMP_ID, LAST_NAME FROM EMPLOYEES;
  EMPLOYEE_RECORD EMPLOYEE_CURSOR%ROWTYPE;
BEGIN
  OPEN EMPLOYEE_CURSOR;
  LOOP
    FETCH EMPLOYEE_CURSOR INTO EMPLOYEE_RECORD;
  END LOOP;
  CLOSE EMPLOYEE_CURSOR;
END
```

Analysis ▼

The preceding example fetches the current row of the cursor into the aggregate variable employee_record, and it uses a loop to scroll the cursor. Of course, the block is not actually accomplishing anything.

Input ▼

```
DECLARE
  CURSOR EMPLOYEE_CURSOR IS
    SELECT EMP_ID, LAST_NAME  FROM EMPLOYEES;
  ID_NUM EMPLOYEES.EMP_ID%TYPE;
  NAME EMPLOYEES.LAST_NAME%TYPE;
BEGIN
  OPEN EMPLOYEE_CURSOR;
  LOOP
    FETCH EMPLOYEE_CURSOR INTO ID_NUM, NAME;
  END LOOP;
  CLOSE EMPLOYEE_CURSOR;
END
```

Analysis ▼

This example fetches the current row of the cursor into the variables id_num and name, which were defined in the DECLARE section.

CLOSE

When you have finished using a cursor in a block, you should close the cursor using the command CLOSE, as you normally close a book when you have finished reading it.

Syntax ▼

```
BEGIN
  open employee_cursor;
  statement1;
  statement2;
  .
  .
  .
  close employee_cursor;
END
```

26

Analysis ▼

After a cursor is closed, the result set of the query no longer exists. You must reopen the cursor to access the associated set of data.

Conditional Statements

Now we are getting to the good stuff—the conditional statements. Conditional statements give you control over how your SQL statements are processed versus the optimizer having control over how they're processed. The conditional statements in PL/SQL resemble those in most third-generation languages, such as C or COBOL.

IF...THEN

The IF...THEN statement is probably the most familiar conditional statement to many programmers. The IF...THEN statement dictates the performance of certain actions if certain conditions are met. The structure of an IF...THEN statement is as follows:

Syntax ▼

```
IF condition1 THEN
  statement1;
END IF;
```

If you are checking for two conditions, you can write your statement as follows:

Syntax ▼

```
IF condition1 THEN
  statement1;
ELSE
  statement2;
END IF;
```

If you are checking for more than two conditions, you can write your statement as follows:

Syntax ▼

```
IF condition1 THEN
  statement1;
ELSIF condition2 THEN
  statement2;
ELSE
  statement3;
END IF;
```

Analysis ▼

The final example states this: If condition1 is met, perform statement1; if condition2 is met, perform statement2; otherwise, perform statement3. IF...THEN statements may also be nested within other statements and/or loops. The END IF statement terminates the entire IF...THEN statement.

Loops

Loops in a PL/SQL block allow statements in the block to be processed continuously for as long as the specified condition exists. There are three types of loops: LOOP, WHILE-LOOP, and FOR-LOOP.

LOOP is an infinite loop, most often used to scroll a cursor. To terminate this type of loop, you must specify when to exit. For example, in scrolling a cursor you would exit the loop after the last row in a cursor has been processed:

Syntax ▼

```
BEGIN
open employee_cursor;
LOOP
  FETCH employee_cursor into employee_record;
  EXIT WHEN employee_cursor%NOTFOUND;
  statement1;
  .
  .
  .
END LOOP;
close employee_cursor;
END;
```

Analysis ▼

%NOTFOUND is a cursor attribute that identifies when no more data is found in the cursor. The preceding example exits the loop when no more data is found. If you omit this statement from the loop, the loop will continue forever.

The WHILE-LOOP executes commands *while* a specified condition is TRUE. When the condition is no longer true, the loop returns control to the next statement.

Input ▼

```
DECLARE
  cursor payment_cursor is
    select cust_id, payment, total_due from payment_table;
  cust_id payment_table.cust_id%TYPE;
  payment payment_table.payment%TYPE;
  total_due payment_table.total_due%TYPE;
BEGIN
  open payment_cursor;
  WHILE payment < total_due LOOP
    FETCH payment_cursor into cust_id, payment, total_due;
    EXIT WHEN payment_cursor%NOTFOUND;
    insert into underpay_table
    values (cust_id, 'STILL OWES');
END LOOP;
  close payment_cursor;
END;
```

26

Analysis ▼

The preceding example uses the WHILE-LOOP to scroll the cursor and to execute the commands within the loop as long as the condition payment < total_due is met.

You can use the FOR-LOOP in the previous block to implicitly fetch the current row of the cursor into the defined variables.

Input ▼

```
DECLARE
  CURSOR PAYMENT_CURSOR IS
    SELECT CUST_ID, PAYMENT, TOTAL_DUE FROM PAYMENT_TABLE;
  CUST_ID PAYMENT_TABLE.CUST_ID%TYPE;
  PAYMENT PAYMENT_TABLE.PAYMENT%TYPE;
  TOTAL_DUE PAYMENT_TABLE.TOTAL_DUE%TYPE;
BEGIN
  OPEN PAYMENT_CURSOR;
  FOR PAY_REC IN PAYMENT_CURSOR LOOP
    IF PAY_REC.PAYMENT < PAY_REC.TOTAL_DUE THEN
      INSERT INTO UNDERPAY_TABLE
      VALUES (PAY_REC.CUST_ID, 'STILL OWES');
    END IF;
  END LOOP;
  CLOSE PAYMENT_CURSOR;
END;
```

Analysis ▼

This example uses the FOR-LOOP to scroll the cursor. The FOR-LOOP is performing an implicit FETCH, which is omitted this time. Also, notice that the %NOTFOUND attribute has been omitted. This attribute is implied with the FOR-LOOP; therefore, this and the previous example yield the same basic results.

The EXCEPTION Section

The EXCEPTION section is an optional part in any PL/SQL block. If this section is omitted and errors are encountered, the block will be terminated. Some errors that are encountered may not justify the immediate termination of a block, so the EXCEPTION section can be used to handle specified errors or user-defined exceptions in an orderly manner. Exceptions can be user-defined, although many exceptions are predefined by Oracle.

An *exception* is an error that is raised during processing when running a PL/SQL program.

Raising Exceptions

Exceptions are raised in a block by using the command RAISE. Exceptions can be raised explicitly by the programmer, whereas internal database errors are automatically, or implicitly, raised by the database server.

Syntax ▼

```
BEGIN
  DECLARE
    exception_name EXCEPTION;
  BEGIN
    IF condition THEN
      RAISE exception_name;
    END IF;
  EXCEPTION
    WHEN exception_name THEN
      statement;
  END;
END;
```

Analysis ▼

This block shows the fundamentals of explicitly raising an exception. First, exception_name is declared using the EXCEPTION statement. In the PROCEDURE section, the exception is raised using RAISE if a given condition is met. The RAISE then references the EXCEPTION section of the block, where the appropriate action is taken.

Handling Exceptions

The preceding example handled an exception in the EXCEPTION section of the block. Errors are easily handled in PL/SQL, and by using exceptions, the PL/SQL block can continue to run with errors or terminate gracefully.

26

Syntax ▼

```
EXCEPTION
  WHEN exception1 THEN
    statement1;
  WHEN exception2 THEN
    statement2;
  WHEN OTHERS THEN
    statement3;
```

Analysis ▼

This example shows how the EXCEPTION section might look if you have more than one exception. This example expects two exceptions (exception1 and exception2) when running this block. The WHEN OTHERS command tells statement3 to execute if any other exceptions occur while the block is being processed. WHEN OTHERS gives you control over any errors that might occur within the block.

Inserting Comments

What would a program be without comments? Programming languages provide commands that enable you to place comments within your code, and PL/SQL is no exception. The comments after each line in the preceding sample block structure describe each command. The accepted comments in PL/SQL are as follows:

Syntax ▼

```
-- This is a one-line comment.

/* This is a
multiple-line comment.*/
```

Executing a PL/SQL Block

PL/SQL statements are normally created using a host editor and are executed like normal SQL script files. PL/SQL uses semicolons to terminate each statement in a block—from variable assignments to data-manipulation commands. The forward slash (/) is mainly associated with SQL script files, but PL/SQL also uses the forward slash to terminate a block in a script file. The easiest way to start a PL/SQL block is by issuing the START command, or @.

Your PL/SQL script file might look like this:

Syntax ▼

```
/* This file is called proc1.sql */
BEGIN
  DECLARE
    ...
  BEGIN
    ...
    statements;
    ...
  EXCEPTION
    ...
  END;
END;
/
```

You execute your PL/SQL script file as follows:

Input ▼

```
SQL> start proc1    or
SQL> @PROC1
```

> PL/SQL script files can be executed using the START command or the character @. PL/SQL script files can also be called within other PL/SQL files, shell scripts, or other programs.

Displaying Output to the User

Particularly when handling exceptions, you might want to display output to keep users informed about what is taking place. You can display output to convey information, and you can display your own customized error messages, which will probably make more sense to the user than an error number. Perhaps you want the user to contact the database administrator if an error occurs during processing, rather than to see the exact message.

PL/SQL does not provide a direct method for displaying output as a part of its syntax, but it does allow you to call a package that serves this function from within the block. The package is called DBMS_OUTPUT.

Input ▼

```
EXCEPTION
  WHEN zero_divide THEN
    DBMS_OUTPUT.put_line('ERROR:  DIVISOR IS ZERO.  SEE YOUR DBA.');
```

26

Analysis ▼

ZERO_DIVIDE is a predefined Oracle exception. Most of the common errors that occur during program processing will be predefined as exceptions and are raised implicitly (which means that you don't have to raise the error in the PROCEDURE section of the block).

If this exception is encountered during block processing, the user would see

Output ▼

```
ERROR:  DIVISOR IS ZERO.  SEE YOUR DBA.
PL/SQL procedure successfully completed.
```

Doesn't that message look friendlier than this:

Output ▼

```
ERROR at line 1:
ORA-01476: divisor is equal to zero
ORA-06512: at line 20
```

Transactional Control in PL/SQL

In Lesson 14, "Controlling Transactions," we discussed the transactional control commands COMMIT, ROLLBACK, and SAVEPOINT. These commands allow the programmer to control when transactions are actually written to the database, how often, and when they should be undone.

Syntax ▼

```
BEGIN
  DECLARE
    ...
  BEGIN
    statements...
    IF condition THEN
      COMMIT;
    ELSE
      ROLLBACK;
    END IF;
    ...
  EXCEPTION
    ...
  END;
END;
```

The good thing about PL/SQL is that you can automate the use of transactional control commands instead of constantly monitoring large transactions, which can be very tedious.

Putting Everything Together

So far, you have been introduced to PL/SQL, have become familiar with the supported data types, and are familiar with the major features of a PL/SQL block. You know how to declare local variables, constants, and cursors. You have also seen how to embed SQL in the PROCEDURE section, manipulate cursors, and raise exceptions. When a cursor has been raised, you should have a basic understanding of how to handle it in the EXCEPTION section of the block.

Now you are ready to work with some practical examples and create blocks from BEGIN to END. By the end of this section, you should fully understand how the parts of a PL/SQL block interact with each other.

Sample Tables and Data

We will be using two tables to create PL/SQL blocks. PAYMENT_TABLE identifies a customer, how much she has paid, and the total amount due. PAY_STATUS_TABLE does not yet contain any data. Data will be inserted into PAY_STATUS_TABLE according to certain conditions in the PAYMENT_TABLE.

Input/Output ▼

```
SQL> SELECT *
  2  FROM PAYMENT_TABLE;

CUSTOMER  PAYMENT  TOTAL_DUE
--------  -------  ---------
ABC         90.50     150.99
AAA         79.00      79.00
BBB        950.00    1000.00
CCC         27.50      27.50
DDD        350.00     500.95
EEE         67.89      67.89
FFF        555.55     455.55
GGG        122.36     122.36
HHH         26.75       0.00
9 rows selected.

SQL> DESCRIBE PAY_STATUS_TABLE
```

Name	Null?	Type
CUST_ID	NOT NULL	CHAR(3)
STATUS	NOT NULL	VARCHAR2(15)
AMT_OWED		NUMBER(8,2)
AMT_CREDIT		NUMBER(8,2)

Analysis ▼

DESCRIBE is an Oracle SQL command that displays the structure of a table without having to query the data dictionary. DESCRIBE and other Oracle SQL*Plus commands are covered on Lesson 25, "Using Oracle SQL*Plus to Satisfy Reporting Needs."

26

A Simple PL/SQL Block

This is how the PL/SQL script (block1.sql) file looks:

Input ▼

```
SET SERVEROUTPUT ON
BEGIN
  DECLARE
    AMTZERO EXCEPTION;
    CCUSTID PAYMENT_TABLE.CUST_ID%TYPE;
    FPAYMENT PAYMENT_TABLE.PAYMENT%TYPE;
    FTOTALDUE PAYMENT_TABLE.TOTAL_DUE%TYPE;
    CURSOR PAYMENT_CURSOR IS
      SELECT CUST_ID, PAYMENT, TOTAL_DUE
      FROM PAYMENT_TABLE;
    FOVERPAID NUMBER(8,2);
    FUNDERPAID NUMBER(8,2);
  BEGIN
    OPEN PAYMENT_CURSOR;
    LOOP
      FETCH PAYMENT_CURSOR INTO
        CCUSTID, FPAYMENT, FTOTALDUE;
      EXIT WHEN PAYMENT_CURSOR%NOTFOUND;
      IF ( FTOTALDUE = 0 ) THEN
        RAISE AMTZERO;
      END IF;
      IF ( FPAYMENT > FTOTALDUE ) THEN
        FOVERPAID := FPAYMENT - FTOTALDUE;
        INSERT INTO PAY_STATUS_TABLE (CUST_ID, STATUS, AMT_CREDIT)
        VALUES (CCUSTID, 'OVER PAID', FOVERPAID);
      ELSIF ( FPAYMENT < FTOTALDUE ) THEN
        FUNDERPAID := FTOTALDUE - FPAYMENT;
        INSERT INTO PAY_STATUS_TABLE (CUST_ID, STATUS, AMT_OWED)
        VALUES (CCUSTID, 'STILL OWES', FUNDERPAID);
      ELSE
        INSERT INTO PAY_STATUS_TABLE
        VALUES (CCUSTID, 'PAID IN FULL', NULL, NULL);
      END IF;
    END LOOP;
    CLOSE PAYMENT_CURSOR;
  EXCEPTION
    WHEN AMTZERO THEN
    DBMS_OUTPUT.PUT_LINE('ERROR: AMOUNT IS ZERO. SEE YOUR SUPERVISOR.');
    WHEN OTHERS THEN
    DBMS_OUTPUT.PUT_LINE('ERROR: UNKNOWN ERROR. SEE THE DBA');
  END;
END;
/
```

Analysis ▼

The DECLARE section defines six local variables, as well as a cursor called payment_cursor. The PROCEDURE section starts with the second BEGIN statement in which the first step is to open the cursor and start a loop. The FETCH command passes the current values in the cursor into the variables that were defined in the DECLARE section. As long as the loop finds records in the cursor, the statement compares the amount paid by a customer to the total amount due. Overpayments and underpayments are calculated according to the amount paid, and we use those calculated amounts to insert values into the PAY_STATUS_TABLE. The loop terminates, and the cursor closes. The EXCEPTION section handles errors that might occur during processing.

Now start the PL/SQL script file and see what happens.

Input/Output ▼

```
SQL> @BLOCK1

Input truncated to 1 characters
ERROR: amount is Zero. See your supervisor.
PL/SQL procedure successfully completed.
```

Now that you know an incorrect amount appears in the total_due column, you can fix the amount and run the script again.

Input/Output ▼

```
SQL> UPDATE PAYMENT_TABLE
  2  SET TOTAL_DUE = 26.75
  3  WHERE CUST_ID = 'HHH';

1 row updated.

SQL> COMMIT;

Commit complete.

SQL> TRUNCATE TABLE PAY_STATUS_TABLE;

Table truncated.
```

26

NOTE

This example truncates the PAY_STATUS_TABLE to clear the table's contents; the next run of the statement will repopulate the table. You might want to add the TRUNCATE TABLE statement to your PL/SQL block.

Input/Output ▼

```
SQL> @BLOCK1

Input truncated to 1 characters
PL/SQL procedure successfully completed.
```

Now you can select from the PAY_STATUS_TABLE and see the payment status of each customer.

Input/Output ▼

```
SQL> SELECT *
  2  FROM PAY_STATUS_TABLE
  3  ORDER BY STATUS;

CUSTOMER STATUS          AMT_OWED AMT_CREDIT
-------- --------------- -------- ----------
FFF      Over Paid                    100.00
AAA      Paid in Full
CCC      Paid in Full
EEE      Paid in Full
GGG      Paid in Full
HHH      Paid in Full
ABC      Still Owes         60.49
DDD      Still Owes        150.95
BBB      Still Owes         50.00
9 rows selected.
```

A row was inserted into PAY_STATUS_TABLE for every row of data that is contained in the PAYMENT_TABLE. If the customer paid more than the amount due, the difference was input into the amt_credit column. If the customer paid less than the amount owed, an entry was made in the amt_owed column. If the customer was paid in full, no dollar amount was inserted in either of the two columns.

A More Extended Example of a PL/SQL Block

This example uses a table called PAY_TABLE:

Input/Output ▼

```
SQL> DESC PAY_TABLE

 Name                            Null?    Type
 ------------------------------- -------- ----
 NAME                            NOT NULL VARCHAR2(20)
 PAY_TYPE                        NOT NULL VARCHAR2(8)
 PAY_RATE                        NOT NULL NUMBER(8,2)
 EFF_DATE                        NOT NULL DATE
 PREV_PAY                                 NUMBER(8,2)
```

First, take a look at the data:

Input/Output ▼

```
SQL> SELECT *
  2  FROM PAY_TABLE
  3  ORDER BY PAY_TYPE, PAY_RATE DESC;

NAME                  PAY_TYPE  PAY_RATE EFF_DATE  PREV_PAY
--------------------  --------  -------- --------- ---------
SANDRA SAMUELS        HOURLY       12.50 01-JAN-99
ROBERT BOBAY          HOURLY       11.50 15-MAY-98
KEITH JONES           HOURLY       10.00 31-OCT-99
SUSAN WILLIAMS        HOURLY        9.75 01-MAY-99
CHRISSY ZOES          SALARY    50000.00 01-JAN-99
CLODE EVANS           SALARY    42150.00 01-MAR-99
JOHN SMITH            SALARY    35000.00 15-JUN-98
KEVIN TROLLBERG       SALARY    27500.00 15-JUN-98
8 rows selected.
```

Situation: Sales are up. Any individual who has not had a pay increase for six months (180 days) will receive a raise effective today. All eligible hourly employees will receive a 4% increase, and eligible salary employees will receive a 5% increase.

Today is

Input/Output ▼

```
SQL> SELECT SYSDATE
  2  FROM DUAL;

SYSDATE
---------
20-DEC-08
1 rows selected.
```

Before examining the next PL/SQL block, we will perform a manual select from the PAY_TABLE that flags individuals who should receive a raise.

Input/Output ▼

```
SQL> SELECT NAME, PAY_TYPE, PAY_RATE, EFF_DATE,
  2         'YES' DUE
  3  FROM PAY_TABLE
  4  WHERE EFF_DATE < SYSDATE - 180
  5  UNION ALL
  6  SELECT NAME, PAY_TYPE, PAY_RATE, EFF_DATE,
  7         'NO' DUE
```

26

```
 8  FROM PAY_TABLE
 9  WHERE EFF_DATE >= SYSDATE - 180
10  ORDER BY 2, 3 DESC;
```

```
NAME                     PAY_TYPE  PAY_RATE  EFF_DATE   DUE
--------------------     --------  --------  --------   ---
SANDRA SAMUELS           HOURLY       12.50  01-JAN-99  No
ROBERT BOBAY             HOURLY       11.50  15-MAY-98  YES
KEITH JONES              HOURLY       10.00  31-OCT-98  YES
SUSAN WILLIAMS           HOURLY        9.75  01-MAY-99  No
CHRISSY ZOES             SALARY    50000.00  01-JAN-99  No
CLODE EVANS              SALARY    42150.00  01-MAR-99  No
JOHN SMITH               SALARY    35000.00  15-JUN-98  YES
KEVIN TROLLBERG          SALARY    27500.00  15-JUN-98  YES
8 rows selected.
```

The DUE column identifies individuals who should be eligible for a raise. Here's the PL/SQL script:

Input ▼

```
SET SERVEROUTPUT ON
BEGIN
  DECLARE
    UNKNOWNPAYTYPE EXCEPTION;
    CURSOR PAY_CURSOR IS
      SELECT NAME, PAY_TYPE, PAY_RATE, EFF_DATE,
             SYSDATE, ROWID
      FROM PAY_TABLE;
    INDREC PAY_CURSOR%ROWTYPE;
    COLDDATE DATE;
    FNEWPAY NUMBER(8,2);
  BEGIN
    OPEN PAY_CURSOR;
    LOOP
    FETCH PAY_CURSOR INTO INDREC;
    EXIT WHEN PAY_CURSOR%NOTFOUND;
    COLDDATE := SYSDATE - 180;
    IF (INDREC.PAY_TYPE = 'SALARY') THEN
      FNEWPAY := INDREC.PAY_RATE * 1.05;
    ELSIF (INDREC.PAY_TYPE = 'HOURLY') THEN
      FNEWPAY := INDREC.PAY_RATE * 1.04;
    ELSE
      RAISE UNKNOWNPAYTYPE;
    END IF;
    IF (INDREC.EFF_DATE < COLDDATE) THEN
      UPDATE PAY_TABLE
      SET PAY_RATE = FNEWPAY,
          PREV_PAY = INDREC.PAY_RATE,
          EFF_DATE = INDREC.SYSDATE
```

```
      WHERE ROWID = INDREC.ROWID;
      COMMIT;
    END IF;
    END LOOP;
    CLOSE PAY_CURSOR;
  EXCEPTION
    WHEN UNKNOWNPAYTYPE THEN
      DBMS_OUTPUT.PUT_LINE('=======================');
      DBMS_OUTPUT.PUT_LINE('ERROR: ABORTING PROGRAM.');
      DBMS_OUTPUT.PUT_LINE('UNKNOWN PAY TYPE FOR NAME');
    WHEN OTHERS THEN
      DBMS_OUTPUT.PUT_LINE('ERROR DURING PROCESSING.  SEE THE DBA.');
    END;
END;
/
```

Are you sure that you want to give four employees a pay raise? (The final SELECT statement has four Yes values in the DUE column.) Why not…let's give all four employees a raise. You can apply the appropriate pay increases by executing the PL/SQL script file, named block2.sql:

Input/Output ▼

```
SQL> @BLOCK2

Input truncated to 1 characters
PL/SQL procedure successfully completed.
```

You can do a quick SELECT to verify that the changes have been made to the pay_rate of the appropriate individuals:

Input/Output ▼

```
SQL> SELECT *
  2  FROM PAY_TABLE
  3  ORDER BY PAY_TYPE, PAY_RATE DESC;
```

NAME	PAY_TYPE	PAY_RATE	EFF_DATE	PREV_PAY
SANDRA SAMUELS	HOURLY	12.50	01-JAN-99	
ROBERT BOBAY	HOURLY	11.96	20-MAY-99	11.5
KEITH JONES	HOURLY	10.40	20-MAY-99	10
SUSAN WILLIAMS	HOURLY	9.75	01-MAY-99	
CHRISSY ZOES	SALARY	50000.00	01-JAN-99	
CLODE EVANS	SALARY	42150.00	01-MAR-99	
JOHN SMITH	SALARY	36750.00	20-MAY-99	35000
KEVIN TROLLBERG	SALARY	28875.00	20-MAY-99	27500

```
8 rows selected.
```

26

Four employees received a pay increase. If you compare this output to the output of the original SELECT statement, you can see the changes. The current pay rate was updated to reflect the pay increase, the original pay rate was inserted into the previous pay column, and the effective date was updated to today's date. No action was taken on those individuals who did not qualify for a pay increase.

Wait—you didn't get a chance to see how the defined EXCEPTION works. You can test the EXCEPTION section by inserting an invalid PAY_TYPE into PAY_TABLE.

Input/Output ▼

```
SQL> INSERT INTO PAY_TABLE VALUES
  2  ('JEFF JENNINGS','WEEKLY',71.50,'01-JAN-99',NULL);

1 row created.
```

The moment of truth:

Input/Output ▼

```
SQL> @BLOCK2

Input truncated to 1 characters
========================
ERROR: Aborting program.
Unknown Pay Type for:  JEFF JENNINGS
PL/SQL procedure successfully completed.
```

An error message told you that JEFF JENNINGS had a pay_type with a value other than SALARY or HOURLY. That is, the exception was handled with an error message.

Using Stored Procedures, Packages, and Triggers

Using PL/SQL, you can create stored objects to eliminate having to constantly enter monotonous code. Procedures are simply blocks of code that perform some sort of specific function. Related procedures can be combined and stored together in an object called a *package*. A trigger is a database object that is used with other transactions. You might have a trigger on a table called ORDERS that will insert data into a HISTORY table each time the ORDERS table receives data. The basic syntax of these objects follows.

Sample Procedure

Procedures are often used to encapsulate more complex queries so that the logic they facilitate is easier to deploy. The following demonstrates the basic syntax of a procedure.

Syntax ▼

```
PROCEDURE procedure_name IS
  variable1 datatype;
  ...
BEGIN
  statement1;
  ...
EXCEPTION
  when ...
END procedure_name;
```

One of the previous PL/SQL blocks has been converted into a procedure as follows. The only difference from the previous example is the first line of code.

Input ▼

```
CREATE PROCEDURE P_PAYMENTS IS
BEGIN
  DECLARE
    AMTZERO EXCEPTION;
    CCUSTID PAYMENT_TABLE.CUST_ID%TYPE;
    FPAYMENT PAYMENT_TABLE.PAYMENT%TYPE;
    FTOTALDUE PAYMENT_TABLE.TOTAL_DUE%TYPE;
    CURSOR PAYMENT_CURSOR IS
      SELECT CUST_ID, PAYMENT, TOTAL_DUE
      FROM PAYMENT_TABLE;
    FOVERPAID NUMBER(8,2);
    FUNDERPAID NUMBER(8,2);
  BEGIN
    OPEN PAYMENT_CURSOR;
    LOOP
      FETCH PAYMENT_CURSOR INTO
        CCUSTID, FPAYMENT, FTOTALDUE;
      EXIT WHEN PAYMENT_CURSOR%NOTFOUND;
      IF ( FTOTALDUE = 0 ) THEN
        RAISE AMTZERO;
      END IF;
      IF ( FPAYMENT > FTOTALDUE ) THEN
        FOVERPAID := FPAYMENT - FTOTALDUE;
        INSERT INTO PAY_STATUS_TABLE (CUST_ID, STATUS, AMT_CREDIT)
        VALUES (CCUSTID, 'OVER PAID', FOVERPAID);
      ELSIF ( FPAYMENT < FTOTALDUE ) THEN
        FUNDERPAID := FTOTALDUE - FPAYMENT;
```

26

```
      INSERT INTO PAY_STATUS_TABLE (CUST_ID, STATUS, AMT_OWED)
      VALUES (CCUSTID, 'STILL OWES', FUNDERPAID);
    ELSE
      INSERT INTO PAY_STATUS_TABLE
      VALUES (CCUSTID, 'PAID IN FULL', NULL, NULL);
    END IF;
  END LOOP;
  CLOSE PAYMENT_CURSOR;
EXCEPTION
  WHEN AMTZERO THEN
  DBMS_OUTPUT.PUT_LINE('ERROR: AMOUNT IS ZERO. SEE YOUR SUPERVISOR.');
  WHEN OTHERS THEN
  DBMS_OUTPUT.PUT_LINE('ERROR: UNKNOWN ERROR. SEE THE DBA');
  END;
END;
/
```

Sample Package

Packages are a further way in which you can encapsulate complex code. It is a group of procedures, functions, variables, and SQL statements that form a single related group of objects. The following syntax demonstrates the basic package implementation:

Input ▼

```
CREATE PACKAGE package_name AS
  PROCEDURE procedure1 (global_variable1 datatype, ...);
  PROCEDURE procedure2 (global_variable1 datatype, ...);
END package_name;
CREATE PACKAGE BODY package_name AS
  PROCEDURE procedure1 (global_variable1 datatype, ...) IS
    BEGIN
      statement1;
      ...
    END procedure1;
  PROCEDURE procedure2 (global_variable1 datatype, ...) IS
    BEGIN
      statement1;
      ...
  END procedure2;
END package_name;
```

Sample Trigger

The basis of database programming deals with set operations. However, often you need also to perform row-based operations as well. This is where the trigger comes in. It provides a methodology for you to perform row-based operations. The following code demonstrates the basic syntax of a trigger.

Input ▼

```
CREATE TRIGGER trigger_name
  AFTER UPDATE OF column ON table_name
  FOR EACH ROW
BEGIN
  statement1;
  ...
END;
```

The following example uses a trigger to insert a row of data into a transaction table when a user updates the PAY_TABLE table. The TRANSACTION table looks like this:

Input/Output ▼

```
SQL> DESCRIBE TRANS_TABLE
```

Name	Null?	Type
ACTION		VARCHAR2(10)
NAME		VARCHAR2(20)
PREV_PAY		NUMBER(8,2)
CURR_PAY		NUMBER(8,2)
EFF_DATE		DATE

Here's a sample row of data:

Input/Output ▼

```
SQL> SELECT *
  2  FROM PAY_TABLE
  3  WHERE NAME = 'JEFF JENNINGS';
```

NAME	PAY_TYPE	PAY_RATE	EFF_DATE	PREV_PAY
JEFF JENNINGS	WEEKLY	71.50	01-JAN-99	

```
1 row selected.
```

Now, create a trigger:

Input/Output ▼

```
SQL> CREATE TRIGGER PAY_TRIGGER
  2    AFTER UPDATE ON PAY_TABLE
  3    FOR EACH ROW
  4  BEGIN
  5    INSERT INTO TRANS_TABLE VALUES
  6    ('PAY CHANGE', :NEW.NAME, :OLD.PAY_RATE,
```

26

```
7      :NEW.PAY_RATE, :NEW.EFF_DATE);
8  END;
9  /
```

Trigger created.

The last step performs an update on PAY_TABLE, which should cause the trigger to be executed.

Input/Output ▼

```
SQL> UPDATE PAY_TABLE
  2  SET PAY_RATE = 15.50,
  3      EFF_DATE = SYSDATE
  4  WHERE NAME = 'JEFF JENNINGS';

1 row updated.

SQL> SELECT *
  2  FROM PAY_TABLE
  3  WHERE NAME = 'JEFF JENNINGS';

NAME                   PAY_TYPE  PAY_RATE  EFF_DATE    PREV_PAY
-------------------    --------  --------  ---------   ---------
JEFF JENNINGS          WEEKLY       15.50  20-MAY-99

1 row selected.


SQL> SELECT *
  2  FROM TRANS_TABLE;

ACTION       NAME                 PREV_PAY   CURR_PAY  EFF_DATE
----------   ------------------   --------   --------  ---------
PAY CHANGE   JEFF JENNINGS            71.5       15.5  20-MAY-99

1 row selected.
```

PREV_PAY is null in PAY_TABLE, but PREV_PAY appears in TRANS_TABLE. This approach isn't as confusing as it sounds. PAY_TABLE does not need an entry for PREV_PAY because the PAY_RATE of 71.50 per hour was obviously an erroneous amount. Rather, we inserted the value for PREV_PAY in TRANS_TABLE because the update was a transaction, and the purpose of TRANS_PAY is to keep a record of all transactions against PAY_TABLE.

<table>
<tr><td>**NOTE**</td><td>If you are familiar with network technologies, you might notice similarities between PL/SQL and Java stored procedures. However, some differences should be noted. PL/SQL is an enhancement of standard SQL because it implements the commands of a procedural language. Java, which is more advanced than PL/SQL, allows programmers to write more complex programs than are possible with PL/SQL. PL/SQL is based on the database-intensive functionality of SQL; Java is more appropriate for CPU-intensive programs. Most procedural languages, such as PL/SQL, are developed specifically for the appropriate platform. As procedural language technology evolves, a higher level of standardization will be enforced across platforms.</td></tr>
</table>

Summary

PL/SQL extends the functionality of standard SQL. The basic components of PL/SQL perform the same types of functions as a third-generation language. The use of local variables supports dynamic code; that is, values within a block may change from time to time according to user input, specified conditions, or the contents of a cursor. PL/SQL uses standard procedural language program control statements. IF...THEN statements and loops enable you to search for specific conditions; you can also use loops to scroll through the contents of a defined cursor.

Errors that occur during the processing of any program are a major concern. PL/SQL enables you to use exceptions to control the behavior of a program that encounters either syntax errors or logical errors. Many exceptions are predefined, such as a divide-by-zero error. Errors can be raised any time during processing according to specified conditions and may be handled any way the PL/SQL programmer desires.

26

This lesson also introduces some practical uses of PL/SQL. Database objects such as triggers, stored procedures, and packages can automate many job functions. This lesson's examples apply some of the concepts that were covered in previous lessons.

Q&A

Q Does this lesson cover everything I need to know about PL/SQL?

A Most definitely not. The introduction just scratches the surface of one of the greatest concepts of SQL. We have simply tried to highlight some of the major features to give you a basic knowledge of PL/SQL. We recommend *Sams Teach Yourself PL/SQL in 21 Days* by Jonathan Gennick and Tom Luers (ISBN 0-672-31798-2) for much more in-depth information on PL/SQL.

Q Can I get by without using PL/SQL?

A Yes, you can get by, but to achieve the results that you would get with PL/SQL, you might have to spend much more time coding in a third-generation language. If you do not have Oracle, seek your implementation documentation for procedural features like that of PL/SQL.

Q Is PL/SQL standard?

A Not completely. Some facets of PL/SQL, such as triggers, are a part of the newly proposed standard, but some features are specific to Oracle.

Q A cursor seems similar to a view. Is this an accurate comparison?

A Cursors are much like views in that they are both defined by queries. Like views, cursors define a subset of data from the database.

Workshop

The Workshop provides quiz questions to help solidify your understanding of the material covered, as well as exercises to provide you with experience in using what you have learned. Try to answer the quiz and exercise questions before checking the answers in Appendix A, "Answers."

Quiz

1. How is a database trigger used?
2. Can related procedures be stored together?
3. True or false: Data Manipulation Language (DML) can be used in a PL/SQL statement.
4. True or false: Data Definition Language (DDL) can be used in a PL/SQL statement.

5. Is the capability of outputting text on the screen contained within a PL/SQL command?

6. List the three major parts of a PL/SQL statement.

7. List the commands associated with cursor control.

Exercises

1. Using the Oracle syntax as shown in this lesson, declare a variable called HourlyPay in which the maximum accepted value is 99.99/hour.

2. Using the Oracle syntax as shown in this lesson, define a cursor whose content is all the data in the CUSTOMER_TABLE, where the CITY is INDIANAPOLIS.

3. Using the Oracle syntax as shown in this lesson, define an exception called UnknownCode.

4. Using the Oracle syntax as shown in this lesson, write a statement that will set the AMT in the AMOUNT_TABLE to 10 if CODE is A, set the AMT to 20 if CODE is B, and raise an exception called UnknownCode if CODE is neither A nor B. The table has one row.

26

LESSON 27

An Introduction to Transact-SQL

This lesson's material covers the Transact-SQL language, which is a supplement to the accepted SQL standard. This lesson's goals are to

- Identify one of the more popular extensions to SQL: Transact-SQL

- Outline the major features of Transact-SQL

- Provide practical examples to give you an understanding of how Transact-SQL is used

An Overview of Transact-SQL

Lesson 19, "Temporary Tables, Stored Procedures, Triggers, and Cursors," briefly covers static SQL. The examples in Lesson 19 depict the use of embedded SQL in third-generation programming languages such as C. With this method of programming, the embedded SQL code does not change and is therefore limited. On the other hand, you can write dynamic SQL to perform the same functions as a procedural programming language and allow conditions to be changed within the SQL code.

As we have mentioned during the discussion of virtually every topic in this book, almost every database vendor has added many extensions to the language. Transact-SQL is the Sybase and Microsoft SQL Server database product. Oracle's product is PL/SQL. Each of these languages contains the complete functionality of everything we have discussed so far. In addition, each product contains many extensions to the ANSI SQL standard.

Extensions to ANSI QL

To illustrate the use of these SQL extensions to create actual programming logic, we are using Microsoft SQL Server's Transact-SQL language. Transact-SQL contains most of the constructs found in third-generation languages (procedural programming languages such as C), as well as some SQL Server–specific features that turn out to be very handy tools for the database programmer. (Other manufacturers' extensions contain many of these features and more.)

Who Uses Transact-SQL?

Everyone reading this book can use Transact-SQL—from casual relational database programmers who occasionally write queries to developers who write applications and create objects such as triggers and stored procedures.

The Basic Components of Transact-SQL

SQL extensions overcome SQL's limits as a procedural language. For example, Transact-SQL enables you to maintain tight control over your database transactions and to write procedural database programs that practically exempt the programmer from exhausting programming tasks.

This lesson covers the following key features of Transact-SQL:

- A wide range of data types to optimize data storage
- Program flow commands such as loops and IF...ELSE statements
- Use of variables in SQL statements

- Summarized reports using computations
- Diagnostic features used to analyze SQL statements
- Many other options to enhance the standard language of SQL

Data Types

In Lesson 9, "Creating and Maintaining Tables," we discussed data types. When creating tables in SQL, you must specify a specific data type for each column.

> NOTE
>
> Data types vary among implementations of SQL because of the way each database server stores data. For instance, Oracle uses certain data types, whereas Microsoft's SQL Server has its own data types.

Microsoft's SQL Server supports the data types described in the next sections.

Character Strings

Character string data types are utilized for storing pure character strings with the following specific types available:

- char stores fixed-length character strings, such as a STATE abbreviation, where the column is always two characters.
- varchar stores variable-length character strings, such as an individual's name, where the exact length of a name is not specified. For example, from AL RAY to WILLIAM STEPHENSON.
- text stores strings with nearly unlimited size, such as a remarks column or description of a type of service.

Numeric Data Types

Numeric data types are designed to hold purely numeric data normally used in calculations. SQL Server provides the following numeric data types:

- int stores integers from -2,147,483,647 to 2,147,483,647.
- smallint stores integers from -32,768 to 32,767.
- tinyint stores integers from 0 to 255.

27

■ `float` expresses numbers as real floating-point numbers with data precisions. Decimals are allowed with these data types. The values range from +2.23E-308 to +1.79E308. (The numeric value to the right of the E in this notation represents the number of times the decimal place is shifted to the right or left, depending on the sign of the number to the right of E. A negative number shifts the decimal place to the left. Scientific notation is used to accommodate very large numeric values.)

■ `real` expresses real numbers with data precisions from +1.18E-38 to +3.40E38.

Date Data Types

Date data types hold date and time specific data. It is important to note that SQL Server does not provide separate date and time types except in SQL Server 2008, which is the latest version. All SQL Server versions provide the following data types:

■ `datetime` values range from Jan 1, 1753 to Dec 31, 9999.

■ `smalldatetime` values range from Jan 1, 1900 to Jun 6, 2079.

Money Data Types

Money data types are special numeric types that are constructed to specifically hold monetary values. SQL Server provides the following types of money data types:

■ `money` stores values up to ±922,337,203,685,477.5808.

■ `smallmoney` stores values up to ±214,748.3647.

Money values are inserted into a table using the dollar sign—for example:

Syntax ▼

```
insert payment_tbl (customer_id, paydate, pay_amt)
values (012845, 'May 1, 1997', $2099.99)
```

Binary Strings

Binary data types are normally used to hold BLOB data for things such as files and images. SQL Server provides for the following binary data types:

■ `binary` stores fixed-length binary strings.

■ `varbinary` stores variable-length binary strings.

■ `image` stores very large binary strings; for example, photographs and other images.

bit: **A Logical Data Type**

The data type bit is often used to flag certain rows of data within a table. The value stored within a column whose data type is bit is either a 1 or 0. For example, the value 1 might signify a true condition, whereas 0 denotes a false condition. The following example uses the bit data type to create a table containing individual test scores:

Syntax ▼

```
create table test_flag
( ind_id int not null,
  test_results int not null,
  result_flag bit not null)
```

The column result_flag is defined as a bit column, where the bit character represents either a pass (true) or fail (false).

Throughout the rest of this lesson, pay attention to the data types used when creating tables and writing Transact-SQL code.

NOTE

The code in this lesson's examples uses both uppercase and lowercase. Although SQL keywords are not case sensitive in most implementations of SQL, always check your implementation.

Accessing the Database with Transact-SQL

All right, enough talk. To actually run this lesson's examples, you will need to build the following database tables in a database named BASEBALL.

27

The BASEBALL Database

The BASEBALL database consists of three tables used to track typical baseball information: the BATTERS table, the PITCHERS table, and the TEAMS table.

The BATTERS Table

The table can be created using the following Transact-SQL statement:

Input ▼

```
1> create database BASEBALL on default
2> go
```

```
1> use BASEBALL
2> go
1> create table BATTERS (
2> NAME char(30),
3> TEAM int,
4> AVERAGE float,
5> HOMERUNS int,
6> RBIS int)
7> go
```

Analysis ▼

Line 1 creates the database. You specify the database BASEBALL and then create the table BATTERS underneath BASEBALL.

Enter the data in Table 27.1 into the BATTERS table.

> **NOTE**
>
> The command go separating each Transact-SQL statement in the preceding example is not part of Transact-SQL. go's purpose is to pass each statement from a front-end application to SQL Server.

Table 27.1   Data for the BATTERS Table

Name	Team	Average	Homeruns	RBIs
Billy Brewster	1	.275	14	46
John Jackson	1	.293	2	29
Phil Hartman	1	.221	13	21
Jim Gehardy	2	.316	29	84
Tom Trawick	2	.258	3	51
Eric Redstone	2	.305	0	28

The PITCHERS Table

The PITCHERS table can be created using the following Transact-SQL statement:

Input ▼

```
1> use BASEBALL
2> go
1> create table PITCHERS (
2> NAME char(30),
3> TEAM int,
```

```
4> WON int,
5> LOST int,
6> ERA float)
7> go
```

Enter the data in Table 27.2 into the PITCHERS table.

Table 27.2   Data for the PITCHERS Table

Name	Team	Won	Lost	Era
Tom Madden	1	7	5	3.46
Bill Witter	1	8	2	2.75
Jeff Knox	2	2	8	4.82
Hank Arnold	2	13	1	1.93
Tim Smythe	3	4	2	2.76

The TEAMS Table

The TEAMS table can be created using the following Transact-SQL statement:

Input ▼

```
1> use BASEBALL
2> go
1> create table TEAMS (
2> TEAM_ID int,
3> CITY char(30),
4> NAME char(30),
5> WON int,
6> LOST int,
7> TOTAL_HOME_ATTENDANCE int,
8> AVG_HOME_ATTENDANCE int)
9> go
```

Enter the data in Table 27.3 into the TEAMS table.

Table 27.3   Data for the TEAMS Table

Team_ID	City	Name	Won	Lost	Total_Home_ Attendance	Avg_Home_ Attendance
1	Portland	Beavers	72	63	1,226,843	19,473
2	Washington	Representatives	50	85	941,228	14,048
3	Tampa	Sharks	99	36	2,028,652	30,278

27

Refer back to Lesson 11, "Manipulating Data," for information regarding populating tables with data. If you have an available SQL Server database, you might want to create the tables and follow along.

Declaring Local Variables

Every programming language enables some method for declaring local (or global) variables that can be used to store data. Transact-SQL is no exception. Declaring a variable using Transact-SQL is an extremely simple procedure. The keyword that must be used is the DECLARE keyword. The syntax looks like this:

Syntax ▼

```
declare @variable_name data_type.
```

To declare a character string variable to store players' names, use the following statement:

Input ▼

```
1> declare @name char(30)
2> go
```

Note the @ symbol before the variable's name. This symbol is required and is used by the query processor to identify variables.

Declaring Global Variables

If you delve further into the Transact-SQL documentation, you will notice that the @@ symbol precedes the names of some system-level variables. This syntax denotes SQL Server global variables that store information.

Declaring your own global variables is particularly useful when using stored procedures. SQL Server also maintains several system global variables. These variables contain information that might be useful to the database system user. Table 27.4 contains the complete list of these variables. The source for this list is the Sybase SQL Server 2005 documentation.

Table 27.4   SQL Server Global Variables

Variable Name	Purpose
@@char_convert	0 if character set conversion is in effect
@@client_csid	Client's character set ID
@@client_csname	Client's character set name

Table 27.4 Continued

Variable Name	Purpose
@@connections	Number of logons since SQL Server was started
@@cpu_busy	Amount of time, in ticks, the CPU has been busy since SQL Server was started
@@error	Contains error status
@@identity	Last value inserted into an identity column
@@idle	Amount of time, in ticks, that SQL Server has been idle since started
@@io_busy	Amount of time, in ticks, that SQL Server has spent doing I/O
@@isolation	Current isolation level of the Transact-SQL program
@@langid	Defines local language ID
@@language	Defines the name of the local language
@@maxcharlen	Maximum length of a character
@@max_connections	Maximum number of connections that can be made with SQL Server
@@ncharsize	Average length of a national character
@@nestlevel	Nesting level of current execution
@@pack_received	Number of input packets read by SQL Server since it was started
@@pack_sent	Number of output packets sent by SQL Server since it was started
@@packet_errors	Number of errors that have occurred since SQL Server was started
@@procid	ID of the currently executing stored procedure
@@rowcount	Number of rows affected by the last command
@@servername	Name of the local SQL Server
@@spid	Process ID number of the current process
@@sqlstatus	Contains status information
@@textsize	Maximum length of text or image data returned with SELECT statement
@@thresh_hysteresis	Change in free space required to activate a threshold
@@timeticks	Number of microseconds per tick
@@total_errors	Number of errors that have occurred while reading or writing
@@total_read	Number of disk reads since SQL Server was started
@@total_write	Number of disk writes since SQL Server was started
@@tranchained	Current transaction mode of the Transact-SQL program
@@trancount	Nesting level of transactions
@@transtate	Current state of a transaction after a statement executes
@@version	Date of the current version of SQL Server

27

Using Variables

The DECLARE keyword enables you to declare several variables with a single statement (although this device can sometimes look confusing when you look at your code later). An example of this type of statement appears here:

Input ▼

```
1> declare @batter_name char(30), @team int, @average float
2> go
```

The following sections explain how to use variables to perform useful programming operations.

Using Variables to Store Data

Variables are available only within the current statement block. To execute a block of statements using the Transact-SQL language, use the go statement to terminate the block. (Oracle uses the semicolon for the same purpose.) The scope of a variable refers to the use of the variable within the current Transact-SQL statement.

You cannot initialize variables simply by using the = sign. Try the following statement and note that an error will be returned.

Input ▼

```
1> declare @name char(30)
2> @name = 'Billy Brewster'
3> go
```

Analysis ▼

You should have received an error informing you of the improper syntax used in line 2. The proper way to initialize a variable is to use the SET command. (Yes, the same command you have already mastered.) Repeat the preceding example using the correct syntax:

Input ▼

```
1> declare @name char(30)
2> SET @name = 'Billy Brewster'
3> go
```

Analysis ▼

This statement was executed correctly, and if you had inserted additional statements before executing the go statement, the @name variable could have been used.

Retrieving Data into Local Variables

Variables often store data that has been retrieved from the database. They can be used with common SQL commands, such as SELECT, INSERT, UPDATE, and DELETE. Example 27.1 illustrates the use of variables in this manner.

Example 27.1

This example retrieves the name of the player in the BASEBALL database who has the highest batting average and plays for the Portland Beavers.

Input ▼

```
1> declare @team_id int, @player_name char(30), @max_avg float
2> select @team_id = TEAM_ID from TEAMS where CITY = 'Portland'
3> select @max_avg = max(AVERAGE) from BATTERS where TEAM = @team_id
4> select @player_name = NAME from BATTERS where AVERAGE = @max_avg
5> go
```

Analysis ▼

This example was broken into three queries to illustrate the use of variables. The first query selects the TEAM_ID into the team_id variable from the TEAMS table for the city of Portland. The second query selects the highest average from the BATTERS table into the max_avg variable, based on the new value of the team_id derived from the first query. The third query uses the value of max_avg to get the player's name from the BATTERS table.

The PRINT Command

One other useful feature of Transact-SQL is the PRINT command. This feature enables you to print output to the display device. The PRINT command has the following syntax:

Syntax ▼

```
PRINT character_string
```

Although PRINT displays only character strings, Transact-SQL provides a number of useful functions that can convert different data types to strings (and vice versa).

Example 27.2

Example 27.2 repeats Example 27.1, but prints the player's name at the end.

27

Input ▼

```
1> declare @team_id int, @player_name char(30), @max_avg float
2> select @team_id = TEAM_ID from TEAMS where CITY = 'Portland'
3> select @max_avg = max(AVERAGE) from BATTERS where TEAM = @team_id
4> select @player_name = NAME from BATTERS where AVERAGE = @max_avg
5> print @player_name
6> go
```

Analysis ▼

Note that a variable can be used within a WHERE clause (or any other clause) just as if it were a constant value. The last example did not accomplish much of anything. In this example, we have added the PRINT command to display the final value derived from the group of queries.

Establishing Flow Control

Probably the most powerful set of Transact-SQL features involves its capability to control program flow. *Flow control* is the programmer's capability to control each step the program takes in processing data. If you have programmed with other popular languages such as C, COBOL, Pascal, and Visual Basic, you are probably already familiar with control commands such as IF...THEN statements and with loops, which enable you to force a series of statements to be executed based on certain criteria that you define within the program. This section contains some of the major commands that allow you to enforce program flow control.

BEGIN **and** END **Statements**

Transact-SQL uses the BEGIN and END statements to signify the beginning and ending points of code blocks. Other languages use brackets ({}) or some other operator to signify the beginning and ending points of functional groups of code. These statements are often combined with IF...ELSE statements and WHILE loops. Here is an example block using BEGIN and END:

Syntax ▼

```
BEGIN
   statement1
   statement2
   statement3...
END
```

IF...ELSE **Statements**

One of the most basic programming constructs is the IF...ELSE statement. Nearly every programming language supports this construct, and it is extremely useful for checking the value of data retrieved from the database. The Transact-SQL syntax for the IF...ELSE statement looks like this:

Syntax ▼

```
if (condition)
begin
     (statement block)
end
else if (condition)
begin
     statement block)
end
.
.
.
else
begin
     (statement block)
end
```

Analysis ▼

Note that for each condition that might be true, a new BEGIN/END block of statements was entered. Also, it is considered good programming practice to indent statement blocks a set amount of spaces, and to maintain this number of spaces throughout your application. This visual convention greatly improves the readability of the program and cuts down on silly errors that are often caused by simply misreading the code.

Example 27.3

Example 27.3 extends Example 27.2 by checking the player's batting average. If the player's average is over .300, the owner wants to give him a raise. Otherwise, the owner couldn't really care less about the player!

27

Input ▼

```
1> declare @team_id int, @player_name char(30), @max_avg float
2> select @team_id = TEAM_ID from TEAMS where CITY = 'Portland'
3> select @max_avg = max(AVERAGE) from BATTERS where TEAM = @team_id
4> select @player_name = NAME from BATTERS where AVERAGE = @max_avg
5> if (@max_avg > .300)
6> begin
```

```
7>      print @player_name
8>      print 'Give this guy a raise! '
9> end
10> else
11> begin
12>      print @player_name
13>      print 'Come back when you''re hitting better! '
14> end
15> go
```

Example 27.3 uses the IF...ELSE statement to evaluate conditions within the statement. If the value of max_avg is greater than .300, the text "Give this guy a raise!" is printed; alternative text is printed under any other conditions (ELSE).

Example 27.4

This new IF statement enables you to add some programming logic to the simple BASE-BALL database queries. Example 27.4 adds an embedded IF...ELSE branch to the code in Example 27.3.

Input ▼

```
1> declare @team_id int, @player_name char(30), @max_avg float
2> select @team_id = TEAM_ID from TEAMS where CITY = 'Portland'
3> select @max_avg = max(AVERAGE) from BATTERS where TEAM = @team_id
4> select @player_name = NAME from BATTERS where AVERAGE = @max_avg
5> if (@max_avg > .300)
6> begin
7>      print @player_name
8>      print 'Give this guy a raise! '
9> end
10> else if (@max_avg > .275)
11> begin
12>      print @player_name
13>      print 'Not bad.  Here's a bonus! '
14> end
15> else
16> begin
17>      print @player_name
18>      print 'Come back when you're hitting better! '
19> end
20> go
```

Here we have added another condition to the IF...THEN statement in the previous example to accommodate any batting averages between .275 and .300. If max_avg falls within this range, "Not bad. Here's a bonus!" is printed.

Transact-SQL also enables you to check for a condition associated with an IF statement. These functions can test for certain conditions or values. If the function returns TRUE, the IF branch is executed. Otherwise, if provided, the ELSE branch is executed, as you saw in the previous example.

The EXISTS Condition

The EXISTS keyword ensures that a value is returned from a SELECT statement. If a value is returned, the IF statement is executed. Example 27.5 illustrates this logic.

Example 27.5

In this example, the EXISTS keyword evaluates a condition in the IF statement. The condition is specified by using a SELECT statement.

Input ▼

```
1> if exists (select * from TEAMS where TEAM_ID > 5)
2> begin
3>      print 'IT EXISTS!! '
4> end
5> else
6> begin
7>      print 'DOES NOT EXIST '
8> end
```

Testing a Query's Result

The IF statement can also test the result returned from a SELECT query. Example 27.6 implements this feature to check for the maximum batting average among players.

Example 27.6

This example is similar to Example 27.5 in that it uses the SELECT statement to define a condition. This time, however, we are testing the condition with the greater than sign (>).

Input ▼

```
1> if (select max(AVERAGE) from BATTERS) > .400
2> begin
3>      print 'UNBELIEVABLE!!'
4> end
5> else
6>      print 'TED WILLIAMS IS GETTING LONELY!'
7> end
```

27

Analysis ▼

This program uses the MAX function to look at all rows of data in the BATTERS table for the highest average. If the highest batting average is greater than .400, "UNBELIEVABLE!" is printed. Otherwise, "TED WILLIAMS IS GETTING LONELY!" is printed.

We recommend experimenting with your SQL implementation's IF statement. Think of several conditions you would be interested in checking in the BASEBALL (or any other) database. Run some queries making use of the IF statement to familiarize yourself with its use.

The WHILE Loop

Another popular programming construct that Transact-SQL supports is the WHILE loop. This command has the following syntax:

Syntax ▼

```
WHILE logical_expression
     statement(s)
```

Example 27.7

The WHILE loop continues to loop through its statements until the logical expression it is checking returns a FALSE. This example uses a simple WHILE loop to increment a local variable (named COUNT).

Input ▼

```
1> declare @COUNT int
2> select @COUNT = 1
3> while (@COUNT < 10)
4> begin
5>      select @COUNT = @COUNT + 1
6>      print 'LOOP AGAIN!'
7> end
8> print 'LOOP FINISHED! '
```

NOTE

Example 27.7 implements a simple FOR loop. Other implementations of SQL, such as Oracle's PL/SQL, actually provide a FOR loop statement. Check your documentation to determine whether the system you are using supports this useful command.

The BREAK **Command**

You can issue the BREAK command within a WHILE loop to force an immediate exit from the loop. The BREAK command is often used along with an IF test to check some condition. If the condition check succeeds, you can use the BREAK command to exit from the WHILE loop. Commands immediately following the END command are then executed. Example 27.8 illustrates a simple use of the BREAK command by checking for some arbitrary number (say, @COUNT = 8). When this condition is met, it breaks out of the WHILE loop.

Example 27.8

Notice the placement of the BREAK statement after the evaluation of the first condition in the IF.

Input ▼

```
1> declare @COUNT int
2> select @COUNT = 1
3> while (@COUNT < 10)
4> begin
5>        select @COUNT = @COUNT + 1
6>        if (@COUNT = 8)
7>        begin
8>              break
9>        end
10>       else
11>       begin
12>             print 'LOOP AGAIN!'
13>       end
14> end
15> print 'LOOP FINISHED!'
```

Analysis ▼

The BREAK command caused the loop to be exited when the @COUNT variable equaled 8.

27

The CONTINUE **Command**

The CONTINUE command is also a special command that can be executed from within a WHILE loop. The CONTINUE command forces the loop to immediately jump back to the beginning, rather than executing the remainder of the loop and then jumping back to the beginning. Like the BREAK command, the CONTINUE command is often used with an IF statement to check for some condition and then force an action, as shown in Example 27.9.

Example 27.9

Notice the placement of the CONTINUE statement after the evaluation of the first condition in the IF statement.

Input ▼

```
1> declare @COUNT int
2> select @COUNT = 1
3> while (@COUNT < 10)
4> begin
5>      select @COUNT = @COUNT + 1
6>      if (@COUNT = 8)
7>      begin
8>          continue
9>      end
10>     else
11>     begin
12>         print 'LOOP AGAIN!'
13>     end
14> end
15> print 'LOOP FINISHED!'
```

Analysis ▼

Example 27.9 is identical to Example 27.8 except that the CONTINUE command replaces the BREAK command. Now instead of exiting the loop when @COUNT = 8, it simply jumps back to the top of the WHILE statement and continues.

Using the WHILE Loop to Scroll Through a Table

SQL Server and many other database systems have a special type of object—the *cursor*—that enables you to scroll through a table's records one record at a time (see Lesson 19). However, some database systems (including SQL Server pre-2000) do not support the use of scrollable cursors. Example 27.10 gives you an idea of how to use a WHILE loop to implement a rough cursor-type functionality when that functionality is not automatically supplied.

Example 27.10

You can use the WHILE loop to scroll through tables one record at a time. Transact-SQL stores the rowcount variable, which can be set to tell SQL Server to return only one row at a time during a query. If you are using another database product, determine whether your product has a similar setting. By setting rowcount to 1 (its default is 0, which means unlimited), SQL Server returns only one record at a time from a SELECT query. You can use this one record to perform whatever operations you need to perform.

By selecting the contents of a table into a temporary table that is deleted at the end of the operation, you can select out one row at a time and delete each row when you are finished. When all the rows have been selected out of the table, you have gone through every row in the table! (As we said, this is a very rough cursor functionality!) Let's run the example now.

Input ▼

```
1> set rowcount 1
2> declare @PLAYER char(30)
3> create table temp_BATTERS (
4> NAME char(30),
5> TEAM int,
6> AVERAGE float,
7> HOMERUNS int,
8> RBIS int)
9> insert temp_BATTERS
10> select * from BATTERS
11> while exists (select * from temp_BATTERS)
12> begin
13>     select @PLAYER = NAME from temp_BATTERS
14>     print @PLAYER
15>     delete from temp_BATTERS where NAME = @PLAYER
16> end
17> print 'LOOP IS DONE!'
```

Analysis ▼

Note that by setting the rowcount variable, you are simply modifying the number of rows returned from a SELECT. If the WHERE clause of the DELETE command returned five rows, five rows would be deleted. Also note that the rowcount variable can be reset repeatedly. Therefore, from within the loop, you can query the database for some additional information by simply resetting rowcount to 1 before continuing with the loop.

Using Transact-SQL Wildcard Operators

27

The concept of using wildcard conditions in SQL was introduced in Lesson 3, "Expressions, Conditions, and Operators." The LIKE operator enables you to use wildcard conditions in your SQL statements. Transact-SQL extends the flexibility of wildcard conditions. A summary of Transact-SQL's wildcard operators follows.

- The underscore character (_) represents any one individual character. For example, _MITH tells the query to look for a five-character string ending with MITH.

- The percent sign (%) represents any number of characters, including zero characters. For example, WILL% returns the value WILLIAMS if it exists. WILL% returns the value WILL.

- Brackets ([ ]) allow a query to search for characters that are contained within the brackets. For example, [ABC] tells the query to search for strings containing the letters A, B, or C.

- The ^ character used within the brackets tells a query to look for any characters that are not listed within the brackets. For example, [^ABC] tells the query to search for strings that do not contain the letters A, B, or C.

Date Conversions

Microsoft's SQL Server can insert dates into a table in various formats and can also extract dates in several different types of formats. This section shows you how to use SQL Server's CONVERT command to manipulate the way a date is displayed.

Syntax ▼

CONVERT (datatype [(length)], expression, format)

The following date formats are available with SQL Server when using the CONVERT function:

Format Code	Format Picture
100	mon dd yyyy hh:miAM/PM
101	mm/dd/yy
102	yy.mm.dd
103	dd/mm/yy
104	dd.mm.yy
105	dd-mm-yy
106	dd mon yy
107	mon dd, yy
108	hh:mi:ss
109	mon dd, yyyy hh:mi:ss:mmmAM/PM
110	mm-dd-yy
111	yy/mm/dd
112	yymmdd

Input/Output ▼

```
select convert(char(15), getdate(), 107) as PayDate

PayDate
---------------
Dec 1, 2008
```

Analysis ▼

The preceding example uses the format code 107 with the CONVERT function. According to the date format table, code 107 displays the date in the format mon dd, yy.

SQL Server Diagnostic Tools—SET Commands

Transact-SQL provides a list of SET commands that enable you to turn on various options that help you analyze Transact-SQL statements. Here are some of the popular SET commands:

- SET STATISTICS IO ON tells the server to return the number of logical and physical page requests.
- SET STATISTICS TIME ON tells the server to display the execution time of a SQL statement.
- SET SHOWPLAN ON tells the server to show the execution plan for the designated query.
- SET NOEXEC ON tells the server to parse the designated query, but not to execute it.
- SET PARSONLY ON tells the server to check for syntax for the designated query, but not execute it.

The following Transact-SQL commands help to control what is displayed as part of the output from your queries:

- SET ROWCOUNT n tells the server to display only the first n records retrieved from a query.
- SET NOCOUNT ON tells the server not to report the number of rows returned by a query.

27

Summary

This lesson introduces a number of topics that add some teeth to your SQL programming expertise. The basic SQL topics that you learned earlier in this book are extremely important and provide the foundation for all database programming work you undertake. However, these topics are just a foundation. The SQL procedural language concepts explained in this lesson build upon your foundation of SQL and give you, the database programmer, a great deal of power when accessing data in your relational database.

The Transact-SQL language included with the Microsoft SQL Server database product provides many of the popular programming constructs found in third- and fourth-generation languages. Its features include the IF statement, the WHILE loop, and the capability to declare and use local and global variables.

Keep in mind that this lesson is only a brief introduction to the features and techniques of Transact-SQL code. Feel free to dive head first into your documentation and experiment with all the tools that are available to you. For more detailed coverage of Transact-SQL, refer to the Microsoft SQL Server Transact-SQL documentation.

Q&A

Q Does SQL provide a FOR loop?

A Programming constructs such as the FOR loop, the WHILE loop, and the CASE statement are extensions to ANSI SQL. Therefore, the use of these items varies widely among different database systems. For instance, Oracle provides the FOR loop, whereas Transact-SQL (SQL Server) does not. Of course, a WHILE loop can increment a variable within the loop, which can simulate the FOR loop.

Q I am developing a Windows (or Macintosh) application in which the user interface consists only of Windows GUI elements, such as windows and dialog boxes. Can I use the PRINT statement to issue messages to the user?

A SQL is entirely platform-independent. Therefore, issuing the PRINT statement will not pop up a message box. To output messages to the user, your SQL procedures could return a predetermined value that indicates success or failure. Based on these return values, the user could be notified of the status of the queries. (The PRINT command is most useful for debugging because a PRINT statement executed within a stored procedure will not be output to the screen anyway.)

Q How much variation actually exists among data types in different implementations of SQL?

A Each implementation of SQL has its own set of available data types and its own way for storing data based on guidelines in the SQL standard. This is one thing that makes each implementation unique. Although different data types exist, the basic storage of data in relational databases is conceptually the same.

Q What exactly is a local variable?

A A local variable is available within the scope of a program. Some implementations allow the use of global variables, which can be shared among programs.

Workshop

The Workshop provides quiz questions to help solidify your understanding of the material covered, as well as exercises to provide you with experience in using what you have learned. Try to answer the quiz and exercise questions before checking the answers in Appendix A, "Answers."

Quiz

1. True or false: The use of the word *SQL* in Oracle's PL/SQL and Microsoft Transact-SQL implies that these products are fully compliant with the ANSI standard.

2. True or false: Transact-SQL is case sensitive.

3. What data type is often used to flag certain rows of data within a table?

4. What statement is used to execute a block of statements in Transact-SQL?

Exercises

1. If you are not using Microsoft SQL Server, compare your product's extensions to ANSI SQL to the extensions mentioned in this lesson.

2. Write a brief set of statements that will check for the existence of some condition. If this condition is true, perform some operation. Otherwise, perform another operation.

3. Examine the following code and identify the errors:

```
1> use BASEBALL
2> go
3> create table TEAMS
4> TEAM_ID int,
5> CITY char(30)
6> NAME char(30),
7> WON int,
8> LOST int,
9> TOTAL_HOME_ATTENDANCE int,
10> AVG_HOME_ATTENDANCE int,)
11> stop
```

27

LESSON 28

Using MySQL on a UNIX-based System

MySQL is a multiuser, multithreaded SQL database client/server implementation. MySQL consists of a server daemon, a terminal monitor client program, and several client programs and libraries. The main goals of MySQL are speed, robustness, and ease of use. MySQL was originally designed to provide faster access to very large databases. Throughout this book, you have been using MySQL for hands-on exercises whenever possible. Most likely, you are using a Windows-based system. This lesson emphasizes the MySQL installation on a UNIX-based system. By the end of this lesson, you should understand

- How MySQL is related to other implementations of SQL

- How to install and set up a MySQL database for use on a UNIX platform

- How to connect to a MySQL database

- How to use MySQL help

- How to enter SQL commands at the prompt

NOTE

The current stable version of MySQL is 5.1. MySQL is basically free for most situations. One example of where a license must be purchased is if you are linking another program to MySQL that only works with MySQL. Check www.mysql.com for current software licensing details.

MySQL Administration

This section covers basic administration of MySQL on a UNIX-based system, including the installation of the product, how to start and stop the daemon, and the initial privileges that come with MySQL. MySQL is available for just about any operating system that exists today. One of the most popular installations of MySQL is on a Linux system, such as Red Hat Linux. However, regardless of the version of UNIX (Solaris, AIX, HP-UX, Red Hat Linux, and so forth), the basic administration tasks covered in this lesson are the same or very similar.

Installing MySQL

MySQL can be downloaded from http://www.mysql.com. To install a MySQL binary distribution, you need GNU gunzip to uncompress the distribution and a reasonable TAR to unpack the distribution. The binary distribution file will be named mysql-*VERSION-OS*.tar.gz, where *VERSION* is the version ID of MySQL, and *OS* is the name of the operating system.

The current version of MySQL is 5.1. You can get the source code, as well as several binary packages depending on the type and version of UNIX required, from the MySQL website. Currently, the versions of UNIX that have precompiled packages are

Linux	AIX
Solaris	SCO
FreeBSD	SGI Irix
MacOS X	DEC OSF
HP-UX	BSDI

If you're adventurous, the source code is also available to compile with different options than the defaults.

> **NOTE**
>
> If the UNIX environment being used is Red Hat Linux or any other environment that supports RPMs, it is easier to download the file MySQL-server-community-5.1.30-0.rhel3.i386.rpm. This is a Red Hat Package Manager file, which can be installed with rpm -Uhv MySQL-server-community-5.1.30-0.rhel3.i386.rpm as the superuser. The package name might be somewhat different depending upon the environment that you are loading it on, as several versions are available.

Pick the correct package for your version of UNIX and download it.

The TAR command archives and extracts files from and to a single file called a tar file.

> **NOTE**
>
> The # sign used in this lesson's examples is the UNIX operating system prompt. Check your version or operating system for your specific prompt. However, the database commands used will remain the same.

The commands you must execute to install and use a MySQL binary distribution are as follows:

```
# cd /usr/local
# gunzip < mysql-VERSION-OS.tar.gz ¦ tar xvf -
# ln -s mysql-VERSION-OS mysql
# cd mysql
# scripts/mysql_install_db
```

These commands install the MySQL directories under the /usr/local/mysql directory:

Directory	Contents of Directory
bin	Client utilities and the mysqld server
data	Log files and databases
include	Include (header) files
lib	Libraries
scripts	mysql_install_db
share/mysql	Error message files
sql-bench	Benchmarks

Starting and Stopping MySQL

After installing MySQL, the mysqld daemon needs to be started.

Input ▼

```
# cd /usr/local/mysql
# ./bin/safe_mysqld &
```

```
Starting mysqld daemon with databases from /usr/local/mysql/data
```

> **NOTE**
>
> Remember to be in the /usr/local/mysql directory when starting the mysqld daemon. This will be the standard location of the MySQL installation on any UNIX-based system. These standards are normally adhered to so that any DBA can easily find the installation when moving from one machine to the next.

28

To stop the `mysqld` daemon, use this statement:

Input ▼

```
# /usr/local/mysql/bin/mysqladmin shutdown
```

Initial MySQL Privileges

After installing MySQL, you set up the initial access privileges by running

Input ▼

```
scripts/mysql_install_db
```

Generally, MySQL then creates default privileges on your system as defined next to get you started:

- The MySQL user *root* is created as a superuser who can do anything.
- An *anonymous* user is created who can do anything with databases that have a name of test or starting with test_. Connections must be made from the local host. This means any local user can connect and be treated as the anonymous user.
- Other privileges are denied.

CAUTION

> The initial password for root is empty, so anyone can connect as root without a password and be granted all privileges.

The easiest way to change MySQL passwords is to use the SET PASSWORD statement, as follows:

Input ▼

```
# mysql -u root mysql

mysql> SET PASSWORD FOR root=PASSWORD('new_password');
```

The MySQL Terminal Monitor

This section provides an introduction to using the MySQL client program `mysql`, also referred to as the *terminal monitor*, or simply the monitor. The monitor is an interactive program that allows you to connect to the MySQL server and run queries. There is also a batch mode for the monitor, which is where you place your queries in a file beforehand, and then tell the monitor to execute the contents of the file.

Connecting to the Database

To connect to the server, you need a MySQL username and password. Additionally, if the server is running on a machine other than the computer you are currently connected to, you need to provide the hostname of the machine's server. After you know the parameters, you should be able to connect using the following syntax:

Input ▼

```
# mysql -h hostname -u username -p

Enter password: *******
Welcome to the MySQL monitor.  Commands end with ; or \g
Your MySQL connection id is 21 to server version: 3.22.23b
Type help for help.
mysql>
```

The ******* represents your password that you type when the Enter Password: prompt is displayed. Some installations allow users to connect as the anonymous user to the server on the local host. If this is so, you can start the monitor without any parameters. After some introductory information, the monitor will display the mysql> prompt, telling you that it is ready for you to enter commands.

To disconnect from the monitor, type QUIT at the mysql> prompt, or press Ctrl+D.

Input ▼

```
mysql> quit

Bye
```

Command-Line Options

A list of the options available with the monitor command is provided with the --HELP option. Note that all of the options can be given in long (--BATCH) or short (--B) form:

Input ▼

```
# mysql --help

Usage: mysql [OPTIONS] [database]
  -A, --no-auto-rehash  No automatic rehashing.
  -B, --batch           Print results with a tab as separator
```

28

```
-C, --compress              Use compression in server/client protocol
-T, --debug-info            Print some debug info at exit
-e, --execute=...           Execute command and quit
-f, --force                 Continue even if we get an sql error.
-i, --ignore-space          Ignore space after function names
-?, --help                  Display this help and exit
-h, --host=...              Connect to host
-H, --html                  Produce HTML output
-n, --unbuffered            Flush buffer after each query
-O, --set-variable var=option
                            Give a variable a value.
-o, --one-database          Only update the default database.
-p[password], --password[=...]
                            Password to use when connecting to server
-P  --port=...              Port number to use for connection
-q, --quick                 Don't cache result, print it row by row.
-r, --raw                   Write fields without conversion.
-s, --silent                Be more silent.
-L, --skip-line-numbers     Don't write line number for errors
-N, --skip-column-names     Don't write column names in results
-S  --socket=...            Socket file to use for connection
-t  --table=...             Output in table format
-u, --user=#                User for login if not current user
-v, --verbose               Write more
                               (-v -v -v gives the table output format)
-V, --version               Output version information and exit
-E, --vertical              Print the output of a query (rows) vertically
-w, --wait                  Wait and retry if connection is down
```

Entering MySQL Monitor Commands

A MySQL command normally consists of a SQL statement terminated by a semicolon or by a \g. (A few commands—such as QUIT and USE—do not need to be terminated by a semicolon.)

Input/Output ▼

```
mysql> select current_date(),version();

+----------------+---------------------+
| current_date() | version()_____ |
+----------------+---------------------+
| 2008-12-19     | 5.067-community-nt  |
+----------------+---------------------+

1 row in set (0.00 sec)
mysql>


sdfsdf
```

The monitor displays the output of the query as a table with rows and columns. Column headings are either the label for the column or the expression being evaluated.

Note that the semicolon determines the end of a command. This means that MySQL will evaluate your command and produce error messages at that time. It also means that you can have a long command stretch over several lines. The monitor will change to the -> prompt to indicate that you are continuing to enter a command.

Input/Output ▼

```
mysql> version
    -> ;
ERROR 1064: You have an error in your SQL syntax near 'version
;' at line 1
mysql> select
    -> version()
    -> ;
```

Note that MySQL commands are not case sensitive, so you can type them in any combination of upper- and lowercase. The only exceptions to this case-sensitivity rule are database names and table names—for example,

Input/Output ▼

```
mysql> sHoW DataBases;
+-----------+
| Database  |
+-----------+
| mysql     |
| test      |
+-----------+
3 rows in set (0.00 sec)
mysql> use Mysql;
ERROR 1049: Unknown database 'Mysql'
mysql> use mysql;
Database changed
```

To abort a command that you are in the process of entering, type \c literally (not Ctrl+C, which will exit the monitor entirely):

Input/Output ▼

```
mysql> select
    -> current_date(),
    -> \c
```

Notice how the prompt changes to `->` when it is expecting the continuation of a command, and then back to `mysql>` to tell you that it is ready for a new command.

The monitor has two additional prompts: `"->` (double quote, dash, greater than) and `'->` (single quote, dash, greater than). Like `->`, these prompts indicate that the continuation of a command is expected by the monitor. In these cases, however, the prompt means that you've entered a line containing a string that begins with a `"` or `'`, but haven't typed in the matching quote yet.

Input ▼

```
mysql> select * from the_table where location="INDIANA
    "> POLIS, INDIANA";
```

Command-Line History

The MySQL client uses the file named in the `MYSQL_HISTFILE` environment variable to save the command-line history. The default value for the history file is `$HOME/.mysql_history`.

While you are in the monitor, you can use the up and down arrow keys to recall previous commands you have entered, line by line. Because everything you enter is saved in the `.mysql_history` file, the recall extends even to your previous sessions.

Batch Mode

In the previous sections, you used `mysql` interactively to enter queries and view the results. You can also run `mysql` in batch mode. To do this, put the commands you want to run in a file, and then tell `mysql` to read its input from the file:

Input ▼

```
# mysql < batch_file_name
```

If you need to specify connection parameters on the command line, the command might look like this:

Input/Output ▼

```
# mysql -h host -u user -p < batch-file
sdfsdfsd
Enter password: ********
```

When you use `mysql` this way, you are creating a script file and then executing the script.

Note that the default output format is different when you run `mysql` in batch mode than when you use it interactively. For example, the output of `SELECT DISTINCT NAME FROM TEAM` looks like this when run interactively:

Output ▼

```
+---------+
¦ name    ¦
+---------+
¦ Fred    ¦
¦ John    ¦
¦ Jim     ¦
¦ Sam     ¦
+---------+
4 rows in set (0.00 sec)
```

But like this when run in batch mode:

Output ▼

```
Name
Fred
John
Jim
Sam
```

If you want to get the interactive output format in batch mode, use `mysql -t`. To echo to the output the commands that are executed, use `mysql -vvv`.

SHOW

`SHOW` provides information about databases, tables, columns, or the server. If the `LIKE` `wild` code segment is used, `wild` can be a string that uses the SQL `%` and `_` wildcard characters.

The syntax for `SHOW` is

Syntax ▼

```
SHOW DATABASES [LIKE wild]
    or SHOW TABLES [FROM db_name] [LIKE wild]
    or SHOW COLUMNS FROM tbl_name [FROM db_name] [LIKE wild]
    or SHOW INDEX FROM tbl_name [FROM db_name]
    or SHOW STATUS
    or SHOW VARIABLES [LIKE wild]
    or SHOW PROCESSLIST
    or SHOW TABLE STATUS [FROM db_name] [LIKE wild]
```

28

SHOW can be used in a number of ways:

- SHOW DATABASES lists the databases on the MySQL server host. You can also get this list using the MYSQLSHOW command.

- SHOW TABLES lists the tables in a given database. You can also get this list using the MYSQLSHOW DB_NAME command.

- SHOW COLUMNS lists the columns in a given table. The DESCRIBE statement provides information similar to SHOW COLUMNS.

- SHOW TABLE STATUS works like SHOW STATUS, but provides a lot of information about each table. You can also get this list using the MYSQLSHOW --STATUS DB_NAME command.

- SHOW FIELDS is a synonym for SHOW COLUMNS, and SHOW KEYS is a synonym for SHOW INDEX. You can also list a table's columns or indexes with MYSQLSHOW DB_NAME TBL_NAME or MYSQLSHOW -K DB_NAME TBL_NAME.

- SHOW INDEX returns the index information in a format that closely resembles the SQLSTATISTICS call in ODBC.

- SHOW STATUS provides server status information similar to MYSQLADMIN EXTENDED-STATUS.

- SHOW VARIABLES shows the values of some of the MySQL system variables. You can also get this information using the MYSQLADMIN VARIABLES command. If the default values are unsuitable, you can set most of these variables using command-line options when mysql starts up.

- SHOW PROCESSLIST shows you which threads are running. You can also get this information using the MYSQLADMIN PROCESSLIST command.

MySQL Utilities

MySQL comes with several utility programs and scripts, located in the /usr/local/mysql/bin and /usr/local/mysql/scripts directories. All the MySQL utilities include a --HELP option that provides a full description of the program's different options.

- isamchk—Utility to describe, check, optimize, and repair MySQL tables.

- mysqlaccess—Script that checks access privileges.

- mysqladmin—Utility for performing administrative operations.

- mysqldump—Dumps a MySQL database into a file as SQL statements or as text.

- mysqlimport—Imports text files into tables.

- mysqlshow—Lists information about databases, tables, columns, and indexes.

Summary

MySQL is a SQL Server client implementation that is freely available for download for a wide variety of platforms. MySQL is easy to use, and designed to run quickly even with very large databases. In this lesson, we showed you some of the basics of MySQL on a UNIX-based system, including basic administration, help commands, available options, and examples of SQL statements. Keep in mind that MySQL, like most other implementations of SQL, has its own features and extensions that might not be available in other implementations. As with any relational database, the exact syntax of commands might vary, but the concepts behind managing data with SQL are the same.

Q&A

Q What was MySQL originally designed for?

A Giving faster access to very large databases.

Q Which platforms is MySQL available for?

A MySQL is available for a variety of operating systems, including AIX, BSDI, DEC UNIX, FreeBSD, HP-UX, Linux, NetBSD, OpenBSD, OS/2 Warp 3, SGI Irix, Solaris, SunOS, SCO OpenServer, SCO UnixWare, Tru64 UNIX, and Windows.

Workshop

The Workshop provides quiz questions to help solidify your understanding of the material covered, as well as exercises to provide you with experience in using what you have learned. Try to answer the quiz and exercise questions before checking the answers in Appendix A, "Answers."

Quiz

1. What are the main design goals of MySQL?
2. How do you start the `mysql` daemon?
3. How do you stop the `mysql` daemon?
4. Which commands/elements in MySQL Terminal Monitor are case sensitive?

28

Exercises

1. Enter the MySQL command to display the database names from the UNIX prompt, as well as from the `mysql` terminal monitor.
2. Enter the MySQL command to display the table names in the test database.

APPENDIX A
Answers

Answers For Lesson 1

Quiz

1. SQL determines what should be done, not how it should be done. The database must implement the SQL request. This feature is a big plus in cross-platform, cross-language development.
2. Apply Dr. Codd's 12 (actually, 13) rules.
3. SQL enables you to select, insert, modify, and delete the information in a database; perform system security functions and set user permissions on tables and databases; handle online transaction processing within an application; create stored procedures and triggers to reduce application coding; and transfer data between different databases.
4. The Relational model is what Dr Codd's RDBMS is based upon and breaks data up into discrete sets.

Answers For Lesson 2

Quiz

1. The only difference between the two statements is that one statement is in lowercase and the other uppercase. Case sensitivity is not normally a factor in the syntax of SQL. However, be aware of capitalization when dealing with data.
2. a. The FROM clause is missing. The two mandatory components of a SELECT statement are SELECT and FROM. Additionally, the semicolon is missing.

   b. The semicolon, which identifies the end of a SQL statement, is missing.

    c. You need a comma between each column name: `Select amount, name, payee FROM checks;`

3. All of the answers work except c, which is missing a semicolon.

4. `SELECT ` check` , amount FROM checks;`

5. `SELECT DISTINCT payee FROM checks;`

6. `SELECT DISTINCT payee, amount FROM checks;`

   No, the ordering does not matter.

7. No. Ordering is only guaranteed when using the `ORDER BY` clause.

Exercises

1. `SELECT CHECK#, REMARKS FROM CHECKS;`

2. `SELECT REMARKS, CHECK# FROM CHECKS;`

3. `SELECT DISTINCT REMARKS FROM CHECKS;`

4.
```
mysql> select `check`, amount
    -> from checks;
+-------+--------+
| check | amount |
+-------+--------+
|     1 | 150.00 |
|     2 | 245.34 |
|     3 | 200.32 |
|     4 |  98.00 |
|     5 | 150.00 |
|     6 |  25.00 |
|     7 |  25.10 |
+-------+--------+
7 rows in set (0.05 sec)
```

5. `mysql> show databases;`

6. `mysql> use mysql`

7. `mysql> show tables;`

8. `mysql> use BOB`

Answers For Lesson 3

Quiz

1. `SELECT * FROM FRIENDS WHERE LASTNAME LIKE 'M%';`

2.
```
SELECT * FROM FRIENDS
WHERE ST = 'IL'
AND FIRSTNAME = 'AL';
```

3. Use `INTERSECT`. Remember that `INTERSECT` returns rows common to both queries.
```
SELECT PARTNO FROM PART1
INTERSECT
SELECT PARTNO FROM PART2;
```

4. `WHERE a BETWEEN 10 AND 30;`

5. Nothing will be returned, as both conditions are not true.

6. The `UNION` clause removes duplicates the `UNION ALL` clause does not.

7. `INTERSECT` displays rows that show up in both groups of queries. `MINUS` shows the rows that are in the first group but not the second.

Exercises

1.
```
SQL> SELECT (FIRSTNAME || 'FROM') NAME, ST
        FROM FRIENDS
        WHERE ST = 'IL'
        AND
        LASTNAME = 'BUNDY';
```

2.
```
SQL>SELECT LASTNAME || ',' || FIRSTNAME NAME,
  2         AREACODE || '-' || PHONE PHONE
  3 FROM FRIENDS
  4 WHERE AREACODE BETWEEN 300 AND 400;
```

3.
```
mysql> select * from price
    -> where wholesale > .50;
+----------+-----------+
| item     | wholesale |
+----------+-----------+
| POTATOES |      0.51 |
| BANANAS  |      0.67 |
| CHEESE   |      0.89 |
+----------+-----------+
3 rows in set (0.01 sec)
```

4.
```
+----------+-----------+
| item     | wholesale |
+----------+-----------+
| TOMATOES |      0.34 |
| POTATOES |      0.51 |
+----------+-----------+
2 rows in set (0.00 sec)
```

5. Yes.

6. The two queries joined by the union need to have the same columns. The second query is missing LASTNAME.

Answers For Lesson 4

Quiz

1. Yes, when using aggregate functions in a query, all columns that are not associated with aggregate functions must be listed in the GROUP BY clause.

2. The GROUP BY clause groups data result sets that have been manipulated by various functions. The GROUP BY clause acts like the ORDER BY clause in that it orders the results of the query in the order the columns are listed in the GROUP BY.

3. No, the syntax is incorrect. The GROUP BY must come before the ORDER BY. Also, all the selected columns must be listed in the GROUP BY.

4. No.

5. Yes, it is not necessary to use the SELECT statement on a column that you put in the ORDER BY clause.

6. The ordering will be by the order of the columns in the GROUP BY statement.

7. Average Salary, then Name.

Exercises

1. Here is your baseline that shows how many people are on each team:
```
SELECT TEAM, COUNT(TEAM)
FROM ORGCHART
GROUP BY TEAM;

TEAM                 COUNT
================ ===========

COLLECTIONS            2
MARKETING              3
PR                     1
RESEARCH               2
```

Compare it to the query that solves the question:

```
SELECT TEAM, COUNT(TEAM)
FROM ORGCHART
WHERE SICKLEAVE >=30
GROUP BY TEAM;
```

A

```
TEAM                 COUNT
=============== ===========

COLLECTIONS              1
MARKETING               1
RESEARCH                1
```

The output shows the number of people on each TEAM with a SICKLEAVE balance of 30 days or more.

2. ```
SQL> SELECT CHECK#, PAYEE, AMOUNT
     FROM CHECKS
     WHERE CHECK# = 1;
```

You can get the same results in several ways. Can you think of some more?

3. ```
mysql> select team, sum(sickleave), sum(annualleave)
    -> from orgchart
    -> group by team
    -> order by 2;
```

4. Yes.

5. No. The salary column is not included in the select list.

6. ```
mysql> select name, team, (sickleave+annualleave)
    -> from orgchart
    -> order by 3 desc;
```

# Answers For Lesson 5

## Quiz

1. 5,000,000.

2. An equi-join.

3. A will not work. The column employee_id exists in both tables. The fourth line should read where e.employee_id = ep.employee_id.
```

B works, but you get a Cartesian product because the tables are not properly joined in the WHERE clause.

C works and returns usable data.

4. You can join on more than one column. For example, sometimes a primary key in a table consists of more than one column.

5. Inner joins only return rows that match the join condition. Outer joins return NULL values for the side that does not match but still returns the rows.

6. LEFT OUTER JOIN.

Exercises

1.
```
SELECT F.PARTNUM, F.DESCRIPTION,
       S.PARTNUM,S.DESCRIPTION
FROM PARTS F, PARTS S
WHERE F.PARTNUM = S.PARTNUM
  AND F.DESCRIPTION <> S.DESCRIPTION
  AND F.DESCRIPTION > S.DESCRIPTION;
```

2.
```
select o.orderedon, o.name, p.partnum,
       p.price, p.description
from orders o, part p
where o.partnum = p.partnum
  and o.orderedon between '1-SEP-96' and '30-SEP-96'
order by p.partnum;
```

3.
```
select o.orderedon, o.name, p.partnum, o.quantity
from orders o,
     Part p
where o.partnum = p.partnum
  And o.orderedon like '%SEP%';
```

Many other queries will also work.

4.
```
mysql> SELECT P.PARTNUM, P.DESCRIPTION,P.PRICE*O.QUANTITY DUE,
    -> O.NAME, O.PARTNUM
    -> FROM PART P, ORDERS O
    -> WHERE P.PARTNUM = O.PARTNUM
    -> ;
```

5.
```
mysql> SELECT P.PARTNUM, P.DESCRIPTION,P.PRICE,
    -> O.NAME, O.PARTNUM
    -> FROM PART P
    -> LEFT OUTER JOIN ORDERS O ON O.PARTNUM = 76
    -> ;
```

PARTNUM	DESCRIPTION	PRICE	NAME	PARTNUM
54	PEDALS	54.25	TRUE WHEEL	76
54	PEDALS	54.25	BIKE SPEC	76
54	PEDALS	54.25	LE SHOPPE	76
54	PEDALS	54.25	AAA BIKE	76
54	PEDALS	54.25	JACKS BIKE	76
42	SEATS	24.50	TRUE WHEEL	76
42	SEATS	24.50	BIKE SPEC	76
42	SEATS	24.50	LE SHOPPE	76
42	SEATS	24.50	AAA BIKE	76
42	SEATS	24.50	JACKS BIKE	76
46	TIRES	15.25	TRUE WHEEL	76
46	TIRES	15.25	BIKE SPEC	76
46	TIRES	15.25	LE SHOPPE	76
46	TIRES	15.25	AAA BIKE	76
46	TIRES	15.25	JACKS BIKE	76
23	MOUNTAIN BIKE	350.45	TRUE WHEEL	76
23	MOUNTAIN BIKE	350.45	BIKE SPEC	76
23	MOUNTAIN BIKE	350.45	LE SHOPPE	76
23	MOUNTAIN BIKE	350.45	AAA BIKE	76
23	MOUNTAIN BIKE	350.45	JACKS BIKE	76
76	ROAD BIKE	530.00	TRUE WHEEL	76
76	ROAD BIKE	530.00	BIKE SPEC	76
76	ROAD BIKE	530.00	LE SHOPPE	76
76	ROAD BIKE	530.00	AAA BIKE	76
76	ROAD BIKE	530.00	JACKS BIKE	76
10	TANDEM	1200.00	TRUE WHEEL	76
10	TANDEM	1200.00	BIKE SPEC	76
10	TANDEM	1200.00	LE SHOPPE	76
10	TANDEM	1200.00	AAA BIKE	76
10	TANDEM	1200.00	JACKS BIKE	76

A

```
30 rows in set (0.01 sec)
```

Answers For Lesson 6

Quiz

1. The result set has no duplicates because of the query that called this subquery
```
SELECT ALL C.NAME, C.ADDRESS, C.STATE,C.ZIP
FROM CUSTOMER C
WHERE C.NAME IN
```

2. a. False. They all return a single value.

b. False. The limit is a function of your SQL implementation.

c. False. Correlated subqueries enable you to use an outside reference.

3. a. No. You are missing the parentheses around the subquery.

b. No. The SQL engine cannot correlate all the columns in the PART table with the operator =.

c. Yes. This subquery is correct.

Exercises

1. SUBQUERY
```
mysql> select name
   -> from orders
   -> where name > 'J';
OUTER QUERY
mysql> select orderedon, name
   -> from orders
   -> where name in (results of the inner query)
```

2. SUBQUERY
```
mysql> select max(price)
   -> from part;
OUTER QUERY
mysql> select description
   -> from part
   -> where price = (result of the subquery);
```

Answers For Lesson 7

Quiz

1. INITCAP.

2. Group functions and aggregate functions are the same thing.

3. Yes, it will return the total of rows.

4. No, the query won't work because LASTNAME is a character field.

5. The CONCAT function and the || symbol.

6. 6 is the number of records in the table.

7. No, we are missing () around LASTNAME,1,5. Also, a better plan is to give the column an alias. The statement should look like this:
```
SQL> SELECT SUBSTR(LASTNAME,1,5) NAME FROM NAME_TBL;
```

Exercises

1. SQL> SELECT NAME FROM TEAMSTATS
   2 WHERE (HITS/AB) < .25;

NAME

HAMHOCKER
CASEY

2. SQL> select substr(firstname,1,1)||'.'||
                 substr(m,1,1)||'.'||
                 substr(lastname,1,1)||'.' INITIALS, code
         from characters
         where code = 32;

3. mysql> select max(hits/ab), min(hits/ab)
          -> from teamstats;

4. mysql> select max(ab) from teamstats;

5. mysql> select min(ab) from teamstats;

6. mysql> select max(ab), min(ab) from teamstats;

7. select concat(lastname,',',' ',firstname,',',' ',m,' ',code)
         from characters;

8. mysql> select firstname, lastname, m
          -> from characters;

9. mysql> select lower(firstname), lower(lastname), lower(m)
          -> from characters;

10. We have combined several concepts here into one SELECT statement.

The mid(firstname,1,1) portion singles out the character we want to be in UPPER case.

upper(mid(firstname,1,1)), the UPPER function, converts that character to UPPER case, if it is not already in that state.

concat(upper(mid(firstname,1,1)), the CONCAT function, allows us to connect the results of this function to the next set of functions.

mid(firstname,2), the MID/SUBSTRING function, written in this manner starts at the second character in the string, and because there is no specification on how many characters to continue, pulls all characters from the second to the end of the string.

`lower(mid(firstname,2))` LOWER converts the characters identified by the MID/SUBSTRING function into lowercase.

Because all of these functions are enclosed within the CONCAT function, they are joined back together in the form of one string.

Answers For Lesson 8

Quiz

1. True.

2. False. Sometimes it is better to denormalize your database a bit to improve performance by decreasing the number of join operations required to retrieve data.

3. True.

4. A denormalized database will typically perform better than a normalized database because fewer join operations are required to retrieve data from tables.

5. Although performance is increased by denormalizing a database, redundant data will be stored, making overall manageability and consistency of data more difficult.

6. You can create foreign key constraints in MySQL, but they have no function as of version 3.23. Foreign key constraints support referential integrity in future releases of MySQL when using the InnoDB database type.

Exercises

1. Note that there is no one correct answer here. Every situation should be treated individually, and situations are handled differently by different people.

```
EMP             EMP_PROFILE        EMP_PAY          EMP_CUST
emp_id          emp_id             emp_id           emp_id
emp_name        emp_dob            emp_pay          cust_id
emp_addr        emp_sex            emp_pay_date
emp_zip         emp_dependents     emp_withholding
emp_phone       emp_position_id    emp_dept_id


POSITIONS       DEPARTMENTS        EDUC_CODES       SEX_CODES
position_id     dept_id            educ_code        sex_code
position        department         education_       sex
                                   desc


STATE_CODES     SERVICES           ZIP_CODES
State           service_id         zip
state_desc      service_type       city
                service_cost       state
```

```
SERVICE_DETAIL      ACCOUNTS_          CUST_COMMENTS
                    RECEIVABLE
invoice_number      invoice_number     invoice_number
service_id          amt_due            rating
cust_id             date_due           comments
service_hours
service_date


CUST
cust_id
cust_name
cust_addr
cust_zip
cust_phone
cust_fax
```

A

2. Primary keys are designated by boldface type. Foreign keys are designated with an asterisk (*). Notice that the primary key in the EMP_CUST table is the combination of the EMP_ID and CUST_ID columns.

EMP	EMP_PROFILE	EMP_PAY	EMP_CUST
emp_id	**emp_id** *	**emp_id** *	**emp_id** *
emp_name	emp_dob	emp_pay	**cust_id** *
emp_addr	emp_sex	emp_pay_date	
emp_zip *	emp_dependents	emp_ withholding	
emp_phone	emp_position_ id *	emp_dept_ id *	

POSITIONS	DEPARTMENTS	EDUC_CODES	SEX_CODES
position_id	**dept_id**	**educ_code**	**sex_code**
position	department	education_ desc	sex

STATE_CODES	SERVICES	ZIP_CODES	
State	**service_id**	**zip**	
state_desc	service_type	city	
	service_cost	state	

SERVICE_DETAIL	ACCOUNTS_RECEIVABLE	CUST_COMMENTS
invoice_number	**invoice_ number** *	**invoice_number** *
service_id *	amt_due	rating
cust_id *	date_due	comments
service_hours		
service_date		
CUST		
cust_id		
cust_name		
cust_addr		
cust_zip *		
cust_phone		
cust_fax		

Answers For Lesson 9

Quiz

1. False. Most systems do not have an ALTER DATABASE command. The ALTER TABLE command is used to modify an existing table's structure.

2. False. The DROP TABLE command is not equivalent to the DELETE FROM `<table_name>` command. The DROP TABLE command completely deletes the table along with its structure from the database. The DELETE FROM... command removes only the records from a table. The table's structure remains in the database.

3. True.

4. This statement has two problems. The first problem is that the name ID is repeated within the table. Even though the data types are different, reusing a field name within a table is illegal. The second problem is that the closing parenthesis is missing from the end of the statement. It should look like this:

   ```
   CREATE TABLE new_table (
   ID NUMBER,
   FIELD1 char(40),
   FIELD2 char(80));
   ```

5. The command to modify a field's data type or length is the ALTER TABLE command, not the ALTER DATABASE command.

6. The owner of the new table is whomever created the table. If you signed on as your ID, your ID would be the owner. If you signed on as SYSTEM, SYSTEM would be the owner.

7. VARCHAR2 would be the best choice. Here's what happens with the CHAR data type when the data length varies:

   ```
   SQL> SELECT *
       2   FROM NAME_TABLE;

   LAST_NAME      FIRST_NAME
   JONES          NANCY
   SMITH          JOHN
   2 rows selected.

   SQL> SELECT LAST_NAME
       2  FROM NAME_TABLE
       3  WHERE LAST_NAME LIKE '%MITH';

   No rows selected.
   ```

You were looking for SMITH, and SMITH does exist in this table. The query finds SMITH because the column LAST_NAME is CHAR and there are spaces after SMITH. The SELECT statement did not ask for these spaces. Here's the correct statement to find SMITH:

A

```
SQL>  SELECT LAST_NAME
  2      FROM NAME_TABLE
  3      WHERE LAST_NAME LIKE '%MITH%';
```

```
LAST_NAME
SMITH
1 row selected.
```

By adding the % after MITH, the SELECT statement found SMITH and the spaces after the name.

When creating tables, plan your data types to avoid this type of situation. Be aware of how your data types act. If you allocate 30 bytes for a column and some values in the column contain fewer than 30 bytes, does the particular data type pad spaces to fill up 30 bytes? If so, consider how this might affect your SELECT statements. Know your data and its structure.

8. Yes. Just as long as the owner or schema is not the same.

9. You can only apply the NOT NULL constraint if none of the current data in the column is NULL. The removal of the constraint can be done regardless of the data.

Exercises

1. N/A . You should just create the table using the statement provided.

2. N/A . You should just create the table using the statement provided.

3.
```
mysql> alter table cust change
    -> cust_id cust_id varchar(5) not null;
       Query OK, 5 rows affected (0.05 sec)
    Records: 5  Duplicates: 0  Warnings: 0
```

4.
```
create table view as
    select c.fname, s.title, m.description
     from cust c, stock s, media m
    where c.stock_id = s.stock_id
    and c.media_id = m.media_id;
```

5. create table age as

```
        select c.fname, c.lname, s.title,
        s.rating, year(now())-year(c.dob) Age
        from cust c, stock s
        where c.stock_id = s.stock_id;
```

6. alter table age add

```
        junk_food varchar(30) not null;
```

7. alter table age change

```
        junk_food snacks varchar(30) null;
```

8. mysql> drop table age;

Answers For Lesson 10

Quiz

1. There is no limit to the number of unique constraints that you can have in a table.

2. A check constraint checks to see whether inserted data in a column meets certain criteria, as specified in the definition of the check constraint.

3. The parent record must always be inserted first.

4. The child record must always be deleted first.

Exercises

1. desc table_name;
   MEDIA table: media_id primary key.
   STOCK table: stock_id primary key.
   CUST table: media_id, stock_id foreign key.

2. ALTER TABLE MEDIA ADD PRIMARY KEY (MEDIA_ID);
       ALTER TABLE STOCK ADD PRIMARY KEY (STOCK_ID);

3. ALTER TABLE CUST
           ADD CONSTRAINT STOCK_ID_FK FOREIGN KEY (STOCK_ID)
           REFERENCES STOCK (STOCK_ID);

4. ALTER TABLE SEX_CODES ADD CONSTRAINT CHECK_SEX_CODE CHECK(SEX IN
   ➥('M','F'));

Answers For Lesson 11

Quiz

1. If you want to delete all records from the COLLECTION table, you must use the following syntax:

   ```
   DELETE FROM COLLECTION;
   ```

   Keep in mind that this statement will delete all records. You can qualify which records you want to delete by using the following syntax:

   ```
   DELETE FROM COLLECTION
   WHERE VALUE = 125
   ```

   This statement deletes all records with a value of 125.

2. This statement was designed to insert all the records from TABLE_2 into the COLLECTION table. The main problem here is using the INTO keyword with the INSERT statement. When copying data from one table in another table, you must use the following syntax:

   ```
   INSERT COLLECTION
   SELECT * FROM TABLE_2;
   ```

   Also, remember that the data types of the fields selected from TABLE_2 must exactly match the data types and order of the fields within the COLLECTION table.

3. This statement confuses the UPDATE function with the INSERT function. To UPDATE values in the COLLECTION table, use the following syntax:

   ```
   UPDATE COLLECTION
   SET NAME = 'HONUS WAGNER CARD',
     VALUE = 25000,
     REMARKS = 'FOUND IT';
   ```

4. Nothing would be deleted because of incorrect syntax. The * is not required here.

5. All rows in the COLLECTION table would be deleted.

6. All values in the COLLECTION table for the WORTH column would be 555, and all remarks in the COLLECTION table would say UP FROM 525. Probably not a good thing!

7. No. The syntax is not correct. The INSERT and the SET do not go together.

8. Yes. This syntax is correct.

Exercises

1. Now do a SELECT from the CHECKS table and view the data.

```
DESCRIBE CHECKS;

INSERT INTO CHECKS VALUES (0,'JETHRO TULL',225,'MUSIC LESSONS');
SELECT * FROM CHECKS;
```

2.
```
UPDATE CHECKS
SET REMARKS = 'CHOIR DUES'
WHERE CHECK = 6;
```

3. `SELECT * FROM CHECKS;`

4. After careful study of the CHECKS table, you notice that several entries need to be corrected.

   There are two rows with check number 6. Get rid of the one you do not want.

```
DELETE FROM CHECKS
WHERE CHECK_NUM = 6
AND REMARKS = 'CHOIR DUES';
```

   Your study of SQL and databases has taught you that the storage of periods (.) or other forms of punctuation in your tables is not a practical use of space. Correct this situation for check number 2.

```
UPDATE CHECKS
SET PAYEE = 'READING RR'
WHERE CHECK = 2;
```

   There is a check number listed as 0. After some research you discover that it in fact should have been check number 10. Make the correction.

```
UPDATE CHECKS
SET CHECK_NUM = 10
WHERE CHECK_NUM = 0;
```

   The data in the CHECKS table now seems to be okay, but you've noticed that three check numbers seem to be skipped. After much frantic searching, you find the receipts and can now put the data into the table.

```
(7,'WE B CATS',,13.42,'SCOOPER')
(8,'JOES STALE & DENT',,4.32,'AIR FRESHENER')
(9,'BLOOMBURGS',7.14,'CAT TOYS')
INSERT INTO CHECKS VALUES
(7,'WE B CATS', 13.42,'SCOOPER');
INSERT INTO CHECKS VALUES
(8,'JOES STALE & DENT', 4.32,'AIR FRESHENER');
INSERT INTO CHECKS VALUES
(9,'BLOOMBURGS', 7.14,'CAT TOYS');
```

5. DELETE FROM CHECKS WHERE CHECK = 9;
   DESCRIBE CHECKS;

Answers for Lesson 12

A

Quiz

1. The system date is derived from the current date and time of the operating system on the host machine.

2. YEAR, MONTH, DAY, HOUR, MINUTE, SECOND.

3. The awareness of time zones might be a concern.

4. An individual's age changes from day to day and with every second of every day. It is better to store more constant values in a database if possible, such as an individual's date of birth. It is very easy to construct a query to determine an individual's age after you have the date of birth.

5. SELECT NAME, TRUNC((SYSDATE - DOB)/365) "AGE"
   FROM STUDENTS;

6. The OVERLAPS operator.

7. You would get the difference between the dates in days shown in a decimal value.

Exercises

1. SELECT TO_CHAR(SYSDATE,'MONTH DD YYYY')
   FROM DATES;

2. SELECT TO_DATE('DECEMBER 31 1997','MONTH DD YYYY')
   FROM DATES;

3. SELECT TO_CHAR('31-DEC-98','DAY')
   FROM DATES;

4. select current_date();

5. select dayname("2002-07-08");

6. select date_format("2002-07-09",'%W, %M %D, %Y');

7. Thursday, Monday, Monday. select dayname("date_value");

8. select date_add("1999-12-31 23:59:59", interval 1 second);

9. select date_add("1991-06-21", interval 10 year);
   select current_date();

Answers For Lesson 13
Quiz

1. No, data can only be manipulated using a view if the view is comprised of only one base table.

2. Yes, the owner of the view automatically has all permissions on the view.

3. The GROUP BY clause must sort data in order to break data into groups.

4. Yes, it is correct although the parentheses are not required.

5. No, the unique keyword is not part of the syntax.

6. No, the syntax is as follows:
   ```
   SQL> drop view debts;
   ```

7. You would just use the following
   ```
   SQL> create view ACCOUNTANT.credit_debts as
      (select * from debts
      where account_id = 4);
   ```

Exercises

1. No answer required.

2. ```
   SQL> CREATE VIEW TEST
        FROM TABLE_NAME;
   SQL> SELECT * FROM TEST;
   ```

3. ```
   SQL> CREATE VIEW TEST1 AS
        SELECT * FROM TEST;

   SQL> DROP VIEW TEST;

   SQL> SELECT * FROM TEST1;
   ```

   You will receive an error; it depends on your particular implementation as to what the error message will read.

Answers For Lesson 14
Quiz

1. When nesting transactions, any rollback of a transaction cancels all the transactions currently in progress. The effect of all the transactions will not truly be saved until the outer transaction has been committed.

2. Yes. Savepoints allow the programmer to save off statements within a transaction. If desired, the transaction can then be rolled back to this savepoint instead of to the beginning of the transaction.

3. A `COMMIT` command can be issued by itself or within the transaction.

4. Yes and no. You can issue the command, but it will not roll back the changes.

5. No. A savepoint comes into play only if a `ROLLBACK` command is issued—and then only the changes made after the savepoint will be rolled back.

A

Exercises

1. ```
SQL> SET TRANSACTION READ WRITE;

SQL> INSERT INTO CUSTOMERS VALUES
   > ('SMITH', 'JOHN');
SQL> COMMIT;
```

2. This statement is correct and will work quite well; however, you have just updated everyone's current balance to $25,000!

3. This statement is correct. Nothing will be inserted.

# Answers For Lesson 15

## Quiz

1. The clustered index would not be created. If there are no non-unique values in the column, the clustered index would be created but would not allow duplicate entries to be created.

2. a. True.

   b. False. In some instances indexes degrade performance, as is the case with data updates.

   c. True.

3. Yes.

4. Additional storage space, maintenance of the indexes, and slowing of data updates (inserts, updates, and deletes).

5. No. Remember that columns with a large percentage of non-unique values are not good candidates for indexes.

6. The index is stored in the same data blocks as the data.

7. You can dropping and then recreate the indexes for the data load process.
```

Exercises

1. a. Small tables should not be indexed, as there would be no performance gain.

   b. A unique index.

   c. A composite or covering index of the columns used in the WHERE clause.

   d. Indexes could be used depending on what types of queries are run. Indexes should be dropped and recreated for the data manipulation jobs.

2. No answer required.

3. No answer required.

Answers For Lesson 16

Quiz

1. Carefully planning your statement and arranging the elements within your clauses to maximize performance.

2. No, you should try to store them separately to avoid disk contention.

3. To provide for more efficient data access.

4. A table's data is read row by row.

5. By creating indexes and arranging the conditions in a SQL statement so that they take advantage of them.

6. Insufficient shared memory, limited number of available disk drives, running large batch loads that are unscheduled, failing to commit or rollback transactions, and improper sizing of tables and indexes.

7. OLAP systems are generally developed for "read-mostly" environments such as reporting or data warehouses. OLTP systems are mainly developed for transactional systems.

8. Backing up the table data, dropping the original table, recreating the original table, and then re-importing the data.

Exercises

1. You should reformat the SQL statement as follows, depending on the consistent format of your choice:

```
SELECT E.LAST_NAME, E.FIRST_NAME, E.MIDDLE_NAME,
       E.ADDRESS, E.PHONE_NUMBER, P.SALARY,
       P.POSITION,E.SSN, P.START_DATE
```

```
FROM EMPLOYEE E,
     PAYROLL P
WHERE E.SSN = P.SSN
  AND E.LAST_NAME LIKE 'S%'
  AND P.SALARY > 20000;
```

2. According to the statistics, your new query should look similar to the following answer. NAME LIKE 'SMITH%' is the most restrictive condition because it will return the fewest rows:

```
SELECT M.INDIVIDUAL_NAME, M.ADDRESS, M.CITY, M.STATE, M.ZIP_CODE,
       S.SEX, S.MARITAL_STATUS, S.SALARY
FROM MAILING_TBL M,
     INDIVIDUAL_STAT_TBL S
WHERE M.INDIVIDUAL_ID = S.INDIVIDUAL_ID
  AND S.MARITAL_STATUS = 'S'
  AND S.SEX = 'MALE'
  AND S.SALARY >= 30000
  AND M.CITY = 'INDIANAPOLIS'
  AND M.NAME LIKE 'SMITH%';
```

Answers For Lesson 17

Quiz

1. There is no Connection role. The proper statement should be
```
SQL> GRANT CONNECT TO DAVID;
```

2. It is only true if the CASCADE option is used with the DROP USER statement.

3. Everyone with access to the database would be able to select from your table.

4. Yes, it will create the user with the default settings.

5. No, the keyword user is missing. The statement should be
```
SQL> alter user RON
identified by RON;
```

6. Yes.

7. Only users who have the SELECT privilege for that table.

8. No, as of yet MySQL does not provide support for roles.

Exercises

1. ```
   mysql> use mysql;
   mysql> show tables;
   mysql> desc user;
   mysql> select host, user, password from user;
   ```

2. No answer needed

3. ```
   mysql> insert into user(host,user,password) values
        > ('localhost','betty','betty');
   ```

4. ```
   mysql> select * from user where user = 'betty';
   update user
   set Select_priv = 'Y',
   Insert_priv = 'Y',
   Update_priv = 'Y',
   Delete_priv = 'Y',
   Create_priv = 'Y',
   Drop_priv = 'Y',
   Reload_priv = 'Y',
   Shutdown_priv = 'Y',
   Process_priv = 'Y',
   File_priv = 'Y',
   Grant_priv = 'Y',
   References_priv = 'Y',
   Index_priv = 'Y',
   Alter_priv = 'Y'
   where user = 'betty';
   ```

5. ```
   mysql> use matt;
   mysql> grant insert, update, delete on emp_tbl to betty;
   ```

6. No answer needed. Just view the results.

7. ```
   mysql> grant alter, drop on emp_tbl to betty;
   mysql> revoke update on emp_tbl from betty;
   ```

8. No answer needed—this is just an individual exercise.

Answers For Lesson 18

Quiz

1. By selecting from USER_CATALOG or CAT. The name of the data dictionary object will vary by implementation, but all versions have basically the same information about objects such as tables and views.
   ```

A

2. Database design, user statistics, processes, objects, growth of objects, performance statistics, stored SQL code, and database security are all stored in the data dictionary.

3. Performance statistics suggest ways to improve database performance by modifying database parameters and streamlining SQL, which may also include the use of indexes and an evaluation of their efficiency.

4. Tables, indexes, synonyms, clusters, and views.

5. INFORMATION_SCHEMA

6. Code is more easily portable to another implementation that adopts the standard, such as SQL Server.

Exercises

1. `mysql`

2. `SHOW CREATE TABLE USER;`

3.
```
SELECT GRANTEE, TABLE_NAME, PRIVILEGE_TYPE
FROM INFORMATION_SCHEMA.TABLE_PRIVILEGES
ORDER BY GRANTEE, TABLE_NAME;
```

4.
```
SELECT USER, TABLE_NAME, GRANTOR, TABLE_PRIV
FROM ALL_TABLES_PRIV
ORDER BY USER, TABLE_NAME;
```

5.
```
SELECT USER, TABLE_NAME, TIMESTAMP
FROM ALL_TABLES_PRIV
ORDER BY USER, TABLE_NAME;
```

6.
```
SELECT USER, TABLE_NAME,
DATE_FORMAT(TIMESTAMP, "%W, %M %D, %Y %T")
FROM ALL_TABLES_PRIV;
SELECT USER, TABLE_NAME,
DATE_FORMAT(TIMESTAMP, "%W, %M %D, %Y %T")
FROM ALL_TABLES_PRIV
ORDER BY USER, TABLE_NAME;
```

7. Your action plan might vary depending on your company policy or individual situation. You must weigh your options as to what course of action to take and determine what course both achieves some desired level of results while still being within the business constraints of your company.

Answers For Lesson 19

Quiz

1. False. Triggers can be fired from INSERT, UPDATE, and DELETE statements only. Not SELECT statements.

2. False. A cursor must be issued the OPEN command for it to be opened for reading.

3. False. Static SQL requires a precompiler. Dynamic SQL is just that: dynamic. The SQL statements used with dynamic SQL can be prepared and executed at runtime.

4. temporary

5. You must deallocate the cursor. The syntax is

   ```
   SQL> deallocate cursor cursor_name;
   ```

6. No. They are executed by the use of UPDATE, DELETE, or INSERT.

7. No. The trigger is automatically dropped when the table is dropped.

Exercises

1. PRODUCTS table
           PRODUCT_ID
           PRODUCT
           COST
           DESCRIPTION
   INVENTORY table
           PRODUCT_ID
           QUANTITY
   ORDERS table
           PRODUCT_ID
           ORDER_DATE
           ORDER_QUANTITY
           CUSTOMER_ID

2. A stored procedure would be needed for each table to handle INSERT, UPDATE, and DELETE operations.

3. A trigger would be needed to update the QUANTITY in the INVENTORY table based on the quantity ordered for each customer order.

Answers For Lesson 20

Quiz

1. The execution statement, the trigger restrictions, and the trigger action.

2. The INSERT, UPDATE, and DELETE events.

3. Many privileges can be granted to a role. Then the role can be granted to many users (instead of many privileges). Privileges are granted and revoked much easier, and you can break your database users into groups, whereby each group is allowed to perform certain actions.

4. Data manipulation, referential integrity enforcement, database auditing and monitoring, and business rules enforcement.

5. User-defined type.

6. VARBINARY().

7. ExtractValue().

8. Validation and accessibility.

9. REGEXP and RLIKE. There is no real difference, as RLIKE is just a synonym for REGEXP.

Exercises

1. ```
   CREATE ROLE ROLE_NAME
   GRANT SELECT TO ROLE_NAME
   GRANT ROLE_NAME TO USERNAME
   ```

2. ```
   CREATE TYPE TYPE_NAME AS OBJECT
   (COLUMN_NAME VARCHAR2(10),
    COLUMN_NAME NUMBER(9))

   CREATE TABLE TABLE_NAME
   (COLUMN1 UDT_NAME,
   COLUMN2 NUMBER(9))

   INSERT INTO TABLE_NAME
   VALUES
   (UDT NAME('COLUMN1',COLUMN2)
   ```

Answers For Lesson 21

Quiz

1. You can generate SQL scripts from database tables and the data dictionary.

2. Yes, the SQL statement will generate a SQL script, but the generated script will not work. You need SELECT 'SELECT in front of COUNT(*):

   ```
   SELECT 'SELECT COUNT(*) FROM ' || TABLE_NAME || ';'
   ```

   Otherwise, your output will look like

   ```
   COUNT(*) FROM TABLE_NAME;
   ```

   which is not a valid SQL statement.

3. Once again, yes and no. The statement will generate a SQL script, but the SQL that it generates will be incomplete. You need to select a comma (,) between the privileges CONNECT and DBA:

   ```
   SELECT 'GRANT CONNECT, DBA TO ' || USERNAME || ';'
   ```

4. Yes. The syntax of the main statement is valid, and the SQL that will be generated will grant CONNECT and DBA roles to all users selected.

5. False. You do not care how many rows are being selected, as that will not be part of the syntax of your generated statements.

6. False. You should spool to a .sql file or whatever your naming convention is for a SQL file. However, you may choose to spool within your generated file.

7. True—just to be safe.

8. The ED command takes you into a full-screen text editor. ED is very similar to vi on a UNIX system and appears like a Windows Notepad file.

9. The SPOOL OFF command closes an open spool file.

Exercises

1.
```
SQL> SET ECHO OFF
SQL> SET FEEDBACK OFF
SQL> SPOOL GRANTS.SQL
SQL> SELECT 'GRANT SELECT ON HISTORY_TBL TO ' || USERNAME || ';'
  2  FROM SYS.DBA_USERS
  3  WHERE USERNAME IN ('JOHN','KEVIN','RYAN','RON','CHRIS')
  4  /
```

```
GRANT SELECT ON HISTORY_TBL TO JOHN;
GRANT SELECT ON HISTORY_TBL TO KEVIN;
GRANT SELECT ON HISTORY_TBL TO RYAN;
GRANT SELECT ON HISTORY_TBL TO RON;
GRANT SELECT ON HISTORY_TBL TO CHRIS;
```

A

2. There are no wrong answers as long as the syntax is correct in your generated statements.

3. `mysql>select concat(`describe `,table_name,`;`) from tables_priv;`

4. `mysql>select concat(`select count(*) from `,table_name,`;`) from` ➥`table_priv;`

Answers For Lesson 22

Quiz

1. The innermost function.

2. NULL values are not recognized by aggregate functions.

3. There are 1,024 bytes in a kilobyte and 1,024 kilobytes in a megabyte.

4. You must first convert the character to a numeric value using a conversion function. In this lesson, we used Oracle's conversion function called TO_NUMBER.

Exercises

1. RESIDENCE
- -
WILLIAM REYNOLDS LIVES AT 1231 FARNSWORTH BLVD IN CARMEL, IN.

HENRY SMITH LIVES AT 33 BEACON CT IN INDIANAPOLIS, IN.

VIRGINIA TAYLOR LIVES AT 1390 DAYTON ST IN NOBLESVILLE, IN.

```
mysql> select concat(first_name, ' ', last_name, ' lives at ', st_add,
➥' in ',
    >         city, ', ', st, '.') residence
    > from emp_tbl;
```

2.
```
SQL> SELECT M.MEM_LAST_NAME || ', ' || M.MEM_FIRST_NAME NAME,
  2     SUM(MO.QTN * PP.COST) "AMT SPENT"
  3 FROM MEMBER_TBL M,
  4 PROD_PROFILE_TBL PP,
  5 MEM_ORDER_TBL MO
  6 WHERE M.MEM_NO = MO.MEM_NO
  7 AND PP.PROD_NO = MO.PROD_NO
```

```
 8 AND MO.DATE_ORD LIKE '%JUL%97%'
 9 AND M.MEM_NO NOT IN (SELECT MEM_NO
10                       FROM RETURNS_TBL)
11 GROUP BY M.MEM_LAST_NAME, M.MEM_FIRST_NAME, MO.QTN, PP.COST
12 HAVING SUM(MO.QTN * PP.COST) > (SELECT AVG(MO.QTN * PP.COST)
13                                 FROM PROD_PROFILE_TBL PP,
14                                      MEM_ORDER_TBL MO
15                                 WHERE PP.PROD_NO = MO.PROD_NO);
```

Answers For Lesson 23

Quiz

1. At first you would think to yourself, "Yeah, sure, you just forgot your password." But this error can be returned if a front-end application cannot connect to the database. However, if you know the database is functional, just change the password by using the ALTER USER command and tell the user the new password.

2. In order for tables not to take the default settings for storage, you must include the storage clause. Otherwise, medium or large tables will fill up and take extents, causing slower performance. They also might run out of space, causing a halt to your work until the DBA can fix the space problem.

3. No, notice that SYSDATE is renamed to TODAY, and TODAY is a reserved word.

4. False. The error message might give you an idea of what is wrong, and every once in a while will tell you exactly what is wrong. Most of the time, error identification comes from experience.

5. False. The CREATE TABLE statement should process. The error might come later if the tables grow and fill up the system tablespace.

Exercises

1. `SQL> DROP TABLE JSMITH.HISTORY;`

2. ```
CREATE TABLE TEAMS
(TEAM_ID   VARCHAR(2)   NOT NULL,
 TEAM_NAME VARCHAR(10) NOT NULL);
```

3. ```
INSERT INTO TEAMS VALUES
('HA', 'HACKERS');
```

4. `SELECT * FROM TEAMS;`

5. ```
SELECT TEAM_ID, TEAM_NAME
FROM TEAMS
WHERE TEAM_ID = 'HA';
```
```

Answers For Lesson 24

Quiz

1. `OracleClient.OracleCommand.`
2. The `Statement` object.
3. A generic database API that can be used with almost any database.
4. JDBC.

Exercise

```
Dim orclConnection As New OracleClient.OracleConnection
➥("Data Source=XE;User ID=test;Password=redshift;Unicode=True")

Dim SQLCommand As String = "UPDATE PART SET PRICE=PRICE/2"

Dim orclCommand As
New OracleClient.OracleCommand(SQLCommand, orclConnection)

orclConnection.Open()

orclCommand.ExecuteNonQuery()

orclConnection.Close()
```

Answers For Lesson 25

Quiz

1. `SET` commands change the settings available with your SQL*Plus session.
2. Yes. SQL*Plus can accept parameters from a user and pass them into variables.
3. You would probably break up your groups by customer because you are selecting from the CUSTOMER table.
4. The only limitations are that the text in your `LOGIN.SQL` file must be valid SQL and SQL*Plus commands.
5. False. `DECODE` is like an `IF...THEN` statement.
6. False. The original file will be overwritten with the new output.

Exercises

1. ```
   compute sum of count(*) on report
        break on report
        select product_id, product_name, unit_cost, count(*)
        from products
        group by product_id, product_name, unit_cost;
   ```

2. ```
   set heading off
   select to_char(sysdate,' "Today is "Day, Month dd yyyy')
   from dual;
   ```

3. ```
   1  select *
   2  from orders
   3  where customer_id = '001'
   4* order by customer_id;

   12
   c/orders/customer

   14
   append   DESC
   ```

Answers For Lesson 26

Quiz

1. A database trigger takes a specified action when data in a specified table is manipulated. For instance, if you make a change to a table, a trigger could insert a row of data into a history table to audit the change.

2. Related procedures can be stored together in a package.

3. True.

4. False. DDL cannot be used in a PL/SQL statement. It is not a good idea to automate the process of making structural changes to a database.

5. Text output is not directly a part of the language of PL/SQL; however, text output is supported by the standard package DBMS_OUTPUT.

6. The DECLARE section, PROCEDURE section, and EXCEPTION section.

7. OPEN, FETCH, and CLOSE.
   ```

Exercises

1.
```
DECLARE
      HourlyPay number(4,2);
```

2.
```
DECLARE
      cursor c1 is
      select * from customer_table
      where city = 'INDIANAPOLIS';
```

3.
```
DECLARE
      UnknownCode EXCEPTION;
```

4.
```
IF ( CODE = 'A' ) THEN
      update AMOUNT_TABLE
      set AMT = 10;
   ELSIF ( CODE = 'B' ) THEN
      update AMOUNT_TABLE
      set AMT = 20;
   ELSE
      raise UnknownCode;
   END IF;
```

A

Answers for Lesson 27

Quiz

1. False. The word *SQL* is not protected by copyright. The products mentioned do comply with much of the ANSI standard, but they do not fully comply with everything in that standard.
2. False. Transact-SQL commands are not case sensitive.
3. bit.
4. The go statement.

Exercises

1. Because nearly all of this lesson deals with Transact-SQL, we did not explore the many other extensions to ANSI SQL. Most of the documentation that accompanies database products makes some effort to point out its SQL extensions. Keep in mind that using these extensions will make porting your queries to other databases more difficult.

2. This operation requires an IF statement. There are no wrong answers as long as you follow the syntax for logical statements (IF statements) discussed in this lesson.

3. There is a missing left parenthesis on line 3, a missing comma on line 5, and an extra comma on line 10, and the word stop on the last line should be the go keyword to terminate the statement.

```
 1> use BASEBALL
 2> go
 3> create table TEAMS (
 4> TEAM_ID int,
 5> CITY char(30),
 6> NAME char(30),
 7> WON int,
 8> LOST int,
 9> TOTAL_HOME_ATTENDANCE int,
10> AVG_HOME_ATTENDANCE int)
11> go
```

Answers For Lesson 28

Quiz

1. Speed, robustness, and ease of use.

2. # cd /usr/local/mysql
   # bin/safe_mysql

3. # /usr/local/mysql/bin/mysqladmin shutdown

4. Database names and table names are case sensitive in the terminal monitor. All other words can be typed in either upper- or lowercase.

Exercises

1. # **/usr/local/mysql/bin/mysqlshow**

```
+-----------+
| Database  |
+-----------+
| mysql     |
| test      |
+-----------+
2 rows in set (0.00 sec)
# mysql -u root
Enter password: *******
mysql> show databases;
```

A

```
+------------+
| Database   |
+------------+
| mysql      |
| test       |
+------------+
2 rows in set (0.00 sec)
```

2. ``# mysql -u root``
   Enter password: ******
   mysql> **show tables;**
   ERROR 1046: No Database Selected
   mysql> **use test;**
   Reading table information for completion of table and column names
   You can turn off this feature to get a quicker startup with -A

   Database changed
   mysql> **show tables;**

```
+----------------+
| Tables in test |
+----------------+
| mytable1       |
| mytable2       |
+----------------+
2 rows in set (0.00 sec)
```

APPENDIX B
Code Examples to Create Tables

This appendix contains the CREATE TABLE statements for the tables that we used for examples in this book. To create these tables in your database, simply log in to your database as a valid user and then execute each of these commands.

Note that the exact syntax of some implementations of SQL may vary slightly from this code. This is basic SQL code to create tables; the implementations used are Oracle and MySQL.

The CREATE TABLE statements are as follows:

```
Oracle
create table checks
(check#          number(6)       not null,
 payee           varchar(20)     not null,
 amount          number(6,2)     not null,
 remarks         varchar(20)     not null);

MySQL
create table checks
('check'         integer         not null,
 payee           varchar(20)      not null,
 amount          decimal(6,2)     not null,
 remarks         varchar(20)     not null);


Oracle
create table deposits
(deposit#        number(8)        not null,
 whopaid         varchar(25)      not null,
 amount          number(6,2)      not null,
 remarks         varchar(20)      not null);

MySQL
create table deposits
(deposit         integer         not null,
 whopaid         varchar(25)      not null,
 amount          decimal(6,2)     not null,
 remarks         varchar(20)      not null);
```

```
Oracle
create table bikes
(name          varchar(15)      not null,
 framesize     number(10,2)     not null,
 composition   varchar(12)      not null,
 milesridden   number(10)       not null,
 type          varchar(8)       not null);

MySQL
create table bikes
(name          varchar(15)      not null,
 framesize     decimal(10,2)    not null,
 composition   varchar(12)      not null,
 milesridden   integer      not null,
 type          varchar(8)       not null);

Oracle
create table price
(item          varchar(15)      not null,
 wholesale     number(4,2)      not null);

MySQL
create table price
(item          varchar(15)      not null,
 wholesale     decimal(4,2)     not null);

Oracle
create table hilow
(state         varchar(10)      not null,
 lows          number(8)        not null,
 highs         number(8)        not null,
 difference    number(10)       null);

MySQL
create table hilow
(state         varchar(10)      not null,
 lows          integer      not null,
 highs         integer      not null,
 difference    integer          null);

Oracle
create table remains
(numerator     number(10)       not null,
 denominator   number(12)       not null);

MySQL
create table remains
(numerator     numeric(10)      not null,
 denominator   numeric(12)      not null);
```

```
Oracle
create table precedence
(n1          number(10)      not null,
 n2          number(10)      not null,
 n3          number(10)      not null,
 n4          number(10)      not null);

MySQL
create table precedence
(n1          numeric(10)      not null,
 n2          numeric(10)      not null,
 n3          numeric(10)      not null,
 n4          numeric(10)      not null);

Oracle
create table friends
(lastname    varchar(15)     not null,
 firstname   varchar(15)     not null,
 areacode    number(9)       null,
 phone       varchar(10)     null,
 st          char(2)         not null,
 zip         varchar(5)      not null);

MySQL
create table friends
(lastname    varchar(15)     not null,
 firstname   varchar(15)     not null,
 areacode    numeric(9)      null,
 phone       varchar(10)     null,
 st          char(2)         not null,
 zip         varchar(5)      not null);

Oracle
create table parts
(name        varchar(15)     not null,
 location    varchar(15)     not null,
 partnumber  number(10)      not null);

MySQL
create table parts
(name        varchar(15)     not null,
 location    varchar(15)     not null,
 partnumber  numeric(10)     not null);

Oracle
create table vacation
(lastname    varchar(15)     not null,
 employeenum number(11)      not null,
 years       number(8)       not null,
 leavetaken  number(11)      null);
```

B

```
MySQL
create table vacation
(lastname         varchar(15)    not null,
 employeenum      numeric(11)    not null,
 years            numeric(8)     not null,
 leavetaken       numeric(11)    null);

Oracle
create table football
(name             varchar(20)    not null);

MySQL
create table football
(name             varchar(20)    not null);

Oracle
create table softball
(name             varchar(20)    not null);

MySQL
create table softball
(name             varchar(20)    not null);

Oracle
create table teamstats
(name             varchar(10)    not null,
 pos              varchar(3)     not null,
 ab               number(3)      not null,
 hits             number(4)      not null,
 walks            varchar(5)     not null,
 singles          varchar(7)     not null,
 doubles          varchar(7)     not null,
 triples          varchar(7)     not null,
 hr               number(2)      not null,
 so               varchar(2)     not null);

MySQL
create table teamstats
(name             varchar(10)    not null,
 pos              varchar(3)     not null,
 ab               numeric(3)     not null,
 hits             numeric(4)     not null,
 walks            varchar(5)     not null,
 singles          varchar(7)     not null,
 doubles          varchar(7)     not null,
 triples          varchar(7)     not null,
 hr               numeric(2)     not null,
 so               varchar(2)     not null);
```

```
Oracle
create table project
(task           varchar(14)  not null,
 startdate      date,
 enddate        date);

MySQL
create table project
(task           varchar(14)  not null,
 startdate      date,
 enddate        date);

Oracle
create table numbers
(a              number(10,4)    not null,
 b              number(10,4)    not null);

MySQL
create table numbers
(a              decimal(10,4)   not null,
 b              decimal(10,4)   not null);

Oracle
create table characters
(lastname       varchar(15)     not null,
 firstname      varchar(15)     not null,
 m              char(1)         null,
 code           number(10)      not null);

MySQL
create table characters
(lastname       varchar(15)     not null,
 firstname      varchar(15)     not null,
 m              char(1)         null,
 code           numeric(10)     not null);

Oracle
create table convert
(name           varchar(15)  not null,
 testnum        number(9)    not null);

MySQL
create table convert
(name           varchar(15)  not null,
 testnum        numeric(9)   not null);

Oracle
create table puzzle
(name           varchar(15)     not null,
 location       varchar(14)     not null);
```

B

```
MySQL
create table puzzle
(name          varchar(15)     not null,
 location      varchar(14)     not null);

Oracle
create table orgchart
(name          varchar(15)     not null,
 team          varchar(11)     not null,
 salary        number(10,2)    not null,
 sickleave     number(10)      not null,
 annualleave   number(11)      not null);

MySQL
create table orgchart
(name          varchar(15)     not null,
 team          varchar(11)     not null,
 salary        decimal(10,2)   not null,
 sickleave     numeric(10)     not null,
 annualleave   numeric(11)     not null);

Oracle
create table part
(partnum       number(10)      not null,
 description   varchar(20)     not null,
 price         number(10,2)    not null);

MySQL
create table part
(partnum       numeric(10)     not null,
 description   varchar(20)     not null,
 price         decimal(10,2)   not null);

Oracle
create table customer
(name          varchar(10)     not null,
 address       varchar(10)     not null,
 state         varchar(6)      not null,
 zip           varchar(10)     not null,
 phone         varchar(10)     null,
 remarks       varchar(30)     not null);

MySQL
create table customer
(name          varchar(10)     not null,
 address       varchar(10)     not null,
 state         varchar(6)      not null,
 zip           varchar(10)     not null,
 phone         varchar(10)     null,
 remarks       varchar(30)     not null);
```

```
Oracle
create table orders
(orderedon       date,
 name            varchar(10)    not null,
 partnum         number(10)     not null,
 quantity        number(10)     not null,
 remarks         varchar(30)    not null);
```

```
MySQL
create table orders
(orderedon       date,
 name            varchar(10)    not null,
 partnum         numeric(10)    not null,
 quantity        numeric(10)    not null,
 remarks         varchar(30)    not null);
```

B

```
Oracle
create table bills
(name            varchar(25)    not null,
 amount          number(6)      not null,
 account_id      number(10)     not null);
```

```
MySQL
create table bills
(name            varchar(25)    not null,
 amount          numeric(6)     not null,
 account_id      numeric(10)    not null);
```

```
Oracle
create table salaries
(name            varchar(30)    not null,
 salary          number(9)      not null,
 age             number(10)     not null);
```

```
MySQL
create table salaries
(name            varchar(30)    not null,
 salary          numeric(9)     not null,
 age             numeric(10)    not null);
```

```
Oracle
create table products
(pro             char(3)        not null,
 product_name    varchar(30)    not null,
 unit_cost       number(9,2)    not null);
```

```
MySQL
create table products
(pro             char(3)        not null,
 product_name    varchar(30)    not null,
 unit_cost       decimal(9,2)   not null);
```

```
Oracle
create table states
(st          char(2)          not null);

MySQL
create table states
(st          char(2)          not null);

Oracle
create table ssn_table
(ssn              varchar(9)     not null);

MySQL
create table ssn_table
(ssn              varchar(9)     not null);

Oracle
create table job_tbl
(name            varchar(30)    not null,
 job             varchar(15)    not null,
 department      varchar(10)    not null);

MySQL
create table job_tbl
(name            varchar(30)    not null,
 job             varchar(15)    not null,
 department      varchar(10)    not null);
```

--Lesson 13 Tables--

```
ORACLE
CREATE TABLE COMPANY
(NAME          CHAR(30)         NOT NULL,
 ADDRESS       CHAR(50),
 CITY CHAR(30),
 STATE CHAR(2));


CREATE TABLE BANK_ACCOUNTS
(ACCOUNT_ID    NUMBER           NOT NULL,
 TYPE          CHAR(30),
 BALANCE       NUMBER,
 BANK CHAR(30));


CREATE TABLE BILLS
(NAME          CHAR(30)         NOT NULL,
 AMOUNT        NUMBER,
 ACCOUNT_ID    NUMBER           NOT NULL);
```

--Lesson 14 Tables--

```
ORACLE
CREATE TABLE CUSTOMERS
(NAME         VARCHAR(30),
 ADDRESS      VARCHAR(50),
 CITY         VARCHAR(30),
 STATE        CHAR(2),
 ZIP          NUMERIC(5),
 CUSTOMER_ID  NUMERIC(2));

CREATE TABLE BALANCES
(AVERAGE_BAL  DECIMAL(8,2),
 CURR_BAL     DECIMAL(8,2),
 ACCOUNT_ID   NUMERIC(2));

MySQL
create table customers
(name         char(30),
 address      char(50),
 city         char(30),
 state        char(2),
 zip          int(5),
 customer_id int(2));

create table balances
(average_bal  decimal(8,2),
 curr_bal     decimal(8,2),
 account_id int(2));
```

--Lesson 19 Tables--

```
create table artists (
      name char(30),
      homebase char(40),
      style char(20),
      artist_id int);

create table media (
      media_type int,
      description char(30),
      price float);

create table recordings (
      artist_id int,
      media_type int,
      title char(50),
      year int);
```

B

```
--Lesson 22 Tables--

CREATE TABLE EMP_TBL
(EMP_ID            CHAR(9)         NOT NULL,
LAST_NAME          VARCHAR(15)     NOT NULL,
FIRST_NAME         VARCHAR(15)     NOT NULL,
MIDDLE_NAME        VARCHAR(15)     NULL,
ST_ADD             VARCHAR(20)     NOT NULL,
CITY               VARCHAR(20)     NOT NULL,
ST                 CHAR(2)         NOT NULL,
ZIP                VARCHAR(5)      NOT NULL,
HOME_PH            VARCHAR(10)     NULL,
EMER_CONT          VARCHAR(30)     NULL,
EMER_PH            VARCHAR(10)     NULL,
CONSTRAINT EMP_PK PRIMARY KEY (EMP_ID));


CREATE TABLE EMP_PAY_TBL
(EMP_ID            CHAR(9)         NOT NULL,
DT_START           DATE            NOT NULL,
POSITION           VARCHAR(15)     NOT NULL,
SALARY             DECIMAL(8,2)    NULL,
HR_PAY             DECIMAL(4,2)    NULL,
COUNTY             VARCHAR(15)     NOT NULL,
DEPARTMENT         VARCHAR(15)     NOT NULL,
CONSTRAINT EMP_PAY_PK PRIMARY KEY (EMP_ID));


CREATE TABLE MEMBER_TBL
(MEM_NO            VARCHAR(30)     NOT NULL,
MEM_LAST_NAME      VARCHAR(20)     NOT NULL,
MEM_FIRST_NAME     VARCHAR(20)     NOT NULL,
MEM_MID_NAME       VARCHAR(20)     NULL,
MEM_ST_ADD         VARCHAR(20)     NOT NULL,
MEM_CITY           VARCHAR(15)     NOT NULL,
MEM_ST             CHAR(2)         NOT NULL,
MEM_ZIP            VARCHAR(5)      NOT NULL,
DT_LAST_ORDER      DATE,
PREFERENCE         VARCHAR(8)      NULL,
MUSIC_STY_1        VARCHAR(15)     NULL,
MUSIC_STY_2        VARCHAR(15)     NULL,
MUSIC_STY_3        VARCHAR(15)     NULL,
CONSTRAINT MEM_PK PRIMARY KEY (MEM_NO));


CREATE TABLE FORMER_MEM_TBL
(FMEM_NO           VARCHAR(30)     NOT NULL,
FMEM_LAST_NAME     VARCHAR(20)     NOT NULL,
FMEM_FIRST_NAME    VARCHAR(20)     NOT NULL,
FMEM_MID_NAME      VARCHAR(20)     NULL,
FMEM_ST_ADD        VARCHAR(20)     NOT NULL,
```

```
FMEM_CITY           VARCHAR(20)     NOT NULL,
FMEM_ST             CHAR(2)         NOT NULL,
FMEM_ZIP            VARCHAR(5)      NOT NULL,
FDT_LAST_ORDER      DATE,
FPREFERENCE         VARCHAR(8)      NULL,
FMUSIC_STY_1        VARCHAR(15)     NULL,
FMUSIC_STY_2        VARCHAR(15)     NULL,
FMUSIC_STY_3        VARCHAR(15)     NULL,
REASON_TERM         VARCHAR(50)     NULL,
CONSTRAINT FMEM_PK PRIMARY KEY (FMEM_NO));


CREATE TABLE MEM_PROFILE_TBL
(MEM_NO             VARCHAR(30)     NOT NULL,
REGION              VARCHAR(10)     NOT NULL,
SEX                 VARCHAR(6)      NULL,
DOB                 DATE,
INCOME              DECIMAL(8,2)    NULL,
CONSTRAINT MEM_PRO_PK PRIMARY KEY (MEM_NO));


CREATE TABLE PROD_PROFILE_TBL
(PROD_NO            VARCHAR(15)     NOT NULL,
VEND_NO             VARCHAR(20)     NOT NULL,
ARTIST              VARCHAR(30)     NOT NULL,
TITLE               VARCHAR(30)     NOT NULL,
COST                DECIMAL(4,2)    NOT NULL,
STYLE               VARCHAR(15)     NULL,
FORMAT              VARCHAR(8),
CONSTRAINT PROD_PRO_PK PRIMARY KEY (PROD_NO));


CREATE TABLE INVENTORY_TBL
(PROD_NO            VARCHAR(15)     NOT NULL,
FORMAT              VARCHAR(8)      NOT NULL,
QTN                 DECIMAL(20)     NOT NULL,
ON_ORDER            DECIMAL(20)     NULL,
DATE_ORDERED        DATE,
DELIVERY_DATE       DATE,
CONSTRAINT INV_PK PRIMARY KEY (PROD_NO));


CREATE TABLE RETURNS_TBL
(PROD_NO            VARCHAR(15)     NOT NULL,
MEM_NO              VARCHAR(30)     NOT NULL,
QTN                 DECIMAL(20)     NOT NULL,
STYLE               VARCHAR(15)     NOT NULL,
FORMAT              VARCHAR(8)      NOT NULL,
DISTRIBUTOR         VARCHAR(20)     NULL,
REASON_RT           VARCHAR(50)     NULL,
CONSTRAINT RTNS_PK PRIMARY KEY (PROD_NO, MEM_NO));
```

```
CREATE TABLE VENDOR_TBL
(VEND_NO           VARCHAR(15)    NOT NULL,
VEND_NAME          VARCHAR(25)    NOT NULL,
VEND_ST_ADD        VARCHAR(20)    NOT NULL,
VEND_CITY          VARCHAR(15)    NOT NULL,
VEND_ST            CHAR(2)         NOT NULL,
VEND_ZIP           VARCHAR(5)     NOT NULL,
VEND_PH            VARCHAR(10)    NOT NULL,
VEND_FAX_PH        VARCHAR(10)    NULL,
CONTACT            VARCHAR(25)    NULL,
TYPE_PROD          VARCHAR(20)    NOT NULL,
CONSTRAINT VEND_PK PRIMARY KEY (VEND_NO));


CREATE TABLE MEM_ORDER_TBL
(MEM_NO            VARCHAR(30)    NOT NULL,
PROD_NO            VARCHAR(25)    NOT NULL,
DATE_ORD           DATE,
STYLE              VARCHAR(15)    NOT NULL,
FORMAT             VARCHAR(8)     NOT NULL,
QTN                DECIMAL(20)     NOT NULL,
SHIP_COST          DECIMAL(5,2)    NOT NULL,
CONSTRAINT MEM_ORD_PK PRIMARY KEY (MEM_NO, PROD_NO));
CREATE TABLE EMP_HIGH_PAY_CITY_TBL AS SELECT * FROM EMP_TBL;
```

APPENDIX C

Code Examples to Populate Tables

This appendix contains the INSERT statements used to populate the sample tables with data. To populate the tables that you created based on Appendix B, "Code Examples to Create Tables," simply log in to your database as the user (schema) who owns the tables created from Appendix B and execute these commands. If you are using MySQL, you might need to issue the use *database* command to ensure that you are working in the correct database.

Note that the exact syntax of some implementations of SQL may vary slightly from this code. This is basic SQL code to insert data into tables; the implementations used are Oracle and MySQL.

Unless specified by the words Oracle only, these INSERT statements work in *both* Oracle and MySQL.

Oracle and MySQL

```
insert into checks values
('1', 'Ma Bell', '150', 'Have sons next time');

insert into checks values
('2', 'Reading R.R.', '245.34', 'Train to Chicago');

insert into checks values
('3', 'Ma Bell', '200.32', 'Celluar Phone');

insert into checks values
('4', 'Local Utilities', '98', 'Gas');

insert into checks values
('5', 'Joes Stale $ Dent', '150', 'Groceries');

insert into checks values
('6', 'Cash', '25', 'Wild Night Out');

insert into checks values
('7', 'Joans Gas', '25.1', 'Gas');
```

```
insert into deposits values
('1', 'Rich Uncle', '200', 'Take off Xmas list');

insert into deposits values
('2', 'Employer', '1000', '15 June Payday');

insert into deposits values
('3', 'Credit Union', '500', 'Loan');

insert into bikes values
('TREK 2300', '22.5', 'CARBON FIBER', '3500', 'RACING');

insert into bikes values
('BURLEY', '22', 'STEEL', '2000', 'TANDEM');

insert into bikes values
('GIANT', '19', 'STEEL', '1500','COMMUTER');

insert into bikes values
('FUJI', '20', 'STEEL', '500', 'TOURING');

insert into bikes values
('SPECIALIZED', '16', 'STEEL', '100', 'MOUNTAIN');

insert into bikes values
('CANNONDALE', '22.5', 'ALUMINUM', '3000', 'RACING');

insert into price values
('TOMATOES', '.34');

insert into price values
('POTATOES', '.51');

insert into price values
('BANANAS', '.67');

insert into price values
('TURNIPS', '.45');

insert into price values
('CHEESE', '.89');

insert into price values
('APPLES', '.23');

insert into hilow values
('CA', '-50', '120',null);

insert into hilow values
('FL', '20', '110',null);
```

```
insert into hilow values
('LA', '15', '99',null);

insert into hilow values
('ND', '-70', '101',null);

insert into hilow values
('NE', '-60', '100',null);

insert into remains values
('10', '5');

insert into remains values
('8', '3');

insert into remains values
('23', '9');

insert into remains values
('40', '17');

insert into remains values
('1024', '16');

insert into remains values
('85', '34');

insert into precedence values
('1', '2', '3', '4');

insert into precedence values
('13', '24', '35', '46');

insert into precedence values
('9', '3', '23', '5');

insert into precedence values
('63', '2', '45', '3');

insert into precedence values
('7', '2', '1', '4');

insert into friends values
('BUNDY', 'AL', '100', '555-1111', 'IL', '22333');

insert into friends values
('MERRICK', 'BUD', '300', '555-6666', 'CO', '80212');

insert into friends values
('MAST', 'JD', '381', '555-6767', 'LA', '23456');
```

C

```
insert into friends values
('BULHER', 'FERRIS', '345', '555-3223', 'IL', '23332');

insert into parts values
('APPENDIX', 'MID-STOMACH', '1');

insert into parts values
('ADAMS APPLE', 'THROAT', '2');

insert into parts values
('HEART', 'CHEST', '3');

Insert into parts values
('SPINE', 'BACK', '4');

insert into parts values
('ANVIL', 'EAR', '5');

insert into parts values
('KIDNEY', 'MID-BACK', '6');

insert into vacation values
('ABLE', '101', '2', '4');

insert into vacation values
('BAKER', '104', '5', '23');

insert into vacation values
('BLEDSOE', '107', '8', '45');

insert into vacation values
('BOLIVAR', '233', '4', '80');

insert into vacation values
('BOLD', '210', '15', '100');

insert into vacation values
('COSTALES', '211', '10', '78');

insert into football values
('ABLE');

insert into football values
('BRAVO');

insert into football values
('CHARLIE');

insert into football values
('DECON');
```

```
insert into football values
('EXITOR');

insert into football values
('FUBAR');

insert into football values
('GOOBER');

insert into softball values
('ABLE');

insert into softball values
('BAKER');

insert into softball values
('CHARLIE');

insert into softball values
('DEAN');

insert into softball values
?('EXITOR');

insert into softball values
('FALCONER');

insert into softball values
('GOOBER');

insert into teamstats values
('JONES', '1B', '145', '45', '34', '31', '8', '1', '5', '10');

insert into teamstats values
('DONKNOW', '3B', '175', '65', '23', '50', '10', '1', '4', '15');

insert into teamstats values
('WORLEY', 'LF', '157', '49', '15', '35', '8', '3', '3', '16');

insert into teamstats values
('DAVID', 'OF', '187', '70', '24', '48', '4', '0', '17', '42');

insert into teamstats values
('HAMHOCKER', '3B', '50', '12', '10', '10', '2', '0', '0', '13');

insert into teamstats values
('CASEY', 'DH', '1', '0', '0', '0', '0', '0', '0', '1');
```

C

These statements are Oracle only to ensure the proper date-time format is used:

```
insert into project values
('KICKOFF MTG', '01-APR-98', '01-APR-98');

insert into project values
('TECH SURVEY', '02-APR-98', '01-MAY-98');

insert into project values
('USER MTGS', '15-MAY-98', '30-MAY-98');

insert into project values
('DESIGN WIDGET', '01-JUN-98', '30-JUN-98');

insert into project values
('CODE WIDGET', '01-JUL-98', '02-SEP-98');

insert into project values
('TESTING', '03-SEP-98', '17-JAN-99');
```

These are the MySQL INSERT statements that properly handle the Date data type format:

```
insert into project values
('KICKOFF MTG', '1998-04-01', '1998-04-01');

insert into project values
('TECH SURVEY', '1998-04-02', '1998-05-01');

insert into project values
('USER MTGS', '1998-05-15', '1998-05-30');

insert into project values
('DESIGN WIDGET', '1998-06-01', '1998-06-30');

insert into project values
('CODE WIDGET', '1998-07-01', '1998-09-02');

insert into project values
('TESTING', '1998-09-03', '1999-01-17');
```

Oracle and MySQL

```
insert into numbers values
('3.1415', '4');

insert into numbers values
('-45', '.707');
```

```
insert into numbers values
('5', '9');

insert into numbers values
('-57.667', '42');

insert into numbers values
('15', '55');

insert into numbers values
('-7.2', '5.3');

insert into characters values
('PURVIS', 'KELLY', 'A', '32');

insert into characters values
('TAYLOR', 'CHUCK', 'J', '67');

insert into characters values
('CHRISTINE', 'LAURA', 'C', '65');

insert into characters values
('ADAMS', 'FESTER', 'M', '87');

insert into characters values
('COSTALES', 'ARMANDO', 'A', '77');

insert into characters values
('KONG', 'MAJOR', 'G', '52');

insert into ssn_table values
('300431117');

insert into ssn_table values
('301457111');

insert into ssn_table values
('459789998');

insert into job_tbl values
('ALVIN SMITH', 'VICEPRESIDENT', 'MARKETING');

insert into `convert` values
('40', '95');

insert into `convert` values
('13', '23');

insert into `convert` values
('74', '68');
```

C

```
insert into puzzle values
('TYLER', 'BACKYARD');

insert into puzzle values
('MAJOR', 'KITCHEN');

insert into puzzle values
('SPEEDY', 'LIVING ROOM');

insert into puzzle values
('WALDO', 'GARAGE');

insert into puzzle values
('LADDIE', 'UTILITY CLOSET');

insert into puzzle values
('ARNOLD', 'TV ROOM');

insert into orgchart values
('ADAMS', 'RESEARCH', '34000.00', '34', '12');

insert into orgchart values
('WILKES', 'MARKETING', '31000.00', '40', '9');

insert into orgchart values
('STOKES', 'MARKETING', '36000.00', '20', '19');

insert into orgchart values
('MEZA', 'COLLECTIONS', '40000.00', '30', '27');

insert into orgchart values
('MERRICK', 'RESEARCH', '45000.00', '20', '17');

insert into orgchart values
('RICHARDSON', 'MARKETING', '42000.00', '25', '18');

insert into orgchart values
('FURY', 'COLLECTIONS', '35000.00', '22', '14');

insert into orgchart values
('PRECOURT', 'PR', '37500.00', '24', '24');

insert into customer values
('TRUE WHEEL', '550 HUSKER', 'NE', '58702', '555-4545', 'NONE');

insert into customer values
('BIKE SPEC', 'CPT SHRIVE', 'LA', '45678', '555-1234', 'NONE');

insert into customer values
('LE SHOPPE', 'HOMETOWN', 'KS', '54678', '555-1278', 'NONE');
```

```
insert into customer values
('AAA BIKE', '10 OLDTOWN', 'NE', '56784', '555-3421', 'JOHN-MGR');

insert into customer values
('JACKS BIKE', '24 EGLIN', 'FL', '34567', '555-2314', 'NONE');

insert into part values
('54', 'PEDALS', '54.25');

insert into part values
('42', 'SEATS', '24.50');

insert into part values
('46', 'TIRES', '15.25');

insert into part values
('23', 'MOUNTAIN BIKE', '350.45');

insert into part values
('76', 'ROAD BIKE', '530.00');

insert into part values
('10', 'TANDEM', '1200.00');
```

These statements are Oracle only to ensure the proper date-time format is used:

```
insert into orders values
('15-MAY-1996', 'TRUE WHEEL', '23', '6', 'PAID');

insert into orders values
('19-MAY-1996', 'TRUE WHEEL', '76', '3', 'PAID');

insert into orders values
('2-SEP-1996', 'TRUE WHEEL', '10', '1', 'PAID');

insert into orders values
('30-JUN-1996', 'TRUE WHEEL', '42', '8', 'PAID');

insert into orders values
('30-JUN-1996', 'BIKE SPEC', '54', '10', 'PAID');

insert into orders values
('30-MAY-1996', 'BIKE SPEC', '23', '8', 'PAID');

insert into orders values
('17-JAN-1996', 'BIKE SPEC', '76', '11', 'PAID');

insert into orders values
('17-JAN-1996', 'LE SHOPPE', '76', '5', 'PAID');
```

C

```
insert into orders values
('1-JUN-1996', 'LE SHOPPE', '10', '3', 'PAID');

insert into orders values
('1-JUN-1996', 'AAA BIKE', '10', '1', 'PAID');

insert into orders values
('1-JUL-1996', 'AAA BIKE', '76', '4', 'PAID');

insert into orders values
('1-JUL-1996', 'AAA BIKE', '46', '14', 'PAID');

insert into orders values
('11-JUL-1996', 'JACKS BIKE', '76', '14', 'PAID');
```

These are the MySQL INSERT statements that properly handle the Date data type format:

```
insert into orders values
('19-MAY-1996', 'TRUE WHEEL', '76', '3', 'PAID');

insert into orders values
('1996-09-02', 'TRUE WHEEL', '10', '1', 'PAID');

insert into orders values
('1996-06-30', 'TRUE WHEEL', '42', '8', 'PAID');

insert into orders values
('1996-06-30', 'BIKE SPEC', '54', '10', 'PAID');

insert into orders values
('1996-05-30', 'BIKE SPEC', '23', '8', 'PAID');

insert into orders values
('1996-01-17', 'BIKE SPEC', '76', '11', 'PAID');

insert into orders values
('1996-01-17', 'LE SHOPPE', '76', '5', 'PAID');

insert into orders values
('1996-06-01', 'LE SHOPPE', '10', '3', 'PAID');

insert into orders values
('1996-06-01', 'AAA BIKE', '10', '1', 'PAID');

insert into orders values
('1996-07-01', 'AAA BIKE', '76', '4', 'PAID');

insert into orders values
('1996-07-01', 'AAA BIKE', '46', '14', 'PAID');
```

```
insert into orders values
('1996-07-11', 'JACKS BIKE', '76', '14', 'PAID');
```

Oracle and MySQL

```
insert into bills values
('Phone Company', '125', '1');

insert into bills values
('Power Company', '75', '1');

insert into bills values
('Record Club', '25', '2');

insert into bills values
('Software Company', '250', '1');

insert into bills values
('Cable TV Company', '35', '3');

insert into bills values
('Joe''s Car Palace', '350', '5');

insert into bills values
('S.C. Student Loan', '200', '6');

insert into bills values
('Florida Water Company', '20', '1');

insert into bills values
('U-O_s Insurance Company', '125', '5');

insert into bills values
('Debtor''s Credit Card', '35', '4');

insert into salaries values
('JACK', '35000', '29');

insert into salaries values
('JILL', '48000', '42');

insert into salaries values
('JOHN', '61000', '55');

insert into products values
('P01', 'MICKEY MOUSE LAMP', '29.95');

insert into products values
('P02', 'NO 2 PENCILS - 20 PACK', '19.9');
```

C

```
insert into products values
('P03', 'COFFEE MUG', '6.95');

insert into products values
('P04', 'FAR SIDE CALENDAR', '10.5');

insert into products values
('P05', 'NATURE CALENDAR', '12.99');

insert into products values
('P06', 'SQL COMMAND REFERENCES', '29.99');

insert into products values
('P07', 'BLACK LEATHER BRIEFCASE', '99.99');

insert into states values
('IN');

insert into states values
('FL');

insert into states values
('KY');

insert into states values
('IL');

insert into states values
('OH');

insert into states values
('CA');

insert into states values
('NY');
```

The following INSERT statements are for the Oracle tables in Lesson 13.

```
INSERT INTO COMPANY VALUES
('Phone Company', '111 1st Street', 'Atlanta', 'GA');

INSERT INTO COMPANY VALUES
('Power Company', '222 2nd Street', 'Jacksonville', 'FL');

INSERT INTO COMPANY VALUES
('Record Club',    '333 3rd Avenue', 'Los Angeles', 'CA');

INSERT INTO COMPANY VALUES
('Software Company', '444 4th Drive', 'San Francisco', 'CA');
```

```
INSERT INTO COMPANY VALUES
('Cable TV Company', '555 5th Drive', 'Austin', 'TX');

INSERT INTO COMPANY VALUES
('Joe''s Car Palace', '1000 Govt. Blvd', 'Miami', 'FL');

INSERT INTO COMPANY VALUES
('S.C. Student Loan', '25 College Blvd', 'Columbia', 'SC');

INSERT INTO COMPANY VALUES
('Florida Water Company', '1883 Hwy 87', 'Navarre', 'FL');

INSERT INTO COMPANY VALUES
('U-O-Us Insurance Company', '295 Beltline Hwy', 'Macon', 'GA');

INSERT INTO COMPANY VALUES
('Debtor''s Credit Card', '115 2nd Avenue', 'Newark', 'NJ');

INSERT INTO BANK_ACCOUNTS VALUES
(1, 'Checking', 500, 'First Federal');

INSERT INTO BANK_ACCOUNTS VALUES
(2, 'Money market', 1200, 'First Investor');

INSERT INTO BANK_ACCOUNTS VALUES
(3, 'Checking', 90, 'Credit Union');

INSERT INTO BANK_ACCOUNTS VALUES
(4, 'Savings', 400, 'First Federal');

INSERT INTO BANK_ACCOUNTS VALUES
(5, 'Checking', 2500, 'Second Mutual');

INSERT INTO BANK_ACCOUNTS VALUES
(6, 'Business', 4500, 'Fidelity');

INSERT INTO BILLS VALUES
('Phone Company', 125, 1);

INSERT INTO BILLS VALUES
('Power Company', 75, 1);

INSERT INTO BILLS VALUES
('Record Club', 25, 2);

INSERT INTO BILLS VALUES
('Software Company', 250, 1);

INSERT INTO BILLS VALUES
('Cable TV Company', 35, 3);
```

C

```
INSERT INTO BILLS VALUES
('Joe''s Car Palace', 350, 5);

INSERT INTO BILLS VALUES
('S.C. Student Loan', 200, 6);

INSERT INTO BILLS VALUES
('Florida Water Company', 20, 1);

INSERT INTO BILLS VALUES
('U-O-Us Insurance Company', 125, 5);

INSERT INTO BILLS VALUES
('Debtor''s Credit Card', 35, 4);
```

The following INSERT statements are for the tables used in Lesson 14.

```
INSERT INTO CUSTOMERS VALUES
('Bill Turner', '725 N. Deal Parkway', 'Washington', 'DC', 20085, 1);

INSERT INTO CUSTOMERS VALUES
('John Keith', '1220 Via De Luna Dr.', 'Jacksonville',    'FL', 33581, 2);

INSERT INTO CUSTOMERS VALUES
('Mary Rosenburg', '482 Wannamaker Avenue', 'Williamsburg', 'VA', 23478, 3);

INSERT INTO CUSTOMERS VALUES
('David Blanken', '405 N. Davis Highway', 'Greenville', 'SC', 29652, 4);

INSERT INTO CUSTOMERS VALUES
('Rebecca Little', '7753 Woods Lane', 'Houston', 'TX', 38764, 5);

INSERT INTO BALANCES VALUES
(1298.53, 854.22, 1);

INSERT INTO BALANCES VALUES
(5427.22, 6015.96, 2);

INSERT INTO BALANCES VALUES
(211.25, 190.01, 3);

INSERT INTO BALANCES VALUES
(73.79, 25.87, 4);

INSERT INTO BALANCES VALUES
(1285.90, 1473.75, 5);

INSERT INTO BALANCES VALUES
(1234.56, 1543.67, 6);

INSERT INTO BALANCES VALUES
(345.25, 348.03, 7);
```

The following INSERT statements are for Lesson 19:

```
insert into artists values('Soul Asylum','Minneapolis','Rock',1);

insert into artists values('Maurice Ravel','France','Classical',2);

insert into artists values('Dave Matthews Band','Charlottesville','Rock',3);

insert into artists values('Vince Gill','Nashville','Country',4);

insert into artists values('Oingo Boingo','Los Angeles','Pop',5);

insert into artists values('Crowded House','New Zealand','Pop',6);

insert into artists values('Mary Chapin-Carpenter','Nashville','Country',7);

insert into artists values('Edward MacDowell','U.S.A','Classical',8);

insert into media values(1,'Record',4.99);

insert into media values(2,'Tape',9.99);

insert into media values(3,'CD',13.99);

insert into media values(4,'CD-ROM',29.99);

insert into media values(5,'DAT',19.99);

insert into recordings values(1,2,'Hang Time',1988);

insert into recordings values(1,3,'Made to Be Broken',1986);

insert into recordings values(2,3,'Bolero',1990);

insert into recordings values(3,5,'Under the Table and Dreaming',1994);

insert into recordings values(4,3,'When Love Finds You',1994);

insert into recordings values(5,2,'Boingo',1987);

insert into recordings values(5,1,'Dead Man''s Party',1984);

insert into recordings values(6,2,'Woodface',1990);

insert into recordings values(6,3,'Together Alone',1993);

insert into recordings values(7,5,'Come On, Come On',1992);

insert into recordings values(7,3,'Stones in the Road',1994);

insert into recordings values(8,5,'Second Piano Concerto',1985);
```

C

The following INSERT statements are for Lesson 22:

```
INSERT INTO EMP_TBL VALUES
('324540787','MERCER','RICHARD','1023 S
➥3RD','LOUSIVILLE','KY','45345','3178234528',NULL,NULL);

INSERT INTO EMP_TBL VALUES
('234566742','SMITH','HENRY','321 GRAND AVE','TERRE
➥HAUTE','IN','47804','8122344434',NULL,NULL);

INSERT INTO EMP_TBL VALUES
('313219830','PIERCE','THOMAS','31
➥MERIDIAN','INDIANAPOLIS','IN','46113','3175462918',NULL,NULL);

INSERT INTO EMP_TBL VALUES
('435663121','REYNOLDS','WILLIAM','342 SOUTH
➥ST','CARMEL','IN','45343','3177926529',NULL,NULL);

INSERT INTO EMP_TBL VALUES
('412331221','TAYLOR','VIRGINIA','12 EAST
➥54TH','INDIANAPOLIS','IN','46112','3179872335',NULL,NULL);

INSERT INTO EMP_TBL VALUES
('143234343','JONES','JOHN','23 WEST
➥38TH','INDIANAPOLIS','IN','46112','3179856734',NULL,NULL);

INSERT INTO EMP_TBL VALUES
('453897657','BENNETT','CHRIS','4268 WEST
➥10TH','INDIANAPOLIS','IN','46112','3179874532',NULL,NULL);

INSERT INTO EMP_TBL VALUES
('412453872','OSBORNE','JASON','35 SOUTH
➥CHESTER','INDIANAPOLIS','IN','46112','3174539876',NULL,NULL);

INSERT INTO EMP_TBL VALUES
('345608124','TAYLOR','JOHN','30 EAST
➥24TH','INDIANAPOLIS','IN','46112','3179561234',NULL,NULL);

INSERT INTO EMP_TBL VALUES
('238513942','NICCOSON','JULIE','5434 EAST
➥5TH','INDIANAPOLIS','IN','46112','3179463248',NULL,NULL);

INSERT INTO EMP_TBL VALUES
('435649765','SCHULER','STEVE','4534
➥GRAND','INDIANAPOLIS','IN','46123','317453654',NULL,NULL);

INSERT INTO EMP_TBL VALUES
('127643652','FERGUSON','JOHN','345 EAST
➥10TH','INDIANAPOLIS','IN','46112','3174534351',NULL,NULL);
```

```
INSERT INTO EMP_PAY_TBL VALUES
('324540787','01-JAN-2006','CLERK',33000.00,NULL,'SMITH','SALES');

INSERT INTO EMP_PAY_TBL VALUES
('234566742','15-JUL-2004','VP MARKETING',250000.00,NULL,'VIGO','MARKETING');

INSERT INTO EMP_PAY_TBL VALUES
('313219830','08-AUG-2005','SALEPERSON',30000.00,NULL,'MARION','SALES');

INSERT INTO EMP_PAY_TBL VALUES
('435663121','01-JAN-2005','CLERK',NULL,9.00,'HAMILTON','HQ');

INSERT INTO EMP_PAY_TBL VALUES
('412331221','01-MAY-2005','CUSTOMER SERVICE',NULL,13.00,'MARION','SALES');

INSERT INTO EMP_PAY_TBL VALUES
('143234343','01-JUL-2004','CUSTOMER SERVICE',NULL,13.15,'MARION','SALES');

INSERT INTO EMP_PAY_TBL VALUES
('453897657','15-OCT-2002','CUSTOMER SERVICE',NULL,14.00,'MARION','SALES');

INSERT INTO EMP_PAY_TBL VALUES
('412453872','01-FEB-2003','CUSTOMER SERVICE',NULL,12.75,'MARION','SALES');

INSERT INTO EMP_PAY_TBL VALUES
('345608124','15-APR-2002','CUSTOMER SERVICE',NULL,13.25,'MARION','SALES');

INSERT INTO EMP_PAY_TBL VALUES
('238513942','01-AUG-2006','CUSTOMER SERVICE',NULL,13.00,'MARION','SALES');

INSERT INTO EMP_PAY_TBL VALUES
('435649765','01-APR-2003','CUSTOMER SERVICE',NULL,18.50,'MARION','SALES');

INSERT INTO EMP_PAY_TBL VALUES
('127643652','01-MAY-2005','CUSTOMER SERVICE',NULL,14.00,'MARION','SALES');

INSERT INTO VENDOR_TBL VALUES
('1234','SONY','2343 NORTH 3RD','TERRE
➥HAUTE','IN','47802','8135451007','8135451002','Robert Mcelroy','MUSIC');

INSERT INTO VENDOR_TBL VALUES
('4563','CAPITOL PACKING','1234 NORTH
➥MERIDIAN','INDIANAPOLIS','IN','46312','2127035888','2127036790','Betsy
➥Conway','BOXES');

INSERT INTO VENDOR_TBL VALUES
('3876','OFFICE DEPOT','23 WEST
➥82ND','INDIANAPOLIS','IN','46113','3175527007',NULL,NULL,'OFFICE');
```

C

```
INSERT INTO VENDOR_TBL VALUES
('9256','UPS','2334 AIRPORT
➡EXPRESSWAY','INDIANAPOLIS','IN','46213','3178982301',NULL,NULL,'SHIPPING');

INSERT INTO VENDOR_TBL VALUES
('3452','APPLE RECORDS','32 MAIN ST','NEW
➡YORK','NY','12543','2132215009','2132215020','Cindy Roberts','MUSIC');

INSERT INTO VENDOR_TBL VALUES
('4352','COLUMBIA RECORDS','32 WEST
➡PACIFIC','SEATTLE','WA','96243',5172996012,NULL,NULL,'MUSIC');

INSERT INTO MEMBER_TBL VALUES
('1111','MOORE','KEITH','D','101 S. KENTUCKY','GREENSBORO','KY','54642',
➡'13-MAY-2007','COUNTRY','COUNTRY','ROCK','CLASSICAL');

INSERT INTO MEMBER_TBL VALUES
('2222','DAVID','RICHARDS','T','30 SOUTH
➡AMARILLO','DALLAS','TX','35246',NULL,'POP','POP','ROCK','COUNTRY');

INSERT INTO MEMBER_TBL VALUES
('3333','LARRY','THOMAS','C','4536 EAST
➡CYCLE','CANTON','OH','10324',NULL,'ROCK','ROCK','POP','COUNTRY');

INSERT INTO MEMBER_TBL VALUES
('4444','PAUL','BAKER','W','32 EASTERLY AVE','BANKFORD','MA','54335',
➡'01-JAN-2009','CLASSICAL','CLASSOCAL',NULL,NULL);

INSERT INTO MEMBER_TBL VALUES
('5555','BEVERLY','STONE','F','1342 NORTH
➡SUTTON','PENNSYLVANIA','PA','34235','01-NOV-2005','POP','ROCK','POP',
➡'COUNTRY');

INSERT INTO MEMBER_TBL VALUES
('6666','JEREMY','WYATT','Q','3254 NORTH CANAL','ERIE','PA','46378',
➡'13-AUG-2007','POP',NULL,NULL,NULL);

INSERT INTO MEMBER_TBL VALUES
('7777','JOHNATHAN','ELLIS','L','34 EAST
➡MAIN','MADESTO','CA','45231',NULL,'POP','POP','ROCK',NULL);

INSERT INTO MEMBER_TBL VALUES
('7777','JAMES','STEWART','G','3245 EAST VALLEY','HOLLYWOOD','CA','46354',
➡'13-MAY-1999','CLASSICAL','CLASSICAL',NULL,NULL);

INSERT INTO MEM_PROFILE_TBL VALUES
('1111','NORTHEAST','MALE','20-NOV-1950',30000.00);

INSERT INTO MEM_PROFILE_TBL VALUES
('2222','WEST','MALE',NULL,NULL);
```

```
INSERT INTO MEM_PROFILE_TBL VALUES
('3333','SOUTH','MALE',NULL,112000.00);

INSERT INTO MEM_PROFILE_TBL VALUES
('4444','MIDWEST','MALE','17-JAN-1980',65000.00);

INSERT INTO MEM_PROFILE_TBL VALUES
('5555','WEST','FEMALER','02-JAN-1960',NULL);

INSERT INTO MEM_PROFILE_TBL VALUES
('6666','SOUTHEAST','MALE',NULL,35000.00);

INSERT INTO MEM_PROFILE_TBL VALUES
('7777','MIDWEST','MALE','15-JUN-1970','40000.00);

INSERT INTO MEM_PROFILE_TBL VALUES
('8888','WEST','MALE','06-JUL-1940',1500000.00);
```

C

APPENDIX D
Using MySQL for Exercises

The instructions for installing MySQL in this appendix have been included for your convenience. These instructions are accurate as of this book's writing. Neither the authors nor Sams Publishing place any warranties on the MySQL software or provide MySQL software support. For any installation problems or to inquire about software support, refer to the MySQL documentation or contact MySQL.

NOTE

> You might want to review the current documentation for MySQL. To get to the online documentation, either select Documentation from the main menu on www.mysql.com, or go directly to www.mysql.com/doc.

Windows Installation Instructions

Use the following instructions if you will be installing MySQL on a computer running Microsoft Windows. Note that steps 1–6 might vary according to the layout of www.mysql.com.

1. Go to www.mysql.com to download MySQL.
2. Select Downloads from the main menu.
3. Select the latest stable version, MySQL 5.1.
4. Review the provided information about version 5.1.
5. Find the appropriate Windows download for your system and click the Download selection.
6. Select a mirror site for download that is close to your location. Save the file to your computer.

7. Create a folder under C:\ called mysql.

8. Double-click the zip file that you downloaded, and then extract all files to your mysql folder.

9. Go to your mysql folder and double-click the setup.exe file.

10. Follow the instructions to install MySQL on your computer.

11. After MySQL is successfully installed, test the software installation by executing mysql.exe under C:\mysql\bin.

12. At the `mysql>` prompt, type **help**. You should see a list of commands.

13. If all of the previous steps were successful, you are ready to use MySQL for exercises in this book.

If you experience problems during the installation, repeat steps 1–13. If you are still unable to obtain or install MySQL, contact MySQL for support.

Linux Installation Instructions

Use the following instructions if you will be installing MySQL on a computer running Linux. Note that steps 1–6 might vary according to the layout of www.mysql.com.

NOTE   If you have Red Hat Linux 7.1, MySQL should already be included.

1. Go to www.mysql.com to download MySQL.

2. Select Downloads from the main menu.

3. Select the latest stable version, MySQL 5.1.

4. Review the provided information about version 5.1.

5. Find the appropriate Linux download for your system and click the Download selection. You will most likely need to download and install the MySQL-client-VERSION.i386.rpm file.

6. Select a mirror site for download that is close to your location. Save the file to your computer.

7. Copy the file MySQL-client-VERSION.i386.rpm to your Linux computer.

8. Execute the following command as root to install MySQL. This is the standard minimal installation:

   ```
   shell> rpm -i MySQL-VERSION.i386.rpm MySQL-client-VERSION.i386.rpm
   ```

9. After installation, MySQL data will be located in /var/lib/mysql.

10. After MySQL is successfully installed, test the software installation by following the instructions in the post-installation portion of the online documentation.

11. If all of the previous steps were successful, you are ready to use MySQL for exercises in this book.

If you experience problems during the installation, repeat the previous steps. If you are still unable to obtain or install MySQL, contact MySQL for support.

> **NOTE**
>
> MySQL is also available for MacOS and most other versions of UNIX.

D

Index

INFOMRATION_SCH
EMA, 461-463

MySQL table
commands, 460-461

objects, 452-456

security, 451-452

sessions, 458-459

space allocation,
457-458

users, 450-451

views, 449-450

DBA_ROLES view, 451

DBA_ROLE_PRIVS view, 451

DBA_SYS_PRIVS view, 451

DBA_USERS view, 451

**DBMS (database
management system), 6,
241, 413**

MODIFY clause, 261

DBMS OUTPUT package, 643

**DDL (Data Dictionary
Language), 631**

commands, PL/SQL, 631

DEALLOCATE command, 475

**DEALLOCATE statement,
syntax, 475**

**decimal values,
deleting, 533**

**DECLARE command, of
PROCEDURE section
(PL/SQL blocks), 636**

**DECLARE cursor_name
CURSOR statement, 473**

**DECLARE keyword,
variables, 670**

**DECLARE section (PL/SQL
blocks), 631-632**

constant assignment, 633

cursor definitions, 633

%ROWCOUNT attribute,
634-635

%ROWTYPE
attribute, 634

%TYPE attribute, 633-634

variable assignment,
632-633

declaring

global variables, 668-669

local variables, 668

variables, table name
conflicts, 635

DECODE function, 616-619

**default storage parameters,
large tables, 569**

**DEFINE command, SQL*Plus
variables, 611-612**

DEL command, 588

**DELETE, INSERT, VALUES
statement, 298**

**DELETE ANY TABLE system
privilege, 424**

DELETE clause, 299

**DELETE command, 332,
418, 440**

views, 343

DELETE event, 490

**DELETE operation, tables
(triggers), 479**

DELETE statement, 285

data, deleting, 298-302

table views, 345

WHERE clause, 300

deleting. See also removing

databases, 263

decimal values, 533

information, 298-302

lines in code, 591

object privileges, 425

records, parent/child
relationships, 279

roles, 420

SQL*Plus settings, 603

stored procedures, 478-479

tables, 262

users from Personal
Oracle, 419

**delimited text files,
exporting, 303**

**denormalizing databases,
237-238**

DEPENDENTS table, 10

**DESC command, table
structure, viewing, 593**

**DESC operator, sorting
indexes, 378**

DESCRIBE command

table structure, 645

table structure, viewing,
593-594

UDTs (User Defined
Types), attributes, 495

designing

databases, 230-231

triggers, 479

designs, databases, 244

Destination dialog box, 303

**development tools for
applications, 575**

Java, 576

.NET, 577

ODBC, 576

Personal Oracle, 576

**diagnostic tools, SQL
Server, 681**

diagrams, syntax, 86

**dictionaries. See also data
dictionary**

data

CASE tools, 245

creating, 244-245

RDBMS packages, 245

MySQL data
dictionary, 440

Oracle data dictionary. See
Oracle, data dictionary

Direct Access Method, 370

direct invocation, 17

**directories, installing
MySQL, 687**

numbers. *See also*
 arithmetic operators
  line, 589-590
numeric data types (T-SQL),
 663-664
numeric values, 541-544

O

object privileges, 424-425
object-orientation, 492
objects
 of databases, scripts,
  maintaining, 279
 DBA of Oracle data
  dictionary, 452-456
 placing in system
  tablespaces, 569-570
obstacles of database
 performance, identifying,
 407-408
ODBC (Open Database
 Connectivity), 16-17, 576
 APIs, 16
 Applications,
  developing, 576
 architecture, 16
 connections, creating, 580
 Data Sources, 580
OLAP (online analytical
 processing), 397
OLAP (online analytical
 processing) databases,
 397-398
OleDB, 577
OLLBACK command, 401
OLTP (online transactional
 processing), 397
 and batch loads,
  comparing, 398-400
OLTP databases
 and OLAP databases,
  comparing, 397
 tuning, 397-398

OMMIT command, 401
online analytical processing
 (OLAP), 397-398
OPEN command of
 PROCEDURE section
 (PL/SQL blocks), 636
Open command (File
 menu), 303
Open Database Connectivity.
 See ODBC
opening cursors, 473
operations
 arithmetic
  ABS function, 195
  CEIL function, 196
  EXP function, 196-197
  FLOOR function, 196
  functions, 195
  LN function, 197-198
  LOG function, 197-198
  MOD function, 198
  POWER function, 199
  SIGN function, 199-200
  SQRT function,
   200-201
 DELETE, tables, 479
 INSERT, tables, 479
 join, 233
 UPDATE, tables, 479
operators
 arithmetic, 42-43
  / (division sign), 48-49
  = (equal sign), 538
  - (minus sign), 46-48
  % (modulo sign), 51-53
  * (multiplication sign),
   49-51
  + (plus sign), 43-46
  precedence, 53-54
 BETWEEN, 78-80
 CAST, converting data
  types, 321
 character

|| (double pipe)
 concatenatation, 67-70
LIKE, 63-65
 _ (underscore), 65-67
comparison, 55-56, 63
 = (equal sign), 56-58
 > (greater than sign), 59
 >= (greater than or
  equal to sign), 59
 < or != (inequalities),
  62-63
 < (less than sign), 60-61
 <= (less than or equal to
  sign), 60-61
 FALSE value, 55
 NULL, 55-57
 TRUE value, 55
 UNKNOWN value, 55
DESC, sorting indexes, 378
|| (double pipe), 338
IN, 78-80
 values, comparing, 538
logical, 70-71, 693
 AND, 71-72
 NOT, 73-75
 OR, 72-73
OR logical, avoiding in
 queries, 396-397
queries, 42
relational, = (equal
 sign), 159
set, 75
 INTERSECT, 77
 MINUS (difference),
  77-78
 UNION, 75-77
 UNION ALL, 75-77
UNION, SELECT
 statement, 343
wildcards (T-SQL),
 679-680
OR logical operator, 72-73
 avoiding in queries,
  396-397

prompts, MySQL terminal monitor, 692

PROMPTs, writing queries, 24

pseudocolumn, SYSDAYE function, 314

PUBLIC keyword, 422

public synonyms, 430

  CREATE PUBLIC SYNONYM privilege, 517

  in multischema databases, 567

Q

QA (quality assurance), 568

qualifying tables, 519

  for Personal Oracle, 427-429

quality assurance (QA), 568

QUARTER function, 321

queries. *See also* SQL queries

  aliases, 46

  ALL keyword, 33

  arithmetic operators, 42-43

    / (division sign), 48-49

    % (modulo sign), 51-53

    * (multiplication sign), 49-51

    - (minus sign), 46-48

    + (plus sign), 43-46

    precedence, 53-54

  BETWEEN operator, 78-80

  [ ] (brackets) wildcard operator (T-SQL), 680

  ^ (caret) wildcard operator (T-SQL), 680

  character operators

    LIKE, 63-65

    || (double pipe) concatenation, 67-70

    _ (underscore), 65-67

CHECKS table, 25

clauses, 85

  AVG(ANNUALLEAVE), 113-115

  AVG(SALARY), 113-115

  AVG(SICKLEAVE), 113-115

  combining, 112

  errors, 109

  GROUP BY, 98-105, 116-117

  HAVING, 105-111, 116-117

  NAME, 113

  ORDER BY, 89-98, 114-116

  PAYEE, 112

  REMARKS, 112

  SELECT, 100

  SELECT statement, syntax, 85-86

  syntax, 86

  TEAM, 113-115

  WHERE, 87-88, 115-116

<column name = alias> syntax, 46

columns

  individual, selecting, 28

  order, changing, 29-32

commands, case sensitivity, 22

comparison operators, 55-56, 63

  = (equal sign), 56-58

  > (greater than sign), 59

  >= (greater than or equal to sign), 59

  < or != (inequalities), 62-63

  < (less than sign), 60-61

  <= (less than or equal to sign), 60-61

  NULL, 55-57

complex, simplifying with views, 347-348

concepts, applying, 25-26

conditions, 40-41

database, PL/SQL, 631

date functions

  applying, 312

  current dates, 313-314

  dates and time periods, comparing, 320

  dates, subtracting, 318-320, 713

  time, 315-318

dates

  current, 313-314

  subtracting, 318-320, 713

  and time periods, comparing, 320

DISTINCT keyword, 33

elements, arranging, 393-395

expressions, 40

FROM keyword, 23-24

full-table scans, 371

IN operator, 78-80

indexes, 378

logical operators, 70-71, 693

  AND, 71-72

  NOT, 73-75

  OR, 72-73

MySQL, 39

NULL, 55-57

operators, 42

OR logical operator, avoiding, 396-397

output, 598-599

% (percent sign) wildcard operator (T-SQL), 680

Personal Oracle8, 39

procedures, 395-396

PROMPTs, 24

How can we make this index more useful? Email us at indexes@samspublishing.com

tables. *See also* columns

aliases, 133, 157, 391

ALTER TABLE command, constraints (on data), 275-276

ALTER TABLE statement
CHANGE option, syntax, 259
table structures, modifying, 257-261

ARTISTS, 469
cursors, creating, 473

backing up, 523

BALANCES, transaction control, 355

BANK ACCOUNTS, data, 254, 334

base, 135

BATTERS, 666

BILLS
ACCOUNT ID field, creating indexes, 373-377
AMOUNT field, creating indexes, 377-378
data, 253-254, 333
data breakdown, 247

CASE tools, 245

CHECKS, 25

child, Oracle SQL*Plus referential integrity reports, 280-281

columns
changing from NOT NULL to NULL, syntax, 259
changing from NULL to NOT NULL to NULL, 260-261
finding, 128-129
lengths, increasing or decreasing, 258
names, 336

in relational databases, 8

renaming, 45, 337-338

selecting and placing, 336

COMPANY, data, 254, 334

composite indexes, 393

constraints, disabling, 516-517

COUNT(*) function, 507

CREATE DATABASE statement, 242
data dictionaries, creating, 244-245
data, breaking down, 247
database design, 244
key fields, creating, 246-247
options, 243
syntax, 242

CREATE statements, 241

CREATE TABLE command, 255, 335

CREATE TABLE statement, 247-248
code example, 248
field data types, 249-250
field names, 249
field NULL value, 250-252
fields (unique), 252-254
storage clause, 254-255
table names, 248-249
tables, creating, 255-257
tables, storing and sizing, 254-255

CREATE TABLE statement examples, 737

create table statements, 269, 731-738

creating, 241, 255-257, 495-496, 577
code examples, 731-738
for Personal Oracle, 425-426

creating and populating, 333

CUSTOMERS, transaction control, 354

data
entering, 577
inserting with INSERT, VALUES statement, 287
summarizing with views, 349

data definition statements, 241

data dictionary, 437

data manipulation statements, 241

data, merging, 233

DBMS, 241

defragmenting, 403

DELETE operation, triggers, 479

deleting, 262

DEPENDENTS, records, 10

DEPENDENTS and EMPLOYEE, retrieving fields, 10

DESCRIBE command, 645

disk space, 244

driving, 135

DROP DATABASE statement, 262-263

DROP TABLE command, 262

DROP TABLE statement, 261-263

dropping, 377

DUAL, 314, 615-616

public synonyms in multischema databases, 567

table or view that does not exist, 552

TNS: Listener could not resolve SID given in connector descriptor, 563

use of DISTINCT when selecting multiple columns, 566

using reserved words in your SQL statement, 564-566

TRUE value, comparison operators, 55

TRUNC command, 533

TRUNC function, 319

truncating

PAY STATUS table, 647

schema tables, 522-523

tables, backing up, 523

truncation (databases), 298

TTITLE command, formatting reports, 604

tuning

databases, 405-407

tools (built-in), 409

OLAP databases, 398

OLTP databases, 397-398

%TYPE attribute of DECLARE section (PL/SQL blocks), 633-634

types. *See also* data types

ALTER TYPE statement, 493-494

CREATE TYPE statement, 492-496

of constraints (on data), 269

check, 276-277

foreign key, 274-276

NOT NULL, 269-271

parent/child table relationships, 275-276

primary key, 271-273

unique, 273-274

U

UDTs (User Defined Types), 493

attributes, 495

creating, 494-495

tables, creating, 495-496

underscore (_) character operator, 65-67

underscore (_) wildcard operator (T-SQL), 679

UNION, relational databases, 9

UNION ALL set operator, 75-77

UNION operator, SELECT statement, 343

UNION set operator, 75-77

unions, relational databases, 9

unique constraints (on data), 273-274

unique fields, 252-254

UNIQUE keyword, CREATE INDEX statement, 381-382

unique values, inserting, 291-292

unit of work (transactions), 354

units, converting with views, 346-347

UNIX, MySQL, 685

administration, 686

initial access privileges, 688

installing, 686-687

isamchk utility, 694

mysqlaccess utility, 694

mysqladmin utility, 694

mysqldump utility, 694

mysqlimport utility, 694

mysqlshow utility, 694

(pound sign), 687

starting, 687-688

stopping, 687-688

terminal monitor, 688-694

utilities, 694

UNKNOWN value, comparison operators, 55

unqualified tables, dropping, 566-567

UPDATE ANY TABLE system privilege, 424

UPDATE command, 332, 418, 440

views, 343-344

UPDATE event, 490

UPDATE function, views, 345

UPDATE operation, tables (triggers), 479

UPDATE statement, 285

data, modifying, 295-298

syntax, 295

WHERE clause, 295

updating

data from banking applications, 355

virtual columns, 345

UPPER function, 203-205

use database command, populating tables, 743

USE ROLLBACK SEGMENT option (SET TRANSACTION statement), 357

usefulness of constraints (on data), 268

USER CATALOG view, 453

User Defined Types. See UDTs